A Complete System of CHRISTIAN THEOLOGY

or,

A Concise, Comprehensive, and Systematic View of the Evidences, Doctrines, Morals, and Institutions of Christianity

by
SAMUEL WAKEFIELD, D.D.

"Go ye into all the world, and preach the Gospel to every creature."

SCHMUL

COPYRIGHT © MCMLXXXV BY SCHMUL PUBLISHING CO.
All rights reserved. No part of this publication may be reproduced or used in any form or by any means—graphic, electronic, or mechanical, including photocopying, recording, taping, or information storage or retrieval systems—without prior written permission of the publisher.

Churches and other noncommercial interests may reproduce portions of this book without prior written permission of the publisher, provided such quotations are not offered for sale—or other compensation in any form—whether alone or as part of another publication, and provided that the text does not exceed 500 words or five percent of the entire book, whichever is less, and does not include material quoted from another publisher. When reproducing text from this book, the following credit line must be included: "From *A Complete System of Christian Theology*, by Samuel Wakefield, DD, © 1985 by Schmul Publishing Co., Nicholasville, Kentucky. Used by permission."

Cover photo: The Garden Tomb, "Place of the Resurrection of Jesus Christ in Jerusalem, Israel," 123RF. Used by permission.

Published by Schmul Publishing Co.
PO Box 776
Nicholasville, KY 40340

This book is a facsimile reprint and may contain imperfections such as marks, notations, marginalia and flawed pages.

ISBN 10: 0-88019-582-7
ISBN 13: 978-0-88019-582-9

Visit us on the Internet at
www.wesleyanbooks.com,
or order direct from the publisher by calling 800-772-6657,
or by writing to the above address.

PREFACE.

In presenting this volume of Christian Theology to the public, it may be necessary that the author should make some prefatory remarks, both in regard to the history of its origin, and to the distinctive character of the work itself.

There is perhaps no system of divinity extant which possesses more real merit than "Watson's Theological Institutes." As a body of purely evangelical theology, both theoretic and practical, it is nowhere surpassed; and in regard to its polemic character, for the clearness of its statements, the candor with which conflicting sentiments are considered, the fairness of its arguments, and the force of its logical conclusions, it has no equal. Its worth has been acknowledged by divines of various denominations both in Europe and America; and wherever it is known it cannot fail to reflect credit upon its able author, and to be regarded as the workings of a *master-mind*.

But notwithstanding its numerous excellencies, and its perfect adaptation to the *mature theologian*, it is not well suited to the wants of those who are *merely commencing* their theological course. The very style in which the work is written is quite too labored for that of a text-book on any subject. Many of its sentences are so long and complicated, that in order to gather their meaning the most rigid attention is required. This not only diminishes the pleasure of study, but prevents, in a great measure, that deep and lasting impression on the memory which the subject would otherwise produce. A considerable portion of the work consists in quotations from various authors. By this means the uniformity of its style is frequently interrupted; and as many of these quotations are from books of comparatively ancient date, the style is occasionally somewhat antiquated. Moreover, as the opinions of different authors are frequently brought to bear upon the same point of doctrine, there is often an uncalled for and wearisome repetition of the same ideas; and sometimes the introduction of matter which has no direct connection with the subject under discussion.

For many years the author entertained the opinion, that by a judicious abridgment of the "Institutes" these defects might be remedied; and that by this means a concise and simple theological text-book might be furnished, which would possess all the intrinsic value of the original, and at the same time conduct students to their desired acquisition by a shorter and easier path. Finding, however, after waiting long, and conversing with many upon the subject, that no one was willing to undertake the task, he finally commenced it himself; and, as his time and ability would allow, prosecuted it to its conclusion.

But at this point a new question arose. It is known by all that there are many topics of vast importance to the students of theology which are not at all discussed in the "Institutes." It became evident, therefore, that a mere abridgment of Watson, however well executed, would not *fully* meet the present wants of the Church. It was this fact, together with corresponding suggestions from an official source, which led to the preparation of the following work in its present form.

And now, in regard to the character of the work itself, it is only necessary to say that it has for its basis an abridgment of "Watson's Theological Institutes," which the author has given in his own style; that to this is added a considerable amount of original matter, for the purpose of completing the system; that the whole is presented in a new and strictly systematic form; and that it assumes to a very great extent, as every candid reader will allow, the character of originality.

As to the design of the author, it was to furnish a clear and comprehensive outline of scriptural theology, which, though especially intended for the benefit of those who are preparing for the Christian ministry, should at the same time be adapted to the wants of all classes of readers, from the aged theologian to the Sabbath-school scholar. How far he has succeeded in the accomplishment of his purpose others must judge. He knows that his work is imperfect, and will need the indulgence of a generous public. But he has done what he could; and now his earnest prayer is, that God may accept the humble offering, and render it subservient to the enlargement and edification of his Church: "To whom be glory for ever and ever. Amen!"

CONTENTS.

INTRODUCTION.
PART I.

	PAGE
OF THEOLOGY IN GENERAL	9
§ 1. The Nature of Theology	9
§ 2. The Objects of Theology	12
§ 3. Divisions of Theology	13

PART II.

	PAGE
OF THE SOURCES OF THEOLOGY	18
§ 1. Of Reason, as a Source of Theology	18
§ 2. Of Revelation, as a Source of Theology	22

BOOK I.

EVIDENCES OF A DIVINE REVELATION 39

CHAPTER I.
EVIDENCES NECESSARY TO AUTHENTICATE A DIVINE REVELATION	40
§ 1. External Evidence	40
§ 2. Internal Evidence	48
§ 3. Collateral Evidence	50

CHAPTER II.
GENUINENESS OF THE HOLY SCRIPTURES 51

CHAPTER III.
THE INTEGRITY OF THE SACRED SCRIPTURES 58

CHAPTER IV.
AUTHENTICITY OF THE SACRED SCRIPTURES 64

CHAPTER V.
DIVINE AUTHORITY OF THE SACRED SCRIPTURES: Inspiration 71

CHAPTER VI.
DIVINE AUTHORITY OF THE SACRED SCRIPTURES: Proof from Miracles 83

CHAPTER VII.
DIVINE AUTHORITY OF THE SACRED SCRIPTURES: Proof from Prophecy 90

CHAPTER VIII.
DIVINE AUTHORITY OF THE SACRED SCRIPTURES: Internal Evidence 98

CHAPTER IX.

DIVINE AUTHORITY OF THE SACRED SCRIPTURES: Collateral Evidence........... 109

CHAPTER X.

DIVINE AUTHORITY OF THE SACRED SCRIPTURES: Miscellaneous Objections answered. 114

BOOK II.

DOCTRINES RESPECTING GOD....................................... 124

CHAPTER I.
THE EXISTENCE OF GOD... 124

CHAPTER II.
THE ATTRIBUTES OF GOD.. 139
§ 1. Unity of God... 140
§ 2. Spirituality of God... 142
§ 3. Eternity of God 145
§ 4. Omnipotence of God 146
§ 5. Omnipresence of God... 149
§ 6. Omniscience of God.. 151
§ 7. Immutability of God 156
§ 8. Wisdom of God 159
§ 9. Truth of God.. 162
§ 10. Justice of God 165
§ 11. Holiness of God 167
§ 12. Goodness of God 170

CHAPTER III.
THE TRINITY IN UNITY 178
§ 1. The Importance of the Doctrine 180
§ 2. Scripture Proofs of the Doctrine 182

CHAPTER IV.
DIVINITY OF CHRIST... 187
§ 1. The Pre-existence of Christ.. 187
§ 2. Christ the Jehovah of the Old Testament 190
§ 3. Divine Titles ascribed to Christ.................................... 195
§ 4. Divine Attributes are ascribed to Christ 199
§ 5. Divine Works are ascribed to Christ 201
§ 6. Divine Worship paid to Christ 205

CHAPTER V.
THE SONSHIP OF CHRIST.. 210

CHAPTER VI.
THE PERSON OF CHRIST 221

CHAPTER VII.
PERSONALITY AND DEITY OF THE HOLY GHOST 227

CHAPTER VIII.
THE DECREES OF GOD... 234

CHAPTER IX.
OF CREATION 242
§ 1. Of Creation in General 242
§ 2. Of Creation in Particular 249

CHAPTER X.
OF DIVINE PROVIDENCE... 261

BOOK III.

DOCTRINES RESPECTING MAN.. 275

CHAPTER I.
Man's Primitive State 275

CHAPTER II.
The Fall of Man 281

CHAPTER III.
The Effects of the Fall 290
   § 1. The Nature of that Death which was made the Penalty of Sin 291
   § 2. The Legal Relation which Adam sustained to his Posterity 292
   § 3. The Moral Condition in which Men are actually Born into the World 296

CHAPTER IV.
Man's Moral Agency 308

CHAPTER V.
Man's Moral Agency: Objections 322

PREFACE
TO THE SECOND EDITION

JUST as John Wesley was the founder of the Methodist Church, Richard Watson was the father of Methodist theology. Mr. Watson, with his advanced knowledge and his scholarly ability, wrote the *Theological Institutes*. When this work was published, it provided the Methodist Church with the purest strain of doctrinal and theological truth which could be found in the Protestant religion. However, it was soon discovered that this excellent work was more suited for the mature, theological mind than for the student beginning a course in theology.

Dr. Wakefield was familiar with Watson's theology. He edited Watson's *Institutes* and added some important material of his own. It was Dr. Wakefield's conviction that there should be a systematic theology textbook suitable for the student preparing for the ministry. Therefore, following in the same vein of scriptural, theological truth which Mr. Watson had pursued, Dr. Wakefield prepared a comprehensive systematic theology textbook with a literary style easy to read and understand. This work presents a clear scriptural concept of regeneration and Christian perfection just as it was taught by John Wesley and the early Methodists.

Wakefield's *Theology* is an abridgement of Watson's *Theological Institutes*. The last edition of Dr. Wakefield's *Theology* was published more than one hundred years ago. This second edition will make available to all who are interested a valuable work unexcelled in the field of Christian theology.

—Charles E. McCormick
El Monte, CA 1985

INTRODUCTION.

BEFORE we enter upon the discussion of the various topics which more strictly belong to the Christian system, we will offer a few introductory remarks in regard to theology in general, and the sources from which it is derived.

PART I.

OF THEOLOGY IN GENERAL.

In our remarks upon theology in general, we will notice its *Nature*, its *Objects*, and its *Divisions*.

§ 1. *The Nature of Theology.*

The term theology is derived from θεός, (*theos*,) GOD, and λόγος, (*logos*,) a *discourse;* and literally signifies a *discourse concerning* GOD.

The ancient Greeks used the term according to its most literal signification, and hence, those who wrote the history of the gods, their works and exploits, were called θεολόγοι, or *theologians*. Pherecydes, of Scyros, was the first who was so denominated, and his work was entitled θεολογία, or *Theology*. Homer and Hesiod were theologians in this sense of the word.

In the writings of the Fathers the term is sometimes employed in a restricted sense to denote some particular doctrine concerning God. Accordingly, they speak of the theology of the sacred Trinity, and of the theology of the Son of God; that is, the doctrine of the Trinity, and of the Divinity of Jesus Christ.

But in the twelfth century Peter Abelard employed the term to denote particularly learned or scientific instruction in religion; and this use of the word was preserved by most of the succeeding theologians. In the seventeenth century, however, many of the Protestant divines gave the name of *theology* to any knowledge respecting God and divine things, thus using the word in its etymological sense.

Theology, in its modern acceptation, is that science which treats of the existence, the character, and the attributes of God; his laws and government; the doctrines which we are to believe, the moral change which we must experience, and the duties which we are required to perform. In this sense *theology* and *divinity* are synonymous, both embracing the whole system of revealed religion, and both signifying learned or scientific instruction respecting God. Hence, a *theologian*, or *divine*, is one who is able thoroughly to explain, prove, and defend the doctrines of religion, and to teach them to others.

When we say that theology embraces the whole system of revealed religion, we do not intend to convey the idea that *theology* and *religion* are terms of precisely the same import; for though they should not be employed in opposition to each other, as some modern writers have done, yet they differ materially in regard to their signification. *Religion*, understood *subjectively* and in its most comprehensive sense, includes, 1. A knowledge of God in regard to his nature, his attributes, his relations to men, and his will respecting them; and, 2. Affections and conduct corresponding with this knowledge. The former, which may be denominated the *theory* of religion, is addressed to the human understanding; while the latter, which is the *practical* part, belongs to the will and affections.

These two essential parts of religion are always united in the teachings of Christ and his apostles. "If ye know these things, happy are ye if ye do them." John xiii, 17. "Be ye doers of the word, and not hearers only, deceiving your own selves." James i, 22. Religion, in this sense of the term, comprehends theology, as a system of doctrines, and also practical piety.

Thus far we have considered religion *subjectively*, or in its relation to those who possess it; but it may also be taken *objectively* to designate the whole sum of doctrines respecting God and his will. In this sense religion is nearly equivalent to theology, but with this difference, that the latter is commonly restricted to the knowledge of the true God, while the former is applied to any system of doctrines respecting either the true God, or false gods and their worship. We therefore speak of the religion of the Romans, of the Turks, of the Hindoos, or of the Indians, as well as of the Christian religion. We speak of *false* religions, as well as of that which is *true;* and also of embracing, professing, changing, or renouncing religion, using the term in the same sense.

It follows, therefore, that religion, as distinguished from theology, consists in practical piety, or the performance of all known duties to God and our fellow-men, in obedience to the divine law; and that theology, as distinguished from religion, is a systematic arrangement of *doctrines* respecting God, his will, and his worship.

As theology consists in a systematic arrangement of the general principles and leading doctrines of revealed religion, it is therefore called a *science;* and it is doubtless as worthy of that distinction as any other department of human knowledge. Indeed, it may be properly called the *science of sciences*, because it comprehends in its wide range every other science. It leads us back to the beginning of the world and the origin of man; and it directs our attention to the arts, manners, customs, religion, and history of ancient nations. It calls into its service language, astronomy, geography, and poetry; it explores the fields of natural, intellectual, and moral philosophy; it leads us to investigate the wonderful construction of our own bodies in the science of anatomy and of physiology; and, in a word, it takes in the entire circle of human knowledge, whether it be addressed to the memory, the understanding, or the imagination.

Many of the topics embraced in theology are abstruse, and nearly all of them have been perplexed by controversies which commenced as soon as our religion was promulgated, and have been continued from age to age with all the arguments that ingenuity and learning could supply.

The private Christian, ignorant of the subtle disputes which have arisen concerning almost every article of faith, humbly takes up the Bible as the word of God, and by a short and easy process acquires that measure of religious knowledge which makes him wise unto salvation. But the minister of religion proceeds more slowly, encounters obstacles at every step, and is often compelled to assume the character of a polemic. He must therefore study theology as a science, that he may be able not only to instruct the simple and illiterate, but also to contend with the wise and learned, whether as infidels they oppose revelation in general, or as heretics they impugn any of its doctrines.

From what has been said of theology in general, we must perceive the transcendent dignity and excellence of this science, and consequently the importance of theological study. Whether we turn our attention to the doctrines which theology embraces, or to the moral influence which it is intended to exert upon mankind, we can hardly fail to see that it claims the preference to every other study. To know God as far as he has revealed himself to us is the noblest aim of our understanding; to love him, the purest and holiest exercise of our affections; and to obey his commandments, the most rational, honorable, and delightful employment to which our time and talents can be devoted.

A man may be comparatively ignorant of human science and of the liberal arts, and yet by the sanctifying light of pure religion he may find his way to life eternal; but he who lives without a knowledge of God, though his mind may be stored with every other kind of knowledge, is living like a fool, and shall die without hope.

§ 2. *The Objects of Theology.*

There are three different objects that men may propose to themselves in the study of theology. They may pursue it, first, merely as a branch of liberal education, in order to gratify a laudable curiosity; or, secondly, to qualify themselves for the practical duties of the Christian life; or, thirdly, to fit themselves for the office of the Christian ministry. The first of these objects requires much more than the second; but more is necessary for the accomplishment of the third than for both the others.

So far as it relates to the first of these objects, it may be remarked that theological science, even apart from its utility, is both ornamental and entertaining; and no good reason can be assigned why theology should not be studied like any other science, purely for its own sake as a branch of liberal education. With regard to the second object, a qualification for the practical duties of the Christian life, every Gospel minister is thus far a professor of theology, and every attentive hearer of the Gospel is thus far a theological student. But it is chiefly for the accomplishment of the third and most comprehensive object—a qualification for the sacred office of the Christian ministry—that men pursue a regular course of theological training.

The least of what is required in the Christian pastor is that he be qualified to discharge the various duties of the Christian life, for in this respect he ought to be an example to his flock. Farther, he should labor to acquire a knowledge of whatever is necessary for the edification, the comfort, and the protection from all spiritual danger, of the people that may be committed to his care, or whatever may be of use in defending the cause of God. Again, whatever may enable him to make a proper application of all his acquisitions in knowledge, so as to turn them to the best account for the benefit of his people, is no less requisite.

To little purpose will it be for the minister to possess even the best materials, if he has not acquired the necessary skill to use them to advantage. The former we may call the *theory* of the profession; the latter the *practice*. The first without the second, however considerable, may be compared to wealth without economy. It will not be near so beneficial to the owner, and to those who depend upon him for support, as a more scanty portion would be where economy is understood and practiced. Nor will the second do entirely without the first, for the best economy can be of no real value where there is no subject on which to exercise it.

It follows therefore, that in the proper qualifications of a Christian minister there are two leading departments: the first regards the *science* of theology alone; the second, the *application* of that science to the purposes of the Christian pastor.

§ 3. *Divisions of Theology.*

Theology is divided, according to the sources from which it is derived, into *Natural* and *Revealed;* and it may be arranged under three general epithets, depending upon the distinctive manner in which it is treated, as *Didactic, Polemic,* and *Practical.*

1. *Natural Theology* is that knowledge of God and of divine things which is supposed to be derived from the light of nature, or from the exercise of reason and the suggestions of conscience. It is taught by the advocates of Natural Theology, that man, by a contemplation of the objects around him in the natural world, will be led to infer the existence of a Great First Cause, by whom these objects were created; and to ascribe to this Invisible Being certain attributes and perfections, the signatures of which are seen upon the works of his hands.

From this great first principle of natural religion other doctrines are deduced, such as that God governs the world; that man, in order to possess the favor of God, must practice piety, justice, and benevolence; that the human soul is immortal; and that there is a future state of retribution, in which the righteous shall be rewarded and the wicked punished. These are generally supposed to be the fundamental articles of Natural Theology; and much reason and eloquence have been employed in illustrating them, and in demonstrating their truth, in opposition to the objections of atheists.

By some theologians the division of Theology into *Natural* and *Revealed* is entirely rejected. They maintain that we owe all our knowledge of God, originally, to Divine Revelation; and that therefore, as to its origin, it cannot be *natural.* But though we allow that God revealed himself to men even in the earliest ages of the world, and that much of that revelation has been transmitted, from age to age, until the present time, yet this division is not to be rejected. The light of nature may not be the *primary source* of religious knowledge; but it is obviously an important means by which this knowledge is confirmed, enlarged, and perpetuated. Men are left to examine, in the diligent use of their natural powers, the grounds of revealed truth, to deduce from it its proper consequences, and to build higher upon this solid foundation. They thus obtain additional knowledge by the study and contemplation of nature; and why may not this religious knowledge, thus obtained, be called *Natural Theology?*

2. *Revealed Theology* is that system of divine truth which is contained in the Holy Scriptures. It is called Revealed, or supernatural, because it is derived exclusively from the word of God, and not from the deductions of human reason. It includes all the articles of natural religion; but it comprehends many other important doctrines, which never could have been known, had not God revealed them to the

world. What, for instance, could the light of nature teach with regard to the existence and character of angels, the origin of moral evil, and the redemption of man by Jesus Christ?

3. *Didactic Theology* consists in a plain exposition of the several doctrines of religion, and the adduction of the proofs by which they are sustained. The theologian who pursues his subject *didactically*, must proceed in the same manner as a teacher of any other science. It is his business to give a clear statement of the constituent doctrines of theology, and the conclusions which may be legitimately drawn from them, together with the train of reasoning upon which these conclusions are founded. He should not only state, explain, and prove the several doctrines of religion, but exhibit them also in their proper order and connection. Didactic Theology should therefore be *systematic*. Such a methodically arranged form of the great truths of religion will enable the student to contemplate them in their natural connection, and to perceive both the mutual dependence of the parts, and the symmetry of the whole.

It is granted that the doctrines of religion, as taught in the Bible, are not arranged in this systematic form, but are disclosed gradually, as providence required, and as Divine Wisdom directed. This circumstance, however, forms no objection either to the perfection of the Sacred Scriptures, or to a systematic arrangement of the doctrines which they contain. It forms no objection to the perfection of the Sacred Scriptures; for if we consider attentively the economy of divine grace in relation to the restoration of man, we can hardly fail to see that, in order to the perfecting of the whole plan, it was necessary that the several parts should be revealed by successive degrees, as the scheme advanced toward its completion. If therefore God has revealed, with sufficient clearness, the doctrines to be believed and the duties to be practiced, we have no reason to complain, nor should we dare to prescribe rules to Infinite Wisdom.

On the other hand, it is no ojection to a systematic arrangement of the doctrines of theology, that they are not thus digested in the Bible. God has given us a revelation of his will, that it may be employed for our spiritual instruction, our moral improvement, and our eternal salvation; he has given us a capacity to make a proper use of this revelation; he requires us to employ this capacity so as to turn the spiritual benefits which he has so graciously bestowed upon us to the best account; and we are therefore at liberty, nay, it becomes our duty, in the proper exercise of our reason, to arrange the doctrines of revealed religion into that form which will best assist us in obtaining the benevolent end that God had in view in revealing his will to man.

But while we admit that the doctrines of the Bible are not arranged in a systematic or scientific form, we are not to suppose, on the other hand, that revealed religion is destitute of all order; or that the Bible is an assemblage of writings which have no relation to one another but that of juxtaposition or collocation in the same volume. There is certainly an approach to system in some parts of the Bible, particularly in the writings of St. Paul. It is a consecutive revelation of the counsels of God toward man; and there is order here, as well as in all his other works, though it may require patient investigation to discover it to its full extent. We should therefore study the Scriptures, not to load the memory with a multitude of unconnected ideas, but that we may be able to bring together and systematize the saving truths which they reveal, and thus "understand what the will of the Lord is."

No intelligent man can be a careful and constant reader of the Bible without forming in his own mind a system of doctrines. And he will observe, moreover, that in proportion as this system advances toward completeness, its parts will reflect increasing light upon one another. Are we then to believe that the utility of such a system is either destroyed or diminished by its being communicated to others? Surely not.

Arrangement in any science is a great help both to the judgment and the memory; and the more simple and natural the arrangement is, the greater is the assistance which it affords. Theology, like any other science, may be digested according to different methods, each of which may have advantages peculiar to itself; but that arrangement is best, upon the whole, in which the order of nature is most strictly followed, and in which nothing is previously taught that presupposes a knowledge of what is afterward to be explained.

4. *Polemic Theology* consists in a vindication of the doctrines, precepts, and institutions of religion, against the opinions and attacks of errorists. The term *polemic* is derived from the Greek πολεμικός, (*polemikos*,) and signifies *warlike*. A polemic divine is therefore a warrior, in opposing error and defending truth.

It is acknowledged that this epithet sounds rather harshly when applied to a minister of the Gospel, who ought to be emphatically a messenger of peace; and it may be partly on this account that Polemic Theology has been often held in disrepute. It is loudly demanded by many that the voice of controversy be no more heard in the Church of God—that Christians bury all their religious disputes and differences of opinion in perpetual oblivion, and that they dwell together in brotherly union. This demand is no doubt often made in sincerity; but it always exhibits a great want of discernment. It proceeds upon the supposition that peace is of more value than truth, and that solid and lasting peace may exist without having truth for its foundation, neither of which can be admitted.

We believe, however, that this demand for peace is sometimes intended to conceal a sinister design under the plausible appearance of great liberality—a design to prevent one party from defending its doctrines, that another may propagate its opinions without opposition. Such cries for peace are like the conduct of Joab, when he took Amasa by the beard, saying, "Art thou in health, my brother?" and smote him in the fifth rib. 2 Sam. xx, 9.

There is nothing more evident than that when truth is assailed it ought to be defended. Thus we see that many of our Lord's discourses were intended to correct prevailing errors. St. Paul declares of himself, that he was "set for the *defense* of the Gospel;" and Jude exhorted those to whom he wrote to "*contend* for the faith which was once delivered to the saints." As it would therefore be base pusillanimity to yield, without a struggle, to the enemies of truth, so it would be disgraceful, as well as criminal, in the professed guardians of truth, not to be qualified to sustain the dignity of their office, and to uphold the sacred interests of Christianity. They should be "able, by sound doctrine, both to exhort and to convince the gainsayers." Titus i. 9.

It is not necessary for the theologian to acquire a knowledge of all the controversies that have ever arisen in the Christian Church. Such a task would be both tedious and unprofitable. But it is a matter of the utmost consequence that he be able to maintain the claims of revealed religion against the attacks of infidels, and to defend its fundamental doctrines against all errorists. He should therefore gain a particular acquaintance with the theological disputes and questions of the age and country in which he lives, and with the distinguishing tenets of the different sects with which he is surrounded.

5. *Practical Theology* is that which states and explains our moral and religious duties. In the two preceding departments of theological science the doctrines of religion are illustrated and defended. These doctrines are the foundation of Practical Theology, and supply the only motives that can lead us to the proper performance of the duties which God requires. In Didactic and Polemic Theology, therefore, the way is prepared for this; for Practical Theology is only the improvement which should be made of the doctrines of the Holy Scriptures.

No truth is more clearly sustained by the word of God than that the doctrines of Theology should be turned to a practical purpose. Christ declares: "Not every one that saith unto me, Lord, Lord, shall enter into the kingdom of heaven; but he that doeth the will of my Father which is in heaven." Matt. vii, 21. With this agree the teachings of the inspired apostles. "For the grace of God that bringeth salvation hath appeared to all men, teaching us that, denying ungodliness and worldly lusts, we should live soberly, righteously, and godly in this present world." Titus ii, 11, 12. "And hereby we know that we know him if we keep his commandments." 1 John ii, 3.

The practical intention of Theology appears, moreover, from the nature of revealed religion. If we take a view of the several parts of Christian doctrine, it will appear that they have a direct reference to piety and practice; and that if this point were given up, religion would be of no utility, and the whole subject might at once and forever be dismissed. But the several articles of Theology are such as tend to produce practical piety. This is particularly true in regard to what it teaches concerning God, his Attributes and his Works; as likewise concerning the Person and Offices of our Lord Jesus Christ. The precepts of religion are given for practice, and would not be precepts if they were given only in order that they might be known, but not obeyed. The promises of Scripture always presuppose pious obedience, as they are made to those only who are truly pious; and they would cease to be promises if there were no established connection between obedience and reward.

It may be observed also that the threatenings of God would have no force, if the necessity of obedience were excluded. It becomes the duty, therefore, of every minister of the Gospel to represent religion as a practical system, to show the tendency of its doctrines to promote holiness of heart and life, and to explain as far as possible the nature of that "holiness without which no man shall see the Lord."

Theology is not a subject which belongs exclusively to the curious to investigate, and in which speculative men may spend their leisure hours; it is one which claims universal attention. Its instructions are addressed to all classes of men; to the learned and the illiterate; to the free and the bond; to them who abound in wealth, and to the children of poverty and want; to the retired student, and to the man of business engaged in the stirring scenes of life. To all it speaks with equal authority, and it should be equally interesting to all, as pointing out the only way that leads to life eternal.

But while this subject claims a share of every man's attention, because it has a direct bearing upon every man's welfare, there is an additional reason why those who have devoted themselves to the Christian ministry should make it the subject of their most careful and thorough investigation. Theology is their *profession*, as really as medicine is the profession of the physician, or law that of the barrister. In this profession they should labor to excel; not, indeed, from the same motives that actuate men of other professions—a desire of fame, and the prospect of worldly emolument; but with a view to the faithful and honorable discharge of the sacred duties of their holy calling.

The nature and responsibilities of this sacred office are concisely and forcibly presented, in the charge which God gave to the prophet Ezekiel. "So thou, O son of man, I have set thee a watchman unto the house of Israel; therefore thou shalt hear the word *at my mouth*, and warn them from me. When I say unto the wicked, O wicked man, thou shalt surely die; if thou dost not speak to warn the wicked from his way, that wicked man shall die in his iniquity, but his blood will I require at thine hand. Nevertheless, if thou warn the wicked of his way to turn from it, if he do not turn from his way, he shall die in his iniquity; but thou hast delivered thy soul." Ezekiel xxxiii, 7–9.

PART II.

OF THE SOURCES OF THEOLOGY.

We now proceed to inquire into the sources from which theological knowledge is derived. These are *Reason* and *Divine Revelation*.

§ 1. *Of* Reason, *as a Source of Theology.*

By *Reason* we understand, in general, that faculty of the mind by which we distinguish truth from falsehood, and good from evil; or by which we are enabled to deduce inferences from facts and propositions. But when Reason is spoken of as a source of Theology, it means the rational and moral faculties of man, exercised, without any supernatural assistance, in the investigation of religion.

There are two aspects in which human reason may be regarded; and what is true of it in one, may not be true of it in the other. *First*, it may be taken for that high intellectual ability with which man was originally endowed, and which was as sufficient to direct him in all the various concerns of life, as instinct is to direct the lower animals. We do not say that even then Reason was man's only guide. The sacred history clearly shows that he lived in familiar intercourse with his Maker, and was favored with occasional communications of the Divine will.

But, *secondly*, Reason may signify the rational and moral powers of man in his fallen, sinful, and enfeebled state. It is to Reason, in this sense alone, that our inquiries are now to be directed; and we will try to ascertain, as nearly as we can, its true relation to the acquisition of theological or religious knowledge. Let us notice the *extent* of its discoveries, its real *use*, and its *limitation*.

1. *The* Extent *of its discoveries as a Source of Theology.*

Whether man, by the mere light of nature, can attain all the religious knowledge which is necessary to conduct him to virtue and happiness, is the great question of controversy between infidels and Christians. Of this question the advocates of natural religion take the affirmative, and contend that their theory is supported by what we know of the Divine Perfections. They assert that it would be inconsistent with the justice and the goodness of God to suppose that he would hold men responsible for their moral and religious conduct, if they had not in themselves sufficient means to acquire a knowledge of the Divine will;

that for this very purpose he endowed men with *Reason*, which must therefore be perfectly sufficient to direct them in every part of their duty; and that the notion of any supplementary means is a reflection upon the wisdom of God, as if he had not originally adapted man to his situation, and was therefore compelled to devise a new expedient for correcting the error.

Without examining these assertions one by one, and showing, as might easily be done, that they are mere gratuitous assumptions, it may be enough to observe, that there is not a single fact in the history of mankind by which they can be confirmed. They are fictions of the imagination, and not sober relations of things as they really exist. They are deductions from false premises, and not conclusions drawn from observation and experience.

It is not our business to inquire what *should be*, according to our own ideas of justice and fitness, but what *actually is;* not what Reason was designed to accomplish, but what it has actually accomplished. It is preposterous to give an arbitrary definition of Reason, and then to conclude that it is capable of exerting all the power which has thus been ascribed to it. It would be more consonant to sound philosophy to judge of the power of Reason by its effects. In a word, we must not waste our time and impose upon ourselves by endeavoring to show beforehand what Reason can do; we ought to proceed according to a different and a safer plan, and inquire what it has actually done.

Viewing the subject in this light, we are forced to the conclusion that it is, to say the least, extremely doubtful whether the doctrines embraced in what is called *Natural Religion* are within the reach of unassisted Reason as original discoveries.* That these doctrines, when clearly proposed to the mind, are approved by Reason, no one will deny. But whether men, by mere rational investigation, could arrive at the conclusion that there is a God, the Creator and Governor of the universe, and if they could, whether they would connect with this primary tenet the other articles of the system, are questions yet to be determined. Nor would it be any more an impeachment of the Attributes of God to affirm the incompetency of Reason in matters of religion, than it is to say that an eye which in consequence of disease does not see at all, or sees very imperfectly, is unfit for the purpose which it was originally intended to serve.

We admit that what is popularly called the *light of nature* may be so understood as to justify the opinion that it is sufficient, independent of a direct revelation, to lead men to a knowledge of God and of divine

---

* The phrase *Natural Religion* is often used equivocally. Some understand by it every thing in Religion, by whatever means it may be discovered, which has a real foundation in the nature and relations of things, and which unprejudiced Reason will approve. Others confine it to that system of Religion which they suppose to be discoverable by men, in the sole exercise of their natural faculties, without higher assistance.

things. But in this view of the light of nature three things are to be taken into the account. *First*, mankind generally possess, to a greater or less extent, a traditional knowledge of the existence, the attributes, and the will of God. *Secondly*, there is, to the eye of Reason, an adaptation in *surrounding nature* to confirm and illustrate these traditional discoveries, and to lead men of reflection to a knowledge of its Author. "The heavens declare the glory of God; and the firmament showeth his handy work." Psalm xix, 1. "For the invisible things of him from the creation of the world are clearly seen, being understood by the things that are made, even his eternal power and Godhead; so that they are without excuse." Romans i, 20. *Thirdly*, man possesses an additional source of the knowledge of God in *himself*, in his own *conscience;* which distinctly acquaints him with a Supreme and Invisible Judge of his thoughts and actions. Thus St. Paul represents the Gentiles, who were without the written law, as having "the law written in their hearts, their conscience also bearing witness, and their thoughts the mean while accusing or else excusing one another." Romans ii, 15.

The light of nature, therefore, as thus understood, includes a degree of supernatural instruction traditionally preserved; the deductions of right Reason from creation and providence, and the dictates of our *moral* nature. It is only in this connection that Reason is sufficient to conduct men to a knowledge of God; but even then it leaves them in perplexing doubts in regard to many very important points. It cannot, therefore, afford them *all* the assistance which they need for their religious instruction and moral improvement. But if Reason, even when thus assisted, is insufficient to discover many religious truths of the highest interest to man, *unassisted* Reason, as a source of theological knowledge, must be wholly inadequate.

We are not to conclude, however, from what has been said respecting the insufficiency of Reason, that it is to be entirely discarded from religion. It has important offices to perform in regard to this subject as well as to every other. If we were not rational creatures we would be as incapable of religion as the beasts that perish; and if we did not employ our Reason in the study of religion it would be addressed to us in vain. But as God has endowed us with rational powers, he requires us to exert them in search of truth; and they are never so worthily employed as in endeavoring to acquire just notions of his character, our relations to him, the duties which he has enjoined upon us, and the hopes which he has authorized us to entertain. Let us then consider,

2. *The* USE *of Reason, as an Instrument of Religious Knowledge.*

The *Use* of Reason in matters of religion is to investigate the evidences on which its claims to truthfulness are founded, and fairly and impartially to interpret its teachings. It belongs to Reason, then,

(1.) *To judge of the evidences of religion.* While reason is thus employed it not only collects proofs from observation and experience, in favor of the doctrines of natural theology, but it examines the grounds upon which any new doctrine claims to be a revelation from God. As various systems of religion claim this high origin, it is necessary that their pretensions should be carefully and critically investigated, and to do this is the legitimate work of human reason. There are two ways in which this investigation may be conducted. We may compare the system which demands our assent with our previous conceptions of the Divine character and will, in order to ascertain whether it harmonizes with them, because it is certain that sound Reason and a genuine Revelation cannot contradict each other. Or, we may consider certain circumstances extrinsic to the system itself, by which its claims to a supernatural origin may be determined.

The external circumstances to which we allude are such as these: The character of the publishers of the system, the nature of their testimony, and the works to which they appeal in attestation of their mission; and of all these Reason is competent to judge. The *doctrines* of the system may be so far beyond the range of Reason that it shall be incapable, by an abstract contemplation of them, to determine whether they are true or false; and yet the marks of truth which accompany the system may be so easy of apprehension as to carry conviction even to an ordinary understanding. For, though a man may be unable to comprehend a revealed truth, he may find no difficulty in estimating the force of the evidence by which its truth is established. We do not then retract what we have said respecting the insufficiency of Reason in matters of religion when we make it the judge of its evidences, for in this office it has nothing more difficult to perform than in the common affairs of life. But it is the office of Reason,

(2.) *To interpret a religious system*, or to ascertain what its real doctrines are. Here the same rules are to be applied as in the interpretation of any other record. The terms employed are to be taken in their plain and commonly received sense; figures of speech are to be interpreted with a reference to the local peculiarities of the country in which the writers resided; idioms are to be understood according to the genius of the language that is used; the key to allegorical or mystical discourses must be sought in the book itself, and not in our own fancies; what is obscure must be interpreted by what is plain; and the scope and tenor of a discourse must be regarded, and no conclusion formed on passages detached from their context, unless they are complete in sense, or evidently intended as axioms or apothegms. Notice is also to be taken of the *time* and *place* in which the record was written, the circumstances of the writer, and also of those to whom he wrote.

Reason may be farther employed in the *exhibition* and *statement* of the doctrines of religion. If these are brought together in a disconnected manner, as they evidently are in the Bible, we may use our Reason in collecting, arranging, and uniting them into such a system as shall suit our own convenience or the advantage of others. We may also illustrate the truth, the excellence, and the fitness of the various parts of the system, by analogies drawn from things around us, by the observation of human nature, by historical facts, and in many other ways which call Reason into exercise.

3. *The* LIMITATION *of Reason.* This is found in the *authority of God.* Reason may canvass the evidence, and proceed to settle by the laws of criticism and common sense the genuine import of Revelation; but here it should stop. The wisdom of God must not be tried by human reason. In the former case it acts as a servant, but in the latter it would assume the authority of a master. When, therefore, God has explicitly revealed any doctrine, that doctrine is to be humbly received, whatever degree of rational evidence may be afforded in its support; and no torturing or perverting criticism can be *innocently* employed to bring a doctrine into accordance with our favorite views, any more than to make a precept bend to our vicious inclinations.

§ 2. *Of* DIVINE REVELATION, *as a Source of Theology.*

A *Divine Revelation* is "a discovery of some proposition to the mind which came not in by the usual exercise of its faculties, but by some miraculous divine interposition, either mediate or immediate."*

In our remarks upon Divine Revelation as a source of theology, we will briefly point out its *Possibility,* its *Necessity,* and its *Probable Character.*

I. A REVELATION IS POSSIBLE.

No one who believes that there is a God, and that he is a Being of infinite knowledge, wisdom, and power, can reasonably deny that he can, if he thinks fit, make a revelation of himself and of his will to men in an extraordinary way, different from the discoveries made by men themselves in the ordinary use of their rational faculties; for if God is almighty his power must extend to whatever does not imply a contradiction, which cannot be pretended in this case.

We cannot distinctly explain the origin of our ideas, or the way in which they are excited or impressed upon the mind, but we know that this is done in various ways. And can it be supposed that the Author of our being has it not in his power to communicate ideas to our mind, in order to instruct us in those things which we are deeply concerned to know? Our inability to explain the manner in which this is done is no just objection against it. This has been acknowledged by Lord Bolingbroke, a distinguished antagonist of Revelation. He observes,

* DODDRIDGE'S Lectures, Part 5, Definition 68.

that "an extraordinary action of God upon the human mind, which the word *inspiration* is now used to denote, is not more inconceivable than the ordinary action of mind on body, or body on mind;" and that "it is impertinent to deny the existence of any phenomenon, merely because we cannot account for it."

As God can, if he sees fit, communicate his will to men in the way of extraordinary revelation, so he can do it in such a manner as to assure those to whom it is made that it is, indeed, a Divine Revelation. This is a natural consequence, for to suppose that God can communicate his will to men, and yet that he is not able to give them this assurance, is evidently absurd and contradictory. It is, in effect, to say, that he can reveal his will, but has no way of making men know that he does so, which is most unreasonable. If men can communicate their thoughts by language, so that we may certainly know who it is that addresses us, it would be a strange thing to affirm that God has no way of causing his rational creatures to know when he reveals to them his will that it is He, and no other, who makes the revelation. To deny that a God of infinite perfection has such a power is a glaring contradiction.

II. A REVELATION IS NECESSARY.

This is a sentiment in which all will concur, except those who regard religious truth as a matter of absolute indifference, and those who believe that Reason is sufficient for all the discoveries which are necessary to guide men to virtue and happiness. Infidels profess to adopt the latter principle, but act according to the former; for, in no part of their conduct is there any indication of reverence for religious truth, or of a sincere desire to discover it. They continually betray symptoms of levity and impiety, a contempt for seriousness, a disposition to cavil, to raise objections, to perplex evidence, to involve everything in doubt, and to turn into ridicule the most solemn of all subjects.

But whatever may be the thoughts of men devoted to pleasure, and living without God in the world, every one who feels that he is an accountable being must desire to know by what means he may fulfill the design of his existence, and obtain the happiness of which he is capable. That a Revelation is necessary is evident,

1. *From the weakness and insufficiency of human Reason in the discovery of religious and moral truth.*

It is not from mere theory but from experiment, not from conjecture but from matters of fact, that we can ascertain what Reason can do in the discovery of religious truth. Let us, therefore, turn our attention to some of the doctrines of Natural Religion, which are supposed to be fairly within its province, that we may discover the results of its researches respecting them. We will notice,

(1.) *The existence of God.* This is the fundamental principle of all true religion. That it is demonstrable by Reason, when once the idea is suggested to the mind, we readily allow, for it has been evinced by arguments so strong and conclusive that it is hard to conceive how any one can resist them and continue to be an Atheist. The metaphysician should be overpowered by the profound reasonings of Clarke; and the man of plainer understanding by the more obvious arguments of Ray, Derham, and Paley. It should not be overlooked, however, that this triumphant demonstration of the Divine Existence is found only in the writings of Christians. For, though a similar train of argument was pursued by some of the heathen philosophers, as Cicero and Socrates, yet the illustration was not so ample as it is now made by the discoveries of modern philosophy, nor was the conclusion to which it naturally led drawn with equal clearness and confidence.

The cause of this difference is obvious. To the Gentile the existence of God was a question involved in doubt, an inference to be deduced from premises; and though he could see clearly some steps in the process, he was not always able, with equal distinctness, to perceive the result. But when Christians attempt to discuss this subject they are fully convinced of the fact; and we must perceive, upon the slightest reflection, that it is much more difficult to discover an unknown truth, by a slow process of induction, than to adduce proofs in support of what is already known. The former is like the voyage of Columbus, when he was in search of the new world. He did not know that there was such a country as America, and consequently he had nothing but *probability* to support him amid the difficulties and perils of the enterprise. But the latter is like a voyage to a well-known port, whither the skillful mariner can shape his course by his chart and his compass.

That nature, in all her works, declares the existence of a God, is readily admitted; but the sages of antiquity either disregarded her voice, or failed to interpret her language. Hence, their notions respecting him are so exceedingly imperfect and erroneous, as to afford indubitable proof that the God of NATURAL THEOLOGY will never be any thing more than the *dumb idol* of philosophy, neglected by the philosopher himself, and unknown to the multitude; acknowledged in the closet, but forgotten in the world.

To heathen philosophers, the idea of the distinct subsistence or *personality* of the Deity was in a great measure unknown. They regarded him, not so much an Intelligent Being, as an Animating Power diffused throughout the world. This notion was introduced into their speculative system, to account for the motion of passive matter, which they supposed to be coeval and co-existent with God himself.

In practice they adopted the polytheism of their country, and paid religious honors to an endless train of gods that were acknowledged by the vulgar. There was not a nation upon the earth, except the Jews, in which the living and true God was adored. Every natural object was mistaken for him, every part of the universe was deified, and fancy exerted its creative power in superadding a multitude of *imaginary* beings as objects of worship. Even in Greece, that seat of refinement and philosophy, there were not less than thirty thousand gods. In modern India, where science has long been cultivated, the number is still greater, for her gods are estimated by millions.

From these facts we have a right to conclude that the existence of *One God*, which is the first principle of what is called Natural Religion, is not discoverable by reason, or, at least, that reason cannot discover it with sufficient clearness to produce a permanent and practical conviction of it on the mind. Philosophers sometimes spoke of the Deity as *One*, but there was no certainty or consistency in their opinions. Though the idea occurred to them, obscurity hung upon it, and to the wisest of them he remained "the unknown God."

(2.) *The creation of the world.* We believe that all things were created by the almighty power of God; and though the production of the universe out of nothing is an event of which we can form no conception, yet we consider the Cause as adequate, Omnipotence being able to do whatever does not imply a contradiction. But among those who had only the light of nature to guide them, very different sentiments were entertained. Unassisted reason never arrived at the conclusion that the universe had a beginning. Nor did it assent to this doctrine, even when it was suggested. *Ex nihilo nihil fit*—nothing is made out of nothing—was an undisputed maxim among all the sages of antiquity. In the details of their systems they differed, in many respects, from one another; but they all concurred in rejecting, as absurd, the idea of a proper creation.

Some believed that the universe was eternal, both in matter and form, that the heavens and the earth had always existed, and that the human race had no beginning, and would have no end. Others maintained that the present order of things had a beginning, but they ascribed it to accident, to a fortuitous concourse of atoms, which, dancing up and down in infinite space, united themselves at last in the present regular system of nature.

Among those philosophers who acknowledged a Deity, some, instead of regarding him as the Creator of all things, confounded him with his works. They supposed him to be the soul of the universe, giving life and motion to its various parts, as the soul of man animates his body. Others, though they distinguished him from the universe, did not believe that he created it, but held the opinion that he only reduced it to order from its previous chaotic state. But according to all of them matter was co-eternal with the Diety, and depended upon him only in this, that his power was exerted in moving and arranging it. Their notions, therefore, of the relation of the universe to God must have been very different from those which we entertain. We hold that he created the earth on which we dwell, and the heavens which shed their influences upon us, and that "in him *we* live, and move, and have our being."

(3.) *Divine Providence.* We could hardly expect those who were so much mistaken, or so imperfectly informed, with respect to the character of God as *Creator* of the world, to entertain just ideas of his *government* of it.

It was natural for such philosophers as attributed the present system of the universe to accident, to deny a Providence altogether. Accordingly, the Epicureans represented the gods as indolently reposing in their own region of undisturbed felicity, and beholding with indifference the affairs of mortals. Aristotle taught that God "observes nothing, and cares for nothing beyond himself." The Stoics contended for a Providence, and occasionally said some fine things respecting it. "Of religion toward the gods," says Epictetus, "this is the principal thing: to form right conceptions of them as existing, and administering all things well and justly; to obey them, and acquiesce in all things that happen, and to follow willingly as being under the conduct of the most excellent mind."

But this elevated language loses much of its value when we remember that the Stoics held the doctrine of *fate*, by which all things were controlled, and to which both gods and men were subject. According to them, therefore, the world was not, properly, governed by the gods, for they, as well as their nominal subjects, were bound by the eternal and inviolable chain of causes and effects. Plato, and the followers of Pythagoras, professed to believe that all things happened according to Divine Providence; but this they overthrew by uniting God with *fortune*. "God, fortune, and opportunity," says Plato, "govern all the affairs of men."

In all the ancient heathen nations there were "gods many, and lords many." But wherever polytheism is admitted it is as destructive of the doctrine of Providence as fate, though by a different process. The fatalist supposes all things to be fixed and certain, and thus excludes the true idea of government; the polytheist gives up the government of the world to the will of contrary deities, and thus makes everything uncertain. If he gains the favor of one deity, the wrath of another equally powerful, or even more so, may be provoked; or the gods may quarrel among themselves. Such is the only Providence which can be discovered in the Iliad of Homer and the Æneid of Virgil.

We see, then, that though the idea of a Providence floated in the minds of heathen sages, they were not able to give it a distinct and consistent shape. All that reason could do was to point out the general truth. It failed to illustrate it, and to erect upon this foundation the superstructure of a rational piety.

(4.) *The immortality of the soul, and a future state of retribution.* Though in some form these doctrines were recognized in most pagan systems of religion, yet their evidence was either very defective, or they were mixed up with notions entirely subversive of that moral effect which they were originally intended to produce.

The doctrine of judicial astrology,* which perhaps originated in Chaldea, but was extensively received by the Egyptians, the Greeks, and the Romans, is so nearly allied to fatalism as to subvert the idea of a probationary state *here*, and of a retribution *hereafter*. But the doctrine which has done more than any other to destroy the moral effect of a belief in man's immortality is, that "God is the soul of the world," from which all human spirits come, and to which they will all return; some immediately at death, and others through a course of transmigration. The Scriptures teach that the human soul is from God by creation. The refinement of pagan philosophy is, that it is from him by a separation of essence, and that it still remains a separate portion of God, seeking its return to him. Revelation shows that at death the souls of the just return to God, not to lose their individuality, but to be united to him in holy and delightful communion. The philosophic perversion is, that the parts so separated from God, and for a time connected with matter, will be reunited to the great Source by *refusion*, as a drop of water to the ocean.

When, therefore, the ancients attributed a proper eternity to the human soul, we must not suppose that they understood it to be eternal in its distinct and peculiar existence, but that it was discerpted from the substance of God in *time*, and would in *time* be rejoined to it again. They only differed about the time of this reunion or resolution, the greater number holding it to be at death; but the Pythagoreans not till after many transmigrations. Those of the Platonic school went between these two opinions, supposing that *pure* souls are joined to the Universal Spirit at death, while those which have contracted much defilement pass through a succession of bodies before they return to their parent substance. This theory is not only incompatible with the doctrine of future rewards and punishments, but it turns the immortality of man, so far as his distinct consciousness and personality are concerned, into absolute annihilation.

Another notion equally at war with the soul's immortality, and with a state of future retribution, was that of a periodical destruction and renovation of all things. This sprung up in the Egyptian schools, and was thence transmitted into Greece and India, and throughout all Asia. This theory is, according to Diodorus Siculus, "that the universe under-

---

* *Judicial astrology* is a science which is based upon the supposition that the heavenly bodies have a ruling influence over the physical and moral world, and which teaches men to judge of the influences of the stars, and to foretell future events by their situation and different aspects.

goes a periodical conflagration, after which all things are to be restored to their primitive form, to pass again through a similar succession of changes."

As the Stoics held that all inferior divinities, and all human souls, were portions separated from the soul of the world, and would return into the first celestial fire, so they supposed that at the same time the whole visible world would be consumed in one general conflagration. "Then," says Seneca, "after an interval the world will be entirely renewed, every animal will be reproduced, and a race of men, free from guilt, will repeople the earth. Degeneracy and corruption are, however, to creep in again, and the same process is to go on forever." This is evidently a corruption of the primitive doctrine of the destruction of the world, and the consequent termination of man's probationary state, preparatory to the general judgment; but it is one which effectually destroys the *moral influence* of that awful and most salutary revelation.

The doctrine of Aristotle and the Peripatetics gives no countenance to the opinion of the soul's immortality, or even of its existence after death. Democritus and his followers taught that the soul is material and mortal; Heraclitus, that when the soul is purified from soft vapors it returns into the soul of the universe, if not it perishes; and Epicurus and his followers, that "*when death is we are not.*" Pliny declares that "the soul and body have no more sense after death than before we were born; and Seneca, "that the day which he fears as his last is the birthday of eternity." The poets, it is true, spoke of the joys of Elysium, and the tortures of Tartarus; but both philosophers and poets regarded them as vulgar fables, as Virgil clearly shows. Thus the light of nature was too feeble to dispel the darkness that rested on all beyond the grave.

(5.) *The systems of heathen morality.* Here, it must be acknowledged, reason has had a degree of success. There are admirable treatises upon morality, which were composed by heathen philosophers, and which we may read both with pleasure and profit; but he who expects to find in any of them a perfect system of morality will be greatly disappointed.

It has indeed been affirmed by Lactantius that everything delivered in the Scriptures on the subject of morals is contained in the writings of one or another of the philosophers; but Lactantius, though a fine reasoner and an elegant writer, is not entitled to much deference in matters of theology, of which he has shown himself to be an incompetent judge. What he has affirmed is not true, for in the moral systems of the philosophers some duties of great importance are omitted, and some things which they call virtues, when brought to the Christian standard, are found to be vices.

Cicero declares that "virtue proposes *glory* as its end, and looks for no other reward;" and Zeno, that "all crimes are equal, and that a person who has offended or injured us should never be forgiven." The

Cynics held "that there was nothing shameful in committing acts of lewdness in public." Aristippus affirmed "that as pleasure was the *summum bonum*, a man might practice theft, sacrilege, or adultery, as he had opportunity." With regard to veracity, the rule of Menander was that "a lie is better than a hurtful truth." Plato said, "He may lie, who knows how to do it *in a fit season;*" and Maximus Tyrius, that "there is nothing decorous in truth, but when it is profitable." Humility, which is a Christian virtue of the first order, was despised by heathen philosophers as an indication of a mean and dastardly spirit; and the direct tendency of their moral lessons was to inspire men with notions of personal dignity, a feeling of self-approbation, a consciousness of worth, which, of all tempers, is most offensive to God.

We see, then, that the systems of heathen morality were exceedingly defective; but, in addition to this, they were entirely destitute of *any authority* that could give them force. Their authors claimed no commission from God; they performed no miracles for the confirmation of what they taught; their doctrines were incapable of a mathematical demonstration, and consequently they could only be regarded as mere human opinions, which every one might receive or reject, as his judgment, his interest, or his passions might dictate. Such systems of morality had therefore no power over the conscience; and the motives to virtue which they contained were insufficient to counteract men's innate propensity to evil, or to overcome the strong temptations to which they were continually exposed. Hence, a general depravity of manners prevailed among the ancient Gentile nations, a depravity which was not confined to the lower and uneducated classes of society, but which extended to the higher and better informed, and even to the very men who professed to be teachers of wisdom.

It would be a great mistake to suppose that the heathen philosophers spent their days in the study and practice of virtue. There is abundant proof that they were, in general, a class of unprincipled declaimers, whose infamous conduct daily contradicted their eloquent harangues. It was in view of this fact that Cicero inquired: "Who is there of all the philosophers whose mind, life, and manners were conformable to right reason? Who ever made his philosophy the law and rule of his life, and not a mere show of his wit and parts? Who observed his own instructions, and lived in obedience to his own precepts?"

This induction of facts must prove to every one that the principles of natural theology are beyond the reach of unassisted reason. It is therefore in vain for any man to contend for its sufficiency till he can point out an instance in which it has discovered and established, by satisfactory arguments, the great truths of natural religion.

But here we may observe, that little as reason has done in the discovery of religious truth, we have no evidence that it could have done even so much had it been left to work out its own discoveries alone.

Indeed, its solitary strength has never been fairly tried, for man has never been entirely destitute of a Revelation. Though this was in a great measure lost among the nations of the world, yet some fragments of it remained, from which the philosophers of antiquity made up their various systems of religion. From this source they derived the idea of a God, and their notions of Providence, of morality, and of a future state. Thus tradition was supplementary to reason; and though its light was faint, yet it led to the knowledge of some truths which the eye of reason, amid the surrounding darkness, could not have discovered.

Another remark to which this investigation leads us is, that those who contend for the sufficiency of reason in matters of morals and religion, owe all their best views to that fountain of inspiration from which they criminally turn away. How otherwise can it be accounted for, that the very principles which modern philosophers regard as demonstrable by unassisted reason were held doubtfully, or connected with some manifest absurdity, or utterly denied by the wisest moral teachers among the ancient Gentiles? They had the same works of God, and the same course of Providence to direct them; and to neither were they inattentive. They had intellectual endowments which have been admired in all subsequent ages; and their reason was rendered acute and discriminative by the discipline of mathematical and dialectic science. They had everything which the moderns have, *except the* BIBLE; and yet, on points which have been generally settled among modern philosophers as fundamental to natural religion, they had no just views, and no settled conviction.

The strongest advocates of natural religion must admit that of the ancient philosophers, some argued themselves into a belief of Atheism; some, by ascribing all things to chance, and others to absolute fatality, subverted all true notions of religion. Some patronized particular vices, while others professed open immorality. Even the better sort of them, who reasoned most correctly concerning the Providence of God, the immortality of the soul, and a future state of retribution, discoursed on all these subjects with much uncertainty and doubtfulness.

Were we even to allow that those just views of God and religion which sometimes appear in the writings of heathen philosophers are to be ascribed to the power of human reason, the argument for its sufficiency would not be greatly strengthened. It would only show that the reason which occasionally reached the truth had not power to hold it fast; that the pinion which sometimes bore the mind into fields of light could not maintain it in its elevation. But facts will not allow us to admit that the truth which they occasionally advanced was the discovery of their own powers. They were evidently indebted to a traditional knowledge much earlier than their own day, and they obtained additional light from the descendants of Abraham, whose sacred books contain noble and just views of God, and a correct morality.

We have now seen how defective Reason is in its application to natural theology; but if we apply it to the peculiar doctrines of Revelation, we shall soon find that here it cannot make a single discovery. It is like the eye, which, though it perceives objects within a given limit, cannot discern, unless aided by art, those parts of creation which lie in the profound abyss of space. To Reason, the line which is drawn between natural and revealed theology is impassable. On the one side of it are some gleams of light; but on the other all is impenetrable darkness.

Revealed theology is founded on that mysterious distinction in the Divine Essence which we call the *Trinity;* a distinction which Reason could never have discovered, and which only God himself could disclose. It also unfolds the wise and benevolent counsels of God respecting our *fallen race,* of which no trace can be looked for in creation, as they relate to a state of things posterior to creation, and differing from that state in which man was originally placed.

It is true some Christian writers have asserted that in the *works* of God there is an obscure revelation of *grace;* and the celebrated infidel, Lord Herbert, has laid it down as one of his five articles of natural religion, that "if men repent of their sins God will forgive them." But nature teaches no such doctrine, for there is nothing in Creation, or even in the dispensations of Divine Providence, which indicates an intention on the part of God to pardon his disobedient creatures. And farther, the principle which is assumed by Lord Herbert, as the dictate of nature, is false, for God does not pardon sinners on mere repentance. He requires an *atonement,* but of this nature gives no indication.

We conclude, then, from all which we have seen, that a Revelation was necessary, if even it had gone no farther than to shed light upon the doctrines of natural religion, and to dissipate the doubts which reason could not solve. These doctrines, which were more or less interesting to all, were especially so to men of reflection; but the success of their inquiries was by no means commensurate with the earnestness of their wishes. To men in these circumstances a Revelation must be as acceptable as is the rising of the sun to the bewildered traveler, who is anxiously seeking the place of his destination, but cannot find it amid the darkness of the night.

This necessity of a Revelation would exist to a very considerable extent, even if reason in some cases were capable of discovering all the religious knowledge that is necessary. The strongest believers in the sufficiency of reason will admit that we cannot gain a knowledge of the principles of natural theology from the investigation of nature itself without close and persevering study; but every one must see that this would place the acquisition beyond the reach of a majority of mankind. There are many whose intellectual faculties are naturally weak, whose minds have not been improved by education, and whose daily occupations afford them but little leisure for inquiry and reflection. Such persons are apt to be misled by false opinions, and distracted by worldly cares, and to neglect those objects which require abstraction of mind and patient investigation. The infidel himself is compelled to acknowledge that Reason has generally failed to lead men to a rational system of religion.

It is manifest, therefore, that a Revelation which should point out at once, and to all, the doctrines which reason could discover only by a tedious process, would be a most invaluable gift to the world. On this subject no doubt can be entertained. Such a Revelation has been granted, and what is the consequence? The doctrines of natural religion are better understood than they could otherwise be: they are known not only to men of contemplative minds, but to the illiterate, and we become acquainted with them in the morning of life. There are thousands of young persons in every Christian country whose religious knowledge far exceeds that of the wisest heathen philosopher. They have learned more by a few lessons of revealed truth than he could acquire by the painful researches of a long life.

The necessity of a Divine Revelation may be farther argued,

2. *From the concessions of heathen philosophers.*

There are many passages in the writings of the heathens which show, that while they were conscious of their ignorance on religious subjects, they were persuaded that there was no remedy for it, except in some Divine interposition. "The various apprehensions of wise men," says Cicero, "will justify the doubtings and demurs of skeptics, and it will then be sufficient to blame them when others agree, or any one has found out the truth. We say not that nothing is true, but that some false things are annexed to all that is true, and that with so much likeness, that there is no certain note of judging what is true, or assenting to it. We deny not that something may be true; but we deny that it can be perceived so to be, for what have we certain concerning good and evil? Nor for this are WE to blame, but NATURE, which has hidden the truth in the deep."*

"The truth is," says Plato, speaking of future rewards and punishments, "to determine or establish anything certain about these matters, in the midst of so many doubts and disputations, is the work of God only." Again, one of the speakers in his Phædo says to Socrates concerning the immortality of the soul: "I am of the same opinion with you, that in this life it is either absolutely impossible, or extremely difficult, to arrive at a clear knowledge in this matter." In his apology for Socrates, he puts these words into his mouth: "You may pass the remainder of your days in sleep, or despair of finding out a sufficient expedient for this purpose, if God, in his providence, do not send you some other instruction."

But there is a most remarkable passage in Plato's dialogue between

* See *De Nat. Deorum*, l. 1, n. 10, 11. *Acad. Qu.*, l. 2, n. 66, 120.

Part II, § 2.] SOURCES OF THEOLOGY: REVELATION.

Socrates and Alcibiades, on the duties of religious worship. The design of the dialogue is to convince Alcibiades that men, on account of their great ignorance, should be exceedingly cautious in their addresses to the gods, and should content themselves with very general prayers, or, what is better, not pray at all. "To me," says he, "it seems best to be quiet; it is necessary to wait till you learn how you ought to behave toward the gods and toward men." "When," exclaims Alcibiades, "when, O Socrates! shall that time be, and who will instruct me? for most willingly would I see this man, who he is." "He is one," replies Socrates, "who cares for you; but, as Homer represents Minerva as taking away darkness from the eyes of Diomedes, that he might distinguish a god from a man, so it is necessary that he should first take away the darkness from your mind, and then bring near those things by which you shall know good and evil." "Let him take away, if he will," rejoins Alcibiades, "the darkness or any other thing, for I am prepared to decline none of those things which are commanded by him, whoever this man is, if I shall be made better."*

This passage is truly curious, and deserves our particular attention as a proof of the longings of the ancient sages for such a Revelation as God has given to the world. The wisest philosopher of antiquity acknowledged its necessity, and ventured to anticipate it, without, however, knowing what he said. His disciple was transported at the thought, and declared his readiness to submit to the lessons of his desired teacher. It is only among unbelievers of modern times—the "men of reason," as they would be accounted—that the idea of a Divine Revelation is held up to ridicule, and the sufficiency of Reason maintained.

But we have a most conclusive proof of the necessity of a Revelation from God,

3. *In the debasing and demoralizing tendency of all pagan religions.*

It cannot be denied that the very systems of religion and established forms of worship among heathens, instead of being calculated to preserve men in the practice of morality and virtue, only served to plunge them into vice and degrading superstition. They paid divine worship to oxen, to crocodiles, to birds, and to reptiles. They metamorphosed beasts into gods, and conversely transformed their gods into beasts, ascribing to them drunkenness, unnatural lusts, and the most loathsome vices. They worshiped *drunkenness,* under the name of Bacchus; and *lasciviousness,* under that of Venus. Momus was to them the god of *calumny,* and Mercury the god of *thieves.* Even Jupiter, the greatest of their gods, they considered to be an *adulterer.* At length the worship of avowedly evil beings became prevalent among them; and hence, many of their rites were cruel and contrary to humanity, and the licentiousness and impurity of their whole religious system became notorious.

* Platonis Alcibiad., II.

Thus, to select a few instances out of many, the rites of the goddess Cybele were no less infamous for lewdness than for cruelty; and the practice of these rites spread far and wide, and formed part of the public worship at Rome. The *aphrodisia*, or festivals in honor of Venus, were observed with lascivious ceremonies in many parts of Greece; and Strabo tells us that there was a temple at Corinth so rich that it maintained more than a thousand harlots, sacred to her service. The feasts of Bacchus were equally impure and licentious; and according to Herodotus, many of the Egyptian rites were cruel and shockingly obscene. The *floralia* among the Romans, or their festivals in honor of Flora, the goddess of flowers, were celebrated for four days together by the most shameful actions, and with the most unbounded licentiousness.

The horrible practice of offering human sacrifices was for many ages very general in the heathen world. It obtained among the Phœnicians, Syrians, Arabians, Carthaginians, and other people of Africa; and among the Egyptians, till the time of Amasis. The same is asserted concerning the Thracians, the ancient Scythians, the Gauls, the Germans, and the Britons. And though this rite was not so common among the Greeks and Romans, as among some other nations, yet they practiced it for a long time on extraordinary occasions, as being the most meritorious sacrifice that could be offered to the gods.*

Indeed, when we examine the history of the ancient pagan world, we are struck with the accuracy of the description which is given of them by St. Paul in the first chapter of his Epistle to the Romans. He asserts that they "changed the glory of the uncorruptible God into an image made like to corruptible man, and to birds, and four-footed beasts, and creeping things." And as they were not willing to retain the knowledge of God, they were judicially given up to uncleanness and a reprobate mind. Hence the apostle tells us that they were "filled with all unrighteousness, fornication, wickedness, covetousness, maliciousness;" that they were "full of envy, murder, debate, deceit, malignity;" and that they were "whisperers, backbiters, haters of God, despiteful, proud, boasters, inventors of evil things, disobedient to parents, without understanding, covenant breakers, without natural affection, implacable, unmerciful."

If we direct our attention to heathen nations of the present age, such as Tartary, the Philippine Islands, and many parts of Africa, China, and Hindoostan, we learn, from the unanimous testimony of navigators and travelers, that they are enveloped in the grossest ignorance and idolatry, and that their religious worship, doctrines, and practices are equally corrupt with those of the pagan nations of antiquity.

With regard to Hindoostan in particular, though her inhabitants are

---

* See Leland's Necess. and Advan. of Revelation; Clarke's Evid. of Nat. and Rev. Religion; Gregory's Letters on Christian Religion; Horne's Introduction, vol. i; and Hartley on Man, vol. ii.

celebrated for their progress in the useful arts, and for intellectual acuteness, yet her polytheism is of the grossest and most debasing kind. There are not fewer than *three hundred and thirty millions of deities* claiming the adoration of their votaries! Her religion enjoins rites the most impure, penances the most toilsome, and modes of self-torture almost innumerable, and as exquisite in degree as human nature can sustain. The burying alive or burning of widows, infanticide, the immersion of the sick and dying in the Ganges, and self-devotement to destruction by the idol Juggernaut, are among the horrid practices which flow from her established system of idolatry, and which have never been exceeded in folly and ferocity by any to which Paganism has given birth.*

Let our argument then, be summed up.

We have seen that the light of human reason was too weak to conduct heathen philosophers to just conclusions, either with respect to the fundamental doctrines of *natural religion*, or to the principles of *a pure morality;* that the heathen sages themselves felt and acknowledged the insufficiency of reason in matters of religion, and strongly desired some direct communication from the gods; and that the religions of all Pagan nations, both ancient and modern, instead of elevating men and purifying their moral nature, have exerted upon them a most corrupting and demoralizing influence.

These are the facts, and they affect not only a small portion of mankind, but all who have not had the benefits of the Holy Scriptures. Where the Bible is unknown there is not, and never has been, since the corruption of the primitive religion, a religious system containing just views of God and of religious truth, or which has enjoined a correct morality, or even opposed any effectual barrier against the deterioration of public manners.

These facts cannot be denied, and the conclusion is therefore irresistible, that an express Revelation of the will of God, accompanied by efficient corrective institutions, had become necessary, and is still demanded by the religious and moral condition of every part of the earth into which Christianity has not been introduced.

Having then shown the possibility and the necessity of a Divine Revelation, we will proceed to consider,

III. ITS PROBABLE CHARACTER.

If there is ground to presume that God, in his compassion for his creatures, would not leave them without a direct and clear communication of his will, there is equal ground to presume that this communication, whenever made, should be of such a nature, and accompanied by such circumstances, as would most effectually meet the wants of the world.

Presumptions as to the nature and manner of such a Revelation, we

---

* Asiatic Researches, vol. viii.

will allow, ought to be guarded; but, without violating this rule, it may, from the obviousness of the case, be presumed, 1. That it should contain explicit information on those subjects which are of most importance to mankind, and in regard to which they have most fatally erred. 2. That it should accord with the principles of former revelations, should any have been given. 3. That it should have a satisfactory external authentication. And, 4. That it should contain provisions for its effectual promulgation among all classes of men. All this, allowing the necessity and the probability of a Divine Revelation, must certainly be expected; but this expectation is fully met in the Christian System.

1. It gives explicit information in regard to *the nature and perfections of* GOD; *his* WILL, *as the rule of moral actions; the means of obtaining* PARDON *and of conquering vice; the true* MEDIATOR *between God and man; Divine* PROVIDENCE; *the* CHIEF GOOD *of man*, respecting which alone more than three hundred different opinions among the ancient sages have been reckoned up; *the accountability and* IMMORTALITY *of man; and a* FUTURE STATE *of retribution*.

2. It accords with the principles of former Revelations. The veracity of God requires, that so far as one Revelation renews, explains, or adds to another, it must agree with the previous communication.

Now whatever direct proof may be adduced in favor of the Divine authority of the Jewish and the Christian Revelations, there is this in their favor: that they have a substantial agreement and harmony among themselves, and with that traditional system which existed in the earliest ages of the world. As to the patriarchal religion, to which reference has several times been made, we have ample information in the book of Job, from which venerable relic a copious body of doctrinal and practical theology might be collected.*

It recognizes in the clearest manner the Being and Attributes of God; the corrupt and helpless condition of man; the offering of propitiatory sacrifices, as of Divine appointment; the expectation of a Divine Redeemer; the immortality of the soul; the resurrection of the body; and a future judgment. It condemns immoral actions and vicious passions, as violations of the laws of God; and speaks of purity of heart, kindness, compassion to the poor, and cheerful submission to the will of God, as virtues of the highest obligation.

Such was the comprehensive system of patriarchal theology; and it would be easy to show that these great principles are all recognized and taken up in the successive Revelations by Moses, and by Christ. Here then are three religious systems, introduced at widely distant periods, and by agents greatly differing in their condition and circumstances,

* There is sufficient evidence that Job lived between the flood of Noah and the calling of Abraham; and that the book which bears his name was written not later than the time of Moses.

but they exactly harmonize in every leading doctrine, and agree in their great moral end—PERFECT PURITY OF HEART AND CONDUCT.

3. It was accompanied by an *external authentication*, of such a nature as to leave no reasonable doubt of its Divine authority.

The reason of this is obvious. A mere impression of truth on the understanding could not be distinguished from a discovery made by the human intellect, and could therefore have no authority as a Revelation from God, either with the person receiving it, or with others to whom he might promulge it. Hence an authentication of revealed truth, *external* to the Revelation itself, is necessary to give it authority, and to create the obligation of obedience.

The authority of the ancient patriarchal religion rested on external evidence. The received opinion was, that the Almighty Lawgiver, under celestial appearances, conversed with our first parents, and with the patriarchs; and that his laws thus delivered were authenticated by his kindness to the obedient and his judgments upon the rebellious. It was in consequence of the deep impress of Divinity which this system received in the earliest ages, from the attestation of singular judgments, and especially the flood, that it was universally transmitted, and waged so long a war against religious corruptions.

But the primitive system, being traditional, was liable to alteration and abuse. Hence, notwithstanding its original authentication as a matter of Divine Revelation, and the effects which it produced in the world for many ages, it was at length so much corrupted by transmission, and its external evidence so greatly weakened by the lapse of time, that some merciful interposition on the part of God was rendered necessary by the general ignorance of mankind. Indeed, the primitive Revelations supposed subsequent ones, and were not, in themselves, regarded as complete.

But if only a republication of the primitive truth had been necessary, it would have required a new authentication, in a form adapted to the circumstances of the world, and the same would be true of every enlarged or additional Revelation. If we presume, therefore, that a new Revelation was necessary, we must presume that, when given, it would have an external authentication as coming from God, from which there could be no reasonable appeal; and we therefore conclude, that as the Mosaic and the Christian Revelations profess both to republish and to enlarge former Revelations, the circumstance of their resting their claims on the external evidence of miracles and prophecy is a presumption in their favor.

4. It contains provisions for its effectual promulgation among all classes of men.

As the Revelation in question was designed to restore and enlarge the communications of truth, and as tradition had become an imperfect medium of conveying it, the fair presumption is, that the persons th ough whom the communication was made should record it in WRITING, as being the most natural and effectual means of preserving it. Any corruption of the record would be rendered impracticable, by its being publicly taught in the first instance; by a standard copy being preserved with care; or by such a number of copies being dispersed as to defy material alteration. This presumption is realized both in the Jewish and the Christian Revelations, as will be seen when the authority of the Holy Scriptures comes to be discussed. They were first publicly taught, then committed to writing, and copies were multiplied.

Another method of preserving and diffusing the knowledge of a Revelation once made would be the institution of public commemorative rites. These also we find in the Revelations of Moses and of Christ, at once preserving the memory both of great events themselves, and of the doctrines connected with them.

If it was reasonable to expect a Revelation, it was equally reasonable to presume that it should contain some injunctions favorable to its propagation among men of *all ranks*. For, as the compassion of God to the moral necessities of his creatures, generally, is the ground on which so great a favor rests, it is not to be restricted to any one class of men, but to be extended to all.

This reasonable expectation is also realized in the Mosaic and the Christian Revelations. Both provide for their general publication; both instituted an order of men, not to conceal, but to *read* and *teach*, the truth committed to them; both recognized a right in the people to search the record, and by it to judge of the ministrations of the priests; both made it obligatory on the people to be taught; and both separated one day in seven to afford leisure for that purpose.

Nothing but such a Revelation, and with such accompanying circumstances, appears capable of reaching the actual case of mankind, and of effectually instructing and bringing them under moral control; and, whether the Bible can be proved to be of Divine authority or not, this at least must be granted: that it presents itself to us under these circumstances, and claims, for this very reason, our most serious and candid attention.

CHRISTIAN THEOLOGY.

BOOK I.

EVIDENCES OF A DIVINE REVELATION.

WE now proceed to inquire whether we have sufficient reason to conclude that the Scriptures of the Old and the New Testament are a Revelation from God. This is a question of the greatest importance; for it is universally acknowledged among us that the Bible is the only book in the world whose claims to Divine authority are worthy of serious examination. If, therefore, the advantage of supernatural and infallible instruction has been afforded to man, it must be found in that alone.

Every humble and sincere man who is conscious of his own infirmity, and who knows the perplexities in which the wisest of men have been involved on religious and moral subjects, will desire to find at length an infallible guide, and will therefore examine the evidences of the Bible with an anxious wish that he may find sufficient reason to acknowledge its Divine authority. And should he be disappointed he will feel that he has met with a painful misfortune, and not a matter of triumph. This temper of mind is perfectly consistent with a full and even severe examination of the claims of Scripture, and he who is destitute of it is neither a *sincere* nor an *earnest* inquirer after truth.

That the Bible is in favor of the highest virtues, cannot be denied. It both prescribes them, and affords the strongest possible motives to their cultivation. It might be confidently put to every candid person, however skeptical, whether the universal observance of the morality of the Scriptures, by all ranks and classes of men, would not produce the most beneficial changes in society, and secure general peace, friendship, and happiness. If, therefore, he who investigates the Divine authority of the Holy Scriptures has had the means of even a superficial acquaintance with their contents, he ought, if a lover of *virtue* as well as of *truth*, to be predisposed in their favor.

In the investigation of the truth of revealed religion we will direct our attention, 1. To the *evidences* which are necessary to authenticate a Divine Revelation; 2. To the *genuineness* of the Holy Scriptures; 3. To their *authenticity;* 4. To their *integrity;* and, 5. To their *Divine authority.*

CHAPTER I.

EVIDENCES NECESSARY TO AUTHENTICATE A DIVINE REVELATION.

The Evidences in proof of the Divine authority of the Sacred Scriptures may be divided into EXTERNAL, INTERNAL, and COLLATERAL. The *External Evidence* consists of miracles and prophecy; the *Internal Evidence* is drawn from the nature and moral tendency of the doctrines taught; and the *Collateral Evidence* arises from a variety of circumstances, which indirectly prove the Revelation to be divinely inspired.

§ 1. *Of External Evidence.*

The principal and most appropriate evidence of a Revelation from God must be *external* to the Revelation itself. If, therefore, any person should profess to have received a Revelation from God to teach to mankind, and that he was directed to command their obedience to it on pain of the Divine displeasure, he would be asked for some *external* authentication of his mission. He might believe that a Divine communication had been made to himself; but *his* belief would have no authority to command *ours*. Nor could we have any means, without *external proof*, of knowing that he had received such communication. *Internal evidence alone* could not be a sufficient proof; for we could not tell whether his doctrines, however excellent, might not be the fruits of his own mental labor. To us, therefore, they could only have the authority of mere human opinions; and though their reasonableness and excellence might entitle him to attention and respect, without some *external* authentication he could not *command*.

Agreeable to this, the authors both of the Jewish and Christian Scriptures profess to have authenticated their mission by the two great external proofs, MIRACLES and PROPHECY; and it remains to be considered whether a mission to teach the will of God to man is sufficiently authenticated when *miracles* are really performed, and *prophecies* unequivocally accomplished.

I. MIRACLES.—In looking at these, as an external and authenticating proof of Divine Revelation, we may consider,

1. *Their Nature.*—In a *philosophic* sense, a miracle is an event which is inconsistent with some known law of nature, or contrary to the settled constitution and course of things. Accordingly, miracles presuppose an established system of nature, within the limits of which they operate, and with the order of which they disagree.

In a *theological* sense, a miracle is an event contrary to the established constitution and course of things, effected by the interposition of God for the proof of some particular doctrine, or in attestation of the authority of some particular person.*

The miracles recorded in the Holy Scriptures agree with the theological meaning of the term. They were wrought immediately by God himself, to attest the Divine mission of particular persons, and to authenticate their doctrines; or by some superior creatures, commissioned by him for the same purpose; or by men, in order to prove that they were invested with Divine authority.

In order to distinguish a real miracle, it is necessary that we should understand the common course of nature, for, without some knowledge of the operations of physical causes, we might deem an event miraculous merely because it is strange and inexplicable. Should an earthquake happen in a country where men had never heard of such a calamity, by the ignorant it might be considered miraculous; whereas, it is a regular effect of the established laws of nature.

But as we have at best only a partial knowledge of these laws, it seems necessary that such miracles as are intended to authenticate a Divine Revelation should be effected upon objects whose properties are well understood, and that they should be evidently contrary to some known laws by which such objects have been uniformly governed; or, that their apparent cause should be known to have no adequate power or adaptation to produce them. When these circumstances concur in any event, there is sufficient ground to conclude that it is miraculous.

Assuming, then, for the present, that the works ascribed to Moses and to Christ were actually performed by them, they are of such a nature as to leave no reasonable doubt of their miraculous character. The rod cast from the hand of Moses became a serpent. Here the subject was well known; it was a *rod;* and it was obviously contrary to the established course of nature that it should undergo so signal a transformation.

---

* Farmer, in his "Dissertation on Miracles," denies to created beings, however high, the power of working miracles when acting from themselves alone. If they perform miracles at all they must do it by a Divine commission, and by the interposition of Divine power. Dr. Taylor, of New Haven, takes the same ground.

The sea is parted at the stretching out of the rod of Moses, and the waters stand upon each side, leaving a passage for the host of Israel. But there is here no adaptation in the apparent cause to produce the effect, which was obviously in direct opposition to the known qualities of water.

It is in the nature of clouds to be carried about by the wind; but the cloud which attended the Israelites in the wilderness rested on their tabernacle, moved when they were commanded to march, and directed their course. It rested when they were to pitch their tents; and by night, when it is the nature of clouds to become dark, it shone with the brightness of fire. In all these cases, therefore, if the facts can be established, there can be no doubt as to their miraculous character.

"Were a physician instantly to give sight to a blind man, by anointing his eyes with a chemical preparation, to the nature and qualities of which we were absolute strangers, the cure would be to us wonderful; but we could not pronounce it miraculous, because it might be the physical effect of the unguent upon the eyes. But were he to give sight to his patient merely by commanding him to receive it, or by anointing his eyes with spittle, we should, with the utmost confidence, pronounce the cure to be a miracle, because we know that neither the human voice nor human spittle has any such power over the diseases of the eye."

"Persons apparently dead are often restored to their families and friends by being treated, during suspended animation, in the manner recommended by the *Humane Society*. To the vulgar, and even sometimes to men of science, these resuscitations appear very *wonderful;* but as they are known to be effected by physical agency, they cannot be miraculous. On the other hand, no one could doubt of his having witnessed a real miracle, who had seen a person that had been four days dead come alive out of the grave at the call of another."*

2. *Their Possibility.*—Those who believe in a Supreme Creator, and in the dependence of all things upon his power and will, cannot deny the *possibility* of miracles; nor is there anything in them inconsistent with the wisdom and the immutability of God, or with the perfection of his works. They are departures from the ordinary course of God's operations; but not to remedy unforeseen evils, or to repair imperfections in the system of nature. The reasons for them are *moral* and not natural reasons; and they are wrought to accomplish *moral ends.* They remind us, when they occur, that the power of God is superior to nature, and that on him all nature depends.

3. *The Circumstances under which Miracles are an authenticating Evidence.*—Granting their possibility, the argument which is drawn from them is this: that as the established and known course of nature has been fixed by the Creator and Preserver of all things, it can never be

* Gleig's edition of Stackhouse's History of the Bible, vol. iii, p. 241.

counteracted but by himself, or by other beings at his command, and by his assistance. To deny this, is to deny the omnipotence and natural government of God.

But miracles, in order to be an authentication of a Divine mission, must be effected by the power of God for this very purpose. The following circumstances are sufficient to establish this fact: 1. When the miracles occur only in connection with an actual profession of certain persons that they have a mission from God, and while they are engaged in the proper functions of their office. In this there would be a strong presumption that the works were wrought by God in order to authenticate this pretension. 2. When they are performed by the persons themselves, at their own will, and for the express purpose of establishing their mission. If the works are real miracles, it is then clear that God is with them, and that his co-operation is an authenticating and visible seal upon their commission.

But though it should be allowed, that when real miracles occur under the circumstances which we have mentioned they are satisfactory evidences of a Divine mission, and that eye-witnesses of such miracles would be bound to admit the proof; it has been made a question, whether their testimony affords to others sufficient evidence that such events actually took place, and whether we are bound to acknowledge the authority of that mission in attestation of which the miracles are said to have been wrought.

If we assume the negative, either the benefits of a Revelation must be confined to those who witnessed its attestation by miracles, or similar attestations must be afforded to every man. But as no religious system can plead the authentication of *perpetual* miracles, either this principle is unsound, or we must abandon all hope of discovering a religion of Divine authority.

These remarks will lead us to notice,

4. *The Competency of human Testimony to establish the Credibility of Miracles.*—As miracles are facts, they, like other facts, may be reported; and, from the nature of the miracles in question, the competency of any man of ordinary understanding to determine whether they were actually wrought, cannot be doubted. If, therefore, the witnesses are credible; and if, in matters of the greatest moment in common life, we should not hesitate to act upon their testimony, it would be mere perverseness to reject it in the case of miracles.

Mr. Hume denies the credibility of miracles on the ground of human testimony. The substance of his objection is this: *Experience* is the ground of the credit which we give to human testimony; but this experience is by no means constant, for men often prevaricate and deceive. It is *experience*, in like manner, which assures us of those laws of nature, in the violation of which the notion of a miracle consists; but this experience is constant and uniform. Hence, it is contrary to experience that miracles should be true, but not contrary to experience that human testimony should be false; and, therefore, no human testimony can, in any case, render them credible.

To this objection, which has been met at large by many authors,* we oppose the following remarks:

There is an ambiguity in the term " experience," and in the phrase " contrary to experience," which ought to be removed. Strictly speaking, the narrative of a fact is contrary to experience when the fact is related to have existed at a time and place, at which time and place we, being present, did not perceive it to exist; as if it should be asserted that in a particular room, and at a particular hour of a certain day, a man was raised from the dead, in which room, and at the time specified, we, being present and looking on, perceived no such event. Here the assertion is contrary to experience in the proper sense of the phrase; and this is a contrariety which no evidence can surmount, whether the fact be miraculous or otherwise.

But is this the experience and contrariety which Mr. Hume intended in the objection? It certainly is not. When, therefore, he asserts that miracles are contrary to experience, he must be understood to mean, either that we ourselves have not experienced them, (which is properly a want of experience, and not a contradiction of it,) or, that they have not been generally experienced by others. We say, "not *generally;*" for to assert that no miracle was *ever* experienced is to assume the subject in controversy.

To argue against miracles from the supposed unalterable course of nature, is a mere begging of the question. It is to argue upon a supposition which is wholly incapable of proof: that the course of nature is indeed so *unalterably* fixed, that even God himself, by whom its laws were ordained, *cannot*, when he sees fit, suspend their operation. On the other hand, to expect that miracles should become a matter of common experience, is to expect what is contrary to their nature, what would make them cease to be miracles, and what would totally destroy the purpose for which they were wrought.

Mr. Hume attempts to adjust, in a sort of metaphysical balance, the degrees of probability resulting from what he is pleased to call " *opposite experiences;*" that is, the experience of men's veracity on the one hand, and of the unalterable laws of nature on the other. But it will at once appear, that he only weighs the experience of those who never had the opportunity of witnessing a miracle, against the experience of those who declare that they were eye-witnesses of the fact. Instead, therefore, of weighing *opposite experiences*, properly so called, he is only balancing total *inexperience* on the one hand, against positive *experience* on the other.

* See Campbell's Dissertations on Miracles; Paley's Evidences; Adam's Essay on Miracles; Bishop Douglas's Criterion; Dwight's Theology, vol. 2; and Chalmers.

There is a palpable fallacy in representing the experience of mankind as being *opposite* to the testimony on which our belief of miracles is founded. For the *opposite* experiences, as they are called, are not contradictory to each other, since there is no inconsistency in believing them both. A miracle necessarily supposes an established and *generally unaltered* course of nature, for in the interception of such a course lies the very essence of a miracle. Our experience, therefore, of the course of nature leads us to expect its continuance, and to act accordingly; but it does not prove that it is absolutely unalterable, nor does it set aside valid testimony of a deviation from it. How can our being personally unacquainted with a matter of fact which took place a thousand years ago, or in a distant part of the world, warrant us in rejecting the testimony of personal witnesses of the event? Common sense revolts at the absurdity of considering one man's ignorance or inexperience as a counterpoise to another man's knowledge and experience of a matter of fact. Yet on no better foundation does this favorite argument of infidelity rest.

But we may also remark, that "the evidence arising from human testimony is *not solely derived* from experience. On the contrary, testimony has a natural influence on belief, antecedent to experience. The early and unlimited assent given to testimony by children, gradually contracts as they advance in life; and it is therefore more consonant to truth to say, that our diffidence in testimony is the result of experience, than that our faith in it has this foundation."

"Besides, the uniformity of experience in favor of any fact is not a proof against its being reversed in a particular instance. The evidence arising from the single testimony of a man of known veracity, will go farther to establish a belief of its being actually reversed. And if his testimony be confirmed by a few others of the same character, we cannot withhold our assent to the truth of it."

"Now, though the operations of nature are governed by uniform laws, and though we have not the testimony of our senses in favor of any violation of them; still, if in particular instances we have the testimony of thousands of our fellow-creatures, and those, too, men of strict integrity, swayed by no motives of ambition or interest, but governed by the principles of common sense, that they were actually witnesses of these violations, the constitution of our nature obliges us to believe them."*

We have now shown the nature and possibility of real miracles; that under certain circumstances they are to be regarded as a sufficient authentication, both of the Divine mission of those who performed them, and of the doctrines which they taught; that as facts they are proper subjects of human testimony, and that credible testimony respecting them lays a competent foundation for our belief in them, and in those

* Reasonableness of Christianity.

Revelations which they were clearly designed to attest. Thus, the way is prepared for the consideration of the miracles recorded in Scripture.

II. PROPHECY. This is the other great branch of the external evidence of a Revelation from God, and its nature and force may be pointed out before we examine either the miracles or the prophecies of the Bible. For, by ascertaining the general principles on which this kind of evidence rests, the consideration of particular cases will be rendered more easy and satisfactory. We will notice,

1. *The Nature of Prophecy.*—It may be defined to be "*a miracle of knowledge.*" It is a declaration, description, or representation of something future, which is beyond the power of human sagacity to discover or calculate.

Prophecy is a *miracle*, because, to foresee and foretell future events, to which no existing cause necessarily and evidently leads, no train of probabilities points, is as much beyond the ability of man as to cure diseases with a word, or even to raise the dead. It is a miracle, too, the proof of which remains within itself. That such actions as may be properly termed *miracles of power* were ever performed, can be proved, at a distant period, only by human testimony, against which cavils may be raised, or causes for doubt advanced. But the man who reads a prophecy, and perceives the corresponding event, is *himself* the witness of the miracle. He sees that thus it was predicted, and that thus it has come to pass.

Prophecies yet unfulfilled are miracles which at present are incomplete. These may be regarded as the seeds of future conviction, ready to grow up and bear their fruit whenever the corresponding facts shall be exhibited on the theater of the world. This kind of evidence has been so admirably contrived by the wisdom of God, that, in proportion as the lapse of ages might *seem* to weaken the argument derived from miracles long since performed, that very lapse serves only to strengthen the argument derived from the fulfillment of prophecy.

2. *The Force of its Evidence.*—The force of the evidence arising from the prediction of such events as human sagacity could not anticipate is at once apparent. Such predictions, whether in the form of declarations, descriptions, or representations of things future, are evidently supernatural, and must be divinely inspired. When, for instance, the events are distant many years or ages from the time of the prediction; when they depend on causes not so much as existing when the prophecy was uttered and recorded, and likewise upon various circumstances and a long arbitrary series of things, and the fluctuating uncertainties of human volitions; and especially when they depend not at all upon any external circumstances, nor upon any created being, but arise merely from the counsels and appointment of God, such events can be foreknown only by an

omniscient Being, and can be foretold by him only to whom the "Father of lights" shall reveal them.

It follows, therefore, that whoever is manifestly endowed with this predictive power must, in that instance, speak and act by Divine inspiration, and what he declares must be received as the *word of God*. The infidel author of "The Moral Philosopher" rather insinuates than attempts fully to establish a dilemma, with which to perplex those who regard prophecy as one of the proofs of a Divine Revelation. He thinks that either prophecy must respect "necessary events, as depending upon necessary causes, which might be certainly foreknown and predicted" without any Divine interposition; or that, if human actions are free, the possibility of prophecy must be given up, as it implies foreknowledge, which, if granted, would render them necessary.

To the first part of this objection we answer, that there are indeed many necessary events, dependent upon necessary causes, the existence and operation of which are within the compass of human knowledge. But to foretell such events would not be to prophesy, any more than to say that on a certain day and hour next year there will be an eclipse of the sun or moon, when that event has been previously ascertained by astronomical calculation.

Were we to allow that *all* events were necessary, yet, in a variety of instances, the argument from prophecy would not be at all affected; for the foretelling of necessary events in certain circumstances is beyond human intelligence, because they can be known to Him only by whose power those necessary causes on which they depend have been arranged, and who has prescribed the times of their operation.

Let us allow, for the sake of illustration, that the prophecy of Isaiah respecting the taking of Babylon by Cyrus was uttered, as it purports to have been, more than a century before Cyrus was born, and that all the actions of Cyrus and of his army, and those of the Babylonian monarch and his people, were necessitated. Is it to be maintained that the chain of necessitating causes, running through more than a century, could be traced by a *human* mind so as to describe the precise manner in which that fatality would unfold itself, even to the turning of the river, the drunken carousal of the inhabitants, and the neglect to shut the gates of the city? This being known to be above all human apprehension, would prove that the prediction was really a communication from God. Were events therefore subject to invincible fate, there might nevertheless be prophecy.

The other branch of the dilemma is founded on the notion that, if we allow the freedom of human actions, prophecy is impossible, because certain foreknowledge is contrary to that freedom, and renders events necessary.

Our reply is, that the objection is founded on a false assumption, the Divine foreknowledge having no more influence in making any future event necessary than human knowledge, in the degree in which it may exist. There is no moral causality in knowledge. This lies in the *will*, which is the determining and acting principle in every moral agent. The infallible judgment of God respecting contingent events no more causes them to be necessary, than our knowledge of a present truth is any cause of its being either *true* or *present*.

Things which depend upon a chain of *necessary* causes must be necessary, and as such God foreknows them; but it by no means follows that, from the foreknowledge of God concerning events which depend upon *free* causes, things otherwise supposed to be *free* will thereby unavoidably become *necessary*. The whole question lies in this: is the simple *knowledge* of an action a necessitating cause of the action? The answer must be in the negative, as every man's consciousness and common sense will assure him.

§ 2. *Of Internal Evidence.*

The second kind of evidence in attestation of a Divine Revelation is called *Internal;* to the nature of which, as also to its rank in the scale of evidence, we will briefly turn our attention.

1. Its Nature.—*Internal evidence* is that kind of evidence which arises from a consideration of the doctrines taught in the Holy Scriptures, as being consistent with the character of God, and promotive of the happiness of man. It is derived from the wonderful sublimity of the sacred volume, the perfect purity of its moral precepts, the profundity and importance of its discoveries, the exact agreement of all its parts, and its obvious tendency to promote the wellbeing of mankind.

2. Its Rank *in the scale of Evidence.*—On this subject very different opinions have been entertained. Some have advanced the notion that internal evidence ought not to be ranked, as a *leading* proof, with miracles and prophecy, because the proof from them is decisive and absolute. But for the same reason prophecy might be excluded from the rank of *leading* evidence, inasmuch as miracles *alone* are decisive and absolute. If there is any force at all in the argument from miracles, it goes the full length of rational proof of a Divine attestation, both to him who witnesses the miracles, and to him to whom they are credibly reported; and nothing more is absolutely necessary to enforce a rational conviction.

But should it please the Author of a revelation to superadd the farther evidence of prophecy, and also that of the obvious truthfulness and beneficial tendency of this revelation, it ought not to be disregarded, or thought to be of trifling import in its favor. For, though this additional evidence may not be necessary to establish a rational proof, it may have a tendency to rouse attention, and to leave objectors more obviously without excuse.

By others, the internal evidence has been placed *first* in order and importance, and upon it the force of the evidence from miracles and prophecy has been made to depend. Nothing, say they, is to be received as a revelation from God which does not contain doctrines worthy of his character and promotive of the good of mankind.

This, we reply, is readily admitted. But are we to try a professed Revelation by our own notions of what is worthy of God and beneficial to mankind? This would be to assume, that, independent of a Revelation, we know what God is, and that we are so perfectly acquainted with the character, relations, and wants of man as to determine what is most for his benefit. This, however, cannot be granted.

But again, to make internal evidence the *primary* test of a Divine Revelation, is to render the *external* testimony comparatively unimportant. For, if a Revelation is to contain an evidence of its truth, which shall be independent of all external testimony, the utility of the evidence of miracles is rendered very questionable. It is either unnecessary, or it is subordinate and dependent. But this notion is contradicted by the whole tenor of the Scriptures; for miracles are everywhere represented as a complete and absolute demonstration of the mission and doctrines of those by whom they were performed.

It is easy to discover the causes which have led to this error in regard to the true *office* and *rank* of the internal evidence of Revelation.

First, a hypothetical case has been assumed, and it has been asked, "If a doctrine absurd and wicked should be attested by miracles, is it to be admitted as Divine upon their authority?" The answer is, that this is a case which in the nature of things can never occur, and which cannot, therefore, be made the basis of an argument. We have seen already that a *real* miracle can be wrought by none but God, or by his commission. Therefore, whenever a real miracle takes place, in *attestation* of any doctrine, that doctrine cannot be either unreasonable or impious.

The *second* cause of the error has been, that the *rational* evidence of a Revelation has been confounded with the *authenticating* evidence. When the character, plans, and laws of God are made known, they carry to the reason of man, so far as they are comprehended, the demonstration which accompanies truth of any other kind. For, as the eye is formed to received light, so the rational powers of man are formed to receive conviction when the congruity of propositions is made evident. This is *rational* evidence, but it is not *authenticating* evidence.

Let us suppose that there is no *external* evidence to attest the Divine mission of those teachers from whom we have received the doctrines which appear to us to be so sublime, so important, so true. It will then follow that they had no means of knowing these doctrines to be from God, or of distinguishing them from the discoveries of their own mind. And if even they had, we can have no means of knowing that they are anything more than mere human opinions. They may be true, but of this we can have no infallible proof; for neither our own rational faculties, nor those of any other human being, are infallible. But even granting them to be true, they cannot be attested to be Divine. Add, then, the *external* testimony, and we have the attestation required. The *rational* evidence of the doctrines, in both cases, is the same; but this evidence is no proof that God revealed them. It is in *external* evidence alone that this proof is found.

From this distinction the relative importance of the External and Internal evidence may be further illustrated.

Rational evidence of the doctrines proposed to us, when it can be had, goes to establish their *truth*, so far as we can depend upon our judgment; but external testimony, if satisfactory, establishes their *Divine authority*, and consequently their absolute truth, leaving no appeal. It is of the most simple and decisive kind, and gives to unbelief the character of obvious perverseness and inconsistency: *perverseness*, because there is a clear opposition of the will rather than of the judgment in the case; *inconsistency*, because men act upon a much lower degree of evidence in the most important concerns of life.

In difficult doctrines, of a kind to give rise to a variety of opinions, rational evidence is accompanied with doubt; but the attestation of miracles rests on principles supported by the universal and constant experience of mankind: 1. That a real miracle is above human power; 2. That men unquestionably virtuous in every other respect are not likely to propagate a deliberate falsehood; and, 3. That they should do so not only without advantage, but at the hazard of reproach, persecution, and death, contradicts all the known motives to action in human nature.

In strict propriety, therefore, miracles may be considered as the *primary* evidence of the truth of a Revelation, and every other species of proof as *confirmatory*. Prophecy and the internal evidence are *leading proofs*, but neither of them stands in the foremost place.

§ 3. *Of Collateral Evidence.*

The third kind of evidence by which a Revelation from God may be confirmed is the *collateral*. But here we will only adduce a few instances, merely to illustrate this kind of testimony.

The collateral evidence of a Revelation from God may be its agreement with former Revelations, should any have been given; its adaptation to the condition of the world at the time of its communication, and to effect the great moral ends which it proposes; the agreement of its record of facts with the credible traditions and histories of the same times; the monuments, either natural or instituted, which may remain to attest the truth of its history; the concessions of adversaries in its favor; and, finally, the continuance of its adaptation to the case of the human family to the present day.

We have now briefly considered the several classes of evidence by which a Divine Revelation may be authenticated; but before we proceed to a practical application of these evidences it will be necessary to establish the *Genuineness*, the *Authenticity*, and the *Integrity* of the Holy Scriptures.

CHAPTER II.

GENUINENESS OF THE HOLY SCRIPTURES.

The genuineness of a book consists in its having been written by the author whose name it bears, and should be distinguished from its authenticity, with which it is often confounded. The former refers exclusively to the authorship of the book in question; the latter, to the correctness of the facts which are detailed in it. A book may therefore be genuine which is not authentic, and one may be authentic which is not genuine.

The history of Sir Charles Grandison is genuine, being indeed written by Richardson, the author whose name it bears; but it is not authentic, being a mere production of fictions. Again, the Account of Lord Anson's Voyages is an authentic book, being a relation of facts; but it is not genuine, for its real author was not Walters, whose name is appended to it, but Benjamin Robins. Hayley's Memoirs of the Life of Cowper are both genuine and authentic. They were written by Mr. Hayley, and the information which they contain is perfectly reliable.

In establishing the genuineness of the sacred Scriptures it will be proper,

I. To ascertain THE EXISTENCE, AGE, *and* ACTIONS *of the leading persons mentioned in them*, as the instruments by whom the Revelations were made.

It is not necessary that our attention should be directed to more than two of these persons, Moses and Christ; because the evidence which establishes their existence and actions, and the period of both, will also establish all that is stated in the same records as to the subordinate and succeeding agents.

The existence and the respective antiquity of Moses and of Christ may be satisfactorily proved,

1. *From the Existence of the Jewish Polity and of the Christian Religion.*—The writings which are ascribed to Moses claim that he was the

leader and legislator of the Jews, near sixteen hundred years before the Christian era, according to the common chronology. That the Jews existed very anciently as a nation cannot be doubted. And that it has been an uninterrupted tradition among them, that Moses led them out of Egypt, and first gave them their system of laws and religion, is equally certain. The history of that event they have in writing, and also the laws attributed to him. This history is uncontradicted by the authentic records of other nations; and as their institutions bear the marks of a systematic arrangement, established at once, they must have been enforced by some political authority, and are to be attributed to one superior and commanding mind. The Jews refer them to Moses, and if this be denied, it cannot be shown that any other person is entitled to that honor. The history therefore can only be denied on some principle of skepticism which would equally shake the foundation of all history.

The same observations may be made in regard to the existence of the Founder of the Christian religion. In the records of the New Testament he is called JESUS CHRIST, and his birth is fixed upward of eighteen centuries ago. This also is at least uncontradicted testimony.

The Christian religion exists, and must have had an author. Like the institutions of Moses, it bears the evidence of being the work of one mind; and, as a theological system, it presents no indications of a gradual and successive elaboration. There was a time when there was no such religion as Christianity, and it follows that there once flourished a teacher to whom it owed its origin. All tradition and history unite in their testimony, that this teacher was JESUS CHRIST.

2. *By the Testimony of Ancient Writers.*—MANETHO, CHEREMON, APOLLONIUS, and LYSIMACHUS are quoted by Josephus as agreeing that Moses was the leader of the Jews when they departed from Egypt, and the founder of their laws. STRABO, JUSTIN, PLINY, TACITUS, JUVENAL, LONGINUS, and DIODORUS SICULUS all speak of Moses; and Justin Martyr expressly says, that most of the historians, poets, lawgivers, and philosophers of the Greeks mention him as the leader and prince of the Jewish nation. From all these testimonies it is clear that it was commonly received among ancient nations generally, as well as among the Jews themselves, that Moses was the founder and lawgiver of the Jewish state.

As TO CHRIST, it is only necessary to give the testimony of two historians, whose antiquity no one ever thought of disputing. SUETONIUS mentions him by name, and says that Claudius expelled from Rome those who adhered to his cause.* TACITUS records the progress which the Christian religion had made; the violent death its founder had

---

* Judæos impulsore Christo assidue tumultuantes Româ expulit.—SUET., Edit. Var., p. 544.

suffered; that he flourished under the reign of Tiberius; that Pilate was then procurator of Judea, and that the original author of this profession was *Christ*.* Thus both the real existence of Christ, and the period in which he lived, are exactly ascertained.

Another important fact in proof of the genuineness of the sacred Scriptures is,

II. THEIR ANTIQUITY.

In establishing the antiquity of the books which contain the Jewish and the Christian Scriptures we will direct our attention,

1. *To those of the Old Testament.* The question before us is, whether the books of the Old Testament were written at the respective times assigned to them. It is not necessary to go into a critical examination of the date of each book separately, for if we can ascertain the period in which the five books of Moses were written it will not be a difficult matter to settle the date of all the rest. To prove, therefore, that the *Pentateuch* was written synchronically with the exodus of the Jews from Egypt, we will present a chain of historical facts which, if duly considered, must prove satisfactory to every candid mind. We will begin with the apostolic age, and travel backward step by step, as the evidence of facts may lead the way.

(1.) Josephus, who was himself a Jewish priest, and also cotemporary with the apostles, gives us a catalogue of the sacred books of the Jews, in which he expressly mentions the five books of Moses, thirteen of the prophets, four of Hymns and Moral Precepts; and if, as many critics maintain, Ruth was added to Judges, and the Lamentations of Jeremiah to his Prophecies, the number agrees with the books of the Old Testament as it is received at the present day.

This threefold division of the Jewish Scriptures into the *Law*, the *Prophets*, and the *Psalms*, mentioned by Josephus, was expressly recognized before his time by Jesus Christ,† as well as by the subsequent writers of the New Testament. We have therefore sufficient evidence that the Old Testament existed at that time; and if we only allow that Jesus Christ was a person of a virtuous character, we are bound to conclude that these Scriptures were not corrupted in his day. For, when he accused the Pharisees of making the law of no effect by their traditions, and when he exhorted his hearers to "search the Scriptures," he could not have failed to mention the corruptions or forgeries of Scripture had any in that age existed.

(2.) The books of the Old Testament were translated into Greek, for the use of the Alexandrian Jews, about two hundred and eighty-seven years before the Christian era. This Greek translation, of which almost every one has some knowledge, is proof positive that the Hebrew Pen-

---

* Auctor nominis ejus Christus, qui Tiberio imperitante, per procuratorem Pontium Pilatum supplicio affectus erat.—Annal., 1, 5.

† See Matt. xi, 13; Luke xvi, 16; Acts xxvi, 22; Rom. x, 5.

tateuch existed at that period. But if it existed two hundred and eighty-seven years before Christ it must have existed in the days of Ezra, five hundred and thirty-six years before Christ; for this simple reason, that the circumstances of the Jews rendered its composition impossible at any point between these two periods. This will appear evident if we weigh the next fact to be adduced.

(3.) The Hebrew language, in which the Old Testament was written, ceased to be the living language of the Jews soon after the Babylonish captivity; and the learned agree that there was no grammar for the language till many ages after that event. It follows, therefore, that every book which is written in *pure* Hebrew must have been composed either before or about the time of the captivity. It is also an important fact, that after that period the writings of the Jews were generally either in Chaldee or Greek. Hence it is utterly impossible that the Hebrew Pentateuch could have been written at any period subsequent to the return of the Jews from Babylon.

(4.) As this cannot be rationally denied, some have thence contended that it was written by Ezra. But to this opinion, however plausible some may think it to be, there are insuperable objections. In the book of Ezra, "*the Law of Moses, the man of God,*" is particularly referred to as a well known *written* document then actually existing.* And in the book of Nehemiah we have an account of the manner in which that same *written* document was openly read to the people, under the precise name of "*the book of the Law of Moses, which the Lord had commanded to Israel.*"† Nor is this all. It was not that Ezra produced a new volume, and then called upon the people to receive it as the authentic Law of Moses; but the *people themselves* called upon Ezra to bring forth and read that book, as a work with which they had long been acquainted.

The Law of Moses, therefore, must have been known to exist as a *written document* previous to the return from Babylon; and as Ezra could not have produced under that name a mere compilation of oral traditions, so neither could he have suppressed the ancient volume of the Law, nor have set forth, in its stead, that volume which the Jews have ever since received as the genuine Pentateuch. Add to this, that when the foundation of the second temple was laid, many persons were there who well remembered the first temple. These, consequently, must have known whether there had or had not been a written Law of Moses anterior to the captivity; nor could they have been deceived by the introduction of a new composition, either by Ezra or by any one else.

(5.) We have now extant two Hebrew copies of the Law of Moses. One is received by the Jews, and the other by the Samaritans; each maintaining that their own is the genuine record. The coincidence of

* Ezra iii, 2; vi, 18. † Neh. viii, 1.

these two copies is such as to demonstrate that they were taken from the same original. But if so, that original must have existed long before the Captivity, as circumstances will show. For, since the Pentateuch was received as the book of the Law both by the ten tribes, and also by the two tribes it follows as a necessary consequence, that they each received it *before* they became divided into two kingdoms, which event took place about nine hundred and seventy years before Christ. Had it been forged in a later age among the Jews, the perpetual enmity that existed between them and the Israelites would utterly have prevented it from being adopted by the Samaritans; and had it been a spurious production of the Samaritans, it would never have been received by the Jews.

(6.) The universal admission of the Pentateuch, as the inspired Law of Moses, throughout the whole commonwealth of Israel, prior to its disruption into two hostile kingdoms—the magnificent temple of Solomon, and the whole ritual attached to it, are plain proofs of the *previous existence* of this sacred document. And as the Law strictly prohibits more than one practice of Solomon, it is incredible either that he should have been its author, or that it should have been written under his sanction and authority.

(7.) And with as little probability can we ascribe it to David. His life was occupied with almost incessant troubles and warfare; and it is difficult to conceive how a book written by that prince could, in the space of a few years, be universally received as the inspired composition of Moses.

(8.) The Pentateuch might be more plausibly ascribed to Samuel than to either of those two princes; but this supposition will not stand the test of rational inquiry. For, besides the impossibility that he should persuade all Israel to adopt, as the inspired Law of Moses, a mere modern composition of his own, there is this additional fact, that in a speech which he made to the assembled Israelites he expressly referred to the well known commandment of Jehovah, and to the Divine legation of Moses and Aaron.

(9.) We have now ascended to within four centuries of the exodus from Egypt, and the alleged promulgation of the Law from Mount Sinai; and, from Ezra to Samuel, we have found no person to whom the composition of the Pentateuch can reasonably be ascribed. The only remaining question is, whether it could have been written during the three hundred and fifty-six years that intervened between the entrance of the Israelites into Palestine, and the appointment of Saul to be their king.

Now, the whole history of that period utterly forbids such a supposition. The Israelites are uniformly described as acknowledging the authority of a written Law of Moses. It is declared that Joshua wrote the book which bears his name as a supplement to a *prior* book, which is denominated the "*book of the* Law." It is likewise asserted that this book of the Law is "*the book of the Law of Moses;*" a copy of which, Joshua declares, he had written in the presence of the children of Israel.

Thus, finally, we come to the *original*, whence the copy of Joshua was taken; for we are told that Moses, with his own hand, wrote the words of THIS LAW in a BOOK, and commanded the Levites to put THIS BOOK into the ark of the covenant, that it might be preserved throughout their generations.

These arguments fully establish the genuineness of the books of Moses. As to those of the Prophets, it can be proved, from Jewish tradition, the list of Josephus, the Greek translation, and from their being quoted by ancient writers, that they existed many ages before some of those events occurred, to which we shall refer in the proper place, as unequivocal instances of prophetic accomplishment.

In pursuing the argument respecting the antiquity and genuineness of the sacred books, we will consider,

2. *Those of the New Testament.*—Of the ancient date of these books we have sufficient proof,

(1.) *In the Quotations which are made from them by early Christian Authors.*—Quotations from the books of the New Testament are found in the writings of *Clement*, of the first century; and also in those of *Ignatius*, of *Polycarp*, of *Justin Martyr*, of *Irenæus*, Bishop of Lyons, of *Athenagoras*, of *Theophilus* of Antioch, and many others. Thus we have the testimony of a series of Christian writers, beginning with those who were cotemporary with the apostles, or who immediately followed them, and proceeding in close and regular succession from their time to the present.

This medium of proof is most unquestionable, and is not to be diminished by the lapse of ages. Bishop Burnet, in the History of his Own Times, inserts various extracts from Lord Clarendon's History. *One* such insertion is a proof that Lord Clarendon's History was extant when Bishop Burnet wrote, that it had been read and received by him as a work of Lord Clarendon's, and that he regarded it as an authentic account of the transactions which it relates, and it will be a proof of these facts a thousand years hence.

The application of this argument to the Gospel History is obvious. If the books in which it is contained have been quoted as genuine, by a series of writers, up to the age in which their authors lived, it is then clear that they must have existed prior to the earliest of those writings in which they are quoted, and that they were then regarded as genuine.

(2.) *In the early Catalogues of the Christian Scriptures.*—Catalogues of the books of the New Testament were drawn up by different persons at an early period, from which we learn that the books which are now acknowledged existed then, and were received as genuine.

The first catalogue is that of Origen in the year 210, who omits the

Epistle of James, and the Epistle of Jude; but he acknowledges both of them in other parts of his writings.

The second is the catalogue of Eusebius in the year 315, which is the same with ours. He says, however, that a few of the books were disputed by some. Of the same date is the catalogue of Athanasius, which exactly accords with ours.

The catalogue of Cyril of Jerusalem, drawn up in 340, that of the Council of Laodicea in 364, and that of Gregory Nazianzen in 375, omit the Revelation, but contain all the other books.

Philostrius, Bishop of Brescia, in 380, leaves out Revelation and the Epistle to the Hebrews; but Jerome in 382, Ruffinus in 390, and Augustine in 394, have all the books of the New Testament, as they are now acknowledged.

Nothing farther is necessary to prove that these books were written at the time assigned for their publication, and by the persons to whom they are ascribed. There seems, indeed, to have been no doubt relative to this matter in the early ages of Christianity. It is true, that by some the genuineness of a few of these books was called in question; but this circumstance supplies additional evidence of the genuineness of the New Testament Scriptures, by showing that the clearest proof was required before any of the books could be acknowledged. When we find that men are far from being credulous, and that while they give assent in some instances they withhold it in others, we rest with the greater confidence in their decisions.

(3.) *In the Testimony of the Enemies of Christianity.*—No public contradiction of the Gospel history was ever put forth by the Jewish rulers, and this silence on their part is important evidence in its favor. But the *direct* testimonies of its adversaries to the facts of the Gospel are both numerous and clear.

CELSUS in the second century, PORPHYRY and HIEROCLES in the third, and JULIAN in the fourth, all wrote against Christianity. They have given evidence that they were well acquainted with the New Testament Scriptures, and that they believed them to have been written by Christ's own disciples. Indeed, they never pretended to call this in question, or to produce any contrary account, as they surely would have done had it been in their power. They quoted passages from the writings of the apostles, touching nearly all the leading facts of the Gospel history; nor did they deny even the *miracles* of our Saviour. True, they mentioned these things only with a design to ridicule and expose them; but they afford incontestible proof, that in their times these Scriptures were in existence.

Among the evidences in support of the genuineness and truth of the Christian Scriptures, perhaps none are of more value than the testimonies of those learned philosophers who wrote against Christianity in its first ages. They express no doubt concerning the authenticity of these

Scriptures, nor do they ever insinuate that Christians were mistaken in regard to the authors to whom they ascribe them. They confirm the prevailing sentiments of the Church respecting those books of the New Testament which are called *canonical;* for their writings show that those very books, and not any others, are the books which Christians then acknowledged as the rule of their faith, as they now are of ours.

These writers proposed to overthrow the arguments for the Christian religion, and to arrest its progress. But in these designs they had very little success in their own times; and their works, composed and published in the early days of Christianity, are now a testimony in its favor, and will be of use in its defense to the latest ages.

We have thus established the genuineness of the books of the New Testament by the testimony of those who had the best opportunities of ascertaining whether they were indeed written by the persons whose names they bear; because they lived in the age when these books were published, or soon after, and were led by their circumstances to make a critical investigation of the whole matter. We receive them, therefore, as the genuine works of their respective authors, for the very same reason that we receive as genuine the writings of Xenophon, of Polybius, of Cesar, or of Tacitus; namely, because we have the uninterrupted testimony of ages to their genuineness, and have no reason to suspect imposition.

CHAPTER III.

THE INTEGRITY OF THE SACRED SCRIPTURES.

HAVING established the genuineness of the Sacred Scriptures, we will proceed, in the next place, to consider their *Integrity.*

By the *Integrity* of the Scriptures is meant, *their entire and uncorrupted preservation.* This implies, *first,* that we have now all the books which formerly belonged to the *Canon;* and, *secondly,* that these books have come down to us without any material alteration. We assert,

I. THE INTEGRITY OF THE CANON.*

We are now in possession of all the books which were ever received as canonical, either by the Jews or by the primitive Christians. This is sufficiently evident,

1. *With respect to the Books of the Old Testament.*—The list of Josephus, the Septuagint translation, and the Samaritan Pentateuch clearly prove that the books which we now receive as sacred are the very same that were received by the Jews and the Samaritans, long before the Christian era. But it is equally evident,

* See the note at the end of this chapter.

2. *In regard to the Books of the New Testament.*—We have already shown, that in the writings of the earliest Christian authors there are numerous quotations from nearly all the books now included in the New Testament, and references to them by name; and also, that catalogues of the books which the ancient Christians received as Divine were drawn up by Origen, Eusebius, and others. These catalogues, which were published at early periods, and in countries distant from one another, differ in no material point, and all contain the four Gospels. It is therefore certain that we have at present the very books which were received by the ancient Christian Church, and that not one of them has been lost.

To this it has been objected, that the Scriptures themselves make mention of books which are not now extant: as "the book of the wars of the Lord," Num. xxi, 14; "the book of Jasher," Josh x, 13; "the book of Nathan" and "the book of Gad," 1 Chron. xxix, 29; and the Epistle from Laodicea," Col. iv, 16.

Our answer is this: It cannot be made appear that these are different books from what are extant under different titles. But if even this could be done, it is not at all requisite to the integrity of the canon of Scripture that we should have all the writings of holy and inspired men, or all the histories quoted in the Bible. This is proved from the consideration that the ancient Jews and Christians had not these books in the canon, and yet they never entertained the least doubt of their having the entire canon of Sacred Scripture.

But we maintain the integrity of the Scriptures,

II. WITH RESPECT TO THE PARTICULAR BOOKS.

These have come down to us without corruption, or any material alteration. This we hold to be true,

1. *With regard to the Old Testament.*—The integrity of these Scriptures will appear both from the impossibility of corrupting them, and from the agreement of numerous ancient manuscripts. We will call attention,

(1.) *To the Impossibility of corrupting the Jewish Scriptures.*— This is put beyond all dispute by the consideration of a few historical facts.

Before the time of Christ, the profound regard which the Jews had for their sacred books rendered any material change in their contents impossible.

The Law being the deed by which the land of Canaan was divided among the Israelites, it is improbable that they would suffer it to be altered or falsified. The distinction of the twelve tribes, and their separate interests, made it more difficult to alter their Law than that of any other nation.

The Samaritans had the Pentateuch as well as the Jews; and the jealousy and hatred which existed between the two nations made it impracticable for either to corrupt or alter the text, in anything of consequence, without certain discovery.

The general agreement between the Hebrew and the Samaritan Pentateuch plainly demonstrates that they were originally the same. Nor can there be any better evidence that the Jewish Scriptures have not been corrupted or interpolated than this very book of the Samaritans, which, after more than two thousand years of discord between the two nations, varies as little from the Jewish Pentateuch as any classic author has varied from itself in less time by the unavoidable mistakes of transcribers.

After the Jews returned from Babylon, the Law and the Prophets were publicly read in their synagogues every Sabbath day, which was an excellent method of securing their purity; and a law was also enacted by them which denounced him to be guilty of inexpiable sin who should presume to make the slightest possible alteration in their sacred books.

Since the birth of Christ the Old Testament has been held in high esteem both by Jews and Christians. They have been a mutual guard upon each other, which must have rendered any material corruption impossible if it had been attempted. For if such attempt had been made by the *Jews*, it would have been detected by the Christians; and if any such attempt had been made by the *Christians*, it would certainly have been detected by the Jews. Nor could such a purpose have been effected by any other body of men without its being exposed by both Jews and Christians.

But as the Jews were dispersed among all the nations of the then known world, and as it was therefore impossible that they should collect all the copies of the Law, with the intention of corrupting them, the accomplishment of such a design was on their part utterly impracticable. But we will notice,

(2.) *The Agreement of Ancient Manuscripts.*—The agreement of all the manuscripts of the Old Testament which are known to be extant, amounting to more than eleven hundred, is a clear proof of its uncorrupted preservation. These manuscripts are not all entire, some containing one part and some another. But it is absolutely impossible that *every* manuscript, whether in the original Hebrew or in any ancient version, should or could be *designedly* altered or falsified in the *same* passages without detection either from Jews or Christians.

These manuscripts are, confessedly, liable to errors and mistakes from the negligence and inaccuracy of copyists; but they are not *all* uniformly incorrect in the same words or passages, for what is incorrect in one is correct in another. And although the various readings which learned men have discovered in the Hebrew Scriptures amount to many thousands, yet these differences are of very little real moment.

Equally satisfactory is the evidence for the integrity of the Scriptures,

2. *With regard to the Books of the New Testament.*—This is manifest,

(1.) *From their Contents.*—For, as early as the first two centuries of the Christian era, we find the very same *facts* and the very same *doctrines* universally received by Christians which we of the present day believe on the authority of the New Testament.

(2.) *From the impossibility of their being universally corrupted.*— They could not be corrupted during the life of their authors; and before their death copies were dispersed among the different communities of Christians, who were scattered throughout the world.

Within twenty years after the ascension, Churches were planted in all the principal cities of the Roman Empire; and in all these Churches the books of the New Testament, especially the four Gospels, were read as a part of their public worship, just as the writings of Moses were read in the Jewish synagogues.

Copies of these books were multiplied and disseminated as rapidly as the boundaries of the Church increased, and translations were made into as many languages as were spoken by its members. This rendered it impossible to corrupt these books in any one important word or phrase; for it is morally impossible that *all* Christians should agree in such a design.

But as these books could not be corrupted during the life of their respective authors, so neither could any material alteration take place after their death while the original manuscripts were preserved in the Churches.

The Christians who were instructed by the apostles, or by their immediate successors, traveled into all parts of the world, carrying with them copies of the apostolic writings, from which other copies were multiplied and preserved. We have therefore an unbroken series of testimonies for the uncorrupted preservation of the New Testament, which can be traced back from the fourth century of the Christian era to the very time of the apostles.

It is known that a division commenced in the fourth century, between the Eastern and the Western Church, which exists to the present day. Now, if it had been possible to alter all the copies in one of these divisions, those of the other would have detected the alteration. But the fact is, that both the eastern and the western copies agree; and this proves that on neither side were they altered or falsified.

The Church was early rent with fierce contentions on doctrinal points; but in all such disputes the New Testament was appealed to by every sect, as being conclusive in all matters of controversy. It was therefore morally impossible that any man or body of men could corrupt this book in any fundamental article.

3. *From the Agreement of Manuscripts.*—Of these upward of three

hundred and fifty were collected by Griesbach for his celebrated critical edition. True, they were not all entire. Most of them contained only the four Gospels; others the Gospels, Acts of the Apostles, and the Epistles; and a few contained the Apocalypse. They were all written in different and distant parts of the world, and some of them are upward of twelve hundred years old; but in all essential points they perfectly agree, as any one may ascertain by examining the critical editions published by Mill, Bengel, Wetstein, and Griesbach.

The thirty thousand various readings by Dr. Mill, and the one hundred and fifty thousand of Griesbach's edition, in no degree whatever affect the general credit or integrity of the sacred text. They consist almost wholly of palpable errors in transcription, grammatical and verbal differences, such as the insertion or omission of an article, the substitution of a word for its equivalent, or the transposition of a word or two in a sentence.

Even the few various readings that do change the sense, affect it almost exclusively in passages relating to unimportant, historical, and geographical circumstances, or other collateral matters; and the still smaller number that make any alteration in things of consequence do not place us in any absolute uncertainty. For, either the true reading may be found by a reference to different manuscripts and versions, or, should these fail, we may explain the point in question by other *undisputed* passages of Scripture.

4. *From the Agreement of the Ancient Versions of the New Testament with Quotations made from it by Christian Writers of the first three centuries, and by the succeeding Fathers of the Church.*—These quotations are so numerous that almost the whole body of the Gospels and Epistles might be compiled from the various passages which appear in the writings of those authors. And though the citations were, in many cases, made from memory, yet they correspond with the original records from which they were extracted. Thus we have an irrefragable argument for the purity and integrity of the New Testament Scriptures.

NOTE.—The word *canon*, in its general sense, means anything which is determined according to a fixed measure, rule, or law. It was employed by the early ecclesiastical writers to designate a catalogue of things that belonged to the Church. Hence they applied the term to a collection of hymns which were to be sung on festival occasions; to a list, in which were introduced the names of Church members; and particularly to a publicly approved catalogue of all the books that might be read in Christian assemblies for instruction and edification. But by modern theologians the word *canon* is usually employed to designate our authorized collection of Inspired Writings.

The establishment of the Jewish canon is by some ascribed to Ezra, and by others to Nehemiah; but it can hardly be doubted that in a work so important the priests, the lawyers, and all the leading men of the nation must have been unitedly engaged, as the grammarians of Alexandria were in determining the canon of the Greek classics. It is probable, however, that in this undertaking both Ezra and Nehemiah had a principal share.

The canon of the Old Testament Scriptures appears to have originated somewhat in the following manner. When the Jews returned from Babylon and re-established Divine worship, they collected the inspired books which they still possessed, and commenced with them a sacred library, as they had done before with the books of the Law. To this collection they afterward added the writings of Zechariah, Malachi, and other distinguished prophets and priests, who wrote during the Captivity, or shortly after; and also the books of Kings, Chronicles, and other historical writings, which had been compiled from the ancient records of the nation. The collection thus made was ever after considered complete, and the books composing it were called THE HOLY SCRIPTURES; or, THE LAW AND THE PROPHETS.

It is evident from the historical information which we possess, that the canon of the New Testament was not finished at once, but was commenced a considerable time before it was made complete. The Gospels were collected as early as the second century, and in the third century were regarded as of undoubted authority throughout the Christian Church. They were prefixed to the other books of the New Testament, because the history of Jesus was considered, at that early period, as the basis of Christian truth; just as the historical writings of Moses were prefixed to the Old Testament as the basis of the Mosaic economy.

As to the *Epistles*, a collection of them was commenced at a very early period, and was gradually enlarged and completed. It appears, indeed, to be of somewhat later origin than the collection of the Gospels; but both of them must have existed before the beginning of the third century. As early as the third century most of the copies of the apostolic Epistles contained all the books which now belong to this collection, as appears from the catalogues of Origen and Eusebius.

CHAPTER IV.

AUTHENTICITY OF THE SACRED SCRIPTURES.

We have produced, in a former chapter, a variety of proofs in support of the genuineness of the sacred books. Should any one still deny that they were written by the persons to whom they are ascribed, we have a right to ask, By whom then were they composed? We do not, however, expect an answer to this question; for, as they never were attributed to any other authors by those who had the best opportunities of knowing their history, it would be ridiculous, at this late day, to attempt to trace them to a different origin. It remains, then, for us to inquire whether they are a faithful record of the facts and transactions of which they give us information.

The authenticity of the Scriptures may be proved,

I. From their Internal Marks of Credibility.

Mr. Leslie has laid down four rules for determining the truth of historical facts in general. These rules are, 1. That the fact be such as that men can judge of it by their outward senses; 2. That it be public; 3. That it be kept in memory both by public monuments and by the performance of some outward actions; 4. That such monuments exist, and such actions be observed, from the time that the matter of fact came to pass.

With these rules in view, let us direct our attention,

1. *To the Books of Moses.*—In these we have a history of the Jewish people from the call of Abraham to the death of Moses, embracing a period of nearly five hundred years, and detailing a succession of the most wonderful events that ever took place in the history of nations. But, in addition to their historical character, they were the standing and municipal law of the Jewish nation, binding both the king and the people. They required the king to prepare himself a copy, and to "read therein all the days of his life;" and the people were commanded to lay up the words of this law in their hearts, and faithfully and diligently to teach them to their children.*

These books teach us moreover that God appointed and consecrated the tribe of Levi as his priests, by whom alone the sacrifices of the people were to be offered and their solemn institutions celebrated; that their high priest wore a glorious miter, and magnificent robes of God's own contriving;† and that at his word the king and the people were to go out and to come in. They teach us that the Levites were the chief judges in all matters, and that it was death to resist their sentence.

* Deut. xi, 18, 19; xviii, 18. † Num. xxvii, 21.

But the books of Moses, while they contain the history of the Jews, together with the laws by which their civil and religious affairs were regulated, give us an account of the institution of various commemorative rites, and of the commemoration of particular actions and events. For examples we may take the *Passover*, in memory of God's passing over the children of the Israelites when he slew all the first-born of Egypt;* the *Rod of Aaron*, which was kept in the ark, in memory of the destruction of Korah, Dathan, and Abiram, and of the confirmation of the priesthood in the tribe of Levi;† the *Pot of Manna*, in memory of their having been fed on manna in the wilderness;‡ the *Brazen Serpent*, which was kept to the days of Hezekiah, as a memorial of their wonderful deliverance from the biting of the fiery flying serpents;§ and the *Feast of Pentecost*, in memory of the dreadful appearance of God upon Mount Horeb.‖

There were other solemn institutions among the Jews in memory of their deliverance out of Egypt; as the Sabbath, their daily sacrifices and yearly expiation, and their new moons, and other feasts and fasts. Of these things, therefore, there were yearly, monthly, weekly, and daily recognitions.

Now, if the books of Moses had not been a faithful record of all these facts, they never could have been received by the Jews as authentic, unless they could have been made to believe that they had received them from their fathers, had been instructed in them when they were children, and had taught them to their children; that they had all been circumcised, and had circumcised their children, in pursuance of what was commanded in these books; that they had observed the yearly passover, the weekly Sabbath, the new moons, and all the several feasts, fasts, and religious ceremonies commanded in these books; and that they had a magnificent tabernacle, with a visible priesthood to administer in it, which was confined to the tribe of Levi, over whom was placed a glorious high priest, clothed with great and mighty prerogatives. Was it possible to have persuaded a whole nation of men that they had known and practiced all these things if they had not done it? or to have received a book for truth, which said that they had practiced them when they knew they had not?

But now let us suppose that these things were practiced before the books of Moses were written, and that the only imposition was in making the people believe that they had kept these observances in memory of certain events recorded in those books; will not the same impossibility appear upon this supposition, as in the former case? It must then be supposed that the Jews kept all these observances in memory of nothing, or without knowing anything of their origin or why they kept them; whereas these very observances express the reason of their

---

* Num. viii, 17, 18.   † Num. xvi; xvii.   ‡ Deut. xvi, 32, 33.
§ Num. xxi, 8, 9; 2 Kings xviii, 4.   ‖ Exod. xix; xx.

being kept; as the Passover, in memory of God's passing over the children of the Jews when he slew all the first-born of Egypt.

But if the Israelites knew no reason at all why they kept these observances, was it possible to make them believe that they had kept them in memory of events of which they had never heard before the time when it is supposed these books were written? Take, for illustration, the Stonehenge in Salisbury Plain. Every body knows it; and yet no one knows by whom, or for what reason, these great stones were placed there. Now, suppose we should write a book, and tell the world that these stones were set up by Hercules, in memory of his catching the stag with golden horns. And suppose we should say in this book that it was written by Hercules himself, or by eye-witnesses, at the time of that event; that it had been received as truth, and quoted by the most reputable authors in all ages since; that it was enjoined by legislative authority to be taught to our children, and that when we were children it was taught to us. We would ask the deist whether he thinks it possible that such a cheat could be palmed upon an enlightened community? or whether, if we should insist upon it, we should not, instead of being believed, be regarded as insane?

Let us now compare this with the twelve stones set up at Gilgal, the history of which is given in the fourth chapter of Joshua. There we learn that these stones were designed for a memorial unto the children of Israel of their miraculous passage over Jordan. The miracle in memory of which they were set up was such as could not possibly be imposed upon that nation when it is said to have been done. It was as wonderful as their passage through the Red Sea. Notice was given to the Israelites the day before this great miracle was performed.* It was done at noonday, before the whole nation. When the waters of Jordan were divided it was not at low ebb, but when that river overflowed all its banks.† And it was done not gradually, as by the action of winds, but suddenly, as soon as "the feet of the priests that bare the ark were dipped in the brim of the water."‡

Now, to form our argument, let us suppose that there never was any such thing as that passage over Jordan—that these stones at Gilgal were set up on some other occasion—and then, that some designing man invented this book of Joshua, saying that it was written by Joshua at that time, and giving these stones for a testimony of its truth. Would not everybody say to him, I know these stones at Gilgal, but I never before heard of this reason for them, nor of this book of Joshua? Where has it been all this time? Besides, this book tells us that our children were to be instructed, from age to age, in regard to this passage over Jordan and this memorial at Gilgal. But we never heard of that event when we were children, nor did we ever teach our children any such thing; and it could hardly have been forgotten while so

* Josh. iii, 5.   † Josh. iii, 15   ‡ Josh. iv, from verse 18.

Chap. 4.] AUTHENTICITY OF THE SCRIPTURES. 67

remarkable a memorial continued. If, therefore, we could not be imposed upon as to the Stonehenge in Salisbury Plain, much less could we be in regard to the twelve stones at Gilgal.

If the books of the Law were written by Moses, as has been shown, it is easy to prove that he could not have deceived the people by a mere pretense of miraculous attestations. The very instances of miracles which he gives renders this impossible. Suppose a man should pretend that yesterday he divided the Thames, in sight of all the people of London, and carried the whole city, men, women, and children, over to Southwark on dry land, the waters standing like walls on both sides; is it not morally impossible that he could persuade the people of London to believe this to be true, when every man, woman, and child would know it to be a notorious falsehood? Equally impossible was it for Moses to persuade six hundred thousand men that he had brought them out of Egypt through the Red Sea, or that he had fed them forty years with manna if it had not been true, because the senses of every man that was then alive must have contradicted it. And, for the same reason, it was impossible for him to make them receive his five books as truth, which declared that these things had been done before their eyes, if they had not been so done.

But Mr. Leslie's four rules for determining the truth of historical facts will apply with equal force,

2. To the Gospel History.—The works and miracles of our Lord were done publicly in the face of the world. He said to his accusers, "I spake openly to the world, and in secret have I said nothing." John xviii, 20. But his works were as public as was his teaching. Some of his most notable miracles were performed in the presence of many witnesses. Take, for instance, his first miracle in Cana of Galilee,* the healing of the paralytic,† the raising of the widow's son from the dead at the city of Nain,‡ and the feeding of five thousand men, besides women and children.§ Equally public were the miracles wrought by the apostles; and as it is impossible that men could have been deceived in regard to what was done thus publicly before their eyes, these facts accord with the first two rules before mentioned.

Then, for the other two, we have Baptism and the Lord's Supper. These were instituted by the Author of the Christian religion, to be observed in his Church to the end of time: the former, as a *sign* and *seal* of God's gracious covenant with his people; and the latter, as a *memorial* of the sacrificial death of Christ. Accordingly, they have been observed, without interruption, down to this time.

Moreover, Christ ordained men to preach his Gospel, administer the sacraments, and govern his Church; and these ministers of religion have continued, in regular succession, until the present day. The exist-

* John ii, 1-10.   † Matt. ix. 2-8.   ‡ Luke vii, 11-15.   § Matt. xiv, 15-21.

ence of the Christian clergy is therefore as notorious a matter of fact as was that of the tribe of Levi among the Jews; and that such an order of men was appointed by Christ the Gospel positively declares.*

But if the Gospel is a fiction, and was invented in some age after Christ, then, at the time when it was invented, there could have been no public sacraments of Christ's institution, and no order of clergy to administer them. For it is impossible that these things could have existed before they were invented; and it is equally impossible that they could have been received, when invented, as matters of fact that had existed long before.

And now, to apply what has been said, we may safely affirm that the Sacred Scriptures never could have been received had not their historical records been true. The institution of the Priesthood of Levi, of the Sabbath, of the Passover, and of circumcision; as also that of the Gospel ministry, of Baptism, and of the Lord's Supper, are there related as having been handed down, without interruption, from the time in which they were severally appointed. But it was impossible to persuade men that they had been circumcised or baptized, that they had circumcised or baptized their children, that they had celebrated passovers, Sabbaths, and sacraments, under the administration of a certain order of priests, if they had done none of these things. And without believing such facts, it would have been impossible for men to receive either the Law or the Gospel.

These public institutions, then, are an appeal to the senses of mankind for the truth of the matters of fact recorded in the Jewish and the Christian Scriptures. For, as it is impossible that the senses of men could have been imposed upon at the time when such public matters of fact took place; so it is equally impossible that any one should have invented such stories in after ages without being detected at the time.

The authenticity of the Sacred Scriptures may be farther argued,

II. FROM THE CREDIBILITY OF THE SACRED WRITERS.

There are four facts which cannot fail to give credibility to any witness: 1. That he is virtuous and sober; 2. That he has had an opportunity to know the truth of what he relates; 3. That he has no interest in making good his story; and, 4. That his account is circumstantial. These guarantees of faithful testimony meet, in the highest degree, in the authors of the New Testament, and to them our remarks shall be principally confined.

1. *They were Men of strict and exemplary Virtue.*—Indeed, this has not been denied even by the most malicious enemies of Christianity. Of their sincerity they gave the utmost proof in the openness of their testimony, never affecting reserve or shunning inquiry. They were so fully convinced of the truth of the Gospel, that they were willing for

* Matt. x, 1–7; xviii, 18–20; xxviii, 19, 20.

its sake to endure all manner of shame, reproach, and persecution. They constantly exhibited, in the bright and faithful mirror of their own behavior, the amiableness and excellence of the religion which they taught; and, in every scene and circumstance of life, were distinguished for their devotion to God, their love for mankind, their sacred regard for truth, their self-government and moderation, and for every social and moral virtue that can adorn and exalt the character of man. They were never dejected or intimidated by their severest sufferings; but when persecuted in one city they fled to another, and there proclaimed their message with intrepid boldness and heaven-inspired zeal. They were patient in tribulation, joyful under reproach and persecution, and, when in dungeons, they cheered the silent hours of the night with hymns of praise to God. They met death itself in some of its most dreadful forms, but with a serenity and exultation that *Stoic philosophy* never knew.

2. *They were in Circumstances certainly to know the Truth of what they relate.*—They were the select companions and familiar friends of the hero of their story. They had free access to him at all times, heard both his public and private discourses, and were spectators of his amazing works. Some of them were his inseparable attendants, from the commencement to the close of his public ministry. No writers ever enjoyed a more favorable opportunity for publishing just accounts of persons and things than did the Evangelists for giving a true history of Jesus Christ.

Most of the *Greek* and *Roman* historians lived long after the persons whom they immortalize and the events which they record; but the sacred writers commemorate actions which they saw and discourses which they heard. They describe characters with which they were familiar and scenes in which they were deeply interested.

And as it was contrary to their character to deceive others, so neither could they be deceived themselves. They could not be deceived in the case of Christ's feeding the five thousand, of his suddenly healing those who were leprous, lame, and blind. They could not but know whether he who professed to be the risen Saviour, and with whom they conversed forty days, was the same Jesus with whom they had daily and familiar intercourse before his crucifixion. They could not be mistaken as to Christ's ascension to heaven; as to their being suddenly endowed with the gift of tongues; and as to their being able to work miracles, and to impart the same power to others.

3. *The Apostles were not influenced by Worldly Interests.*—Not only were they *disinterested* in their testimony, but their interests were on the side of concealment. One of the Evangelists, Matthew, occupied a lucrative situation when called by Jesus, and was evidently an opulent man. The fishermen of Galilee were at least in circumstances of comfort, and never had any worldly inducement held out to them by their

Master. St. Paul, from his education, connections, and talents, had encouraging prospects in life. But they voluntarily abandoned every temporal expectation, and embarked in a cause which the world regarded as wretched and hopeless to the last degree.

The *earthly* rewards which the apostles of our Lord obtained for their devotedness to his cause are thus graphically presented by St. Paul: "Even unto this present hour we both hunger and thirst, and are naked, and are buffeted, and have no certain dwelling-place; we are made as the filth of the world, and are the offscouring of all things unto this day." 1 Cor. iv, 11, 13. Finally, they sealed their testimony with their own blood; a circumstance of which they had been forewarned by their Master, and in the daily expectation of which they lived. From such facts the conclusion is irresistible, that these men *could not be deceivers.*

4. *Their Testimony was in the highest degree circumstantial.*—The writings of the Evangelists are full of references to persons then living, many of whom were persons of consequence, and to places in which miracles and other transactions had publicly taken place. If these things had not been true they would have been contradicted; and if contradicted on good evidence, the authors must have been overwhelmed with confusion.

This argument is strengthened by the consideration that "these things were not done in a corner;" nor was the age dark and illiterate, or prone to admit fables. The *Augustan Age* was the most learned that the world had ever seen. The love of arts, sciences, and literature was the universal passion in almost every part of the Roman Empire, where Christianity was first taught in its doctrines and proclaimed in its facts. In this inquisitive and discerning age it rose, flourished, and established itself, with much resistance to its doctrines, *but without being once questioned as to the truth of its historical facts.* And yet how easily might they have been disproved had they been false.

But we may add, finally, that the history of the Evangelists is impressed with every feature of credibility. An artless simplicity characterizes all their writings. They use no studied arts to adorn their story; but record the most astonishing events in as plain a manner, and with as much dispassionate coolness, as if they had been the most common transactions. They are distinguished above all other writers for their sincerity and integrity. Impostors never proclaim to the world the defects of their own character. But the Evangelists inform us of the lowliness and poverty of their condition, their dullness of apprehension, and of their ambitious views and warm contentions among themselves. They even tell us that they basely deserted their Master when he was seized by his enemies; and that, after his crucifixion, they returned to their former secular employments, abandoning the cause in which they had been so long engaged, notwithstanding the conviction which they had before entertained that Jesus was the *Messiah.*

Such men could neither suffer themselves to be deceived, nor be capable of imposing a falsehood upon others. We have therefore as much reason to believe that they have given us a true history of the life and transactions of JESUS, as that Xenophon and Plato have given a faithful narrative of the character and doctrines of SOCRATES. Their sacred regard for truth appears in everything which they have written; and to reject such a history is to insult the common understanding of mankind, and to renounce all faith in history. As well might we reject everything that is related in *Herodotus, Thucydides, Diodorus Siculus, Livy,* and *Tacitus,* and confound all history with fable, truth with falsehood, and veracity with imposture.

We have now considered the Genuineness, the Integrity, and the Authenticity of the Sacred Scriptures, and it only remains for us to show that these Scriptures are of DIVINE AUTHORITY. This question, therefore, will now be examined.

———————

CHAPTER V.

DIVINE AUTHORITY OF THE SACRED SCRIPTURES: INSPIRATION.

WHEN we say that the Sacred Scriptures are of Divine authority, our meaning is that they are *an inspired Revelation from God to man.* But before we attempt to adduce the evidences by which this proposition is infallibly established, we will inquire into the nature and extent of that Divine inspiration which is claimed for the sacred writers, and to this subject the present chapter will be devoted.

It has been shown that the sacred writers were men of the utmost integrity, and entitled to the most implicit confidence of mankind. But since it is possible that honest men may be mistaken, if we had nothing more to urge in behalf of these writers than the excellence of their character their writings would only be of human authority. Something more was therefore required than a pious life, and a mind purified from prejudice and passion, to qualify them for being infallible teachers of the will of God, namely, *Divine inspiration.*

This may be defined to be that extraordinary influence of the Holy Spirit upon the human mind by which men are qualified to communicate to others religious knowledge without error or mistake.

In the discussion of this subject it will be necessary, 1. To offer a few preliminary observations; 2. To show that the sacred writers claimed to be divinely inspired; and, 3. To ascertain, as nearly as we can, in what sense and to what extent they were supernaturally assisted in writing the Holy Scriptures.

I. WE WILL OFFER A FEW PRELIMINARY OBSERVATIONS.—It will be proper to observe,

1. *That Inspiration is possible.*—The Father of spirits may act upon the mind of his creatures, and this action may be extended to any degree which the purposes of God may require. He may superintend those who write, so as to prevent the possibility of error in their writings, which is the lowest degree of inspiration. He may enlarge their understanding, and elevate their conceptions beyond the measure of ordinary men, and this is the second degree. Or, he may suggest to them the thoughts which they should express, and the very words which they shall employ, so as to make them merely the vehicles of conveying his will to others. This is the highest degree of inspiration, and no sound Theist will deny that all these degrees are possible.

2. *It is reasonable,* that the sentiments and doctrines developed in the Holy Scriptures should be suggested to the mind of the writers by the Supreme Being himself. They are every way worthy of his character, and promotive of the highest interests of man; and the more important the communication is, the more it is calculated to preserve men from error, to stimulate them to holiness, and to guide them to happiness, the more reasonable it is to expect that God should make the communication free from every admixture of error. Indeed, the notion of inspiration enters essentially into our ideas of a revelation from God, so that to deny it is the same as to affirm that there is no revelation.

3. *Inspiration is necessary.*—This is evident from the nature of the *subjects* which the Scriptures unfold. Some past facts are recorded in the Bible which could not possibly have been known if God had not revealed them in a supernatural way. How, for instance, could Moses have given a correct history of the creation of the world, and of antediluvian times, if he had not been divinely inspired? The Scriptures contain predictions of future events which God alone could foreknow and foretell; and many of the doctrines which they unfold are so far above the capacity of the human mind to discover, that they must have been delivered by Divine inspiration.

The authoritative language of the Scriptures, too, if we admit the veracity of the writers, argues the necessity of inspiration. They propose things, not as matters for consideration, but for adoption. They do not grant us the alternative of receiving or rejecting their instructions. They do not present to us their own thoughts, but preface their communications by "*Thus saith the Lord,*" and on this ground demand our assent. It follows, therefore, either that the sacred writers spoke and wrote "as they were moved by the Holy Ghost," or that they were impostors. But as the latter is too absurd to be admitted, we must adopt the former.

If the Scriptures were not divinely inspired they could not claim our entire confidence as an infallible standard of religious truth. For, however fully we might be convinced of the honesty of the sacred writers, and of the general truthfulness of our religion, when we should proceed to examine its nature, and to investigate its doctrines, its precepts, its promises, and its institutions, we could not have perfect confidence in the detailed account, unless we had reason to believe that its authors had been so assisted by supernatural influence as to be infallibly preserved from all error.

4. *Divine Inspiration has always been ascribed to the sacred penmen*, both by the Jewish and the Christian Church. By the Jews the Law of Moses was accounted the Law of God himself, and their other canonical books were held in like veneration. Accordingly Josephus tells us that they were accustomed, from their infancy, to call these Scriptures *the doctrines of God;* and that they were ready, at any time, to lay down their life in vindication of them.

The primitive Christians entertained the same respect for the writings of Moses and the Prophets that the Jews did; but they received also, by universal consent, the Scriptures of the New Testament as being composed by the direction and Inspiration of the Holy Spirit. They regarded, therefore, both the Jewish and Christian Scriptures as *Oracles*, to decide all differences in matters of religion; and every sentence in them was looked upon as a Divine *axiom*, from which there was no appeal. And thus the case was viewed for nearly seventeen centuries, for it is only in modern days that the plenary inspiration of the Scriptures has been called in question.

The opinion of the Church in the first centuries, respecting the inspiration of the sacred writers, is explicitly set forth in the testimony of the Christian Fathers.

Clemens, Bishop of Rome, a cotemporary with the apostles, tells us that "the apostles preached the Gospel, being filled with the Holy Ghost;" that "the Scriptures are the true words of the Spirit;" that "Paul wrote to the Corinthians things true by the aid of the Spirit;" and that "he, being divinely inspired, admonished them by an epistle concerning himself, Cephas, and Apollos."

Justin Martyr says that "the Gospels were written by men full of the Holy Ghost."

Irenæus declares that "all the apostles received the Gospel by Divine revelation; that the Scriptures were dictated by the Spirit of God; and that, therefore, it is wickedness to contradict them, and sacrilege to make any alteration in them."

Theophilus, citing the authors of the Old and the New Testament, says that "both the one and the other spake, being inspired by one and the same Spirit." And again he says, "These things the Holy Scriptures teach us, and all who were moved by the Holy Spirit."

Clemens Alexandrinus says that "the whole Scriptures are the law of God—that they are all Divine; and that the evangelists and apostles wrote by the same Spirit that inspired the prophets."

Origen tells us that "the Scriptures proceeded from the Holy Spirit; that there is not one tittle in them but what expresses a Divine wisdom; that there is nothing in the Law, or the Prophets, or the Gospels, or the Epistles which did not proceed from the fullness of the Spirit; that we ought, with all the faithful, to say that the Scriptures are divinely inspired; that the Gospels are admitted as Divine in all the Churches of God; and that the Scriptures are no other than the organs of God."

II. THE SACRED WRITERS THEMSELVES CLAIMED TO BE DIVINELY INSPIRED. This is true,

1. *With regard to the Writers of the Old Testament Scriptures.*—The Jewish lawgiver often reminded those whom he addressed of the Divine authority of his communications by the well known declaration, "the Lord spake unto Moses;" and the language of David is, "the Spirit of the Lord spake by me, and his word was in my tongue." 2 Sam. xxiii, 2. Thus, too, the Jewish prophets delivered their predictions, not only in the name of Jehovah, but also as being received directly from him. Isaiah introduces many of his prophetic messages by the declaration, "Thus saith the Lord;" and Jeremiah, Ezekiel, and others by asserting, "The Lord said unto me," or, "The word of the Lord came unto me."

But the plenary inspiration of the Old Testament Scriptures is most distinctly asserted by Christ and his apostles. They recognize the whole Jewish Canon in their threefold division of the LAW, the PROPHETS, and the PSALMS. It is upon the evidence of these Scriptures that our Lord proves himself to be the Messiah; and to them he constantly appeals, both in proving his own doctrines and in refuting the errors of the Jews. But farther, what Moses wrote in the Pentateuch is expressly declared by Christ to have been spoken by God himself. "Have ye not read that which was *spoken unto you by God*, saying, I am the God of Abraham, and the God of Isaac, and the God of Jacob?" Matt. xxii, 31, 32.

What David wrote in the Psalms is declared by St. Peter to have been spoken by the Holy Ghost. "This Scripture must needs have been fulfilled, which the Holy Ghost by the mouth of David spake before concerning Judas." Acts i, 16. He tells us, moreover, that what the prophets delivered was by the Spirit of Christ speaking in them; and that they spoke "as they were moved by the Holy Ghost."*

St. Paul also bears the most unequivocal testimony to the inspiration of the Jewish prophets. "Well spake the Holy Ghost by Esaias the prophet unto our fathers." Acts xxviii, 25. And again, enlarging the terms which he employs to their utmost latitude, but undoubtedly hav-

* 1 Peter i, 11; 2 Peter i, 21.

ing a special reference to the Jewish Canon, he declares, "All Scripture is given by inspiration of God." 2 Tim. iii, 16. Thus we see that the writers of the New Testament Scriptures bear witness to the inspiration of those of the Old. But,

2. *They claim the same kind of Inspiration for themselves.*—The proof of this is seen,

(1.) *In the general tone of Confidence and Authority with which they delivered their Discourses.*—To feel the force of this argument, we must take a view of the apostles, first in themselves, and then in their changed condition, when the gifts of the Spirit had qualified them for the duties of their office.

Behold these weak, dismayed, and timid fishermen of Galilee, who had fled at the apprehension of their Master, and had with difficulty been persuaded of his resurrection. The day of Pentecost arrives, and they are all together in one place, waiting for the promised Comforter. The house is shaken where they are assembled, and the Divine Spirit descends and rests upon each of them under the external appearance of "cloven tongues like as of fire." They are suddenly endowed with new and surprising powers, assume a new character, and speak with new tongues. Unlearned as they were, and discouraged and cowardly as they had proved themselves to be, they discourse with the greatest readiness and propriety, and with a boldness which nothing could daunt, in every tongue and dialect of the assembled crowds. New courage, discernment, skill in argument, and fortitude in bearing testimony to the truth, appear in all their discourses. "With *great power* gave the apostles witness of the resurrection of the Lord Jesus, and great grace was upon them all." Acts iv, 33. But the apostles give us additional proof of their claim to Divine inspiration,

(2.) *In classing their own Teachings with the Scriptures of the Old Testament, as being of equal Authority with them.*—Hence St. Paul, in speaking of believers as "the household of God," declares that they "are built upon the foundation of the apostles and prophets." Eph. ii, 20. St. Peter occupies the same ground when he says, "I stir up your pure minds by way of remembrance; that ye may be mindful of the words which were spoken before by the holy prophets, and of the commandment of us the apostles of the Lord and Saviour." 2 Peter iii, 1, 2.

Again, they apply to the writings of the New Testament, as well as to those of the Old, the peculiar and solemn title of *Scripture*. "For the *Scripture* saith, Thou shalt not muzzle the ox that treadeth out the corn; and, the laborer is worthy of his reward." 1 Tim. v, 18. Here it is seen that the first part of the authoritative citation is taken from the Law of Moses; the second, from the Gospel of St. Luke.* Peter speaks of the Epistles of St. Paul as being indited by more than human

* Deut. xxv, 4; Luke x, 7.

wisdom, and evidently claims for them Divine authority. They are revelations of Divine truth, " which they that are unlearned and unstable wrest, as they do also the other Scriptures, unto their own destruction." 2 Peter iii, 16. To these considerations it may be added that the claim of the apostles to Divine inspiration is evinced,

(3.) *By their own positive and express Declarations.*—If the prophets began their discourses with the solemn formula, " Thus saith the Lord," the apostles begin with the same claim of a Divine command: " Paul, an apostle of Jesus Christ, by the commandment of God our Saviour." 1 Tim. i, 1. " If any man think himself to be a prophet, or spiritual, let him acknowledge that the things that I write unto you are the commandments of the Lord." 1 Cor. xiv, 37.

In the fifteenth chapter of the Acts of the Apostles we have the account of an epistle which was addressed by the College of Apostles to the brethren of the Gentiles. In this short letter we have this remarkable passage: " For it seemed good *to the Holy Ghost and to us* to lay upon you no greater burden than these necessary things." Hence it follows that the Apostolical Epistles claim to be inspired by the Holy Ghost.

St. Paul, in his First Epistle to the Corinthians, uses this language : " My speech and my preaching was not with enticing words of man's wisdom, but in demonstration of the Spirit and of power, that your faith should not stand in the wisdom of men, but in the power of God." He then declares that his doctrine was " the wisdom of God in a mystery ;" that it was what " none of the princes of this world knew ;" but that God had revealed it to him " *by his Spirit.*" Here the apostle evidently claims Divine inspiration ; but to put this beyond all possibility of doubt, he expresses himself in terms which cannot be misunderstood : " Which things also we speak, not in the words which man's wisdom teacheth, but which the *Holy Ghost teacheth,* comparing spiritual things with spiritual," or, as some render it, adapting spiritual expressions to spiritual things.

Again, the apostle's solemn injunction to the Galatians to adhere strictly to his doctrines demands our attention. On a particular point of prudential discipline, such as the marriage of Christians under certain circumstances, he had received no inspired communication, and he mentions the exception. But on all the truths of the Christian revelation he had received the most positive command. What then is his language when he approaches the doctrines of Christianity? "I marvel that ye are so soon removed from him that called you into the grace of Christ, unto another Gospel. But though we, or an angel from heaven, preach any other Gospel unto you than that which we have preached unto you, let him be accursed. I certify you, brethren, that the Gospel which was preached of me is not after man ; for I neither received it of man, neither was I taught it, but by the revelation of Jesus Christ. It pleased God to reveal his Son in me, that I might preach him among the heathen." Gal. i, 6–16.

Correspondent to these declarations is the language of the apostle, when, in his Epistle to the Ephesians, he is speaking of the revelation of Gospel privileges to the Gentile world. "If ye have heard of the dispensation of the grace of God which is given me to you-ward: how that by *revelation he made known unto me the mystery*, as I wrote afore in few words; whereby, when ye read, ye may understand my knowledge in the mystery of Christ, which in other ages was not made known unto the sons of men, as *it is now revealed unto the holy apostles and prophets by the Spirit.*" Eph. iii, 2–5.

We have now seen that Divine inspiration is possible, reasonable, and necessary; that the Church, in all ages, has ascribed it to the sacred writers; and that they have claimed it in terms which cannot be mistaken. Let us then proceed to inquire,

III. *In what sense and to what extent they were supernaturally assisted in writing the Holy Scriptures?*

This question has given rise to a diversity of opinions. Some have had the boldness to deny inspiration altogether, while others have circumscribed it within very narrow limits. "I think," says Dr. Priestley, "that the Scriptures were written, without any particular inspiration, by men who wrote according to the best of their knowledge, and who, from their circumstances, could not be mistaken with respect to the greater facts, of which they were proper witnesses." He assumes, however, that they were liable, like other men, "to adopt a hasty and ill-grounded opinion concerning things which did not fall within the compass of their own knowledge." But it is a sufficient refutation of this theory that it directly contradicts what the sacred writers declare of themselves, and is an impeachment of their veracity.

Some who advocate the doctrine of Divine inspiration limit it to the prophetical parts of Scripture; while others extend it to the *doctrinal* parts also, but not to the historical. There are many who maintain that the inspiration of the sacred writers was only occasional; that they were not always under that immediate and plenary influence of the Holy Spirit which renders their writings the unerring word of God; and that consequently, as they were sometimes left to themselves, they then thought and reasoned like ordinary men. According to this notion, an intermixture of human infirmity and error is by no means excluded from the Sacred Scriptures. But if it is once granted that they are in the least degree alloyed with error, an opening is made for every imaginable corruption. And to admit that the sacred writers were only occasionally inspired, would involve us in the greatest perplexity; because, not knowing when they were or were not inspired, we could not determine what parts of their writings should be regarded as the infallible word of God. To tell us, therefore, that they were inspired only on certain occasions, while we have no means of ascertaining what those occasions were, is the same as to say that they were not inspired at all.

Many learned men have held the *plenary* inspiration of the Scriptures; the import of which is that every part of them is inspired. This doctrine has been violently opposed, and even treated with ridicule; but the objections against it have arisen, in some cases at least, from misconception. It has been supposed to imply that every part of the sacred books was immediately communicated to the mind of the writers. Hence it has been argued that as some parts of them relate to things which might have been known from other sources, it is absurd to suppose a revelation where the bodily senses and natural reason were adequate to the purpose. But this is not the true idea of plenary inspiration. It extends, indeed, to every part of the Scriptures; but it admits of degrees suited to the nature of the various subjects which the writers were employed to record, and did not supersede the use of their natural faculties, so far as these could contribute to the general design.

We do not then apply the term inspiration in the same sense to every portion of Scripture, because the same degree of Divine assistance was not necessary in the composition of every part. When the prophets predicted future events, or when the apostles made known the mysteries of redemption, it was God alone who spoke, and they were employed merely as instruments for the communication of his will. When Moses related the miracles of Egypt and the journeyings of the Israelites in the wilderness, and when the Evangelists related the history of Christ, they only declared what they had previously known; but without the assistance of the Holy Spirit they could not have performed their work so well.

The true doctrine of plenary inspiration may be drawn from the special promises which our Lord made to his apostles respecting the gift of the Holy Spirit. "But the Comforter, which is the Holy Ghost, whom the Father will send in my name, he shall teach you all things, and bring all things to your remembrance, whatsoever I have said unto you." John xiv, 26. And again, "When he, the Spirit of truth, is come, he will guide you into all truth; for he shall not speak of himself; but whatsoever he shall hear, that shall he speak; and he will show you things to come." John xvi, 13.

If we examine these promises we can hardly fail to see that they must have related to those supernatural endowments which were necessary to render the apostles infallible teachers of the doctrines of Christianity. The Holy Ghost is here promised, not as a *Spirit of Miracles* but as a SPIRIT OF TRUTH; an expression which, if taken in connection with other terms of the passages, manifestly includes an unerring direction in the communication of religious instruction. The Spirit was also promised to abide with them "*for ever;*" and this promise secured to them his constant operations, without change or intermission, whenever and wherever they were engaged in the execution of their office.

Again, the Holy Ghost is called "*another* Comforter," from which phraseology the apostles must have drawn the conclusion that he would fully supply the place of their Master's personal presence; and with the distinct promises before them that the Comforter would teach them all things, bring all things to their remembrance, guide them into all truth, and show them things to come, they could not, from the most obvious meaning of these declarations, expect anything less than the constant help of the Holy Spirit to secure them from all error in the communication of religious instruction.

But we have a more particular account of the nature and extent of that supernatural influence which these promises imply in the language of our Saviour on another occasion. "When they bring you unto the synagogues, and unto magistrates and powers, take ye no thought how or what thing ye shall answer, or what ye shall say; for the Holy Ghost shall teach you in the same hour what ye ought to say." Luke xii, 11, 12. To this it is added by Matthew: "For it is not ye that speak, but the Spirit of your Father which speaketh in you." Matt. x, 20. Such, then, is the nature of Divine inspiration; it is the Spirit of God speaking in or by men, and teaching them what they ought to say. But if the apostles were thus divinely assisted in defending themselves before their persecutors, we surely have a right to conclude that they were at least equally assisted in composing their sacred books, as these were to be the rule of faith and practice to the Church in all succeeding ages.

The different degrees of Inspiration which theologians have usually mentioned are *superintendence, elevation,* and *suggestion.* Let us briefly inquire into the nature of each.

1. *Superintendence* signifies that controlling influence of the Holy Spirit by which the sacred writers, in relating what they knew by ordinary means, were preserved from error, and directed to what they should record.

There are many things in the Scriptures which the writers must have known without any direct communication from God. They did not need a revelation to inform them of what passed before their eyes, or to point out those inferences and moral maxims which were obvious to every attentive observer. Moses could record, without a Divine afflatus, the deliverance of the Israelites from bondage, and the history of their journeyings toward the Promised Land. So Solomon could remark that " a soft answer turneth away wrath, but grievous words stir up anger;" or, that "better is a dinner of herbs where love is, than a stalled ox and hatred therewith." In such cases as these no supernatural influence was required to enlighten the mind of the writers. It was necessary, however, that they should be infallibly preserved from error.

But the true notion of superintendence implies also that the sacred penmen were moved or excited by the Holy Ghost to record particular events, and to set down particular observations. They were not like common historians, who introduce facts and reflections into their narratives according to their own judgment and sense of propriety; but they were rather like amanuenses, who commit to writing such things only as are selected by their employers. Passages which are thus recorded under the direction and superintendence of the Spirit are, in a proper sense, divinely inspired. But if the writers had recorded them at the suggestions of their own minds they would be mere human compositions, and, though free from error, would be exactly on a level with profane history, so far as it is agreeable to truth.

2. *Elevation* denotes that Divine influence by which the mental faculties of the sacred writers, though acting in a natural way, were raised and invigorated to an extraordinary degree; so that their compositions were more truly sublime, noble, and pathetic than what they could have produced merely by the force of their natural genius.

By some this kind of inspiration is restricted to such parts of Scripture as are lofty and sublime; but it is easy to perceive that there must have been, in some cases at least, an elevation of the mind above its ordinary state, even when the province of the writer was simple narrative. This may be seen in the case of the Evangelists. It is not to be supposed that illiterate men, unskilled in the art of composition, such as we may conceive Jewish fishermen and publicans to have been, could, if they had not been supernaturally assisted, have expressed themselves with that perspicuity and dignity of language by which their writings are so eminently characterized. It must be granted, therefore, that a Divine influence was exerted upon the mind of the Evangelists by which they were enabled to relate the discourses and miracles of our Lord, and to record the facts of his history, not only with fidelity, but in that manner also which was most appropriate and impressive.

Further, in many passages of Scripture there is such a grandeur, such a sublimity of ideas and expressions, as must inevitably lead us to conclude that the faculties of the writers were elevated far above their ordinary capacity. " Should a person of moderate talents give as elevated a description of the majesty and attributes of God, or reason as profoundly on the mysterious doctrines of religion, as a man of the most exalted genius and extensive learning, we could not fail to be convinced that he was supernaturally assisted; and the conviction would be still stronger if his composition should transcend the highest efforts of the human mind. In either of these cases it would be impossible to account for the effect by the operation of any ordinary cause; and yet sentiments so dignified, and representations of Divine things so grand and majestic occur in their writings, that the noblest flights of human genius, when compared with them, appear cold and insipid."*

3. *Suggestion* is the highest degree of inspiration, and includes all those direct revelations which were made to the sacred writers, of such things as they could not have discovered by ordinary means. It is manifest, with respect to many passages of Scripture, that the subjects of which they treat must have been matters of direct revelation. They could not have been known by natural means, nor was the knowledge of them attainable by a simple elevation of the mental faculties. They were founded on the free determinations of God and his prescience of human affairs, and with the abilities of an angel we could not explore the thoughts and purposes of the Divine mind. Such subjects, therefore, could not have been known but by a direct communication from the "Father of lights." This degree of inspiration is properly ascribed to those who were employed to predict future events, to those who were sent with particular messages from God to his people, and to those who were empowered to make known the mysteries of the Gospel.†

From the preceding account of inspiration, it is easy to perceive in what sense the Scriptures, taken as a whole, may be called the *Word of God*. We give them this denomination because they were written by persons who were moved, directed, and assisted by the Holy Spirit, and who were, therefore, infallibly preserved from error. Hence we are authorized to consider all the doctrines, precepts, promises, and threatenings which they contain, as true, righteous, and faithful; and to believe also that the events which are said to have happened did so happen, and that the words which are said to have been spoken were so spoken.

We are not to conclude, however, that all the sentiments contained in the Scriptures are just, and that all the examples are worthy of imitation. Some, from the want of reflection, fall into a mistake in this matter. They quote a sentiment as authoritative because they read it in the Scriptures, without waiting to consider by whom it was uttered. They draw arguments for the regulation of their own conduct and that of others from some recorded action, without inquiring into its moral quality. Yet it is certain that the sacred writers recorded not only the imperfections and misdoings of those who were confessedly pious, but also the words and actions of wicked men and devils. No moral action, therefore, is proved to be right merely from its being recorded in the Scriptures. This only proves that the action did really take place, and that it was the will of God that we should know it; but its conformity or disconformity to the standard of truth and rectitude must be determined by the judgment pronounced in the Scriptures themselves on par-

---

* Dick's Theology, vol. i, Lecture xi.
† See Gal. i, 12; Eph. iii, 3, 5; 1 Cor. ii, 9, 10.

ticular cases, or by applying those principles and general rules which are laid down in them to regulate our decisions.

Whether inspiration extended to the *language* of the Scriptures, as well as to the subjects recorded, is a question which has engaged a considerable share of attention. In answering this question it may be of some importance to distinguish one part of Scripture from another. We cannot rationally suppose that in those commands, messages, and communications which were delivered in the name of God the writers were left to choose their own language; but the very words, as well as the thoughts, must have been dictated by the Holy Spirit. This was evidently the case when they announced new and mysterious doctrines, of which they could have had no conception if the words had not been suggested to them; and when they delivered predictions which they did not understand, the inspiration consisted solely in presenting the words to their mind. That the prophets did not always understand their own predictions is obvious from the language of Peter, who represents them as trying to search out their meaning: "Searching what, or what manner of time the Spirit of Christ which was in them did signify when it testified beforehand the sufferings of Christ, and the glory that should follow." 1 Peter i, 11. Thus far, therefore, it must be allowed that inspiration extended to the words.

With regard to other parts of Scripture, consisting of histories, moral reflections, and devotional pieces, we would not contend for the inspiration of the language in the same sense. It is reasonable to believe that the writers were permitted to exercise their own faculties to a certain extent, and to express themselves in their natural manner; but, at the same time, we have no right to suppose that even when they were most at liberty, they were in no degree directed by a secret influence in the selection of words and phrases.

It was of the utmost importance that the facts and observations which God intended for the instruction of mankind in all ages should be properly expressed. But if we had nothing to depend upon for the accuracy of Scripture language but the skill and attention of the writers themselves, most of whom were illiterate and ignorant of the art of composition, we could have no certainty that it is always correct; and our faith would be frequently disturbed by the suspicion, that what is only a difficulty might be a mistake. It must be granted, therefore, that the sacred writers, even in relating what they knew, what they had seen, and what they had learned from the testimony of others, were divinely assisted in the words which they employed; and consequently, their very language bears the seal of God's approbation.

To this it is objected, that each of the sacred penmen has written in his own peculiar *style*, and therefore the *language* of Scripture cannot be a matter of inspiration. We admit the statement, but deny the inference, because the diversity of style observable in the sacred writers is by no means inconsistent with the inspiration of their language. It is possible, and in the highest degree probable, that God, in communicating his will to mankind, accommodated himself to the character and genius of those whom he employed as his instruments; and surely no man in his senses will affirm that there was only one style in which he could communicate his will.

"God employs second causes in all his operations so far as we can trace them. In employing these second causes he conforms to the laws to which he himself has subjected them. God waters the earth, but how? Here, by gentle and oft-repeated showers; there, by the silent and refreshing dews; and yonder, by the overflowing river. God destroys the wicked nation: in this instance, by turning the waters of the river and sending an invading army through the channel; in that, by the crow and the battering-ram; in another, by the bomb-shell and the bayonet. God, in condescension to human infirmities, uses human *language*. Is it any more wonderful that he should avail himself of human *peculiarities?* that, in conveying truth to the prophet's lips, he should take the route of the prophet's imagination, emotions, and mental habits? Truly, there is nothing incredible in this to him who knows that the hearts and minds of men are in the hands of God, as well as all the modifications of external nature."*

CHAPTER VI.

DIVINE AUTHORITY OF THE SACRED SCRIPTURES: PROOF FROM MIRACLES.

It has already been proved that Miracles are possible; that they are appropriate, necessary, and satisfactory evidences of a revelation from God; and that, like other facts, they are capable of being authenticated by credible testimony. These points having been established, the main questions before us are, whether the facts alleged as miraculous in the Old and the New Testament have sufficient claim to that character, and whether they were wrought in confirmation of the doctrines and mission of the founders of the Jewish and the Christian religion.

As miracles are manifestly above human power, and as no created being can effect them, unless empowered by the Author of nature, when they are wrought in proof of some particular doctrine, or in attestation of the authority of some particular person, they are authentications of a Divine mission by a special and sensible interposition of God himself.

* Dr. Thomson's Lectures.

Let us, then, in examining the miracles of Scripture, turn our attention, 1. To those of Moses; and, 2. To those of Christ.

I. THE MIRACLES OF MOSES.

From the numerous miracles wrought by the agency of Moses we will select only a few. We notice,

1. *The Plague of* DARKNESS.*—Two circumstances are to be noted in this event. It continued three days, and it afflicted none but the Egyptians; for "all the children of Israel had light in their dwellings." The phenomenon was not produced by an eclipse of the sun, for no eclipse of that luminary can continue so long. Some of the Roman writers mention a darkness by day so great that persons were unable to know each other; but we have no account of any other darkness so long-continued as this, which was so intense that the Egyptians "rose not up from their places for three days."

But if any such circumstance had again occurred, and a natural cause could have been assigned for it, yet even then the miraculous character of this event would remain unshaken; for the distinction made between the Israelites and the Egyptians, while they inhabited the same district of country, must be attributed to a supernatural cause. "Moses stretched out his hand," and the darkness prevailed everywhere except in the dwellings of his people. The fact being allowed, the *miracle* of necessity follows. We will consider,

2. *The destruction of the* FIRST-BORN *of Egypt.*†—This judgment was threatened in the presence of Pharaoh, *before* any of the other plagues were brought upon him and his people. The Israelites also were forewarned of it, and were directed to slay a lamb, to sprinkle the blood upon their door-posts, and to prepare for their departure that same night. The stroke was inflicted only upon the first-born of the Egyptians, and not upon any other part of the family—it occurred in the same hour; but the first-born of the Israelites escaped, without a single exception.

The history, therefore, being established, the *miracle* must be admitted; for if a pestilence were to be assumed as the agent of this calamity, every one knows that an epidemic disease comes not upon the threat of a mortal, and makes no such selection as the first-born of every family.

3. *The dividing of the* RED SEA.‡—This miracle has already been mentioned, but merits a more particular consideration. The miraculous character of this event is strongly marked. An expanse of water from nine to twelve miles broad, known to be exceedingly subject to agitations, is divided, and a wall of water is formed on each side, affording a passage on dry land for the Israelites. The instrument is a strong east wind, which begins its operation upon the waters at the stretching out of the hand of Moses and ceases at the same signal. The phenomenon

* See Exod. x, 21-23.   † See Exod. xii, 29, 30.   ‡ Exod. xiv, 21-23.

occurs just as the Egyptians are on the point of overtaking the Israelites, and ceases when the latter reach the opposite shore in safety; and when the former are in the midst of the passage, and in the only position in which the closing of the waters could insure the entire destruction of so large a host.

It has been asked whether there were not some ledges of rocks where the water was shallow, so that an army, at particular times, might pass over; and whether the *Etesian* winds might not blow so violently against the sea as to keep it back " on a heap." But if there were any force in these questions, such suppositions would not account for the destruction of the Egyptians.

At the place where the passage of the Red Sea was effected its depth, according to Bruce, is about fourteen fathoms, and its breadth between three and four leagues. But there is no "ledge of rocks;" and as to the *Etesian* winds, if they could keep the sea as a wall on one side, still the difficulty would remain of building the wall on the other. It is also worthy of remark, that the *monsoon* of the Red Sea blows the summer half of the year from the north and the winter half from the south, neither of which could have produced the miracle in question. For the wind which actually did blow, according to the history, was an "*east wind*," and, as Dr. Hales observes, "seems to be introduced, by way of anticipation, to exclude the *natural* agency which might be afterward resorted to for solving the miracle."

4. *The Miracle of the* MANNA.—The falling of the manna in the wilderness for forty years is another unquestionable miracle. That this event was not produced by the ordinary course of nature is rendered certain by the fact that the same wilderness has been traveled by individuals and by large bodies of men from the earliest ages to the present, but no such supply of food was ever found, except on this occasion. Its miraculous character is marked by the following circumstances: 1. It fell but six days in the week; ·2. It was so abundant as to sustain three millions of people; 3. A double quantity fell on every Friday, so as to serve the Israelites for the next day, which was their Sabbath; 4. What was gathered on the first five days of the week bred worms and became offensive if kept over one day, but that which was gathered on Friday kept sweet for two days; and, 5. It continued to fall while the Israelites remained in the wilderness, but ceased as soon as they obtained corn to eat in the land of Canaan. Let these very extraordinary particulars be considered and they will unequivocally establish the miracle.

II. THE MIRACLES OF CHRIST.

When we proceed to the examination of these we find that their miraculous character becomes, if possible, still more indubitable. Even a slight investigation of the feeding of the multitudes in the desert, the healing of the paralytic, the raising from the dead of the daughter of Jairus, of the widow's son, and of .Lazarus, and many other such instances of miraculous power, will be sufficient to convince any ingenuous mind that all the characters of real and adequately attested miracles meet in them. But to complete this branch of external evidence it is only necessary to adduce that greatest of all miracles, the resurrection of our Lord from the dead.

That it is a miracle, in its highest sense, for a person actually dead to raise himself again to life cannot be doubted; and when wrought, as the raising of Christ was, in attestation of a Divine commission, it is evidence of the most irrefragable kind. So this miracle has been regarded by unbelievers, who have bent all their force against it; and so God himself regarded it, rendering its proofs ample and indubitable in proportion to its importance. That we may perceive it in its true light, let us attend to the following remarks:

1. *There can be no dispute in regard to the Reality of Christ's Death.*—His execution was public, where all could witness the tragedy. When the soldiers who broke the legs of the two malefactors came to Jesus they saw that he was already dead. Pilate refused to deliver the body for burial until he had learned, from the officer on duty, that he was really dead. But if no such circumstantial evidence could be adduced, it is not to be supposed that they who had sought his death with so much eagerness would be inattentive to the full execution of the sentence for which they had clamored. The reality of Christ's death is therefore established.

2. *He was not taken away to some unknown or distant place of interment.*—Joseph, of Arimathea, made no secret of the place where he had buried him. It was in his own family tomb, "which was nigh at hand;" and the Pharisees knew where to direct the watch which was appointed to guard the sepulcher.

3. *It is agreed on all hands that the Body of Christ was removed from the Tomb,* and that in a state of death it was never more seen. How then is this fact accounted for? The disciples affirm that in the midst of a great earthquake, and while the affrighted keepers became as dead men, an angel descended from heaven and rolled back the stone from the door of the sepulcher, proclaiming that Jesus Christ had risen from the dead; that they examined the tomb for themselves, and saw his grave-clothes, but found not his body; that at different times he appeared to them, both separately and when assembled; that he continued to make his appearance among them for about forty days, allowing them to converse with him and to handle his body; and that he finally led them out to Bethany and, in the presence of them all, ascended to heaven.

The manner in which the Jewish Sanhedrim accounted for the absence of our Lord's body from the sepulcher is, that "his disciples came by night and stole him away," while the Roman soldiers were sleeping. As we have no other account, we are warranted in the conclusion that

PROOF FROM MIRACLES.

the Pharisees had nothing but this to oppose to the positive testimony of the disciples. But it must be seen that in this attempt they fell far below their usual subtilty, for the story which they circulated carries with it its own refutation. This, however, may be accounted for from the hurry and agitation of the moment, and from the necessity under which they were laid to invent *something* to amuse the populace, who were rather inclined to charge them with the death of Jesus.

This absurd rumor was not only hastily gotten up, but it was almost as hastily abandoned; for it is remarkable that it was never adverted to by the Pharisees in any of those legal proceedings which were instituted against the first preachers of Christ as the risen Messiah. Peter and John were first brought before the great council, then the whole body of the apostles twice. On all these occasions they affirmed the resurrection of Christ before the very men who had originated the tale of the stealing away of his body; but in none of these instances did the chief priests oppose their story to the explicit testimony of the disciples, or bring forward even *one* of the sixty soldiers to disprove what they asserted.

That a Roman guard should be found off their watch, or asleep, a fault which the military law of that people punished with death, is most incredible. Or that the timid disciples of Christ should dare to steal away his body, even if the guard were asleep, is very improbable. The soldiers were either awake or asleep: if awake, why did they suffer a few unarmed men and women to take away the body? and if asleep, how came they to know that the disciples had done it?

There is really, therefore, no testimony whatever against the resurrection of Christ. The very inability of the Jewish rulers to account for the absence of his body, which had been entirely in their own power, affords strong presumptive evidence in favor of the statement of the disciples. The tomb was carefully closed and sealed by officers appointed for that purpose, a guard was set, and yet the body was removed. The story of the Pharisees does not at all account for the fact, being too absurd to be for a moment credited; and unless the history of the Evangelists be admitted, that singular fact remains still to be accounted for.

But, in addition to this presumption, let the circumstances of credibility in the testimony of the disciples be collected, and the evidence will become indubitable.

(1.) *Their own account sufficiently proves that they were incredulous as to the fact of the Resurrection of Christ when it was first announced*, and therefore they were not likely to be imposed upon by a mere conceit. Indeed this, under all the circumstances, was *impossible;* for the appearances of Christ were too numerous, and continued for too long a time, forty days. And it was equally impossible that they should persuade upward of five hundred persons that they had seen and conversed with Christ, or to agree, not only without reward, but in renunciation of all interests, and in hazard of all dangers and of death itself, to continue to assert a falsehood.

(2.) *The account given by the disciples is highly probable;* for if we allow the miracles wrought by Christ during his life, his resurrection follows as a *natural* conclusion. Before that event can be maintained to be in the lowest sense improbable, the whole history of his public life, in opposition not to the Evangelists merely, but to the testimony of Jews and heathens also, must be proved to be a fable.

(3.) *The manner in which their testimony is given is in its favor.* They give an account of the transaction so variant as to make it clear that they wrote independent of one another; and yet so agreeing in the leading facts, and so easily capable of reconcilement in those minute circumstances in which some discrepancy at first sight appears, that their evidence in every part carries with it the air of honesty and truth.

(4.) *A long period did not elapse before the fact of the Resurrection was proclaimed;* nor was a distant place chosen in which to make the first report of it. These would have been suspicious circumstances. But, on the contrary, the disciples testified the fact *from the very day of the resurrection.* One of them, in a public speech at the feast of Pentecost, addressed to a mixed multitude, affirmed it; and the same testimony was given by the whole college of apostles, before the great council, twice. This, too, was done *at Jerusalem,* the scene of the whole transaction, and in the presence of those most interested in detecting the falsehood had it indeed been false. Their evidence was given before magistrates and tribunals; before philosophers, rabbies, and lawyers; before people expert in examining and cross-examining witnesses; and yet they were never convicted of prevarication, nor were they ever confronted with others who could contradict them, as to this or any other matter of fact.

(5.) *To this testimony of the Apostles was added the seal of Miracles.* The gift of tongues was in proof of the resurrection and ascension of Jesus Christ; and the miracles of healing, which were wrought by the apostles in their Master's *name,* were proofs both of his resurrection and of their Divine commission.*

We may close this chapter by observing that the miracles which the Scriptures record, while they prove the Divine authority of the sacred books, are connected, in a most remarkable manner, with that system of human recovery which has been carried on in the world from the fall of Adam to the present time.

The mark set upon Cain served as a memorial of the first apostacy from the true religion under a dispensation of grace. The general

---

* See West on the Resurrection; Sherlock's Trial of the Witnesses; and Dr. Cook's Illustration of the Evidence of Christ's Resurrection.

deluge was an awful instance of Divine vengeance against an ungodly world. The confusion of tongues was intended to preserve the worship of the true God from the influence of atheism and idolatry. The wonders wrought in Egypt, by the hand of Moses, were manifestly designed to expose the senseless and abominable idolatries of that devoted country; and the subsequent miracles in the desert had an evident tendency to wean the Israelites from an attachment to the false deities of the surrounding nations. The wonders connected with the settlement of the Israelites in Canaan, and with their subsequent history, all conspired to the separation of that people from a wicked and apostate world, and to the preservation of a chosen seed, through whom all the nations of the earth should be blessed. Every miracle wrought under the Jewish theocracy appears to have been intended, either to correct the superstitions and impieties of the neighboring nations, or to reclaim the Jews whenever they betrayed a disposition to relapse into heathenish abominations and to forsake the true religion.

In the miracles of our Lord he not only evinced his Divine power, but fulfilled many important predictions relating to himself as the Messiah, and thus afforded a twofold evidence of his authority. And in those of the apostles there is nothing done for mere ostentation, but all have a direct reference to the great purpose of the Gospel, that of turning men "from darkness to light, and from the power of Satan unto God."

Whoever will take this view of the peculiar design and use of Scripture miracles must perceive in them the unerring counsels of Infinite *Wisdom*, as well as the undoubted exertions of Infinite Power. He will be compelled to acknowledge that they exhibit proofs of *Divine agency*, carried on in one continued series, such as no other system can claim; and that such agency is not only beyond the power of created beings, but demonstrates the impossibility of imposture in any part of the proceeding.

On miracles, therefore, like those which attest the mission of Moses and of Christ, we may safely rest the proof of the authority of both, and say to each of them, though with a due sense of the superiority of the "SON" to the "SERVANT," "*Rabbi, we know that thou art a teacher come from God, for no man can do these miracles that thou doest, except God be with him.*" John iii, 2.

CHAPTER VII.

DIVINE AUTHORITY OF THE SACRED SCRIPTURES: PROOF FROM PROPHECY.

The nature and force of the argument from Prophecy have already been stated,* and it has been proved that *real predictions* can be uttered only by inspired men, and that the author of such communications can be no other than the infinite and omniscient God, showing to his servants things to come in order to authenticate their mission, and to fix upon their doctrines the stamp of his own infallible authority.

The only subject of inquiry proper to this chapter is, therefore, the *prophetic character* of the predictions contained in the Old and the New Testament. In order to place this subject in as clear a light as possible, it will be necessary, 1. To make a few general observations; and, 2. To adduce some examples of Scripture prophecy which prove themselves to be real predictions.

I. General Observations in regard to the Prophecies of the Holy Scriptures.

1. *The instances to be considered by those who would fully satisfy themselves on this point are numerous.* There are prophecies relative to individuals, to cities and states, to the person and offices of Christ, and to the Christian Church. Some of these have been unequivocally fulfilled; and there are others which are now taking place, or which are to be fulfilled hereafter.

2. *Men may differ in regard to the fulfillment of some particular prophecies;* but there are many others the accomplishment of which has been so evident as to defy rational doubt. Nor can it be shown that any clear prediction of the Holy Scriptures has ever been falsified by the event.

3. *The Predictions of Scripture chiefly relate to a grand scheme for the moral recovery of the human race from ignorance, vice, and wretchedness.* They speak of the agents to be employed in it, and especially of the Redeemer himself; and of those mighty and awful proceedings of Providence, as to the nations of the earth, by which judgment and mercy are exercised with reference both to the ordinary principles of moral government, and especially to this restoring economy.

Prophecy is of very great extent. It commenced at the fall of man, and reaches to the consummation of all things. For many ages it was delivered darkly to but few persons, and with long intervals from the date of one prophecy to that of another; but at length it became more

* See chapter i of this book, § 1.

clear and more frequent. It was uniformly carried on in the line of one people, who were separated from the rest of the world that they might be the repository of the Divine Oracles; and, with some intermission, the spirit of prophecy subsisted among them to the coming of the Messiah. But Christ and his apostles exercised this power in the most conspicuous manner, leaving behind them many predictions, recorded in the New Testament, which profess to respect very distant events, and even to run out to the end of time.

Farther, besides the extent of this prophetic scheme, the dignity of the *Person* whom it mainly concerns deserves our consideration. He is described in terms which excite the most august and magnificent ideas. He is indeed spoken of as "*the seed of the woman*," and as "*the Son of man ;*" yet so as being at the same time of more than mortal extraction. He is represented as the Word and the Wisdom of God; as the eternal Son of the Father; and the "brightness of his glory, and the express image of his person." Such is the transcendent excellence of that Jesus to whom all the prophets bear witness.

But we may add, that the declared purpose for which the Messiah came into the world corresponds to all the rest of the representation. It was not to deliver an oppressed nation from civil tyranny, or to erect a great civil empire. It was another and far sublimer purpose—a purpose, in comparison of which all our policies are poor and little, and all the performances of man as nothing. It was to deliver a world from ruin; to abolish sin and death; to purify and immortalize human nature; and thus, in the most exalted sense, to be the Saviour of men and a blessing to all nations. Such is the scriptural delineation of that economy which we call prophetic.

4. *Prophecy in this peculiar sense, and on this ample scale, is found nowhere but in the Holy Scriptures*, and to them therefore the advantage of this species of evidence exclusively belongs. It is a *growing* evidence, gathering strength by length of time, and affording from age to age fresh proofs of its Divine origin. Heathenism never made any clear and well-founded pretensions to it; and Mohammedanism, though it stands as a proof of the truth of Scripture prophecy, is unsupported by a single prediction of its own.

5. *The Objection raised to Scripture Prophecy from its supposed obscurity has no solid foundation.* There is, it is true, a prophetic language of symbol, or emblem; but it is a language which is definite in its meaning, and as easily understood as that of poetry. This, however, is not always used. The style of prophecy often differs in nothing from that of the Hebrew poets, or sinks into the plainness of historical narrative.

The two great ends of prophecy are, to excite expectation before the event, and to confirm the truth by an unequivocal fulfillment; and it is a sufficient answer to the allegation of the obscurity of prophecy, that it has abundantly accomplished both these objects. It cannot be denied, for instance, that by means of predictions an expectation of the advent of a *Divine Restorer* was kept up among the Jews; that as these predictions multiplied their expectation became more intense; and that at the time of our Lord's coming this expectation prevailed, not only among the Israelites, but also among other nations. This purpose then was sufficiently answered, and the objection is met. It is in this way that prophecy serves as a basis for our hope in regard to things yet to come, such as the final triumph of truth and righteousness, the universal establishment of the kingdom of our Lord, and the ultimate rewards of the righteous.

The second end of prophecy is, to confirm the truth by the subsequent event. Here the question of the actual fulfillment of Scripture prophecy is involved, to which we shall immediately advert.

6. *From what theologians call the "double sense" of prophecy* an objection of another kind has been raised, as though no definite meaning could be assigned to the prophecies of Scripture but that they resembled the ambiguity of the pagan oracles. Nothing, however, can be more unfounded. The equivocations of the heathen oracles arose from their ignorance of future events, and from their endeavors to conceal that ignorance by such indefinite expressions as might be equally applicable to two or more events of a *contrary* description. But the double sense of Scripture prophecy springs from a foreknowledge of its accomplishment in *both* senses; whence the prediction is purposely so framed as to include both events, the one being *typical* of the other.

So far, then, are these seeming ambiguities of meaning from forming any valid objection to the credibility of Scripture prophecies, that we may urge them as additional proofs that these predictions came from God. For, who but the Being who is infinite in knowledge and in counsel could so construct predictions as to give them a twofold application to events not only distant from one another, but to *human* foresight, unconnected with each other?

II. EXAMPLES OF PROPHECY WHICH PROVE THEMSELVES TO BE REAL PREDICTIONS.

We now proceed to enumerate a few predictions contained in the Scriptures which most unequivocally show a perfect knowledge of future events, and which, therefore, as certainly prove that they were uttered by men who spoke "as they were moved by the Holy Ghost." Let us notice,

1. *The Prophecy respecting the Seed of the Woman.*—"I will put enmity between thee and the woman, and between thy seed and her seed; it shall bruise thy head, and thou shalt bruise his heel." Gen. iii, 15. In vain is it attempted to resolve the whole of the transaction with which this prediction stands connected into *allegory*, or to show that the language expresses a mere fact of natural history, the enmity

between the human race and serpents. In no intelligible sense can the passage be understood but in that fixed upon it by other portions of the sacred volume.

The serpent and the seed of the woman are representatives of two invisible and mighty powers, the one good, the other evil; the one Divine, though incarnate, the other diabolic. Between them enmity is placed, which is to express itself in a long and fearful struggle, in the course of which the seed of the woman shall sustain a temporary wound; but the conflict shall issue in the infliction of a fatal blow upon the power of the serpent.

The scene of this contest is our globe, and *generally* the visible agents in it are men under their respective leaders. The serpent is endeavoring to render dominant error, vice, and rebellion against the Divine government; while the seed of the woman is advocating truth, virtue, and obedience to God.

Now, that such a contest of principles and powers has existed in the world no one can deny. It commenced with Cain and Abel, and was continued in the wickedness and punishment of the antediluvians, and in the prevalence of idolatry and the judgments of God upon idolatrous nations; and we trace it in the history of the Jews down to the coming of our Lord. We witness the sufferings and death of the incarnate Redeemer, the bruising of his *heel;* but he died only to revive again, more visibly and powerfully to establish his kingdom and to commence his spiritual conquests. The history of the Christian Church is but the history of this mighty struggle between light and darkness. The contest still continues, but with increasing zeal on the part of Christianity, and with a success which warrants the hope that the time is not far distant when the *head of the serpent shall be bruised* throughout the entire world, and the idols of modern heathenism be displaced to introduce the worship of the universal Saviour.

Infidels may scoff at a redeemer, and deride the notion of a tempter; but they cannot deny that such a contest as is here foretold has actually taken place and still continues. This contest, so extended, so continued, and so to be terminated, no human foresight could have foretold; and the fact is therefore established that no one could have uttered this first promise made to fallen man but He whose eye looks through the depths of future ages.

2. *The Prediction of Jacob in regard to the coming of* "SHILOH."— "The scepter shall not depart from Judah, nor a lawgiver from between his feet, until Shiloh come." Gen. xlix, 10.

The word "*Shiloh*" signifies *the Peacemaker*, or *he who is to be sent.* In either sense it is applicable to the Messiah. Nor is this application an invention of Christians, for it was so understood by the ancient Jews, and the modern ones are unable to resist the evidence drawn from the passage in favor of the claims of our Lord. That the prophecy has received a singular accomplishment in the person of Christ is certain, and it is equally certain that in no other person has it been accomplished in any sense whatever.* Judah, *as a tribe*, remained till after the advent of Christ, which cannot be said of the long-dispersed ten tribes, and scarcely of Benjamin, which was merged into the tribe of Judah.

It has been asked, Where was the supremacy of Judah when Nebuchadnezzar carried the whole nation captive to Babylon, when Alexander subdued Palestine, and when it was a tributary province of the Roman empire? We reply that the prediction does not convey the idea of either independent or supreme power, but that the tribe of Judah should retain its *ensigns*, its *chiefs*, and its *tribeship* until the coming of Shiloh. During the captivity in Babylon this tribe was kept distinct, and had its own internal government and chief. Under the dominion of the Asmonean kings the Jews had their rulers, their elders, and their council; and so under the Romans.

It is, therefore, matter of unquestionable historic fact, that until our Lord came and had accomplished his work on earth the tribe of Judah continued; and that in a short time afterward it was dispersed, and mingled with the common mass of the Jews of all tribes and countries. We see, then, that this prediction implies a prescience of countless contingencies, occurring in the lapse of successive ages, which can only belong to God.

3. *Predictions respecting the Jewish Nation.*—These predictions, beginning with those of Moses and running through all the Jewish prophets, are too numerous to be adduced; but there are three prominent topics contained in them which demand consideration. These are, the frequent and gross departures of the Jews from the Divine Law, their signal punishments, and their final restoration to their own land. All these have taken place. Even the last was accomplished by the return of the Jews from Babylon, though, in its highest sense, it is still future.

(1.) *Their Apostasies.*—These were foretold by Moses. "I know," said he, "that after my death ye will utterly corrupt yourselves, and turn aside from the way which I have commanded you." Deut. xxxi, 29. This prediction proves very clearly that Moses was an inspired prophet. The rebellious race whom he had led into the wilderness had died there, the new generation were much more disposed to obey their leader, and when these words were written appearances were all in favor of the future obedience of that people.

But even if this had not been the case, it would have been the last thought with Moses, as a merely political man, that his favorite institutions should fall into disuse and contempt. Nor is it to be supposed that he would have closed his public life by declaring that he foresaw

* See Newton on the Prophecies.

such an event if even he had feared it. Nothing, therefore, but the spirit of prophecy could have influenced him to make such an announcement.

(2.) *Their threatened Punishments.*—The Jews were threatened with signal punishments in famines, pestilences, invasions, dispersions, captivities, and subjugations to foreign enemies; and these are represented as being solely the consequences of their vicious departures from God and from his laws.

It may be said that Moses uttered his predictive menaces to deter the people from departing from institutions which he was anxious, for the sake of his own fame, that they should observe. To this we answer, that he could not expect the Israelites to attach any weight to his threats, unless their former rebellions had been punished by such visitations. For forty years his laws had been often disobeyed, and if no infliction of Divine displeasure had followed, what reason had they to credit the menaces of Moses as to the future? But if such inflictions had resulted from their disobedience, everything in regard to these threatenings is rational and consistent.

The infidel may choose which of these positions he pleases. If he thinks that Moses aimed to deter the people from departing from his institutions by empty threats, he ascribes an incredible absurdity to a man of unquestionable wisdom and policy; but if his predictive threatenings were enforced by former marked and acknowledged interpositions of Divine Providence, he was God's inspired prophet. Who but an inspired man could foresee that no famine, no blight, no invasion would befall the Jews, except in obvious punishment for their offenses? What was there in the common course of things to prevent them, though observant of their laws, from falling under the dominion of more powerful nations but the special protection of God? And what but this could guard them from the plagues and famines to which their neighbors were liable?

If we turn to matters of fact as recorded in the sacred history, we will find that every instance of singular calamity is consequent on a previous departure from the laws of Moses; the one following the other with almost as much regularity and certainty as natural effects follow their causes. In this the predictions of Moses and the Prophets are strikingly fulfilled, and a more than human foresight is proved.

Let us look farther into the detail of these threatened punishments of the Jews. Besides the ordinary inflictions of failing harvests and severe diseases in their own country, they were, according to the predictions of Moses, (Deut. xxviii,) to be scattered "among all people, from the one end of the earth even unto the other." And where is the trading nation in Asia, Africa, Europe, or America in which they are not? Who could foresee this but God; especially when their singular preservation as a distinct people, a solitary instance in the history of nations, is implied ?

This remarkable chapter, written more than three thousand years ago, contains other predictions equally striking, and as evidently accomplished. The siege of Jerusalem by the Romans is pointed out with that particularity which demonstrates, in the most unequivocal manner, the prescience of Him to whom all events are known with absolute certainty. That the Romans are intended in verse 49, by the nation brought from "*the end of the earth*," distinguished by their well-known ensign, "*the eagle*," and by their fierce and cruel disposition, is exceedingly probable. And it is remarkable, that the account of Moses in regard to the horrors of the siege of which he speaks is exactly paralleled by those well-known passages in Josephus, in which he describes the siege of Jerusalem by the Roman army.

(3.) *Their final Restoration.*—Moses and other prophets agree, that after all the captivities and dispersions of the Jews they shall again be restored to their own land. This was in one instance accomplished, as we have seen, in their restoration by Cyrus and his successors, after which they became a considerable state. Jeremiah had fixed the captivity so unequivocally to seventy years, that the Jews in Babylon, when the time drew near, began to prepare for their return. But there was nothing in the circumstances of the Babylonian empire, when the prediction was uttered, to warrant the hope of such a deliverance. No one therefore but He who determines the affairs of the world by his power and wisdom could foretell that event.

A future restoration, however, awaits this people, and will be to the world a glorious demonstration of the truth of prophecy. This being future, we cannot argue upon; but three things are certain : the Jews themselves expect it; they are preserved by the providence of God as a distinct people *for their country;* and their country, which in fact is possessed by no one, is preserved *for them.*

4. *Prophecies respecting the Messiah*—the great end and object of the prophetic dispensation. Divines have selected more than *one hundred* predictions, generally of very clear and explicit meaning, and each referring to some different circumstance connected with the appearing, the person, or the history of Jesus Christ. How are all these to be disposed of, if the inspiration of the Scriptures which contain them be denied ?

These predictions are in books written many ages before the birth of our Saviour; and that no interpolations have taken place to accommodate them to him is evident, for the same predictions are found in copies which are in the hands of the Jews, and which have descended to them from before the Christian era. On the other hand, the history of Jesus answers to these predictions, and exhibits their exact accomplishment.

The Messiah was to be of the seed of David; born in Bethlehem; born of a virgin; an incarnation of deity, *God* with us; and an eminent but unsuccessful teacher. He was to open the eyes of the blind, heal the diseased, and raise the dead. He was to be despised and rejected of his own countrymen, arraigned on false charges, denied justice, and condemned to a violent death. He was to rise from the dead, ascend to the right hand of God, and being there invested with power and authority, he was to punish his enemies, and to establish his own spiritual kingdom, which shall never end.

We need not enter into more minute predictions, for the argument is irresistible when founded on these alone. If we deny that the prophets were divinely inspired, how shall we account for the fact that these circumstances, strange as they are, have all met in one person, and in one only of all the millions of men, and that person Jesus of Nazareth? We may assert that no man, or number of men, could have made such conjectures. It is therefore impossible to evade the evidence in favor of the prophetic character of these predictions, which their fulfillment affords, unless it could be shown that Jesus and his disciples, by some kind of concert, made the events of his life and death to correspond with the prophecies in order to substantiate his claim to the Messiahship.

No infidel has ever been so absurd as to hazard this opinion except Lord Bolingbroke. He asserts that Jesus Christ brought on his own death, by a series of willful and preconcerted measures, merely to give his disciples the triumph of an appeal to ancient prophecies! But this hypothesis does not reach the case. He ought to have shown that our Lord preconcerted his descent from David, his being born of a virgin, and in the town of Bethlehem; and that he contrived not only his death, but his resurrection and ascension also, and the spread of his religion in opposition to human opinion and human power, in order to give his disciples the triumph of an appeal to the Prophecies!" Thus men do violence to their own understanding by denying the truth.

That wonderful series of particular prophecies respecting our Lord, contained in the fifty-third chapter of Isaiah, will illustrate the foregoing observations, and may properly close this chapter.

The style of this portion of Scripture is that of *narrative;* it is also entire in itself, and unmixed with any other subject; and it evidently refers to one single person. So the ancient Jews understood it, and applied it to the Messiah; and though modern Jews, in order to evade its force in the argument with Christians, allege that it describes the sufferings of their nation, and not of an individual, the objection is refuted by the terms of the passage.

The Jewish people could not be the *sufferer*, because he was to bear *their* griefs, to carry *their* sorrows, and to be wounded for *their* transgressions; so that the person of the sufferer is clearly distinguished from the Jewish nation. Moreover, his death and burial are spoken of, which in no sense can be applied to the Jews. To some *individual* it must be applied; to no one but our Lord can it be applied; and applied to him, the prophecy assumes the appearance of real history.

Let the infidel meditate thoroughly and soberly upon these predictions. Their priority to the events admits of no question, and their fulfillment is obvious to every competent inquirer. Here, then, are facts, and we must account for these facts on rational and adequate principles. Is human foresight equal to the task? Is conjecture? Is chance? Is political contrivance? If none of these can account for the facts, neither can any other principle that may be devised by the sagacity of man. As, therefore, every effect must have a cause, true philosophy, as well as true religion, will ascribe them to the inspiration of the Almighty.

CHAPTER VIII.

DIVINE AUTHORITY OF THE SACRED SCRIPTURES: INTERNAL EVIDENCE.

The Internal Evidence of a revelation from God has been stated to be that which is drawn from the nature and moral tendency of the doctrines taught.* This is at least its chief characteristic, though other particulars may also be included in this species of proof.

There are some truths, made known to us through the medium of a revelation from God, which, though not discoverable by the unassisted reason of man, yet, when once revealed, are attended by strong *rational* evidence, so far as we can understand them. Of other truths revealed to us in the Bible, and those in many instances fundamental to the Christian system, we have no proof of this kind; but they stand alone on the firm basis of Divine attestation as their *authenticating* evidence. Such are the doctrines of the Trinity, of the hypostatic union of the two natures in Christ, and of his Divine and eternal Sonship.

The Internal Evidence of the Holy Scriptures, so far as *doctrines* are concerned, is restrained to truths of the former class; but there are facts and circumstances connected with all Scripture from which this kind of evidence may be drawn. Our remarks, however, will be confined to the *excellence of the doctrines*, their *moral tendency*, the wonderful *agreement of the sacred* writers, and their *style and manner*.

I. The Excellence of the Doctrines of Scripture.

In presenting this feature of the subject we will not attempt to do

* See chap. i, § 2.

anything more than to consider a few of the more prominent doctrines of the Bible. We will notice,

1. *The Scripture Doctrine respecting the Nature and Attributes of God.*—That this doctrine presents itself to the mind of man with strong rational evidence is clearly shown by that astonishing change of opinion on this great subject which took place in pagan nations on the promulgation of Christianity, and which continues to this day. The discoveries of revelation have satisfied the human mind on this great and primary doctrine, and have given it a resting-place which it never before found. A class of ideas the most elevated and sublime, and which the most profound philosophers in former times sought without success, have thus become familiar to the most illiterate in Christian nations.

2. *The Moral Condition of Man.*—Of this, as it is represented in the Scriptures, the evidence from fact and from our own consciousness is very copious. What man is in his relations to God we never could have discovered without revelation; but now, as this is made known, confirmatory facts crowd in on every side, affording evidence of the truth of the doctrine. The Scriptures represent the human race,

(1.) *As absolutely vicious, and capable, without moral check and control, of the greatest enormities.*—To this the history of all ages bears witness, and present experience gives its testimony. All the states of antiquity crumbled down or were suddenly destroyed by their own vices; and the general character and conduct of the people who composed them may be read in the works of their historians, poets, and satirists, which have been transmitted to our times.

These testimonies fully bear out the dark coloring of man's moral condition as it is found in the first chapter of St. Paul's Epistle to the Romans, and in other passages of the Scriptures; and to this day the same representation depicts the condition of almost all pagan countries. Even where the redeeming influence of revealed religion has been most powerfully exerted, the same appetites and passions may be seen in perpetual contest with the laws of the state, the example of the virtuous, and the commands of God. The Scriptures therefore characterize man as he has been found to be in all ages and in all places. But they assume,

(2.) *That Man is vicious in consequence of a Moral Taint in his Nature.*—This assumption is the basis of the whole scheme of moral restoration through Jesus Christ. Accordingly the Scriptures constantly remind him that he is "*conceived in sin and shapen in iniquity,*" and that being "*born of the flesh,*" he "*cannot please God.*" That man is strongly inclined to do evil cannot be denied, for the doctrine appeals to our reason through the evidence of unquestionable facts. It is supported by every penal law in civil legislation; by every legal deed, with its seals and witnesses; and by the history of nations, which is chiefly a record of human crime.

This tendency to evil, the Scriptures tell us, arises from "*the heart;*" nor is it otherwise to be accounted for. It cannot be the result of association and example, as some have supposed; for if men were naturally inclined to good and averse to evil, how is it that the whole race have become evil by association? This not only involves the absurdity of supposing the weaker cause to be more efficient than the stronger, but it is also contrary to the reason of the case; for with persons *naturally* well disposed, example and association can produce no other effect than that of maturing and confirming their good dispositions.

Nor is there any plausibility in the opinion that this general corruption is the result of bad education. If man in all ages had been rightly affected in his moral inclinations, how could a course of deleterious education have commenced? and if it could have commenced, why was it not arrested and a better system introduced? The Scriptures, therefore, assign the only rational cause for this phenomenon: that man is by NATURE *prone to evil.* But as it is unreasonable to suppose that this disposition was implanted in him by his Maker, we are bound to admit the Scripture doctrine of the FALL of the human race from a higher and better state.

The Scriptures also teach,

(3.) *That the Divine Administration in regard to Man is of a mixed Character, exhibiting both Severity and Kindness.*—As he is corrupt in his nature and tendencies, he is placed under a rigidly *restraining* discipline; and as he is an actual offender, he is under correction and a penal dispensation. But, on the other hand, as he is a being for whose pardon and recovery Divine Mercy has made provision, moral ends are connected with these severities, and the administration of God is crowned with instances of benevolence to the sinning race.

The proof of these different relations of man to God surrounds us in that admixture of good and evil, of indulgence and restraint, of felicity and misery, to which he is so manifestly subject. Life, in all ordinary circumstances, is felt to be a blessing; but it is short and uncertain, and subject to numerous evils. Many enjoyments fall to the lot of men, yet with the majority they are attained by means of great and exhausting labors; or they are accompanied with so many disappointments, fears, and cares, that their number and quality are greatly lessened.

The globe itself, the residence of man, bears evident marks of the mixed character of the Divine government. It is subject to destructive earthquakes, volcanoes, and inundations; to blights and dearths, the harbingers of famine; and to those atmospheric changes which induce wide-wasting epidemic disorders. These and many other instances show a course of discipline very incongruous with the most enlightened views of the Divine character, if man be considered as an innocent being.

On the contrary, he cannot be under an unmixed *penal* administration; for the earth yet ordinarily yields her increase to industry; the destructive convulsions of nature are but occasional; and, generally, the health of men predominates over sickness, and their animal enjoyments exceed their positive misery.

To those *diverse* relations of man to God, as stated in the Bible, the *contrarieties* of nature and providence bear an exact adaptation. Assume man to be anything else than what the Scriptures represent him to be, and they would be discordant and inexplicable; but in this view they harmonize. Man is neither *innocent* nor *finally condemned*—he is fallen and guilty, but not excluded from the compassion and benignity of his God.

3. *The Doctrine of Atonement.*—The great article of Christianity is, the restoration of man to the Divine favor, through the merits of the VICARIOUS AND SACRIFICIAL DEATH OF CHRIST, the incarnate Son of God. The rational evidence of this doctrine, we grant, is partial and limited; but this does not affect its *authority*. It is indeed not unreasonable to suppose that the internal evidence of such a doctrine should be somewhat obscure, for we must not expect as clear information in regard to the Divine conduct as concerning our own duty. There is nevertheless a reasonableness in this doctrine, when fairly understood, and a wonderful adaptation to the moral condition of man, which strongly commend it to every sober and thoughtful mind.

The doctrine of the atonement is grounded upon man's liability to be eternally punished in a future life for sins committed in this. That men are capable of committing sin, and that sin is productive of misery and disorder, cannot be denied; for the great sum of human misery is the effect of actual offense. And as it is a principle in human legislation to estimate the guilt of individual acts by their general tendency, and to proportion their punishment by that consideration, the same reason of the case is in favor of that future and eternal punishment which the Scriptures declare to be the penalty of the Divine law.

That atonement for sin which was made by the death of Christ is represented in the Christian system as the means by which mankind may be delivered from this awful catastrophe. This end it proposes to accomplish by means which preserve the character of the Supreme Governor from mistake, and maintain the authority of his government; and which give to man the strongest possible reason for hope, and render most favorable the circumstances of his earthly probation.

How sin may be forgiven without leading to such misconceptions of the Divine character as would encourage disobedience, and thereby weaken the influence of the Divine government, is a problem of very difficult solution. A government which never punishes offense is a contradiction—it cannot exist; but one which admits no forgiveness sinks the guilty to inevitable destruction, and where all are guilty, makes the destruction universal.

The Ruler of the world is not careless in regard to the conduct of his creatures; for that penal consequences are attached to offense is manifest from daily observation. It is a principle already laid down, that the authority of God must be maintained; and it ought to be observed, that in the kind of administration which restrains evil by penalty, and encourages obedience by favor and hope, we and all moral creatures are the interested party, and not the Divine Governor. The reasons therefore which move him to maintain his authority do not terminate in himself. If he becomes a party against offenders it is for our sake, and for the sake of the moral order of the universe. And if the granting of pardon be strongly and even severely guarded, we are to refer it to the moral necessity of the case in order to secure the general welfare; and not to any reluctance on the part of God to forgive, or to anything vindictive in his nature.

If, then, the interests of the moral universe require that man's restoration to the Divine favor ought to be so granted that no license shall be given to offense, that the holiness and justice of God shall be as clearly manifested as his compassion, and that the awful authority of his government shall be fully maintained, we ask, on what scheme, save that which is developed in the New Testament, are these necessary conditions provided for?

But may not sin be pardoned in the exercise of the Divine prerogative? The reply is, that if this prerogative were exercised toward a part of mankind only, the passing by of others could not be reconciled to the character of God; but if the benefit were extended to all, government would be at an end. Nor is this scheme improved by confining the act of grace to *repentant* criminals. What offender, in the immediate view of danger, feeling the vanity of guilty pleasures now past forever, and beholding the approach of delayed but threatened punishment, would not repent? Were this principle to regulate human governments every criminal would escape, and judicial forms would become a subject for ridicule.

Nor is this the principle on which the Divine Being governs men in the present state. Repentance does not restore health injured by intemperance, property wasted by profusion, or character once stained by dishonorable practices. If repentance alone can secure pardon, then all must be pardoned and government dissolved, as in the case of forgiveness by mere prerogative; but if a selection be made, then different and discordant principles of government are introduced into the Divine administration.

To avoid the force of these obvious difficulties some have added *reformation* to repentance, and would restrain forgiveness to those only who to their penitence add a course of future obedience to the Divine law. But a change of conduct does not, any more than repentance, repair the mischiefs of former misconduct. The sobriety of the reformed man does not always restore health; and the industry and economy of the formerly negligent and wasteful do not repair the losses of extravagance. This theory is in direct opposition to the principles and practice of human governments, which in flagrant cases never suspend punishment in anticipation of a change of conduct; but in the infliction of the penalty look steadily to the crime actually committed, and to the necessity of vindicating the majesty of violated law.

But we may go farther and show that the reformation anticipated is *impracticable*. To make this clear, it must be recollected that they who advocate this theory leave out of it, not only the vicarious sacrifice of Christ, but also that agency of the Holy Spirit which awakens the thoughtless to consideration, and prompts and assists their efforts to attain a higher character. Man is therefore left, unassisted and uninfluenced, to his own endeavors, and in the unalleviated circumstances of his morally depraved state. How then is this supposed reformation to commence? If man is totally corrupt, the only principles from which reformation can proceed do not exist in his nature; and if only his propensity to evil is stronger than it is to good, it would be absurd to suppose that the weaker propensity should resist the stronger, that the rivulet should force its way against the tides of the ocean. The *reformation*, therefore, which is to atone for his vices is impracticable.

How then can mercy be extended to our guilty race consistent with the character and government of God and with the highest interests of his moral creatures? The only answer is found in the Holy Scriptures. They alone show, and indeed they alone *profess* to show, how God may be *just*, and yet the *justifier* of the ungodly. Other schemes show how he may be *merciful;* but the difficulty lies not there. This meets it by declaring " the righteousness of God," at the same time that it proclaims his mercy. The voluntary sufferings of an incarnate Divine person " for us," in our room and stead, magnify the justice of God, display his hatred to sin, proclaim the " exceeding sinfulness " of transgression by the deep and painful agonies of the Substitute, warn the persevering offender of the terribleness and certainty of his punishment, and open the gates of salvation to every true penitent.

The same Divine plan secures the influence of the Holy Spirit to awaken the wanderer to repentance and lead him back to God; to renew his fallen nature in righteousness at the moment he is justified through faith, and to qualify him to " walk not after the flesh, but after the Spirit." *All the ends of government are here answered.* No license is given to sin, the moral law is unrepealed, the day of judgment is still appointed, future and eternal punishments still display their awful sanctions, a new and singular manifestation of the Divine purity is afforded, pardon is offered to all who seek it, and the whole world may be saved!

With such evidence of suitableness to the case of mankind, and under such lofty views of connection with the principles and ends of moral government, does the doctrine of THE ATONEMENT present itself. But other important considerations are not wanting to mark the united wisdom and goodness of this method of extending mercy to the guilty. All that can most powerfully illustrate the united tenderness and awful majesty of God, and the odiousness and destructive tendency of sin; all that can win back the heart of man to his Maker and Lord, and render future obedience a matter of affection and delight as well as duty; all that can extinguish the angry and malignant passions of man toward man; all that can inspire a mutual benevolence, and dispose to a self-denying charity for the benefit of others; and all that can arouse by hope, or tranquilize by faith, may be found in the vicarious death of Christ, and in the principles and purposes for which it was endured.

4. *The Doctrine of the Influence of the Holy Spirit.*—The Scriptures represent man as being influenced, in his moral course, by spiritual agencies, as being solicited to persevering rebellion by the seductions of *evil spirits*, and to obedience by the influences of the Holy Spirit.

It would be easy to show, if it were at all necessary, that no valid objection, either *physical* or *moral*, can be urged against the Scripture doctrine of Divine influence. But assuming for the present what we know to be true, that the doctrine itself is not *unreasonable*, we will inquire at once into some of its excellencies.

(1.) *It is suited to Man's Moral Condition.*—The moral helplessness of man has been universally felt and universally acknowledged. To see the good, and to follow the evil, has been the complaint of all; and precisely to such a state is the doctrine of Divine influence adapted. As the atonement of Christ stoops to the *judicial* destitution of man, the promise of the Holy Spirit meets the case of his *moral* destitution. One finds him without any means of satisfying the claims of justice, the other without either inclination or strength to avail himself of offered pardon. The one relieves him from the penalty, the other from the disease of sin. The former restores him to the favor of God, the latter renews him in the Divine image.

(2.) *It gives an affecting view of the Divine Character.*—That tenderness and compassion of God to his offending creatures; that reluctance that they should perish; that sympathizing anxiety to accomplish their salvation, which were displayed by the "cross of Christ," are here in continued and active manifestation. It is the office and work of the Spirit to convince the mistaken, to arouse the conscience of the guilty, to comfort the penitent and humble, and to plant, foster, and bring to maturity in the hearts of the obedient every grace and virtue. These are views of God which we could not have but for this doctrine; and their obvious tendency is, to fill the heart with gratitude for a condescension so wonderful and a solicitude so tender.

(3.) *It elevates our Aspirations, and encourages our Virtuous Efforts.*—
Were we left wholly to our own resources we should despair; and
perhaps it is exactly in proportion to the degree in which this promise
of the Holy Spirit is apprehended by those who truly receive Christianity that they advance the standard of possible moral attainment. If
God works in us "both to will and to do of his own good pleasure," it
is a reason why we should "work out our own salvation with fear and
trembling;" for, as our freedom is not destroyed by the operations of
the Spirit, and as even the Spirit may be *grieved* and *quenched*, our fall
would be unspeakably aggravated by our advantages. Surely no one
who cordially embraces this doctrine can despair of conquering any
evil habit, of being fully renewed in the image of God, or of being
sustained in the performance of any duty to which he may be called,
even the most difficult and painful. Such are the practical effects of this
doctrine. It prompts to attainments in inward sanctity and outward
virtue which it would have been chimerical to consider possible but
for the aid of a Divine influence, and it leads to exertion for the benefit
of others the success of which would otherwise be too doubtful to encourage the undertaking.

It would be easy to adduce many other doctrines of our religion
which, from their obvious excellence and correspondence with the
experience and circumstances of mankind, furnish much interesting
internal evidence in favor of its divinity. But as this would greatly
exceed the limits of a chapter, and as those doctrines have been considered against which the most strenuous objections from pretended
rational principles have been urged—the moral state and condition of
man, the atonement made by the death of Christ for the sins of the
world and the influences of the Holy Spirit—it is sufficient for the argument to have shown that even such doctrines are accompanied with
important and interesting reasons, and that they powerfully commend
Christianity to universal acceptance. What has been offered is only a
mere specimen of the rational proof which accompanies many of the
doctrines of revelation; but a considerate mind may extend the argument at pleasure.

II. THE MORAL TENDENCY OF THE SACRED SCRIPTURES.

If these Scriptures declare to us the before "*unknown God*,"
unknown even to the wisest of the heathen philosophers; if they reveal
man's true moral condition, and the only means by which he can be
restored to the favor of God and renewed in his image; if they contain
every moral direction which can safely guide us, every promise which
is suitable to our condition, and every hope which can animate us to
run our course of probation and aspire to the high rewards of another
life, then must their moral influence be as powerful as their doctrines
are lofty and important. That the Bible, in this respect, is superior to
every other system of religion, will appear evident from a few observations.

1. *A perfect System of Morals is nowhere to be found but in the Holy Scriptures; and the deficiencies of Pagan morality only exalt the purity, comprehensiveness, and practicability of ours.*—The character of the Being acknowledged as supreme must always impress itself upon that morality which rests upon his will for its obligation. We have seen the views entertained by pagans on this all-important point, and their demoralizing effects. But the God of the Bible is "*holy*," without spot; "*just*," without intermission or partiality; "*good*," boundlessly benevolent and beneficent; and his law is the image of himself, "*holy, just*, and *good*."

2. *With Pagans the great Principles of Morality, so far as they comprehend them, were mere Abstractions, and therefore comparatively feeble in their influence.* But in the person of Christ, our God incarnate, they are exemplified in *action*, displaying themselves amid human relations, and the actual circumstances of human life. With them the authority of moral rules was either the opinion of the wise or the tradition of the ancient, confirmed, it is true, in some degree by observation and experience; but to us they are given as commands immediately from the Supreme Governor, and ratified as his by the most solemn and explicit attestations. With them many great moral principles, being indistinctly apprehended, were matters of doubt and debate; but with us the clear and authoritative manner in which they are revealed excludes both.

3. *Those who never had the benefit of Revelation have no just conception of that moral state of the heart from which alone pure morality can flow.* When, therefore, they speak of the same virtues as those enjoined in the Scriptures they attach to them a lower idea, and in this we see the great superiority of Christianity. It forbids not only the overt acts of vice, but even the very thoughts and desires of the heart from which they spring. It enjoins humanity, meekness, placability, and charity as clearly and solemnly as the grosser vices are prohibited. Nor are the injunctions feeble; they are strictly LAW, and not mere *advice* and *recommendations*.

4. *The Superiority of Christian Morality is also seen in the number and strength of its motives.*—A sense of duty to God and the fear of his displeasure are the highest motives of heathen morality. But to these Christianity adds the motive of tender and supreme love to God, excited by his infinite compassion to us in the gift of his Son; and another, which heathen moralists never knew, the testimony that we please God, manifested in the acceptance of our prayers and in spiritual and felicitous communion with him. A pagan could draw, though with imperfect lines, a *beau ideal* of virtue which he never thought to be attainable; but to all who seek the renovation of their moral nature the religion of Christ gives the "*full assurance of hope*" that they shall obtain the desired object.

What, then, is the moral tendency of Christianity? It is this: to free man from every passion which wastes, and burns, and frets, and enfeebles his spirit; and to lead him to the possession of that new nature, that peace of mind, and that joy unspeakable which will render his obedience voluntary, cheerful, and entire. On vast numbers of men it has superinduced these moral changes; its way is still onward, and he who would arrest its progress, were he able, would quench the only hope which remains to our world and prove himself to be an enemy to mankind.

We conclude, therefore, that the Scriptures are worthy of God, and that they propose the very ends which rendered a revelation necessary. To this whole system of practical religion we may apply the language of Mr. Wesley, in relation to our Lord's Sermon on the Mount: "Behold Christianity in its native form, as delivered by its great Author. See a picture of God, as far as he is imitable by man, drawn by God's own hand. What beauty appears in the whole! How just a symmetry! What exact proportions in every part! How desirable is the happiness here described! How venerable, how lovely is the holiness!"*

III. THE WONDERFUL AGREEMENT OF THE SACRED WRITERS.

The Bible contains the compositions of a vast variety of writers, men of every rank and condition, of every diversity of character and turn of mind. Among them are the monarch and the plebeian, the learned and the illiterate, the talented and the moderately gifted, the historian and the legislator, the orator and the poet. Some of them lived in ages distant from one another, under different modes of civil government and in different dispensations of the Divine economy, filling a period of time which reached from the first dawn of heavenly light to its meridian glory. Each had his peculiar province; "some *apostles*, and some *prophets*, and some *evangelists* and *teachers*." Here we have the writers of the Old Testament and of the New, the prophets predicting future events and the Evangelists recording them; the doctrinal yet didactic epistolary writers, and him who closed the sacred canon in the Apocalyptic vision. These writers furnished their respective portions of the sacred volume under circumstances as varied as we can possibly imagine; and yet in all its bearings, parts, and designs we find a most striking harmony, fitness, and adaptation of its component parts to one beautiful, stupendous, and united whole.

"This instance of uniformity without design, of agreement without contrivance; this consistency maintained through a long series of ages, without a possibility of the ordinary methods for conducting such a plan; these unparalleled congruities, these unexampled coincidences, form altogether a species of evidence of which there is no other instance in the history of all the other books in the world." The inevitable conclusion from all this is, that these sacred writings, of which the Bible is

* Wesley's Sermons.

composed, were dictated by one and the same *omniscient and eternal* SPIRIT.

IV. THE STYLE AND MANNER OF THE SACRED WRITERS.

The *style* of the sacred writers is *various*, and thus accords with the profession that the Bible is a collection of books by different authors. Each has his own peculiarity so strongly marked and so equally sustained throughout the book ascribed to him as to be a forcible proof of genuineness. The writers of the New Testament employ Hebrew idioms, words, and phrases. The Greek in which they wrote is not classic Greek, but is such a dialect as would be used by persons acquiring the language, by frequent intercourse with strangers, where Chaldee or Syriac was spoken as the vernacular tongue. This affords an argument, from internal evidence, that the books were written by the persons whose names they bear. And as this particular style was changed after the destruction of Jerusalem, they must have been written in the first century.

The *manner* of the sacred writers is in proof that they were conscious of the truth of what they related. The whole narrative is simple and natural. Even in the accounts given of the creation, the flood, the exodus from Egypt, and the events of the life and death of Christ, where designing men would have been most inclined to heighten the impression by glowing and elaborate description, the same chastened simplicity is preserved. "These sober recorders of events the most astonishing are never carried away, by the circumstances they relate, into any pomp of diction or use of superlatives. Absorbed in their holy task, no alien idea presents itself to their mind. The object before them fills it. They never digress; are never called away by the solicitations of vanity or the suggestions of curiosity. They never fill up the intervals between the events which they record. They leave circumstances to make their own impression, instead of helping out the reader by reflections of their own. They preserve the gravity of history and the severity of truth without enlarging the outline or swelling the expression."*

* See Mrs. More's Character of St. Paul.

CHAPTER IX.

DIVINE AUTHORITY OF THE SACRED SCRIPTURES: COLLATERAL EVIDENCE.

MUCH of the *Collateral Evidence* of the Divine authority of the Scriptures has been anticipated in the course of this discussion, and need not again be resumed.

The *agreement* of the final revelation of the will of God, by the ministry of Christ and his apostles, with former authenticated revelations, has been pointed out; so that the whole constitutes one body of harmonious doctrines, gradually introduced, and at length fully unfolded and confirmed.

The *suitableness* of the Christian revelation to the state of the world, at the time of its communication, follows from the view we have given of the necessity, not only of a revelation generally, but of such a revelation as God has granted to the world through his Son.

It has also been shown that its historical facts accord with the credible histories and traditions of the same time, that monuments remain to attest its truth in the institutions of the Christian Church, and that adversaries have made concessions in its favor.

These sources of Collateral Evidence having been sufficiently considered, we must confine our further remarks upon this subject to two particulars, but each of very convincing character. The first is, the marvelous diffusion of Christianity in the first three centuries; the second is, its ameliorating influence upon the condition of mankind.

I. ITS MARVELOUS DIFFUSION IN THE FIRST THREE CENTURIES.

How are we to account for the fact, that the first preachers of the Gospel, though unaided by human power or philosophic wisdom, and even in opposition to both, effected a revolution in the opinions and manners of a great portion of the civilized world to which in the history of nations there is no parallel.* In the face of all opposition, and in a short period of time, they induced multitudes in various nations, distinguished both by the peculiarity of their manners and the diversity of

---

* The success of Mohammed, though sometimes presented as a parallel, is, in fact, both as to the means employed and the effect produced, a perfect contrast. The *means* were conquest and compulsion; the *effect* was to legalize and sanctify the natural passions of man for plunder and sensual gratification; and it is indeed strange that a contrast so marked should ever have been regarded as a correspondence. Men were persuaded, when they were not *forced*, to join the ranks of the Arabian impostor by the hope of plunder, and a present and future life of brutal gratification; but they were persuaded to join the apostles by the evidence of truth and by the hope of future spiritual blessedness, but with the certainty of present disgrace and suffering.

their language, to forsake the religious institutions of their ancestors, though sanctified by age, defended by vigorous authority, and associated with the most alluring gratification of the passions, and to embrace the religion of the despised Nazarene. Let us look both at the historical proof of the fact, and the evidence which it affords of the Divine authority of our holy religion.

1. *The Historical Proof of the Fact.*—We have the testimony of Tacitus, about thirty years after the crucifixion, to the extensive propagation of Christianity even in the apostolic age. Speaking of the Christian religion, he says: "This pernicious superstition, though checked for a while, broke out again, and spread not only over Judea, but reached the city of Rome also. At first they only were apprehended who confessed themselves to belong to that sect; afterward a *vast multitude* were discovered and cruelly punished."* This testimony is of great value, because it shows in how short a period of time Christianity had passed from the distant province of Judea to Rome, and with what success it was attended in the capital of the world.

We learn from the younger Pliny, who presided over Pontus and Bithynia in the beginning of the second century, that in his province the Gospel could boast of numerous disciples. "The contagion of this superstition," says he, in his well-known letter to Trajan, "has not only invaded cities, but the smaller towns also, and the whole country." He tells us, moreover, that until he began to use severities against the Christians the temples of the heathen gods were almost deserted, and that those who sold victims for sacrifice could hardly find purchasers.†

These are testimonies of heathens, who could have no interest in magnifying the number of the Christians; but they agree substantially with the testimony of the Christian fathers, as a few quotations will show. About the middle of the second century Justin Martyr writes: "There is not a nation, Greek or Barbarian, or of any other name, even of those who wander in tribes and live in tents, among whom prayers and thanksgivings are not offered to the Father and Creator of the universe in the name of the crucified Jesus." Near the close of this century Tertullian, in his Apology, appeals thus to the Roman governors: "We were but of yesterday, and we have filled your cities and towns; the camp, the senate, and the forum." Origen, in the early part of the third century, says: "By the good providence of God the Christian religion has so flourished and increased that it is now preached freely, and without molestation."

But the great fact in connection with this subject is, that in the year A. D. 300 *Christianity became the established religion of the Roman empire*, and Paganism was abolished. It follows from this event that the religion which thus became triumphant must have been embraced

---

* Annal., lib. xv, cap. 44. † Plin., Ep. x, 97, 98.

by a large majority of *the one hundred and twenty millions* supposed to be contained in that empire; for otherwise no emperor would have attempted to change the religion of so vast a state, nor could such a change have been effected had the attempt been made. Let us then look at this wonderful success of the Christian cause,

2. *As a Proof of the Divine Authority of the Holy Scriptures.*—To present the argument in its true light a few remarks will be necessary.

(1.) *We do not affirm that mere success is a decisive proof of the truth and divinity of a religion;* for this success may not be owing to the justice of its claims, but to other causes. A religion may spread, not indeed as rapidly as did Christianity, but gradually, through its adaptation to the opinions, prejudices, inclinations, and worldly interests of men. Great effects may be produced in the course of time, by the united influence of artifice and authority, when there is a disposition to yield to them. We can account in this manner for the progress of idolatry in the heathen world, and in the Christian Church during the dark ages. A religion may be rapidly and extensively propagated by *force.* Of this we have an example in that of Mohammed, which diffused itself in a short time over several countries in the East.

(2.) *But to none of these causes can we attribute the success of the Christian Religion during the first three centuries.*—We know of one religion which was propagated by the sword; but our Lord, unlike Mohammed in this, as in every other part of his character, made no use of carnal weapons to disseminate his religion, and positively disclaimed them. "My kingdom," said he, "is not of this world. If my kingdom were of this world then would my servants fight, that I should not be delivered to the Jews: but now is my kingdom not from hence." John xviii, 36. Hence said the apostle, "The weapons of our warfare are not carnal;" but still these weapons were "mighty through God." 2 Cor. x, 4.

(3.) *Nor did its success depend upon any support or protection which it received from the civil authority.*—It is a well-authenticated fact, not only that Christianity was unaided by the secular arm, but that it made its way in the face of strong and persevering opposition. Those who professed this despised religion were exposed to the loss of property, of country, of liberty, and of life. They were tortured with every species of cruelty, and accounted the enemies of the human race. The emperors armed the magistrates with authority, and the fury of the populace supplied additional means of destruction. Neither age nor sex was spared; and for centuries a succession of sanguinary persecutions, with only short intervals of repose, marked the progress of the Christian Church. The struggle was prolonged nearly three hundred years, during which the blood of Christian martyrs flowed in torrents in almost every part of the Roman empire. But truth ultimately prevailed, and the religion of the man whom his countrymen rejected was established in every Roman province.

(4.) *It was not because Christianity was suited to the opinions, the prejudices, the carnal inclinations, and the worldly interests of men that it so wonderfully prevailed.*—The Gospel was "to the Jews a stumbling-block, and to the Greeks foolishness." Each of these classes found something in it which was irreconcilable with their preconceived opinions. It was a stumbling-block to the Jews, because it proclaimed a suffering Messiah, a spiritual kingdom, and salvation to the Gentiles, as well as to the sons of Abraham. It was foolishness to the Greeks, because, setting aside their learned speculations and splendid superstitions, it called upon them to acknowledge a God unknown to their ancestors, and a Mediator of whom they had never before heard, and to yield an unhesitating assent to doctrines which were new, strange, and inexplicable by the principles of philosophy. It demanded of its votaries the renunciation of all sinful habits and pursuits, the sacrifice of worldly honors and pleasures, and, conditionally, of life itself. It prescribed humility, the mortification of appetite, and a course of circumspect and persevering obedience; and the promised recompense lay in another world, of which they could have no knowledge but by implicitly depending upon the word of its Author.

(5.) *But who were the immediate instruments in this marvelous diffusion of Gospel truth?*—Were they the wise, the learned, and the eloquent? These, according to human policy, would have been regarded as the fittest persons to accomplish the work; but with such our Lord had no connection. He used no means to secure their assistance, nor did he seem to desire it. He selected, for the execution of this great enterprise, those whom every other person would have rejected as being destitute of the necessary qualifications. They were fishermen and tax-gatherers, without learning, reputation, or friends. They were men whose appearance was ungainly, whose manners were unpolished, and who, instead of drawing attention to their doctrines by the arts of oratory, would render it still more revolting by the rudeness of their speech. Yet these are the persons who were chosen to propagate a religion which was unacceptable to all classes of men; but which nevertheless aimed at universal dominion, requiring the priest, the philosopher, and the statesman to bow to its authority and become its lowly disciples.

(6.) *Now, as the human means employed in the propagation of the Gospel were manifestly inadequate, we must attribute its success to supernatural agency.*—It is a species of miracle which does not strike the eye, but the mind. Something has been done, not indeed without means, but above them; and it is as truly wonderful as was the flowing of water from the rock when Moses smote it with his rod. A power was exerted beyond that which resided in the means employed: it was the power of God. And if means and instruments were selected apparently incompetent in themselves, it was for the express purpose of making that power manifest, and of furnishing a decisive evidence that Christianity is Divine. This thought is forcibly presented by St. Paul. "God hath chosen the foolish things of the world to confound the wise; and God hath chosen the weak things of the world to confound the things which are mighty; and base things of the world, and things which are despised, hath God chosen, yea, and things which are not, to bring to naught things that are: that no flesh should glory in his presence." 1 Cor. i, 27-29. The same writer, in speaking directly of the Gospel, says: "We have this treasure in earthen vessels, that the excellency of the power may be of God, and not of us." 2 Cor. iv, 7.

We come now to consider,

II. THE AMELIORATING INFLUENCE OF CHRISTIANITY UPON THE CONDITION OF MANKIND.

The actual effects which Christianity produced in the world, and which it is still producing, are strong arguments in support of its Divine authority. In every pagan country where it has prevailed it has abolished *idolatry* with its sanguinary and polluted rites. It has raised the standard of *morality;* and by that means, even where its full effects have not been exerted, it has insensibly improved the manners of every Christian state. It abolished *infanticide* and *human sacrifices*, which were so prevalent among ancient and modern heathens.

Christianity has borne its testimony against *polygamy* and *divorce;* and, by the institution of marriage in an indissoluble bond, has given birth to a felicity and sanctity in the domestic circle which it never before knew. It has exalted the character and condition of *woman*, and by that means has humanized *man*. He no longer imposes upon her feeble shoulders the meanest and most servile occupations of life, thus treating her with injustice, cruelty, and ungenerous contempt; but, inspired by the refining and ennobling principles of the Gospel, he feels in his breast a *new and important affection*, which Christianity alone can create, the love of woman, founded on *esteem*.

Christianity abolished domestic slavery in ancient Europe, and from its principles the struggle which is now maintained against this great evil draws its energy and promises a triumph as complete. It has given a milder character to *war*, and taught modern nations to treat their prisoners with humanity, and to restore them by exchange to their respective countries. It has laid the basis of a *jurisprudence* more just and equal, given civil rites to subjects, and placed restraints on absolute power, and crowned its achievements by its *charity*. Hospitals, schools, and many other institutions for the benefit of the aged and the poor, are almost exclusively its own creations; and they abound most where its influence is most powerful.

The same effects are still resulting from its influence in every heathen country into which it has been carried. In some of them idolatry has been renounced; infants, and widows, and aged persons, who would have been immolated to their gods or abandoned by their cruelty, have been preserved, and are now "*living to praise its Divine Author, as they do at this day.*" In other instances the light is prevailing against the darkness, and those systems of dark and sanguinary superstition which have stood for ages only to pollute and oppress, without any symptom of decay, now betray the shocks which they have sustained by the preaching of the Gospel of Christ and nod to their final fall.

Such are the leading evidences of the truth of the Holy Scriptures, and of the religious system which they unfold, from the first promise made to the first fallen man to its perfected exhibition in the New Testament. The Christian will review these solid and immovable foundations of his faith with unutterable joy. They leave none of his moral interests unprovided for in time, and they set before him a certain and felicitous immortality.

The infidel may be entreated by every compassionate feeling to a more serious consideration of the evidences of this Divine system, and the difficulties and hopelessness of his own; and we would remind him that "if Christianity be true it is *tremendously* true." Let him turn to an insulted, but yet merciful Saviour, who even now prays for his enemies as once he prayed for his murderers: "FATHER, FORGIVE THEM; FOR THEY KNOW NOT WHAT THEY DO!"

CHAPTER X.

DIVINE AUTHORITY OF THE SACRED SCRIPTURES: MISCELLANEOUS OBJECTIONS ANSWERED.

IN meeting the objections which are urged against the Bible, it will be our purpose to expose them, in as few words as possible, to the sunlight of truth. The mere cavils of infidel writers may be hastily dismissed, but the most plausible objections shall be considered more at large.

1. It is objected that reason is a sufficient guide in religion, that revelation is therefore unnecessary, and that it reflects upon the wisdom of the Creator, as if he had not at first duly fitted man for the end of his being, and consequently found it expedient afterward to supply the defect.

This specious infidelity, called "*deism,*" or "*the religion of nature,*" made its appearance in France and Italy about the middle of the sixteenth century, and was first advocated in England early in the seventeenth century by Lord Herbert of Cherbury. He lays down five primary articles of religion which, he says, are all discoverable by our natural faculties, and contain everything that is necessary to be believed. They are, that there is a supreme God, that he is chiefly to be worshiped, that piety and virtue are the principal parts of his worship, that repentance expiates offense, and that there is a state of future rewards and punishments.

The history of infidelity from this time is, however, a striking comment upon the words of St. Paul, that "evil men and seducers shall wax worse and worse, deceiving and being deceived;" for in the progress of this deadly error every one of Lord Herbert's five articles has been called in question or given up. HOBBES regarded our duty to God as a chimera, the civil magistrate being supreme in all things. SHAFTESBURY denied the doctrine of future rewards and punishments. HUME attempted to overthrow the argument for the existence of God from the frame of the universe, by denying the relation between cause and effect. By some the worship of God has been rejected as unreasonable because he needs not *our praises*, and is not to be turned from his purposes by *our* prayers.

And as to future rewards and punishments, philosophy has discovered, since the days of Lord Herbert, that the human soul, being a mere result of organization, dies with the body. The great principle of the English proto-infidel, "the sufficiency of our own natural faculties to form a religion for ourselves," is, however, the foundation of all these theories; and this being conceded, the instances just given are a sufficient refutation of the objection. Nothing, therefore, can be more absurd than to wrangle about the sufficiency of reason when it has proved itself to be insufficient in every trial. The fact is a stubborn one, and no speculation can set it aside.

Nor does this fact imply a reflection upon the wisdom of the Creator. With us there is no difficulty in accounting for it. We believe that reason, when first conferred, was fully adequate to all the purposes which it was intended to serve; but that it has since been impaired and perverted by sin, which has both darkened the understanding and corrupted the heart. It is, therefore, subject to be led astray by the imagination and the passions, to adopt false principles, and to draw erroneous conclusions.

2. It is alleged, as an objection to the Divine authority of the prophetic Scriptures, that some of the prophecies have failed. The following are the principal instances referred to:

(1.) It has been said that a false promise was made to Abraham when he was told that his descendants should possess the territory which lies between the Euphrates and the river of Egypt. But this objection is evidently made in ignorance of the Scriptures; for the fact is that

David conquered that territory, and that the dominions of Solomon were thus actually extended.*

(2.) Voltaire objects that the prophets made promises to the Jews of the most unbounded riches, dominion, and influence; but they have lost their possessions instead of obtaining either property or power, and therefore the prophecies are false. But the case is here unfairly stated, for the prophets never made such exaggerated promises. They predicted many spiritual blessings, to be bestowed in the times of Messiah, under figures drawn from worldly opulence and power, which no attentive reader can mistake. They also promised many civil advantages, but conditionally, on the obedience of the nation; and they spoke in high terms of the state of the Jews upon their final restoration, for which objectors must wait before they can determine the predictions to be false.

Moreover, Voltaire should have known that the reverses of the Jews of which he speaks were clearly predicted, and that his very objection acknowledges the truth of prophecy. The promises of the prophets have not been falsified, while their threatenings have been signally fulfilled.

(3.) Paine asserts that the prophecy of Isaiah to Ahaz was not verified by the event. The history of this prophecy, as delivered in the seventh chapter of Isaiah, is this: Rezin king of Syria, and Pekah king of Israel, made war upon Ahaz king of Judah, with the declared purpose of making an entire revolution in the government of Judah, of destroying the royal house of David, and of placing another family on the throne. Their purpose is thus expressed: "Let us go up against Judah, and vex it, and let us make a breach therein for us, and set a king in the midst of it, even the son of Tabeal." Now what did Isaiah say to Ahaz? Did he say, The kings shall not vex thee? shall not conquer thee? shall not succeed against thee? No: but he said, "It (*the purpose of the two kings*) shall not stand, neither shall it come to pass." Did it stand? did it come to pass? Was there any revolution effected? Was the house of David dethroned and destroyed? Was Tabeal ever made king of Judah? No. The prophecy was therefore perfectly accomplished.

(4.) The same writer attempts to fix a charge of false vaticination upon Jeremiah. He refers to a prediction which the prophet delivered to King Zedekiah, and which is recorded in the thirty-fourth chapter of his prophecies, in these words: "Thine eyes shall behold the eyes of the king of Babylon, and he shall speak with thee mouth to mouth, and thou shalt go to Babylon. Thou shalt not die by the sword; but thou shalt die in peace. And with the burnings of thy fathers, the former kings which were before thee, so shall they burn odors for thee."

* See 2 Sam. viii; 1 Chron. xviii.

Mr. Paine alleges that this prediction was not fulfilled; but that the very reverse was the case, according to the eleventh verse of the fifty-second chapter. It is there stated that the king of Babylon "put out the eyes of Zedekiah, and bound him in chains, and carried him to Babylon, and put him in prison till the day of his death." He asks, therefore, "What can we say of these prophets but that they are impostors and liars?" This, however, can be said in truth, that the prophecy was fulfilled in all its parts. Zedekiah beheld the eyes of the king of Babylon when he was brought before him at Riblah. The king spoke with Zedekiah mouth to mouth when he gave judgment upon him, or, as the margin has it, "*spake judgments with him.*" He was carried to Babylon. He did not die by the sword, nor did he fall in battle. He died in peace, for he neither expired upon the rack nor on the scaffold; he was neither strangled nor poisoned; he died upon his bed, though that bed was in a prison. It cannot be shown from the history that the prediction in regard to the funeral burnings was fulfilled, nor can it be proved that it was not; but as every other part was accomplished, the fair conclusion is that this was also.*

(5.) Mr. Paine quotes also a passage from the twenty-ninth chapter of Ezekiel, where, speaking of Egypt, the prophet said: "No foot of man shall pass through it, nor foot of beast shall pass through it, neither shall it be inhabited forty years." This, he says, "never came to pass, and consequently is false."

Now, as the history of Egypt at that remote period is very imperfectly known, it is at least hasty to conclude, even if we had no evidence in support of the prophecy, that it never was accomplished. But that the predicted invasion of Egypt by Nebuchadnezzar did come to pass we have the testimony of Megasthenes and Berosus, two heathen historians, who lived about three hundred years before Christ. This invasion was as devastating in its character as was that of Judea; and we know that the greater part of the inhabitants of that country were destroyed or led captive, and that the land, though not absolutely left without inhabitants, generally remained uncultivated for seventy years. In such circumstances, from the total cessation of all former intercourse between the different parts of the kingdom, it might without exaggeration be said that the foot of man and of beast did not "PASS THROUGH IT," their going from one part to another on business or for worship at Jerusalem being wholly suspended. And as we have no reason to suppose that Nebuchadnezzar was more merciful to Egypt than to Judea, the same expressions might be used, in a popular sense, in regard to that country.

It is admitted that no period can be pointed out, from the time of Ezekiel to the present, in which there was *no* foot of man or of beast to be seen in all Egypt for forty years. The language is evidently hyper-

* See 2 Kings xxv, 5-7; Jer. lii, 10, 11.

bolical, and we are not to expect a literal accomplishment of a hyperbolical expression. We only claim for the prediction that it denotes a great desolation; importing that the trade of Egypt, which was carried on by caravans—by the foot of man and of beast—should be suspended for forty years. No one, however, can prove that the prophecy was not so fully accomplished that the expression might be used without violent hyperbole.

3. It is objected that the Bible has a demoralizing influence upon society, and therefore cannot be divinely inspired. In proof of this various facts and circumstances are urged, the strongest of which we will consider.

(1.) It records the failings and vices of some of its leading characters. The fact is not denied; but the objectors suppress what is equally true, that these vices are never mentioned with approbation; that the characters stained with them are not, in those respects, held up for our imitation; and that such things are recorded for our admonition. They dwell upon the crimes of David, and sneer at his being called "*a man after God's own heart.*" But they seem not to know that this character was ascribed to David long before he committed those crimes; that, even if this were not so, the language had respect to his qualifications as a king, and not to his moral character, and that those very crimes were tremendously visited by the displeasure of the Almighty. This objection to the Bible has therefore no force in the direction intended, but it furnishes a strong argument in favor of the honesty and sincerity of the sacred writers. Had they been cunning impostors no such acknowledgments of crimes and frailties would have been made.

But what has been the effect of infidelity upon the morals of its advocates? Blount committed suicide because he was prevented from an incestuous marriage; Tyndal was notoriously infamous; Hobbes changed his principles with his interests; Morgan continued to profess Christianity while he wrote against it; the moral character of Voltaire was mean and detestable; Bolingbroke was a rake and a flagitious politician; Collins and Shaftesbury qualified themselves for civil office by receiving the Lord's Supper, while they were endeavoring to prove the religion of Christ to be an imposture; Hume was revengeful, disgustingly vain, and an advocate of adultery and self-murder; Paine was the slave of low and degrading habits; and Rousseau was an abandoned sensualist, and guilty of the basest actions. Was it ever found that a truly virtuous and humble man was an infidel? Does infidelity abound among the devout, the pure, the modest, and the dispassionate inquirers after truth? Or, are not rather its advocates profane and dissipated, smatterers in knowledge, false pretenders to philosophy and self-conceited speculatists, who, from their imaginary eminence, look down with contempt upon the opinions and pursuits of the multitude.

(2.) The extermination of the Canaanites by the Jews, according to the Divine command, is urged as an act of the greatest cruelty and injustice. But this objection cannot be urged upon the mere ground that it is contrary to Divine justice or mercy to cut off a people indiscriminately, for this has been done by earthquakes and pestilences. What is here ascribed to the God of the Bible, does not therefore contradict the character of the God of nature.

But was it consistent with the character of God to employ *human agents* in this work of destruction? Who can prove that it was not? Surely no one; and yet here lies the whole stress of the objection. The Jews were not rendered more cruel by their being so commissioned, for we find them much more merciful in their institutions than other ancient nations. Nor can this instance be pleaded in favor of exterminating wars; for there was in the case a special commission for a special purpose, and by that it was limited.

Moreover, the sins of the Canaanites were of so gross a nature that it was necessary to mark them with signal punishments for the benefit of surrounding nations. And the employing of the Israelites as instruments, under a special and publicly proclaimed commission, connected the punishment more visibly with the offense than if it had been inflicted by the array of warring elements; while the Israelites themselves would be more deeply impressed with the guilt of idolatry, and its ever accompanying polluted and sanguinary rites.

(3.) That law in the twenty-first chapter of Deuteronomy, which authorizes parents to bring a rebellious and intemperate son before the elders of the city that, if guilty, he might be stoned to death, has been called inhuman and brutal. In point of fact, however, it was a merciful regulation. In almost all ancient nations parents had the power of taking away the life of their children. This was a branch of the old patriarchal authority which did not all at once merge into the kingly governments which were afterward established. There is reason, therefore, to believe that it was possessed by the heads of families among the Israelites, and that this was the first attempt to control it, by requiring the crimes alleged against their children to be proved before regular magistrates, that the effects of unbridled passions might be prevented.

(4.) The intentional offering of Isaac by Abraham has also had its share of censure. The answer is: 1. That Abraham had no doubt of the Divine command in the case, and of the right of God to take away the life which he had given. 2. That he proceeded to execute the command of God in *faith*, as St. Paul has stated, that God would raise his Son from the dead. Had this transaction been so stated as to encourage human sacrifices it might be fairly objected to, but here are sufficient guards: an indubitable Divine command was given, the sacrifice was prevented by the same authority, and the history stands in a book which prohibits human sacrifices.

(5.) *Indelicacy* and *immodesty* have been charged upon some parts of the Scriptures. We reply, that in no instance is any statement made *in order* to incite impurity; and nothing throughout the whole Scriptures is represented as being more offensive to God than the unlawful gratification of the senses. It is also to be noted, that many of the passages objected to are in the *laws* and *prohibitions* of both Testaments; and as well might the laws of the land be held up as tending to encourage vices of various kinds because they must, in order to prohibit them, describe them with more or less circumstantiality.

We must also take into the account the simplicity of manners and language in early times. We observe, even among the peasantry of modern states, a language on the subject referred to which is more direct, and what refined society would call gross; but greater real indelicacy does not follow.

These cases have been adduced as specimens of the objections which infidels urge against the Scriptures, and of the ease with which they may be met. For others of a similar kind, and for answers to objections founded upon supposed contradictions between different passages of Scripture, reference must be made to commentators.* A little skill, however, in the original languages of the Scriptures, and in the times, occasions, and scope of the sacred books, as also in the antiquities and customs of those countries in which the recorded transactions took place, will always clear the main difficulty.

4. It is objected to the Bible that it contains mysteries and doctrines contrary to reason. It has been a favorite practice with unbelievers to institute a contrast between natural philosophy and revelation, the book of nature and the book of God, and to set the plainness and simplicity of the one against the mysteriousness of the other. The ground of all this is an unwillingness to receive as authorized doctrine what is incomprehensible. They contend that if a revelation has been made there can be no mysteries in it; and that to hold things incomprehensible to be a part of it is a contradiction, and fatal to its claims as a *revelation*.

The sophism here is easily answered. There are many doctrines and duties in which no mystery at all is involved; and as to incomprehensible subjects, nothing is more certain than that a fact may be clearly revealed, as that God is eternal and omnipresent, and still remain mysterious and incomprehensible. The fact is not revealed in a difficult, obscure, or mysterious manner, the only sense in which the objection could be valid. As a fact, it is clearly revealed that these are attributes of the Divine nature; but notwithstanding this clear and indubitable revelation they are still incomprehensible. It is not revealed HOW God is eternal and omnipresent, nor is such a revelation pretended; but

---

* See a copious collection of these supposed contradictions, with judicious explanations, in the Appendix to volume i of Horne's Introduction.

that HE IS SO. The same remarks will apply to the doctrine of the Trinity, and to many other doctrines of the sacred Scriptures. But if men hesitate to admit incomprehensible subjects as matters of faith, they cannot be permitted to fly for relief from revelation to philosophy, much less to claim that the latter is superior to the former in the clearness of its manifestations. Here too it will be seen that mystery and truth go inseparably together, and that he who embraces *facts* embraces at the same time the mystery of their *causes*. For instance, attraction, gravitation, cohesion, electricity, and magnetism are all admitted facts; but though the experimental and inductive philosophy of modern times has led to many discoveries of the *relations*, and in some cases of the *proximate causes* of these phenomena, yet their *real causes* are all confessedly hidden. And here it may be added, that if we turn our attention to the science of mechanics, or even to that of pure mathematics, we will still meet with much that is incomprehensible.

5. Analogical reasoning has made it probable that the planets of our system, and those of others, may be inhabited by moral beings like ourselves. Hence, infidels have argued the improbability that a Divine Person should have been sent into this world for its instruction and salvation, when, in comparison with the solar system, it is but a point, and that system itself, in comparison with the universe, may be nothing more.

Plausible as this may appear, nothing can have less weight, even if only the philosophy and not the theology of the case be considered. The intention with which man is thus compared with the universe is, to prove his insignificance; and the comparison must be made either between man and the *vastness* of planetary and stellar matter, or between the *number* of mankind and the *number* of supposed planetary inhabitants. If the former, we make corporeal magnitude the standard of real worth. It will therefore follow that a mountain is of more value than a man, in proportion as its magnitude is greater than his; that the smaller the disproportion between the man and the mountain, the less would be the relative insignificance of the former; and that if the smaller object be increased in magnitude, its dignity must be proportionately increased in the *true nature of things*. The *Irish giant*, therefore, whose altitude exceeded eight feet, would exceed in relative dignity, by the same proportion, BACON or NEWTON, whose height did not attain to six feet. But if this is *nonsense*, then must that also be *nonsense* from which these conclusions are legitimately drawn.

If we consider the dignity of an intelligent being, and put that in the scale against mere matter, we may affirm, without overvaluing human nature, that the soul of one virtuous man is of greater worth and excellence than the sun and his planets, and all the stars in the universe. Let us not then make bulk the standard of value, nor judge of the importance of man from the weight of his body, or from the size or situation of the planet which is now the place of his abode. If, therefore, man possesses *another magnitude*, which can be brought to another and different scale of computation, a scale which determines him to be of more value than the material universe, then it would not be irrational to suppose that the highest mountains and the widest regions, and the entire system to which they pertain, may be made subservient to his interests.

Such a scale is that by which the *intelligent, moral,* and *immortal* nature of MAN is to be measured, and which the sacred historian calls a formation "*after the image and likeness of God;*" a scale but little regarded in the science of *mere physics.* As soon, however, as the mind clearly apprehends this moral scale of magnitude, and perceives that though man's present existence is bounded by a very short period, yet his *moral nature* is unlimited in time, and will outlast all the mountains of the globe, it then perceives, at the same moment, the deceitful character of the objection which was urged with so much apparent humility.

If the comparison of man with mere material magnitude will not then support this effort to effect his degradation and to shame him out of his trust in the lovingkindness of his God, so neither will the argument which may be drawn from the supposed *number* of other intelligent beings. Their number cannot alter his character; for, though there may be myriads of immortal beings besides himself, yet he is still immortal, and still has his immense capacity for pleasure and for pain. Unless, therefore, it could be proved that the care of God for *each* of his creatures must be diminished as their number is increased, the argument can have no force. But such a supposition would be a base and unworthy reflection upon the supreme Creator himself, as though he could not bestow upon *all* the beings he has made a care and a love adequate to their circumstances.

That man is governed by the providence of God none but an atheist will deny; but any argument drawn from such premises as the preceding would conclude as forcibly against Providence as it can be made to conclude against redemption. And if, by a stupendous exuberance of animal, vegetable, and mineral productions, and the wonderful distribution of light and heat, God supplies the means of life and comfort to the short-lived inhabitants of this globe, can it be incredible, nay, does not this consideration render it in the highest degree probable that he has also prepared the means of eternal happiness for beings whom he has formed for endless duration?

There is, however, another consideration, which gives a sublime and overwhelming grandeur to the Scripture view of redemption, but of which infidel philosophers appear never to have entertained the least conception. It is the moral connection of this world with the whole universe of intelligent creatures, and the intention of God to convey moral instruction to other beings by the history of his moral government in regard to man. Intimations of this great and impressive view are found in various passages of the New Testament, and it opens a scene of inconceivable moral magnificence, " to the intent that now unto the principalities and powers in heavenly places might be known by the Church the manifold wisdom of God."*

* See Dr. Beattie's Evidences of the Christian Religion, and Dr. Chalmers's Discourses on Modern Astronomy.

BOOK II.

DOCTRINES RESPECTING GOD.

THE Divine Authority of the Sacred Scriptures having been established, our next step is to examine their contents, and to collect from them that religious and moral instruction which they contain.

CHAPTER I.

THE EXISTENCE OF GOD.

A BELIEF in the *existence* of God lies at the foundation of all religion, and is the only basis of true morality. This will appear evident if we inquire into the meaning of the terms *religion* and *morality*. By religion is meant either a system of doctrines of which God is the subject, or a system of affections and conduct of which he is the object. Morality sometimes denotes the practice of moral duties merely from motives of convenience or from a regard to our own reputation, and in this sense it may be distinguished from religion; but when it is understood in its true light it means the practice of moral duties from love to God and in obedience to his will, and consequently it is necessarily included in the idea of religion.

It follows, therefore, that if there were no God there could be no religion, no moral obligation, no hope of reward, no fear of punishment. There could in reality be neither virtue nor vice; for men would be under no law but that of stern necessity, and could propose to themselves no higher end than the securing of their temporal happiness by every possible means. But if there is a God of infinite power, wisdom, and goodness, he ought to be loved, worshiped, and obeyed by all his intelligent creatures.

The opinion has been entertained that it is irreverent to adduce proofs in favor of the Divine existence, because it seems to call in question a truth which it is impiety to doubt. There are considerations, however, that will show the propriety and the utility of an investigation of this kind.

Though it is true that mankind generally believe in the existence of God, yet it is equally true that a large proportion of them have embraced the tenet upon the ground of mere authority, without any careful examination of the evidence on which it rests. Such persons would be unable to give a rational account of their faith, or to defend themselves against the attacks of infidelity. Hence it is necessary for every man to examine the ground of his faith, that he may be able to give a reason of his hope.

Moreover, it is of the utmost importance that a truth on which the hopes and happiness of mankind are suspended should be deeply impressed upon the mind. But there is nothing so well suited to produce this result, in relation to the Divine existence, as a thorough and frequent review of the evidences of this fact by which men are everywhere surrounded.

It may also be added that no one knows to what severe trials his faith may be subjected through the temptation of the devil. Men of deep piety have sometimes experienced moments of darkness, in which they have entertained doubts, not only of the providence and goodness of God, but even of his very existence. This is a subject, therefore, which every man should examine for himself, and in regard to which he should obtain clear and enlightened views.

The word God is supposed to be derived from the Icelandic *godi*, which signifies Supreme Magistrate, or Governor of the Universe. It is also a pure Anglo-Saxon term, which among our ancestors literally signified *good*. When, therefore, they thought or spoke of the being whom we call God, they were taught by the primary meaning of the term employed to regard him as being emphatically *the Good Being*, the fountain of infinite benevolence.

The Hebrew word which is translated God is *Elohim*. This, the learned say, is derived from the Arabic *alaha*, which means *to worship, to adore*. Thus God is characterized as the only proper object of worship and adoration. In Greek the name of God is *Theos*, and in Latin, *Deus;* both of which signify the *Supreme Divinity*, or Ruler of the Universe.

The question has been asked, Can God be defined? To this we reply, *first*, that if a definition must necessarily contain a complete description of the nature and attributes of the object defined a definition of God is impossible, because no definition can be given which will fully exhaust the idea in question. But, *secondly*, if it is only necessary that a definition should present so many characteristics of the object defined as will enable us to distinguished it from all others, then, in this sense, God can be defined.

A definition of this great First Cause may be given thus: God is an

Eternal, Independent, Immutable, Omnipotent, Omniscient, Omnipresent, Just, Holy, and Infinitely Benevolent Spirit; the Creator, Preserver, and Governor of all things.

Before we enter upon an examination of the arguments by which the Divine Existence is sustained, we may inquire,

I. BY WHAT MEANS IS THE IDEA OF GOD ORIGINATED? On this subject the three following opinions have been advanced: 1. That the idea is innate; 2. That it is the result of rational investigation; and, 3. That it depends alone upon Divine Revelation. Let us examine each of these briefly.

1. *That the Idea is innate.*—If the notion of a supreme First Cause were an innate idea, it would be as natural for man to believe that there is a God, as to believe in the existence of an external universe. Such an idea would have all the force of a self-evident proposition, and could be doubted by no one possessing rationality. But how does this theory correspond with matters of fact? Is it not evidently inconsistent with the existence of atheism? I am aware some suppose that no man can be an atheist, but this is assuming what cannot be proved. That there are those who profess atheism, and who manifest all possible zeal in its propagation, no one will deny; and, until we can claim the ability to discern the thoughts and purposes of the human heart, we have no right to call in question the truth of their profession or the sincerity of their zeal.

The theory in question is also at war with the true philosophy of mind. The doctrine of innate ideas is a mere hypothesis, which no man has ever been able to prove; but which is contradicted by all experience, and is, therefore, unworthy of our confidence. It is now generally admitted that we gain all our ideas by the use of our natural faculties, sensation and reflection; and if so, we have no reason to believe that our idea of God forms an exception to the general rule.

2. *There seems to be a degree of plausibility in the opinion that men may acquire an idea of God by rational induction, or from the light of nature;* but however plausible this theory may at first sight appear to be, we will find, on further examination, that it is wholly untenable. It is true, *nature* is a volume of theological instruction to those who are capable of reading it. But, as a book may be stored with wholesome and important matter, and yet be of no benefit to the man who understands not the language in which it is written; so the volume of nature may contain a thousand arguments in favor of the Divine existence, and yet men, for the want of a sufficient degree of moral instruction, may be unable in the slightest degree to feel their force or follow their tendency.

To the Jew it is evident that " the heavens declare the glory of God," and that " the firmament showeth his handiwork." To the Christian philosopher it is equally evident that "the invisible things of him from the creation of the world are clearly seen, being understood by the things that are made, even his eternal power and godhead." And to deists and heathen sages, who enjoy a light which they are either unable to trace to its proper source or unwilling to acknowledge, the voice of nature proclaims the existence of a supreme First Cause.

These facts, however, have no direct bearing upon the present subject. The question to be investigated is not, whether the light of nature sustains the proposition that there is a God, for of this there can hardly be a doubt; but it is simply this: Is the light of nature sufficient of itself to lead men to the knowledge of God? In other words, Can men who are entirely destitute of the idea of a God derive that idea from rational investigation? Of the question as understood in this sense we feel disposed to take the negative, and in support of our position we offer the following arguments.

(1.) *The Opinion is not supported by a single matter of fact.*—The history of ages does not afford a single instance in which any man, by a course of philosophic research, obtained the idea of God as an original discovery. On the other hand it is worthy of remark, that the wisest among heathen philosophers confessed themselves to be indebted to *tradition* for the ideas which they entertained upon this point; and no one, in any age or country, has ever pretended to have arrived at an original idea of God by rational investigation.

Had such a discovery ever been made by any man, there would most certainly have been preserved, in some way or other, a notice of so wonderful an event. This is true in regard to all the great discoveries of mankind in arts and science. Thus, the name of *Copernicus* is associated with the present system of astronomy. The name of *Hervey* is connected with the common theory of the circulation of the blood. *Fulton* stands at the head of steam power; and the memory of *Morse* runs with lightning speed along every telegraphic wire. So it is with almost every important discovery. But nothing of this kind marks the discovery of a great First Cause; and the only reason is, that such a discovery was never made by any human being. In every case, where a process of reasoning upon this subject has been instituted, it has been to corroborate the belief in the being of a God, and not to gain a knowledge of him as an original discovery. But,

(2.) *This Theory is incredible in itself, because it is absurd and contradictory.*

To suppose that a man can commence a rational investigation of this kind without an idea of God, and as the result of his researches to arrive at such an idea, is to suppose that he will put forth an effort without any object in view. Or, which is the same thing, to inquire after an object of which he has no conception—a subject of which he has not the least idea. It is, in a word, to have an idea of an object and no idea at the same time; and to suppose that of which he has no knowledge to be the subject of his thought and reasoning.

How, then, is a man to come by the first idea of God, with regard to whose existence he is to decide? Were we to suppose human beings to be without such an idea, is it probable that they would ever institute an inquiry respecting him? Or, if such an intention should somehow or other be formed by them, is it likely that they would be able to prosecute it? No one who understands the philosophy of the human mind will answer these questions in the affirmative. Every one knows that it requires more intellectual strength and effort to discover an unknown truth than to comprehend it when fairly stated, or to see the force of the evidence on which it rests. But,

(3.) *The opinion supposes a degree of mental culture that never has existed, and never can exist, where there is no idea of a God;* and, therefore, the discovery is not probable.

Man, without some degree of education, is wholly a creature of appetite. The gratification of his animal nature occupies all his thoughts, and he is therefore unqualified for rational investigation. If we suppose that God is at all discoverable by the light of nature, we must look to those whose civilization and intellectual culture have fitted the mind for the investigation of abstract and philosophic truth. For, to a people who have never heard of God, his existence must be a question of mere philosophy.

But where is such a state of mental cultivation found? Is it among those from whose mind the idea of God is entirely obliterated? To suppose this is to suppose that men can be raised from a state of barbarism to one of civil and scientific cultivation without the influence of religion; for no religious motives can exist where the foundation of all religion is unknown. It is to suppose that civil and scientific cultivation can exist independent of moral control, without a sense of the principle of justice, without hope or fear in regard to another life.

This is what never was. No civilized nation ever existed under such circumstances. It is utterly impossible to raise any body of men, by mere civil improvement, to that degree of mental cultivation which will fit them for philosophic research without the aid of religion in some form. Accordingly, wherever there has been a sufficient amount of mental improvement to prepare men for the investigation of moral and spiritual truth, there the idea of a great First Cause has been previously known and acknowledged.

Under the influence of religion in one form or other, all states or civil communities, both ancient and modern, have been formed and maintained. It has entered essentially into all their legislative and gubernative institutions. Even the atheists of Greece and Rome acknowledged the necessity of maintaining the public religion as the means of restraining the multitude. We conclude, therefore, that where no idea of a Supreme Ruler or Creator has been suggested to the mind, either by instruction or tradition, it is not to be supposed that men could gain a knowledge of such a truth even in an imperfect form.

We admit that to us, who enjoy the light of Divine instruction, the existence of God may appear to be exceedingly evident and easily demonstrated. Its rational evidence is so abundant, so easily collected, and so convincing, that we may hardly be able to see how any one can fail to discover it from the light of nature; but all this does not prove that the human mind, unaided by any supernatural means, can make the discovery.

If it were possible for the mind to institute an inquiry upon the principle of *cause* and *effect*, in order to arrive at a knowledge of the great First Cause, would it not be as likely to embrace the notion of an eternal succession of causes and effects as to believe in creation and an almighty Creator? The philosophers of Greece and Rome, whether deistical, atheistical, or polytheistical, all agreed that matter is eternal; and though they possessed a traditionary knowledge of God, yet they had no conception of the creation of the world out of nothing. Among them it was a settled point that matter is uncreated.

Were we to admit that on the principle of induction some knowledge of the Creator might be gained by the most contemplative, by what means could they demonstrate to themselves that the world had but *one* Creator? This is an inquiry which the mere light of nature can never answer. But by means of revealed truth, philosophy is so aided in her operations that she can employ arguments which are strong and satisfactory, not only in opposition to the eternity of matter and an eternal succession of causes and effects, but in proof of the unity of the world's Creator.

(4.) *The question before us is one which cannot be settled by an appeal to facts,* for the human family have never been in circumstances to render the experiment possible; they have never been entirely destitute of a knowledge of God. If any one supposes that this knowledge is not coeval with man, or that the idea of God was first obtained by rational investigation, let him show, by some tangible proof, that his theory is true; or if he cannot do this, let him confess that the idea of a God is as old as the race.

It is worthy of remark, that neither Moses, the first of the inspired penmen, nor any of the writers of the succeeding canonical books, enter into any formal *proof* of this first principle of religion, *the existence of a God.* They all assume it as a well-known and commonly admitted fact. Nor is there in the sacred volume any allusion to atheistical sentiments till some ages after Moses. From this circumstance we learn that, previous to the time of Moses, the idea of one supreme and infinitely perfect God was familiar to men in general; that it had descended to them from the earliest ages; and also, that it was originally a truth of revelation, and not one which had been discovered by any of the sages of preceding times.

The progenitor of our race was made in the image and likeness of

God, and he must therefore have known him by sensible manifestations. It was as impossible for Adam not to know his Creator as to doubt his own existence. Equally clear demonstrations were made to Abel, to Noah, to Abraham, to Isaac, to Jacob, and to Moses. Thus, through a period of more than two thousand years, "God at sundry times and in divers manners" revealed himself to his servants. When Moses wrote there were persons still living who had conversed with those who had conversed with God, or who had descended from those to whom God had appeared in visible glory or in angelic forms. These Divine manifestations were matters of public notoriety among the primitive families of mankind. From them the tradition was transmitted to their descendants; and the idea, once communicated, was readily embraced as a necessary truth, and was confirmed by every natural object on which the eye could rest.

It was thus that God was made known to the ancient world. Whether, therefore, such a discovery is within the reach of mere human reason, is a question which has never been determined by experiment; because, as mankind have never been without this knowledge, they have never been in circumstances in which such an experiment could be made. There may have been some uncivilized tribes, such as the Kamtschatkadales of the north, and the Hottentots of southern Africa, among whom the idea of a Supreme Being has been nearly, if not entirely, obliterated; but in no case among such tribes of men has the knowledge of God been recovered, except by the instruction of others. Hence, matter of fact stands opposed to the notion that God is discoverable by the unassisted faculties of man.

From the whole of this reasoning we are conducted to the conclusion,

3. *That we owe our knowledge of God, both in regard to his Existence and his Attributes, to Divine Revelation.*

We do not mean that all who are destitute of a *direct revelation* must necessarily be without this knowledge, but that revelation is the *primary source* of all our knowledge of God, whether it comes to us *directly*, by means of inspired truth, or *indirectly*, by tradition or uninspired instruction.

But now, since God has so clearly revealed himself to man in the volume of Divine inspiration, rational evidence in support of his existence is both copious and irresistible, so much so that atheism has never been able to make much progress where this revelation has been preserved. "Tell men," says Ellis, "that there is a God, and their mind embraces it as a necessary truth; unfold his attributes, and they will see the explanation of them in his works."

Let us then proceed to consider,

II. SOME RATIONAL ARGUMENTS IN SUPPORT OF THE BIBLE DOCTRINE, THAT THERE IS "ONE LIVING AND TRUE GOD."

Theologians have employed two modes of argumentation in demonstrating the Divine existence. One is, to argue from *cause* to *effect*, and is called the argument *à priori*. The other is, to argue from *effect* to *cause*, and is called the argument *à posteriori*. The latter is the only mode on which any dependence can be placed, and its demonstrations are too strong to need a doubtful auxiliary.

Logicians have distributed *causes* into Efficient, Material, Formal, and Final. An *efficient* cause is the agent that produces an effect; a *material* cause is the subject on which the agent acts; a *formal* cause is the effect produced by the agent; and a *final* cause is the end for which a thing is done.

It is according to the common sense, and the common observation and experience of mankind, that the connection between efficient causes and their effects is a *necessary* connection, since without the operation of the cause the effect never takes place. It is, therefore, an *axiom* in philosophy, that for every *effect* there must be an adequate *cause;* that nothing exists or comes to pass without a *cause*. This fact being established, we may proceed to the arguments which are founded upon it in proof of the Divine existence. This may be argued,

1. *From the common consent of mankind.*

It is a generally admitted fact that all the nations of the earth have acknowledged, in one form or other, the being of a God; in proof of which we need only appeal to the history of the human race.

To this it is objected, that some nations or tribes of men have been found who had no idea of a Supreme Being. But our answer is, *first*, that the objection is based upon insufficient grounds; for, though the allegation has been made in regard to certain tribes, it has been, at least in some cases, by persons who were ignorant of their language, customs, and opinions; and, consequently, a more intimate knowledge of them has demonstrated that the account was a hasty and unjust assumption. But, *secondly*, were we to grant that there are tribes of human beings who are so far brutified as to be entirely destitute of all religious knowledge, still our argument would not be greatly impaired; for this would no more prove that men do not commonly consent to the being of a God, than the actual blindness of some would prove that sight is not common to the race.

It may be objected further, that mankind have not agreed in the belief of *one* God, but of *many;* and that, with the exception of the Jews, polytheism was the system of all nations in ancient times, as it still is where neither Christianity nor Mohammedanism has been introduced. But to object to our argument on account of the errors of Paganism, is as unreasonable as to deny the existence of a true coin because it has been extensively counterfeited. It is true, men have held very different notions in regard to the number and character of the objects of their worship. Some have maintained the doctrine of *one*

Supreme Being, while others have swelled the number of their gods to thousands; but in all that mass of inconsistency, contradiction, and absurdity which characterizes the idolatrous worship of pagan nations, there is a harmony on one point: they all agree that the universe is under Divine control.

When we see that distant nations of men, separated by mountains and oceans, by burning sands and drifting snows, holding no intercourse with one another for ages, and differing widely in their language, manners, customs, and modes of thinking, all testify with united voice their belief in a Divine and superintending Power, we are constrained to inquire, How is this harmony of sentiment to be accounted for?

The atheists of the school of Epicurus attempted to account for this general belief by the principle of fear; but this is evidently to put the effect before the cause. Other men would have supposed that fear proceeded from the previous belief of a power or powers superior to mortals, and able to injure them. But in this case it is supposed that men began to be afraid of something, they knew not what; and thinking this to be very unreasonable, as it doubtless was, they set about finding out an adequate cause of their fear, and luckily lighted upon the idea of *gods*—terrible beings, whom it was hazardous to offend. We need say nothing more about this theory, as it clearly refutes itself.

Others account for this general belief by ascribing it to the artifice of statesmen, who contrived in this manner to give greater authority to their laws, and to retain men in subjection by the sanctions of religion. But this notion is altogether destitute of proof. Who was the first legislator that propagated the story of the existence of the *gods?* How did he succeed in persuading a whole people to give credit to a dogma of which they had no evidence but his affirmation, and of which they had never before heard a whisper? If one legislator was the inventor of it, how did it spread so rapidly over the whole earth? Did all the princes and statesmen of the world assemble in congress, agree upon this expedient for maintaining their authority, and then return to their respective countries to put it in practice? And how did it happen that they became the dupes of their own stratagem, and believed in the gods as firmly as their subjects?

We have now seen that this *almost* universal agreement of men with regard to the Divine existence is a fact which cannot be set aside; that the theories which are commonly adopted to account for this fact are insufficient and absurd; and, consequently, that the real cause of this wide-spread effect is still to be ascertained. The only rational ground on which we can account for this general agreement is that of *tradition*, to admit that all nations originally had a common origin, and that, previous to their dispersion, they were in possession of a system of religious doctrine and worship which, in all their long-continued and extensive wanderings, they have never entirely forgotten. But then we must also account for the origin of this *tradition*. Whence originally came this religious knowledge? this idea of a God? this belief in a superior and superintending Providence? We have only to admit that God originally made a revelation of himself to man, and at once we solve the problem. But if we deny this, we may wander in uncertainty and conjecture forever. This view of the subject must, therefore, be acknowledged to furnish an argument of some weight in proof of the existence of God. But this doctrine may be argued,

2. *From our own actual existence, and that of other things around us.*

Every man knows with absolute certainty that he himself and other beings exist. But since beings now exist, either there was a time when all beings began to exist, or otherwise some being must have existed from all eternity. If there was a time when all beings *began* to exist, until that time there was *nothing;* and it will hence follow, that the first being must have started up out of nothing and caused itself to be. If this is too absurd to be admitted, we must believe that a Being has existed from all eternity. Hence, the existence of an eternal Being, the cause of all other beings, is as certain as that anything now exists.

It is also evident that some being has always existed of itself, without any cause; for either all being was caused or some being was uncaused. But if all being was caused, then some one at least was the cause of itself, which is a contradiction.

It is further evident that some being must be independent upon any other being. To say that *all* being is dependent, is to say that it depends on nothing; for there is nothing beyond the compass of being on which it may depend. A being that never depended on any other as a *producing* cause cannot depend on any other as a *sustaining* or *conserving* cause.

It consequently follows that such a being exists *necessarily*. An uncaused being cannot be dependent upon its own choice, nor upon the choice of any other being, for its existence; and, therefore, its existence is not owing to choice at all, but to the necessity of its own nature. To such a being it is impossible ever not to have been or ever to cease from being.

We may now advance another step, and add, that this eternal, uncaused, independent, and necessary Being is *self-active*. Such a Being must be either self-active or entirely inactive; for it is absurd to say that an independent being can derive its activity from another. If we suppose it to be *inactive*, we fall into the inconsistency of ascribing attributes of the most inconceivable excellency and dignity to a being as good as nothing; for there is but little difference between *being* nothing and *doing* nothing. But if, in order to account for the present existence of things, we must allow the existence of an eternal uncaused

Being, the efficient cause of all other beings, as has been shown, we must, on the very same principle, allow that this eternal Being is *self-active;* for an inactive efficient cause is a contradiction. That which can *do nothing* can no more be the producing cause of other beings than that which is nothing. It is therefore evident that there is a necessary, self-active Being, the cause and author of all created beings.

And hence, since we can form no notion of *life* which self-active power does not comprehend, we must consequently allow that this Being is also originally *vital*, having life in and of itself; and being the root of all vitality, whence life is propagated to every living creature.

We argue the existence of God,

3. *From the evidences of* DESIGN *in the works of creation.*

As the dependence of all things around us proves that they must have originated from an independent Cause, and as their actual existence proves his power, so every object in nature affords undeniable proof that the world, and all things therein, are the effects of an intelligent and designing Cause. For, as nothing can be produced without a *cause*, so no cause can work above or beyond its own capacity. Whatever, therefore, is ascribed to any cause above and beyond its ability, is ascribed to no cause at all. If it then follows that when an effect is produced it has a cause, why does it not equally follow, when an effect is produced, having manifest characters of wisdom and design upon it, that it has a wise and designing Cause.

It may be said that there are some productions which look like the effects of wisdom and contrivance, but which are not; as the nests of birds, the comb of bees, and the web of the spider. But who can demonstrate that these creatures are incapable of design? And if even that could be done, it would not prove that there is not a universal designing Cause, from whose directive and operative influence no imaginable effect or event can be exempted. It is no more necessary that a creature which steadily works toward an *end* should itself design and know that end, than that the tools of a mechanic should know what he is doing with them; but if they do not, it is plain that he must.

There are thousands of things produced by man which every one at first sight would pronounce to be the effects of skill, and not of chance. But if men will soberly consider the characters or footsteps of wisdom and design which are everywhere manifest in what are called *the works of nature*, they will be constrained to acknowledge that these works are the effects of an almighty and designing Cause. Indeed, *universal nature*, as it is seen in the variety, order, beauty, and wonderful contrivance of things, and in their adaptation to their proper and respective *ends*, is only the exercise of that almighty power which is everywhere active in the world, in conjunction with that infinite wisdom which directs and governs all its operations. If, therefore, the marks of design in works of *art* are proofs of a designing cause, the same must be true in regard to the works of *nature*.

We will suppose that one who had never seen a *watch*, or anything of the kind, has now, for the first time, this little engine offered to his view. Is it not almost certain that he would, upon the mere sight of its figure, structure, and curious workmanship, at once acknowledge the artificer's hand? And if he were also made acquainted with the object for which it was constructed, and with the manner in which all its parts contribute to the exact measurement of time, would he not most assuredly both confess and admire the ingenuity of the inventor?

But now suppose that a bystander, beholding him in his admiration, and undertaking to show a profounder knowledge, should say, Sir, you are mistaken concerning the composition of this watch. It was neither designed by the skill, nor made by the hand of any one. It had its origin from innumerable little atoms, which were busily frisking and playing to and fro about the place of its nativity; and which, according to the laws of matter and motion, formed themselves into this little fabric. Some of those busy particles agreed to form one wheel, and others another, in that order and with those proportions which you see. Others of them formed the figures upon the dial plate, and also those little moving fingers which point out the hours of the day and the days of the month; and thus all its parts were so happily arranged as to secure its regular motion. Who could be made to believe this piece of natural history? Should any one give this account of the production of a watch we would conclude that he was either jesting or insane.

The mechanism of the watch being once understood, the inference is irresistible that it must have had a maker who both comprehended its construction and designed its use. Nor would it weaken our conclusion that we had never witnessed the making of a watch, or known an artist capable of making one; or that we ourselves could neither execute such a work nor understand the manner in which it was performed. All this is true of some exquisite remains of ancient art, and to most men of the more curious productions of modern manufacture. Ignorance of this kind may lead to a more exalted opinion of the skill of the artist; but it cannot raise a single doubt in regard to his existence and agency.

But if the argument from design is so convincing when based upon a mere work of *art*, it ought to be much more so when transferred to the works of *nature*. In an infinite number of instances ends more singular are there proposed, and are accomplished by contrivances which demonstrate the existence, not only of *intelligence*, but of intelligence of an *infinitely superior order*.

The field of illustration into which this argument leads us is quite too extensive to be explored in a work like this. The entire universe, from the smallest portion of organized matter up to man, and from man to the immense spheres that roll in boundless space, is full of examples of wise design. We must, however, confine ourselves to a few particulars.

(1.) Let us suppose that in some part of the air near this earth, and within such limits as would allow the whole scene to be conveniently viewed, there should suddenly appear a little globe of light resembling that of the sun; and suppose it to be fixed as a center to another body, which we could plainly perceive to be a proportionably little earth, beautified with trees and woods, with flowery fields and flowing streams, and with lakes and seas into which these streams discharged themselves; and suppose there were other planets, all proportioned to the narrow limits assigned them, placed at their due distances, and playing about the supposed sun so as to measure their days, and months, and years; would we not with readiness and amazement confess that the contriver and maker of such a system must possess intelligence far above that of any mortal? And have we not in the present frame of nature a demonstration of wisdom and counsel as far exceeding that which we have now supposed, as the contrivance and execution of something that is of universal benefit to man is greater than the making of the most insignificant toy?

(2.) We may ask those who know anything about the composition of the human body, whether there is not as much evidence of contrivance in that wonderful structure as there is in the most admired productions of human skill? Who can think for a moment that the eye was not intended to serve as the organ of vision? Let us compare it, for example, with a telescope. As far as we can examine there is precisely the same proof that the eye was made for vision as there is that the telescope was made to assist it. They are constructed upon the same principles, both being adjusted to the laws by which the transmission and refraction of the rays of light are regulated.

Some may think that there is no similitude between the eye and the telescope, because the former is a *perceiving organ*, while the latter is only an *unperceiving instrument*. The fact is, however, that they are both instruments; and, so far as their *mechanism* is concerned, this circumstance does not destroy their analogy. It is well known that in order to distinct vision an image of the object must be formed at the bottom of the eye. How this image is connected with the sensation we may not be able to explain, nor is the present question concerned with that inquiry. But the formation of such an image being necessary to the sense of sight, how is it produced? We answer, by means which correspond exactly with those employed in the telescope, but which exhibit infinitely more art. So far as it regards the production of this image, the eye and the telescope are therefore instruments of the same kind. The lenses of the telescope and the humors of the eye bear a complete resemblance to one another in their figure, their position, and their power over the rays of light. They bring each pencil to a point at the proper distance from the lens, and in the eye at the exact place where the retina is prepared to receive it. How, then, is it possible, under such circumstances, to exclude contrivance from one, while we so readily acknowledge it in the other?

We may now turn our attention to that bony column called the *spine*. It is composed of twenty-four bones of very wonderful construction, and is evidently intended to perform various, difficult, and almost inconsistent offices.

It is necessary, in the *first* place, that it should possess both *firmness* and *flexibility:* firmness, to support the body in an erect position; and flexibility, to allow the trunk to bend in all degrees of curvature. Accordingly, the breadth of the bases upon which the parts severally rest, and the closeness of their junction, give to the chain its firmness and stability; while the number of its parts, and the consequent frequency of its joints, impart to it flexibility. This flexibility varies in different parts of the column. It is least in the back, where strength more than flexure is wanted; greater in the loins, where greater flexure is required; and greatest of all in the neck, for the free motions of the head.

This column is intended, *secondly*, to form a safe passage for the spinal marrow. To this end there is a hole in the middle of each vertebra, and when the several bones are put together they form a close and uninterrupted channel. The vertebræ, by means of their processes and projections, and the articulations which some of these form with one another at their extremities, are so locked in and confined as to prevent them from shifting out of their proper position when the body is moved or twisted; and thus, as the relative position of these bones remains nearly unaltered, the line of the canal for the spinal marrow is preserved unbroken.

To prevent the joints from gaping externally when the body is bent forward they are supplied with intervening cartilages, whose yielding nature admits all the motion that is necessary without producing any chasm by a separation of the parts. The spine's being composed of so many bones contributes also to the end in view. Had it consisted of only three or four, the bending of the body must have bruised the spinal marrow at every angle; but now, though we bend our back to almost every degree of inclination, the motion of each vertebra is very small.

But, *thirdly*, the spine affords convenient holes or openings, through which a supply of nerves is sent out from the medullary canal to different parts of the body; and, *fourthly*, it forms a basis for the insertion of muscles, and a support for the ends of the ribs. But we will decline a further consideration of particular parts of the body, and turn our attention,

(3.) To some of its principal *functions*. Let us begin with that of *growth*. Men have invented and constructed many curious and complex machines; but who ever made one that could grow, or that had in it a self-improving power? This is infinitely beyond the ingenuity and ability of man.

Who that has reason enough to be serious is not amazed at the miracle of *nutrition*? The body is constantly throwing off particles of matter which once entered into its composition, and is therefore subject to perpetual waste; but is as constantly receiving a gradual supply and renovation, by which it continues in the same state. It is easy to frame a work of art that shall gradually decay; but who can compose a thing that, like our bodies, shall be continually melting away, and yet be continually repaired for so many years? Nay, who can tell how this reparation is effected? We know how food is received, concocted, and separated; how so much as must serve for nourishment is turned into chyle, and that into blood; how this blood is distributed to all parts of the body for the purpose of nutrition; but how it loses its own nature, and assumes that of the different living tissues, to repair their losses and support their strength, is beyond our comprehension.

And what shall we say of *spontaneous motion*, with which we and other animals are endowed? We know that we have power to move ourselves, or to stop our own motion at pleasure; but how far have all attempted imitations of animated nature fallen short of this perfection? How much more excellent a thing is the smallest insect than the most admired machine of which we ever heard? And is it no proof of a wise and designing Creator that there are innumerable living creatures which, with the greatest facility, can move themselves at their own pleasure, in every possible direction, and with every variety of motion? This, surely, cannot be the work of blind fate or chance.

(4.) We will close this argument by adverting to the nature and powers of the human soul. Men know that they can think, understand, and frame notions of things; that they have a consciousness of all that passes in their own mind; that they can apprehend the future existence of what now is not, and the future appearance of that which is now invisible; that they have a power to compare things with one another, and to judge of their agreement or disagreement; and that they can infer one thing from another, so as from one plain principle to draw out a long chain of logical consequences. They know, too, that they are endowed with a power of choice which we call the *will*, a faculty which is freely exercised in deciding among different objects which shall be pursued.

But there is another and a still higher view to be taken of the human soul. We have considered it only in relation to its *intellectual* endowments, but it is also to be regarded as a *moral* being. Every man is conscious of moral perception. He finds a law within his own bosom by which he judges his feelings, his actions, and his whole moral character. This law commands his obedience so imperatively that he is compelled to regard it as the standard to which his conduct must be brought, and by which it must be tried, independent of human opinions; and he acquits or condemns himself, according to this law, as if he stood before a judicial tribunal. But to acknowledge this law is to acknowledge at the same time that there is an invisible Lawgiver and Judge, who annexes rewards to what is morally good, and punishment to what is morally evil. In this way man comes to the knowledge of a *moral order* of things to which he himself is conscious of belonging, and from which he cannot but infer the existence of a moral Cause, on which this order depends.

If, then, the human soul is a caused being, and consequently had a beginning, and if it is furnished with such wonderful powers and faculties, how came it into existence? To this question no rational answer can be given, but that it owes its being to an intelligent and moral Cause.

Instances of design and wonderful contrivance are as numerous as there are organized bodies in nature and relations between bodies not organized. The subject is, therefore, inexhaustible, but the cases which have been stated are sufficient for the illustration of this species of argument.

Nothing that is contrived can, in a strict and proper sense, be eternal, because the contriver must have existed before the contrivance. Hence it follows, after all the schemes and struggles of a reluctant philosophy, that the necessary resort is a *Deity*. The marks of *design*, which are everywhere to be seen, are too strong to be disregarded. Design must have had a *designer*, and that designer is GOD.

CHAPTER II.

ATTRIBUTES OF GOD.*

HAVING established, as we believe, the doctrine of the *existence* of God, we will proceed, in the next place, to a consideration of the *Attributes* or *Perfections* which are ascribed to him in the sacred Scriptures. We do not presume to enumerate *all* the perfections of Jehovah, or to give a full and adequate idea of *any one* of them. Our notions of Him who is infinite and eternal are very limited and obscure, and must be so

---

* The *Attributes* of God are so denominated because God attributes them to himself. They are called *Perfections*, because they are essential qualities of an infinitely perfect Being. They are also called *Properties*, because we conceive them to be *proper* to God, as distinguishing him from every other being.

from our mental imbecility. "Canst thou by searching find out God? canst thou find out the Almighty unto perfection? It is as high as heaven; what canst thou do? deeper than hell; what canst thou know? The measure thereof is longer than the earth, and broader than the sea." Job xi, 7-9.

Divines have sometimes divided the Attributes of God into different classes. Thus they have been considered as Absolute or Relative; Positive or Negative; Natural or Moral; and Communicable or Incommunicable. But these divisions we consider unnecessary, and will, therefore, adopt no such classification, but will consider the Divine Perfections in that order which seems to us most natural. Those commonly enumerated are the following: *Unity, Spirituality, Eternity, Omnipotence, Omnipresence, Omniscience, Immutability, Wisdom, Truth, Justice, Holiness,* and *Goodness.*

§ 1. *The Unity of God.*

The proper scriptural notion of the Unity of God may be thus presented. A thing may be one by virtue of composition, as a watch, a house; but God is one *uncompounded* and *purely simple* being. A thing may be one of a class or kind, as a man, an angel; but God is *so one* that there is *no other being of the same kind.* A thing may be the only one of the kind, as the sun, the moon; yet there might have been more if the Creator had so willed it. But God is *so one* that there *cannot* be another. In proof of the Unity of God we may appeal,

1. To THE HOLY SCRIPTURES.—Their testimony upon this subject is express and unequivocal. "The Lord our God is ONE Lord." Deut. vi, 4. "Thou art God ALONE." Psa. lxxxvi, 10. "I am God, and there is NONE ELSE." Isa. xlv, 22. "To us there is but ONE God." 1 Cor. viii, 6. Nor is this stated in the Scriptures merely to exclude all other creators, governors, or deities in connection with this system of created things which we behold; but *absolutely,* so as to exclude the idea of the existence, anywhere, of more than *one* Divine nature.

The scriptural argument in proof of this important doctrine is short and simple. We have undoubted evidence of a revelation from the Maker and Governor of the world. Granting him to be wise and good, it is impossible that he should declare what is not true. His own testimony assigns him exclusive deity; and if we admit the authority of the Scriptures, we must admit also that there is only ONE God. But this doctrine may be supported,

2. BY RATIONAL ARGUMENTS.—These are either *metaphysical,* or such as are drawn from the *contemplation of nature.*

(1.) *The arguments of a metaphysical character are based upon the nature of the Divine Being.* The idea of God is appropriated to an individual, and does not admit of application to more than *one*. There cannot be any thing above God, or equal to him, or which is not dependent upon him. He is not only the *first* and the *best*, but the *greatest* of beings; and, consequently, he stands alone in the universe. What do we mean by the term *God* but a being who is infinitely and absolutely perfect? The idea of two equal gods is therefore a chimera. There may be more kings than one, because royalty only implies that each is vested with sovereign authority in his own dominions; but there cannot be a plurality of gods, because, from the nature of things, only one can be possessed of all possible perfections.

If two or more independent beings are supposed to exist, their natures must be the same or different. If different, they are either contrary or various. If contrary, each must destroy the operations of the other; and if various, one must have what the other has not; and so neither of them can have all possible perfection. But if they are the same, having equal perfections, neither of them can be absolutely perfect, because it is not so great to have equal perfections with another as to be superior to all other beings. It is, therefore, impossible that there can be more than ONE absolutely perfect being; and if God is infinitely perfect, his UNITY must be admitted as a necessary consequence.

(2.) *But proofs of the Unity of God are to be drawn from his works, as well as from his nature.* The frame and constitution of the world present to us a harmony, an order, and a uniformity of plan which show that their Creator and Preserver is ONE. We see evidences of but *one will* and *one intelligence;* and, therefore, there is but *one God.*

The universe itself is a system, the parts of which are united together by one common bond, and governed by the same common laws. One law of gravitation causes a stone to drop toward the earth, the moon to move round it, and all the different planets to revolve round the sun; and it is highly probable that the same attracting influence, acting according to the same rule, reaches to the fixed stars. The planets are all subject to the same vicissitudes of days, and nights, and seasons. They all, at least Jupiter, Mars, and Venus, have the same advantages from their atmospheres as we have. The same element of light reaches every planet and every fixed star; and in all cases, from whatever source it emanates, it affects our eyes in the same manner, moves with the same velocity, and is refracted and reflected according to the same laws.

In our own globe the case is still clearer; for the same order of things attends us wherever we go. We never meet with modes of existence so totally different as to indicate that we are in the province of a different creator, or under the direction of a different will. The elements act upon one another, the tides rise and fall, and the magnetic needle elects its position in every part alike. One atmosphere invests all parts of the globe; one sun illuminates; one moon exerts its specific attraction upon all parts. If there be a variety in natural effects, as, for example, in the tides of different seas, that very variety is the result of the same cause, acting under different circumstances.

By the inspection and comparison of living forms we might add to this argument examples without number. Of all large terrestrial animals, the structure, the senses, and the natural functions are nearly alike. Digestion, nutrition, and circulation go on in a similar manner in all; and the great circulating fluid, the *blood*, is in all the same. The resemblance between quadrupeds and birds is somewhat less, yet sufficiently evident; for they are alike in five respects for one in which they differ, and their differences are such only as their different circumstances require.

If a perfectly regular and uniform administration of government in a commonwealth proves the unity of the governing power, will not that uniformity which is everywhere observable in the laws and operations of *nature* prove that its Maker and Governor is ONE? The only rational conclusion from all these sources of evidence is, therefore, that "the Lord our God is ONE."

§ 2. *The Spirituality of God.*

By the Spirituality of God is generally understood his *immateriality;* but, as Dr. Paley very justly remarks, the term expresses an idea which is made up of both a negative and a positive part. The negative part consists in the exclusion of the common properties of matter, such as solidity, inertia, divisibility, and gravitation. The positive part comprises perception, thought, will, power, and action, or the origination of motion.

The terms *spirit* and *matter* denote substances which are perfectly distinct in kind, and are manifested by properties which are not only distinct, but in many respects opposite and incommunicable. The former can perceive, think, reason, will, and act; while the latter is passive, impercipient, divisible, and corruptible. Under these views, and in this popular language, God is characterized in the Scriptures. He is a *Spirit*, not body; *Mind*, not matter. He is a *pure Spirit*, unconnected even with bodily form or organs; "the invisible God whom no man hath seen or can see;" an immaterial, incorruptible, and impassible substance, wholly above the perception of bodily sense. He is free from the imperfections of matter, and all the infirmities of corporeal beings; a self-acting, self-moving, and *Infinite Mind*. He is more excellent than created spirits, because he is their *Creator*, and is therefore styled "the Father of Spirits," and "the God of the spirits of all flesh."

The *immateriality* of God is a point of great importance, not only as it affects our views of his nature and attributes, but because, when once it is established that there exists a pure Spirit, living and intelligent, and invested with moral properties, the question of the immateriality of the human soul may be regarded as almost settled.

The *spirituality* and, consequently, the *immateriality* of God may be argued,

1. FROM THE EXPRESS TESTIMONY OF SCRIPTURE.

Thus, "God is a Spirit." John iv, 24. "Now the Lord is that Spirit." 2 Cor. iii, 17. The same truth is substantially taught in those numerous passages which speak of the "Spirit of God," for the "Spirit" is God himself. But we may argue this doctrine,

2. FROM OUR IDEA OF GOD AS AN ABSOLUTELY PERFECT BEING.

Our first and most natural idea of God is that he possesses all possible perfection. Accordingly, when any property is ascribed to him we are led to inquire, in the first place, whether it is a *perfection* or an *imperfection*. If the former, it belongs to him; but if the latter, it is to be separated from him, as being incompatible with his absolute perfection.

It will hardly be denied that spiritual substances are more excellent than such as are merely material, that the human soul is more excellent than the spiritual nature of the lower animals, and that angels are more excellent than men. But God must have an excellency above all these, and must, therefore, be infinitely removed, not only from the condition of the most refined corporeal substance, but also from that of the highest angelic nature. Hence we are led, by this mode of reasoning, to the attribution of pure spirituality to God. The same result follows,

3. FROM THE INTELLIGENCE OF GOD.

If we allow a First Cause at all, we must allow that cause to be *intelligent*, as we have already shown; but intelligence is not a property of *matter*. We know that every unorganized portion of it, at least, is wholly unintelligent. Its essential properties are impenetrability, divisibility, passiveness, and gravity. In all its forms and mutations, from the granite rock to the yielding atmosphere and the rapid lightning, these properties are discovered; and though they take an infinite variety of accidental modes, they never give the least indication of intelligence.

If, then, intelligence be a property of matter at all, it must be an *accidental* property and not an essential one, because vast masses of matter exist without it. As it cannot, therefore, be an essential property of matter, if we suppose God to be a material being we may suppose, with equal propriety, that he is wholly unintelligent. For, take away any property from a subject which is not essential to it and its essence still remains; and if intelligence, which in this view is only an accident of deity, were annihilated, a God without perception, thought, or knowledge might still remain. A conclusion so monstrous shows, that if a God be at all allowed the absolute spirituality of his nature must follow; for if intelligence is an essential attribute of deity, as all must admit, then that substance to which it is essential cannot be material.

Two objections have been urged against the doctrine of the pure spirituality of God. The *first* is, that the Scriptures ascribe to him material parts or members, such as belong to the human body. This, however, is simply an accommodation to our modes of thinking, and is designed to assist the weakness of our comprehension in regard to the Divine attributes by directing our attention to correspondent properties in ourselves. When, therefore, any bodily member is ascribed to God it must be taken in a figurative sense. By his eyes and ears we are to understand his *infinite knowledge;* by his face, the *manifestation of his favor;* by his mouth, the *revelation of his will;* by his bowels, the *tenderness of his compassion;* and by his hand, his *almighty power.*

The *second* objection is based upon those Scriptures which speak of God as the object of *vision.* There are, indeed, many passages of this kind; in some of which it is declared that God has been seen by men, and in others, that they shall see him in a future life. But there are a few facts, in the light of which all such Scriptures may be easily reconciled with the spirituality of God. The *first* is, that in the economy of redeeming grace God renders himself visible to man in the *person of Jesus Christ.* It is on this principle that the apostle calls him "the image of the invisible God;" and that our Saviour himself declares, "He that hath seen me hath seen the Father." But we are to remember, that even under the Old Testament dispensation Christ sometimes appeared in human form, prelusive of his subsequent incarnation. By this means Abraham saw Jehovah, and conversed with him on the plains of Mamre. In like manner Jacob saw God "face to face," and wrestled with him; and in the person of this Redeemer Job expected to see God in the world to come.

The *second* fact to be noticed is, that God has often revealed himself to men by some visible symbol, or glorious appearance, indicative of his special presence. It was in this way that Moses saw him in the burning bush, and that he and all Israel beheld him when, amid the terrible displays of majesty and glory, he revealed his law from the burning summit of Mount Sinai. Thus, too, God accompanied his chosen people in a pillar of cloud by day and in a pillar of fire by night; and when they made him a sanctuary, that he might dwell among them, he took possession of it in a visible form, which was called "the glory of the Lord."

There is, therefore, a distinction to be made between the *essential* presence of God and what may be called his *majestic* presence. The former regards the Divine *essence*, which, in the most absolute sense, is present everywhere, but which is everywhere invisible; while the latter denotes merely a *visible indication* of the presence of God in some particular place. This we know has been accommodated to the perception even of mortal eyes.

But a *third* fact, which will aid us in the true interpretation of this class of Scriptures, is, that the phrase "to see God" is often employed in a merely figurative sense, and means nothing more than to know him or to enjoy him. Thus, "Blessed are the pure in heart, for they shall see God." Matt. v, 8.

§ 3. *The Eternity of God.*

When this attribute is ascribed to God the meaning is that to his existence there was no *beginning* and there will be no *end*. As all things were made by him he was before all things, and, consequently, there was a time when he existed alone; but there never was a time when he did not exist. And as his existence is not contingent, but *necessary*, it is impossible that he ever should cease to exist. He is, therefore, eminently BEING; according to his own peculiar appellation, "I AM," *self-existent* and ETERNAL.

THIS DOCTRINE IS CLEARLY ASSERTED IN THE SCRIPTURES.—"From everlasting to everlasting thou art God." Psalm xc, 2. "Of old hast thou laid the foundation of the earth; and the heavens are the work of thy hands. They shall perish, but thou shalt endure; yea, all of them shall wax old like a garment; as a vesture shalt thou change them, and they shall be changed; but thou art the same, and *thy years shall have no end.*" Psalm cii, 25-27. He fills and occupies the whole round of boundless duration, and is "the *first* and the *last.*"

In these representations of God's eternity something more than the mere idea of infinite duration is conveyed. Even a created being may be the subject of endless duration in as strict a sense as God himself; but as its existence is derived from the Creator, it is dependent upon him, and must continue so forever. But the language in which the Scriptures speak of the eternity of God suggests a meaning deeper than that of mere duration. They contrast the stability of the Divine existence with the changing nature of all his works; representing them as reposing on him for support, while he lives by virtue of his own nature, and is essentially *unchangeable.*

It is taught by some *that the idea of successive time is not to be allowed in our conceptions of the duration of God;* that as he fills all space with his immensity, so he fills all duration with his eternity; and that with him eternity is *nunc stans,* a permanent *now,* incapable of the relations of past, present, and future. Such, however, is not the doctrine of the Scriptures on this mysterious subject; and if it should be said that they are accommodated to the infirmity of the great body of mankind, we may reply that philosophy, with all its boasting of superior light, has not conducted us a single step beyond the light of revelation; but, in attempting to do so, it has obscured the conceptions of its disciples. "Filling duration with his eternity" is a phrase without meaning. How can any man conceive a permanent instant which coexists with a perpetually flowing duration? One might as easily comprehend a mathematical point coextended with a line, or with all dimensions.

Whether we gain our idea of time from the motion of bodies without us, or from our own consciousness, or from both, we must conceive it to be divisible. Its artificial divisions are years, months, days, hours, minutes, and seconds. That duration is something distinct from these artificial measures is not denied; and yet of this every man is conscious that he can form no idea of duration but in this successive manner.

We are told that the duration of God is a fixed eternal *now*, from which all ideas of succession are to be excluded; and we are required to conceive of eternal duration without any reference to past or future time. But the proper abstract idea of duration is, simply *continuance of being*, without any reference to the exact degree or extent of it. It may be finite or infinite, momentary or eternal; but that depends upon the substance of which it is the attribute, and not upon its own nature.

Duration, then, as applied to God, is no more than an extension of the idea as applied to ourselves; and to exhort us to conceive of it as something essentially different, is to require us to conceive what is inconceivable, or to think without ideas. It follows, therefore, that we must either apply the term duration to the Divine Being in the same sense in which it is applied to creatures, with this difference, that the duration of God is unlimited; or blot it from our creed as a word to which we can attach no meaning. To say that the duration of God does not admit of past, present, and future, is to impugn the Scriptures; for they speak of him as the Being "which *is*, and which *was*, and which *is to come*."

§ 4. *The Omnipotence of God.*

The Omnipotence of God is that unlimited power which he possesses to do whatever is consistent with the other perfections of his nature. Of this attribute we have an ample revelation, and that in the most sublime and impressive language, and connected with illustrations of the most striking character.

From the annunciation in the Scriptures of a Divine Being who *was* "in the beginning," the very first step is the display of his almighty power in the creation of the "*heavens* and the *earth*," and in arranging them in order and perfection. By this is meant, not only our globe with its atmosphere, or with its own celestial system, but the entire universe; for "he made the stars also." We are thus at once placed in the presence of an Agent of unbounded power, the strict and correct conclusion being, that he who could create such a world as this must be almighty. Let us then look at the *manner* in which the Scriptures exhibit the Divine Omnipotence.

1. THIS ATTRIBUTE WAS PROCLAIMED IN THE SIMPLE FACT OF CREATION —the creation of all things out of nothing. This itself, though it had been confined to a single object, however minute, exceeds finite comprehension and overwhelms our faculties. But with God this required no effort: "He spake, and it was done; he commanded, and it stood fast." Psalm xxxiii, 9.

2. THE VASTNESS AND VARIETY OF HIS WORKS ENLARGE THE CONCEPTION.—"The heavens declare the glory of God, and the firmament showeth his handiwork." Psalm xix, 1. "He alone spreadeth out the heavens, and treadeth upon the waves of the sea; he maketh Arcturus, Orion, and Pleiades, and the chambers of the south; he doeth great things past finding out; yea, wonders without number." Job ix, 8, 9. "He stretcheth out the north over the empty place, and hangeth the earth upon nothing. He bindeth up the waters in the thick clouds; and the cloud is not rent under them. He hath compassed the waters with bounds, until the day and night come to an end." Job xxvi, 7-10.

3. THE EASE WITH WHICH GOD SUSTAINS, ORDERS, AND CONTROLS THE MOST POWERFUL AND UNRULY ELEMENTS, *presents his Omnipotence under an aspect of ineffable dignity and majesty.*—He says to the mighty ocean, "Hitherto shalt thou come, but no farther; and here shall thy proud waves be stayed." "Who hath measured the waters in the hollow of his hand, and meted out the heaven with a span, and comprehended the dust of the earth in a measure, and weighed the mountains in scales, and the hills in a balance?" Isaiah xl, 12. "He stood and measured the earth; he beheld, and drove asunder the nations; and the everlasting mountains were scattered, the perpetual hills did bow." Hab. iii, 6.

4. THE SAME ABSOLUTE SUBJECTION TO HIS DOMINION IS SEEN AMONG HIS MORAL CREATURES.—Angels, men, and devils are swayed with as much ease as the least resistless elements. He "maketh his angels spirits, and his ministers a flame of fire." Heb. i, 7. They vail their faces before his throne, and acknowledge themselves his servants. "It is he that sitteth upon the circle of the earth, and the inhabitants thereof are as grasshoppers." Isa. xl, 17. "All nations before him are as nothing; and they are counted to him less than nothing, and vanity." Isa. xl, 2. "He spared not the angels that sinned, but cast them down

to hell, and delivered them into chains of darkness, to be reserved unto judgment." 2 Peter ii, 4.

5. *To complete these transcendent conceptions of the Almighty Power of God, our attention is directed* TO THE CLOSING SCENE OF TIME.—The dead of all nations and ages " shall hear his voice, and shall come forth." John v, 28. Before his *face* heaven and earth shall flee away; "the stars shall fall from heaven, and the powers of the heavens shall be shaken." Matt. xxiv, 29. "And before him shall be gathered all nations, and he shall separate them one from another, as a shepherd divideth his sheep from the goats." Matt. xxv, 32. The wicked " shall go away into everlasting punishment; but the righteous into life eternal." Matt. xxv, 46.

Of these amazing views of the omnipotence of God, the power lies in their *truth*. They are not Eastern exaggerations, mistaken for sublimity. Everything in nature answers to them, and renews from age to age the impression which they must make upon every reflecting mind. The order of the astral revolutions, and the controlment of the ocean's billows, exemplify the almighty power of God. "He toucheth the hills, and they smoke," is not mere imagery. Every volcano is a testimony in nature to that inspired truth, and earthquakes teach, that before him " the pillars of the earth tremble."

Ample, however, as are the views which the Scriptures afford us of the power of God, we are not to consider the subject as bounded by them, or to measure his omnipotence by the actual displays of it which have been made. They are *manifestations* of the principle, but not the *measure* of its capacity. "Lo, these are parts of his ways, but how little a portion is heard of him?" Job xxvi, 14. His power is, therefore, truly *almighty* and *measureless*.

There are some things which, to superficial thinkers, may seem to be inconsistent with infinite power, and to prove that though the power of God far transcends that of the mightiest creatures, it is nevertheless subject to certain limitations. Of these we shall briefly take notice, and show that such supposed limitations detract nothing from this perfection of the Divine nature.

First, God cannot do that which implies a contradiction, as to make a thing to be and not to be at the same time — to make a part greater than the whole — because such contradictions are in their own nature impossible. Nor is it derogatory to the power of God to say that such things cannot be done; for as the object of the eye must be that which is *visible*, and of the ear that which is audible, so the object of power must be that which is *possible*. The reason, then, that God cannot work contradictions, is not that he is deficient in power, but that they are in their own nature impossible.

Secondly, God cannot do that which is repugnant to any of his perfections. He cannot lie, or deceive, or deny himself, for to do so would be injurious to his *truth*. He cannot love sin, for this would be inconsistent with his *holiness*. He cannot punish the innocent, for this would destroy his *goodness*. This, however, is not a physical, but a moral impossibility, and is, therefore, no limitation of omnipotence; but to ascribe a power to God which is inconsistent with the rectitude of his nature, is not to magnify, but to abase him.

§ 5. *Omnipresence of God.*

The *Omnipresence* or *Ubiquity* of God is his being everywhere present at the same time.

A distinction is sometimes made between the *omnipresence* of God and his *immensity*. The latter is regarded as an *absolute* perfection of the Divine nature, which is necessarily unlimited; while the former is viewed as a *relative* perfection, having respect only to created things. This distinction, however, if not improper, is at least unnecessary; for omnipresence and immensity are the same perfection under different aspects.

There is no part of the universe, no portion of space, in which God is not essentially present. Could we, with the swiftness of a sunbeam, travel beyond the limits of the creation, and for ages continue our progress in infinite space, we should still be surrounded with the Divine presence, nor ever be able to reach that space where God is not. His presence also penetrates every part of our world. The most solid portions of matter cannot exclude it, for it pierces as easily the center of the globe as the yielding air. Neither the inmost recesses of the human heart, nor the deepest caverns of the earth, can for a moment exclude his presence.

Proofs in support of this doctrine may be drawn from the Scriptures, and from the absolute perfection and works of God.

1. FROM THE SCRIPTURES.

The declarations of the Holy Scriptures, in proof and illustration of the omnipresence of God, are at once clear and sublime. "Behold the heaven, and the heaven of heavens, cannot contain thee." 1 Kings viii, 27. "Whither shall I go from thy Spirit, or whither shall I flee from thy presence? If I ascend up to heaven, thou art there; if I make my bed in hell, behold thou art there; if I take the wings of the morning and dwell in the uttermost parts of the sea, even there shall thy hand lead me, and thy right hand shall hold me." Psa. cxxxix, 7–10. "Do not I fill heaven and earth, saith the Lord?" Jer. xxiii, 24. God is "not far from every one of us; for in him we live, and move, and have our being." Acts xvii, 27, 28.

2. FROM THE IDEA OF ABSOLUTE PERFECTION.

Every sound theist ascribes infinite perfection to God, and consequently he must believe his essential essence to be infinite; for it would be manifest absurdity to suppose a being to have infinite perfections and a finite nature, to be limited and unlimited at the same time. It is one of our clearest conceptions, that the degree of any quality must be relative to the nature in which it inheres. If, therefore, we allow the essence of God to be infinite, his omnipresence will necessarily follow. But to circumscribe his essence within any boundaries, however widely extended, would be to conceive of him as a limited and imperfect being, which is incompatible with every rational idea of God. Thus reason, as well as revelation, sustains the doctrine of the Divine omnipresence. But we may argue it,

3. FROM THE WORK OF CREATION.

It is a truth which is most evident to all, that a being cannot act where it is not. If, therefore, we admit that God is the sole creator of the world, we cannot but allow that he must be present in every part of it. For, as no attribute of God can be separated from his *essence*, wherever his *power* is exerted there must his essence be. Consequently, if all things in the vast universe were created by him, he must be essentially present with all created things. This doctrine is proved also,

4. FROM THE WORK OF DIVINE PROVIDENCE.

Reason and revelation both declare that the system of nature is sustained by the same power that raised it out of nothing. We are not to suppose that after it was created and made subject to certain laws, it was left to itself to move on, like a well-constructed machine, without the interference of the Architect. This would be to suppose that the universe is independent of its Maker. The laws of nature, then, to which its order and preservation are ascribed, are only the established and uniform modes according to which the power of God is exerted in his providential government of created things. But if God is the preserver of all things, as well as their creator, and if he exercises a universal providence over all his creatures, then must he necessarily be present everywhere.

It was on this principle that the apostle argued when he disputed with the learned Athenians. God is "not far from every one of us;" that is, he is intimately near and present with us; "for in him we live, and move, and have our being." If things *live*, God is in them, and gives them life. If things *move*, God imparts to them their motion. If things have a *being*, that being is in God. Every object that meets our eye on the surface of the earth, or in the expanse above us, announces his presence. By him the sun shines, the winds blow, the earth is clothed with vegetation, and the tides of the ocean rise and fall. Everywhere he exists in the fullness of perfection. The universe is a magnificent temple, erected by his own hands, in which he manifests himself to his intelligent creatures. The Divine Inhabitant fills it, and every part shines with his glory.

It will be said, perhaps, that these arguments prove no more than that God is present throughout the whole creation. This is admitted; but surely no one who has gone so far as this will choose to stop here, and conclude that the limit of the creation is the limit of the Divine *essence*. No reason can be assigned for circumscribing it; but as we have found it in every step of our progress through the universe, we naturally conclude that if we could pursue the search we should find it where it exists alone. He who believes that the power of God is almighty, will admit that he could create new worlds; and he must, therefore, admit, that as he could not act where he is not, he must be present where no sun shines and where no planets roll. For all practical purposes, it is enough to know that he fills heaven and earth; but truth requires us to acknowledge the absolute immensity of his nature, for if he were bounded by creation he would not be infinite.

Among metaphysicians it has been a matter of dispute whether God is present everywhere by an *infinite extension of his essence*. This opinion, which was advocated by Dr. S. Clarke and others, appears to be most in harmony with the Scriptures; though the term *extension*, through the inadequacy of language, is too suggestive of materiality. But it is best to confess that there is an incomprehensibleness in the *manner* of the Divine ubiquity concerning which we ought not to dispute. That we cannot comprehend *how* God is fully, and completely, and undividedly present everywhere, need not surprise us; for the manner in which the human mind is present with the body is as incomprehensible as the manner in which the supreme mind is present with everything in the universe.

§ 6. *The Omniscience of God.*

Omniscience is boundless knowledge; and when it is ascribed to God the meaning is, not merely that he has power to know everything, but that he *actually knows all things*, past, present, and future. In proof that this attribute belongs to God, the following arguments may be adduced:

1. IT IS NECESSARILY INCLUDED IN THE VERY IDEA OF A GOD.

Every one who believes that there is such a being readily admits that he must possess intelligence. What excellence could we perceive in a God without knowledge? We might suppose him to be eternal, immutable, and omnipresent; but if he were ignorant of everything, even of his own existence and attributes, as he would be if knowledge were not one of the number, the meanest creature who is conscious of his own thoughts, and capable of observation and reasoning, would be superior to him. In fact, we could hardly distinguish such a being from the material universe. The ancient Egyptians, who expressed their conceptions by hieroglyphics, made an *eye* the symbol of the

Deity; intimating thereby that all things are open to his inspection. Though many, in the absence of supernatural instruction, have conceived their gods to be material beings, and have ascribed to them human passions and human infirmities, yet all have supposed them to be acquainted with the actions of men, and with the events which take place in the world.

2. THIS DOCTRINE IS EXPRESSLY TAUGHT IN THE WORD OF GOD.

"Hell is naked before him, and destruction hath no covering." Job xxvi, 6. "O Lord, thou hast searched me, and known me. Thou knowest my down-sitting and mine uprising; thou understandest my thought afar off. Thou compassest my path and my lying down, and art acquainted with all my ways. . . . If I say, Surely the darkness shall cover me; even the night shall be light about me. Yea, the darkness hideth not from thee; but the night shineth as the day: the darkness and the light are both alike to thee." Psa. cxxxix, 1–3, 11, 12. "Known unto God are all his works from the beginning of the world." Acts xv, 18. How just, therefore, is the conclusion of the Psalmist, that "*His understanding is* INFINITE." Psa. cxlvii, 5.

3. THE OMNISCIENCE OF GOD MAY BE INFERRED FROM THE EXISTENCE OF KNOWLEDGE AMONG HIS CREATURES.

We know, both from consciousness and observation, that there is intelligence among created beings. We know, likewise, that intelligence is a perfection, and that to possess it is better than to be without it. We know, moreover, that the intelligence of creatures must have had a beginning, and, consequently, some efficient cause. Now, as a cause cannot communicate a perfection which it does not itself possess, if we allow God to be the cause of intelligent creatures we must allow him to be possessed of knowledge. And if he is the *First Cause*, his knowledge must be infinite or unlimited; since limitation without a limiter would be an effect without a cause.

To assist our understanding, the *objects* of the Divine knowledge have sometimes been divided into several classes.

(1.) *God knows himself.*—He knows what is his own essence, of which we can only say that it is *spiritual*, without being able to affix any positive idea to the term. He knows his own perfections, with some of which we have a partial acquaintance, while he may possess others of which we have no knowledge whatever. He knows the harmony of his attributes, which we are often unable to reconcile. He knows his own counsels and plans, which are too extensive and complicated to be comprehended by any finite mind. He knows, in a word, all the mysteries of his nature, at which human reason stands amazed and confounded.

(2.) *God knows all things* EXTRINSIC *to himself*, whether past, present, or future.

First, he knows all things that are *past*. Though they have gone by, and no memorial of them remains, they are still present to him, as if they continued to exist, and not one of them is forgotten. By the faculty of memory we retain a knowledge of many past events. Though the sunbeam leaves no trace of its path, nor the cloud of its place in the sky, yet our sensations and thoughts make an impression upon our mind which lasts for years, and sometimes for life. Since, then, creatures possess the power of remembering the past, we must allow that the Creator possesses a similar power; but with this difference, that in him it is free from all the imperfections to which human memory is subject.

Without a knowledge of the past, God could not be the judge of the human race. At the close of time all the generations of men shall appear before him, to receive their final award; but the justice of the sentence will depend upon his perfect knowledge of their character and actions. As he was witness to their conduct during its course, so he will recall the minutest parts of it, though after an interval of thousands of years. To impress this more deeply upon the mind, and to assure us that no mistake will be committed, the Scriptures declare, in allusion to the proceedings of earthly courts, that "*the books*" shall be opened, and that the dead shall be judged according to what is written in them.

Secondly, God knows all things that *now are*. In this respect his knowledge resembles our own, but is infinitely superior in degree. He tells the number of the stars, and calls them by their names. He sees in one view the various orders of living creatures by which the universe is peopled. He knows every human being, however obscure. He observes the most insignificant objects in animated nature. "Are not five sparrows sold for two farthings? and not one of them is forgotten before God." Luke xii, 6. Nothing can be more unimportant than a single hair; and yet our Lord says, "The very hairs of your head are all numbered." Matt. x, 30. The humblest person upon earth has therefore no right to fear that, amid the innumerable objects which engage the Divine attention, he shall be overlooked; nor may he whose interest it would be to remain unnoticed, hope that he shall be concealed from the eye of Omniscience.

Thirdly, God knows all things that will be *in futurity*. In this respect there is no resemblance of his knowledge in man; nor, we presume, in any created being. That God sees the future, as well as the past and the present, is fully established by the predictions of the Scriptures, many of which have been most circumstantially fulfilled. This subject may be seen in its true light by reference to Book I, chap. 7.

The knowledge of God in regard to future events is called FORE-KNOWLEDGE or PRESCIENCE. Its objects are, 1. *Necessary events*, or those things which result from the established course of nature, or from a fixed Divine decree; 2. *Conditional events*, or those things which will take place only on certain conditions, as the good or evil that will be done by persons under given circumstance; and, 3. *Contingent events,* or those which depend upon the *will* of moral agents.

Some have supposed it to be difficult, if not impossible, to reconcile this view of the Divine foreknowledge with the freedom of human actions and man's accountability. Hence they have adopted various modifications of opinion as to the knowledge of God, in order to avoid this supposed difficulty and to remove objections. Two of these theories we may here examine, that the true doctrine of Scripture may be fully brought out and established.

The *first* theory is that of Chevalier Ramsay, who held it to be "a matter of choice in God to think of finite ideas;" and similar opinions, though variously worded, have been occasionally adopted. In substance his theory is this: that though the knowledge of God is infinite, as his power is infinite, there is no more reason to conclude that his knowledge should be always exerted to the full extent of its capacity, than that his power should be employed to the extent of his omnipotence; and that if we suppose him to *choose* not to know some contingencies, the infiniteness of his knowledge is not thereby impugned.

To this it may be answered, 1. That the Scriptures represent the *power* of God, as in the nature of things it must be, as an infinite *capacity,* and not as an infinite *act;* while they speak of the knowledge of God, not as a capacity to know, but as *actually* comprehending all things. 2. That if God chooses not to know some things, the *reason* why he refuses to know them can only arise out of their nature and circumstances; and this supposes at least a partial knowledge of them, from which the reason of his choosing not to know them arises. The doctrine is therefore somewhat contradictory. But, 3. It is fatal to this opinion that it does not meet the difficulty which it was intended to obviate. We are sure that some contingent actions, for which men have been made accountable, were *foreknown* by God, because by his Spirit in the prophets they were *foretold;* and if the freedom of man can in these cases be reconciled to the *prescience* of God, so it may in every other case which can possibly occur.

The *second* theory is, that the *foreknowledge of contingent events* is in its own nature impossible, because it implies a contradiction; and that, therefore, it does not dishonor God to affirm that of such events he can have no prescience whatever. Thus, the prescience of God as to moral actions being wholly denied, the difficulty of reconciling it with human freedom and human accountability has no existence.

Our first answer to this scheme is, that while we acknowledge the authority of the Scriptures, it does not remove the difficulty. That man is accountable to God for his conduct, and therefore free, are doctrines clearly contained in the Bible; and to the notion of necessity we have here a full and satisfactory reply. Whether we hold, therefore, that the knowledge of God, like his power, is arbitrary, or that the prescience of contingencies is impossible, so long as the Scriptures are allowed to contain predictions respecting the moral conduct of men the difficulty of reconciling such conduct with the foreknowledge of God remains in all its force.

That the Bible contains many predictions which involve the free actions of men, no one can deny. It was predicted, for instance, that Babylon should be taken by Cyrus in the midst of a midnight revel; that the Messiah should be taken away by a violent death, inflicted by men in defiance of all the principles of justice; and that Jerusalem should be utterly destroyed by the Roman army. If the moral actions connected with these events were contingent, what comes of the principle that it is impossible to foreknow contingencies? They were foreknown, because the results of them were predicted. But if they were not contingent they must have been *necessary*, and, consequently, neither virtuous nor vicious. It must be evident to every careful observer, that the whole body of prophecy is founded on the certain prescience of contingent actions; for otherwise it would not be prophecy, but guess and conjecture. Such are the fearful results to which a denial of the Divine prescience leads.

On the main principle of the theory, that the prescience of contingent events is impossible, because their nature would thereby be destroyed, we may add a few remarks.

We acknowledge that the *manner* in which God foreknows future events of any kind is incomprehensible; but that such a property exists in the Divine nature is too clearly stated in the Scriptures to allow of any doubt. It is equally clear that the moral actions of men are not necessitated, because human accountability is the main pillar of that moral government which the Scriptures unfold. Whatever, therefore, becomes of human speculations, these points are sufficiently settled, and our inability to perceive their congruity is no proof that the facts do not exist.

But the position, that *certain prescience* destroys *contingency*, is a mere sophism. The fallacy lies in the supposition that *contingency* and *certainty* are opposites; whereas the term contingency is used in this controversy in the sense of *freedom*. An action which results from the choice of the agent is distinguished from a *necessary* action in this, that it might not have been, or might have been otherwise, according to the self-determining power of the agent. To express this freedom of moral actions the term contingency is used, and it is, therefore, opposed to *necessity*, and not to certainty. The very nature of the controversy fixes this as the precise meaning of the term. The question is not, in point of fact, about the *certainty* of moral actions, that is, whether they *will* happen or not, but about their *nature*, whether they *must* happen or not. Accordingly, those who deny the prescience of moral actions do not do so because they care anything about their *cer-*

tainty; but because they conclude that such a prescience renders them *necessary.*

If contingency meant *uncertainty*, the dispute would be at an end. But though an *uncertain* action cannot be foreseen as *certain*, yet a *free unnecessitated* action may; for there is nothing in the *knowledge* of the action which can in the least affect its nature. Necessitated actions are not made *voluntary*, nor are free actions made *necessary* by their being foreknown. Consequently the certain prescience of free actions does not destroy their contingency.

But how stands the case as to the *certainty* of contingent events? Precisely on the same ground as that of others. The certainty of a *necessary* action results from the operation of its necessitating cause; and that of a *free* action, from the determination of a voluntary cause. Whether, therefore, an action is necessary or free, its being foreknown has nothing to do with its *certainty.* Nor will it alter the case to say, that a voluntary action might have been otherwise; for had it been otherwise, the knowledge of it would have been otherwise also. The foreknowledge of God, then, has no influence upon either the *freedom* or the *certainty* of actions, for this plain reason, that it is *knowledge* and not *power;* nor does certain foreknowledge render actions necessary.

But here it is objected, that if the result of an absolute contingency is certainly foreknown it *cannot* happen otherwise. This is not the true inference. It *will not* happen otherwise; but why *could* it *not* happen otherwise? What deprives it of that power? It may be said of a necessary action that it could not otherwise happen; but then that would arise from its necessitating cause, and not from the prescience of the action. If, however, the action is free, and if it enters into the very nature of a voluntary action to be unconstrained, then it might have happened in a thousand other ways or not have happened at all. The foreknowledge of it no more affects its nature in this case than in the other.

But then we are told, that according to this view of contingent events the prescience of them must be uncertain. Not unless it can be proved that the Divine prescience is unable to dart through all the workings of the human mind, all its comparisons of things in the judgment, all the influences of motives on the affections, all the hesitancies and haltings of the will, to its final choice. "Such knowledge is too wonderful for us," but it is the knowledge of Him who " understandeth the thoughts of man afar off."

§ 7. *The Immutability of God.*

When we say that God is *immutable*, the meaning is that he is *unchangeable;* that he always was, is, and will be to all eternity, *the same;* that he is subject to no change either in his *essence* or in his *perfections.* The Immutability of God may be proved,

1. From the Holy Scriptures.

This is indicated in his august and awful title, "I am." All other beings are dependent and mutable, and thus stand in striking contrast to him who is independent, and, therefore, incapable of change. "The counsel of the Lord standeth forever, the thoughts of his heart to all generations." Psa. xxx, 11. "Of old hast thou laid the foundations of the earth, and the heavens are the work of thy hands. They shall perish, but thou shalt endure; yea, all of them shall wax old like a garment, as a vesture shalt thou change them, and they shall be changed; but thou art the same, and thy years shall have no end." Psa. cii, 25–27. "I am the Lord, I change not." Mal. iii, 6. He is "the Father of lights, with whom is no variableness, neither shadow of turning." James i, 17. But of this truth, which is so important to religion and morals, we have a confirmation,

2. In the uniformity of the Laws by which the Natural World is governed.

The ample universe, with its immense aggregate of individual beings, displays not only the all-comprehending and pervading power of God, but, as it remains from age to age subject to the same laws, and fulfilling the same purposes, it is a visible image of the existence of a Being of steady counsels, free from caprice, and liable to no control.

3. The Moral Government of God gives its Evidence to the same Truth.

The laws under which we are now placed are the same as those which were prescribed to the earliest generations of men. What was vice then is vice now, and what was virtue then is virtue now. Miseries of the same kind and degree have been consequent on the former, and peace and blessedness have accompanied the latter in every age of the world. God has manifested his will to men by successive revelations, as the Patriarchal, the Mosaic, and Christian; but though these revelations were many ages distant from one another, the *moral principles* on which they rest are precisely the same, as are also the *moral ends* which they propose. Their differences are merely circumstantial, varying according to the age of the world, the condition of mankind, and the plans of Infinite Wisdom; but the identity of their *spirit*, their *influence*, and their *character*, shows their Author to be an unchangeable being of holiness, truth, justice, and mercy.

4. The Immutability of God may be inferred from the Perfection of his Nature.

The stability of the Divine operations and counsels, as indicated by the laws of the material universe and the revelations of the Divine will, only shows the immutability of God through those periods within which these operations and dispensations have been in force; but in

Scripture this attribute is represented as one which arises out of the Divine nature itself, and which is therefore *essential* to it. " I am the Lord, I change not." He changes not *because* he is "the Lord." To suppose him capable of change is to suppose him an imperfect being; for if he change, it must be to a higher or a lower degree of perfection. If to a higher, it will argue a previous imperfection, and show that he is not God; and if to a lower, he will not be perfect after the change, and so not God. The sovereign and absolute perfection of the Deity is therefore an invincible bar against all mutability. In his being and perfections he is eternally THE SAME. He cannot cease to be. He cannot become more perfect, because his perfection is *absolute*. He cannot become less so, because he is *independent* of all external power, and has no internal principle of decay.

We must not, however, so interpret the immutability of God as to conclude that his operations admit no change; or that he is incapable of different *regards* and *affections* toward the same creatures under different circumstances. He creates, and he destroys; he wounds, and he heals; he works, and he ceases from working; he loves, and he hates; but these, as being under the direction of his immutable wisdom, holiness, goodness, and justice, are the proofs of the unchanging principles of his nature. Thus in Scripture language, "The Lord loveth the righteous," but "he is angry with the wicked." If, however, the righteous turn away from their righteousness, they will cease to be the objects of God's love; and if the wicked turn from their wickedness, his anger against them will be averted.*

There is a sense in which this may be called change in God; but it is not the change of imperfection and defect. It argues precisely the contrary. If the love or the anger of God toward his moral subjects did not correspond with their moral character, he could not be the unchangeable lover of holiness, and hater of iniquity. By these scriptural doctrines, therefore, the Divine immutability is confirmed.

Allied to the immutability of God is his LIBERTY. This enables us to conceive of his unchangeableness in a suitable manner—to view it as the result of his will and infinite moral excellence, and not as the consequence of a blind and physical necessity. He is a God "who worketh all things after the counsel of his own will." Eph. i, 11. A being who does not possess *liberty* cannot properly be called an *agent*, or the *cause* of anything; for to act necessarily is really and properly not to act at all, but only to be acted upon. If the Supreme Cause is a mere necessary agent, whose actions are all as absolutely necessary as his existence, then it follows that nothing which is not could possibly have been; that nothing which is could possibly not have been; and that no circumstance of anything that exists could possibly have been otherwise than it now is. But if these conclusions are evidently false and absurd,

* See Ezek. xviii, 26, 27.

it will necessarily follow that the Supreme Cause is not a necessary agent, but a being who possesses *liberty* and *choice*. "He doeth according to his *will* in the army of heaven, and among the inhabitants of the earth." Dan. iv, 35.

§ 8. *The Wisdom of God.*

The *Wisdom* of God is that grand attribute of his nature by which he knows and orders all things for the promotion of his glory and the good of his creatures.

Wisdom, considered merely as a mental attribute, is the faculty of discerning what is most proper and useful; but when viewed in a practical light, it is the choice of laudable ends, and of the best means to accomplish them. *Wisdom* may easily be distinguished from *knowledge*. The latter is simply the apprehension of things as they are; the former is the arrangement of our ideas in proper order, and in such a train as to produce some practical and useful result. Wisdom cannot exist without knowledge, but knowledge may exist without wisdom. Accordingly, there are men possessing very extensive knowledge who in their conduct give many proofs of a great want of wisdom. In an all-perfect being, however, these attributes are necessarily conjoined. Omniscience supplies the materials of Infinite Wisdom.

That God possesses the attribute of wisdom in its highest perfection is proved,

1. From the Sacred Scriptures.

"With him is *wisdom* and strength; he hath counsel and understanding." Job xii, 13. "He is mighty in strength and *wisdom*." Job xxxvi, 5. "O Lord, how manifold are thy works! in *wisdom* hast thou made them all." Psalm civ, 24. God has performed everything by nice and delicate adjustment—by number, weight, and measure. "He looketh to the ends of the earth, and seeth under the whole heaven to make the *weight* for the winds; and he *weigheth* the waters by *measure*. When he made a *decree* for the rain, and a *way* for the lightning of the thunder, then did he see it, and declare it; he prepared it, yea, and searched it out." Job xxviii, 24–27. "Now unto the King eternal, immortal, invisible, *the only wise God*, be honor and glory for ever and ever. Amen." 1 Tim. i, 17. But the wisdom of God is proved also,

2. From the works of Creation.

Our general design will not allow us to pursue this argument to any great length, nor will it be necessary here to call up particular instances illustrative of the Divine Wisdom. This was done to a sufficient extent in the first chapter of this book, in proof of an *intelligent* and *designing* Cause. We can only, therefore, notice a few leading *principles*, according to which the works of God seem to be regulated, and in the operations of which his wisdom is signally manifested. We may remark, then,

(1.) *That God performs all his works for worthy ends.*—To act with *design*, is a sufficient proof of *intelligence;* but *wisdom* requires that the exercise of the understanding should be *fit* and *proper*. We acknowledge our inability to enter fully into the designs of God even after they are revealed; but since he has endowed us with some portion of understanding, there is no arrogance in venturing to say, when we see him pursuing certain ends, that they appear to us to be suitable to the dignity of his character. For many of his acts the *reasons* are at least partially given in his own word; and they command at once our admiration and gratitude, as worthy of himself and benevolent toward us.

The reason of the creation of the world was the manifestation of the perfections of God to his rational creatures, and to confer on them a felicity equal to their largest capacity. The *end* was important, and the means by which it was to be accomplished evidently *fit*. *To be*, was itself made a source of satisfaction. God was revealed to man as his Maker, Lord, and Friend; and though he was invisible, every object was fitted to make him present to the *mind* of his creature, and to be a remembrancer of his power, glory, and care. The understanding of man was called into exercise by the number, the variety, and the curious structure of the works of God; while their sublimity, beauty, and harmony contributed to his pleasures of taste.

God manifested himself to man, not only in his creative munificence and preserving care, but also in the directions of his holy law; thus arraying himself in the full splendor of his natural and moral attributes, the object of love and awe, of trust and submission. The great moral end of man's creation, and of his residence in the world, and the means by which this end was accomplished, were, therefore, displays of the Divine wisdom.

(2.) *That in the works of God numerous and great effects are produced by few and simple means.*—From one material substance, possessing the same essential proprieties, all the visible beings which surround us are made: the granite *rock*, and the central *sun;* the moveless *clod*, the rapid *lightning*, and the transparent *air*. *Gravitation* unites the atoms which compose the world, combines the planets into one system, and regulates their motions. And though its power is vast, and its influence all-pervading, it submits to an infinite number of modifications which allow of the motion of individual bodies, and give place even to contrary forces, which yet it controls and regulates.

One act of Divine power, in giving a certain inclination to the earth's axis, produces its vicissitudes of seasons, giving laws to its temperature, and covering it with an increased variety of productions. To the composition of light, and a few simple laws impressed upon it, every object owes its color, and thus the heavens and the earth are invested with beauty. A combination of earth, water, and the gases of the atmosphere forms the strength and majesty of the oak, and the grace, beauty, and odor of the rose; and from the principle of *evaporation* are formed clouds which drop fatness upon the earth, dews which refresh the languid fields, and springs and rivers which cause the valleys to rejoice through which they flow.

(3.) *That in the works of God there is an endless variety of equally perfect operations.*—" O Lord, how manifold are thy works!" All the three kingdoms of nature pour forth the riches of *variety*. It is seen in the varied forms of crystalization and composition in *minerals;* in the colors, forms, and qualities of *vegetables;* and in the kinds, properties, and habits of *animals*. No two things are exactly alike, even when of the same kind. Plants of the same species, and the leaves and flowers of the same plant, have all their varieties. Animals of the same kind have their individual character. The wisdom of this appears more strongly marked when we consider that important ends often depend upon it. The *resemblance* of various natural things in greater or less degree becomes the means of acquiring a knowledge of them with greater ease, because it is made the basis of their arrangement into kinds and sorts, without which the human memory would fail and the understanding be confused.

But a *difference* in things is as important as their resemblance. I domestic animals did not differ individually, no property could be claimed in them, nor when lost could they be recovered. The countenance, the voice, and the manner of every man differ from all the rest of his species. This is not only an illustration of the resources of creative power and wisdom, but of design and intention, to secure a practical end. Parents, children, and friends could not otherwise be distinguished, nor the criminal from the innocent. No felon could be identified by his accusers, and courts of judgment would not only be obstructed, but often rendered of no avail for the protection of life and property.

To variety of kind and form we may add that of *magnitude*. In the works of God we have the extremes of minuteness and magnificence, and those extremes filled up in perfect gradation from the one to the other. We adore the mighty sweep of that power which scooped the bed of the fathomless ocean, moulded the mountains, and filled space with innumerable worlds; but the same hand formed the animalcule which requires the strongest magnifying power of optical instruments to make it visible. The workmanship, however, is as complete in the smallest as in the most massive object. But we may add,

(4.) *That the connection and dependence of the works of God are as wonderful as their variety.*—Every created object fills its place, not by accident, but by design. The meanest weed that grows stands in intimate connection with the mighty universe. It depends upon the atmosphere for moisture, which atmosphere supposes an ocean, clouds, winds, and gravitation. It depends upon the sun for its color, and for its required degree of temperature; and this supposes the revolution of the earth, and the adjustment of the whole planetary system.

We have, however, the highest manifestation of the Divine Wisdom,
3. IN THE PLAN OF HUMAN REDEMPTION.

It is in this that God "hath abounded toward us in all *wisdom* and prudence." Herein does the perfection of his wisdom shine forth, in his reconciling the exercise of mercy with the claims of justice, and in his doing this by such an expedient as is perfectly consistent with the ends of his moral government. There is Divine wisdom reflected even from the cross of Christ. His ignominious death was no doubt intended by his enemies, to defeat the benevolent purpose for which he came into the world; but in the wisdom of God it was made the means by which he triumphed over men and devils, overturning the powers of darkness, and filling heaven and earth with wonder and joy.

§ 9. *The Truth of God.*

By the *Truth* of God we understand his perfect and undeviating *veracity* in all his communications to mankind. When we speak of him as the *True God*, we mean to distinguish him from the imaginary gods of the heathen, and to ascribe to him supreme divinity. But when we say that he is a *God of Truth*, our design is, not directly to assert his divinity, but to declare his veracity. We virtually say, that all his communications to us are in exact accordance with the real nature of things; and that there is the utmost sincerity in all his declarations, and faithfulness in all his promises and purposes. This attribute of God may be proved,
1. FROM THE SACRED SCRIPTURES.

To this it may be objected, that it is absurd to bring God's own declarations to evince his truth, since this is to take for granted the very doctrine to be proved and to reason in a circle. We acknowledge this objection to be a specious one, but contend that it is unsound. It must be granted, that the mere declaration on the part of any being that *he is sincere*, furnishes, by itself, no evidence of his sincerity; for we know that insincere persons will as readily claim sincerity as those who are sincere. But the uniform agreement of a man's declarations *with facts* is justly regarded by his fellow-men as a satisfactory proof of his sincerity and truthfulness. In the same manner God may evince his veracity by his own declarations, and this he has done in the Scriptures, as may easily be shown.

(1.) *God has declared himself to be a God of Truth.*—"For the word of the Lord is right, and all his works are done in *truth*." Psa. xxxiii, 4. "My covenant will I not break, nor alter the thing that is gone out of my lips." Psa. lxxxix, 34. "The *truth* of the Lord endureth forever." Psa. cxvii, 2. "God is not a man, that he should lie; neither the Son of man, that he should repent. Hath he said, and shall he not do it? or hath he spoken, and shall he not make it good?" Num. xxiii, 19. "It was impossible for God to lie." Heb. vi, 18. These passages are adduced, not to *prove* the veracity of God, but to show that he *claims* to be a God of truth.

(2.) *The declarations of God are all in strict agreement with the facts professedly declared.*—The history which the Scriptures contain is, even at this day, capable of being satisfactorily examined as to its accordance with facts. Some parts of it are, indeed, beyond the reach of a direct examination; but, as almost all of it can be thus examined, and can at any time be proved to be true, the truth of the rest cannot reasonably be called in question. In these declarations we have as convincing evidence of the truth of God, as we can have of the veracity of men from the agreement of their declarations with the real state of things.

(3.) *God has uttered numerous predictions which have been exactly fulfilled.*—In this manner he has not only proved his omniscience, but also his truth; especially in the exact accomplishment of such predictions as appeared, at the time when they were uttered, altogether unlikely to be fulfilled. Such were those which related to the advent, the character, and the mediation of the Messiah. Such, also, were those which respected his dispensations to the Jewish Church and nation, and the establishment and progress of Christianity. Of the fulfillment of these and other similar predictions no explanation can be given which will not firmly establish the truth of God.

(4.) *God has verified both his promises and his threatenings in regard to men.*—So far as he has promised blessing to them in this life, or threatened them with punishments, he has not failed, in the course of his providence, to bestow those blessings and to inflict those punishments. In this, therefore, we have another strong scriptural argument in support of the Divine veracity. But the truth of God may be argued,

2. FROM HIS OTHER PERFECTIONS.

If he possesses in himself all power, wisdom, justice, holiness, and goodness, he must be at an infinite distance from all those influences which lead men to practice deceit and falsehood. Men sometimes speak what is not agreeable to truth from ignorance, or misconception of the subject of discourse; but with God there can be no such defect. He knows perfectly the nature of all things, with all their various relations; and, therefore, he cannot be deceived or err in judgment. "God is light, and in him is no darkness at all." 1 John i, 5.

The declarations of men may be made rashly, without a foresight of consequences, or they may not be distinctly remembered; and, therefore, they are not always, nor with full confidence, to be received and depended on. But the perfect knowledge and wisdom of God, which must, under all circumstances, be the same, infallibly secure him from precipitancy, instability, and forgetfulness. Men may violate their engagements for the want of ability to fulfill them; but the omnipotence of God precludes every idea of difficulty where his word is concerned. Men may be disposed to deceive one another, or violate their promises through malevolence of nature, or from selfish motives; but "the Holy One of Israel," being self-existent, and perfectly independent, cannot be liable to such temptations. The veracity of God may be inferred,

3. FROM HIS HAVING IMPLANTED IN MAN A DISPOSITION TO ESTEEM TRUTH AND DESPISE FALSEHOOD.

This respect for truth and contempt for falsehood are irresistible, from two causes: *First*, they are the necessary dictates of the understanding, and are perfectly independent of any feeling or influence on the heart. Knaves, as truly and irresistibly as honest men, despise knavery and falsehood; and no other dictate of the understanding was ever found or can ever exist among men. But, *secondly*, truth is known to be absolutely necessary to the *happiness* of mankind, and invariably productive of it; and falsehood utterly inconsistent with our happiness, and invariably productive of misery. We see, then, in this great practical lesson that men are compelled to respect truth, without a possibility of its being otherwise, and to despise deceit and falsehood.

It is unreasonable to suppose that God, as a perfectly independent being, would impress on the mind of his creatures any character which is not in strict accordance with his own. But if the necessary dictates of the human understanding, in regard to truth and falsehood, are in accordance with the character of God, he must be a God of truth. Moreover, as God has so constituted us that we are compelled to esteem truth and to despise falsehood; and as he has commanded us to "love him with all the heart, and with all the understanding, and with all the soul," it follows, as a necessary consequence, that he is a God of absolute veracity; for if he were not we could not love him at all, much less as he requires. But the veracity of God is proved,

4. FROM THE CONSEQUENCES WHICH WOULD FOLLOW A DENIAL OF IT.

If no confidence could be placed in God, none could be placed in any other being. Every thought, purpose, interest, and hope would be afloat on the waves of a boundless and perpetually disturbed ocean, where rest and safety could never be found. Suspicion and jealousy would make all men strangers and enemies to one another. Suspense would fill every mind, and hang, as a dark cloud, over every enjoyment. Truth would be known, if known at all, only as a thing unattainable;

and, wandering in endless doubt and perplexity, we should close our comfortless existence without being able to tell whence we had come, or whither we were going. A Divine revelation would afford no satisfaction; because, amid the subversion of all evidence, it would be impossible to ascertain that it had proceeded from the Author of our being. But if even this point could be settled, that would not prove its statements to be worthy of credit.

It is by the *truth of God* that this restless and stormy ocean is hushed to peace. All men know, or may know, that the purposes, the declarations, and the promises of God are immutable; and that he can neither deceive their confidence nor disappoint their reasonable hopes. However fluctuating and uncertain the state of things may be with respect to creatures, the soul rests on God with perfect reliance and final safety.

It only remains to be observed that the truth of God, when we consider it in its relation to the accomplishment of his predictions, his promises, or his threatenings, is denominated FAITHFULNESS. In this God manifests his veracity by declaring beforehand what his subsequent conduct will be; and afterward, by acting according to his previous declarations. The *truth* and the *faithfulness* of God are, then, in reality the same moral perfection, only viewed under different circumstances; nor can we conceive of his possessing the one and not the other. There is, therefore, no reason for making them separate subjects of examination.

§ 10. *The Justice of God.*

The *Justice* of God is defined by Dr. Ryland to be, "the ardent inclination of his will to prescribe equal laws as the Supreme Governor, and to dispense equal rewards and punishments as the Supreme Judge." It is that attribute by which God actively manifests his approbation of what is good, and disapprobation of what is evil. It is, therefore, the same in essence with his *holiness*. So far as God *takes pleasure* in what is good, he is called *holy;* so far as he *exhibits* this pleasure, in his actual procedure in the government of the world, he is called *just.* The term *holiness*, accordingly, refers rather to the internal disposition of God; and *justice*, to the display or outward manifestation of this disposition.

The *justice* of God may be considered as *general* or *particular*. The *general* or *universal* justice of God is that perfection of his nature which leads him, on all occasions, to do what is right and equal, and is often expressed by the term *righteousness*. His *particular* justice consists in his perfect rectitude as a moral governor. His justice, in this sense, is either *legislative* or *judicial*.

LEGISLATIVE JUSTICE determines man's duty and binds him to the performance of it. It also defines the rewards of the obedient and the punishments of the rebellious. God has unquestionably an absolute right to the entire and perpetual obedience of his creatures; and in pursuance of this all moral agents are placed under *law*, and are subject to rewards and punishments.

JUDICIAL JUSTICE is that which respects a righteous retribution. God "will render to every man according to his deeds." Rom. ii, 6. This branch of justice is either *remunerative*, as when God rewards the obedient, or *vindictive*, as when he punishes the guilty. Rewards, properly speaking, are of *grace*, and not of debt; for God cannot be a debtor to his creatures. But since he binds himself by engagements in his law, "this do, and thou shalt live," or attaches a particular promise of reward to some duty, it becomes a part of *justice* to perform the engagement. "If we confess our sins, he is faithful and *just* to forgive us our sins." 1 John i, 9.

VINDICTIVE or PUNITIVE JUSTICE consists in the infliction of punishment. In the first place, it renders the punishment of unpardoned sin *certain*, so that no criminal shall escape; and, secondly, it graduates the exact proportion of punishment to the nature and circumstances of the offense. Both these facts are marked in numerous passages of Scripture, the testimony of which on this subject may be summed up in the words of Elihu: "For the *work* of man shall he render unto him, and cause every man to find *according* to his ways; yea, surely God will not do wickedly, neither will the Almighty pervert judgment." Job xxxiv, 12.

There are many circumstances in the administration of the affairs of the world which appear to be irreconcilable to that strict exercise of justice which is ascribed to God as our Supreme Ruler. We see, for instance, that the notoriously wicked, in some cases, enjoy a long life and great worldly prosperity, while those who are truly pious are subjects of poverty and affliction. But if we take these two facts into the account, 1, that offending man is under a dispensation of mercy, which provides for his pardon and moral renovation; and, 2, that God has "appointed a day in which he will judge the world in righteousness," a satisfactory light will be thrown upon all those cases in the Divine administration which have been thought most difficult.

The doctrine of a *future and general judgment*, which alone explains so many difficulties in the dispensations of Providence, is grounded solely on the doctrine of redemption. Under an administration of *strict justice*, punishment must follow offense without delay. This is clearly indicated in the sanction of the first law, "in the day thou eatest thereof thou shalt surely die;" a threat which would have been fully executed but for the immediate introduction of the redeeming scheme. Under such an administration no reason would seem to exist for a general judgment. This has its reason in the circumstances of trial in which men are placed by the introduction of a method of recovery. Justice, in virtue of the *atonement*, admits of the suspension of punishment for offense, of long-suffering, of the application of means of repentance and conversion, and that through the whole term of human life. But the judgment, the examination, and the public exhibition of the use or abuse of these appliances are deferred to an appointed day, in which he who now offers grace will administer justice, strict and unsparing.

However difficult it may be, without taking these things into consideration, to trace the manifestations of justice in God's moral government, or to reconcile certain circumstances with the character of a righteous governor, by their aid all difficulty is entirely removed. Indeed, the single fact of a general judgment is enough to rectify all the inequality of present dispensations were it a thousand times greater.

From these remarks respecting the nature and characteristics of Divine justice several important conclusions may be drawn.

1. It is no impeachment of a righteous government that external prosperity should be the lot of great offenders. This may be part of a gracious adminstration to bring them to repentance by *favor*; or it may be designed to make their fall and final punishment more *marked*, and to show the light value of outward advantages, separate from holy habits and a thankful heart.

2. It is not inconsistent with the rectitude of God that the pious should be afflicted and oppressed, since their defects may require chastisement, and since, also, afflictions are made to work out for them "a far more exceeding and eternal weight of glory."

3. As the administration under which man is placed is one of *grace* in harmony with *justice*, the dispensation of what is purely matter of favor may have a great variety, without any impeachment of Divine justice. Of this fact the parable of our Lord respecting the laborers in the vineyard is a fit illustration.*

4. But with *nations* the case is very different. Their rewards and punishments, being of a civil nature, may be fully administered in this life; for, as bodies politic, they have no posthumous existence. National retribution has, therefore, in all ages, been visible and striking. In succession all vicious nations have perished; and always by means so marked, and often so singular, as to bear upon them a broad and legible *punitive* character.

§ 11. *The Holiness of God.*

Holiness, considered as an attribute of God, is his *perfect moral purity*. It is that perfection of his nature by which he is infinitely averse to all moral evil, and inclined to love all that is good and right. The

* See Matt. xx, 1-16.

holiness of God, then, implies the absence of all moral impurity and imperfection, and the possession, in an infinite degree, of all that is morally pure, lovely, and excellent.

It may be proper to remark, that the term *holy*, when applied to God, is sometimes used to signify *august* and *venerable*. Thus, when the Psalmist pronounces his name to be "Holy and Reverend," the second epithet may be understood to be exegetical of the first. And when he says that "his *holy arm* hath gotten him the victory," there is no direct reference to *moral excellence*, but to majestic force, to irresistible power. The command to "sanctify the Lord," is a command to treat him with the most profound reverence, and is thus explained by Isaiah: "Sanctify the Lord God of hosts himself, and let him be your fear, and let him be our dread." Isa. viii, 13. He is a Being separated or distinguished from all other beings by his infinite excellence, as sacred things are separated from things that are common. He is possessed of every perfection, intellectual and moral, in the highest possible degree, and is, therefore, entitled to the veneration of angels and of men.

But while the holiness of God does certainly suggest, in many instances, the idea of *greatness* or *majesty*, it is equally certain, that in others it is expressive of the purity of his nature. This is obviously the case in the following passage: "As he which hath called you is *holy*, so be ye holy in all manner of conversation, because it is written, Be ye holy, for I am *holy*." 1 Pet. i, 13. There would be no force in the exhortation if the holiness ascribed to God were not of the same nature as that which is required of us; for the former is referred to as the reason and pattern of the latter. Hence, when we call God *holy*, we mean that there are in his nature certain moral qualities or principles analogous to those on account of which men are pronounced holy, that he is perfectly free from the slightest taint of moral pollution, and that his will is always conformable to the rectitude of his nature, so that he invariably hates sin and loves righteousness.

The holiness of God is commonly regarded as an attribute distinct from all his other perfections; but this, we think, is a mistake. Holiness is a complex term, and denotes, not so much a particular attribute, as that *general character* of God which results from all his moral perfections. The holiness of a man is not a distinct quality from his virtuous dispositions, but signifies the state of his mind and heart as influenced by these. When we proceed to analyze his holiness, or to show in what it consists, we say that he is a devout man; a man of integrity, a man faithful to all his engagements and conscientious in all his relative duties, a man who abhors sin and loves righteousness. In like manner, the holiness of God is not, and cannot be, something different from the moral perfections of his nature, but is the general term under which all these perfections are comprehended.

The holiness of God is proved,

1. FROM THE SCRIPTURES.

"Ye shall be holy, for I the Lord your God am *holy*." Lev. xix, 2. "Exalt the Lord our God, and worship at his holy hill; for the Lord our God is *holy*." Psa. xcix, 9. This attribute was the subject of praise to the seraphim who surrounded the throne of Jehovah when he appeared in the temple to the prophet Isaiah. "And one cried unto another, and said, Holy, holy, holy is the Lord of hosts; the whole earth is full of his glory." Isa. vi, 3. It is said in the Apocalypse, of the four living creatures, that "they rest not day and night, saying, Holy, holy, holy, Lord God Almighty." Rev. iv, 8.

2. FROM THE MORAL NATURE WITH WHICH MAN WAS ENDOWED AT HIS CREATION.

Man was not only made a living soul, and endowed with intellectual powers, but there was impressed upon him the image of his Maker, consisting in the perfect rectitude of his mind, in the order and harmony of his faculties, and in pure and heavenly affections. Thus man, in his primitive state, was resplendent with the glory of God's moral excellence. This state he might have retained; for, to suppose that his power was not adequate to his circumstances, would be to make God the author of sin. The fall of man was not owing to the want of anything which God ought to have done for him, but he voluntarily yielded to temptation, disregarding the considerations which would have counteracted its influence.

3. FROM THE NATURE AND DESIGN OF THE LAW WHICH WAS ORIGINALLY GIVEN TO MAN.

As to the *nature* of this law, it is pure and holy. It forbids sin in all its modifications: in its most refined as well as in its grossest forms, the taint of the mind as well as the pollution of the body, the secret approbation of sin as well as the external act, the transient look of desire, and every irregular emotion. While it commands us to place a guard upon the avenues by which temptation might enter, it enjoins the strictest care of the heart, and calls upon us to destroy the seed before it has grown. "The law is holy, and the commandment holy." Rom. vii, 12.

The *design* of the law was to retain man in a state of innocence and purity. It was sanctioned by promises and threatenings, and thus, while it taught him his duty, it actuated him to obedience by the hope of reward, and deterred him from sin by the fear of punishment. In this, therefore, we see a proof both of God's care for man and of his regard to holiness.

4. FROM THE INDICATIONS OF PROVIDENCE IN THE GOVERNMENT OF THE MORAL WORLD.

Let us here notice, in the *first* place, the natural checks which God has placed upon sin, and the natural encouragements which he has held out to the practice of virtue, for in these we clearly perceive his regard to the interests of holiness. It is certain that various affections and actions have been enjoined upon all rational creatures under the general name of *righteousness*, and their contraries have been prohibited. It is also a matter of constant experience and observation, that the good of society is promoted only by what is commanded, and injured by what is forbidden; and that every individual derives, by the very law of his nature, benefit and happiness from rectitude, and injury and misery from vice. This constitution of human nature is, therefore, an indication that the Maker and Ruler of men formed them with the intent that they should avoid vice and practice virtue; and that the former is the object of his aversion, the latter of his regard.

We notice, *secondly*, that God has manifested his holiness, and his infinite abhorrence of sin, by the exercise of his punitive justice. When angels rebelled against him they were cast down to hell. When our first parents disobeyed the Divine command they were expelled from Paradise. When the antediluvian world sinned against God he overwhelmed them in the waters of the deluge. Upon Sodom and Gomorrah he rained down fire and brimstone; and when his chosen people indulged in vice, or forsook his worship, he delivered them into the hands of their enemies. Truly, then, God is *holy*.

5. From the work of Redemption.

It is this that dispelled the cloud which sin had spread over the character of God, revealing him in all his glory as the moral governor of the world. In the person of the Redeemer we have an exemplification of that holiness in which man was created, and to which he must be restored, in order that he may be admitted to eternal life. In the sufferings and death of Christ, as an atonement for sin, we have a demonstration both of the inflexible justice of God and of his infinite compassion toward the guilty. The immediate design of the atonement was to meet the claims of God's holy law; but the ultimate design was to restore men to that state of holiness from which they had fallen. The means were of the most wonderful and unexpected kind—the substitution and sufferings of a Divine person—the obedience and crucifixion of the Lord of glory. He "gave himself for us, that he might redeem us from all iniquity, and purify unto himself a peculiar people, zealous of good works." Titus ii, 14. It follows, therefore, that holiness must be infinitely acceptable to God, and that he is an infinitely holy being, since he resorted to this extraordinary method of re-establishing holiness in our world.

§ 12. *The Goodness of God.*

In the investigation of this Divine attribute it will be proper, in the first place, to make some general observations explanatory of its *nature;* and, secondly, to adduce the *proofs* by which the goodness of God is established.

I. THE NATURE OF THE DIVINE GOODNESS.

Goodness, when it is considered as a distinct attribute of God, signifies *benevolence*, or a disposition to communicate happiness. From an inward principle of good-will, God exerts his omnipotence in diffusing happiness through the universe in proportion to the different capacities with which he has endowed his creatures, and according to the direction of his infinite wisdom. Here we may observe,

1. *That the goodness of God, according as it terminates upon different objects, admits of different denominations.* When it confers happiness without merit, it is called *grace;* when it commiserates the distressed, it is *pity;* when it supplies the indigent, it is *bounty;* when it bears with offenders, it is *patience* or *long-suffering;* and when it pardons the guilty, it is *mercy.* These, therefore, are not to be regarded as distinct attributes of God, but as various modes according to which he manifests his *goodness* to his creatures.

2. *That goodness in God is represented as goodness of* NATURE, as one of his essential perfections, and not as an accidental or occasional affection. He is thus set infinitely above the imaginary gods of the heathen, whose benevolence was occasional, limited, and often disturbed by contrary passions. Such were the best views of pagans; but to us a being of a far different character is manifested as our Creator and Lord. One of his appropriate and distinguishing names, as proclaimed by himself to Moses, signifies, "*The gracious One,*" and imports *goodness* in the *principle;* and another, "*The all-sufficient and all-bountiful pourer forth of all good,*" and expresses goodness in *action.*

3. *That the goodness of God is* EFFICIENT *and* INEXHAUSTIBLE. It reaches every fit case, it supplies all possible want, and endures forever. As the sun sheds his rays upon the surrounding worlds, and enlightens and cherishes the whole creation without being diminished in splendor, so God imparts without being exhausted, and though ever giving, has yet infinitely more to give.

4. *That God* TAKES PLEASURE *in the exercise of his goodness.* It is not reluctantly or coldly imparted, nor is it stintedly measured out. He "is rich unto all that call upon him." He "giveth to all men liberally, and upbraideth not." He is ready to do for us "exceeding abundantly above all that we ask or think." It is under these views that the Scriptures afford so much encouragement to *prayer*, and lay so strong a ground for absolute *trust* in God. His goodness throws a mild and tranquilizing luster over the majestic attributes of his nature, and presents them to us under a friendly aspect. It enables us to regard him not only as a Sovereign, but as a Father. It causes us to feel emotions of gratitude and love, rising in harmony with sentiments of veneration, and encourages us to supplicate his favor and submit to his control.

II. PROOFS BY WHICH THE GOODNESS OF GOD IS ESTABLISHED.

These are so numerous that they cannot all be adduced, nor will our limits allow us to pursue the argument to any great length. The most that we can do is to present a few of the most obvious proofs in support of the Divine goodness. We may argue it,

1. *From the plain and positive declarations of Scripture.*—When Moses prayed, "I beseech thee, show me thy glory," Jehovah replied, "I will make all my goodness pass before thee," as if he accounted this attribute most glorious to himself. Thus he proclaimed his own name: "The Lord, the Lord God, merciful and gracious, long-suffering, and abundant in goodness and truth." Exod. xxxiv, 6. This description of the Divine character is confirmed throughout the whole system of revelation. "O give thanks unto the Lord, for he is good; for his mercy endureth forever." 1 Chron. xvi, 34. "The earth is full of the goodness of the Lord." Psa. xxxiii, 5. "O taste and see that the Lord is good." Psa. xxxiv, 8. "For thou, Lord, art good, and ready to forgive, and plenteous in mercy unto all them that call upon thee." Psa. lxxxvi, 5. "The Lord is good to all; and his tender mercies are over all his works." Psa. cxlv, 9.

2. *From the fact of creation.*—When we consider God as possessing in himself all possible perfection and felicity, and as being independent of all creatures, we may ask, What motive could have induced him to exert his power in giving life to so many orders of beings, and in fitting up the earth to be a convenient habitation for them, but pure and unmixed goodness—a desire to communicate happiness to other beings? He did not perform the work of creation by a necessity of nature, as the sun gives light, or as a fountain pours out its waters; but in consequence of counsel and design. As a free agent, he exerted his power to such an extent, and in such a variety of ways, as seemed agreeable to himself. Of the counsels of God we are not competent judges, and it would, therefore, be presumptuous in us to affirm that benevolence was the *only* motive to the work of creation; but we are safe in concluding that the diffusion of happiness was its *primary* design. What other idea is suggested by the contemplation of a system so regular and beautiful in all its parts, and teeming with life and enjoyment? Had not the nature of God been communicative he would have remained alone; but now he beholds from his throne a scale of beings, ascending from the insect to the archangel, all rejoicing in conscious existence, and partaking of the riches of his liberality.

3. *From the state in which living creatures are made.*—They are relatively perfect; that is, they are all perfectly fitted for their various places in creation, their peculiar modes of life, and the purposes which they were designed to serve. They possess everything that is necessary for the preservation of life, for defense, for the procuring of food, and for motion from place to place. Had we found living creatures

that were destitute of any of those members and organs of sense on which their safety and comfort depended, as birds without wings, fishes without fins, or beasts without legs, we might have supposed that the Creator intended them to languish in misery and perish; but the contrary conclusion must be drawn from the provision which has been evidently made for the comfortable subsistence of animated nature. He who has bestowed life has rendered it a gift worthy of himself, by associating with it a variety of conveniences and pleasures.

4. *From the abundant provision which God has made for the wants of his creatures.*—"The eyes of all wait upon thee; and thou givest them their meat in due season. Thou openest thine hand, and satisfiest the desire of every living thing." Psa. cxlv, 15, 16. With the care and bounty of a father, he provides for all the members of his family. The various species of animals differ from one another as much in their taste as in their form. The food that sustains one will not nourish another; and what one eagerly seeks another rejects with disgust. Substances offensive to *our* senses, and which if taken into our stomachs would be noxious, furnish wholesome and delicious nutriment to creatures differently constituted. Thus God manifests his goodness in providing for every living creature its appropriate aliment; for, though the guests at the table of Providence have no community of interests and feelings, yet they all find suitable entertainment. Not one of them goes away disappointed, for our "heavenly Father feedeth them."

5. *From the variety of natural pleasures which God has provided for the animal creation.*—Every creature capable of happiness, that comes immediately from the forming hand of God, is placed in circumstances of positive felicity; and by associating happiness with animal existence he has made life truly a blessing, and has acted in the character of benevolence. There seems, indeed, to be a high degree of pleasure attached to simple existence, as we may judge from the lively motions of young animals. These motions appear to have no specific object, as the friskings of a lamb, for example, but to proceed from an indescribable satisfaction which animals experience in the possession of life and activity. The goodness of God is farther displayed in the pleasures which animals derive from the gratification of their natural appetites, and from pursuing their instinctive propensities. When in summer the air is filled with myriads of insects, which are almost constantly on the wing, wheeling in sportive circles, we have an evidence of the delight with which they pass their transitory duration, and a proof of the Divine beneficence. Their enjoyment is merely sensitive, but it is the only kind of which they are capable; and it is goodness, rich in its treasures and minute in its attentions, which thus adapts itself to every living nature.

What has been said relates chiefly to the condition of the lower animals; but we will now proceed to argue the goodness of God,

6. *From his dispensations to Man.*—As this is a subject of vast extent, the reader will at once perceive that we can only present a hasty sketch of the argument, leaving him to fill up the outline by his own reflections. Let us then notice,

(1.) *Man's original state and condition.*—Though created last, he was not least. A high rank was assigned to him in the scale of being. As to his body, it was "fearfully and wonderfully made." In his *intellectual* powers he was placed infinitely above every other terrestrial creature. He possessed understanding and reason, and had a knowledge of himself and his Maker, and of the various relations which subsisted between them. He was also endowed with a *moral* nature, with innate rectitude, a love of holiness, and a strong desire to know and serve God. He therefore enjoyed, under the smile of his Maker, a felicity incomparably greater, both in kind and degree, than that of the inferior creatures. The *place* of his abode corresponded with the dignity of his character and with the peculiarities of his constitution. In the garden of Paradise, which the hand of God prepared for man, there was nothing wanting that could minister to his good or afford him comfort—all was beauty, and melody, and delight.

Again, God placed man under moral government. He gave him a good and holy law, promising to reward his obedience with everlasting felicity. Obedience, indeed, was a debt which he owed his Creator; so that, though he had fulfilled the whole law, he should have had no claim to remuneration. True, man lost the noble prize which was set before him; but that event does not in any degree obscure the evidence of benignity in God, from which the promise of it proceeded. Even at this distance we ought to look back with grateful emotions upon the hope which animated our first progenitor in the commencement of his career, and the blessedness which might have descended as an inheritance to his children. Now, if we look at these facts, either separately or taken together, we will be forced to the conclusion that God intended the happiness of man, and that, therefore, he is rich in goodness. But we may look at man,

(2.) *In his present fallen condition.*—When he transgressed the law of his Creator a dispensation of unmixed wrath might have commenced. And when for wise reasons God suspended the infliction of the threatened penalty, and permitted the offender to live, he might have doomed him and his posterity to a life of extreme misery; but we find it far otherwise. Though our world is a world of sinners, yet it is one in which the goodness of God is gloriously displayed. It is especially for man that the sun pours out a flood of light and genial heat; that the earth is endowed with unceasing powers of fertility; and that life and health are borne upon the wings of the wind. What a delightful view of the Divine goodness is given by the regular succession of the seasons, the opening buds and blossoms of spring, the luxuriant growth of summer, and the matured fruits and rich harvests of autumn! Surely God has not left "himself without witness, in that he did good, and gave us rain from heaven, and fruitful seasons, filling our hearts with food and gladness." Acts xiv, 17.

The goodness of God appears also in the provision which he has made for the gratification of our senses. We experience that food not only satisfies the appetite of hunger and nourishes our bodies, but also gratifies our taste. Now this pleasure is not at all necessary to the great design of food. It might be perfectly tasteless, without any diminution of its nutritive quality; but the taste is superadded by our Maker to render it pleasant as well as useful, and clearly shows his attention to our animal comfort. The same conclusion may be drawn from the gratification of other senses. There is beauty prepared for the eye, music for the ear, and sweet perfumes for the sense of smelling. But why is it that we are thus so agreeably affected by natural objects? Not because it renders them more useful, but more attractive; not because it sustains life, but imparts to it a higher relish.

It is here urged, as an objection to the doctrine which we have advocated, that the globe, as the residence of man, has its inconveniences and positive evils. This is admitted. It has its extremes of cold and heat; its earthquakes, volcanoes, tempests, and inundations; its sterility in some places, which wears down man with labor; and its exuberance of vegetable and animal life in others, which generates diseases, or gives birth to annoying and destructive animals. The diseases of the human race, their general poverty, their universal sufferings and cares, and their short life and painful dissolution, must all be acknowledged.

It was to account for such evils as these that the ancient philosophers supposed the world to be governed by two contrary deities. They could not see how a benevolent being could be the author of natural evil, and hence they ascribed everything of this kind to an evil god. We, however, who enjoy the light of the Scriptures, can solve this question without difficulty. We acknowledge that there are real evils in the world; but we contend that their existence is not inconsistent with the benevolence of the Author of nature, because the world in which they are found is inhabited by sinful beings. Physical evil is the consequence of moral evil. Had man continued in his original state, natural evil would be unaccountable; but no one who believes that God is just can wonder that suffering should be the attendant of guilt. God is holy as well as benevolent, and his goodness ought to be considered, not as a disposition to confer happiness indiscriminately, but to confer it upon proper objects. We are placed under a mixed dispensation of mercy and judgment. God exercises much patience and long-suffering toward men, but he also gives tokens of his displeasure; and the true ground of surprise is, not that there is a portion of evil in their lot, but that there is so much good; because they deserve the former, but are altogether unworthy of the latter.

But with all the evils which belong to our condition, we cannot but acknowledge that physical good greatly preponderates. In general the days of health are many, and those of pain and sickness few. Enjoyment of one kind or other is within the reach of all; and even in conditions which seem to be most unfavorable to it, there are sources of satisfaction of which others are not aware. The poor have their pleasures as well as the rich; the laboring classes as well as those who are living at ease. All esteem existence a blessing, and suicide is committed only when the mind is diseased, or when the instinctive love of life is overcome by the extremity of pain, or the dread of some intolerable evil. The state even of fallen man bears ample testimony to the goodness of his Maker. It is, upon the whole, a happy world in which we live, although it is a world of sinners. God displays before our eyes the riches of his goodness, forbearance, and long-suffering.*

There are two other considerations which ought not to be overlooked in this connection. The *first* is, that positive evils are mitigated by various alleviations, and are often connected with beneficent ends. The necessity of *labor* obliges us to occupy time usefully, which is both a source of enjoyment and a preventive of much evil. *Familiarity* and *habit* render many circumstances tolerable which at first sight we conceive to be necessarily the sources of wretchedness. Pain teaches vigilance and caution, and renders its remission in returning health a source of higher enjoyment; while the process of mortal diseases mitigates our natural horror of death. In all this there is surely an ample proof and an adorable display of the Divine goodness.

The second consideration is, that man himself is chargeable with far the largest share of the miseries of the present life. View men *collectively*. Sin, as a *ruling habit*, is not necessary. The means of repressing its inward motions, and of restraining its outward acts, have been furnished to all mankind; and if the miseries which are the effects of voluntary vice were all removed, comparatively few would remain in the world. Oppressive governments, private wrongs, wars, jealousies, intemperance, and all their consequent evils, would disappear.

But besides the removal of so many evils, how greatly would the sum of positive happiness be increased! Peace, security, and industry would cover the earth with fruits in sufficient abundance for all. Intellectual improvement would yield the pleasures of knowledge. Arts would multiply the comforts, and mitigate many of the most wasting toils of life. General benevolence would unite men in warm affections and friendships, productive of innumerable reciprocal offices of kindness, and piety would crown all with the pleasures of pure devotion, remov-

* See Dick's Theology, Lecture 24.

ing every annoying passion and tormenting fear, and inspiring its subjects with a blissful hope of a better state of being. All this is *possible*. If it is not *actual*, it is the fault of the human race, not of their Maker; and his goodness is not to be questioned because they are perverse. We may direct our attention,

(3.) *To what God has done for Man's recovery.*—It is in the plan of human redemption, that he has most gloriously evinced the perfection of his goodness—goodness beyond all calculation, immense and infinite! It is on this subject, more than on any other, that we are constrained to cry out in profound admiration, "*God is love.*" The whole scheme originated from this source, and every part of it declares "the exceeding riches of his grace, in his kindness toward us, through Christ Jesus." Eph. ii, 7.

It is impossible to set a *proper* estimate upon the goodness of God, as manifested in the work of human redemption; but if we would make any considerable approach toward it we must consider, 1. The gift bestowed: "He gave his only begotten Son." John iii, 16. 2. The manner in which Christ effected our redemption: "He took upon him the form of a servant, and was make in the likeness of men; and being found in fashion as a man, he humbled himself, and became obedient unto death, even the death of the cross." Phil. ii, 7, 8. 3. The depth of misery from which we were rescued: "Christ hath redeemed us from the *curse of the law.*" Gal. iii, 13. 4. The height of bliss to which we are raised: "peace with God" here, and "everlasting life" hereafter. And, 5. The means which are still in operation to bring men to the enjoyment of this great salvation, the institutions of the Gospel, and the saving influences of the Holy Spirit. Who can take a survey of this wonderful system of human recovery and call in question the goodness of God?

Such are the adorable perfections of the ever-blessed God, which are distinctly revealed to us in his Word; but in addition to these there are other excellences, ascribed to him in a more general way, which serve to heighten our conceptions of his character, and to set before the humbled and awed spirit of man an overwhelming height and depth of majesty and glory.

God is PERFECT. We are thus taught to ascribe to him every natural and moral excellence which we can conceive. Every attribute in him is perfect in its *kind*, and is the most elevated of its kind. It is perfect in its *degree*, not falling in the least below the standard of the highest excellence either in our conceptions, or those of angels, or in the possible nature of things.

God is ALL-SUFFICIENT. This is another of those declarations of Scripture which exalt our views of God into a mysterious, unbounded, and undefined amplitude *from himself*, eternally rising out of his own perfection, *for himself*, so that he is ALL to himself, and depends upon no other being, and *for all that communication*, however large and however lasting, on which the whole universe depends. The same vast thought is expressed by St. Paul in the phrase, "ALL IN ALL."

God is UNSEARCHABLE. All that we see or hear of him is but a faint and shadowy manifestation. Beyond the highest glory there is yet an unpierced and unapproachable light, a track of intellectual and moral splendor, untraveled by the thoughts of the adoring spirits who are nearest his throne. "Canst thou find out the Almighty unto perfection?" Job xi, 7. "Great is the Lord, and greatly to be praised, and his greatness is unsearchable." Psa. cxlv, 3.

We cannot close this chapter in a more suitable manner than in the adoring language of the psalmist: "*Blessed* be the *Lord God*, the God of Israel, who only doeth wondrous things. And *blessed* be his glorious *name* forever: and let the whole earth be filled with his *glory; Amen, and Amen*. Psa. lxxii, 18, 19.

CHAPTER III.

THE TRINITY IN UNITY.

WE now approach this great mystery of our faith, the doctrine of the *Trinity*, for the declaration of which we are exclusively indebted to the Sacred Scriptures. Not only is it incapable of proof *à priori*, but it derives no direct confirmatory evidence from the existence and wise and orderly arrangement of the works of God. It stands, however, on the unshaken foundation of his own word, that revelation which he has given of himself in both Testaments; and if we see no traces of it in the works of creation, as we do of his existence and perfections, the reason is, that creation in itself could not be the medium of manifesting or of illustrating it.

Among the leading writers in defense of the Trinity there are some shades of difference in opinion as to what constitutes the *Unity* of the three persons in the Godhead. The scheme which seems to comport most exactly with Scripture is that of Bishop Pearson, with whom Bishop Bull and Dr. Owen also agree. It is thus expressed by Dr. Doddridge: "Though God the Father is the fountain of the Deity, the whole Divine nature is communicated from the Father to the Son, and from both to the Spirit, yet so as that the Father and the Son are not separate, nor separable from the divinity, but do still exist in it, and are most intimately united to it."

The term *person* signifies in ordinary language an intelligent being.

Two or more persons, therefore, in the strict philosophical sense, would be two or more distinct intelligent beings. If the term *person* were so applied to the Trinity in the Godhead a plurality of gods would follow; while if taken in what has been called a *political* sense, personality would be no more than *relation*, arising out of office. Personality in God is, therefore, not to be understood in either of the above senses if we pay respect to the testimony of Scripture. God is *one being*. But he is more than one being in three *relations;* for *personal acts*, such as we ascribe to distinct persons, and which most unequivocally characterize personality, are ascribed to each person of the Trinity. The Scripture doctrine therefore is, that the persons are not *separate*, but distinct, and that they are so united as to be but *one God*. In other words, that the Divine nature exists under the personal distinction of Father, Son, and Holy Ghost, and that these three have equally, and in common with one another, the nature and perfections of supreme divinity. This appears to be the true simple doctrine of the Trinity, when stripped of refined and learned distinctions. As to the *manner* in which three persons are united in the Godhead, it is granted to be incomprehensible; but so is God himself, as is also every essential attribute of his nature.

It is objected by some that the term *person* is not used in the Scriptures, and that, therefore, we should not employ it in connection with this subject. To such it may be sufficient to reply, that if what is clearly taught in Scripture is compendiously expressed by this term, and cannot so well be expressed, except by an inconvenient periphrasis, it ought to be retained. But is there not a scriptural warrant for the term itself? Our translators so concluded when in Heb. i, 3, they called the Son "the express image" of the Father's "*person*." The original word is ὑπόστασις, which signifies substance, essence, being; something of which we can say, it is, in opposition to mere appearance, and was understood by the Greek fathers to signify a *person*, though not exclusively so used.

The sense of ὑπόστασις in this passage must be considered, by all who allow the divinity of the Son of God, as fixed by the apostle's argument. For the Son being called "the express image" of the Father, a *distinction* between the Son and the Father is thus unquestionably expressed; but if there is but *one* God, and if the Son is Divine, the distinction here expressed cannot be a distinction of essence, and must, therefore, be a *personal* distinction.

Having made these preliminary remarks, we are now prepared to enter upon a more particular investigation of the doctrine of the Trinity. We will consider, *first*, its vast importance in the system of revealed truth; and, *secondly*, the Scripture proofs by which it is established.

§ 1. *The Importance of the Doctrine.*

To consider the importance of the doctrine of the Trinity is the more necessary because it has been represented as of little consequence, or as a matter of useless speculation. Thus Dr. Priestley: "All that can be said for it is, that the doctrine, however improbable in itself, is necessary to explain some particular texts of Scripture; and that, if it had not been for those particular texts we should have found no want for it."* That the reader may see the importance of this revealed doctrine, he is requested to weigh the following considerations:

1. THE KNOWLEDGE OF GOD IS FUNDAMENTAL TO RELIGION; and as we know nothing of him but what he has revealed, and as these revelations have all *moral ends*, and are designed to promote *piety*, and not to gratify *curiosity*, all that he has revealed of himself in *particular* must partake of that character of fundamental importance which belongs to the knowledge of God in the aggregate. Nothing, therefore, can disprove the fundamental importance of the Trinity in Unity but that which will prove that it is not a doctrine of Scripture.

2. IT ESSENTIALLY AFFECTS OUR VIEWS OF GOD AS THE OBJECT OF OUR WORSHIP, whether we regard him as one in essence and one in person, or admit that in the unity of the Godhead there are three equally Divine persons. These are two very different conceptions, both of which cannot be true. The God of those who deny the Trinity is not the God of those who worship the Trinity in Unity, so that either the former or the latter worship a being which does not exist; and, so far as it respects any *reality* in the object, they might as well worship a pagan idol.

But as the *object* of our worship is affected by our respective views on this great subject, so also is its *character*. For if the doctrine of the Trinity is true, then those who deny it do not worship the God of the Scriptures, but a fiction of their own framing, and are, therefore, guilty of idolatry. If it is false, Trinitarians, by paying Divine honors to the Son and to the Holy Ghost, are equally guilty of idolatry, though in another mode. The importance of the doctrine must, therefore, be obvious to all.

3. THE DOCTRINE OF THE TRINITY HAS AN INTIMATE CONNECTION WITH THE SUBJECT OF MORALS. What is morality but conformity to the Divine law, which law must take its character from that of its Author? The Trinitarian scheme is essentially connected with the doctrine of atonement, which depends on the divinity of Christ. It acknowledges the fallen and helpless condition of man, the exceeding sinfulness of sin, and the inflexible justice of God. The Unitarian theory necessarily excludes atonement, and regards sin as a matter of

* History of "Early Opinions."

comparatively trifling moment. It supposes that God is not strict to punish sin, and that if punishment does follow it will not be eternal. Whether, under these soft and easy views of the law of God, and of the evil of transgression, morals can have an equal sanction, or human conduct be equally restrained, are points too obvious to be argued.

But we must not forget that faith in the testimony of God is an essential part of morality. To *believe* is so much a Divine *command* that the highest sanction is connected with it. "He that believeth shall be *saved;* and he that believeth not shall be *damned.*" It is, therefore, an act of *duty* to believe, because it is an act of *obedience;* and hence St. Paul speaks of "the obedience of faith." It is of the utmost importance, then, that we should know what God has revealed as the object of our faith, since the rejection of any revealed truth must certainly be visited with punishment; the *law of faith* having the same authority and the same sanction as the *law of works.* Thus we see the connection of this doctrine with Christian morality, and, consequently, its great value.

4. *But the importance of the doctrine of the Trinity may be finally argued* FROM THE MANNER IN WHICH A DENIAL OF IT WOULD AFFECT THE CREDIT OF THE HOLY SCRIPTURES. Dr. Priestley allows that this doctrine "is necessary to explain some particular texts of Scripture." This fact alone is sufficient to mark its importance and to establish its truth, especially as it can be shown that these "*particular* texts" comprehend a very large portion of the sacred volume. If the doctrine of a Trinity of Divine persons in the Godhead is true, the style and manner of the Scriptures are in perfect accordance with the facts in the case; but if the Son and the Holy Spirit were creatures, then would the language of the sacred books be most deceptive and dangerous. It would be so well adapted to lead men to the belief of falsehood, even in fundamental points, and to idolatry itself, that "abominable thing" which the Lord hates, that they would lose all claim to be regarded as a revelation from the God of truth, and ought rather to be shunned than studied.

If the doctrine of the Trinity is denied, how is it to be accounted for, that in the Old Testament God should be spoken of in plural terms, and that this plurality should be restricted to *thee?* How is it that the very name *Jehovah* should be given to each of them, and that repeatedly on the most solemn occasions? How is it that the incarnate Messiah should be invested with the loftiest attributes of God; and that acts and characters of unequivocal divinity should be ascribed to the *Holy Spirit* also? How is it that in the New Testament the name of God should be given to both, and that without any intimation that it is used in an inferior sense? How is it that, in the very form of initiation by baptism into the Church of Christ, the ordinance, which itself is a public and solemn profession of faith, is to be performed in the *one name* of Father, Son, and Holy Ghost? This, if Socinianism were true, would be to administer baptism in the name of one God and two *creatures;* as though the very door of entrance into the Christian Church should have been purposely made the gateway into the temple of idolatry!

§ 2. *The Scripture Proofs.*

In deducing from the sacred volume the doctrine of a Trinity of Divine persons in the Unity of the Godhead, our attention will be directed to the important fact,

1. THAT THE ONE JEHOVAH OF THE BIBLE IS FREQUENTLY DESIGNATED BY PLURAL APPELLATIONS, AND PLURAL FORMS OF SPEECH.

The very first name under which he is made known to us as the Creator of the world is in the plural form. " In the beginning אלהים," ELOHIM, *the Gods,* " created the heavens and the earth." Gen. i, 1. That the word is plural, is made certain by its being often joined with adjectives, pronouns, and verbs plural. But when it can mean nothing else than the true God, it is usually joined in its plural form with a singular verb; as ברא אלהים, BARA ELOHIM, *the Gods created.*

This name is plural throughout the whole first chapter of Genesis, where it is so often employed, and in a thousand other places. In fact, it is rarely used in the singular אלה, ELOAH. The plural is preferred even when the design is to assert, in the most solemn manner, the Unity of God. Thus, " Hear, O Israel, the Lord אלהינו," ELOHAYNU, *our Gods,* " is one Lord." Deut. vi, 4. But this is not the only name which is applied in its plural form to the Divine Being. "If I be אדונים," ADONIM, *Masters,* " where is my fear?" Mal. i, 6. "Remember את בוראיך," ETH BOREKA, *thy Creators,* "in the days of thy youth." Eccl. xii, 1. " For בעליך עשיך," BOALAIK OSAIK, *thy Makers is thy husbands.* Isa. liv, 5.

Other plural forms of speech also occur when the ONE true God only is spoken of. "And God said, Let *us* make man in *our* image, after *our* likeness." Gen. i, 26. "And the Lord God said, Behold, the man is become as *one of us.*" Gen. iii, 22. These instances need not be multiplied; they are common forms of speech in the sacred Scriptures, which no criticism has been able to resolve into mere idioms, and which only the doctrine of a plurality of persons in the Unity of the Godhead can satisfactorily explain.

This argument, however, does not contain the strength of the case; for if these plural titles and forms of expression were blotted out, the evidence of a plurality of Divine persons in the Godhead would still remain in its strongest form. This evidence is found in the fact,

2. THAT THE SCRIPTURES SPEAK OF THREE PERSONS, AND THREE PERSONS ONLY, UNDER DIVINE TITLES.

It is a remarkable fact, that while the Scriptures maintain, as their leading principle, that there is but ONE God, they so frequently speak of *three* persons, to each of whom they ascribe the peculiar attributes of divinity. This being once established, it may be asked which of the hypotheses, the Orthodox, the Arian, or the Socinian, agrees best with what the Scriptures so plainly teach upon this subject; and whether those who confide in the testimony of God, rather than in the opinions of men, have not sufficient reason to distinguish their faith from the unbelief of others by avowing themselves *Trinitarians.**

(1.) *This doctrine is indicated in that solemn form of benediction in which the Jewish high priests were commanded to bless the children of Israel*, and which singularly answers to the apostolic benediction that so appropriately closes the solemn services of Christian worship. It is given in Num. vi, 24–27 :

"Jehovah bless thee, and keep thee;
Jehovah make his face to shine upon thee, and be gracious unto thee;
Jehovah lift his countenance upon thee, and give thee peace."

If the three members of this form of benediction be attentively considered, they will be found to agree respectively to the three persons of the Trinity, taken in the usual order of Father, Son, and Holy Ghost. The first member of the formula expresses "the love of God," the Father of mercies and Fountain of all good; the second well comports with the redeeming and reconciling "grace of the Lord Jesus Christ;" and the last is appropriate to the purity, consolation, and joy which are received from "the communion of the Holy Ghost."

The connection of certain blessings in this form of benediction with the Jehovah, mentioned three times distinctly, and those which are represented as flowing from the Father, Son, and Holy Ghost in the apostolic form, would be a singular coincidence if it even stood alone ; but the light of the same eminent truth breaks forth from other partings in the clouds of the early morning of revelation. Hence,

(2.) *The inner part of the Jewish sanctuary was called the* HOLY OF HOLIES, that is, the holy place of the *Holy Ones.* The number of these is indicated, and limited to *three*, in that celebrated vision of Isaiah which took place in the very abode of the *Holy Ones.* Before them the seraphim vailed their faces, " and one cried unto another, and said, Holy, holy, holy is the Lord of hosts." Isa. vi, 3. Here let it be observed, that this *trine* act of adoration, which has been supposed to mark a plurality of persons in the object of it, is answered by a voice from the excellent glory which overwhelmed the mind of the prophet, responding in the same language of plurality in which the doxology of the seraphim is expressed. " Also I heard the voice of the Lord, saying, Whom shall I send, and who will go for US ?"

But this is not the only evidence that the *persons* who were addressed,

* The word τριας, *trinitas*, came into use in the second century.

each by his appropriate and equal designation of *holy*, were the *three* Divine substances in the Godhead. The Being addressed is the "Lord of hosts." This phrase, all acknowledge, designates the Father; but the Evangelist John, in manifest reference to this same transaction, observes, "These things said Esaias, when he saw his (Christ's) glory and spake of him." John xii, 41. In this vision, therefore, we have the *Son* also, whose glory on this occasion the prophet beheld; and St. Paul bears testimony to the presence of the Holy Spirit. "Well spake the *Holy Ghost* by Esaias the prophet unto our fathers, saying, Go unto this people and say, Hearing ye shall hear, and shall not understand; and seeing ye shall see, and shall not perceive." Acts xxviii, 25, 26. These words, quoted from Isaiah, the apostle declares to have been spoken by the Holy Ghost; but Isaiah tells us, that they were spoken on this very occasion by the "Lord of hosts."

Now let all these circumstances be placed together—THE PLACE, the holy place of the Holy Ones; the repetition of the homage, THREE times Holy, holy, holy; the ONE Jehovah of hosts, to whom it was addressed; the plural pronoun used by this ONE Jehovah, US; the declaration of St. John, that on this occasion Isaiah saw the glory of CHRIST; and the testimony of St. Paul, that the Lord of hosts who spoke on that occasion was the HOLY GHOST; and the conclusion will not be without most powerful authority, both circumstantial and declaratory, that the adoration Holy, holy, holy, referred to the Divine *three* in the one essence of the Lord of hosts. Accordingly, in the book of Revelation, where "*the Lamb*" is associated with the Father as the object of *equal* homage, the *living creatures*, corresponding to the seraphim of the prophet, are heard in the same strain, and with the same *trine* repetition, saying, "Holy, holy, holy, Lord God Almighty, which was, and is, and is to come." Rev. iv, 8.

(3.) *The prophet Isaiah makes this threefold distinction and limitation.* "And now the *Lord God*, and his Spirit, hath sent *me*." Isa. xlviii, 16. The words are manifestly spoken by Messiah, who declares himself to be sent by the *Lord God*, and by his *Spirit*. Some render it, hath sent *me* and his *Spirit*, the latter term being also in the accusative case. This strengthens the application by bringing the phrase nearer to that which is so often used by our Lord when he speaks of *himself* and the *Spirit* as being sent by the Father.

Again, "I am with you, saith the *Lord of hosts:* according to the word that I covenanted with you when ye came out of Egypt, so *my Spirit* remaineth among you; fear ye not. For thus saith the Lord of hosts; I will shake all nations, and the Desire of all nations shall come." Hag. ii, 4-7. Here also we have three persons distinctly mentioned, the *Lord* of hosts, his *Spirit*, and the *Desire* of all nations.

(4.) *This doctrine is most explicitly taught in the New Testament.* The passages commonly adduced are familiar to all: "Baptizing them in the name of the *Father*, and of the *Son*, and of the *Holy Ghost*." Matt. xxviii, 19. " The grace of the *Lord Jesus Christ*, and the love of *God*, and the communion of the *Holy Ghost*, be with you all." 2 Cor. xiii, 14. There are other passages in which the sacred *three*, and *three* only, are thus collocated as objects of *equal* trust and honor, and as being *equally* the *fountain* and *source* of grace and benediction. But the strongest proof which the Scriptures afford of the doctrine of the Trinity is in the fact,

3. THAT IN NUMEROUS INSTANCES TWO PERSONS ARE SPOKEN OF AS BEING ASSOCIATED WITH GOD IN HIS PERFECTIONS.

We have now shown that while the Unity of God is to be considered a fundamental doctrine of the Scriptures, the very names of God, as given in the revelation which he has made of himself, have plural forms, and are connected with plural modes of speech; that other indications of plurality are given in various passages; and that this plurality is restricted to *three*. On those texts, however, which in their terms denote a plurality and a Trinity, we do not wholly or chiefly rely. There are multiplied instances in which *two* distinct persons are spoken of, sometimes connectedly and sometimes separately, as being associated with God in his incommunicable perfections, and as performing works of unequivocal Divine majesty and infinite power; and thus that *triunity* of the Godhead is manifested which the Church has, in all ages, adored and magnified. This, then, is the great proof upon which the doctrine mainly rests. The first of these two persons is the *Son*, the second the *Holy Spirit*.

(1.) *Of the* SON, *it may be observed that he is invested with all the titles and attributes of God;* that he is eminently known, both in the Old Testament and in the New, as the Son of God; that he became incarnate in our nature, and wrought miracles by his own power; that he authoritatively forgave sin; that he is seated upon the throne of the universe, in the possession of all power in heaven and in earth; that he is worshiped both by men and angels; and that he will raise the dead at the last day, judge the world, and, finally, determine the everlasting state of the righteous and the wicked.

(2.) *As to the Divine character of the Holy Spirit, it is equally explicit.* To him also are ascribed the names, the attributes, and the works of Jehovah; and, finally, he is associated with the Father and the Son in the Christian form of baptism, and in the apostolic form of benediction, as being, equally with them, the source and fountain of grace and blessedness. These decisive points we shall soon proceed to establish by express declarations both of the Old and the New Testament. When that is done, the argument will then be, that as, on the one hand, there is but ONE GOD; and as, on the other, *three persons* are, in unequivocal language, and by unequivocal circumstances, declared to be *Divine;* therefore, these THREE PERSONS ARE ONE GOD. This is the only conclusion that can harmonize the declarations of Scripture on this important subject.

Thus the Trinity is asserted, but the Unity of God is not obscured; while his Unity is confessed without a denial of the Trinity. It is not, however, the Socinian notion of Unity. Theirs is the Unity of *one*, ours the Unity of *three*. Nor do we believe, as they seem to suppose, that the Divine Essence is *divisible*, or that it is *participated* by three persons, and *shared among* them; but that it is wholly and undividedly *possessed* by each. Whether, therefore, we address our prayers and adorations to the Father, the Son, or the Holy Ghost, we address *the same adorable Being, the one living and true God*.

A few remarks on the *difficulties* in which the doctrine of the Trinity is supposed to involve its advocates may properly close this chapter.

Mere difficulty in conceiving of what is wholly proper and peculiar to God forms no objection to a doctrine. It is more rationally to be considered as a presumption of its truth, since in the nature of God there must be mysteries far above the reach of the human mind. All his natural attributes, though of some of them we have images in ourselves, are utterly incomprehensible; and the *manner* of his existence cannot be less so. All attempts, however, to show that the doctrine implies a contradiction have failed. A contradiction is only where two contraries are predicated of the *same thing*, and in the *same respect*. Let this be kept in view, and the sophism of our opponents will be easily detected. They urge that the same thing cannot be *three* and *one;* that is, if the proposition has any meaning at all, not in the *same respect*. The three *persons* cannot be one *person*, nor can the one *God* be three *Gods*. But it is no contradiction to say that in *different respects* the three may be one; that is, that in respect to *persons* they may be *three*, and in respect to *Godhead, essence,* or *nature*, they may be *one*.

As for *difficulties*, we shall certainly not be relieved by running either to the Arian or the Socinian hypothesis. The one ascribes the creation and government of the world, not to the Deity, but to a *creature;* for however exalted the Arian inferior Deity may be, he is a creature still. The other makes a mere man the creator of all things; for whatever is meant by the Word that "was made flesh," he is the very same Word by whom "all things were made."

CHAPTER IV.

THE DIVINITY OF CHRIST.

The result of our observations on the doctrine of the Trinity is, that there are three persons in the Divine Essence, or that the Father, Son, and Holy Ghost are the same in substance, and equal in power and glory. If we have succeeded in proving that a Trinity is revealed in the Scriptures, we might proceed without delay to the consideration of other subjects, fully assured that he who redeemed us with his own blood, and he who is the Author of our holiness and consolation, are not to be ranked among creatures, but are entitled to the same religious honor which is due to the Father. There are, however, various considerations which point out the propriety of suspending our progress, and of engaging in a more minute inquiry into the divinity of the Son and of the Holy Spirit.

The Supreme Divinity of our Lord Jesus Christ will be made the subject of this chapter. In proof of this doctrine we will proceed to show that he existed previous to his incarnation; that he was the Jehovah of the Old Testament; that to him are ascribed Divine titles, Divine attributes, and Divine works; and that he is the object of Divine worship.

§ 1. *The Pre-existence of Christ.*

By establishing, on scriptural authority, the pre-existence of our Lord, we take the first step in the demonstration of his absolute divinity. His pre-existence, indeed, simply considered, does not evince his Godhead, and is not, therefore, a proof against the *Arian* hypothesis; but it destroys the *Socinian* notion, that he was a *mere man*. To prove that he existed prior to his incarnation, it will only be necessary to weigh the following scriptural propositions.

1. He was before John the Baptist.—" He that cometh after me is preferred before me, for *he was before me*." John i, 15.

The Socinian exposition is: "The Christ, who is to begin his ministry after me, has, by the Divine appointment, been preferred before me, because he is my chief or principal." Thus they interpret the last clause, "For he was before me," in the sense of *dignity*, and not of *time*; though St. John uses the same word to denote priority of time in several places in his Gospel.* The verb in this clause sufficiently fixes πρωτός in the sense of priority of time. Had it referred to the

---

* See in the original, John viii, 7; xv, 18; xx, 4, 8.

rank and dignity of Christ it would not have been ην, "he WAS," but εστι, "he IS before me."

2. HE WAS BEFORE ABRAHAM.—Thus our Lord declared: "Before Abraham was, I am." John viii, 58.

Whether the verb ειμι, "*I am*," may be understood to be equivalent to the incommunicable name *Jehovah*, shall be considered in another place. The obvious sense of the passage is, Before Abraham was, or was born, I was in existence. Our Lord had declared that Abraham rejoiced to see his day. "Then said the Jews unto him, Thou art not yet fifty years old, and hast thou seen Abraham?" To this he solemnly replied, "Verily, verily, I say unto you, before Abraham was, I am." I had priority of existence, with a continuation of it to the present time. Nor did the Jews mistake his meaning, but being filled with indignation at so manifest a claim to divinity, "they took up stones to stone him."

How, then, do the Socinians dispose of this passage? The two hypotheses on which they have rested, for one would not suffice, are, *first*, "that Christ existed before Abraham had become, according to the import of his name, the Father of many nations; that is, before the Gentiles were called." But this was as true of the Jews with whom Christ was conversing as it was of himself. The *second* is: "Before Abraham was born, I am *he;* that is, the Christ, in the destination and appointment of God." But this was not declaring anything that was peculiar to Christ; since the existence, and the part which every one of his hearers was to act, were as much in the destination and appointment of God as his own. These opinions, therefore, are too absurd to require a formal refutation.

3. CHRIST CAME DOWN FROM HEAVEN.—Thus he declares: "I am the living bread which came down from heaven." John vi, 51. "No man hath ascended up to heaven, but he that came down from heaven, even the Son of man, which is in heaven." John iii, 13. Socinius and his early disciples, in order to account for these phrases, supposed that Christ, between the time of his birth and entrance upon his office, was translated to heaven, and remained there some time, that he might see and hear what he was to publish to the world. But modern Socinians, finding the unreasonable position of their elder brethren to be entirely destitute of proof, resolve the whole into *figure*. They tell us that our Lord's words do not necessarily imply a literal ascent and descent, but merely "that he alone was admitted to an intimate knowledge of the Divine will, and was commissioned to reveal it to men."*

In these passages, which so clearly teach the pre-existence of Christ, there are two phrases to be accounted for: *ascending into heaven*, and *coming down from heaven*. If to be "admitted to an intimate knowledge of the Divine will" were the sense of the former, it would not

* BELSHAM'S "Calm Inquiry."

be true that "*no man*" had thus ascended but "the Son of man;" since Moses and all the prophets in succession had been admitted to a knowledge of the Divine counsels, and had been commissioned to reveal them to men. Allowing, therefore, the principle of the Socinian gloss, it is totally inapplicable to the texts in question, and is, in fact, directly refuted by them.

But their principle of interpretation is false. For, whatever the phrase, *ascending into heaven*, may be supposed to signify, *coming down from heaven* must signify the opposite if we abide by the figure. But the latter phrase, they say, means, "to be commissioned to reveal the will of God to man."* If so, the two phrases, which are manifestly opposed to each other, lose all their opposition in the interpretation, which is sufficient to show that it is, as to both, entirely gratuitous, arbitrary, and contradictory. Now, allowing Socinians all they wish to establish as to the first clause—that *to go up into heaven* means *to learn and become acquainted with the counsels of God*—what must follow if they were to reason justly upon their own principles? Plainly this: that *to come down from heaven* being precisely the opposite of the former, must mean *to unlearn or to lose the knowledge of those counsels.*

Another passage which may be quoted in this connection is John vi, 62. Our Lord had told the Jews that he was the bread of life which "*came down from heaven.*" This they understood *literally*, and therefore asked: "Is not this the son of Joseph, whose father and mother we know? how is it, then, that he saith, *I came down from heaven.*" His disciples, too, so understood his words, for they also "murmured." But our Lord, so far from removing that impression, strengthens the assertion, and makes his profession a stumbling-block still more formidable. "Doth this offend you? What and if ye shall see the Son of man ascend up WHERE HE WAS BEFORE?" The occasion, therefore, fixes the sense of the passage beyond all perversion.

4. CHRIST CLAIMS A GLORIOUS EXISTENCE ANTECEDENT TO THE WORLD.—" And now, O Father, glorify thou me with thine own self, *with the glory which I had with thee before the world was.*" John xvii, 5. Whatever this glory was, it was possessed by Christ "before the world was;" or, as he afterward expresses it, "before the foundation of the world." But if he was with the Father, and had a glory with him "before the world was," then had he an existence, not only before his incarnation, but before the very "foundation of the world."

The Socinian gloss is, "The glory which I had with thee, in thy immutable decree, before the world was, or which thou didst decree before the world was, to give me." But the words rendered "which I had with thee" cannot bear any such sense, and the occasion was too peculiar to admit of any mystical, forced, or para-

* BELSHAM's "Calm Inquiry."

bolic modes of speech. It was in the hearing of his disciples, just before he went out into the garden, that these words were spoken. There, in a solemn act of devotion, he declares to the Father that he had a glory with him before the world was, and prays that he might be reinstated in that former glory. The language is so explicit, that if there were no other proof in the whole New Testament of the pre-existence of Christ, this single passage would establish it.

Whatever, therefore, the true nature of our Lord Jesus Christ may be, we have at least discovered, from testimonies which no criticism and no unlicensed and paraphrastic comments have been able to shake or obscure, that he had an existence previous to his incarnation, and previous to the very "foundation of the world."

§ 2. *Christ, the Jehovah of the Old Testament.*

In reading the Scriptures of the Old Testament, it is impossible not to mark with serious attention the frequent visible appearances of God to the patriarchs and prophets, and, what is still more singular, his visible residence in a cloud of glory, both among the Jews in the wilderness, and in their sacred tabernacle and temple. The fact of such appearances cannot be disputed, and in order to point out its bearing upon the divinity of Christ it will be necessary to establish three propositions, namely:

1. THE PERSON WHO MADE THESE APPEARANCES WAS TRULY A DIVINE PERSON.—The proofs of this are, that he bears the name of Jehovah, God, and other Divine appellations; and that he dwelt among the Israelites as the object of their supreme worship.

(1.) *He bears the name of Jehovah and God.*—When the angel of the Lord found Hagar in the wilderness, "she called the name of *Jehovah* that spake unto her, Thou God seest me." Gen. xvi, 13. One of the three persons in human form who appeared to Abraham in the plains of Mamre is called Jehovah. "And JEHOVAH said, Shall I hide from Abraham that thing which I do?" Two of the three departed, but he to whom this high appellation is given remained; for "Abraham stood yet before JEHOVAH." This Jehovah is also called by Abraham "the Judge of all the earth," and the account of the solemn interview is thus given by the sacred historian: "The Lord (JEHOVAH) went his way, as soon as he had left communing with Abraham." Gen. xviii, 33.

This Divine person appeared to Jacob on several occasions. After one of these manifestations he said, "Surely the Lord (JEHOVAH) is in this place;" and after another, "I have seen God face to face." Gen. xxviii, 16; xxxii, 30. The same Jehovah was made visible to Moses, and gave him his commission. "God said unto Moses, I AM THAT I AM: and he said, Thus shalt thou say unto the children of Israel,

I AM hath sent me unto you." Exod. iii, 14. The same Jehovah went before the Israelites in a pillar of cloud by day, and in a pillar of fire by night; and by him the law was given, amid terrible displays of power and majesty, from Mount Sinai. "Did ever people hear the voice of *God* speaking out of the midst of the fire, as thou hast heard, and live?" Deut. iv, 33.

(2.) *This Jehovah dwelt among the Israelites as the object of their supreme worship.*—He commanded them to build him a sanctuary, that he might reside among them; and when it was erected he took possession of it in a visible form, which was called "the glory of the Lord." There the SHECHINAH, the visible token of the presence of Jehovah, rested above the ark. There he was consulted on all occasions, and there he received their worship from age to age. Both in their tabernacle and temple services he was constantly celebrated as JEHOVAH, the God of Israel, the God of their fathers, and the object of their own exclusive *hope* and *trust*.

To this it is objected, that this personage is also called "the ANGEL of the Lord." This is true; but if "the angel of the Lord" is the same person as he who is called Jehovah, the same as he who gave the law in *his own name*, then it is clear that the term "angel" does not, in this application of it, indicate a created being, that it is not a designation of *nature* but of *office*, and that it is not inconsistent with absolute divinity.

It will be easy to show that Jehovah and "the angel of the Lord," when used in this eminent sense, denote the same person. Jacob says, "The angel of God spake unto me in a dream, saying, I am the God of Bethel." Gen. xxxi, 11, 12. Upon his death-bed he calls this same Divine person both *God* and *Angel*. "The *God* which fed me all my life long unto this day, the angel which redeemed me from all evil, bless the lads." Gen. xlviii, 15, 16. The prophet Hosea says of Jacob that "He had power with *God;* yea, he had power over the *angel*, and prevailed. He found him in Bethel, and there he spake with us; even the *Lord God of hosts.*" Hos. xii, 3–5. Here the same person is called God, Angel, and Lord God of hosts. "The *angel of the Lord* called unto Abraham out of heaven the second time, and said, By myself have I sworn, saith the *Lord*, (JEHOVAH,) for because thou hast done this thing." Gen. xxii, 15, 16. It was the *angel of the Lord* that appeared to Moses in a flame of fire, but it was this same angel that said to him, "I am the *God* of thy father, the *God* of Abraham, the *God* of Isaac, and the *God* of Jacob." Exod. iii, 6. St. Stephen, in alluding to this part of the history of Moses, in his speech before the council, says, "There appeared to him in the wilderness of Mount Sinai *an angel of the Lord* in a flame of fire," showing that this phraseology was in use among the Jews in his day, and that this angel was regarded as the Jehovah who gave the law; for he adds, Moses "was in the

Church in the wilderness, with the *angel* which spoke to him in Mount Sinai."

These Scriptures prove, beyond the shadow of a doubt, that the angel of Jehovah is constantly represented as Jehovah himself, and, therefore, as a Divine person. Those, however, who deny the divinity of our Lord, endeavor to evade the force of this argument, according to their respective creeds. The Arians, who think the appearing angel to have been Christ, but who yet deny his being Jehovah, assume that this glorious but created being personated the Deity, and as his embassador and representative, spoke by his authority, and took his name.

The answer to this is, that though embassadors speak in the name of their masters, they do not apply the names and titles of their masters to themselves; that *created* angels, mentioned in Scripture as appearing to men, declare that they were sent by God, and never personate him; that the prophets uniformly acknowledge their commission to be from God; that God himself asserts, "Jehovah is my name, and my glory *will I not give to another;*" and yet, that the appearing angel calls himself, as we have seen, by this incommunicable name in almost innumerable instances; and that he claims and receives the *exclusive* worship both of the patriarchs, to whom he occasionally appeared, and the Jews, among whom he visibly resided for ages. To suppose him therefore to to be a created being, is to suppose the religion of the Bible to be a system of idolatry.

If the Arian account of the angel of Jehovah is untenable, the Socinian notion will be found to be equally unsupported, and indeed ridiculous. Dr. Priestley assumes the marvelous doctrine of "occasional personality," and thinks that "in some cases angels were nothing more than *temporary appearances*, and no permanent beings, the mere organs of the Deity, assumed for the purpose of making himself known." He speaks therefore of "a power occasionally emitted, and then taken back again into its source;" of this power being vested with a *temporary personality*, and thinks this possible! Little cause had the doctor and his adherents to talk of the mystery and absurdity of the doctrine of the Trinity, who can make a *person* out of a *power*, emitted and then drawn back again to its source; a *temporary person*, without individual subsistence! The wildness of this fiction is its own refutation. But that the angel of Jehovah was not this temporary occasional person, is made evident by Jacob's calling him the angel of the Lord who had fed him all his life long; and by this also that the same *person* who was called by himself and by the Jews "the God of Abraham, of Isaac, and of Jacob," was the God of the chosen people in *all* their generations.

Mr. Belsham's theory is that "the angel of the Lord was the visible symbol of the Divine presence;" and this opinion commonly obtains among Socinians. This notion, however, involves a whole train of absurdities. The phrase, the "angel of Jehovah," is not accounted for by a visible symbol, unless that symbol be considered as distinct from Jehovah. We have then the name Jehovah given to a cloud, a light, a fire. The fire is the *angel of the Lord*, and yet the angel of the Lord calls to Moses *out of the fire*. This visible symbol says to Abraham, "By MYSELF I have sworn," for these are said to be the words of the angel of Jehovah; and this angel, the visible symbol, spake to Moses on Mount Sinai. Such are the absurdities which flow from error! Most clearly, therefore, is it determined on the testimony of several Scriptures, and by necessary induction from the circumstances attending the numerous appearances of the angel of Jehovah in the Old Testament, that the person thus manifesting himself, and thus receiving supreme worship, was not a created angel, as the Arians would have it, nor an *atmospheric appearance*, the theory of modern Socinians, but that he was a DIVINE PERSON.

2. THIS DIVINE PERSON WAS NOT GOD THE FATHER.—We do not claim that the Father never manifested himself to men, as distinct from the Son; for this is contradicted by Scripture testimonies.* It is amply sufficient for the argument with which we are now concerned to prove that the angel of the Lord, whose appearances are so often recorded, is *not* the Father. This is clear from his appellation *angel*, with respect to which there can be but two interpretations. It is either a name descriptive of *nature* or of *office*. In the first view it is generally employed in the sacred Scriptures to designate one of an order of intelligences superior to man, but still *finite* and *created*. We have, however, already proved that the angel of the Lord is not a *creature;* and he cannot therefore be called an angel with reference to his *nature*.

The term must then be considered as a term of *office*. He is called the *angel* of the Lord because he was the *messenger* of the Lord—because he was *sent* to do his will and to be his visible image and representative. His office, therefore, under this appellation, was ministerial; but ministration is never attributed to the Father. He who was *sent* must be a distinct person from him *by whom* he was sent; the *messenger* from him whose *message* he brought, and whose will he performed. The angel of Jehovah is therefore a different person from the Jehovah whose messenger he was; and yet the angel himself is Jehovah, and, as we have proved, truly Divine. Thus does the Old Testament most clearly reveal to us, in the case of Jehovah and the angel of Jehovah, *two Divine persons*, while it still maintains its great fundamental principle, that there is but *one God*.

3. THE DIVINE PERSON SO OFTEN CALLED THE ANGEL OF THE LORD WAS THE PROMISED MESSIAH, *and is consequently* THE LORD AND SAVIOUR OF THE CHRISTIAN CHURCH.—We have seen that it was the angel of

* See Exod. xxiii, 20; Matt. iii, 17; xvii, 5.

the Lord who gave the law to the Israelites, and that in his *own name*, though still an *angel*, a *messenger* in the transaction; being at once servant and Lord, angel and Jehovah—circumstances which can only be explained on the hypothesis of his divinity, and for which neither Arianism nor Socinianism can give any solution. He was therefore the person who made the Mosaic covenant with the children of Israel. But the prophet Jeremiah says that the *new* covenant with Israel was to be made by the same person who had made the old. "Behold, the days come, saith the Lord, that *I will make* a new covenant with the house of Israel, and with the house of Judah; not according to the covenant that *I made* with their fathers, in the day that I took them by the hand, to bring them out of the land of Egypt." Jer. xxxi, 31, 32. The angel of Jehovah, who led the Israelites out of Egypt and gave them their law, is here plainly introduced as the author of the new covenant. But this new covenant, as we learn from the Epistle to the Hebrews,* is the Christian dispensation; and if Christ is its author, the Jehovah of the Old Testament and Christ of the New are the same Divine person.

Equally striking is the celebrated prediction of Malachi, the last of the Jewish prophets: "Behold, I will send my messenger, and he shall prepare the way before me; and the Lord, whom ye seek, shall suddenly come to his temple, even the messenger of the covenant whom ye delight in; behold, he shall come, saith the Lord of hosts." Mal. iii. 1. Here the prophet describes the coming Messiah, not only as the messenger of the covenant, but also as the Lord and Owner of the Jewish temple; and, consequently, as a Divine prince or governor—he shall "come to *his temple*." The Lord of any temple is the divinity to whose worship it is consecrated. The temple at Jerusalem, of which the prophet here speaks, was consecrated to the true and living God; and we have therefore the express testimony of Malachi that the Christ, the Deliverer, whose coming he announced, was no other than the Jehovah of the Old Testament.

This prophecy is expressly applied to Christ by St. Mark. "As it is written in the prophets, Behold, I send my messenger before thy face, which shall prepare thy way before thee." Mark i, 2. It follows from this that Jesus Christ is the Lord, the Lord of the temple, the messenger of the covenant mentioned in the prophecy. The appearing Jehovah of the Old Testament was the *King* of the Jews; their temple was HIS, because he resided in it; and he was the *messenger* of *their covenant*. But as all these characters are ascribed to Jesus Christ, the identity of the persons cannot be mistaken. One coincidence is singularly striking. It has been proved that the Angel Jehovah had his residence in the Jewish tabernacle and temple, and that he took possession of both at their dedication, suddenly filling them with his glory. On one occasion Jesus himself, though in his state of humiliation, came

* Heb. viii, 8–13.

in public procession to the temple at Jerusalem, and called it *his own;* thus at once declaring that he was the ancient and rightful Lord of the temple, and appropriating to himself this eminent prophecy.

It would be easy to multiply quotations in which the name Jehovah and other Divine titles are applied to the Messiah; and to show, moreover, that these very passages are applied, in the New Testament, to our Lord Jesus Christ. We will, however, notice only two others. The first is Isaiah xl, 3: "The voice of him that crieth in the wilderness, Prepare ye the way of the LORD, (JEHOVAH,) make straight in the desert a highway for our GOD." This prediction is applied, in the Christian Scriptures, to John the Baptist, as the harbinger of Christ; and it is, therefore, evident that our Lord is the person whom the prophet calls JEHOVAH and "*our* GOD."

The other passage is 1 Cor. x, 9: "Neither let us tempt Christ, as some of them (that is, the Jews in the wilderness) also tempted, and were destroyed of serpents." The pronoun αυτὸν, *him*, must be understood after "tempted," as referring to Christ just before mentioned. The Jews in the wilderness are here said to have tempted some person; and to understand by that person any other than Christ, who is just before mentioned, is against all grammar, which never allows, without absolute necessity, any other accusative to be understood with the verb than that of some person or thing previously mentioned in the same sentence. The conjunction καὶ, *also*, establishes this interpretation beyond a doubt. Neither let us tempt CHRIST as some of them ALSO tempted—tempted whom? The obvious answer is, *Christ.* If, therefore, the Israelites tempted Christ in the wilderness he is the Jehovah of the Old Testament.

It has now been established that the Angel Jehovah and Jesus Christ our Lord are the same person; and this is the first great argument by which his divinity is proved. He not only existed before his incarnation, but is seen at the head of the religious institutions of his Church up to the earliest ages. In every manifestation of himself he has given evidence that he "thought it not robbery to be equal with God." No name is given to the Angel Jehovah which is not given to Jehovah Jesus. No attribute is ascribed to the one which is not ascribed to the other. The worship which was paid to the one by patriarchs and prophets was paid to the other by evangelists and apostles; and the Scriptures declare them to be the same august person, *the Redeeming Angel, the Redeeming Kinsman, and the Redeeming* GOD.

§ 3. *Divine Titles ascribed to Christ.*

The next argument in support of the divinity of Christ is drawn from the titles which are ascribed to him in the sacred volume. If they are such as can designate a Divine Being, and a Divine Being *only*, then is

Christ truly Divine. To deny this conclusion would be to charge the word of truth with direct deception, and that, too, in a fundamental article of religion. This is our argument, and we will proceed to the illustration. Our attention will be directed to only four of the Divine titles which are ascribed to our Lord. These are, *Jehovah, Lord, God,* and *King of Israel.*

1. JEHOVAH.—That this name is applied to the Messiah in many passages of the Old Testament is admitted even by our opponents. But Dr. Priestley attempts to destroy the force of the argument deduced from this fact, by alleging that "several things in the Scriptures are called by the name of Jehovah; as, Jerusalem is called Jehovah our righteousness."* It is, however, a miserable pretense to meet this argument by asserting that the name Jehovah is sometimes given to places. It is so, but only in composition with some other word; as Jehovah-Jire, Jehovah-Nissi, Jehovah-Shallum. Such names are used, not as descriptive of particular localities, but as *memorials* of events connected with them, which mark the interposition and character of Jehovah himself. Thus: "Jehovah-Jire," *the Lord will see* or *provide,* referred to HIS interposition to save Isaac, and probably to the *provision* of the sacrifice of Christ. Nor is it true that Jerusalem is called "Jehovah our righteousness." The parallel passage clearly shows that this is the name, not of Jerusalem, but of "THE BRANCH."†
No instance can be given in which a created being is called Jehovah in the Scriptures, or was so called among the Jews. The peculiar sacredness attached to this name among them was a sufficient guard against such an application of it in their common language; and as for the Scriptures, they explicitly represent it as peculiar to divinity itself. "I am JEHOVAH, that is my name, and my glory will I *not* give to *another.*" Isa. xlii, 8. "Thou, whose NAME ALONE is JEHOVAH, art the Most High above all the earth." Psa. lxxxiii, 18.

We see, then, that this is the peculiar and appropriate name of God, that name by which he is distinguished from all other beings, and which imports perfections so exclusively belonging to the living and true God that it cannot, in truth, be applied to any other being. This name, however, is *solemnly* and *repeatedly* given to the *Messiah;* and, unless we can suppose Scripture to contradict itself, by making that a peculiar name of God which is not peculiar to him, and by establishing an inducement to that idolatry which it so sternly condemns, then this adorable name itself declares the absolute divinity of him who is invested with it.

2. LORD.—Our Lord's disciples not only applied to him those passages of the Old Testament in which the Messiah is called Jehovah, but they saluted and worshiped him by the title κυριος, LORD, which is of precisely the same original import. We admit that it is sometimes

* History of "Early Opinions." † Jer. xxiii, 5, 6; xxxiii, 16.

used as the translation of other names of God, which import simply dominion, and that it is applied also to merely human masters and rulers; but, in its *highest sense*, it is universally allowed to belong to God. If in this *highest sense* it is applied to Christ, then are we to regard it as denoting true and absolute divinity.

The *first* proof of this is, that both in the Septuagint and by the writers of the New Testament, κύριος is the term by which the name Jehovah is translated. In all those passages, therefore, in which the Messiah is called by that peculiar title of divinity, we have the authority of the LXX for applying it in its full and highest signification to Jesus Christ, who is that Messiah. Accordingly, the New Testament writers apply this appellation to their Master when they quote these prophetic passages as fulfilled in him. They found it used in the Greek version of the Old Testament, in its *highest possible import*, as a rendering of Jehovah. Had they thought Jesus to be less than God, they could not have given him a title which would have misled their readers, unless they had intimated that they did not use it as a title of divinity, but in its lowest sense, as a term of merely human courtesy, or at most, of human dominion. But we have no such intimation; and, if they wrote under Divine inspiration, it follows that they used it as being fully equivalent to the title JEHOVAH itself, as their quotations will show.

St. Matthew quotes, and applies to Christ, Isaiah xl, 3: "The voice of one crying in the wilderness, Prepare ye the way of the LORD, κυρίου." The other Evangelists make the same application of it, representing John as the herald of Jesus, the Jehovah of the prophet, and their κύριος, *Lord*. On this point St. Paul also adds his testimony, Romans x, 13: "Whosoever shall call on the name of the LORD (κυρίου) shall be saved," which is quoted from Joel ii, 32: "Whosoever shall call on the name of JEHOVAH shall be delivered."

But, *secondly*, even when the title κύριος, LORD, is not employed as the rendering of the name JEHOVAH, but is used as a common appellation of Christ, it is so connected with other terms, and with circumstances which clearly imply divinity, as to afford additional proof that the disciples themselves considered it as a Divine *title*, and intended that it should be so understood by others. It is put *absolutely*, and by way of *eminence*, "THE LORD." Christ is called by St. Luke "the LORD GOD;" and Thomas adoringly addresses him, "My LORD and my GOD." When κύριος is used to express dominion, that dominion is represented as *absolute* and *universal*, and therefore *Divine*. Hence Peter declares of Jesus Christ that "he is (κύριος) LORD of all." Acts x, 36.

3. GOD.—That this title is ascribed to Christ, even the adversaries of his divinity are obliged to confess. It is indeed said, that the term is sometimes used in an inferior sense; but this proves nothing against the Deity of Christ, for it must still be allowed that it is *generally* used in

Scripture to designate the Divine Being. The question is, therefore, limited to this: Is our Lord called *God* in the highest sense of that appellation?

Before we proceed to the examination of this question, it will be necessary to show that the term *God*, in its highest sense, involves the idea of absolute divinity. This has been denied by Sir Isaac Newton and Dr. Samuel Clarke, who considered it a *relative* term, importing nothing more than dominion. But if we trace the Scripture notion of what is *truly* and *properly* God, we shall find it made up of these several ideas: infinite wisdom, invincible power, immutability, all-sufficiency, and the like. These are the foundation of *dominion*, which is a secondary consideration; but it must be nothing less than dominion *supreme*, which will accord with the Scripture notion of *God*. It is not merely that of a *ruler*, a *governor*, a *lord*, or a *protector;* but a *Sovereign* Ruler, an *Omniscient* and *Omnipresent* Governor, an *Almighty* Lord, an eternal, immutable, and all-sufficient *Creator, Preserver*, and *Protector*. Whatever falls short of this is not *properly* God, in the Scripture import of that term, and cannot be so denominated, except by way of figure.

If *God* were merely a relative term, having reference to *subjects*, it would necessarily follow, either that some of those subjects had an eternal existence, or that there was a time when there was no God. We have, however, the express testimony of Divine truth, that it is not dominion *only*, but absolute divinity, that is designated by the term. Thus, "Before the mountains were brought forth, or ever thou hadst formed the earth or the world, even from everlasting to everlasting, thou art GOD." Psa. xc, 2. Here the term *God* is applied to that eternal Being who "formed the earth and the world." He is declared to be GOD "from everlasting," and consequently before any creature existed, and so before he had any *subjects*, or exercised any *dominion*.

The import of the term GOD, in its highest sense, being thus shown to include all the excellences and glories of the Divine nature, if in this sense it is ascribed to Christ, it will prove, not as Arians would have it, his *dominion* only, but his divinity. Nor will it set aside this conclusion to say, that men are sometimes called gods; for in the New Testament the term God is never applied in the singular to any man.

Let us then adduce a few passages of Scripture in which this appellation is applied to Jesus Christ. Matt. i, 23: "Behold, a virgin shall be with child, and shall bring forth a son, and they shall call his name EMMANUEL, which being interpreted is, GOD with us."

John i, 1: "In the beginning was the WORD, and the WORD was with GOD, and the WORD was GOD."

John xx, 28: "And Thomas answered and said unto him, My Lord and my GOD."

Romans ix, 5: "And of whom, as concerning the flesh, Christ came, who is over all, GOD blessed forever."

Titus ii, 13: "Looking for that blessed hope, and the glorious appearing of the great GOD and our Saviour Jesus Christ."

Hebrews i, 8: "But unto the Son he saith, Thy throne, O GOD, is for ever and ever."

1 John v, 20. "And we are in him that is true, even in his Son Jesus Christ. This is the true GOD, and eternal life."

4. KING OF ISRAEL.—This title has an allusion to Christ's pre-existence, and to his sovereignty over Israel under the law. It has been already established that the "*Jehovah*," "the *Holy One of Israel*," "the *Lord of hosts*," "the *King of the Jews*" of the Old Testament, is not the Father, but another Divine person, who, in the New Testament, is affirmed to be *Jesus Christ*. This being the view of the sacred writers of the evangelical dispensation, it is evident that they could not use the appellation "KING OF ISRAEL" in a lower sense than that in which it stands in the Old Testament, and it is equally evident that the Jews understood it to imply divinity.

Nathanael, upon a satisfactory proof of Christ's Messiahship, exclaimed, "Thou art the Son of God, thou art the KING OF ISRAEL." John i, 49. While our Saviour hung upon the cross, the chief priests, the scribes, and the elders said, "If he be the KING OF ISRAEL, let him now come down from the cross, and we will believe in him." Matt. xxvii, 42.

§ 4. *Divine Attributes are ascribed to Christ.*

Having considered the import of some of the titles applied to our Lord in the Scriptures, and having proved that they imply divinity, we may next consider the *attributes* which are ascribed to him. If, to names and lofty titles which imply divinity, we find added attributes never given to creatures, and from which all creatures are excluded, the Deity of Christ will be established beyond reasonable controversy. No argument can be more conclusive than this. Of the essence of Deity we know nothing, but that he is a Spirit. He is made known to us by his attributes, and it is from them we learn that there is an *essential* distinction between him and his creatures. He has attributes which they have not, and those which they have in common with him he possesses in an absolutely perfect degree. From this it follows, that HIS is a *peculiar* nature, a nature *sui generis*, to which no creature can possibly approximate. Should, then, these same attributes be found ascribed to Christ as explicitly and literally as to the Father, it will follow of necessity that, the attributes being the same, the essence must be the same, and that this essence is the exclusive nature of the θεοτης, or Godhead.

Of the peculiar attributes of Deity which are ascribed to Jesus Christ we may notice,

1. ETERNITY.—Isaiah calls him "The mighty God, the *Everlasting Father*, the Prince of Peace." Isa. ix, 6. The phrase "Everlasting Father" is variously rendered by the best orthodox critics; but every rendering is consistent with the application of a positive eternity to the Messiah, of whom this is evidently a prediction. Christ declares of himself, "I am THE FIRST and THE LAST;" and again, "I am Alpha and Omega, the beginning and the ending, saith the Lord, which is, and which was, and which is to come, the Almighty." Rev. i, 8, 17. Now, it is by these very terms that the eternity of God is declared. "Before me there was no God formed, neither shall there be after me." Isa. xliii, 10. "I am the first, and I am the last; and besides me there is no God." Isa. xliv, 6. These titles clearly indicate that the Being to whom they properly belong had no beginning, and will have no end; and as they are explicitly and absolutely claimed by Christ, they are proofs of his eternity.

2. OMNIPRESENCE.—Our Lord declares himself to be, at the same time, both in heaven and upon the earth; which is surely a property of divinity alone. "No man hath ascended up to heaven, but he that came down from heaven, even the Son of man which is in heaven." John iii, 13. Again, "Where two or three are gathered together in my name, *there am I in the midst of them.*" Matt. xviii, 20.

How futile is the Socinian comment on this text, that this promise is to be "limited to the apostolic age!" Were that even granted, what would the concession avail? In that age the disciples met in the name of their Lord many times in the week and in many parts of the world at the same time. He, therefore, who could be "in the midst of them," whenever and wherever they assembled, must be *omnipresent*. The text is as literal a declaration of Christ's presence everywhere with his true worshipers, as that similar promise of Jehovah to the Israelites: "In all places where I record my name, I will come unto thee, and I will bless thee." Exod. xx, 24. At the very moment, too, of Christ's ascension, and when, as to his bodily presence, he was about to leave his disciples, he promised still to be with them, calling their attention to this promise by an emphatic exclamation: "Lo, I AM WITH YOU ALWAY, even to the end of the world." Matt. xxviii, 20.

3. OMNISCIENCE.—This is an attribute which cannot be ascribed to a creature; for though it may be difficult to say how far the knowledge of the highest order of intelligent creatures may be extended, yet there are two kinds of knowledge which God solemnly and exclusively claims as peculiar to himself. The *first* is a perfect knowledge of the thoughts and purposes of the human heart. "I the Lord search the heart, I try the reins." Jer. xvii, 10. "Thou, even thou only, knowest the hearts of all the children of men." 1 Kings viii, 39. This knowledge is

attributed to our Lord, and claimed by him; not, however, as a supernatural *gift*, but as an original attribute. Hence St. John declares that "HE KNEW ALL MEN, and needed not that any should testify of man; for HE KNEW WHAT WAS IN MAN." John ii, 24, 25. After his exaltation he claimed this prerogative, in the full style and majesty of the Old Testament Jehovah. "And all the Churches shall know that *I am he which* SEARCHETH THE REINS AND HEARTS." Rev. ii, 23.

The *second* kind of knowledge, to which reference has been made, is the knowledge of *futurity;* which is so peculiar to Deity that God distinguishes himself from all the false divinities of the heathen by this circumstance alone. "I am God, and there is none else; I am God, and there is none like me; declaring the end from the beginning, and from ancient times the things that are not yet done." Isa. xlvi, 9, 10. This kind of knowledge is also ascribed to Christ. All the predictions which he uttered are in proof that he possessed this attribute; for they are nowhere referred to *inspiration*, the source to which all the prophets and apostles ascribed their prophetic gifts, but resulted from his own prescience. He "*knew from the beginning* who they were that believed not, and who should betray him." John vi, 64.

4. OMNIPOTENCE.—This also is peculiar to the Godhead; for, though power may be communicated to a creature, yet a finite capacity must limit the communication; nor can it exist in an infinite degree any more than wisdom, except in an infinite nature. Christ claims "all power in heaven and in earth;" and in Rev. i, 8, he is expressly styled "THE ALMIGHTY." To the Jews he said, "What things soever he [the Father] doeth, THESE ALSO DOETH THE SON LIKEWISE." John v, 19.

Thus we have seen that the Scriptures ascribe to our Lord Jesus Christ *Eternity, Omnipresence, Omniscience,* and *Omnipotence*—attributes which prove him to be "The true God;" and we may now close the argument with his own remarkable declaration: "ALL THINGS which the Father hath ARE MINE." John xvi, 15. If the Son possess all things that belong to the Father, then he possesses all the attributes and perfections of the Father, and must necessarily be of the same nature, substance, and Godhead.

§ 5. *Divine Works are ascribed to Christ.*

This argument is confirmatory of the foregoing; for if acts have been done by Christ which, in the nature of things, cannot be performed by any creature, however exalted, then must he be truly God. That such works are ascribed to him in the Holy Scriptures, we will now proceed to show.

1. CREATION.—The Socinians themselves acknowledge that the production of things out of nothing is possible only to Divine power; and they, therefore, attempt to prove that the creation of which Christ is

said to be the author, is a *moral* creation. To correct this error it is only necessary to exhibit two or three passages of Scripture which evidently ascribe to him the whole physical creation. St. John affirms, in the introduction of his Gospel, that "all things [without limitation or restriction] were made by" the Divine Word; and that "without him was not *anything* made that was made." If he had reference to a *moral*, and not a *physical* creation, he could not have expressed himself in this manner without intending to mislead: a supposition which is equally contrary to his piety and to his inspiration. His meaning must, therefore, be, that there is no created object which had not Christ for its creator.

But the apostle shows most clearly that the physical creation was the work of Christ, by asserting that "THE WORLD WAS MADE BY HIM;" that world into which he came as "the light;" that world *in* which he was when he was made flesh; that *world* which "knew him not." It matters nothing to the argument whether "the world" be understood of men or of the material world. On either supposition "the world was made by him," and the creation was, therefore, *physical*. In neither case could the creation be a *moral* one, for the *material* world is incapable of a moral renewal; and the world which "knew not" Christ, if understood of *men*, was not renewed by a moral creation, but was unregenerate.

Another passage, equally explicit in ascribing to Christ the physical creation, is found in Heb. i, 2: "By whom also HE MADE THE WORLDS." "God," says the apostle, "hath in these last days spoken unto us by his SON, whom he hath appointed heir of all things;" and he then proceeds to give *farther* information in regard to the nature and dignity of the personage thus denominated the "SON" and "HEIR." In order to prove him greater than angels, who are the greatest of all created beings, the apostle declares that "by him also God made the worlds." That the term "worlds" is here to be understood of the material universe, is evident from Heb. xi, 3: "Through faith we understand that the WORLDS were framed by the word of God, so that things which are seen were not made of things which do appear:" words which can only be understood of the physical creation.

Another consideration which fixes the meaning of the clause, "by whom also he made the worlds," is, that in the same chapter the apostle reiterates the doctrine of the creation of the world by Jesus Christ. "But unto THE SON he saith," not only, "Thy throne, O God, is for ever and ever;" but also, "Thou, Lord, [Jehovah,] in the beginning hast laid the foundation of the earth; and the heavens are the works of thine hands." This language is, beyond all controversy, addressed to Christ, and will forever attach to him, on the authority of inspiration, the title of "*Jehovah*," and array him in all the majesty of creative power and glory.

The only additional passage which it is necessary to adduce, in order to show that Christ is the creator of all things, and that the creation of which he is the author is not a *moral* but a *physical* creation; not the framing of the Christian dispensation, but the forming of the whole universe of creatures out of nothing, is Colossians i, 16, 17: "For by him were all things CREATED, that are in heaven, and that are in earth, visible and invisible, whether they be thrones, or dominions, or principalities, or powers; all things were created BY him and FOR him; and he is BEFORE all things." The terms here employed are an abundant refutation of the notion, that the creation mentioned is to be understood in a *moral* sense. The objects created are "all things in heaven and in earth;" and lest immaterial beings should be thought to be excluded, the apostle adds, "visible and invisible." And, lest things *invisible* should be understood of *inferior* angels only, to the exclusion of those of the higher orders, the apostle becomes still more particular, and adds, "whether they be thrones, or dominions, or principalities, or powers;" terms by which the Jews expressed the different orders of angels, and which are thus employed in the Scriptures.* The passage shows, moreover, that in the creation of all things Jesus Christ was both the *efficient* and the *final* cause, and not merely the *instrumental* cause, working by and for another. "All things were created BY him and FOR him."

2. PRESERVATION.—The sacred Scriptures declare that Jesus Christ is the preserver of all things as well as their creator, for "by him all things CONSIST," (συνεστηκε, *sunesteke*,) are kept together, or preserved from falling into confusion or annihilation. This is surely a Divine work; nor could it be said, consistent with reason and piety, that the universe is sustained by a created being. The same doctrine is taught in Heb. i, 3, where Christ is spoken of as "*upholding all things*" by the word of his power." Τὰ πάντα (*ta panta*) signifies the universe, which the Son of God bears up, or sustains, by his almighty word. If, then, to preserve the created universe is the work of JEHOVAH, as the Scriptures declare,† and if this work is ascribed to our Lord, there can remain no doubt whatever that he also is JEHOVAH.

3. THE FORGIVENESS OF SINS.—This is unquestionably one of the peculiar acts of God. In the manifest reason of the thing, no one can forgive but the party offended; and, as sin is the transgression of the law of God, he alone is the offended party, and, therefore, he only can forgive. *Mediately* others may *declare* his pardoning acts, or the conditions on which he proposes to forgive; but *authoritatively*, there can be no actual forgiveness of sins but by God himself.

But Christ forgives sins by his own authority, and therefore he is God. One single passage will prove this. "He said to the sick of the palsy, Son, be of good cheer, *thy sins be forgiven thee.*" Matt. ix, 2.

* See Eph. i, 21; Col. ii, 10.   † Neh. ix, 6; Psa. xxxvi, 6.

The scribes understood that he did this *authoritatively*, and that he thereby assumed a Divine prerogative. They, therefore, said among themselves, "This man blasphemeth." What then was the conduct of our Lord on that occasion? Did he admit that he only ministerially *declared*, in consequence of some revelation, that God had forgiven the sins of the paralytic? On the contrary, he performed a miracle to prove that the very right which they disputed was vested in him. "That ye may KNOW that the Son of man hath power on earth to forgive sins, then saith he to the sick of the palsy, Arise, take up thy bed, and go unto thine house." Matt. ix, 6.

4. THE RAISING OF THE DEAD.—It will be acknowledged by all, that to raise the dead is a Divine work. He only who first framed the human body, and connected with it a living spirit, can restore that body again to life, and bring back the soul from the invisible world to its original abode. It is "God who quickeneth the dead." Rom. iv, 17. But this power is claimed by Jesus Christ: "As the Father raiseth up the dead, and quickeneth them; even so the Son quickeneth whom he will." John v, 21. Here Christ explicitly assumes equal power with the Father, and the same uncontrolled and sovereign exercise of it in the restoration of life. This power was exerted by our Lord, while he sojourned upon the earth, in raising to life the daughter of Jairus, the widow's son, Lazarus, and others; but it will be more gloriously displayed at the end of time, in restoring to life the millions of the human race who shall then be sleeping in the dust. "The hour is coming, in which all that are in the graves shall hear his voice, and shall come forth." John v, 28, 29.

It may be objected that this work is not a decisive proof of divinity, because the dead were raised by some of the prophets and by the apostles of our Lord. To this it is only necessary to reply, that the prophets raised the dead *in the name* of the God of Israel, and the apostles *in the name* of Jesus Christ; but he performed this miracle of power in his own name, and spoke of himself in terms which no prophet or apostle would have dared to employ: "I am the resurrection and the life; he that believeth in me, though he were dead, yet shall he live." John xi, 25.

5. THE FINAL JUDGMENT IS ASCRIBED TO CHRIST.—The Scriptures declare that "the *Lord* (JEHOVAH) is our Judge," and that "every one of us shall give account of himself to *God;*" but they declare also, that "we must all appear before the judgment-seat of *Christ;*" that "before him shall be gathered all nations;" and that "he shall separate one from another, as a shepherd divideth his sheep from the goats."* To him who will pronounce the final sentence omniscience is necessary as well as omnipotence to execute it; for it will proceed not merely upon the external actions of men, but upon their motives and their

* See Isa. xxxiii, 22; Rom. xiv, 12; 2 Cor. v, 10; Matt. xxv, 32.

thoughts, which are known to him alone who searches the heart. Christ will indeed act in concurrence with the Father, who is hence said to judge the world by him; but this high office necessarily supposes him to be truly God.

§ 6. *Divine Worship is paid to Christ.*

It will be our business in this section, *first*, to establish the fact that Jesus Christ is the object of worship; and *secondly*, to consider the bearing which this fact has upon the doctrine of his Supreme Divinity.

1. CHRIST IS THE OBJECT OF WORSHIP.—Of this fact there are numerous proofs in the sacred Scriptures, a few of which we will notice.

(1.) *He was worshiped by his disciples prior to his ascension to heaven.*—" When he was come down from the mountain, great multitudes followed him; and behold, there came a leper and WORSHIPED HIM, saying, Lord, if thou wilt, thou canst make me clean." Matt. viii, 1, 2. When Jesus said to the man whom he had previously cured of blindness, "Dost thou believe on the Son of God? he answered and said, Who is he, Lord, that I might believe on him? And Jesus said unto him, Thou hast both seen him, and it is he that talketh with thee. And he said, Lord, I believe; and he WORSHIPED HIM." John ix, 35-38. He worshiped Christ, be it observed, under the character, "Son of God," a title which the Jews regarded as implying actual divinity. The worship paid by this man must, therefore, in its intention, have been supreme, for it was offered to a person who was acknowledged to be Divine, "the Son of God." Again, when the disciples, fully yielding to the demonstration of our Lord's Messiahship, arising out of a series of splendid miracles, recognized him *also* under his personal character, "they WORSHIPED HIM, saying, Of a truth thou art the Son of God." Matt. xiv, 33.

It is admitted that the word προσκυνέω, (*proskuneo,*) *to worship,* is sometimes used to express that lowly reverence with which, in the East, it has been always customary to salute persons of rank, and especially rulers and sovereigns; but it is frequently used to express also the worship of the Supreme Jehovah. Whether, then, it denotes an act of civil respect or of Divine adoration, the circumstances of the case must determine.

Our Lord could not have received the worship which was paid to him in the character of a civil governor. He had cautiously avoided the least intimation that he had any civil pretensions, or that his object was to make himself a king; and, therefore, to have suffered himself to be saluted with the homage proper to civil governors would have been a marked inconsistency. Nor could he have received it in compliance with the custom of the Jewish Rabbins, who exacted great external reverence from their disciples, for he sharply reproved their haughtiness, and their love of adulation and honor. The circumstances, then, which accompany these instances make it evident that the worship which the disciples paid to Christ was of the highest order—they *worshiped him as* GOD.

(2.) *Christ was worshiped by his disciples subsequent to his resurrection and ascension.*—When "he was parted from them, and carried up into heaven, they WORSHIPED HIM." Luke xxiv, 51, 52. Here the act must necessarily have been one of Divine adoration, since it was performed *after* "he was parted from them," and, therefore, it cannot be resolved into the customary token of *personal* respect paid to superiors, which was always exhibited in their *presence.*

When the apostles were assembled to fill the place of Judas, the lots being prepared " they prayed, and said, Thou, Lord, which knowest the hearts of all men, show whether of these two thou hast chosen." Acts i, 24. That this prayer was addressed to Christ is clear, from its being his special prerogative to choose his own apostles. They are, therefore, styled "apostles," not of the Father, but "of Jesus Christ." Here, then, is a direct act of worship, because it is an act of prayer, and our Lord is addressed as one who knows "the hearts of all men."

When Stephen, the protomartyr, was stoned, he prayed, "LORD JESUS, RECEIVE MY SPIRIT;" and again, "LORD, LAY NOT THIS SIN TO THEIR CHARGE." Acts vii, 59, 60. In the former petition he acknowledges Christ to be the disposer of the eternal states of men; in the latter, he acknowledges him to be the governor and judge of men, having power to remit, pass by, or visit their sins. These are so manifestly Divine acts that Stephen must have prayed to Christ, believing him to be truly GOD.

St. Paul, in that affliction which he metaphorically describes by "a thorn in the flesh," "besought the Lord thrice, that it might depart from" him; and the answer shows that "*the Lord*" to whom he addressed his prayer was CHRIST; for he adds, "And he said unto me, My grace is sufficient for thee: for my strength is made perfect in weakness. Most gladly therefore will I rather glory in my infirmities, that the POWER OF CHRIST may rest upon me." 2 Cor. xii, 7–9. The invoking of Christ was not only practiced by the apostle himself, as several passages show;* but is adduced by him as a distinctive characteristic of Christians, so that among all the primitive Churches this practice must have been universal. "Unto the Church of God which is at Corinth, with all that IN EVERY PLACE CALL UPON THE NAME OF JESUS CHRIST our Lord." 1 Cor. i, 2.

To these instances are to be added all the *doxologies* to Christ, in common with the Father and the Holy Spirit, and all the *benedictions* made in his *name* in common with theirs, for all these are forms of wor-

---

* See 2 Thes. ii, 16, 17; 2 Tim. iv, 22.

ship. The first consist of ascriptions of equal and Divine honors, with grateful recognitions of the Being addressed as the author of benefits received. The following may be given as a few out of many instances: "But grow in grace, and in the knowledge of our Lord and Saviour Jesus Christ. To him be GLORY, both now and for ever. Amen." 2 Pet. iii, 18. "Unto him that loved us, and washed us from our sins in his own blood, and hath made us kings and priests unto God and his Father, to him be GLORY and DOMINION for ever and ever. Amen." Rev. i, 5, 6. When we consider the serious and reverential manner in which these doxologies are introduced, and the superlative praise which they convey, so far surpassing what humanity can deserve, we must suppose that the Being to whom they refer is really Divine. The ascription of eternal glory and everlasting dominion, if addressed to any creature, however exalted, would be idolatrous and profane.

Benedictions are blessings solemnly pronounced upon persons in the name of God, and were derived from the practice of the Jewish priests, and the still older patriarchs, who blessed others in the name of Jehovah, as his representatives. These are so regular in their form as to make it clearly appear that the apostles constantly *blessed* the people *ministerially* in the name of Christ as one of the blessed Trinity. "Grace to you, and peace from God our Father, and the Lord Jesus Christ." Rom. i, 7. "The grace of the Lord Jesus Christ, and the love of God, and the communion of the Holy Ghost, be with you all." 2 Cor. xiii, 14.

In answer to the Socinian perversion, that these are mere "wishes," or "expressions of good-will," it may be observed that this objection overlooks, or notices very slightly, the main point on which the whole question turns, the *nature* of the blessings sought, and consequently, the *qualities* which they imply in the Person who is desired to bestow them. The blessings sought are *grace, mercy,* and *peace;* which are the highest gifts that Omnipotent Benevolence can bestow, or a dependent nature receive. To desire such blessings, either in the mode of direct address, or in that of precatory wish, from any being who is not possessed of omnipotent goodness, would be absurd, and sinful in the highest degree.

(3.) *The worship of Christ is practiced among heavenly beings.*— "When he bringeth in the first-begotten into the world, he saith, And let ALL THE ANGELS OF GOD WORSHIP HIM." Heb. i, 6. The Apocalypse, in its scenic representations, exhibits Christ as, equally with the Father, the object of the worship of angels and glorified saints; placing every creature in the universe, except the inhabitants of hell, in prostrate adoration at his feet. "And every creature which is in heaven and on the earth, and under the earth, and such as are in the sea, and all that are in them, heard I saying, Blessing, and honor, and glory, and power, be unto him that sitteth upon the throne, AND UNTO THE LAMB forever and ever." Rev. v, 13. Having now established the fact, that Jesus Christ is the object of *worship*, we will proceed to consider,

2. THE BEARING WHICH THIS FACT HAS UPON THE DOCTRINE OF HIS SUPREME DIVINITY.—To perceive this clearly, we should first inquire into the religious principles and practice of the early disciples of our Lord. As to their religious principles, they were Jews; and Jews, too, of an age in which their nation had shaken off its idolatrous propensities, and which was distinguished by its zeal against all worship or religious trust of which any creature was the object. The great principle of the law was, "Thou shalt have no other gods before (or *beside*) me."* It was, therefore, commanded by Moses, "Thou shalt fear the Lord thy God, and *him* shalt thou serve;"† which words are quoted by our Lord in his temptation, when solicited to worship Satan, so as to prove that to *fear* God and to *serve* him are expressions which signify *worship*, and that all other beings but God are excluded from it. "Thou shalt WORSHIP the Lord thy God, and him *only* shalt thou serve." Luke iv, 8. Accordingly, we find the apostles teaching and practicing this as a first principle of their religion.

St. Paul charges the heathen with not *glorifying* God when they *knew* him, and with worshiping and serving "the *creature* more than (or *besides*) the Creator." Rom. i, 25. Again, when he mentions it as one of the crimes of the Galatians, previous to their conversion to Christianity, that they "did service unto them which by *nature* are no gods," he plainly intimates that no one has a title to religious *service* but he who is by *nature* God; and if so, he himself could not have worshiped Christ had he not believed him to be truly Divine.

The *practice* of the apostles was in strict accordance with this principle. Thus, when worship was offered to Peter by Cornelius, who certainly did not take him to be God, he forbade it. So also Paul and Barnabas prevented the people at Lystra from offering to them religious honors with expressions of horror. An eminent instance is recorded, also, of the exclusion of all creatures, however exalted, from the honor of religious worship, in Rev. xix, 10, where the angel refused to receive so much as even the outward act of adoration. His language is, "See thou do it not: *worship God*," clearly intimating thereby that all acts of religious worship are to be appropriated to God alone.

From the known and avowed religious sentiments, then, of the apostles, both as Jews and as Christians, as well as from their practice, it follows that they could not have paid religious worship to Christ, a fact which has already been established, unless they had considered him as a Divine person, and themselves as bound on that account, according to his own words, to *honor the* SON, *even as they honored the* FATHER. It is the testimony of St. Paul that he, "being in the form of God, thought it not robbery to be equal with God,"—a passage which inci-

* Exod. xx, 4. † Deut. x, 20.

dentally teaches the Godhead of Christ, and which cannot be reconciled to any hypothesis that excludes his essential Deity.

Arians devised the doctrine of *supreme* and *inferior* worship, and a similar distinction was maintained by Dr. Samuel Clarke, to reconcile the worship of Christ with his semi-Arianism. The same sophistical distinction is resorted to by Roman Catholics to vindicate the worship of angels, the Virgin Mary, and departed saints. But it is a sufficient refutation of this theory,

(1.) *That it has no countenance in the Sacred Scriptures.*—We often read of prayer; but there is not a word respecting absolute and relative, supreme and inferior prayer. We are commanded to pray fervently and incessantly, but never to pray sovereignly or absolutely. Nor have we any rules left us about raising or lowering our intentions, in proportion to the dignity of the object.

(2.) *That the Scriptures are directly opposed to it.*—Sacrifice was a mode of worship required under the law, and was doubtless not more solemn in its character than the exercise of prayer; but it is said, "He that sacrificeth unto any god, save unto the Lord only, he shall be utterly destroyed." Exod. xxii, 20. Now suppose any person, considering that this law referred only to absolute and sovereign sacrifice to God, had sacrificed to other gods, and had been convicted of it before the judges. His apology for the act must have run thus: "I did, indeed, sacrifice to other gods, but it was not absolute or supreme sacrifice, which is all that the law forbids. I considered the gods to whom I sacrificed as inferior beings, and I offered them, therefore, only a relative and inferior service; reserving all sovereign sacrifice to the Supreme God of Israel." But is it likely that such an apology would have saved him from the penalty of the law? If it would not, which we think is evident, then the law appropriated all sacrifice to God.

Such being the case with respect to sacrificial worship, we may ask, What is there so peculiar in invocation and adoration that they should not be governed by the same law? Why should not absolute and relative prayer and prostration appear as absurd as absolute and relative sacrifice? They are, like the other, acts of religious worship, and are appropriated to God in the same manner, by the same laws, and upon the same grounds and reasons. We are not at liberty to fix what signification we please to the acts of religious worship, making them high or low at discretion; for God himself has determined their signification to be supreme by claiming to be their only lawful object. It follows, therefore, that we can never use them in any other sense without being guilty of profaneness or idolatry.

CHAPTER V.

THE SONSHIP OF CHRIST.

That the title "Son of God" is applied to Jesus Christ is not denied. His disciples, occasionally before and frequently after his resurrection, gave him this appellation, and he assumed it himself. The question, therefore, is, In what sense is this title to be understood? In answering this question we will, *first*, notice several false theories that have been adopted respecting the Sonship of Christ; *secondly*, adduce the testimony of Scripture in support of the doctrine that the title "Son of God" is a designation of his Divine nature; and, *thirdly*, make some remarks on the importance of maintaining the orthodox view upon this subject.

I. We are to notice several false theories that have been adopted respecting the Sonship of Christ.

1. Various attempts have been made to restrict the title "Son of God" to the mere humanity of our Saviour, and to rest its application upon his *miraculous conception*. It is true that this opinion is held by some who hesitate not to acknowledge that Jesus Christ is a Divine person; but, by denying his Deity as "the Son of God," they both depart from the faith of the early Christian Church, and give up to Socinians the whole argument for the divinity of Christ, which is founded upon that eminent appellation.

Those who think that it was assumed by Christ, and given to him by his disciples because of his miraculous conception, are obviously in error. Our Lord, when he adopted the appellation, never urged his miraculous birth as a proof of his Sonship; but when he called God his Father, he grounded the proof of his claim upon the *miracles* which he performed. The Jews clearly conceived that, in making this profession of Sonship with reference to God, he assumed a Divine character, and made himself "*equal with God.*" They, therefore, took up stones to stone him.

Nor did the disciples themselves give him this title with reference to his conception by the Holy Ghost. Certain it is, that Nathanael did not know the circumstances of his birth, for he was announced to him by Philip as Jesus of *Nazareth*, "the *Son* of *Joseph;*" and he, therefore, asked, "Can any good thing come out of *Nazareth?*" He did not know but that Jesus was the son of Joseph; he knew nothing of his being born in Bethlehem; and yet he confessed him to be "the Son of God" and "the King of Israel."

It may also be observed that in the celebrated confession of Peter,

"Thou art the Christ, the SON of the LIVING GOD," there is no reference at all to our Lord's miraculous conception. Nor did this form any part of the ground on which he confessed "the *Son of Man*" to be the "SON OF GOD;" for our Lord replied, "Flesh and blood hath not revealed this unto thee, but my Father which is in heaven." Peter had, therefore, been taught the doctrine of the Sonship of Christ by a special revelation from God the Father, an unnecessary thing, certainly, if the miraculous conception had been the only ground of that Sonship; for the evidence of that fact might have been collected from Christ and his virgin mother.

2. This ground, therefore, not being tenable, it has been urged that "SON OF GOD" was simply an appellation of Messiah, and is, consequently, an *official*, and not a *personal* designation. Against this, however, the evangelic history affords decisive proof.

That the Messiah was the Jehovah of the Old Testament has been shown in a former chapter; and this is to be regarded as the faith of the ancient Jewish Church. But it is certain that at the period of our Lord's advent the great body of the Jews had given up the Divine character of the Messiah, and held the opinion that he was to be a *temporal monarch*. The true doctrine was retained only among the faithful few, as Simeon, who expressly ascribed divinity to the Messiah, and Nathanael, who connected "SON OF GOD" and "KING OF ISRAEL" together, one the designation of the Divine *nature*, the other of the *office* of the Messiah.

Three things are therefore clear, from the writings of the Evangelists: 1. That the Jews recognized the existence of such a being as the "Son of God." 2. That they regarded it blasphemy for any created being to claim this designation. 3. That for a person to profess to be the Messiah simply was not considered blasphemy, and did not exasperate the Jews. Our Lord certainly professed to be the Messiah; many of the Jews also, at different times, believed on him *as such;* and yet these same Jews were not only offended, but took up stones to stone him as a blasphemer when he declared himself to be the "Son of God." We cannot, therefore, account for the use of this title among the Jews of our Lord's time, whether by his disciples or his enemies, by considering it as synonymous with Messiah. The Jews regarded the former as *necessarily* involving a claim to divinity, but not the latter; and the disciples did not conceive that they fully confessed their Master by calling him the Messiah without adding to it his higher designation. "Thou art Christ," said Peter; but he immediately added, "THE SON OF THE LIVING GOD." So Nathanael, under the influence of a recent proof of his omniscience, and, consequently, of his divinity, salutes him, first, as the "SON OF GOD," and then as Messiah, "THE KING OF ISRAEL."

We conclude, therefore, that the title "Son of God," as it is applied to Jesus Christ, is a *personal* designation, and not one of office; that it was *essential* in him to be a Son, and only *accidental* that he was the Messiah; that he was the first by *nature*, the second by *appointment;* and that, in constant association with the name *Son*, as given to him alone, and in a sense which shuts out all creatures, however exalted, are found ideas and circumstances of full and absolute divinity.

3. Another opinion is, that the title "*Son of God*" is applied to Christ because God raised him from the dead. Those who adopt this theory rest it mainly on a passage in the second Psalm: "The Lord hath said unto me, Thou art my Son; this day have I begotten thee." They suppose that the *day* spoken of in the text is the day of Christ's resurrection, and interpret his being "begotten" of the Father as denoting the act of raising him from the dead, thus making his resurrection the ground of his Sonship.

From apostolic authority we know that the "*Son*" here represented as speaking is Christ, for to him this passage is explicitly applied at least twice in the New Testament.* But he is so frequently called the Son, when there is no reference to his resurrection, that this cannot be the ground of that relation. This point, however, may be settled by the following considerations:

(1.) It is clearly indicated in the Scriptures that Christ raised himself from the dead by his own power. He explicitly declared, when speaking of his *life*, "I have power to lay it down, and I have power to take it again." John x, 18. Accordingly he said to the Jews, "Destroy this temple, and in three days *I will raise it up*." John ii, 19. Hence it would follow, if the preceding interpretation were true, that our Lord begat himself, and is therefore his own son, which is absurd.

(2.) He was declared from heaven to be the beloved Son of the Father at his very entrance upon his public ministry, and, consequently, before his resurrection. "And lo, a voice from heaven, saying, This is my beloved *Son*, in whom I am well pleased." Matt. iii, 17.

(3.) St. Paul tells us (Rom. i, 4) that the resurrection of Christ was the DECLARATION of his Sonship, and not the ground of it— "DECLARED to be the Son of God with power, by the resurrection from the dead." This was, therefore, the declaration of an *antecedent* Sonship.

(4.) The titles and honors ascribed in this Psalm to the extraordinary person who is the chief subject of it far transcend what the Scriptures ascribe to any mere creature. He is the Lord's *Anointed*, the *King of Zion*, and the rightful *Sovereign of the nations*. Accordingly, kings and judges of the earth are exhorted to "kiss the Son;" and all are pronounced blessed who "*put their trust in him*." This is surely an unequivocal declaration of divinity; for it is written, "Cursed be the man that trusteth in man and maketh flesh his arm." Jer. xvii, 5.

* See Acts xiii, 33; Heb. i, 5.

THE SONSHIP OF CHRIST.

(5.) It is also to be noted that St. Paul employs the very passage under consideration to prove that Christ is superior to angels: "For unto which of the angels said he at any time, Thou art my Son, this day have I begotten thee?" Heb. i, 5. The force of this argument lies in the expression "begotten," importing that the person addressed is the Son of God, not by creation, but by generation. Christ's pre-eminence over the angels is here stated to consist in this, that whereas they were *created*, he was *begotten;* and the apostle's reasoning would be fallacious if the expression did not intimate a proper and peculiar filiation. The argument shows, therefore, that the title SON, which is given to the Messiah in this Psalm, implies real divinity.

·Having noticed and refuted some of the false theories respecting the Sonship of Christ, we will now proceed,

II. To ADDUCE THE TESTIMONY OF SCRIPTURE IN SUPPORT OF THE DOCTRINE THAT THE TITLE "SON OF GOD" IS A DESIGNATION OF HIS DIVINE NATURE.

We will direct our attention,

1. *To a few passages in the Old Testament in which a Divine Son is spoken of.*—We have seen that the term *Son*, in the second Psalm, is applied to Jesus Christ, and that it denotes real divinity. To this we may add Prov. viii, 22, in which Solomon introduces, not the personified, but the *personal* wisdom of God, under the same relation of a Son, and in that relation ascribes to him Divine attributes. "The Lord possessed me in the beginning of his way, before his works of old. I was set up (appointed) from everlasting, from the beginning, or ever the world was. When there were no depths I was brought forth," or *born*. Here, from a consideration of the excellence of wisdom in the abstract, there is an easy transition to that of its infinite Source; and hence the inspired writer proceeds to delineate a Divine Being, who is portrayed in colors of such splendor and majesty as can be attributed to no other than the eternal Son of God.

To say of wisdom, as an attribute, that God possessed it in the beginning of his way, is certainly too trifling an observation to be attributed to the wise monarch of Israel. In what way can it be predicated of a quality that it was set up or appointed from everlasting? But every attribute which is here ascribed to wisdom is strictly applicable to the divine *Logos*, who "was in the beginning with God," and in whom "dwelleth all the fullness of the Godhead bodily."

The eternal Sonship of Jesus Christ is most unequivocally expressed in the prophecy of Micah: "But thou, Bethlehem Ephratah, though thou be little among the thousands of Judah, yet out of thee shall he come forth unto me that is to be Ruler in Israel; whose goings forth have been from of old, from everlasting;" or, as it is in the margin, "from the days of eternity." Micah v, 2. There is here ascribed to the person spoken of a twofold birth or going forth. By a natural birth he was to come forth from Bethlehem of Judah; but by another and higher birth he had been "from the days of eternity."*

This passage is so signal a description of Christ, the eternal Son of God, who assumed our nature and was born in Bethlehem, that it evidently belongs to him, and to no other being; and it is so decidedly indicative of that peculiar notion of his divinity, which is marked by the term and the relation of SON, that Socinians have resorted to the utmost violence of criticism to escape its powerful evidence. Dr. Priestley says "that it may be understood concerning the promises of God, in which the coming of Christ was signified to mankind from the beginning of the world."

To this we reply that the word which is rendered "goings forth" never signifies the work of God in predicting future events, but is often used to express natural birth and origin. It is unquestionably so used in the preceding clause, and cannot be taken in a different sense in that which immediately follows, and especially when a clear antithesis is marked and intended. He was born in time, but was not, on that account, merely human; for though born in Bethlehem, his "goings forth," his production, his heavenly birth or generation, was from *everlasting*.

Others refer the phrase, "his goings forth," to the purpose of God that Christ should come into the world; but this is too absurd to need refutation. It would be mere trifling solemnly to affirm of the Messiah what is just as true of every other man born into the world. This passage is, therefore, an irrefutable proof of the faith of the ancient Jewish Church, both in the divinity and the Divine Sonship of the Messiah.

The same relation of SON, in the full view of Supreme Divinity, and where no reference appears to be had to the office and work of the Messiah, is found in Prov. xxx, 4: "Who hath ascended up into heaven, or descended? who hath gathered the wind in his fists? who hath bound the waters in a garment? who hath established all the ends of the earth? what is his name, and what is his SON's name, if thou canst tell?" Here the Deity is contemplated, not in his redeeming acts, but in his works of creation and providence, managing at will and ruling the operations of nature; and yet, even in these peculiar offices of divinity alone, he is spoken of as having a SON, whose "name," that is, according to the Hebrew idiom, whose *nature* is as *deep*, *mysterious*, and *unutterable* as *his own*. "What is HIS name, and what is his SON's name; canst thou tell?"

It was thus that the Scriptures of the Old Testament furnished the Jews with the idea of a personal Son in the Divine nature. They were

---

* The word יָצָא, YATZA, *to come forth*, is frequently used in reference to *birth*, or *generation*, as in Gen. xvii, 6; 2 Kings xx, 18; and so the Jews understood it, when they replied to the inquiry of Herod in regard to the place where Christ should be born, by quoting this very passage. According to a common Hebraism in order to denote *eminency*, the word for birth, which is rendered "goings forth," is used in its plural form.

not only acquainted with the phrase "Son of God," but in a good degree they understood its true import. Nor is it any objection to this, that among their ancient writers it was sometimes applied to the Messiah. It is granted that the Messiah is the Son of God; but that the phrase *Son of God* ceases, on that account, to be a personal designation, or that it imports the same as *Messiah*, is what we deny. David was the son of Jesse and the king of Israel. He, therefore, who was king of Israel was the son of Jesse; but the latter is the *personal*, the former only the *official* description. The latter marks his origin and family; for before he was king of Israel he was the son of Jesse. In like manner "Son of God" marks the *natural* relation of the Messiah to God, and the term *Messiah* his *official* relation to men. This relation to God subsists not in the human, but in the *higher* nature of the Messiah; and this higher nature being proved to be Divine, it follows that the phrase "Son of God," as applied to Jesus Christ, is a title of absolute divinity, importing his participation in the very nature and essence of God.

2. *The same ideas of a* DIVINE SONSHIP *are suggested by almost every passage in which the phrase occurs in the New Testament.*—When Jesus was baptized "the heavens were opened unto him, and he saw the Spirit of God descending like a dove, and lighting upon him; and lo, a voice from heaven, saying, This is my BELOVED SON, in whom I am well pleased." Matt. iii, 16, 17. The circumstances of this testimony are of the most solemn and impressive kind, and there can be no rational doubt but that they were designed authoritatively to invest our Lord with the title "Son of God" in its fullest sense—rendered stronger and more emphatic by the epithet "*beloved*," and by the declaration that in him the Father was "*well pleased*." It is evident that the title was applied to him on grounds independent of the circumstances of his *birth*, or of his *official relation* to men; and that he was in a higher *nature* than his human, and for a higher reason than an *official* one "the Son of God." Accordingly, as soon as John the Baptist had heard the testimony of the Father respecting our Lord, and had seen the descent of the Holy Spirit upon him, he declared him to be "the SON OF GOD."

To the transaction at his baptism our Lord himself adverts in John v, 37 : "And the Father himself, which hath sent me, hath borne witness of me." He had just adverted to the evidence of his divinity arising from his miraculous works, and, in addition to this, he introduces that distinct personal testimony of the Father which was given at his baptism. Now, the witness of the Father on that occasion is that Christ is his "*beloved* SON;" and it is remarkable that our Lord introduces this testimony of the Father at a time when his claim to be the Son of God was a matter of dispute with the Jews. They denied that God was his Father in the high sense in which he was obviously to be understood; and "they sought to kill him, because he had said that

God was his Father, *making himself equal with God.*" What then, in this case, was the conduct of our Lord? He reaffirmed his Sonship even in this very objectionable sense, claiming the power to perform the works of God, to raise the dead, and to exercise all judgment, and the right to be honored of all men, " even as they honor the Father."*

The epithet " ONLY BEGOTTEN," which several times occurs in the New Testament, affords further proof of the Sonship of Christ in his Divine nature. One of these instances *only* need be selected : " The Word was made flesh, and dwelt among us, and we beheld his glory, the glory as of the ONLY BEGOTTEN of the Father, full of grace and truth." John i, 14. If the term " only begotten " referred to Christ's miraculous conception, then the glory " as of the only-begotten " must be a glory of the human nature of Christ only, for that alone was capable of being thus conceived. This, however, is clearly contrary to the scope of the passage, which does not speak of the glory of that nature which the Word assumed, but of the glory of the WORD HIMSELF, who is here said to be the " only-begotten of the Father." It is, therefore, the glory of his Divine nature that is here intended.

It is also clear that the miraculous conception of Christ could not constitute him a Son, except as it consisted in the immediate formation of his manhood by the power of God; but, in this respect, he was not the "*only-begotten,*" not the *only Son,* because Adam was thus also immediately produced, and for this very reason is called by St. Luke " the son of God." The note in the Socinian version tells us, " that this expression," only-begotten, " does not refer to any particular mode of derivation or existence; but is used to express merely a higher degree of *affection,* and is applied to Isaac, though Abraham had other sons." Isaac, however, was so called because he was the only child which Abraham had by his wife Sarah; and this instance is therefore against the Socinian theory. It would be easy to show that μονογενης, *only-begotten,* does not anywhere import the affection of a parent, but the peculiar relation of an *only son,* and as this peculiarity does not apply to the production of the mere humanity of our Lord, the first man being in this sense, and for this very reason, a " son of God," the epithet must be applied to his Divine nature, in which alone he is at once *naturally* and *exclusively* " the SON OF THE LIVING GOD."

Those passages which declare that " all things were made by " the SON,† and that " God *sent* his Son into the world," ‡ may be considered as declarations of a Divine Sonship. The former imply that the CREATOR was a SON at the very period of creation, and the latter, that he was the SON OF GOD before he was *sent* into the world ; and thus both will prove that this relation is independent of his incarnation, or of his official appointment as Messiah.

* See John v, 18–29.   † See John i, 3 ; Col. i, 16 ; Heb. i, 2.
‡ See John iii, 17 ; Gal. iv, 4 : 1 John iv, 9, 10, 14.

Chap. 5.]   THE SONSHIP OF CHRIST.   217

The only plausible objection to this is, that a person may be said to perform actions under a title which he subsequently receives. Thus we ascribe the "*Principia*" to *Sir* Isaac Newton, though that work was written before he received the honor of knighthood. Accordingly, we are told by those who allow the divinity of Christ, while they deny his Divine Sonship, that the sacred writers ascribed creation and other Divine acts to the SON merely by an interchange of appellations between his human and his Divine nature; meaning thereby, that they were done by that same Divine Person who, in consequence of his incarnation and miraculous conception, became the Son of God. Thus it is said that "the Lord of glory" was crucified, and that God purchased the Church "with his *own blood*." So, also, in familiar style, we speak of the divinity of JESUS, and of the Godhead of the SON OF MARY.

To this our reply is, that though an interchange of appellations is acknowledged, yet even this supposes that some of them are designations of our Lord's Divine nature, while others describe the nature which he assumed. But the simple circumstance of such an interchange will no more prove the title SON OF GOD to be a human designation than it will prove SON OF MARY to be a *Divine* one. If "SON OF GOD" does not relate to the divinity of our Lord, then, as God, he has no distinctive name in all the Scriptures. The title "GOD" does not distinguish him from the other persons of the Trinity, and the term "WORD" stands in precisely the same predicament as "SON;" for the same kind of criticism may reduce it to merely an *official* appellative.

But the notion that the title "Son of God" is an appellation of the human nature of our Lord, and that it is applied to him in his Divine character merely by a customary interchange of designations, is an assumption which cannot be proved; while all those passages which connect the title "*Son*," immediately and by way of eminence, with his divinity, remain wholly unaccounted for on this theory, and are therefore contrary to it. It is evident, that in direct relation to his Divine nature, and without reference to any other circumstance, he claimed God as his Father. When he said to the Jews, "My Father worketh hitherto and I work," they understood him to assert that in this high sense "God was his Father, [πατερα ιδιον, HIS OWN PROPER FATHER,] making himself EQUAL with God." John v, 17, 18. And when our Lord said, "I and my Father ARE ONE," the "Jews took up stones to stone him," saying, "For a good work we stone thee not, but for blasphemy; and because thou, being a man, makest thyself God." John x, 31-33.

His unequivocal answer to the direct question of the Jewish council, when he was on his trial before them, is also in point here. "Then said they all, Art thou then the Son of God? And he said unto them, Ye say that I am." Luke xxii, 70. The obvious meaning of our Lord's reply is, *I am that*, or *what ye say ;* thus declaring that, in the very sense in which they put the question, he was the Son of God. But in confessing himself to be in that sense the SON, he did more than claim to be the Messiah, for the counsel judged him to be guilty of blasphemy, and therefore worthy of death; a charge which could not lie against any one, by the Jewish law, for professing to be the Messiah. His blasphemy was alleged to consist in his making himself "THE SON OF GOD," which was, in their view, an assumption of positive divinity; and the conduct of our Lord shows that they did not mistake his intention, for he suffered them to proceed against him without lowering his claims or correcting their opinion.

The whole argument of the apostle in the first chapter of Hebrews is designed to prove that our Lord is superior to angels, and he adduces, as conclusive evidence on this point, that to none of the angels did God ever say, "Thou art my SON, this day have I begotten thee." He argues, therefore, on this very ground of *Sonship* that Christ is superior to angels; that is, superior in *nature* and in *natural relation* to God; for in no other way is the argument conclusive. He has his title SON by way of INHERITANCE; that is, by *natural* and *hereditary* right. "He hath by *inheritance* obtained a more excellent name than they;" that is, by his being OF the Father, and therefore by virtue of his Divine filiation. Angels may be, in an inferior sense, the sons of God by *creation;* but they *cannot inherit* that title for this plain reason, that they are *created,* not *begotten;* while our Lord inherits "the more excellent name" because he is *begotten,* not *created.* "For, unto which of the angels said he at any time, Thou art my SON, this day have I BEGOTTEN thee?" The same ideas of absolute divinity connect themselves with this title throughout the chapter. "The SON," by whom "God hath in these last days spoken unto us," is "the brightness of his glory and the express image of his person;" but it is only to the Divine nature of our Lord that these expressions can refer.

As in none of these passages the title "Son of God" can possibly be considered as a designation of his human nature or office, so we find proof of equal force that it is used even by way of *opposition* and *contradistinction* to the inferior nature. Thus St. Paul says of the "Son Jesus Christ" that he "was made of the seed of David according to the flesh; and declared to be the Son of God with power, according to the Spirit of holiness, by the resurrection from the dead." Rom. i, 3, 4. A very few remarks will be sufficient to point out the force of this passage. The apostle is speaking not of what Christ is officially, but of what he is personally and essentially, for the truth of all his official claims depends upon the truth of his personal ones. If he is a Divine person he is everything else that he assumes to be. He is, therefore, considered by the apostle in his twofold nature. As a man he was "of the seed of David according to the flesh;" but in a superior nature he was "declared to be the Son of God." That an opposition is expressed between what Christ is "according to the flesh," and what he is according to a higher nature, must be allowed, or else there is no force in the apostle's observation; and it must be equally clear that the nature put in *opposition* to Christ's fleshly nature can be no other than his Divine nature, which the apostle calls "the SON OF GOD."

We also learn, from Romans viii, 3, that God sent "his own Son in the likeness of sinful flesh." The person who is here entitled the SON was sent "in the likeness of sinful flesh;" but in what other way could he have been sent if he were *Son* only as a *man?* It is, therefore, most clearly intimated that he was a SON before he was sent, and that FLESH was the nature which the Son *assumed*, but not the nature in which he was "the Son of God."

With the same idea of the absolute divinity of the SON, as distinguished from his humanity, the apostle applies that lofty passage from the forty-fifth psalm. "But unto the Son he saith, Thy throne, O God, is for ever and ever." Heb. i, 8. It is allowed by all who hold the Deity of Christ that he is here addressed as a being composed of two natures, Divine and human. As man, he is anointed " with the oil of gladness," and elevated above his "fellows;" while the stability of his throne, and the unsullied justice of his government, declare his GODHEAD. He is, however, called the SON; but this term could not characterize the being here introduced, unless it agreed with his higher and Divine nature. The SON is addressed—that Son is addressed as GOD, and as God whose throne is *for ever and ever.*

Thus we think it fully established, that the title "SON OF GOD" is not given to Christ on account of his miraculous conception; that it is not an appellative of his human nature, occasionally applied to him by metonymy, when Divine acts and relations are spoken of, as any other human title might be applied; that it is not ascribed to him simply because of his assuming our nature, as is supposed by some who admit the divinity of our Lord but deny his eternal filiation; and that the use of the title cannot be fully explained by any *office* with which he is invested, or any *event* in his mediatorial undertaking. It follows, therefore, that it is a title characteristic of his mode of existence in the Divine essence, and of the relation which exists between the first and the second person in the ever blessed Trinity.

It only remains for us now,

III. To MAKE SOME REMARKS ON THE IMPORTANCE OF MAINTAINING THE ORTHODOX VIEW RESPECTING THE SONSHIP OF JESUS CHRIST.

It is granted that some divines, truly decided on the question of our Lord's divinity, have rejected the Divine Sonship; but in this they have gone contrary to the judgment of the Church of Christ in all ages, and would certainly have been ranked among heretics in her earliest and purest times. This consideration alone is worthy of attention, and ought to induce caution; but there are many considerations to show that points of great moment are involved in the denial or maintenance of the doctrine in question. A few of these we will present in the following remarks:

1. The loose and general manner in which many passages of Scripture, which speak of Christ as a Son, must be explained by those who deny the Divine filiation of Christ, seems to sanction principles of interpretation which would be highly dangerous, or rather absolutely fatal, if generally applied to the Scriptures.

2. The denial of the Divine Sonship destroys all *relation* among the persons of the Godhead. No other relation of the Divine persons is mentioned in Scripture except those which are expressed by *paternity*, *filiation*, and *procession*. If these *natural* relations are removed, we must then conceive of the *persons* in the Godhead as perfectly independent of each other, a view which is incompatible with the *unity* of the Divine *essence*.

3. It is the doctrine of the Divine paternity only which preserves the Scripture idea that the Father is the *fountain* of deity, and as such, the *first*, the *original*, the *principle*. He must have read the Scriptures to little purpose who does not perceive that this is their constant doctrine—that "OF him are all things;" that though the Son is Creator, yet BY the Son the Father made the worlds, and that "as the Father hath life in himself, so hath he given to the Son to HAVE LIFE IN HIMSELF," which can only refer to his Divine nature, nothing being the source of life in itself but what is *Divine*. But where the essential paternity of the Father and the correlative filiation of the Son are denied, these Scriptural representations have no foundation in fact, and are incapable of interpretation.

4. The perfect EQUALITY of the Son with the Father, and, at the same time, the SUBORDINATION of the Son to the Father, are to be equally maintained only by the doctrine of the Divine Sonship. Deny this, and the Son might as well be the *first* as the *second* person in the Godhead, and the *second* as well as the first. The Father might have been *sent* by the Son without incongruity, or either of them by the Holy Spirit. These are most absurd and repulsive conclusions, which the doctrine of the Sonship avoids, and thus proves its accordance with the Holy Scriptures.

5. A denial of the Divine filiation of Christ is derogatory to the *love* of the Father in the gift of his Son. It insensibly runs into the Socinian heresy, and restricts the Father's love to the gift of a *mere man*, if the Sonship of Christ is only *human;* and in that case, the permission of the sufferings of Christ was no greater manifestation of God's love to the world than if he had permitted any other good man to die for the benefit of his fellow-creatures.

CHAPTER VI.

THE PERSON OF CHRIST.

In the present day the controversy respecting the person of Christ is almost wholly confined to the question of his divinity; but in the early ages of the Church it was necessary to establish his proper humanity. The denial of this seems to have existed as early as the time of St. John, who, in his epistles, excludes from the pale of the Church all who denied that "Christ is come in THE FLESH." As his Gospel, therefore, proclaims his Godhead, so his epistles defend also the doctrine of his humanity.

As the Divine nature of Christ has been fully established, it is only necessary in this chapter to prove his true humanity, and to show that the two natures, the human and the Divine, are united in *one person*. But before we proceed to the discussion of these points it will be proper for us to notice, very briefly,

I. A FEW OF THE LEADING ERRORS WHICH HAVE BEEN MORE OR LESS DISSEMINATED IN THE CHURCH RESPECTING THE PERSON OF CHRIST.— These have related both to his human and his Divine nature.

1. *Errors in regard to the human nature of our Lord.*—The *Gnostics* denied the real existence of the *body* of Christ. The things which the Scriptures attribute to his human nature they did not deny, but affirmed that they took place in appearance only. The source of this error appears to have been a philosophical one. Both in the Oriental and Greek schools it was a favorite notion, that whatever was joined to *matter* was necessarily contaminated by it; and that the highest perfection of this life was abstraction from material things, and in another, a total and final separation from the body.

While the Gnostics denied the real existence of the *body* of Christ, the *Apollinarians* maintained that his body was endowed with a sensitive and not with a rational soul, and that the Divine nature supplied the place of the intellectual principle in man. Thus both these views denied to Christ a proper humanity, and both were, accordingly, condemned by the general Church.

Even among those who held the union of the Divine and the human nature in Christ, which in theological language is called the *hypostatical* or *personal* union, several distinctions were also made which led to a diversity of opinion. The *Nestorians* acknowledged two *persons* in our Lord, mystically and more closely united than any human analogy can explain. The Monophysites contended for one person and one nature, the two being supposed to be, in some mysterious manner, confounded. The Monothelites two natures and one will.

2. *Errors respecting the Divine Nature of Christ.*—Among the various errors of this class, which formerly sprung up in the Church, three only can be said to have much influence in the present day, Arianism, Sabellianism, and Socinianism. The two former are now almost entirely merged into the last, whose characteristic tenet is the simple humanity of Christ. Arius, who gave his name to the first, seems to have wrought some of the floating errors of previous times into a kind of system, which, however, underwent various modifications among his followers. The distinguishing tenet of this system was that Christ was the first and most exalted of creatures; that he was produced in a peculiar manner, and endowed with great perfections; that by him God made the worlds; that he alone proceeded immediately from God, while other things were produced mediately by him; and that all things were put under his administration.

The semi-Arians divided from the Arians, but still differed from the orthodox in refusing to admit that the Son was ὁμοούσιος, or of the *same substance* with the Father; but they acknowledged him to be ὁμοιούσιος, or of a *like* substance with the Father. It was only in appearance, however, that they came nearer to the truth than the Arians themselves, for they contended that this *likeness* to the Father in essence was not by *nature*, but by peculiar privilege. In their system, therefore, Christ was but a creature.

A still further refinement on this doctrine was advocated by Dr. Samuel Clarke. His theory was that there is one Supreme Being who is the Father, and two subordinate, derived, and dependent beings. But he objected to call Christ a creature, thinking him something between a created and a self-existent nature. This hypothesis, however, still implies, unless an evident absurdity be admitted, that Christ is a created being.

The *Sabellian* doctrine stands equally opposed to Trinitarianism and to the Arian system. It asserts the divinity of the Son and the Holy Spirit against the latter, and denies the personality of both in opposition to the former. Sabellius taught that the Father, Son, and Holy Ghost are only denominations of one hypostasis; in other words, that there is but one person in the Godhead, and that the Son and the Holy Spirit are virtues, emanations, or functions only; that under the Old Testament God delivered the law as Father; under the New dwelt among men, or was incarnate as the Son; and descended on the apostles as the Holy Spirit. In the early ages they were often called *Patripassians*, because their scheme, by denying a real Sonship, obliged them to acknowledge that it was the Father who suffered for the sins of men.

On the refutation of these errors it is not now necessary to dwell, both because they have at present but little influence, and chiefly because both are involved in the Socinian question, and are decided by the establishment of the scriptural doctrine of a Trinity of Divine persons in the Unity of the Godhead. If Jesus Christ is the Divine Son of God; if he was "sent" from God and "returned" to God; if he distinguished himself from the Father both in his Divine and human nature, saying, as to the former, "I and my Father are ONE," and as to the latter, "My Father is GREATER than I;" if there is any meaning at all in his declaration, that "no man knoweth the Son but the Father, neither knoweth any man the Father save the Son," words which cannot, by any possibility, be spoken of *official* distinction, or of an *emanation* or *operation;* then all these passages prove a real personality, and are incapable of being explained by a *modal* one. This is the answer to the Sabellian opinion; and as to the Arian hypothesis, it falls, with Socinianism, before that series of proofs which has already been adduced from the Scriptures to establish the eternity of our Lord, his consubstantiality and coequality with the Father, and, consequently, his Supreme Divinity. But,

II. WE ARE TO PROVE THAT OUR LORD WAS TRULY MAN AS WELL AS GOD.

That he assumed *humanity*, in the full and proper sense of that term, is, we think, abundantly evident from the following considerations:

1. *The prophets who predicted the coming of the Messiah often spoke of him as a Man.* Hence he is represented as being the seed of the woman;* the seed of Abraham;† a prophet like unto Moses;‡ and "the son of David."§

2. *He is called a* MAN, *and the* SON OF MAN, *in a multitude of instances.*—He is designated by the latter appellation no less than seventy-one times in the sacred Scriptures. In sixty-seven of these instances the title is employed by our Lord *himself*, once by *Daniel*, once by *St. Stephen*, and twice by *St. John*. It must surely be acknowledged that in giving this appellation to himself he disclosed his true character, and that he was therefore, in reality, what he called himself, *the Son of Man*. When spoken of as a man he is ascribed with just such characteristics as belong to other men, those only excepted which involve error or sin. He is exhibited as meek, lowly, and dutiful to his parents; as hungering, thirsting, and being weary; as sustained and refreshed by food, drink, and sleep; as the subject of temptations, infirmities, and afflictions; as weeping with tenderness and sorrow; and, in general, as having all the innocent characteristics of our nature.

3. *The history of the birth, life, and death of our Lord is unanswerable proof that he was really Man.*—He was born, he lived, and he died essentially in the same manner as other men. He "increased in wisdom

* Gen. iii, 15.   † Gen. xxii, 18.   ‡ Deut. xviii, 15.   § Matt. xxii, 42.

and stature;" wrought with his hands; ate, drank, slept; suffered on the cross; gave up the ghost, and was buried, as other men.

4. *The humanity of Christ is argued at large and proved by St. Paul in the second chapter of Hebrews.*—In the passage containing this argument are the following declarations: "Forasmuch then as the children are partakers of flesh and blood, he also himself likewise took part of the same;" and again, "in all things it behooved him to be made like unto his brethren." That Christ had a human body cannot be denied. It is equally undeniable that to increase in wisdom, to be sorrowful, to be tempted, to be obedient to parents, together with many other things of a similar nature, cannot be attributed either to *God* or to *a mere human body*, but are appropriate characteristics of *the human soul*. Christ, therefore, possessed a human *soul* as well as a human body, and was perfectly *man;* or, as it is very properly expressed in the Shorter Catechism, he "became man by taking to himself a true body and a reasonable soul."

While we maintain the integrity of Christ's human nature, we admit that he assumed it with all its *innocent infirmities.* He was not subject to any of the *sinful* infirmities of man, nor was there any stimulus or incentive to sin in the constitution or temperament of his body. The Scriptures declare that he was "without sin;" that "in him is no sin;" and that, though he came "in the likeness of sinful flesh," he was "holy, harmless, undefiled," and "separate from sinners." Nor does it appear that he was subject to any of those bodily diseases which are the portion of man. Infirmities of this kind would have discommoded him in the discharge of his duty, and he was exempted from them on account of his personal purity. But he was subject to hunger and thirst, to cold and heat, to pain of body arising from external injuries, and to distress of mind, from various causes. Against all such annoyances he might have been defended by the order of Omnipotence; but this would not have accorded with the design of his mission. He submitted to our infirmities that he might acquire an experimental knowledge of our sufferings, both corporeal and mental, and that we might be more fully assured of his sympathy. "We have not a high priest which cannot be touched with the feeling of our infirmities; but was in all points tempted like as we are." Heb. iv, 15.

III. WE ARE TO SHOW THAT THE HUMAN AND THE DIVINE NATURE OF OUR LORD ARE UNITED IN ONE PERSON.

The true sense of Scripture appears to have been very accurately expressed by the Council of Chalcedon, in the fifth century, that in Christ there is *one person,* in the unity of person *two natures,* the Divine and the human; and that there is no change, or mixture, or confusion of these two natures, but that each retains its own distinguishing properties. With this agrees the Athanasian Creed; and the Church of England professes, in her second article, that "The Son, which is the word of the Father, begotten from everlasting of the Father, the very and eternal God, of one substance with the Father, took man's nature in the womb of the blessed Virgin of her substance; so that two whole and perfect natures, that is, the Godhead and manhood, were joined together in one person, never to be divided, whereof is one Christ, very God and very man."

Whatever objections may be raised against these views by the mere reason of man, unable to comprehend mysteries so high, but often bold enough to impugn them, they certainly exhibit the doctrine of the New Testament on this important subject though expressed in different terms. That Christ is very God has been fully proved, and that he became truly man no one can reasonably deny. That he is but *one person* is sufficiently clear from these considerations: 1. That no distinction into two was ever made by himself or by his apostles. 2. That actions peculiar to the Godhead are sometimes ascribed to him under his human appellations; and, 3. That actions and sufferings peculiar to humanity are also predicated of him under Divine titles.

That in him there is no confusion of the two natures is evident from the absolute manner in which both are spoken of in the Scriptures. His Godhead was not deteriorated by uniting itself with a human body, for he "is the true God;" nor was his humanity, while on earth, exalted into properties which made it differ in kind from the humanity of his creatures; for, "as the children were partakers of flesh and blood, he also took part of THE SAME." If the Divine nature in him had been imperfect it would have lost its essential character, for it is essential to Deity to be perfect; if any of the essential properties of human nature had been wanting he would not have been man; and if the Divine and the human nature had been mixed or confounded in him he would have been neither God nor man. Nothing was deficient in his divinity, nothing in his humanity, and yet he is *one Christ.*

It is only in the light of these two circumstances, *the completeness of each nature* and *the union of both in one person,* that the testimony of God concerning his Son can be consistently explained. Some things which are spoken of Christ relate to his Divine, others to his human nature; and he who takes with him this principle of interpretation will seldom find any difficulty in apprehending the sense of the sacred writers, though the subjects themselves may be inscrutable.

1. Does any one ask, for instance, If Jesus is truly GOD how could he be born and die? how could he be subject to law? how could he grow in wisdom and stature? how could he be tempted, or stand in need of prayer? how could his soul be "exceeding sorrowful even unto death?" how could he purchase the Church with "his own blood?" The answer is, that he was also MAN.

But if, on the other hand, it be a matter of surprise that a VISIBLE MAN should heal diseases at his will, and by his own power, still the winds and the waves, know the thoughts of men, authoritatively forgive sins, be with his disciples, wherever two or three are met in his name, claim universal homage from all creatures, and be associated with the Father in solemn ascriptions of glory and thanksgiving: what is the answer? The *only* one explanatory of all these statements is, that our Lord Jesus Christ is GOD as well as MAN. But,

2. The *union* of the two natures of Christ in *one person* is as essential as the completeness of each nature to the full exposition of the Scriptures. Without it many passages lose all force, because they lose all meaning. In what possible sense could it be said that "THE WORD was made FLESH" if no such personal unity existed? Without the hypostatical union, how could the argument of our Lord be supported, that the Messiah is both David's SON and David's LORD? If this is asserted of *two persons*, then the argument is gone; if of *one*, then two natures, one which had authority as *Lord*, and the other capable of natural descent, were united in one person.

By this doctrine we also learn how it was that "the Church of God" was "purchased with his OWN BLOOD." Even if we concede the genuine reading to be "the Lord," instead of "God," the concession yields nothing to the Socinians, unless the term *Lord* were a human title, which has already been disproved; and unless a mere *man* could be "Lord both of the dead and living," could wield universal sovereignty, and be entitled to universal homage. If, then, the title "LORD" be an appellation of Christ's superior nature, in no other sense could it be said that the Church was "purchased with HIS OWN blood" than by supposing the existence of that union which we call personal, a union which alone distinguished the sufferings of Christ from those of his martyred followers, gave to his sufferings a merit which theirs had not, and made his blood capable of PURCHASING the Church.

Again: "Who being the brightness of his glory, and the express image of his person, and upholding all things by the word of his power, when he had BY HIMSELF purged our sins, sat down on the right hand of the Majesty on high." Heb. i, 3. To this passage, also, the hypostatical union is the only key. Of whom does the apostle speak when he says, "when he had BY HIMSELF purged our sins," but of HIM who is "the brightness of" the Father's glory, "and the express image of his person?" HE "BY HIMSELF purged our sins;" yet this was done by the shedding of his blood. In that higher nature, however, he could not suffer death, and nothing could make the sufferings of his humanity a purification of sins BY HIMSELF but such a union of the two natures as should constitute one person. For, unless this be allowed, either the characters of divinity in this passage are characters of a being merely human, or else Christ's higher nature was capable of suffering death; or, if not, the purification was not made by HIMSELF, which yet the text affirms.

Another passage of Scripture which may be noticed in this connection is Col. i, 14, 15: "In whom we have redemption through HIS blood, even the forgiveness of sins: WHO is the image of the invisible God, the first-born of every creature." In this passage the lofty description which is given of the person of Christ stands in immediate connection with the mention of the efficacy of "his blood," and is to be considered as the reason why, through that blood, redemption and remission of sins became attainable. Thus, "without shedding of blood" there could be "no remission;" but the blood of Jesus only is thus efficacious, who is "the image of the invisible God," the "Creator" of all things. His blood it could not be but for the hypostatical union, and it is equally true that were it not for this union he could not have had any blood to shed; because, as "the image of the invisible God," that is, God's equal, or God himself, he was incapable of death.

Thus it is by the union of the Divine and the human nature in one person that our Lord is qualified to be the Saviour of the world. He became man that, with the greatest possible advantage to us, he might teach us the nature and the will of God; that his life might be our example; that his acquaintance with human infirmities might assure us of his sympathy; that by suffering on the cross he might atone for our sins; and that in his glorious reward we might behold both the earnest and the pattern of ours.

But had Jesus been *only* a man, or had he been even one of the spirits that surround the throne of God, he could not have accomplished the work of human redemption. For, the entire obedience of every creature being due to the Creator, no part of that obedience can be placed to the account of other creatures so as to supply the defects of their service, or to rescue them from deserved punishment. But the Scriptures declare that the Redeemer who appeared upon earth as *man* is also *God*, mighty to save; and by this revelation we are taught that the efficacy of his interposition in our behalf depends upon the hypostatical union.

CHAPTER VII.

PERSONALITY AND DEITY OF THE HOLY GHOST.

THE discussion of this point of Christian doctrine may be included in much narrower limits than those which have been assigned to the divinity of Christ, because many of the principles on which it rests have been already closely considered, and because the Deity of the Holy Spirit, in several instances, inevitably follows from that of the Son. It will, however, be necessary to show that the Holy Ghost is a PERSON, and that he is GOD.

As to the *manner* of his being, the Orthodox doctrine is, that as Christ is God by an eternal *filiation*, so the Holy Spirit is God by *procession* from the Father and the Son; which procession rests on direct scriptural authority. It is expressly asserted that the Holy Ghost proceeds from the Father. "But when the Comforter is come, whom I will send unto you from the Father, even the Spirit of truth which *proceedeth from the Father*, he shall testify of me." John xv, 26. And though the Scriptures do not expressly declare that the Holy Ghost proceeds from the Father *and the Son*, yet they evidently teach that doctrine. Because he proceeds from the Father, he is called the Spirit of the Father and the Spirit of God.* But the same Spirit is also called the Spirit of the Son and the Spirit of Christ;† and, therefore, there must be the same reason presupposed in reference to the Son as is expressed in reference to the Father. If the Holy Ghost is called the Spirit of the Father because he proceeds from the Father, it will follow that he is called the Spirit of the Son because he proceeds also from the Son.

Again, because the Holy Ghost proceeds from the Father he is spoken of as being *sent* by the Father. "The Comforter, which is the Holy Ghost, whom the *Father will send* in my name, he shall teach you all things." John xiv, 26. But the same Spirit which is sent by the Father is also sent by the Son, as he said, "When the Comforter is come, *whom I will send* unto you." As, therefore, the Scriptures expressly declare that the Holy Spirit proceeds from the Father, so do they also virtually teach that he proceeds from the Son.

ARIUS regarded the Spirit not only as a creature, but as created by Christ; thus making him the creature of a creature. Some time afterward his personality was wholly denied by the Arians, and he was considered as the *exerted energy* of God. This appears to have been the notion of Socinus, and, with occasional modifications, has been adopted by his followers. They sometimes regard him as an *attribute*, and at others they resolve the passages in which he is spoken of into a figure of speech.

Having made these preliminary remarks, we will proceed to establish the proper Personality and Deity of the Holy Ghost.

I. HIS PERSONALITY.

With respect to the Personality of the Holy Ghost, it may be observed,

1. *That it follows from the mode of his subsistence in the Sacred Trinity.*—He proceeds from the Father and the Son, and, therefore, cannot be either. To say that an *attribute* proceeds or comes forth from God would be a gross absurdity. Accordingly, our Lord most clearly represents the Holy Ghost as the third *person* of the Divine

---

* See Matt. x, 20; 1 Cor. ii, 12.   † See Rom. viii, 9; Gal. iv, 6.

essence, and as distinguished *personally* from the Father and the Son. His language is, "I will pray the Father, and he shall give you another Comforter, that he may abide with you forever." This "Comforter," said he, "is the Holy Ghost, whom the Father will send in my name." John xiv, 16, 26. Here he calls the *first* person, most expressly and undeniably, "the Father," and the *third* person, as expressly, "the Holy Ghost." It is, therefore, most evident, and beyond even the possibility of a doubt, that he does not, by these two appellatives, mean one and the same Divine person.

2. *That many Scriptures are wholly unintelligible, and even absurd, unless the Personality of the Holy Ghost is allowed.*—Those who understand the phrase as ascribing merely a figurative personality to the *energy* or *power* of God, reduce such passages as the following to an utter want of meaning: "God anointed Jesus of Nazareth with the Holy Ghost and with power;" that is, with the *power of God* and with power. "That ye may abound in hope, through the power of the Holy Ghost;" that is, through the power of *the power of God*. "It seemed good to the Holy Ghost," that is, to *the power of God*, "and to us."

3. *That in some passages in which the Holy Ghost is spoken of personification of any kind is impossible.*—The reality, which this supposed figure of speech is said to represent, is either an attribute of God, or else the doctrine of the Gospel. Let this theory, then, be tried upon a few passages. "He (the Spirit) shall not speak of *himself*, but whatsoever he shall *hear*, that shall he speak." What attribute of God can here be personified? And if the doctrine of the Gospel be arrayed with personal attributes, where is there an instance of so monstrous a prosopopœia as this passage would present? the doctrine of the Gospel not speaking "of himself," but speaking "whatsoever he shall hear!" "The Spirit maketh intercession for us." What Divine attribute is capable of interceding, or how can the doctrine of the Gospel intercede?

Personification, too, is the language of poetry, and takes place naturally only in excited and elevated discourse; but if the Holy Ghost is a personification, we find it in the New Testament, in the cool and ordinary strain of mere narration and argumentative discourse, and in the most incidental conversations.*

4. *That there have been distinct symbolical representations of the Holy Ghost.*—At the baptism of our Lord, while the Father, by an audible voice declared, "This is my beloved Son," the Spirit "descended like a dove, and lighted upon him." Matt. iii, 16, 17. And on the day of Pentecost also, the communication of the Spirit to the apostles was represented by "cloven tongues like as of fire." Acts ii, 3. St. Peter's exposition of this miracle proves that the Spirit, though act-

* See Acts viii, 29; xix, 2.

ing in union with the Father and the Son, was yet a different person. "This Jesus," said he, "being by the right hand of God exalted, and having received of the Father the promise of the Holy Ghost, hath shed forth this which ye now see and hear." Acts ii, 33. These appearances, we allow, were merely emblematical of the Spirit's operations, and cannot convey to us any adequate conception of his real nature, or the mode of his existence, but they are nevertheless strong indications of his distinct personality.

5. And finally, *that the Holy Ghost is a person, and not an attribute, is proved by the use of masculine pronouns and relatives in the Greek of the New Testament*, in connection with the neuter noun πνευμα, Spirit, and by so many distinct personal acts being ascribed to him; as, to come, to go, to be sent, to teach, to guide, to comfort, to make intercession, to bear witness, to give gifts, "dividing them to every man as HE WILL," to be vexed, grieved, and quenched. These cannot be applied to the mere fiction of a person, and they therefore establish the true personality of the Holy Spirit.

II. THE DEITY OF THE HOLY SPIRIT.

That the Holy Spirit is really God, admits of so little doubt that his divinity is acknowledged even by many who deny his personality. But to place this doctrine in as clear a light as possible, we will adduce the leading arguments by which it is supported. And,

1. *The names which are applied to the Holy Spirit clearly indicate his Divine character.*—He is denominated GOD. "Why hath Satan filled thine heart to lie to the Holy Ghost? Thou hast not lied unto man, but unto God." Acts v, 3, 4. The spiritual gifts which the Corinthians received are all declared to be the work of "that self-same Spirit;" and yet concerning these operations St. Paul as expressly asserts, that "it is the same *God* which worketh all in all." 1 Cor. xii, 6–11. Moreover, to be "born of the Spirit," and to be "born of God," are convertible phrases.* He is also called LORD. "Now the Lord is that Spirit." 2 Cor. iii, 17.

2. *The Attributes which are ascribed to him proclaim his Divinity.*—ETERNITY is his, for he is called "the Eternal Spirit." Heb. ix, 14. He is OMNIPRESENT. "Your body," says the apostle, "is the temple of the Holy Ghost which is in you." 1 Cor. vi, 19. And again, "As many as are led by the Spirit of God, they are the sons of God." Rom. viii, 14. Now, as all true Christians are temples of the Holy Ghost, and are led by him, he must be present with them at all times and *in all places*. He is also OMNISCIENT; for, "the Spirit searcheth all things, yea, the deep things of God." 1 Cor. ii, 10. The moral attributes of God are also given to him. HOLINESS, which includes all in one: the HOLY Ghost is his eminent designation. GOODNESS: "Thy Spirit is good." GRACE: he is "the Spirit of Grace." TRUTH also, for he is "the Spirit of Truth."

* See John iii, 5, 6, 8; 1 John v, 1, 4, 18.

3. *His works are unequivocal attestations of his Divinity;* for they are such as no finite being can perform.

(1.) CREATION *is ascribed to him.* "He garnished the heavens," and "moved upon the face of the waters," to reduce the chaotic mass to order, and to impregnate dead matter with life and animation.* Nor is it an objection to the argument, that creation is ascribed to the Father, and also to the Son, but a confirmation of it, for that creation should be effected by all the three persons of the Godhead, so that each should be a *Creator*, and, therefore, a *Divine Person*, can be explained only by their unity in one essence. If the Spirit of God were a mere influence or attribute he could not be a *Creator*, distinct from the Father and the Son. But that creation is ascribed to him is evident, not only from the passages just quoted, but also from the language of the Psalmist: "By the Word of the Lord were the heavens made, and *all the host of them by the* BREATH (Heb. SPIRIT) *of his mouth.*" Psa. xxxiii, 6. This is further confirmed by Job xxxiii, 4 : "The SPIRIT OF GOD hath made me, and the BREATH *of the Almighty* hath given me life." Here, the latter clause is obviously exegetical of the former, and the whole text proves, that in the patriarchal age believers in the true religion ascribed creation to the Spirit, as well as to the Father; and that one of his appellations was "the BREATH of the Almighty." But as we have seen him acting in the material creation, so he is the author of the *new creation*, which is as evidently a work of Divine power as the former.

(2.) PRESERVATION, *which has been well denominated a continued creation*, is also ascribed to the Holy Spirit.—This is beautifully presented in the following passage: "Thou SENDEST FORTH THY SPIRIT, they are created, (or *reanimated*,) and thou renewest the face of the earth." Psa. civ, 30. It cannot here be meant that the Spirit, by which the generations of animals are perpetuated, is *wind;* nor can the term denote a mere attribute of God, for the Scriptures nowhere teach that he *sends forth* his attributes to renew the face of the earth.

(3.) *It belongs to the Spirit to* RAISE THE DEAD.—"It is the Spirit," said our Lord, "that quickeneth." John vi, 63. Peter testifies that Christ was "put to death in the flesh, but quickened by the Spirit." 1 Peter iii, 18. St. Paul assures us that at the last day our scattered dust shall be collected and reanimated by the same Divine agent. "He that raised up Christ from the dead shall also quicken your mortal bodies by his Spirit that dwelleth in you." Rom. viii, 11.

(4.) *He is the source of* INSPIRATION *to the prophets.*—St. Paul says that "GOD spake unto the fathers by the prophets." Heb. i, 1. St. Peter declares that these "holy men of God spake as they were moved by the HOLY GHOST;" 2 Peter i, 21; and also that it was "the SPIRIT of CHRIST which was in them." 1 Peter i, 11. We may defy any Socin-

---
* See Gen. i, 2; Job xxvi, 13.

ian to interpret these three passages, by making the Spirit an influence or attribute, and thereby reducing the term Holy Ghost to a figure of speech. "*God*," in the first passage, is unquestionably God the Father, and the "holy men of God," the prophets, would then, according to this view, be moved by the influence of the Father; but according to the third passage, the source of their inspiration was "the Spirit of Christ." Thus the two passages contradict each other. Allow the Trinity in Unity, and there is no impropriety in calling the Spirit the Spirit of the Father and the Spirit of the Son, or the Spirit of either. But if the Spirit were an influence, that influence could not be the influence of two persons, one God and the other a creature. If, however, the Holy Ghost is the Spirit of the Father and of the Son, united in one essence, the passages are easily harmonized; for, in conjunction with the Father and the Son, he is the source of prophetic inspiration, and is therefore Divine.

4. The last argument for the divinity of the Holy Ghost is founded on the fact *that he is the object of supreme worship.* We are taught throughout the Scriptures to seek for the influences of the Spirit by fervent prayer; to depend upon him for the mortification of sin, and for our growth in holiness; and to yield ourselves with unfeigned submission to his direction.*

We have an example of prayer to him in the following words, which are still used in the solemn benediction of the Church: "The grace of the Lord Jesus Christ, and the love God, and the *communion of the Holy Ghost*, be with you all. Amen." 2 Cor. xiii, 14. Here the Holy Ghost is acknowledged as the source of spiritual blessings, as well as the Father and the Son, and is invoked in the same spirit of devotion. It is vain to call this merely a wish. It is as distinctly a prayer as any other that occurs in the Scriptures; and there would be no question about its nature if there were no design to evade the force of its evidence.

The form of baptism is also demonstrative of the divinity of the Holy Spirit. It is the form of *covenant* by which the sacred Three become our ONE and ONLY GOD, and we become HIS people. "Go ye, therefore, and teach all nations, baptizing them in the NAME of the FATHER, and of the SON, and of the HOLY GHOST." Matt. xxviii, 19. How is this text to be disposed of if the divinity of the Holy Ghost is denied? Does the form of baptism imply that persons are to be baptized in the name of one *God*, one *creature*, and one *attribute?* An opinion so grossly absurd is its own refutation; for, in the case before us, there can be no personification. If, then, all the Three are *persons*, is Christian baptism to be administered in the name of one *God* and two *creatures?* This would be downright idolatry. It follows, therefore, that in this single passage of Scripture we have a most convincing proof of the divinity of the *Spirit*, as well as of the Father and the Son.

* See Luke xi, 13; Rom. viii, 13, 14; Gal. v, 25.

It may also be observed in this connection that what the Scriptures declare respecting the sin against the Holy Ghost proves him to be the object of supreme worship, and therefore Divine. "But whosoever speaketh against the Holy Ghost, it shall not be forgiven him, neither in this world, neither in the world to come." Matt. xii, 32. This crime consisted in ascribing to Satan the miracles which our Lord wrought by the power of the Holy Ghost. But if to "speak against the Holy Ghost" was a sin in the proper sense, and of so malignant a kind as to place it beyond the reach of mercy, he can be no other than the very and eternal God.

It follows, therefore, in conclusion, that our regards are justly due to this DIVINE PERSON as the object of worship and trust, of prayer and blessing—duties to which we are especially called, both by the general consideration of his divinity and by that affectingly benevolent and attractive character under which he is presented to us in the holy Scriptures. In *creation* we see him moving upon the face of chaos, and reducing it to beauty and order; in *providence*, renewing the earth, garnishing the heavens, and giving life to man. In *grace* we behold him expanding the prophetic scene to the vision of the seers of the Old Testament, and making a perfect revelation of the doctrines of Christ to the apostles of the New. He reproves the world of sin, working in the human heart a secret conviction of its evil and danger. He is "the Spirit of grace and supplication;" and from him are the softened heart, the yielding will, and all heavenly desires and tendencies. He hastens to the troubled spirit of penitent men, who are led by his influences to trust in Christ, with the news of pardon; bearing witness with their spirit that they are the children of God. He helps their infirmities; makes intercession for them; inspires thoughts of consolation and feelings of peace; plants and perfects in them whatsoever things are pure, lovely, honest, and of good report; dwells in the soul as in a temple; and, after having rendered the spirit to God, without "spot, or wrinkle, or any such thing," finishes his benevolent and glorious work by raising the bodies of the saints, at the last day, to immortality and eternal life. So powerfully does "the Spirit of glory and of God" claim our love, our praise, and our obedience! Hence, in the forms of the Christian Church he has been constantly associated with the Father and the Son in equal glory and blessing; and this recognition of the Holy Spirit ought to be made in every gratulatory act of devotion, that so equally to each person of the eternal Trinity glory may be given "in the Church throughout all ages. Amen."

CHAPTER VIII.

THE DECREES OF GOD.

WE have hitherto considered God with regard to his existence, his nature and attributes, and the manner of his subsisting in a Trinity of Persons; but we will now proceed to contemplate him in his *acts* or *efficiency*.

The *acts* of God are, in theological language, either *internal* or *external*. His *internal* acts are either those which belong to himself alone, as the generation of the Son, and the procession of the Holy Ghost; or those which take place in himself with respect to external objects. Such are his *decrees* "which he hath purposed in himself." Eph. i, 9.

The *external* acts of God are those exertions of his power which terminate upon his creatures. These are comprehended in his works of *creation* and *providence*.

As it is reasonable to believe that God does nothing without previous deliberation, and thence resolving upon what his infinite wisdom perceives to be best, which resolves have obtained among divines the name of *decrees*, it will be proper, before we consider his external acts, to present a scriptural view of these decrees; and to this subject our attention will be directed in the present chapter. We will *first* prove their existence, and *secondly*, inquire into their nature and properties.

I. THE EXISTENCE OF THE DIVINE DECREES.

No one who believes God to be an intelligent being, and who considers what intelligence implies, will deny that there are Divine decrees. As God knew all things that his power could accomplish, there were undoubtedly reasons which determined him to do certain things in preference to others, and his choice, which was founded upon those reasons, was his purpose or decree.

It will certainly be admitted, that God intended to create the world before he actually created it; that he intended to make man before he fashioned his body, and breathed into him the breath of life; and that he intended to govern the world according to certain laws. It will be admitted also, that when he resolved to create the world, to make man, and to establish laws physical and moral, he had some ultimate object in view. Having constructed a machine and set it in motion, he knew what would be the result; and this result was the true reason or the final cause why the machine was constructed. This intention of God is, therefore, his decree.

To this general idea of the Divine decrees it would be unreasonable to object, because it is as necessarily forced upon our mind as the idea of a purpose in the mind of a wise man previous to his entering upon any important enterprise; and with this idea the teachings of the holy Scriptures are in perfect harmony. They speak of the purpose of God, his will, his good pleasure, his determinate counsel, and his predestination. "All things work together for good to them that love God, to them who are called according to his *purpose*." Rom. viii, 28. "Paul, an apostle of Jesus Christ by the *will* of God." 2 Cor. i, 1. "Having made known unto us the mystery of his will, according to his *good pleasure* which he hath *purposed* in himself." Eph. i, 9. "Him being delivered by the *determinate counsel* and foreknowledge of God, ye have taken," etc. Acts ii, 23. "Having *predestinated* us unto the adoption of children by Jesus Christ to himself." Eph. i, 5. But it is unnecessary to multiply quotations. These Scriptures clearly prove, as do many others, that the operations of God are not the effects of necessity, but of *counsel* and *design*.

II. THE NATURE AND PROPERTIES OF THE DIVINE DECREES.

The decrees of God may be defined to be, *his purposes or determinations respecting his creatures*. For this reason they are sometimes called the *counsel*, and sometimes the *will* of God; terms which are never applied to necessary things, but only to the determinations of free agents.

When the Scriptures represent the decrees of God as his *counsel*, the word is not to be taken in its common acceptation, as implying consultation with others; nor is it to be understood as denoting reflection, comparison, and the establishment of a conclusion by logical deduction. But the decisions of an infinite mind are instantaneous; and they are called *counsel*, to signify that they are consummately wise.

Nor are we to conclude, because the decrees of God are denominated his *will*, that they are arbitrary decisions; but merely, that in making them he was under no control, but acted according to his own sovereignty. When a man's own will is the rule of his conduct, it is in many instances capricious and unreasonable; but *wisdom* is always associated with *will* in the Divine proceedings. Accordingly, the decrees of God are said to be "the counsel of his will."

But in considering more particularly the nature and properties of the Divine decrees, it may be remarked,

1. *That they are eternal.*—This is virtually taught by the apostle when he says, "Known unto God are all his works from the beginning of the world." Acts xv, 18. The passage clearly imports, that at the commencement of time the plan was arranged according to which the works of God were to be executed. To suppose any of the Divine decrees to be made in time, is to suppose that the knowledge of God is limited; that he receives accessions to it in the progress of time, and that he forms new resolutions as new occasions require. Surely no one who believes that the Divine understanding is infinite, comprehending the past, the present, and the future, will ever assent to the doctrine of

temporal decrees. If God has any plan at all, it must be eternal; and hence St. Paul speaks of "the *eternal purpose* which he purposed in Christ Jesus our Lord." Eph. iii, 11.

2. *The decrees of God are free.*—By this we are to understand, that his determinations were not necessitated by any external cause, that he was at liberty to decree or not to decree, and to decree one thing and not another. This liberty we must ascribe to Him who is supreme, independent, and sovereign in all his dispensations. "Who hath directed the Spirit of the Lord, or being his counselor hath taught him? With whom took he counsel, and who instructed him, and taught him in the path of judgment, and taught him knowledge, and showed to him the way of understanding?" Isa. xl, 13, 14.

To deny the *freedom* of the Divine decrees is the same as to assert that they could not have been different from what they are. But are we prepared to adopt this sentiment? As well might we affirm that God could not have performed the work of creation sooner or later than he did; that he could not have made the world in any respect different from what it is; that he could not have placed man in a higher or lower degree in the scale of being; and that, when he had fallen, he could not have done otherwise than to redeem him by the death of his Son. Such a view of necessity, however, in regard either to the operations or the purposes of God, is both contrary to Scripture, and injurious to the feelings of piety, and must, therefore, be rejected.

We assert, then, that the decrees of God are *free.* No necessity can be supposed to influence the procedure of a self-existent and independent Being, except the necessity arising from his own perfections, of always acting in a manner worthy of himself. To his infinite understanding there must have appeared more than one way of doing this; and though there were doubtless reasons for the choice which he made, it would be boldness, not to be vindicated from the charge of impiety, to say that he could not have made a different choice.

3. *The decrees of God are immutable.*—This characteristic of the Divine decrees results from the infinite perfection and immutability of God; for if the least change should take place in his plans and determinations, it would be an instance of imperfection. The mutability of human purposes is owing to the uncertainty and defectiveness of human knowledge; but God knows with absolute certainty all things that ever were, now are, or ever shall be, and his purposes must therefore continue the same, amid all the changes of created things. "He is of one mind, and who can turn him?" Job xxiii, 13. "The counsel of the Lord standeth forever; the thoughts of his heart to all generations." Psalm xxxiii, 11. He declares, "My counsel shall stand, and I will do all my pleasure." Isa. xlvi, 10.

To the immutability of the Divine decrees it has been objected that the Scriptures represent God, in some cases at least, as changing his purpose. For instance, he said to King Hezekiah, "Set thine house in order; for thou shalt die and not live." But afterward he said to him, "I will add unto thy days fifteen years." 2 Kings xx, 1, 6. Again, God commanded Jonah to say to the people of Nineveh, "Yet forty days, and Nineveh shall be overthrown." But when he saw that "they turned from their evil way," he "repented of the evil that he had said that he would do unto them; and he did it not." Jonah iii, 10.

To meet the objection, and to reconcile these and all similar cases with the immutability of God's purposes, it is only necessary to observe, *first*, that the objector confounds two things which are essentially different, the Divine *purpose*, and the Divine *administration*. The former is nothing more than the *plan* according to which God operates as the Creator and Governor of the world; while the latter consists in his *actual operation* in accordance with this plan. *Secondly*, that man is a free moral agent, and is, therefore, governed by laws and motives adapted to his moral constitution; and that the purpose of God extends to the whole duration of his existence, and not merely to some particular period of it. Hence it is easy to conceive, in view of the conditionality of God's moral government and of the mutability of man, that the Divine administration respecting him may at one time be very different from what it is at another; while in both cases it accords with the immutability of the Divine decrees.

For the sake of illustration, we may remark that the law which at one time protects a man in the possession of civil liberty may, at a subsequent period, condemn him to death. Would this imply a change in the law? By no means. The *law* would continue the same—the only change would be in the *subject* who should incur its penalty. When man was created he was placed under a law, in obedience to which he enjoyed life in its highest sense; but under the operation of that same law he became liable to death spiritual, temporal, and eternal. Did the law change? No; but man changed by disobeying it, and thus subjected himself to its curse. If, then, it is consistent with the immutability of God's *law* that the same moral agent should at one time be acquitted and at another time condemned, it may be equally consistent with the immutability of his *decrees*; for of these his revealed will is only the formal declaration.

When, therefore, we meet with passages of Scripture in which a change of the Divine purpose seems to be indicated, as in the case of Hezekiah, or in which God is said to repent, as it is asserted of him in regard to the inhabitants of Nineveh, we must understand them to imply a change of the Divine *administration*, but not of the Divine purpose. It is to be remembered that in many of the most positive declarations of Scripture there are implied conditions. Thus, when God said to the Jewish king, "Thou shalt die, and not live," it was only the announcement of what must have been the inevitable consequence of his sickness had it not been divinely prevented. But as Hezekiah did not believe the sentence to be unconditional, he "prayed unto the Lord" and "wept sore;" and God regarded his supplications, removed his disease, and added to his "days fifteen years." So also in the case of the Ninevites the threatening was conditional, as the event clearly proves; consequently, when they "turned from their evil way" they escaped the threatened judgment.

4. *The decrees of God have been considered by theologians as either Absolute or Conditional.*

(1.) *Absolute* decrees are such as relate to those events in the Divine administration which have no dependence upon the free actions of moral creatures. These decrees are not called absolute, however, because they were made in the exercise of mere arbitrary power; but because, though made in view of wise and good reasons, the execution of them is not suspended upon any condition that may or may not be performed by moral creatures, but is to be ascribed to Divine agency. Thus, the purpose of God to create the world, to send his Son to redeem it, to bestow Gospel privileges upon one people and to deny them to another, and all his determinations of this nature, are called *absolute decrees*.

(2.) *Conditional* decrees are those in making which God had respect to the free actions of his moral creatures. Of this class are the purposes of God respecting the eternal welfare of men. They are founded upon that foreknowledge of men's moral actions which we are compelled to ascribe to God, and are never absolute, but always conditional. We must not conclude, however, as some have done, that conditional decrees are necessarily uncertain and mutable. They no more involve the idea of mutability than do those that are absolute. To the mind of God the end is as certain in one case as in the other, the only difference being in the means by which it is brought about. In *absolute* decrees God has respect to his own agency alone; in those that are *conditional*, to the agency of his free moral subjects; but in neither case can uncertainty or mutability be justly ascribed to them. God foresaw from eternity how every man would act, and whether he would comply with the conditions under which the designs of God concerning him would take effect or would reject them; and upon this perfect foreknowledge were his decrees founded. It is on this account, therefore, and this alone, that they are denominated *conditional*.

It is maintained by some that the foreknowledge of God is dependent upon his decrees. "If we allow the attribute of *prescience*," says Mr. Buck, "the idea of a decree must certainly be allowed also; for how can an action that is really to come to pass be foreseen if it be not determined? God knew everything from the beginning; but this he could not know if he had not so determined it." This notion, though advocated by high authority, we must regard as both absurd in itself and contrary to Scripture. It is absurd in itself, because it makes an essential attribute of God depend upon his efficiency. "God could not have known everything from the beginning if he had not so determined it." Thus the Divine prescience is brought into existence by an exercise of the Divine mind, in decreeing "whatsoever comes to pass." Again, if "God foresees nothing but what he has decreed, and his decree precedes his knowledge," as Piscator tells us, then it follows that, as the cause cannot be dependent on the effect, God must have made his decrees and contrived his plans independent of his knowledge, which only had an existence as the effect of these decrees. But if these conclusions are absurd, so must that doctrine be also of which they are the legitimate consequences.

This notion is, moreover, contrary to Scripture. St. Paul says, Rom. viii, 29, "For whom he did *foreknow*, he also did *predestinate* to be conformed to the image of his Son;" and St. Peter, in addressing believers, calls them "elect *according to the foreknowledge* of God the Father." 1 Peter i, 2. In these passages the decree of predestination or election is clearly founded on the foreknowledge of God. He foreknew in order to predestinate, but he did not predestinate in order to foreknow. Now as St. Paul tells the Christians at Rome that they were predestinated according to Divine foreknowledge, and St. Peter informs those in Asia Minor that they were elected in the same way, it follows either that all the elect are thus chosen, or that God pursued one plan in electing the Christians of Rome and Lesser Asia, and a different one for the rest of the world. But as the latter cannot be true, the former must be admitted. It is therefore evident that, in the order of cause and effect, the *exercise* of the Divine attributes is consequent upon their *existence;* that the plan of the Almighty is the result of his infinite knowledge; and that the decrees of his throne flow forth from the eternal fountain of his wisdom.

The conditionality of the Divine decrees, so far as they relate to the eternal destiny of men, may be argued, *first*, from the manner in which God actually saves sinners. Does he effect their salvation *unconditionally?* We answer, that he never would have saved men had not Christ died for them. This, then, is a *condition* of human salvation, the grand event on account of which God forgives sin. But does God actually save sinners without any condition *on their part?* The Bible furnishes the answer: "Except ye repent, ye shall all likewise perish." Luke xiii, 3. "He that believeth and is baptized shall be saved; but he that believeth not shall be damned." Mark xvi, 16. "If thou wilt enter into life, keep the commandments." Matt. xix, 17. The conditions, then, of eternal life are repentance, faith, and obedience. These conditions, it is true, are of a different nature from the atonement; but they are equally necessary. Hence we come to the conclusion, that, as the actual salvation of men is *conditional*, the decrees of God respecting it are *conditional* also.

It must be admitted, that the manner in which God will distribute happiness and misery in the future world is the precise mode which he eternally intended to pursue. If, then, it can be made appear that he certainly will reward men according to their works, it will follow that he eternally purposed to do so. But the Scriptures do most explicitly declare that God "will render to every man according to his deeds;" that every man shall "receive the things done in his body, according to that he hath done, whether it be good or bad;" and that "whatsoever a man soweth, that shall he also reap." Therefore, as it is certain that God will, in the world to come, treat men according to their moral conduct here, it follows that he always intended to do so; and if the decrees of God relative to men's future destiny were thus based upon their foreseen voluntary actions, they may be properly denominated *conditional*.

Secondly, the view which we have taken of this subject is further confirmed by what we know of the *character of God*. The Scriptures declare that "God is love;" that he "is good to all, and his tender mercies are over all his works;" and that he has "no pleasure in the death of him that dieth." How, then, could he have decreed to consign millions of the human family to endless perdition regardless of their conduct? Or, how could he place men under circumstances in which they must inevitably continue in sin, and then punish them in hell forever for not exercising that repentance and faith which he determined never to give them? The Scriptures assert that God is "long-suffering to usward, not willing that any should perish, but that all should come to repentance." But how could his bearing with the non-elect be properly an act of long-suffering, if he had determined to withhold forever from them that special grace by which alone they could repent, however long he might wait with them? How could the inspired apostle say that God is "not willing that any should perish," if from all eternity he had doomed, unconditionally, a large portion of the human family to endless misery? How could he assert the willingness of God "that *all* should come to repentance," if he had unconditionally determined to leave millions of our race in that moral condition in which true repentance is impossible?

Moreover, what *sincerity* could there be in the proclamation of the "Gospel to every creature," if God had determined by an absolute decree the eternal destiny of all men? The Gospel would offer a free and full salvation to those for whom no provision had been made in the redeeming plan, and life eternal to those who had been ordained to eternal death. And how can we reconcile with the *justice* and *impartiality* of God the opinion, that while he calls men into existence with a fallen and depraved nature, he should, irrespective of their conduct, elect some to everlasting life and consign others to hell? "God is no respecter of persons; but in every nation he that feareth him, and worketh righteousness, is accepted with him." How could this be said if God had made among his creatures a distinction of such incalculable magnitude and eternal duration as would be implied in the unconditional salvation of some, and unavoidable damnation of others?

The conclusion, then, of the whole matter is this: that though we ascribe to God decrees which are absolute and unconditional, yet, so far as they relate to the eternal destiny of men, they were formed in full view of men's free moral actions, and are, therefore, *conditional*. Properly speaking, however, these decrees cannot be said to depend on any thing but God himself, who perfectly knew from the beginning what would be the nature and consequences of every future occurrence.

We will close this chapter by a brief notice of the distinction which some theologians make between the revealed will of God, and what they are pleased to call his *secret* will. If this distinction were based upon the opinion, that God has plans and purposes which he has not fully revealed to mankind, it might very readily be allowed; for the Scriptures declare that "secret things belong unto the Lord our God; but those things which are revealed belong to us and to our children." Deut. xxix, 29. It is generally assumed, however, by the advocates of this distinction, that the *secret* will of God is, in many cases, directly contrary to what he has revealed in his word. For instance, God "will have all men to be saved, and to come unto the knowledge of the truth." 1 Tim. ii, 4. This is acknowledged to be his *revealed* will; but it is nevertheless contended that his *secret* will is, that many of the human race should *not* "be saved," or "come to the knowledge of the truth," but perish forever.

To this view of the secret will of God we object, for several reasons: 1. It is wholly gratuitous. There is not a single passage of Scripture which, when fairly interpreted, teaches the doctrine that the *will* of God is in any case contrary to his *word*. 2. It is absurd in itself. We can become acquainted with the purposes of God only so far as they are revealed. Of his secret or unrevealed will we can know nothing. If, therefore, we assume, in any given case, that the *secret* will of God is contrary to what he has revealed, we virtually assume that we know, by some means or other, what the secret will of God is, and consequently that it is both secret and revealed at the same time, which is a contradiction. But, 3. This opinion is dishonorable to the Divine character. It represents God as having two wills, which are in many cases contrary to one another, as declaring in the most solemn manner that he has "no pleasure in the death of him that dieth," while it is according to his *secret will* that multiplied thousands should die eternally. We conclude, therefore, that this theory is untenable, and that we can only judge of the will of God by what he has revealed.

CHAPTER IX.

OF CREATION.

HAVING considered in the preceding chapter the decrees of God, we are naturally led to speak, in the next place, of those exertions of his power which terminate upon created objects. Our attention shall be directed, in this chapter, to the work of *Creation;* which we will consider, *first*, in general, and *secondly*, in particular.

§ 1. *Of Creation in General.*

In the investigation of this part of the subject it will be proper to inquire into the *nature*, the *date*, and the *extent* of creation.

I. THE NATURE OF CREATION.

Here it is necessary to ascertain what the precise idea of creation is, or the sense in which the term *create* is to be understood, when it is employed to denote the agency of God in the production of the universe. The original word is ברא, which signifies, in its primary sense, to cause a thing to exist or spring forth from nothing. But it means also, to form a thing out of existing materials, to revive or reinvigorate, and to effect a change in our moral nature, as when a new heart is said to be created within us.

When it is said, in the first of Genesis, that "God *created* the heavens and the earth," the word is to be taken in its primary sense, as denoting the original production of matter by Almighty power; while the subsequent verses inform us by what steps God formed this mass of rude matter into that beautiful system of nature which excites the admiration of every beholder. "In the beginning," or at the commencement of time, he made out of nothing the matter of which the heavens and the earth were composed, and upon which their present form was afterward superinduced. This seems to be the natural way of explaining this part of sacred history; and according to this view, the Bible opens with an ascription to God of the act of creation in the highest sense of the term.

There is another passage of Scripture which will assist us in ascertaining the sense in which God is said to have created the world. "Through faith we understand that the worlds were framed by the word of God, so that things which are seen were not made of things which do appear." Heb. xi, 3. Here we learn that the visible creation was not formed out of pre-existent matter. For, if it had been so formed, that matter, however extended or modified, would still *appear* in the present system; but the apostle asserts, that "the things which are seen [the visible creation] were *not* made of *things which do appear.*" It follows, therefore, that he virtually denies the eternity of matter, and asserts the creation of all things out of nothing, "by the word of God."

By *creation*, then, we are to understand *that act of God by which he gave existence to the world*, or to things extrinsic to himself; or, as it is commonly expressed, *by which he made the world* OUT OF NOTHING. Accordingly, the holy Scriptures constantly describe God as the creator of the world; not merely in regard to its present form, but of the materials themselves from which it is formed.*

The Grecian philosophers and other ancient writers, being ignorant of Divine revelation, and guided only by the wild speculations of their own imagination, had no just idea of creation in its proper sense. They insisted upon the principle, *ex nihilo nihil fit;* and could not admit, therefore, that it was possible for God to create the world out of nothing. Accordingly they believed almost universally that matter, in a chaotic state, existed from all eternity; and that God only arranged and moulded the discordant materials, so as to bring order out of confusion, and cause the universe to appear in its harmony and beauty. With them God was merely the *builder*, and not the *creator* of the world.

It is easy to show, however, that this notion of the eternity of matter is absurd and untenable. To suppose that matter existed from eternity is to ascribe to it self-existence. For, that which existed from eternity could not have been produced by anything else. The only cause of its existence, therefore, must be in itself; and this implies that it is self-existent and independent.

Again, if matter is self-existent and independent, as its eternity clearly implies, it must exist *necessarily.* For, if the cause of its existence has always been in itself, it could not but have existed; otherwise, the necessary connection between cause and effect would be destroyed.

But if matter exists necessarily, this necessity must be the same everywhere. Consequently, upon this supposition, matter must have existed everywhere, or must have filled every portion of space, and have been infinitely extended; which is absurd, and contrary to fact.

There is another consequence which is equally absurd, that, if matter exists necessarily, that necessity must extend to all its properties. But if so, the particular *state* in which it exists must be necessary; and then, the same eternal necessity which determined the *state* of its existence must determine its *continuance* in that state. Consequently, if

---

* The phrase, *to create from nothing*, does not occur in the canonical Scriptures, though the idea itself is scriptural. It seems to have been taken from 2 Macc. vii, 28, in the Vulgate; "*ex nihilo fecit Deus cœlum et terram.*"

matter had existed from eternity in a chaotic state, it must have continued in that state until now; and upon this hypothesis the worlds could not have been produced from chaotic matter.

Some have adopted the theory that the material universe has existed from eternity in its organized condition; but this hypothesis is as unreasonable as the former. For,

1. *It is inconsistent with the nature of time, which is a succession of moments.*—" We can conceive time to commence at any given period, and to run on *ad infinitum*, or never to come to an end; but we cannot conceive it to be actually infinite. An infinite duration can never be made up of finite parts; because as each of those parts has an end, the sum which they compose must also have an end. As it is impossible that an infinite succession of moments can be past, it is impossible that the universe can have existed from eternity."*

2. *The eternity of the world in its organized state is disproved by the history of arts and sciences.*—It is but reasonable to suppose that each generation would profit by the labors and experience of preceding generations, and that human society should be characterized from age to age by progressive improvement. But we know that civilization and learning can be traced back only to a period which is but as yesterday, and that all the great and important discoveries in the arts and sciences are of comparatively recent date. These facts strongly indicate, therefore, that only a few thousand years have elapsed since our earth and its inhabitants came into existence.

3. *Another argument against the eternity of the world in its organized state is founded on the comparatively modern date of authentic history.*—No credible history reaches further back than the period which Moses has assigned for the creation; and profane history has nothing to relate but fables and rumors till the age of Herodotus, who flourished about five hundred years before the Christian era. These facts would be unaccountable if the earth and man had existed from eternity; for then we might readily suppose that history, either recorded or monumental, would carry us back for thousands of centuries.

Such are some of the speculations of heathen philosophers in regard to the visible creation, and of the numerous difficulties in which their theories are involved. But if we follow the principles of philosophy in its present improved state, or rather, if we follow the Bible, to which alone our modern philosophy is indebted for its improvement, we will not admit the maxim *ex nihilo nihil fit* in reference to the creation of the world. This maxim is indeed incontrovertible, when applied to material causes;† but it is not true, if understood of an *efficient* cause

---

* Dick's Theology, Lecture 37.

† The *material* cause of a thing is that out of which it is made. For example, the marble out of which a statue is made is its *material* cause; but the sculptor who forms the statue is its *efficient* cause.

to which omnipotence is ascribed. Consequently, if our theory respecting God and his attributes is well established, this principle applied to him as the efficient cause of the world must be regarded as false. For, if God is omnipotent, he can from nothing produce something, or bring into existence what did not exist before. Moreover, if it is true that matter is *not necessary*, it cannot exist *of itself*, but must derive its existence from God, or depend upon him, who at first created it out of nothing.

The truth that God created from nothing everything that exists, is the uniform doctrine of the Bible; but it is a doctrine which was unknown to the ancient philosophers long after it had been taught by the writers of the Jewish Scriptures. Indeed, it is from these Scriptures that our modern philosophers have derived, however unwilling they are to confess it, all their better views upon this subject. To the sacred writers, therefore, we owe the doctrine that God gave existence to what was not.

II. THE DATE OF CREATION.

According to the Hebrew chronology, as ascertained by Archbishop Usher, the creation took place four thousand and four years before the Christian era; but according to the Septuagint, five thousand two hundred and seventy years. It is easy to determine which of these computations should be preferred. The *original*, when all the copies agree, is surely higher authority than any translation; and especially the Septuagint, which is probably the most inaccurate of all translations. Accordingly the computation of Usher has been generally received as reliable.

But here we are encountered by the pretended discoveries of modern science. The observations which geologists have made upon the structure of the earth are supposed to contradict the Mosaic account, by proving that it must have been created at a more distant period, if it was created at all; and that it must have undergone many revolutions prior to what we call the beginning. By some the Mosaic account is rejected entirely; while others suppose it to be a record, not of the original creation of the earth, but of the changes which took place upon it after some terrible convulsion. Thus, in the language of Cowper,

"Some drill and bore
The solid earth, and from the strata there
Extract a register, by which we learn
That He who made it, and revealed its date
To Moses, was mistaken in its age."

Geologists talk much of primitive formations. They ascribe the origin of rocks to precipitation and crystallization. Looking at a piece of granite they point out the characters of aqueous or igneous fusion, and say that it was formed by the agency of water or fire, carried on through a long process, which it required ages to complete; and from such data they come to the conclusion that a much longer period was necessary to form the rocks and strata of the earth than the Scriptures assign. Thus puny mortals, with but a spark of intellect, and only a moment for observation, deem themselves fully authorized, from a mere glance at a few superficial appearances, to contradict the account which Moses gives of the world's creation. "Where wast thou," said the Almighty to Job, "when I laid the foundations of the earth? Declare, if thou hast understanding." Job xxxviii, 4.

It is easy to show that the main geological argument for the great age of the world is without any solid foundation. It is not denied that the various formations of the earth, so far as they have been examined, appear as if they had been produced by chemical laws. But is it therefore certain that they were so produced? Why may we not suppose that God created everything in agreement with the action of those natural laws which he imparted to matter, and which he evidently intended to operate in the physical world? Why may we not suppose, for instance, that rocks were at first formed so as to correspond with all the phenomena of precipitation and crystallization? No one but an Atheist will deny that this was possible; but if it was possible the argument from primitive formations, against the comparatively modern date of the earth, falls to the ground.

That there was a first man will be admitted by all who believe in the existence of a great First Cause. Now, if we had the opportunity of examining one of his bones we should doubtless perceive that it resembled, in all respects, the bones of other men; and, reasoning according to our geologists, we should conclude that its fibers were at first soft, that they gradually became cartilage, and that they finally acquired the hardness of their perfect state. But we should reason falsely, because that bone was at once made solid and firm. Could we examine the first tree that God created, we should perceive that it indicated, like any other tree, the growth of successive years. We would naturally conclude, therefore, if we had no knowledge of its history, that it had originally sprung from a seed, and that it had come to a state of maturity by the usual process; while the fact would be that it had been produced in a moment. In the former case we would have all the *apparent effects* of ossification, and in the latter, of lignification, while it is certain that these processes never took place. It follows, then, that sensible phenomena cannot alone determine the age of the world, or the mode of the earth's formation.

Some, unwilling to reject the history of Moses in regard to the origin of the world, have attempted to reconcile it with the popular theory, by supposing that the six days of creation were not natural days of twenty-four hours, but so many periods of indefinite length. They assume that the world must have been created at an earlier date than the literal interpretation of the history assigns to it, and that ages were necessary to give rise to those appearances which are observed in its structure.

CREATION IN GENERAL.

To this notion we reply, *first*, that there is no necessity for such an interpretation of the days of Moses, or for supposing the original chaos to have been an immense laboratory, from which, after the operations of ages, the earth came forth as we now see it. There was a Power adequate to create it at once—a Power which formed the primeval rocks without the aid of fire or water, as it made perfect bones and perfect trees, independent of those second causes by which they are now produced. But, *secondly*, this view of the subject is objectionable because it puts a meaning upon the word day which it bears nowhere else in simple narrative, and for which there is no authority in the Bible. Indeed, when we consider the distinct manner in which the day is defined, as "the evening and the morning," if the term were not to be taken in its literal sense, we could hardly vindicate the sacred historian from an intention to mislead.

It must not be forgotten in our geological investigations that the earth was at first in all probability in a fluid state; and, also, that it must have undergone various and great changes at the time of the deluge. It is impossible to conceive the modifications which must have been produced in its structure by the breaking up of "the fountains of the great deep," and by the irresistible action of such an immense body of water as submerged the entire globe. We may not be able to answer all the objections which geologists urge against the literal interpretation of the Mosaic history; but neither can they prove that the appearances upon which they found their theories did not result from those facts.

We conclude, therefore, that the language of Moses is to be taken in its literal sense when he says, "In *six days* the Lord made heaven and earth;" and that the account which he gives of the origin of the world is the only rational theory that has ever been presented. If in any opposing scheme philosophers were generally united, their opinion would have great force; but their theories are different and contradictory. What one builds up another destroys; while the narrative of Moses stands unmoved, like a rock amid the waves of the ocean, resting on the solid basis of all the proofs by which its Divine authority is established.

Thus the heavens and the earth were created about four thousand years before the birth of Christ. The materials themselves were produced out of nothing in an instant by the power of God; but six days were employed in moulding them into that harmonious and beautiful system of nature which we call the universe. On the first day light was created; on the second the atmosphere; on the third the water was collected into lakes and seas, and the dry land appeared, which was immediately covered with grass, herbs, and trees; on the fourth the sun, the moon, and the stars became visible; on the fifth the waters and the air were replenished with inhabitants; and on the sixth terrestrial animals and man were created.

III. THE EXTENT OF THE CREATION.

The sacred historian, in speaking of the creation of the universe, adopts the common and obvious division of it into two parts, the *earth* and the *heavens*. The earth, indeed, is but a small part of the universe; but as it is the allotted habitation of the human race, it was proper that it should be distinctly noticed and particularly described.

All the other parts of creation are comprehended under the term *heavens*, which signifies, in the language of the Jews, the atmosphere; the region of the sun, moon, and stars; and lastly, the habitation of the blessed. The atmosphere properly belongs to the earth, and appears to have been the work of the second day, when God said, "Let there be a firmament in the midst of the waters; and let it divide the waters from the waters." Gen. i, 6. The word רקיע, which is rendered *firmament*, signifies an *expanse* or *space;* a term which very aptly denotes the atmosphere as surrounding the earth, and extending to a great distance from its surface. This is the region in which clouds and meteors are formed, and in which the water exhaled from the earth and the sea is suspended till, condensed by cold, it falls down in dew and rain.

But the term *heavens* includes the sun, moon, and stars. The sun is the great source of light to our system; and the moon, though probably created as soon as the earth, is said to have been made on the fourth day, because it then only became visible by reflecting the rays of the sun.* Under the denomination of the stars are included, not only those luminaries which are properly so called, but the planets also which belong to our system. The Bible gives no further account of these heavenly bodies than that some of them were appointed "for signs, and for seasons, and for days and years." Any additional information respecting them is derived from observation and reasoning; and though the discoveries of modern science make no part of theology, yet they are worthy of attention because they have a tendency to exalt our ideas of the power and beneficence of the Creator.

As the planets are removed from us many millions of miles, they

---

* Though the sun is the principal source of light, yet he is not the only source from which it flows. There is light produced by the ignition of combustible substances, light struck out from hard bodies by percussion or friction, phosphoric light, and electric light. As there is at present light without the sun, there may have been light without him in the beginning, as recorded by Moses; nor can we now tell whether light proceeds from his body or from his atmosphere. But, however this may be, it seems reasonable to suppose that the sun was created at the same time with the earth, though he was not made the grand repository of light until the fourth day. It is asserted that "in the beginning God created the heaven" as well as "the earth." Moreover, the earth could not have occupied its proper place in the system if it had been created before the sun, for by the latter the former is retained in its orbit. But this matter is perfectly plain if we suppose that the sun was created at the same time with the earth, and that it was not till the fourth day that he was made a luminous body; for the influence which he exerts upon the earth depends upon his solid mass, not upon his light.

would not be visible if their magnitude were not great. But how much greater must be the magnitude of the fixed stars, the distance of which from the earth is immense, when compared with that of the utmost planet which revolves around the sun! It is natural to inquire, For what purpose were these fixed stars placed in the heavens? It was surely not to give light to the earth, for their light is of but little account to us. Nor was it to mark the progress of the seasons and the revolution of the year, for this is done by the sun and the changes which take place on the face of the earth. Were they then created in vain? Shall we suppose that He who made the earth for great and benevolent purposes, and made the sun to give it light, could have created millions of suns for no assignable end? Such a conclusion would charge the God of nature with folly, and be at variance with the proofs of intelligence and design which are so amply supplied by all his other works.

The opinion, therefore, that around those suns planets revolve, the inhabitants of which rejoice in their light and are cheered by their influence, is not a mere flight of fancy, but rests upon strong grounds of belief; and while this theory vindicates the wisdom of God, it leads us to admire his infinite goodness, which diffuses life and happiness far beyond the reach of the eye or even the range of imagination. Thus the universe presents itself to our view in all its magnificent and immeasurable extent; and while we raise our thoughts to Him who spoke it into being, we are constrained to exclaim, "O Lord, how manifold are thy works! in wisdom hast thou made them all." Psa. civ, 24.

But in the last place the term *heavens* includes that region of peace, and purity, and joy, where God manifests himself in all his glory to his perfect creatures. This must be a *place*, because human beings now dwell in it, and because it is to be the abode of the righteous after the resurrection. Jesus said to his disciples, "I go to prepare a *place* for you. And if I go and prepare a *place* for you, I will come again and receive you unto myself; that *where* I am, *there* ye may be also." John xiv, 2, 3. This is sometimes called the *third* heaven, of which the holy of holies in the Jewish tabernacle and temple was an interesting type. Where this place is, however, cannot be determined, and conjectures respecting its location are more curious than edifying.

§ 2. *Of Creation in Particular.*

Creation, considered particularly, respects those *intelligent* and *moral* beings whom God has brought into existence. They are comprehended in two general classes, *angels* and *men*. As the Bible furnishes some account of both these classes of beings, we will endeavor to ascertain, to some extent, the important information which is thus placed within our reach. But as the doctrines respecting man will constitute a separate book, we will confine our remarks, in this section, to that class of created intelligences called ANGELS.

The word ANGEL is derived from the Greek $αγγελος$, and is a name not of *nature*, but of *office*. It corresponds with מלאך in Hebrew, and literally signifies a messenger, or one sent on an embassy. The term is sometimes applied to men who are invested with authority over others, as "the Angels of the seven Churches," who were probably their bishops or presidents; but it is generally used in Scripture to designate a superior order of intelligences who inhabit the heavenly world.

That there are such beings as those whom we call angels, in the common acceptation of the term, is evidently taught in the Bible. It might, therefore, seem impossible for any one to deny their existence who believed the Scriptures to be worthy of credit; and yet, as St. Luke informs us, the Sadducees asserted that there was "neither angel nor spirit." There have been some in modern times also who have coincided with the Sadducees in denying the existence of angels, affirming that when they are spoken of as real beings the term is to be understood in a figurative sense. Thus we are told that good angels signify good thoughts, and evil angels sinful thoughts. But with such as make thus free with the Scriptures, and subvert their plainest teachings, it would be useless to reason; for if the Bible history of the existence and doings of angels is to be understood in a figurative sense, we may as well discard the whole volume of revelation as an idle dream.

But relying upon what God has revealed concerning this class of his moral creatures, and understanding this revelation in its plain and obvious sense, we will proceed to offer such remarks as will elicit all the leading features of their history.

From the Bible we learn that angels are divided, in reference to their moral condition, into *holy* and *unholy*, or into *good* and *evil*. Let us, then, inquire briefly concerning each of these classes.

I. OF HOLY ANGELS.

These are so denominated because they have continued in that state of holiness or moral purity in which they were originally created; and also, to distinguish them from the apostate "angels which kept not their first estate." In our remarks respecting them we will notice,

1. *The time of their Creation.*—To the question, When were the angels created? we can return only a general answer. Of this event Moses has given us no information, unless, with some, we suppose angels to be included in the *host of heaven;* but this phrase seems rather to signify the celestial luminaries, the sun, moon, and stars. We have no reason to think, however, that the creation of angels preceded the time to which Moses refers in the first chapter of Genesis. A prior date has been assigned by many; but it is a mere conjecture, and seems

to be at variance with the general language of Scripture. The sacred historian does most certainly teach that the *heavens* were created at the same time with the earth; and though he takes no notice of the *inhabitants* of the heavenly world, yet there is ground to believe that they also were created at the same time. On what day they were created is a question of mere curiosity; but it is supposed by many that God spoke of the angels when he said to Job, "Where wast thou when I laid the foundations of the earth? when the morning stars sang together, and all the sons of God shouted for joy?" Job xxxviii, 4, 7. If by the *morning stars*, and the *sons of God*, the angelic host is meant, which seems to be probable, it will follow that the angels were present when the mighty fabric of the universe was completed, and that they celebrated, on that occasion, the praises of the Divine Architect.

2. *Their Natural Attributes.*—Of angels it may be affirmed that they are spiritual beings, that they are immortal, that they are highly intelligent, and that they possess astonishing power and activity.

(1.) *They are* SPIRITUAL *beings.*—As such they are represented in the fourth verse of the hundred and fourth Psalm, which is quoted in Heb. i, 7: "Who maketh his angels *spirits*, and his ministers a flame of fire." Angels, then, are spirits; and no better definition of a spirit can be given than the one presented by our Lord, though it is of the negative kind, when he said to his terrified disciples, "Handle me, and see; for a spirit hath not flesh and bones, as ye see me have." Luke xxiv, 39. It would be in vain for us to inquire into the *essence* of a spirit, because it is perfectly beyond our grasp; but it is not more so than is the essence of matter, of which we know only the properties.

(2.) *They are* IMMORTAL.—The immortality of angels may be inferred from the language of our Lord respecting the future condition of the righteous. "Neither can they die any more; for they are equal unto the angels." Luke xx, 36. It may be supposed that their immortality is the natural consequence of their immateriality; but the proper ground is the will of God. He willed that the angels should never die, even though they should sin; but in this respect they have no pre-eminence above the souls of men, which are not injured by the stroke of death, but merely separated from those portions of matter which they had animated for a time, and are destined to animate again.

(3.) *They are highly* INTELLIGENT.—The superior intelligence of angels may be argued: 1. From their spirituality. Their spiritual nature is not weighed down by the frailties of weak and perishing bodies. 2. From their superior order. They are confessedly creatures of a higher order than men; and it is, therefore, reasonable to believe that the degree of intelligence which they possess is in proportion to the superiority of their rank. 3. From the place of their abode. Their proper home is the heaven of heavens, where they ever behold the face of God, and dwell amid the effulgence of heavenly light. The angel who appeared to Zachariah in the temple said, "I am Gabriel, that stand in the presence of God." 4. From their long observation and experience. A capacity to increase in knowledge enters into the very nature of rational creatures, and this is surely as true of angels as it is of men. For multiplied ages they have been gazing upon the unfolding attributes of God, and winging their unwearied flight to various and distant parts of heaven's dominions, to execute the Divine will, and to witness the wonders of the Divine administration. To what lofty heights, then, must they be elevated in regard to knowledge and wisdom! That the Jews believed in the superior knowledge of angels, is evident from the words of the woman of Tekoah to David: "My lord is wise, according to the wisdom of an angel of God, to know all things that are in the earth." 2 Sam. xiv, 20.

(4.) *They possess astonishing* POWER *and* ACTIVITY.—In Psalm ciii, 20, David exclaims, "Bless the Lord, ye his angels, that *excel in strength;*" and St. Paul tells us that "the Lord Jesus shall be revealed from heaven with his *mighty angels.*" 2 Thess. i, 7. *Strong angel* and *mighty angel* are phrases in the Apocalypse which are expressive of the same character.

Proofs of the power with which these exalted beings are endowed are in several instances recorded in the Scriptures. It is highly probable that when "the Lord slew all the first born in the land of Egypt" in a single hour it was done by the ministry of an angel, who is, therefore, called "the destroyer." Exod. xii, 23. An angel destroyed seventy thousand persons in three days in consequence of the sin of David in numbering the people. And an angel put to death in one night of the army of Sennacherib a hundred and eighty-five thousand. These instances show that angels possess a power which to us is utterly incomprehensible.

But their *activity* is equally wonderful. Their nature, in this respect, is briefly described in Psalm civ, 4: "Who maketh his angels spirits, and his ministers a flaming fire." The word here rendered *spirits* most commonly signifies *winds.* But in either sense the phraseology forcibly declares the eminent activity of angels, who are thus represented as moving with the swiftness of winds, or of that which is peculiar to spirits, and as operating with the astonishing energy of flaming fire. Moreover, they are represented as flying on wings; and as they are purely spiritual in their nature, we may suppose that they can travel from world to world with the velocity of thought. Of this we have a striking instance recorded in the ninth chapter of Daniel. From this remarkable passage we learn that Daniel set himself to seek the Lord in fasting and prayer; that after his prayer was begun the Angel Gabriel was commanded to visit him with a message of Divine instruction; and that ere his supplication was closed the angel touched him "about the time of the evening oblation." Hence, during the time in which Daniel was employed in uttering his prayer, Gabriel came to him from the heavenly world. This is a rapidity of motion which exceeds all comprehension of the most active imagination; surpassing, beyond any comparison, the amazing swiftness of light.

3. THEIR MORAL CONDITION.—In regard to the moral condition of angels we may remark,

(1.) *That they are* HOLY *beings.*—Such they must have been when they came from the hand of the Creator; and such they have continued to be, though others have fallen into sin. Hence they are expressly denominated by our Lord "*the holy angels.*" Matt. xxv, 31. They are also called the "ministers of" God, "that do his pleasure," (Psa. ciii, 21;) and they are placed before us, in the prayer which Christ taught his disciples, as patterns of holy obedience. "Thy will be done in earth *as it is in* heaven." Matt. vi, 10.

The holiness of angels may be inferred from their place of residence. Heaven is a holy place, and no unholy being can ever dwell in that holy habitation. This has been the home of the holy angels for almost six thousand years, and in no instance have they done anything displeasing to God. They were no doubt tempted; but they indignantly resisted the solicitation of counsel and example. They have witnessed many a foul display of human and angelic depravity, but they have not received the slightest moral taint.

(2.) *Angels are* BENEVOLENT *beings.*—It is in general true that the more men are advanced in holiness the more pleasure they take in the welfare of others, and in the diffusion of morality and piety. But if this is the case with men it must be eminently so with the holy angels. We see here why the plan of human redemption engages their attention, and fills them with delight and wonder. It is a subject which "the angels desire to look into." 1 Pet. i, 12. The chorus in which "the heavenly host" united, when celebrating the nativity of our Lord, is beautifully expressive of angelic piety and benevolence. "Glory to God in the highest, and on earth peace, good-will toward men." Luke ii, 14. Our Lord tells us that "there is joy in the presence of the angels of God over one sinner that repenteth." Luke xv, 10.

(3.) *They are* HAPPY *beings.*—This may be inferred from the holiness of their nature. With them the recollection of the past creates no remorse, and the prospect of the future awakens no fear or anxiety. They have always served God with fidelity, and they will always enjoy his love. They drink immortal joys from the pure fountain of bliss, and feast continually on the enrapturing visions of the Divine glory.* Nor is their happiness impaired by their visits to earth. The offensive scenes which they here behold must excite their strong disapprobation, but they cannot produce the least disquieting emotion. They have acts of vengeance to perform; but as they detest sin, and glow with zeal

* See Matt. xviii, 10.

for the honor of God, they perform with pleasure any service which he requires.

4. THEIR GREAT NUMBER.—The numerousness of angels is most clearly taught in the Scriptures, which everywhere represent God as being surrounded by a great multitude of heavenly servants, or, as they are called by Jacob, "God's host."* "The chariots of God," says the psalmist, "are twenty thousand, even thousands of angels: the Lord is among them, as in Sinai, in the holy place." Psa. lxviii, 17. The same truth is set forth in the language of our Lord. "Thinkest thou that I cannot now pray to my Father, and he shall presently give me more than twelve legions of angels?" Matt. xxvi, 53. St. John tells us that he "beheld, and heard the voices of many angels round about the throne, and the beasts and the elders;" and that "the number of them was ten thousand times ten thousand, and thousands of thousands." Rev. v, 11.

5. THEIR EMPLOYMENT.—It is the employment of the holy angels,

(1.) *To glorify God, and to celebrate his praise.*—When God laid the foundations of the earth these morning stars rejoiced together and shouted for joy. When on Mount Sinai, amid thunderings and lightnings, and a flame of devouring fire, he published his holy law, "the chariots of God, even the thousands of angels," attended him at this awful solemnity. When the Son of God became incarnate an angel proclaimed his birth to the shepherds of Bethlehem, and "a multitude of the heavenly host" praised God on that occasion in the noblest hymn that earth ever heard. And when he ascended on high; having finished the work of redemption, the same exalted beings attended him, singing, as they approached the heaven of heavens, "Lift up your heads, O ye gates! and be ye lifted up, ye everlasting doors! and the King of Glory shall come in." Psa. xxiv, 7. So, also, their constant employment in their heavenly home is to praise and worship God.†

(2.) *Angels are employed in studying God's works and dispensations.*—St. Paul tells us that "God created all things by Jesus Christ; to the intent that now unto the principalities and powers in heavenly places might be known by the Church the manifold wisdom of God." Eph. iii, 9, 10. And as God designed that a knowledge of his dispensations to the Church should be made known to the angelic host, "the principalities and powers in heavenly places," so we learn that the disposition of angels is in perfect accordance with this design. "Which things the angels desire to look into."

(3.) *Angels are employed in executing the judgments of God upon men.*—The first judgment inflicted upon man—his exclusion from Paradise—appears to have been committed to the ministry of angels. In like manner they were the immediate instruments in the infliction of Divine vengeance on the Israelites, on the army of Sennacherib, on

* Gen. xxxii, 2. † See Rev. v, 11, 12; vii, 11, 12.

Nebuchadnezzar, and on Herod. In the same manner, also, they are represented in the Apocalypse as pouring out the vials of Divine wrath upon the nations of our guilty world.

(4.) *Angels are also employed in ministering to the people of God.*—"Are they not all ministering spirits, sent forth to minister for them who shall be heirs of salvation?" Heb. i, 14. Here we are plainly taught that to minister to the saints is a standing employment of angels. Accordingly they are exhibited in Jacob's vision of the ladder (Gen. xxviii, 12) as ascending from earth to heaven, and descending from heaven to earth, in the discharge of this great duty; and the Scriptures furnish numerous examples of their actual ministry to the children of God.

First, in revealing to them the Divine will. An angel instructed Abraham, Joshua, David, Elijah, Daniel, Zechariah the prophet, Zachariah the father of John the Baptist, the Virgin Mary, and others. It was an angel that conducted Joseph and Mary to Egypt, Philip to the eunuch, and Cornelius to Peter. So also it was by the ministry of an angel that God revealed his will to John in the isle of Patmos.

Secondly, in protecting and delivering them from evil. "There shall no evil befall thee, neither shall any plague come nigh thy dwelling; for he shall give his angels charge over thee, to keep thee in all thy ways." Psa. xci, 10, 11. The angel of the Lord encampeth round about them that fear him, and delivereth them." Psa. xxxiv, 7. Thus angels delivered Lot from Sodom, Jacob from Esau, Daniel from the lions, his three companions from the fiery furnace, and Peter from Herod and the Jewish Sanhedrim. We are not to conclude, however, that ministering angels are to preserve the saints from every calamity of life; for it is the will of God that they should sometimes suffer affliction for their own good. But we have reason to believe that these guardian spirits are continually about our path, encircling us with an invisible wall of protection.

Thirdly, in affording them comfort. Thus they comforted Jacob at the approach of Esau; Daniel in his peculiar sorrows and dangers; Joseph and Mary in their perplexities; CHRIST in his agony in the garden; the apostles and their companions after our Lord's resurrection; and St. Paul immediately before his shipwreck.

Fourthly, in conveying the souls of the saints to the mansions of bliss. Having attended them through the journey of life, they will not forsake them in their dying hour; and when their spirits leave the earthly tenement they will bear them in triumph to the upper sanctuary. When Lazarus died he "was carried by the angels into Abraham's bosom." Luke xvi, 22. We look upon death as a scene of sorrow and distress. But if the spiritual world were not hidden from us, we should behold, in the presence of the dying Christian, ministering angels; and we should hear them commingling their sweetest songs with the groans of the sufferer, and the lamentations of weeping friends, and softly whispering, "Sister spirit, come away."

Lastly, the angels will minister for the saints at the second coming of Christ. At the great harvest of the world, as our Lord has taught us, the angels will be the reapers; and as they will then pluck up the tares and cast them into the fire, so they will gather the wheat into the garner. Christ " shall send his angels with a great sound of a trumpet; and they shall gather together his elect from the four winds, from one end of heaven to the other." Matt. xxiv, 31.

Thus we have given a faint outline of the creation, the nature, the moral condition, and the employment of the holy angels as revealed in the Scriptures. How noble and exalted a portion are these celestial beings of the wonderful works of the great Creator! How large and extended must be their views of the infinite wisdom and goodness of God! How profound must be their adoration! How glorious is their employment! Day and night they are fulfilling their Maker's will, not as a dull task, but as a most delightful service. Lord, help us to do thy will on earth as angels do it in heaven!

II. OF UNHOLY OR EVIL ANGELS.

That this class of created spirits were originally both holy and happy, may be clearly inferred from the Divine character. He who is perfectly holy and good could not have produced unholy and miserable beings. It follows, therefore, that they were once holy angels, and in every respect similar to those who now stand in the presence of God; that they are distinguished from the latter, not in their origin nor in their natural attributes, but in their moral character and condition; and that their present character and condition can only be accounted for on the principle that they are fallen creatures. Let us then direct our attention to their fall, their moral condition, their employment, and their destiny.

1. *Their Fall.*—That these unholy angels were once holy and happy, and fell from that exalted state, is clearly taught in the following passages: "Ye are of your father the devil, and the lusts of your father ye will do. He was a murderer from the beginning, and abode not in the truth." John viii, 44. " God spared not the angels that sinned, but cast them down to hell." 2 Pet. ii, 4. "The angels which kept not their first estate, but left their own habitation, he hath reserved in everlasting chains." Jude 6. Thus we learn that the devil "abode not in the truth," which implies that he was once in it; and that the sinning angels "kept not their first estate, but left their own habitation."

Of this wonderful event—a revolt in the heavenly world, and among the highest order of created intelligences—we have no regular history in the Scriptures. Still we are abundantly assured by them that this event did actually take place. By various declarations and allusions which they contain we are taught that Satan, an angel of pre-eminent distinction in heaven, rebelled against his Maker; and that in this deplorable enterprise a multitude of the heavenly host united with him, and, with the same disposition, violated the law of God, and revolted from his government.

There is a diversity of opinion with respect to the first sin of the fallen angels. Some suppose that it consisted in tempting our first parents; but this opinion is refuted by the consideration that they must have been sinful themselves before they could be inclined to lead others into sin. Some have thought that their sin was *envy*—envy either of those angels who were superior to them in rank and dignity, or of man whom God had created in his own image, and invested with dominion over this lower world. But the most probable opinion is that it consisted in *pride* and *ambition*. St. Paul, in speaking of a bishop, says that he must not be "a novice, (νεοφυτος, *a new convert*,) lest being lifted up with pride he fall into the *condemnation of the devil.*" 1 Tim. iii, 6. Here it is clearly implied that the devil was condemned for *pride;* and it is fairly presumable that the same sin was the source of condemnation to his companions.

How it was that these angels sinned without being tempted, or, if self-tempted, how they could have originated the temptation within their own nature, which was at first pure, we cannot fully comprehend; but the facts are revealed, and we are compelled to believe them. That they were under a law is clear from the fact that they sinned. But if they were under a law which it was possible for them to violate, they must have been in a state of trial, and of accountability to God; and, to such a state, the possibility of sinning is essential. To say that holy creatures could not have sinned without a tempter, is the same as to assert the eternity of moral evil, which is absurd; or, that God is its author, which is blasphemous.

2. *Their Moral Condition.*—The fall of angels destroyed none of their natural attributes. With respect to their essence they are still spiritual beings. They are also immortal, highly intelligent, and possessed of great power and activity. But their *moral* qualities have undergone a total change. Of their original holiness not a vestige remains. Sin is now so natural to them that it seems almost to be their essence. It is the element in which they live and move.

The depravity of men is, in some degree, checked and concealed by certain natural feelings and affections, which, though not virtuous, have the effects of virtue in restraining them from acts of malice and cruelty, and in leading them to perform deeds of justice and beneficence. But we have no ground to believe that there is anything analogous to these affections and feelings in apostate angels. Sin rages in them unrestrained. It is the subject of their thoughts, and gives character to all their actions.

We may judge how sin produced immediately its full effect upon fallen angels from the conduct of the tempter. After being expelled from heaven, what was his first work? He visited our earth with the most nefarious and vindictive design to mar its beauty, and to poison and destroy human nature in its source; and he accomplished it by a train of deliberate falsehood and systematic cruelty. There was no relenting at the thought of plunging our whole race into eternal misery. His dark mind rejoiced in the expectation that myriads of human beings should forever endure the same agonies with himself. "He was a murderer from the beginning, and abode not in the truth, because there is no truth in him. When he speaketh a lie, he speaketh of his own, for he is a liar, and the father of it." John viii, 44. This passage illustrates, in a very striking manner, the depravity of fallen angels, for what is true of one is true of them all.

Various names are given to these fallen spirits in the Scriptures, which are descriptive of the depravity of their nature. They are called *evil* spirits, *unclean* spirits, *lying* spirits, the *rulers of the darkness* of this world, and spiritual wickedness. Their leader is denominated *Satan*, or the destroyer; the *devil*, or the accuser; *Apollyon*, or the destroyer; the old serpent; and "the prince of the power of the air."

But the fallen angels are as *unhappy* as they are unholy. This may be inferred from the place of their habitation. Peter says, that "God spared not the angels that sinned, but cast them down to *hell*," or *Tartarus;* for the apostle uses the verb ταρταρωσας, thrusting them down to Tartarus. Neither the verb, nor the noun ταρταρος, from which it is formed, occurs in any other place in the New Testament; but they are both frequently employed by Greek writers, from whom we must learn their meaning. By Tartarus, they understood the lowest of the infernal regions, where the souls of the wicked were supposed to be imprisoned and tormented. The word, as adopted by the apostle, conveys the same general idea. It answers to the Jewish word גיא חנם, and to the Greek γεέννα, and is, therefore, properly rendered *hell*, the place of punishment "prepared for the devil and his angels."

But these unhappy beings are also in a state of *penal suffering*, for God "delivered them into chains of darkness." Having incurred the wrath of their Creator, they can experience only evil, and are bound, as with a chain of iron, to the darkness and misery of their gloomy abode. Their positive misery is very forcibly expressed by our Lord when he represents them as "seeking rest, and finding none;" but still more so when he speaks of their proper abode as a place of "everlasting fire." We are not to conclude, however, that they are constantly confined to that place. It appears from their history that they are prisoners at large; and that they are permitted frequently to visit the home of man, which seems to be the principal theater of their nefarious operations.

3. *Their employment.*—It will appear that the employment of fallen

angels corresponds with the depravity of their nature and the malevolence of their dispositions. It is their constant aim to dishonor God and to injure men, and in prosecuting their wicked designs they submit to no restraint but Almighty power. We learn from the Scriptures,

(1.) *That they are permitted to exercise power over the bodies of men and other material objects.*—In proof of this we may appeal to the history of Job, which fully sustains and illustrates the proposition. But we may appeal to the writings of the Evangelists, also, as furnishing numerous instances of demoniacal possessions, and of the power of evil spirits over the bodies of men.

By some it has been alleged that these were not cases of real possession; that the patients labored under common diseases, such as palsy, epilepsy, and madness; and that they were said to be "possessed of devils," either in a figurative sense, or in accommodation to the opinions of the Jews. But when we consider that the number of demons in particular possessions is given, that their actions are expressly distinguished from those of the persons possessed, that their language in regard to their expulsion is recorded, and that accounts are given of the manner in which they were actually disposed of, it is impossible to deny their reality without admitting that the sacred historians were either deceived themselves or intended to deceive others.

(2.) *That they have power to exercise an evil influence over the human mind.*—This alarming truth is proved, in the first place, by the history of the fall; and in the second place, by many facts and declarations and admonitions in the Scriptures.

It was Satan who tempted Judas to betray his Master,* and who put it into the heart of Ananias and Sapphira "to lie to the Holy Ghost."† Our Lord told his disciples that Satan had desired to have them, that he might sift them as wheat.‡ He is called "the spirit that now worketh in the children of disobedience." Eph. ii, 2. St. Peter says, "Your adversary the devil, as a roaring lion, walketh about seeking whom he may devour." 1 Peter v, 8. And St. Paul says, in the name of all his brethren, "We are not ignorant of his devices." 2 Cor. ii, 11.

These and many other passages fully prove that evil spirits are employed in tempting men to sin. Of the mode of their agency we can have no certain knowledge, and to indulge in conjectures would serve no valuable purpose. One thing is certain, that they cannot compel men to sin, for such a power would be destructive of man's moral agency, and would, therefore, defeat their own design, which is to involve us in guilt.

4. *Their* DESTINY.—The degradation and punishment of the fallen angels are not yet completed. They are delivered "into chains of darkness, *to be reserved unto judgment.*" They will then be tried and con-

* John xiii, 2. † Acts v, 3. ‡ Luke xxii, 31.

demned for all the evils which they will have wrought during the history of time. These evils, however gratifying to them in the perpetration, will, after the judgment of the great day, return upon their own heads, and will cover them with eternal shame, and overwhelm them with endless ruin. The chains which they now wear will confine them unto the judgment, so that they cannot escape; and will confine them forever in the sufferance of that misery to which they have destined themselves by a voluntary devotion. For them, therefore, there is no redemption, no mercy, no hope.

The question has been proposed, Why might not provision have been made for the recovery of fallen angels as well as for that of man? but to this no decisive answer can be returned. It is enough for us to know that God, who always does right, and is too good to be unkind, has passed them by. Still, there are some circumstances connected with their history, as also with the history of our race, which may reflect some light upon this mysterious subject, and which are therefore worthy of our attention. 1. They were doubtless superior to man in intellectual endowments, and, therefore, less liable to be deceived. 2. As man was partly material, and subject to the influences of the senses, his attention might have been diverted and his judgment biased by allurements addressed to them. But angels were purely *spiritual* beings, and therefore could not have been liable to any such temptations. 3. The progenitor of the human race sustained a federal relation to all his posterity. In him they stood; in him they fell. But among the angels no such relation existed. Each one stood or fell for himself alone. 4. Man sinned, in the earthly paradise, through the subtilty of a tempter; but angels sinned, in the heavenly paradise, without a tempter. For, though we do not possess a history of their apostasy, yet we know that they were not solicited, as man was, by some being of superior artifice, because they were the sole inhabitants of heaven.

Whether these considerations are sufficient to account for the fact that angels were not redeemed we will not pretend to say; but one thing appears to be evident, that their apostasy, under all the circumstances of the case, was more unprovoked and atrocious than that of man. We conclude, then, that the eternal destruction of fallen angels is no more incompatible with the character of God than will be the eternal punishment of wicked men. They had their day of trial; but they chose the evil, and must eat the fruit of their doings.

CHAPTER X.

OF DIVINE PROVIDENCE.

DIVINE *Providence* is that care and superintendence which God exercises over his creatures. As he is the *Creator* of all things, he possesses the power and the right to use them according to his own pleasure; and to cause them, and all which is done by them, to promote his own designs. In the discussion of this subject three things demand our attention: 1. The proofs of a Divine Providence; 2. Its nature; and, 3. Its objects.

I. PROOFS OF DIVINE PROVIDENCE.

The doctrine of Providence may be established by a variety of arguments, which may be drawn both from reason and from revelation. We begin with the former.

1. *Proofs from Reason.*—This class of proofs depends upon the truth of the proposition that God created the world. Presuming that this position may now be considered as fully established, we derive proofs of the Providence of God,

(1.) *From his Nature and Attributes.*—That God is both able and willing to take care of his creatures is demonstrable from the idea of an absolutely perfect being. That he is *able* to do this appears from his *omniscience*, by which he knows the circumstances and wants of all his creatures; from his *wisdom*, by which he understands in what manner and by what means the world may be sustained and governed; and from his *omnipotence*, by which he can accomplish all his purposes. That he *will* do this follows alike from his *wisdom* and *goodness*. Can it be supposed that God, after he had created all things, should abandon his own works and be indifferent to the well-being of the countless myriads of creatures that he brought into existence, and formed with desires and a capacity for happiness? It is certainly more reasonable to believe that he will take care of them, and provide for them according to their respective wants. But as God is *just* and *righteous* in all his doings, he must exercise a moral government over his rational creatures, and reward or punish them according to their actions; and, in the course of his providence, so overrule them as to promote the ultimate end of his administration.

(2.) *From the dependent nature of creatures.*—God alone exists by necessity of nature, or, in other words, has the ground of existence in himself. The existence of all other beings is therefore dependent upon the will and power of God; and as they might or might not have been created, so they may cease to be, there being nothing in the nature of things to insure their continuance. Nothing can be more expressive of the dependent nature of all created things than the following words of Scripture: "In him we live, and move, and have our being." Acts xvii, 28. Of the same import is the language of the apostle, when he speaks of the Son of God as "upholding all things by the word of his power." Heb, i, 3. The assertion of divines, that the preservation of existence is a *continual creation*, is not merely a rhetorical figure, importing that the power of God is as truly admirable in preserving all things as in creating them, but is a literal statement of an important fact. For, as all things were created by the power of God, so their preservation depends upon a continued exertion of the same power, as the flowing stream depends upon an uninterrupted supply of water from the fountain.

(3.) *From the order and harmony observable in the course of nature.*—Though the universe is composed of many parts, they are all retained in their proper places, and perform their peculiar functions with such order and harmony as to promote the general good. In this immense and complicated machine no part ever goes wrong. Its motion is never suspended or embarrassed, and its operations are carried on with such regularity that they are made the subject of definite calculation. The heavenly bodies perform their revolutions in their appointed times, without ever interfering with one another. The sun, the source of light and heat, though he has ministered to the system of which he is the center for thousands of years, has lost no portion of his splendor or of his influence. The seasons succeed each other in their regular order. The earth still retains its native fertility, though many generations have been supported by its products. The sea continues within its ancient boundaries, and leaves the dry land to be the abode of terrestrial animals. The various classes of animals and vegetables have continued to propagate themselves, so that the earth is still stocked with inhabitants and with a full supply for their wants. When, therefore, we contemplate this immense system of nature, so wonderful in its contrivances, so constant in its movements, and proceeding from age to age without the slightest confusion, we must necessarily conclude that it is under the *continual government* of an all-controlling Mind.

It may be objected, that the order which prevails throughout the universe may be accounted for by the laws of nature, without an immediate interposition of the Deity; and that it only proves the wisdom of its original constitution. But what is meant by the *laws of nature?* A *law*, in its primary signification, is a rule established and enforced by authority, and obviously implies intelligence and power. But when the term is applied to inanimate things, it signifies nothing more than the *stated and regular order* in which they are found to subsist. Thus, finding that bodies on or near the surface of the earth tend toward its center, and that the planets of our system tend toward the sun, we call this the law of gravitation; and in like manner we speak of other laws by which matter is governed, as the laws of motion and the laws of light. But the truth is that these are only *facts*, and are called laws solely on account of their uniformity.

From observation and experience we know that bodies gravitate toward a center, and that the rays of light are subject to refraction and reflection; but we know not the true cause of these phenomena. Are we to suppose that nature possesses intelligence, or activity, or power of any kind? Let us not forget that matter is inert, and totally incapable of exertion. It can neither put itself in motion, nor stop itself when in motion. Every modification which it undergoes is the effect of some external power. What, then, are the *laws of nature?* They are the *particular modes in which God exerts his power*, which, being uniform, are accounted natural, while any deviation from them is pronounced to be miraculous. It follows, therefore, if this is a just description of what are called the laws of nature, that so far from their accounting for the order which is maintained in the universe, they necessarily imply the actual and constant interposition of the Creator, and as irresistibly suggest the idea of a lawgiver as do the laws of any human society.

(4.) *From those moral sentiments and feelings which are common to men.*—St. Paul tells us, that even the Gentiles who "have not the law, are a law unto themselves;" and that they "show the work of the law written in their hearts." Rom. ii, 14, 15. There is a principle in every man who has received any degree of cultivation which distinguishes between right and wrong, and which lies at the foundation of all our moral feelings. This principle, which we call *conscience*, never fails to remind us that we are subjects of moral government, and accountable to God for our actions; and to pronounce a sentence of approbation or disapprobation upon our conduct, according as we believe it to be good or bad. If there were no Providence, conscience would be an illusive faculty; its decisions would have no better foundation than the hopes and terrors of superstition; but if it is an original principle of our nature, as we may infer from its universality, it is God's own testimony within us to his moral administration and superintending Providence. But we may argue the truth of this doctrine,

(5.) *From its necessity to piety and virtue, and to the happiness of human life.*—Were it not that God exercises a constant and watchful care over his works all piety would immediately cease. A God who did not concern himself in the affairs of the world, and especially in the actions of men, would be to us the same as no God at all. In that case the pious and virtuous could not hope for his approbation, and the guilty would have no punishment to fear. The persecuted could think of him only as the idle spectator of their wrongs, and the suffering and sorrowful could find no consolation. But if, on the other hand, we have a right to believe that God, as a Father, cares for us, that he guides and protects us, and supplies all our wants, and that "in him we live, and move, and have our being," we may then be composed and unshaken even in times of the greatest adversity, "casting all our care upon him" who cares for us.

There are several other arguments which might be advanced in proof of a Divine Providence, such as the experience of every individual, the judgments which are occasionally executed upon notorious transgressors, the great historic events which have taken place in the world, the proportion which exists between the two sexes, and the variety in the human countenance, which answers so many valuable purposes.

2. *Proofs from Scripture.*—The Bible establishes the doctrine of Divine Providence,

(1.) *By express declarations.*—"O, Lord, thou preservest man and beast." Psa. xxxvi, 6. "The eyes of all wait upon thee; and thou givest them their meat in due season. Thou openest thine hand, and satisfiest the desire of every living thing." Psa. cxlv, 15, 16. "The eyes of the Lord are in every place, beholding the evil and the good." Prov. xv, 3. In the New Testament we may consult Matt. vi, 25-32; x, 29-31; and Acts xvii, 24-28. These, and many other passages, clearly prove the Providence of God.

(2.) *By Prophecies.*—This argument is of great weight, and might be very extensively applied, but our limits will only permit its mere adduction. The rise of mighty kingdoms from small beginnings to extensive dominion, and their subsequent fall into decay and dissolution, may be accounted for, to some extent, by the operation of second causes; but they are often accompanied by circumstances which manifestly point to the hand of Divine Providence. This is particularly the case in the revolutions of the great monarchies of ancient times, when viewed in connection with the prophecies concerning them; for who can doubt that they were accomplished by Him who foretold them ages before they took place? Who can read the predictions of Scripture respecting the captivity and restoration of the Jews, the coming of the Messiah, and the spread of the Gospel, and compare them with their actual fulfillment, without being convinced that in all these events God exercised a special Providence?

(3.) *By Miracles.**— As miracles can be performed only by Divine power, to admit the truth of the Scripture history respecting them is, in effect, to admit that God exercises a particular providence over the affairs of men. Even the magicians of Egypt, though employed to oppose the servants of the Lord, were forced to exclaim, on witnessing one of the miracles of Moses and Aaron, "This is the finger of God!"

* See Book I, chap. 1, Miracles; also chap. 6.

The same is true in regard to every miracle which the sacred Scriptures record.

(4.) *By extraordinary events in the life of individuals.*—This argument, if it were followed out to its full length, would involve the entire subject of sacred biography; a subject which fully exhibits the Providence of God in its most interesting light. How clearly is this seen in the history of Noah, of Abraham, of Lot, of Joseph, of Elijah, of Daniel, and a host of others! Time would fail us "to tell of Gideon, and of Barak, and of Samson, and of Jephtha; of David also, and Samuel, and of the prophets."

II. NATURE OF DIVINE PROVIDENCE.

The *nature* of Divine Providence respects the *manner* in which it is concerned in the affairs of the universe. Divines are generally united in the opinion that Providence includes two acts, that is, *preservation* and *government.*

1. *Of Preservation.*—By *preservation* we mean, that efficient agency of God by which all creatures, with their respective essences, powers, and faculties, are kept in being. No idea can be more false than to suppose that the creation of beings renders them independent of the Creator, for what is derived must always be dependent. Created things, it is true, are perfectly distinct from their Creator, as any other work is from the workman; but they are as dependent on him for the continuance of their being, as vitality in the branch is dependent upon the juice which flows from the trunk, or as the growth and life of the human body is dependent upon the blood which is propelled from the heart. Hence the Scriptures declare, not only that God created all things, but that "by him all things consist;" and that he upholds "all things by the word of his power." This absolute dependence upon God for preservation is as true of man as it is of the lower orders of creation; "for in him *we* live, and move, and have our being."

It has been objected, that the absolute dependence of all things upon God implies a reflection upon his wisdom; as if he had executed a work so imperfect as to require his constant interference to prevent it from perishing. Men, it is said, construct works which, when finished, have no further need of their care. A house will stand though the builder should never see it again; and a watch or a clock will point to the hour after it has passed out of the hands of the maker. But it should be considered, that in such cases men merely give a particular form or arrangement to certain pre-existent materials. They neither make them nor uphold them in being, and consequently the durability of their works plainly depends upon some other cause than their own power. With respect to the operations of any piece of machinery, as a watch or clock, let it be further considered that the process does not depend upon the mechanic in any other sense than that he made a proper disposition of all the parts. The real cause of motion is not in the machine itself, but in some weight, or spring, or other power, which is continually acting upon it, and from which all its motions are derived. So likewise the motivity in the immense machine of the universe does not belong to itself, but is to be ascribed to God. Hence the objection leads us to the very conclusion which it is brought to overthrow.

2. *Of Government.*—The *government* of God is that exercise of his agency by which he so overrules all creatures and all events, that nothing can come to pass but what he either wills or permits.*

The actions of God himself, and those of his creatures, embrace all the phenomena which occur in the universe. Every motion or action of any inanimate creature which is not produced by the voluntary effort of a moral agent is to be ascribed to God; but if the motion or action is caused by some moral agent, it is to be attributed directly to the agent who exerts this influence. If my house is consumed by lightning, it is a direct visitation from God; but if I am prostrated upon the ground by the club of a highwayman, God indeed permits it, but it is the robber, a moral agent, who is the *efficient* cause of the crime.

God is perfectly acquainted with all the *efficient causes* which exist, both those which are free in their agency and those which are otherwise. He knows every *act* of these causes, and all the *effects* which they produce, and he guides and controls them all so as to make them subservient to his own designs, and promotive of the highest good of the whole. But though he governs all his creatures, he does not govern them all after the same manner. With respect to such as are irrational he only applies his power; but he governs his rational creatures partly by his power and partly by moral laws—we say partly by his power, because as to life and faculties they are as dependent upon God as other creatures are. But, to be a little more particular, we may observe,

(1.) That God governs the physical universe according to those general and established laws which are usually called the laws of nature, but which are more properly styled *mode of Divine agency.* He keeps the sun in his place as the center, and wheels the planets round him in their respective orbits. He fixes the mountains on their bases, and confines the ocean within its ancient boundaries. Hence, in figurative language, he is said to command the sun to rise, the stars to shine, and other natural events to take place. And, as the laws by which he governs the material universe are only the regular modes of his agency

---

* When we say that God *permits* any event, we are not to understand the term to indicate that he allows it, or consents to it; but rather, that *he does not exert his power to prevent it.* God permits sin, but he does not approve of it; for, as he is infinitely holy, sin must always be the object of his abhorrence. Accordingly, he testifies against the very sins into which he permits men to fall, denouncing his threatenings against them, and actually punishing them for their crimes.

in the production of effects, it is evident that he governs it by an immediate exertion of his power.

(2.) God governs the lower animals by periodical appetites, by instincts, and by some traces of intellect, not amounting, however, to responsibility. Impelled by these principles of animated nature, they propagate their species, seek the food that is provided for them, and perform the various functions for which they are qualified. Thus the ant "provideth her meat in the summer, and gathereth her food in the harvest." "The stork in the heaven knoweth her appointed times; and the turtle, and the crane, and the swallow observe the time of their coming." God sometimes employs irrational animals as instruments to accomplish his will. Thus, frogs, lice, and flies were his instruments in punishing the Egyptians; and ravens were his ministers to carry food to the prophet Elijah. These and other similar facts, recorded in the Scriptures, show that all animated creatures are under the government of that Being who gave them existence. But,

(3.) *God governs the voluntary actions of men by moral laws.*—Of the physical, the intellectual, and the moral constitution of men God is the efficient cause; but with respect to their moral actions the case is quite different. Of these he could not become the efficient cause without destroying their very nature; for no action can be *moral* unless it is *free*. If men were not free to choose and to act they could not be accountable for their actions, for in that case their actions would not be within their own power. If, then, we would not overturn the first principles of morality, if we would not degrade ourselves below the standard of moral beings, and if we would not falsify the dictates of that moral feeling which God himself has so deeply implanted in our hearts, we must firmly maintain the doctrine that man is *morally free*. We are not to expect, therefore, that the government of God over moral beings will be shown by his *compelling* them to perform either good or bad actions.

But while, on the one hand, the freedom of the human will is unimpaired by the government of God, on the other the government of God is unobstructed and undisturbed by the free actions of men. For, though men are free in what they do, their actions are nevertheless under his most perfect control. This will appear evident if we consider, 1. That the moral actions of men depend upon their *moral powers*, of which God alone is both the author and the preserver, and of which he can deprive them at any moment; 2. That the external circumstances connected with those actions are all under the Divine control; and, 3. That God will reward the obedient and punish the disobedient, in exact accordance with their moral character, in the retributions of the eternal world. If to these considerations we add that God foresees the free actions of his moral creatures, and all the consequences of them, as well as those which result from necessary causes, and that the plans and purposes of his providence were formed in full view of all these events, we shall find no great difficulty in reconciling the unobstructed operation of the Divine government with the free-agency of man.

We must not, then, lose sight of the fact that the government of God over the voluntary actions of men is purely of a moral character. He defines their duty by moral laws. He enforces these laws by moral motives, such as the authority of the lawgiver, the equity of the laws themselves, the advantages of obedience, and the evil consequences of sin. He, moreover, lays upon men such external restraints, and affords them such internal assistances of grace as are sufficient, if properly improved, to withhold them from evil and to lead them to what is right. But still it is within their power to yield obedience to the laws of God or to transgress them; and in either case they are the authors of their own free actions.

III. THE OBJECTS OF DIVINE PROVIDENCE.

The objects of Divine Providence, so far as we know, consist of three classes—inanimate things, creatures endowed with life and activity, but possessing no rational or moral powers, and moral beings. Providence, in relation to its objects, is divided into *general, special*, and *particular*. The *general* providence of God extends to all creatures; his *special* providence has respect to men and human affairs; and his *particular* providence is restricted to men of virtue and piety.

1. *The General Providence of God.*—This extends to all created things in the universe—to the small and most insignificant, as well as to the great and most important. "Though the Lord be high, yet hath he respect unto the lowly." Psa. cxxxviii, 6. "O Lord, thou preservest man and beast." Psa. xxxvi, 6. "Are not two sparrows sold for a farthing? and one of them shall not fall to the ground without your Father. But the very hairs of your head are all numbered." Matt. x, 29, 30.

Some talk of a general providence, by which they mean that God upholds the general system of nature without attending to matters of minor importance. Hence they tell us that he takes care of the species, but not of the individuals; not perceiving that it is hardly possible, in so many words, to express a greater absurdity. A species is a general name by which the common and distinguishing properties of a number of individuals are denoted. The species is nothing but the individuals under a particular classification. How, then, can the species be taken care of if the individuals are neglected? If all things, even the smallest, were not subject to the providence of God, scarcely anything could be said to be governed by him; for such is the order, connection, and dependence of causes and effects that in many cases the least causes produce the greatest results. The providence of God, therefore, either extends to *all* things, even to those which we denominate small, or there is no providence; but as the latter is most absurd and impious, the former must be admitted.

Men are accustomed to regard many things as small, insignificant, useless, and even injurious, because they are unable to see their use and importance in the connection of things. This, however, is only a proof of the weakness of the human understanding, and of the great imperfection of human knowledge. But as God *created* all these things, and continually prolongs their existence, he must regard them as useful and necessary, and as adapted to promote his designs in their connection with the whole. How, then, can it be inconsistent with the majesty of God to watch over the most minute things in creation and to preserve them? If it was not dishonorable for him to give them existence, it cannot be dishonorable for him to preserve to them the existence which he has given them. And, indeed, his wisdom, power, and goodness are as evident in his least as in his greatest works.

2. *The Special Providence of God.*—This, we have said, has respect to men and human affairs. Men are the only creatures upon the earth who possess a moral nature, or who have reason and freedom of will; and as possessing these, they are capable of a far higher degree of perfection and happiness than the lower orders of creation. Hence the care of God for them is more apparent, and seems to be more active and efficient than for his other creatures. Of this special providence, or watchful care of God over man, we have abundant proof in the history of our race.

(1.) *It extends to human Life.*—This is true in regard both to its *origin* and to its *termination.*

First, it extends to the *origin* of human life; for though our parents, as the instruments of God, are the means by which we come into the world, yet God is truly our Creator, and the author of our existence. This doctrine is most clearly taught in the sacred Scriptures. Job says, in addressing God, "Thine hands have made me, and fashioned me together round about. Thou hast clothed me with skin and flesh, and hast fenced me with bones and sinews. Thou hast granted me life and favor, and thy visitation hath preserved my spirit." Job x, 8, 11, 12. "My substance," says David, "was not hid from thee, when I was made in secret, and curiously wrought in the lowest parts of the earth. Thine eyes did see my substance, yet being unperfect; and in thy book all my members were written, which in continuance were fashioned, when as yet there was none of them." Psa. cxxxix, 15, 16.

Secondly, Providence is concerned in the *termination* of human life. The causes of death are various, as accident, old age, and disease, either slow or rapid in its progress; but all these causes are under the control of Divine Providence. And as nothing is more precious than human life, it cannot be by chance that men are deprived of it, that their day of trial is terminated, and that their spirits are called into the presence of God to give an account of the deeds done in the body. If a sparrow cannot fall to the ground without the notice of our heavenly Father, it would be most unreasonable to suppose that his providence should not be concerned in the dissolution of every human being. But on this point the Scriptures are clear: "Seeing his days are determined, the number of his months are with thee, thou hast appointed his bounds that he cannot pass." Job xiv, 5. "Thou turnest man to destruction; and sayest, Return, ye children of men." Psa. xc, 3.

It has long been a question of considerable controversy, whether the *time* of every man's death is so fixed and determined that his life can neither be prolonged nor contracted. Some divines think that the affirmative of this question is established by Job xiv, 5, and by some other passages; but others entertain a very different opinion. This much, however, we may safely affirm: 1. That God knows, with absolute certainty, the time of every man's death; 2. That with respect to some the term of life was immutably fixed, as in the case of Moses and of Hezekiah; and, 3. That in regard to all men the term of life is limited, and confined within certain bounds. "The days of our years are threescore years and ten; and if by reason of strength they be fourscore years, yet is their strength labor and sorrow; for it is soon cut off, and we fly away." Psa. xc, 10.

But that God has determined the time of every man's death by an immutable decree is not so evident. Against this opinion various passages of Scripture may be objected. Take, for instance, the promise which is annexed to the fifth commandment, "that thy days may be long upon the land which the Lord thy God giveth thee." Exod. xx, 12. Likewise Psa. lv, 23: "Bloody and deceitful men shall not live out half their days." Another passage is 2 Samuel xxiv, 12–15, where the option which was granted to David seems to imply that God had *not* predetermined the time and manner of the death of those seventy thousand persons who were cut off by pestilence, for if he had there could have been no choice in the case.

It may be objected, also, that this theory leads to the fearful consequence of making God the author of sin. For, where the end is absolutely intended, there the means must also be absolutely intended. Consequently, if God has predetermined the time of every one's death, and if in some cases it is effected by intemperance and murder, these means must likewise have been predetermined.

Moreover, where this doctrine is thoroughly believed, and consistently carried out into action, it must lead to the neglect of the necessary precautions against danger, and of the proper means of recovery from sickness. For, one who is of this opinion may say, If the fixed time of my death has now arrived, these precautions and remedies can be of no service to me; and if it has not yet come, they are wholly unnecessary. If any one should reply that the means of preserving and of losing life

Chap. 10.]   DIVINE PROVIDENCE.   271

are likewise determined, then nothing more remains but that we should wait until God effects within us, and without us, whatever he has decreed.

(2.) *It is concerned in the events of human life.*—It has been said that man is the artificer of his own fortune, and this saying is founded upon the influence which his conduct is frequently observed to have upon his temporal condition. But the remark is more worthy of a heathen or an atheist than of a believer in the Bible. We find, indeed, that certain actions are commonly followed by certain consequences, and it is important that it should be so, because we should otherwise have no motive to act in one way rather than in another. This regularity, however, like the order maintained in the material system, is so far from invalidating the argument for the Divine interference in human affairs that it confirms it. But in the history of men this order does not everywhere prevail. There are frequent deviations from it, which compel us to acknowledge the controlling power of God. "The race is not" always "to the swift, nor the battle to the strong." In many cases industry is frustrated of its reward, and the plans of wisdom prove abortive. Worldly wealth is not apportioned according to any fixed law. It often falls to the lot of the weak and the worthless, while men of superior talents contend for it in vain. The same remarks may be applied to earthly honors, and hence, in the language of worldly men, temporal blessings are called the gifts of fortune, to intimate that they are distributed blindly and without regard to merit. But the true doctrine is, that all these things are controlled by the sovereign will of God. " Promotion cometh neither from the east, nor from the west, nor from the south. But God is the judge: he putteth down one, and setteth up another." Psa. lxxv, 6, 7.

(3.) *It extends to human actions.*—The moral actions of men are regarded as being either good or bad; but whatever their character may be, they are all, in one way or other, under the control of Divine Providence.

First, that God is concerned with the *good* actions of men will not be denied. Their goodness may seem to justify his interference, and the assistance which he gives will be deemed worthy of the purity and benevolence of his character. It will be readily acknowledged that God excites men to good actions, that he presents to them proper objects and proper motives, that he imparts to them spiritual strength and spiritual comfort, that he encourages them to persevere in well-doing, and that he enables them, in many instances at least, to accomplish what they intend. " It is God which worketh in you," says the apostle, " both to will and to do of his good pleasure," and on this fact he grounds the exhortation, " Work out your own salvation with fear and trembling." Phil. ii, 12, 13. But,

Secondly, the providence of God is to be considered in its relation to *moral evil.* The discussion of this question will be attended with some more difficulty; for as, on the one hand, we must be under the strictest guard lest God should be represented as the author of sin, so, on the other, we should be cautious, lest it should be totally removed from under the control of his providence. In the first place, then, this ought to be laid down as a principle of indubitable truth, and as the foundation of all religion, that God is not, in any sense whatever, the author of sin. He neither wills sin nor commits it, otherwise he would be neither holy, just, nor good. "Thou art not a God that hath pleasure in wickedness; neither shall evil dwell with thee." Psa. v, 4. "Let no man say when he is tempted, I am tempted of God: for God cannot be tempted with evil, neither tempteth he any man." James i, 13.

But though God is not the author of sin, yet it is still subject to his control and superintending providence. He permits sin; he limits it; and he overrules it for good.

First, God *permits* sin. This is not a *moral* permission, as if he approved of sin, but physical, by which he suffers it to be committed. The meaning is that he does not interfere in the exercise of his power, as he doubtless might do, to prevent sinful actions. If God should thus prevent his moral creatures from sinning he would force their will and destroy their agency and accountability. Therefore, for wise and holy ends he permits sin. "My people would not hearken to my voice; and Israel would none of me. So I gave them up to their hearts' lust; and they walked in their own counsels." Psa. lxxxi, 11, 12. "Who in times past suffered all nations to walk in their own ways." Acts xiv, 16.

Secondly, God *limits*, or sets bounds to sinful actions. We are not to suppose that when he permits men to sin he exempts them entirely from his control. Such a supposition would be inconsistent with the dependent condition of creatures, and with the character of God as the governor of the world. Wicked men, therefore, are at all times under the superintendence of Divine Providence, and subject to such restraints as God in his wisdom may see proper to impose. He can say to them, as he says to the raging waves of the sea, "Hitherto shall ye come, but no further." Means are always at the command of Providence to circumscribe the wicked actions of sinners. "Surely the wrath of man shall praise thee," said the psalmist; "the remainder of wrath shalt thou restrain." Psa. lxxvi, 10.

Thirdly, God *overrules* sinful actions so as to bring good out of evil. The introduction of sin into the world, though followed by most dreadful consequences, has nevertheless given rise to the brightest manifestation of the glory of God; as also to the highest exercise of his benevolence in the mediation of Christ and the salvation of the guilty through his blood. The sons of Jacob, in selling their brother Joseph into Egypt, committed a great sin; but God overruled it for good both to

Joseph himself and to all his father's family. "As for you," said he to his brethren, "ye thought evil against me; but God meant it unto good, to bring to pass, as it is this day, to save much people alive." Gen. 1, 20. But though God can bring good out of evil, it by no means follows that men may commit sin that good may come. The natural tendency of sin is only to evil; and under the management of creatures, nothing but evil can result from it. The process by which good is deduced from it can be carried on *only* by infinite wisdom and almighty power.

We are not yet done, however, with this important and mysterious subject. The most difficult part remains—the physical agency of God in sinful actions. To understand this matter clearly it will be necessary to distinguish between the moral *powers* with which God has endowed man, and the *exercise* of these powers in voluntary actions. The powers of action come from God, but the use and exercise of these powers he has left to men. This is involved in the very idea that man is a moral being; for, if he were subject to the control of necessity, and not suffered to choose and to do what he sees best, according to the laws of freedom, he would cease to be a moral agent. God is not, therefore, the efficient cause of the free actions of men. He gives them the powers of action, and preserves these powers every moment; but the actions themselves are their own. Thus, for instance, when a man opens his mouth to lie or to blaspheme, God grants him the power at that very moment to open his mouth and to speak; but the *use* of the power is left to the man himself, and he might open his mouth to speak the truth and to glorify God. The action, therefore, whatever it may be, is his own, and for it he alone is accountable; which could not be the case if it proceeded from another.

3. *The Particular Providence of God.*—This has respect to the virtuous and pious, or, in other words, to the people of God, and is therefore sometimes called his *peculiar* or *gracious* providence. No careful reader of the Bible can avoid the conclusion that, though God takes care of all his creatures, and especially of men, yet he exercises a more particular providence toward those who are employed in his service. We do not claim that it is miraculous. It does not suspend the laws of nature in favor of its objects, though it occasionally did so in former times; nor does it consist in visible interpositions. The righteous, so far as we can see, are placed in the same external circumstances with other men. They are rich or poor; they are sick or in health; they meet with successes and disappointments; they have their sorrows and their comforts; but in all God's providential dispensations toward them there is this peculiarity, that in his wisdom and goodness they are rendered subservient to their most important interests. "We know that all things work together for good to them that love God."

The providence of God toward his people is a uniform dispensation of love. He protects them from a thousand evils into which others are permitted to fall. "Whoso hearkeneth unto me shall dwell safely, and shall be quiet from fear of evil." Prov. i, 33. "He shall deliver thee in six troubles; yea, in seven there shall no evil touch thee." Job v, 19. He supports them in times of trial. "When thou passeth through the waters, I will be with thee; and through the rivers, they shall not overflow thee. When thou walkest through the fire, thou shalt not be burnt; neither shall the flame kindle upon thee." Isa. xliii, 2. He bestows upon them his richest spiritual blessings. "For the Lord God is a sun and shield; the Lord will give grace and glory: no good thing will he withhold from them that walk uprightly." Psa. lxxxiv, 11. And finally, if he chastises them, it is the correction of a Father. "For whom the Lord loveth he chasteneth, and scourgeth every son whom he receiveth." Heb. xii, 6. In a word, the ultimate end of providence is the glory of God in the salvation of his people. To this end the evils of life, as well as its good things, are mysteriously made to contribute. This might be illustrated by an appeal to the Scriptures, which are a history of Divine Providence in relation to the world at large, but particularly of its procedure toward the Church and its genuine members.

BOOK III.

DOCTRINES RESPECTING MAN.

The scriptural character of God having been adduced from the inspired writings, we now proceed, in pursuance of our plan, to consider their testimony respecting MAN, both in the estate in which he was created, and in that lapsed condition into which the first act of disobedience plunged the primitive pair and their whole posterity.

CHAPTER I.

MAN'S PRIMITIVE STATE.

In turning our attention to the primitive character and condition of *man*, we will consider him, not so much in a physical, as in a moral light. In order to this we will inquire, in the first place, into the nature of that law under which man was originally placed; and secondly, his moral condition and capabilities, as they are exhibited in the history of his creation.

I. The Nature of the Law under which Man was originally placed.

Here we may remark,

1. That besides the natural government which God exercises over all the various parts of the great visible creation, there is evidence of an administration of another kind. This we call *moral* government, because it has respect to the actions of rational creatures, considered as good and evil, which qualities are necessarily determined by the law of God.

2. All the moral and accountable creatures with which the Scriptures make us acquainted are ANGELS, DEVILS, and MEN, and there is reason to believe that the LAW under which all are placed is substantially the same, and that it is included in this epitome: "Thou shalt love the Lord thy God with all thy heart, and with all thy soul, and with all

thy mind; and thy neighbor as thyself." Matt. xxii, 37, 39. For, though this is addressed to men, yet as it is founded, in both its parts, upon the natural relation of every intelligent creature to God and to all other intelligent creatures, it may be presumed to be universal. Every rational creature owes obedience to God, and a benevolent Creator could only seek, in the first instance, the obedience of love.

From the revealed character of the Creator we must conclude that every rational creature was made, not only to show forth his glory, but that itself might enjoy happiness. The love of God is that affection which unites a created intelligent nature to the Creator, the source of all true happiness, and prevents, in all cases, obedience from being felt as a burden, or regarded under the cold conviction of mere duty. If, therefore, a cheerful obedience from the creature be required, as that which would constantly promote the felicity of the agent, this law of love is to be considered as the law of all moral beings, whether angels or men. Its comprehensiveness is another presumption of its universality; for, unquestionably, it is a maxim of universal import, that "love is the fulfilling of the law," since he who loves must choose to obey every command issued by the sovereign, or the father beloved, and when this love is supreme and uniform the obedience must be absolute and unceasing.

The second commandment is like the first in these respects; it is founded on the natural relations which exist among the creatures of God, and it comprehends every possible relative duty. Thus by these two great first principles of the Divine law, the rational creatures of God would be united to him as their common Lord and Father, and to each other as fellow-subjects and brethren. Indeed, if rational creatures are under a law at all, it cannot be conceived that less than this could be required by their Creator. They are bound to render all love, honor, and obedience to him by a natural and absolute obligation; and, as it has been demonstrated in the experience of man, anything less would be not only contrary to the Creator's glory, but fatal to the creature's happiness.

3. From these views it follows, that all particular precepts, whether they relate to the duties which we owe to God or to other rational creatures, arise out of one or other of these two great commandments, and that every particular law supposes the general one. Our Lord has told us that "on these two commandments *hang* all the law and the prophets;" and St. Paul teaches the doctrine, that all relative duties are briefly comprehended in this saying, " Thou shalt love thy neighbor as thyself."

It was not, therefore, when the law of Moses was engraven on tables of stone by the finger of God, that LAW was first introduced into the world. Men were accounted righteous or wicked between the giving of the law and the flood and before the flood, and were dealt with accordingly. Noah was "a righteous man," Abel was "righteous," and Cain was "wicked." Now as the moral quality of actions is determined by law, and that law the revealed will of God; and as every punitive act on his part, and every bestowment of rewards on account of righteousness, supposes a regal administration, men were under law up to the time of the fall, which law, in all its particular precepts, presupposed the two great commandments.

That our first parents were under law is evident; nor are we to conclude that the command which was given them in the form of a prohibition was the sole measure of their obedience. It was a particular command, which, like those of the Decalogue, and in the writings of the prophets, presupposed a general law of which this was but one manifestation.

Thus are we conducted to a more ancient date of the Divine law than the solemnities of Sinai, or even the creation of man. It is a law coeval in its declaration with the existence of rational creatures, and in its principles with God himself. Under this condition of rational existence must Adam and every other moral creature have come into being, a condition, of course, to which he could not be a party, and to which he had no right to be a party had that been possible. He was *made* under law, as all his descendants are born under law.

But that we may more exactly understand man's primitive state, condition, and capabilities, considered morally, and the nature, extent, and consequences of his fall, it is necessary to consider,

II. THE HISTORY OF HIS CREATION.

The manner in which this event is narrated indicates something peculiar and eminent in the being to be formed, and gives us an intimation of a trinity of persons in the Godhead, all *Divine* because all equally possessed of *creative power*, and to each of whom man was to sustain sacred and intimate relations. "And God said, Let us make man in our image, after our likeness." In what, then, did this "*image*" and "*likeness*" consist?

Human nature has two essential constituent parts: the BODY, formed from the earth, and a LIVING SOUL, breathed into the body by an *inspiration* from God. Did, then, the image or likeness of God in which man was created relate to his body? Certainly not, for "God is a Spirit," without bodily shape or parts, and, therefore, the body of man could not, as such, be in the Divine image.

Nor did this image consist, as some have supposed, in his having *dominion* over the other creatures. Limited dominion may, it is true, be an image of absolute dominion; but it is not said that man was in the image of God's dominion, but in the image and likeness of God himself—of something which constituted *his nature*. Still further, man was evidently made in the image of God *in order to* his having dominion, as the Hebrew imports. His dominion, then, was subsequent to his being made in the Divine image, and could not be that image itself.

It is in vain to say that this image consisted in some *one essential* quality of human nature which *could not be lost;* for we shall find that it comprehended more qualities than *one*, and that while revelation places it, in part, in what was essential to human nature, it included also what was not essential, and what might be both lost and regained. It consisted in what divines have called the *natural* and the *moral* image of God.

1. *His* NATURAL *image.*—The natural image of God in which man was created was essential and ineffaceable, and comprised his *spirituality*, his *immortality*, and his *intellectual powers*. It consisted,

(1.) *In spirituality.*—When God is called "the Father of spirits," a likeness is intimated between man and God in the spirituality of their nature. This is also implied in the argument of St. Paul, Acts xvii, 29: "Forasmuch, then, as we are the offspring of God, we ought not to think that the Godhead is like unto gold, or silver, or stone, graven by art and man's device." Here the apostle argues the spirituality of God, and, consequently, his immateriality, from the spirituality of man; for if man possesses a spiritual nature, that nature must be also immaterial. The argument of the apostle is this: as man is a spiritual and immaterial being, if he is the offspring of God, then God must be a spiritual and immaterial being; consequently, the Godhead cannot be "like unto gold, or silver, or stone."

Nor is it a valid objection to say that immateriality belongs to the lower animals as well as to man; for though we allow them to be actuated by an immaterial principle, it is obviously of an inferior *kind*. The spirit which is incapable of rational induction, and of moral knowledge, must be of an order greatly inferior to the spirits which possess these capabilities; and this is the kind of spirituality which is peculiar to man. But this image consisted,

(2.) *In immortality.*—This applied originally to man's entire compound nature; for even his body would not have died had not sin entered into the world. This is the irresistible conclusion from the reasoning of St. Paul, where he shows that "by one man sin entered into the world, and *death by sin.*" Rom. v, 12. The same fact is implied in the original penalty of the law: "In the day thou eatest thereof, thou shalt surely die." In this there was most certainly a promise implied that if man would continue in obedience he should live.

Again, we may clearly infer that immortality was included in the image of God in which man was created from Gen. ix, 6: "Whoso sheddeth man's blood, by man shall his blood be shed; for in the image of God made he man." The criminality of homicide seems here to be measured by the value of life to an immortal being, whose probationary state is to end in eternal happiness or misery, and whose life, on this very account, is not to lie at the sport of human passions.

Though we allow, as the Scriptures seem clearly to teach, that the immortality of man related originally to his entire being, yet, without running into the absurdity of what is called the "natural immortality" of the human soul, that essence must have been constituted immortal in a high and peculiar sense. Hence it has ever retained its immortality amid the universal death, not only of inferior animals, but of the bodies of all human beings. Men may "kill the body, but are not able to kill the soul." Matt. x, 28.

(3.) *Man's intellectual powers were also included in this image.*—This we prove from Col. iii, 10: "And have put on the new man, which is renewed in *knowledge* after the image of him that created him." Here is a plain allusion to the image of God in which man was originally created. He was made capable of knowledge in regard both to natural and moral subjects, and endowed also with *liberty* of *will*.

As to the *degree* of knowledge which man originally possessed commentators have widely differed. Some have represented him as having been, in this respect, almost in a state of infancy; while others have exalted him to almost, if not altogether, angelic perfection. The truth lies between these two extremes. That his knowledge was exceedingly great, may be inferred from the purity and perfection of his nature, and from his capability of holding converse with his Maker. But that he was in this respect inferior to angels, is clearly implied in that declaration of the psalmist: "Thou hast made him a little *lower* than the angels." Psa. viii, 5.

2. *His* MORAL *image.*—The natural image of God in which man was created was the foundation of that MORAL IMAGE by which also he was distinguished. Unless he had been a spiritual being, possessing knowledge and the power of volition, he would have been wholly incapable of *moral* qualities. That he had such qualities eminently, and that in them consisted the image of God, as well as in the natural attributes just stated, may be argued,

(1.) *From the express testimony of Scripture.*—"Lo, this only have I found," said Solomon, "that God made man UPRIGHT." Eccl. vii, 29. There is also an express allusion to the *moral image* of God in which man was at first created in Eph. iv, 24: "Put on the new man, which after God is created in righteousness and true holiness." In this passage the apostle represents the change produced in true Christians, by the Gospel, as a *renewal* of the image of God in man; as a new or second creation of that image; and he explicitly declares that this image consists in "righteousness" and in "true holiness." It follows, therefore, that man was created in the *moral* image of his Maker. But this may be argued,

(2.) *From that satisfaction with which the Creator viewed the works of his hands.*—"And God saw *everything* that he had made, and behold, it was very good." Gen. i, 31. But, as to man, this goodness must have implied moral qualities as well as physical. Without them he would have been imperfect as *man;* and had they existed in him perverted and sinful he could not have been pronounced "very good."

As to the *degree* of moral perfection in the first man, there are two extreme opinions. Some have placed it at an elevation which renders it exceedingly difficult to conceive how he should have fallen into sin at all, and especially how he should have fallen so soon as seems to be represented in the narrative of Moses. On the other hand those who either deny, or hold very slightly, the doctrine of our hereditary depravity, delight to represent Adam as little, if at all, superior in moral perfection and capability to his descendants.

We may not be able to ascertain the exact degree of his moral perfection; but it is evident, from the Scriptures above quoted, that there is a certain standard below which it cannot be placed. Generally, he was made in the *image of God;* which, as we have proved, is to be understood *morally* as well as *naturally.* We must conclude, therefore, that man, in his original state, was SINLESS, both in *act* and in *principle.* "God made man UPRIGHT."

The Hebrew word ישר, which is here translated *upright,* signifies just, upright, perfect, righteous, and is, therefore, indicative of moral rectitude. It expresses the *exactness* of truth, justice, and obedience; and comprehends both the state of the heart and the habit of the life. Such, then, was the state of primitive man. There was no obliquity in his moral principles—his mind and affections; none in his conduct. He was perfectly sincere and exactly just, rendering from the heart all that was due both to God and to the creatures. All this is fully implied in the language of the apostle, when he places the image of God in which the new man is created in "*righteousness* and *true holiness.*"

It may be proper to observe here, that the "*knowledge*" in which the apostle places the image of God in the renewed man does not merely imply the faculty of the understanding, which is a part of the natural image of God, but that which might be lost, because it is that in which the new man is "*renewed.*" It is, therefore, to be understood as designating more particularly the knowledge of *God;* that knowledge of God which is the result of holy communion and fellowship with him, that knowledge of God which may be fitly denominated *experimental.*

We see, then, that in the primeval condition and character of man the "kindness and love of God" eminently appeared. He was made a rational and immortal spirit, with no limits to the constant enlargement of his powers. He was made holy and happy, and was admitted to intercourse with God. He was not left alone, but had the pleasures of society. He was placed in a world of grandeur, harmony, beauty, and utility, which was canopied with other distant worlds, to exhibit to his very senses a manifestation of the extent of space and the vastness of the universe, and to call into vigorous and salutary exercise his reason, his fancy, and his devotion. He was placed in a paradise where probably all that was sublime and gentle in the scenery of the whole earth was exhibited in *pattern*, and all that could delight the innocent sense, and excite the curious inquiries of the mind, was spread before him. He had labor to employ his attention without producing weariness, and time for his highest pursuits in the knowledge of God, his will and his works. Such was our world and its rational inhabitants, the first pair; and thus did its creation manifest, not only the power and wisdom of the Creator, but also his benevolence.

CHAPTER II.

THE FALL OF MAN.

The Mosaic account of this sorrowful event is given in the third chapter of Genesis, and is substantially this: that man was placed in the garden of Eden to dress and to keep it; that in this garden two trees were especially distinguished, one as "the tree of life," the other as "the tree of the knowledge of good and evil;" that of the fruit of the latter Adam was commanded not to eat, and the command was enforced by the announcement of the penalty, "In the day thou eatest thereof thou shalt surely die;" that through the temptation of the serpent the woman was induced to eat of the forbidden fruit, and through her the husband also; and that for this act of disobedience they were expelled from the garden, made subject to death, and laid under other maledictions.

Interpreters of this account may be divided into three classes: those who deny the literal sense of the relation entirely; those who take it to be in part literal and in part allegorical; and those who, while they contend for the literal interpretation of every part, consider some of the terms used and some of the persons introduced as conveying a meaning more extensive than the letter, and as constituting several symbols of spiritual things and of spiritual beings.

In directing our attention to the scriptural account of the fall we will first prove that it is to be understood in its *literal sense;* and in the second place we will consider some objections which have been urged against the Divine administration, as connected with the circumstances of the fall of man.

I. THE MOSAIC ACCOUNT OF THE FALL IS TO BE UNDERSTOOD IN ITS LITERAL SENSE.

That this account is to be taken as a matter of real history, and according to its literal import, may be established by the following considerations:

1. *That it is a part of a continuous history.*—To select from a regularly conducted narrative a particular portion, as allegorical, when all the other parts in the connection are admitted to be plain history, is contrary to all rules of interpretation. If we may make thus free with the third chapter of Genesis why not the first, and thus deny the reality of the creation? Why not make a similar disposition of the Mosaic history from Abel to Noah, or from Noah to Abraham? One of these consequences must therefore follow: either that the account of the fall must be taken as a history of facts, or that the historical character of the five books of Moses must be given up. But the literal sense of this history is established by the consideration,

2. *That as a simple relation of events it is referred to in various parts of the Scriptures.*—The prophets frequently speak of "the garden of Eden," and of "the garden of God." We have "the tree of life" mentioned several times in the book of Proverbs and in the Revelations. The enemies of Christ and of his Church are spoken of under the name of "the serpent," and the habit of the serpent to "lick the dust" is also referred to by Micah.

If the history of the fall as recorded by Moses were an allegory, or anything but a literal history, several of the above allusions would have no meaning; but the matter is put beyond all possible doubt in the New Testament, unless the same culpable liberties be taken with the words of our Lord and St. Paul as with those of the Jewish lawgiver. Our Lord says, Matt. xix, 4, 5 : "Have ye not read, that he which made them at the beginning, made them male and female, and said, For this cause shall a man leave father and mother, and shall cleave to his wife: and they twain shall be one flesh?" Here, although he does not quote immediately from the history of the fall, yet he quotes a portion of the same continuous narrative; consequently he must have regarded it as a real history.

St. Paul says, "By one man sin entered into the world;" "In Adam all die;" and again, "I fear, lest by any means, as the serpent beguiled Eve through his subtilty, so your minds should be corrupted from the simplicity that is in Christ." 2 Cor. xi, 3. In this passage the instrument of the temptation is said to be a *serpent*, [ὄφις,] which is a sufficient answer to those who would make it any other animal; and Eve is represented as being first seduced, according to the Mosaic account. This the apostle repeats in 1 Tim. ii, 13, 14 : "Adam was first formed, then Eve. And Adam was not deceived, but the woman being deceived was in the transgression."

When we consider that these passages are made the basis of grave reasonings in regard to some of the most important doctrines of Christianity, and of important social duties and points of Christian order and decorum, it would be to charge the sacred writers with the grossest absurdity, nay, with even culpable and unworthy trifling, to suppose that they would argue from the history of the fall as a narrative, when they knew it to be a mere allegory. We must allow, therefore, that our Lord and his apostles regarded it as a real history. This view of the subject will be strengthened if we consider,

3. *The absurdity of supposing the account of the fall to be partly allegorical.*—No writer of true history would mix allegory with plain matter of fact in one continued narrative without any intimation of a transition from one to the other. If, therefore, any part of this narrative is matter of fact, no part is allegorical. On the other hand, if any part is allegorical, no part is naked matter of fact; and the consequence of this will be, that everything in every part of the whole narrative must be allegorical. Thus the whole history of the creation would be an allegory, of which the real subject is not disclosed, and in this absurdity the scheme of allegorizing would end.

4. Though the literal sense of the history is thus established, yet *that it has in several parts, but in perfect accordance with the literal interpretation, a* MYSTICAL *sense*, is equally to be proved from the Scriptures.

It is a matter of established history that our first parents were prohibited from the tree of knowledge, and after their fall were excluded from the tree of life; that they were tempted by a serpent, and that various maledictions were passed upon them and upon the instrument of their seduction. But, rightly to understand this history, it is necessary to recollect that man was in a state of trial; that the prohibition of a certain fruit was but one part of the law under which he was placed; that the serpent was but the instrument of the real tempter, and that the curse on this instrument was symbolical of the punishment reserved for the real agent.

(1.) That man was in a state of trial appears on the very face of the history; but to a state of trial the power of moral freedom is essential. That our first parents possessed this power is as evident as that they were placed under rule and restraint. They are contemplated throughout the whole transaction, not as mere instruments, but as voluntary agents, and as such, capable of reward and punishment. Commands were issued to them which supposes a power to obey; but a power to obey necessarily implies a power to refuse and rebel. The power to obey and disobey being then mutually involved, that which determines a moral agent to the one or to the other is the *will*. For, if it were some power *ab extra*, operating necessarily, he would be no longer an *actor* but a mere passive instrument, and, therefore, in order to man's accountability we must allow his free-agency.

In that state of excellence in which man was created his *will* must have exerted an absolute sovereignty over his thoughts, desires, words, and conduct. This, however, did not exclude solicitation or strong influence from without, provided we allow that it was resistible, either by man's own strength, or by means of assistance from a higher source. But though freedom of will is essential to a rational creature in a state of trial, yet the circumstances of the trial may be varied, and made more easy or more difficult, according to the will of the Divine Governor.

Our first parents, in their primitive state of trial, were evidently subject to temptation from *intellectual pride*, from *sense*, and from *passion*. The first two operated on Eve, and, probably, on Adam also; to which was added, in his case, a passionate subjection to the wishes of his wife. If, then, these were the facts of their temptation, the circumstances of their trial are apparent. Their passions and appetites, so far from being in themselves sinful, were doubtless intended, under the control of reason, to be the instruments of great good; but it was at the same time possible that they should yield to those appetites and passions contrary to the dictates of reason, and thus suffer them to become the occasions of much mischief. To this cause the commission of the first transgression is evidently ascribed. "The woman saw that the tree was good for food, and that it was pleasant to the eyes, and a tree to be desired to make one wise." This view of its qualities, together with the suggestions of the tempter, induced her to act contrary to the express command of God.

It is therefore manifest, that the state of trial in which our first parents were placed required of them, in order to the preservation of their virtue, vigilance, prayer, and the active exercise of the dominion of the *will* over solicitation. No creature can be absolutely perfect, because every creature is finite; and it would appear, from the example of the first pair, that an innocent rational being, though perfect in its *kind*, is kept from falling only by *taking hold on God*. As this is an act, there must be a determination of the will to it; and so, when the least carelessness, the least tampering with the desire of forbidden gratifications is induced, there is always an enemy at hand. Thus, "when lust hath conceived, it bringeth forth sin; and sin, when it is finished, bringeth forth death." James i, 15.

This is the only rational account of the origin of moral evil, and it resolves itself into three principles: 1. The necessary imperfection, in *degree*, of finite creatures. 2. The liberty of choice, which is essential to rational, accountable beings. 3. The influence of temptation on the *will*. That Adam might have resisted the temptation is a sufficient proof of the *justice* of God throughout this transaction; and that the circumstances of his trial were made precisely what they were, is to be resolved into a *wisdom*, the full manifestation of which is not to be expected in this life.

(2.) The prohibition of a certain fruit was but one part of the law under which man was placed. We have already seen that all rational creatures are under a law which requires supreme love to God and entire obedience to his commands; and that, consequently, our first parents were placed under this equitable obligation. We have also seen that all specific laws emanate from this general law, and are manifestations of it. The Decalogue was such a manifestation of it to the Jews, and the prohibition of the *tree of knowledge* is to be considered in the same light. This restraint presupposed a right in God to command, and an obligation in his creatures to obey.

But it would be absurd to suppose that this prohibition was the only rule under which our first parents were placed; for then it would follow that had they become sensual in the use of any other food than that which was forbidden, or had they refused to worship their Creator, it would not have been sin. This precept was, however, made prominent by special injunction; and it is enough to say that it was, as the event shows, a sufficient test of their obedience.

(3.) The visible agent in man's seduction was the serpent, but the real tempter was that evil spirit called the Devil and Satan. It is evident, from the attributes and properties ascribed to the serpent, that some superior intelligence was identified with it in the transaction. Surely the use of speech, reasoning powers, a knowledge of the divine law, and seductive artifice, are not the faculties of an irrational animal. The solemn manner, too, in which God addressed the serpent in pronouncing the curse, proves that an intelligent and free agent was arraigned before him; and it would indeed be ridiculous to suppose the contrary.

This shows that the ridicule of some, as to the serpent, is quite misplaced, and that one of the most serious doctrines is involved in the whole account—the liability of man to diabolical influence. Though we have but general intimations of the existence of an order of apostate spirits, and know nothing of the date of their creation, or of the circumstances of their probation and fall, yet this is clear, that they are permitted to have influence on earth; to war against the virtue and the peace of man, though under constant control and government; and that this was one circumstance in the trial of our first parents, as it is also in ours. Here, then, without giving up the literal sense of the history, we must look beyond the letter, and regard the serpent as only the *instrument* of a superhuman tempter.

(4.) In like manner the sentence pronounced upon the serpent, while it is to be understood literally as to that animal, must be considered as teaching more than is expressed by the letter, and the terms of it are therefore to be regarded as symbolical. The cursing of the serpent was a symbol of the malediction which fell upon the devil—the real agent in the temptation; while the prediction respecting the bruising of the serpent's head by the *seed of the woman* was indicative of man's redemption from the malice and power of Satan by our Lord Jesus Christ. This symbolical interpretation of the passage is confirmed by two considerations:

First, if the serpent was only a mere instrument employed by Satan, as was obviously the case, justice required that the curse should fall with its greatest weight upon the real seducer. But to interpret the history in a *merely* literal sense would confine the punishment entirely to the serpent, and leave the prime mover of the offense without any share of the malediction.

Secondly, it would be ridiculous to suppose, under the circumstances, that the prediction respecting the bruising of the serpent's head was intended to be understood in no other than a literal sense. We see the offenders before God in the utmost distress; and we hear him pronouncing upon them pains, and sorrows, and misery, and death. But are we to imagine that we hear him foretelling with great solemnity, in the midst of all this scene of calamity and woe, that at some future period a serpent should wound the heel of one of Adam's posterity, and that he should revenge himself by bruising its head? What had this trivial circumstance to do with man's fallen condition? What comfort could the condemned offenders have derived from such a prediction? Adam surely could not have understood the prophecy in this light, though some of his sons have so understood it.

II. WE WILL CONSIDER SOME OBJECTIONS WHICH HAVE BEEN URGED AGAINST THE DIVINE ADMINISTRATION AS CONNECTED WITH THE CIRCUMSTANCES OF THE FALL OF MAN.

1. It is asked by way of objection, *Could not God, who certainly foresaw man's apostasy, have prevented so great an evil?* And if so, *how can we reconcile the fall of man with Divine goodness?* That God foresaw the fall we firmly believe, for he declares " the end from the beginning;" and that he could have prevented it we freely admit, for he can do whatever does not imply a contradiction and is consistent with his own perfections.

We do not suppose that God was necessarily compelled to create man. The fact that he did not perform this work till a few thousand years ago is sufficient evidence that he might, had he seen proper, have suspended it even till now. If, then, he was not compelled to create man at first, but acted with perfect freedom, it would follow that he might still continue to exercise the same freedom and unmake what he had made, or so change it as to constitute it something entirely different. So far, then, as the simple question of *power* is concerned, God could have prevented the fall. He could have prevented it by omitting to create man. He could have prevented it by making man anything else than a moral agent. But that he could have prevented it consistent with his own attributes without destroying the moral agency of man is what cannot be proved.

But if the only way by which God could have rendered the apostasy of man impossible was, to withhold from him the power of moral agency, the question then amounts to this : Was it best, upon the whole, that moral agents should be brought into existence? Before the Divine administration in this case can be justly impugned, it must be shown either that it was improper to create moral agents, or that the possibility of transgressing is not essential to the character of a moral agent. That it was improper to create moral agents is contradicted by the fact that God did create such beings. We are, therefore, compelled to allow, that in the judgment of God more good than evil would result from their creation, and that it was best, upon the whole, that such beings should be created.

That the possibility of apostasy is essential to the character of a moral agent is easily proved. 1. A moral agent is one who is capable of performing moral actions. 2. Moral actions imply a law by which they are determined to be right or wrong. 3. A law for the government of moral actions must necessarily be such as may be either obeyed or disobeyed by the subject, otherwise there could be neither virtue nor vice ; there could be no praise attached to obedience, no blame to disobedience. Thus it is clear that moral agency necessarily implies the power to obey or disobey ; consequently, God could not have prevented the possibility of man's apostasy without destroying his moral agency.

2. *The prohibition under which our first parents were placed has often been made the subject of ridicule.*—" What harm could there be in eating an apple," it is asked, " that they should be placed under a restraint so strict and unreasonable ?"

Here it may be observed that the objection does not lie against the fact of man's being placed under law ; for the propriety of this is generally acknowledged. The ground of complaint is in the peculiar character of the law itself; and particularly in its being a *positive* precept, and not a *moral* one. The difference between positive and moral precepts is, that " moral precepts are those the reasons of which we see ; positive precepts those the reasons of which we do not see. Moral duties arise out of the nature of the case itself prior to external command ; positive duties do not arise out of the nature of the case, but from external command. Nor would they be duties at all, were it not for such command received from Him whose creatures and subjects we are."*

But as the obligation of all duties, whether moral or positive, rests

* Butler's Analogy.

upon their being made *law* by the authority of God, no valid objection can lie against the making of a positive precept the special test of man's obedience. To see or not to see the reasons of the Divine enactments, whether moral or positive, is a circumstance which does not affect the question of duty. But that God has sufficient reasons for all that he requires of us, though we may not see them, is a conclusion as rational as it is pious; and to slight *positive* precepts, therefore, is to refuse obedience to the Lawgiver only on the proud and presumptuous ground that he has not made us acquainted with his own reasons for enacting them.

Nor was this positive injunction without some obvious moral reason, which is probably the case with all positive precepts of Divine authority. That all moral creatures should acknowledge subjection to the Creator is equally required by the Divine glory, and by the benefit of the creatures themselves. Man was required to do this by a free and voluntary obedience, in abstaining from the fruit of a single tree, thus acknowledging the common Creator to be his Supreme Lord, and himself to be dependent upon his bounty and favor. The prohibition was simple and explicit, it was not difficult to observe, it accorded with the circumstances of those on whom it was enjoined, and as a test of obedience no injunction could have been more suitable. This view of the transaction in Paradise gives it an aspect so noble and dignified that we may well shudder at the impiety of that poor wit by whom it has been sometimes ignorantly assailed.

3. It has also been objected, that *if the serpent was but the mere instrument of the real seducer, the sentence pronounced upon it was unjust.*—To this the reply is, that it could not be a matter of just complaint to the serpent that its form should be changed, and its species lowered in the scale of being. To its former superior rank it had no original right, but held it at the pleasure of the Creator. If special pain and suffering had been inflicted upon the serpent there would be a semblance of plausibility in the objection; but it suffered no more in consequence of the fall than other irrational animals.

Its degradation was evidently intended as a memento to man; and the real punishment, as we shall show, fell upon the real transgressor, who used the serpent as his instrument. But the enmity of the whole race of serpents to the human race, their cunning, and their poisonous qualities, appear to have been wisely and graciously intended as standing warnings to us to beware of that spiritual enemy who ever lies in wait to wound and destroy.

4. *The penalty annexed to the Adamic law has been made a ground of complaint, as being excessively rigorous and entirely disproportionate to the offense.*—To understand this subject it will be necessary for us to take into the account,

(1.) *Man's primitive condition as a responsible being.*—In order that he might be a proper subject of moral government he was made a rational being, capable of understanding his duty and the reasons of it. He was made capable of perceiving and feeling the influence of motives, and was endowed with every attribute of a free moral agent. His duty was plainly prescribed; while light, like the unobstructed rays of the sun, flowed into his soul by a direct communication from God. No necessity impelled him to transgress the Divine law, for he was in possession of every necessary faculty to enable him to obey. Such was his primitive condition, and such were the circumstances by which he was rendered accountable for his actions.

(2.) *The nature of that authority by which he was bound, and to which he was held responsible.*—It was the supreme authority of the infinite God, enforced by the strong obligations of truth, justice, holiness, and gratitude. Such obligations, as high as heaven and as sacred as God himself, could not be relinquished or disregarded. The honor of the eternal throne forbade it.

(3.) *The character of man's offense.*—Surely, it could not have been so trivial a thing as those seem to suppose who speak so flippantly of the mere circumstance of tasting an apple. The eating of the forbidden fruit was the external act of the transgression; but the seat of the crime lay deep in the soul. There, where all had been holiness and love, pride and lust and unbelief were allowed to reign in triumph. The word of God was contradicted, his authority was thrown off, man's allegiance to heaven was relinquished, and the claims of gratitude were entirely disregarded. How exceedingly defective, then, must be the views of those who represent the first sin as a venial impropriety, of scarcely sufficient magnitude to merit the notice of God!

In view of all these circumstances we have no room to complain that the penalty of death was annexed to the Divine law. The whole history of the case, when properly understood, proves that the penalty, so far from being an evidence of cruelty on the part of the Lawgiver, was a benevolent enactment. In all good governments the object of penal sanctions is not primarily the punishment of the subjects, but the prevention of crime. So, likewise, that Adam might be deterred from transgression, and thereby be preserved in his primitive state of holiness and happiness, the penalty was annexed to the Divine precept, "In the day thou eatest thereof thou shalt surely *die.*" If the prime object of the penalty was the prevention of crime, then the *severity* of the penalty, if such it may be called, is an evidence of Divine *goodness*, which made the inducements to obedience as strong as possible without destroying man's accountability.

CHAPTER III.

THE EFFECTS OF THE FALL

HAVING investigated, in the preceding chapter, the circumstances of the *fall*, we turn to the consideration of its EFFECTS. On this subject three leading opinions are entertained :

First, the view of Pelagius and of the modern Socinians is, that though Adam, by his transgression, exposed himself to the displeasure of his Maker, yet neither he nor his posterity sustained any *moral* injury by his disobedience; that the only evil he suffered was expulsion from Paradise, and subjection to severe labor; that he was created mortal, and would have died had he not sinned; that his posterity, like himself, are placed in a state of trial; and that we may maintain our innocence amid surrounding temptations, and may also daily improve in moral excellence by the proper use of reason and other natural powers.

The *second* opinion is the psuedo-Arminian or semi-Pelagian theory of Dr. Whitby and several other divines of the English Church. It is this: that though Adam was naturally mortal, yet his life would have been forever preserved by the bounty of his Creator had he continued obedient; and that he was a kind of natural representative of his posterity, so that all the effects of his fall, to some extent, are visited upon them; not, however, as penal, but as natural consequences, and as children are often compelled to suffer by the negligence or fault of their parents.

The *third* opinion, and, as we believe, the only rational and scriptural view of this subject, is that Adam, by his transgression, incurred the Divine displeasure, lost the moral image of God in which he was created, and became subject to temporal death, and exposed to death eternal; that as he was the federal head and legal representative of his posterity they fell in him as really as he fell in himself, and thus became liable to all the penal consequences of his transgression; that man, in his fallen condition, "is very far gone from original righteousness, and is of his own nature inclined to evil, and that continually ;" and that he has no power, without divine grace, to do anything that is really good or acceptable to God.

This is the view which was entertained by Arminius, and which is held by that large body of Christians who follow the theological opinions of Mr. Wesley. Nor is there any material discrepancy between this statement of man's fallen condition and the doctrine of the Augsburg Confession, the Church of England, the French Churches, the Calvinistic Church of Scotland, and, so far as this doctrine alone is concerned, of Calvin himself. True Arminianism, therefore, as fully as Calvinism, admits the total depravity of human nature in consequence of the fall of our first parents; and to represent this doctrine as being exclusively Calvinistic, which has often been done, it an entire delusion.

But in order to a further investigation of this subject is will be necessary to consider, 1. The nature of that DEATH which was made the penalty of sin; 2. The legal relation which Adam sustained to his posterity; and, 3. The moral condition in which men are actually born into the world.

§ 1. *The Nature of that Death which was made the penalty of Sin.*

That this penalty includes the very "fullness of death," as divines have justly termed it, death *bodily*, *spiritual*, and *eternal*, is a doctrine which cannot be puffed away by mere sarcasm, but which stands upon the firm basis of inspired truth. A few remarks will show the justness of this conclusion.

1. The Pelagian and Socinian notion that Adam would have died had he not sinned, requires no other refutation than the words of St. Paul: "By one man sin entered into the world, and *death by sin*." Rom. v, 12. It evidently follows, therefore, that if sin had not "entered into the world," so far at least as man is concerned, there would have been no death.

2. In addition to that death which stands opposed to animal life, and which consists in the separation of the rational soul from the body, the Scriptures speak of death in a *moral* sense. This consists in a separation of the soul from communion with God, and is manifested by the dominion of earthly and corrupt dispositions and habits, and an entire indifference or aversion to spiritual and heavenly things. All who have not been made alive by the power of divine grace are regarded as being in this state of spiritual death. "And you hath he quickened, who were DEAD in trespasses and sins." Eph. ii, 1.

In accordance with this view, that moral change which unites the soul to God is represented as a resurrection from the dead, and a passage "from death unto life." To interpret, then, the death pronounced upon Adam as including moral death, is in perfect agreement with the language of Scripture. For, if a state of sin in the unregenerate is a state of spiritual death, then a state of sin in him was a state of spiritual death; the same cause producing the same effect. And, as God withdraws himself from all communion with the guilty, they are thereby separated from the only source of spiritual life, and thus suffer a *deprivation* from which a *depravation* consequently and necessarily follows.

3. But the highest sense of the term death, in the Scriptures, is the punishment of the soul in a future state by a loss of happiness, a separation from God, and a positive infliction of Divine wrath. It was in this sense that our Lord used the term when he said, "If a man keep my sayings, he shall never see death." John viii, 51. This state of hope-

less misery is also called "the second death," and is evidently included in the penalty of the Divine law; for it is to be regarded as an axiom in the jurisprudence of heaven, that "the wages of sin is DEATH." Nor do the Scriptures give us the least intimation that any sin whatever is exempt from this penalty; or that some sins are punished in this life only, and others in the life to come. The degree of punishment will doubtless be proportionate to the offense; but death is the penalty attached to all sin, unless it is averted by pardon. What was there, then, in the case of Adam to take him out of this rule? His act was a *transgression* of the law, and therefore *sin;* and, as such, its wages was *death*, which means, in its highest sense, future and eternal punishment.

§ 2. *The Legal Relation which Adam sustained to his Posterity.*

The question now to be considered is, whether Adam is to be regarded as a mere individual, the consequences of whose conduct terminated in himself, or no otherwise affected his posterity than incidentally, as the misconduct of an ordinary parent may affect his children; or whether he was the legal *head* and *representative* of the human race, who in consequence of his fall have fallen with him. The latter opinion seems best to accord with the teachings of the holy Scriptures, as we will immediately proceed to show.

1. The testimony of the Scriptures in support of this position is so explicit that all attempts to evade it have been in vain. St. Paul, in the fifth chapter of his epistle to the Romans, evidently contrasts the public or federal character of Adam with that of Christ. He shows that the evils which mankind suffer are the consequences of Adam's transgression, and that the benefits which are graciously bestowed upon them are the effects of Christ's obedience. It is with allusion to this representative character that Adam is called "the figure ($\tau\acute{v}\pi o\varsigma$, *type* or *model*) of him that was to come."

The apostle also adopts the phrases "the first Adam" and "the second Adam," which mode of speaking can only be explained on the ground that as sin and death descended from one, so righteousness and life flow from the other; and that what Christ is to all his spiritual seed Adam was to all his natural descendants. On this, indeed, the parallel is founded, 1 Cor. xv, 22: "For as in Adam all die, even so in Christ shall all be made alive;" words which on any other hypothesis can have no natural signification.

2. The condition in which this federal connection between Adam and his posterity placed the latter is next to be considered. This involves what theologians call "the imputation of Adam's sin to his posterity," in regard to which three leading views have been taken.

(1.) Some hold the doctrine of MEDIATE *imputation*, which is, that in virtue of our derivation from Adam, our bodies are mortal and our moral nature is corrupt. This opinion, however, though embracing truth, does not go to the length of Scripture, which must not be warped by the reasonings of erring man.

(2.) Another view is, that Adam's sin is accounted *ours* in the sight of God by virtue of our federal relation. This is called IMMEDIATE *imputation*, and is supported by the assumption that Adam and his posterity constitute *one moral person*, and that the whole human race was in him, its head consenting to his act. But this opinion is inconsistent with that individual agency which enters into the very notion of an accountable being, while it destroys the distinction between original and actual sin. It asserts the imputation of the actual commission of Adam's sin to his descendants, which is false in fact; it makes us chargeable with the full latitude of his transgression and all its attendant circumstances, and it constitutes us separate from all actual voluntary offense, equally guilty with him, all which are equally repugnant to our consciousness and to the equity of the case.

(3.) The other view of this subject, and that which we believe to be in accordance with the Scriptures, is, that the *imputation* of Adam's sin to his posterity is confined to its LEGAL RESULTS. If a man has committed treason, and has thereby lost his estate, his crime is so imputed to his children that they, with him, are made to suffer the penalty of his offense. We do not mean, however, that the *personal act* of the father is charged upon the children, but that his guilt or liability to punishment is so transferred to them that they suffer the legal consequences of his crime.

Thus the sin of Achan was so imputed to his children that they were stoned to death on account of it.* In like manner the covetousness of Gehazi was imputed to his posterity, when God declared, by the mouth of his prophet, that the leprosy should cleave unto him and his seed for ever.† So also the Jews: "His blood be on us and on our children;" that is, let us and our children be punished for it.

In this sense, then, we may safely contend for the imputation of Adam's sin to his posterity; and this agrees precisely with the apostle Paul, who speaks of the imputation of sin to those "who had not sinned after the similitude of Adam's transgression;" that is, to all who lived between Adam and Moses, and consequently to infants, who personally had not offended. He also declares, that "by one man's disobedience many were made," constituted, accounted, and dealt with as "sinners," and treated as though they themselves had actually sinned. For that this is his sense is clear from what follows: "So by the obedience of one shall many be made righteous;" constituted, accounted, and dealt with as such, though not actually righteous, but in fact pardoned criminals. The legal consequences, then, of this imputation are as previously shown, death *temporal, spiritual,* and *eternal.*

* See Josh. vii, 25. † See 2 Kings v, 27.

An objection has been raised against this view of the imputation of Adam's sin to his posterity on the ground of its supposed *injustice*. Before we give a direct reply to the objection it may be proper to remark, that if this imputation is unjust in any of its parts it must be unjust in every part. If it is unjust to make the descendants of Adam liable to eternal death because of his offense, the infliction of temporal death is unjust also; the *duration* of the punishment making no difference in the simple question of justice. If punishment, whether of *loss* or of *pain*, is unjust, its measure and duration may be greater or less injustice, but it is unjust in every degree. If, then, we confine the legal result of Adam's transgression to bodily death, we are in precisely the same difficulty, as to the equity of the proceeding, as when it is extended further. The only way out of this dilemma is to consider death not as a punishment but as a blessing, which involves the absurdity of supposing that God pronounced a blessing upon Adam as the consequence of sin.

But in meeting this objection it is only necessary to show that it rests upon a false foundation. It supposes, contrary to truth, that the legal consequences of Adam's transgression are to be considered apart from that evangelical provision of mercy which includes the whole human race. The redemption of man by Christ was certainly not an after thought, brought in upon man's apostasy. It was a *provision*, and when man fell he found justice hand in hand with mercy. If we look at the subject in this light every difficulty will be removed.

As to the case of Adam and his *adult* descendants, it will be seen that all became liable to bodily death. Here was *justice*. But by means of the atonement, which effectually declares the justice of God, this sentence is reversed by a glorious resurrection. Again, when God, the fountain of spiritual life, withdrew himself from Adam, he died a spiritual death and became morally corrupt; and, as "that which is born of the flesh is flesh," all his posterity are in the same condition. Here is *justice*. But spiritual life visits man from another quarter and through other means. The second Adam "is a quickening Spirit." Through the atonement which he has made the Holy Spirit is given to man, that he may again infuse into his corrupt nature the heavenly life and regenerate and sanctify it. Here is the *mercy*. And as to a future state, eternal life is promised to all who perseveringly believe in Christ, which reverses the sentence of eternal death. Here, again, is the manifestation of *mercy*.

In all this it is impossible to impeach the equity of the Divine administration, since no man suffers any loss or injury ultimately by the sin of Adam but by his own willful obstinacy. The "abounding grace" by Christ has placed before all men upon their believing, not merely compensation for the loss and injury sustained by Adam, but infinitely higher blessings, both in kind and degree, than were forfeited in him.

As to *adults*, then, the objection taken from Divine justice is unsupported.

We come now to the case of *infants*. The great consideration which leads to a solution of this case is found in Romans v, 18: "Therefore, as by the offense of one judgment came upon all men to condemnation, even so by the righteousness of one the free gift came upon all men unto justification of life." In these words the sin of Adam and the merits of Christ are pronounced to be co-extensive, the words applied to both being precisely the same. " *Judgment* came upon ALL MEN,"— "the *free gift* came upon ALL MEN." If the whole human race is meant in the former clause, the whole human race is meant in the latter also; and then it follows, that as all are benefited by the obedience of Christ, so all children dying in infancy must be partakers of this benefit.

The "free gift" which "came upon all men" is said to be "unto justification of life," a full reversal of the penalty of death, and a title to life eternal. But the benefit did not so come "upon all men" as to relieve them immediately from the penalty of the law; for they are by nature still both morally dead, and liable to the death of the body. This is true, not only of adults, but of children also, whether they die in infancy or not; for we have no reason to conclude that children dying in infancy were born with a purer nature than those who live to maturity. The fact of their being born liable to temporal death, a part of the penalty, is sufficient to show that they are born under the whole malediction.

It is, therefore, incorrect to suppose, as some have done, that children are born in a justified and regenerate state; but they are all born under "the free gift," the effects of which extend to "all men," $εἰς$, *in order to* "justification of life." It follows, then, that, in the case of infants, this gift may be connected with the end for which it was given, as well as in the case of adults, or it would be given in vain. All the mystery of the subject arises from this, that in adults we see the "free gift" connected with the *end*, actual justification, by a voluntary acceptance of its benefits; but as to infants, the same end is reached without their voluntary consent, and by a process which is entirely hidden from us. If, however, an infant is not capable of a voluntary acceptance of the benefits of the "free gift," neither, on the other hand, is it capable of a voluntary rejection of them, and it is by rejecting them that adults perish.

We must not overlook the fact that the benefits of this "free gift" are bestowed largely even upon adults, independent of anything they do. This is seen in the longsuffering of God, the instructions of his word, the corrective dispensations of his providence, and, above all, in *preventing grace* and the *influences of the Holy Spirit*, exciting in men various degrees of religious feeling, and enabling them to repent and believe the Gospel. In a word, "justification of life" is offered to them; nay, more, it is pressed upon them, and they fail of it only by rejecting it.

If, then, the very power and inclination to seek "justification of life" is thus prevenient, and in the highest sense *free*, it follows, by the same rule of Divine conduct, that the Holy Spirit may be given to children; that a divine and effectual influence may be exerted on them, which, meeting with no voluntary resistance, shall cure the spiritual death and corrupt tendency of their nature; and that the principle of administration, in their case, does not greatly differ from that in the case of adults.

When, therefore, the doctrine of imputation is considered in this its *whole* and *scriptural* view, the objection which is urged against it, on the ground of its supposed injustice, entirely vanishes; and, at the same time, the evil of sin is manifested, and also the justice of the Lawgiver.

§ 3. *The Moral Condition in which Men are actually born into the World.*

Having established the import of the *death* threatened as the penalty of Adam's transgression, and having shown that the sentence included the whole of his posterity, our next step is to ascertain that moral condition in which men are actually born into the world notwithstanding the gracious provision of redemption. This subject involves the entire question of HUMAN DEPRAVITY, the full discussion of which our limits will not allow; but we will state the doctrine as we believe it to be taught in the Scriptures, and adduce the leading proofs by which man's native depravity is established.

Pelagians, Socinians, and others of kindred sentiments, deny the doctrine of man's native depravity altogether. They hold that the human soul, at its entrance upon the stage of life, is as pure as Adam was when he came from the hand of his Creator.

There are others who teach that all men have suffered to some extent in their moral powers by Adam's transgression; but they define this result to be, not the total depravity of their moral nature, but merely a greater liability to go astray, and to lose that degree of moral purity which they by nature possess.

But as neither of these opinions has any foundation in the sacred Scriptures, nor can be established by any rational argument, we will direct our attention,

I. *To a statement of what we believe to be the true scriptural doctrine respecting the moral condition of man.*

This doctrine is thus expressed in our seventh article of religion: "Original sin standeth not in the following of Adam, (as the Pelagians do vainly talk,) but it is the corruption of the nature of every man, that naturally is engendered of the offspring of Adam, whereby man is very far gone from original righteousness, and of his own nature inclined to evil, and that continually."

Here we have a clear recognition of *human depravity* under the denomination of ORIGINAL SIN—a subject which we will now examine, both as to its *nature* and its *degree*.

1. *Its* NATURE.—As to the *nature* of original sin, some divines have supposed that it consists in a *positive evil*, infused into man's nature by a judicial act of God, which has been transmitted to all Adam's posterity. Others, and those the greater number, both Calvinistic and Arminian, have resolved it into *privation*. Arminius himself calls it "a privation of the image of God," and asserts that the "absence alone of original righteousness is original sin." But he so explains this privation as to include in it both the forfeiture "of the gift of the Holy Spirit" by Adam, for himself and his descendants, and the loss of original righteousness as the consequence. He tells us, therefore, that this state of destitution renders "all men obnoxious to death temporal and eternal;" and that it is "sufficient for the commission and production of every actual sin whatever."

This is by some divines called, with great aptness, "a depravation arising from a deprivation," and is certainly much more consonant with the Scriptures than the opinion that God infused evil qualities into the nature of man. The resulting of moral evil from a mere privation may be fitly illustrated by the consequences of temporal death. For, as the mere privation of animal life causes the extinction of heat, and sense, and motion, and surrenders the body to the operation of chemical decomposition; so from the loss of *spiritual* life followed moral inability, the dominion of irregular appetites and passions, aversion to restraint, and estrangement from God, and even enmity against him.

To perceive this subject in its scriptural light it may be proper to remark,

(1.) *That the life which the Holy Spirit supplies is the only source of righteousness in Man.*—This may be inferred from the *new creation*, which is the renewal of man "in righteousness and true holiness," and which is the work of the Holy Spirit; for, before man is thus quickened by the Spirit he is "dead in trespasses and sins." But even after this change, this being "born again," he is not able to preserve himself in the renewed condition into which he is brought but by the continuance of the same quickening and aiding influence.

(2.) *That the loss of spiritual life included in it the retraction of God's Spirit from offending man.*—For, if "Christ hath redeemed us from the curse of the law, that we might receive the promise of the Spirit," as the apostle declares, then it follows that the loss of God's Spirit was included in the curse which fell on apostate Adam.

(3.) *That the necessary consequence of this privation was the total corruption of Man's moral nature.*—If our spiritual life is supplied alone by the spirit of God, it is reasonable to conclude that the withdrawing of that Spirit from Adam when he willfully sinned, and, consequently, from all his posterity, was the cause of the death and depravation which followed.

2. *The* DEGREE *of human depravity.*—In regard to this we may safely affirm, as being the doctrine of the Bible, that man is by nature *totally depraved.* Some, it is true, who are generally reputed as orthodox, have hesitated to adopt the phrase *total depravity* merely because the *term* is not in the Scriptures. But if it expresses, when properly defined, the Scripture doctrine upon this subject, to reject it merely on this account is perfectly puerile.

Others have rejected this phrase because they have attached to it an improper meaning. They have represented it as implying depravity in the greatest possible degree and in every possible sense. They have, therefore, argued that if all men are totally depraved, no one even in practice can be worse than another, and no one can ever become worse than he is. To these conclusions they have opposed the obvious fact that some are more wicked and depraved than others, as likewise the testimony of Scripture, that "evil men and seducers wax worse and worse;" and they have supposed these arguments to be a triumphant refutation of the doctrine of total depravity.

It is worthy of remark, however, that those who have taken this view of the subject have represented the doctrine of depravity in a very distorted light, and hence their arguments have been directed against a mere fiction of their own imagination, leaving the doctrine in its true sense undisturbed. No sensible advocate for total depravity ever contended that all men are wicked in the same degree, or that wicked men may not still become worse; nor can any such inference be fairly drawn from the doctrine when correctly understood.

Human depravity may be justly denominated *total*, because,

(1.) *It extends to all the powers and faculties of the soul.*—The judgment, the memory, the will, the imagination, the affections, and all the moral powers of our nature, are depraved and polluted by sin. "The whole head is sick, and the whole heart faint." Isa. i, 5.

(2.) *It implies the absence of all positive good.*—"For I know," says St. Paul, "that in me (that is, in my flesh) dwelleth no good thing." Rom. vii, 18. In this sense the doctrine of total depravity is very clearly taught in our eighth article of religion: "The condition of man after the fall of Adam is such that he cannot turn and prepare himself by his own natural strength and works to faith, and calling upon God, wherefore we have no power to do good works, pleasant and acceptable to God, without the grace of God by Christ preventing us, that we may have a good-will, and working with us when we have that good-will." This implies a total loss by the fall of all spiritual good; a complete and total erasure of that moral image of God in which man was created.

(3.) *The entire capacity and powers of the soul abstract from grace are filled and continually employed with evil.*—That this is one sense in which the doctrine of total depravity is to be understood may be seen by a reference to our seventh article of religion, already quoted: "Man is very far gone from original righteousness, and of his own nature inclined to evil, and that continually." This is in exact accordance with the testimony of Divine truth. " God saw that the wickedness of man was great in the earth, and that every imagination of the thoughts of his heart was only evil continually." Gen. vi, 5.

Having stated the doctrine of man's native depravity as held by the great body of orthodox Christians, and having inquired to some extent into its nature and degree, we will proceed,

II. *To adduce the leading proofs* by which *it is established*.

The native and total depravity of all mankind may be argued,

1. *From the penalty of the Adamic law, and the relation which Adam sustained to his descendants.*—That the penalty of the law included death *temporal, spiritual,* and *eternal,* and that Adam was the *federal head* and *representative* of his posterity, have been fully established. But if this relationship existed between Adam and his posterity, it will necessarily follow that all the penal consequences of his transgression must legally fall upon all mankind. In him we were seminally created, and as all mankind were represented in him, our common nature was identified with him in the offense. Had he been annihilated the moment he transgressed, the millions of his posterity would have perished with him, and never could have realized a state of conscious existence. As Adam was the *natural* head of all our race, it is not unreasonable, nay, it appears almost necessarily to follow, in view of the law under which he was placed, that he should have been constituted our *federal* head also. As such, by his one offense he "brought death into the world and all our woe;" and, therefore, whatever the penalty of the law may have been, he incurred it not only for himself, but for all his posterity.

It may here be inquired whether the posterity of Adam stand chargeable with his actual transgression. To this our reply is, that as God looks upon things as they really are, and as the transgression of Adam was not personally committed by his posterity, therefore it cannot be imputed to them as their *personal act*. But as Dr. Watts has remarked, "Sin is taken either for an *act of disobedience* to a law, or for the *legal result* of such an act; that is, the *guilt* or *liableness to punishment.*" Hence it is clear that the full penalty of Adam's sin may be justly charged upon his posterity without making his transgression their personal act. A nation or a community may be justly chargeable with all the consequences of the act of their legal representative, as fully as though they had done the same thing personally; even so, if Adam was the legal head and representative of his posterity, they are justly chargeable with all the legal consequences of his offense. The act was theirs, not personally, but through their representative, and they, therefore, incurred the guilt and the penalty which legally and necessarily resulted from his act of disobedience.

This we believe to be the scriptural view of the subject, and one which necessarily results from the federal relation that Adam sustained to all his descendants. If he had not been their federal head, his guilt could not have been imputed to them without violating the principles of justice; and if his guilt had not been imputed to them, it would be impossible to justify the Divine administration in executing upon them the dreadful penalty. But if we admit, as we must, that Adam was our federal head and representative, then our guilt and subjection to the penalty of death will necessarily follow as legal consequences.

2. *This doctrine is confirmed by experience and observation.*—In entering upon this feature of the subject it may be proper to state that there are several facts of history and experience which must be accounted for in any theory that we may adopt respecting man's moral condition.

(1.) That in all ages great, and even general wickedness has prevailed among those large masses of men called *nations*.

As to the immediate descendants of Adam, a murderer sprung up in the first family, and the world became increasingly corrupt, until "God saw that the wickedness of man was great in the earth, and that every imagination of the thoughts of his heart was only evil continually;" that "all flesh had corrupted his way upon the earth;" and that it "was filled with violence." Gen. vi, 5, 12, 13. Only Noah was found righteous before God; and because of the universal wickedness—a wickedness which spurned all warning and resisted all correction—the flood was brought upon the *world of the ungodly.*

The same course of increasing wickedness was pursued after the flood; and from Abraham to Moses idolatry, injustice, oppression, and gross sensuality characterized the people of Canaan, Egypt, and every other country mentioned in the Mosaic narrative.

The obstinate inclination of the Israelites to idolatry through all their generations until the Babylonish captivity, their abounding wickedness after their return from Babylon, and their general corruption in the time of our Lord, are prominently set forth in the sacred writings, and in those of Josephus, their own historian.

In all heathen nations religious error, idolatry, superstition, fraud, oppression, and vice of almost every description show the general state of society to be exceedingly and even destructively corrupt. And, though Mohammedan nations escape the charge of idolatry, yet pride, avarice, oppression, injustice, cruelty, sensuality, and gross superstition are all prevalent among them.

The case of Christian nations, though in them immorality is more powerfully checked than in any other, and many bright and influential examples of the highest virtue are found among their inhabitants, sufficiently proves that the majority are corrupt and vicious in their habits. It is, therefore, evident that men in all ages and in all places have been generally wicked.

(2.) Another fact to be accounted for is the *strength* of this tendency to general wickedness. This can only be measured by the consideration of two circumstances. The *first* is, the greatness of the crimes to which men have abandoned themselves. If the corrupting principle had only led to trifling errors and practical infirmities, a softer view of man's moral condition might be taken; but in every age, and among all nations, men have been guilty of the most atrocious crimes, both against God and their fellow-men.

The *second* circumstance to be considered is the *number* and *character* of the checks and restraints against which this tide of wickedness has urged on its almost resistless course. It has opposed itself against the law of God, which is in some degree found among all men; against the voice of conscience; against the restraints and penalties of human laws; against the known and acknowledged fact that vice is a never-failing source of misery; against the terrible judgments of God upon wicked nations and individuals; and against the counteracting and reforming influences of God's various dispensations of grace and mercy to our fallen world. We cannot consider the number and power of these checks without acknowledging that the principle in human nature which triumphs over them, and gives rise to so much moral evil, is one of great strength and fearful tendency.

(3.) The third fact to be accounted for is, that the seeds of the vices which exist in society are discoverable in children in their earliest years. We see in them selfishness, pride, envy, deceit, resentment, falsehood, and often cruelty; and to restrain and correct these evils is the principal object of moral education.

(4.) The fourth fact is, that every man is conscious of a natural tendency to many evils. Some are inclined to pride, ambition, and excessive love of honor; some to anger, revenge, and implacableness; some to cowardice, meanness, and fear; some to avarice, care, and distrust; and others to sensuality and prodigality. Where is the man who has not his peculiar constitutional tendency to some evil in one or other of these classes? But there are also evil tendencies which are common to all men. These are, to forget God; to be indifferent to our obligations to him; to love created objects more than the Creator; to desire the praise of men more than the Divine approbation; and to be more influenced by visible things which surround us than by those which are invisible and eternal.

(5.) The last fact which we shall name in this connection is, that even after men have seriously resolved to live "soberly, righteously, and godly," they meet with strong and constant resistance at every step from evil passions, appetites, and inclinations. This is so clearly a matter of universal experience that, in the moral writings of every age and country, and in the very phrases and turns of all languages, virtue is associated with difficulty, and represented under the notion of a warfare.

As these five facts of universal history and experience cannot be denied, and as it would be most absurd to discuss the moral condition of human nature without any reference to them, they must be accounted for. The advocates of man's natural innocence have no way of accounting for these moral phenomena but by referring them to bad example and a vicious education.

Let us take the *first*. To account for general wickedness they refer it to bad example. But we remark,

First, That this does not account for the *introduction* of moral evil. It was not till after the repentance of our first parents, and their restoration to the Divine favor, that their children were born. From what example, then, did Cain learn malice, hatred, and murder? Nor will example account for the fact that the children of virtuous parents often become immoral. If they were naturally good, the good example always present ought to be more influential than bad examples at a distance and only occasionally seen.

Secondly, Example will not account for the general prevalence of vice. If man's natural disposition is more in favor of good than evil, then there ought to have been more good than evil in the world, which is contradicted by fact. But if it is indifferent to good and evil, then the quantum of virtue and vice in society ought to have been pretty equally divided, which is also contrary to fact; and on neither supposition can the existence of general wickedness be accounted for.

Thirdly, This very method of explaining the viciousness of society admits the superior power of bad example, which is almost giving up the matter in dispute; for, why should it be more influential than good example, unless there is a proneness in man to be corrupted by it?

Fourthly, Example does not account for that strong bias to evil in men which in all ages has borne down the most powerful restraints; nor for the early manifestation of wrong principles, tempers, and affections in children, since they appear at an age when example can have no influence; nor for the conflict which always attends a virtuous life.

Let us, then, see whether a bad education, the other cause usually alleged to account for these facts, will be more successful. In regard to this we may observe,

First, That this cause will no more account for the introduction into the family of Adam of passions so hateful as those of Cain than will example. As there was no example of these evils in the primeval family, so certainly there was no education that could incite and encourage them. We are also left still without a reason why, in well-ordered and religious families, where both education and example are good, so many instances of their inefficacy should occur. If bad education corrupts a naturally well-disposed mind, then a good education ought still more powerfully to affect it and give it a right tendency.

Secondly, No reason can be assigned why education as well as example should become generally bad if men are not predisposed to evil. Of education men are usually more careful than of example. The lips are often right when the life is wrong; and many practice evil who will not go so far as to teach it. If human nature is born pure, or at worst, equally disposed to good and evil, then the existence of a generally corrupting system of education in all countries and among all people cannot be accounted for.

Thirdly, It is not the fact that education is directly and universally corrupting in its influence. In many cases it is, indeed, defective; but it has only in a few instances been employed to encourage those vices into which men have commonly fallen. It is in those very vices, against which all education, even the most defective, is designed to guard us, that the world has most obviously displayed its depravity.

Fourthly, If we come to the other facts which must be accounted for, education is placed upon the same ground in the argument as example. The evil dispositions of children appear before education commences, and that opposition to good and proneness to evil of which every man is conscious are in direct opposition to those very principles with which education has furnished his judgment.

It is only, then, by the scriptural account of the natural and hereditary corruption of the human race, commonly called *original sin,* that these facts are fully accounted for, and as the facts themselves cannot be denied, they are strongly confirmatory of the doctrine of man's total depravity.

3. *This doctrine is fully established by the direct testimony of Scripture.*—It has already been shown that the full penalty of Adam's offense passed upon his posterity, and consequently that part of it which consists in spiritual death. A full provision has been made, as we have seen, to meet this case; but that does not affect the state in which men are born. It is a cure for an actually existing disease, and not a preventive.

If, then, we are all born in a state of spiritual death, that is, without that Divine influence upon our faculties which is necessary to give them a holy tendency and to maintain them in it, and if that influence is restored to man only by a dispensation of grace and favor, it follows that by nature he is born with sinful propensities, and is incapable in his own strength of anything that is good.

When it is said (Gen. v, 3) that "Adam begat a son in his own likeness," there seems to be an implied opposition between the likeness of God in which Adam was made, and Adam's "own likeness," in which his son was begotten. It is not said that he begat a son in the likeness of God; which would have been an appropriate declaration, and one apparently called for, if human nature had suffered no injury by the fall.

It is asserted (Gen. viii, 21) that "the imagination of man's heart is evil from his youth." Here it is to be observed, 1. That these words were spoken when there were no human beings upon the earth but righteous Noah and his family. 2. That they were spoken of *man* AS MAN; that is, of human nature, and, consequently, of Noah himself and those saved with him in the ark. 3. That it is affirmed of MAN, that is, of mankind, that the imagination of his heart "is evil from his youth." This passage, therefore, affirms the natural and hereditary tendency of man to evil.

The book of Job, which embodies the patriarchal theology, gives ample testimony to this, as the faith of those ancient times. Thus, Job xi, 12: "Vain man would be wise, though man be born like a wild ass's colt." He is "*born*," literally, "*the colt of a wild ass.*" Again, "Who can bring a clean thing out of an unclean?" Job xiv, 4. The word *thing* is supplied by our translators, but *person* is evidently understood. In Scripture language, cleanness signifies holiness, and uncleanness, sin; and, therefore, the text clearly asserts the natural impossibility of any man's being born sinless, because he is the offspring of guilty and defiled parents. The same doctrine is taught, only more fully, in Job xv, 14: "What is man, that he should be clean; and he which is born of a woman, that he should be righteous?"

Psalm li, 5: "Behold, I was shapen in iniquity; and in sin did my mother conceive me." What possible sense can be given to this passage on the hypothesis of man's natural innocence? Again, Psalm lvii, 3: "The wicked are estranged from the womb; they go astray as soon as they be born, speaking lies."

Prov. xxii, 15, and xxix, 15: "Foolishness is bound up in the heart of a child; but the rod of correction shall drive it far from him." "The rod and reproof give wisdom, but a child left to himself bringeth his mother to shame." These passages put together are a plain testimony of the inbred corruption of young children. "Foolishness" in the former is not barely appetite, or a want of knowledge attainable by instruction, as some have said; for neither of these deserves the correction which is recommended. But it is an indisposedness to what is good, and a strong propensity to evil.

Jeremiah xvii, 5: "Cursed be the man that trusteth in MAN." But why this if he were not, by nature, unworthy of trust? On the scheme of man's natural innocence it would surely have been more appropriate to say, Cursed be the man that trusteth indiscriminately in men, some of whom may have become corrupt. But here human nature itself, *man* in the abstract, is held up to suspicion and caution. "The heart," proceeds the same prophet, verse 9, "is deceitful above all things, and desperately wicked: who can know it?" which is the reason adduced for the preceding caution against trusting in man.

Mark vii, 21-23: "Out of the heart of men proceed evil thoughts, adulteries, fornications, murders, thefts, covetousness, wickedness, deceit, lasciviousness, an evil eye, blasphemy, pride, foolishness; all these evil things come from within, and defile the man." But this representation would not be true on the scheme of natural innocence; for it assumes that "all these evil things" come from *without*, and not "from *within*," as their original source.

John iii, 5, 6: "Except a man be born of water and of the Spirit, he cannot enter into the kingdom of God. That which is born of the flesh is flesh; and that which is born of the Spirit is spirit." Our Lord here declares the necessity of a spiritual birth, in contradistinction to our natural birth, in order to our entrance into the kingdom of God; and he places the necessity of this moral change in the fact that "that which is born of the flesh is *flesh*." The term *flesh* is often used in the Scriptures to denote man's depraved nature. Thus, "In my *flesh* dwelleth no good thing." "They that are in the *flesh* cannot please God." "If ye live after the *flesh* ye shall die." "The *flesh* lusteth against the Spirit." These passages serve to fix the meaning of the term *flesh* as it is used by our Lord in his conversation with Nicodemus, and to confirm the opinion of those who understand him to teach that man is by *nature* corrupt and sinful, and, consequently, unfit for the kingdom of heaven unless he is "*born again;*" and that all amendment of his case must result, not from himself, but from the regenerating influence of the Holy Spirit.

The universal corruption of mankind is strongly set forth in the third chapter of Paul's Epistle to the Romans. His language, as quoted from the fourteenth Psalm, is, "They are all gone out of the way, they are together become unprofitable; there is none that doeth good, no, not one." He shows that "both Jews and Gentiles are all under sin," and that all men are "guilty before God." He then proposes the means of salvation by faith in Christ, on the express ground that "*all* have sinned and come short of the glory of God." Whoever reads the apostle's argument, and considers the universality of the terms employed—ALL, EVERY, ALL THE WORLD, BOTH JEWS AND GENTILES—must conclude, in all fairness of interpretation, that the whole human race, of every age, is intended.

We have now seen that the doctrine of man's total depravity rests upon a solid foundation—that it is clearly implied in the penalty of the Adamic law, and the relation which Adam sustained to his posterity; that it is confirmed by experience and observation; and that it is explicitly taught in the sacred Scriptures. It would, therefore, be the greatest absurdity to call in question the truth of this doctrine, since it is so fully established by evidence which cannot be rejected.

We will close this chapter by considering two objections which have been urged against the doctrine of man's native and total depravity. It has been objected,

1. That "as we have our souls immediately from God, if we are born sinful he must either create sinful souls, which cannot be supposed without impiety, or send sinless souls into sinful bodies, to be defiled by the unhappy union, which is as inconsistent with his goodness as his justice. Add to this, that nothing can be more unphilosophical than to suppose that a body, a mere lump of organized matter, is able to communicate to a pure spirit that moral pollution of which itself is as incapable as the murderer's sword is incapable of cruelty."

To this objection we reply, that however weighty it may have been regarded by some, it rests entirely upon an assumption which cannot be proved; that is, that we have our souls immediately from God by *creation*. This objection will fall to the ground if we can prove that our souls, as well as our bodies, have descended from Adam by *traduction*. And that this is the fact we are led to believe from the following considerations:

(1.) It is said that God "rested on the seventh day from *all* his work" of creation. It is, therefore, unscriptural as well as unreasonable to suppose that he is still engaged in *creating souls*, as the bodies of mankind multiply upon the earth.

(2.) Eve was originally created *in* Adam. God breathed no breath of life into her, to make her "a living soul," as he did into her husband. Therefore, when Adam saw her he said, "She shall be called Woman, because she (her whole self, not her body only) was taken out of man." If, then, the soul of the first woman sprung from the soul of Adam, as her body did from his, what reason is there to believe that the souls of their posterity are produced by immediate creation?

(3.) It is admitted by all that, under God, we receive *life* from our parents. But if so we must derive from them our *soul*, which is the *principle of life;* for " the body without the *spirit* is dead."

(4.) Other animals have power to propagate animated beings like themselves. Why, then, should man be but half a father? When did God restrict him to the propagation of the mere *shell* of his person—the body without the soul? It surely was not when "he blessed him and said, "Be fruitful and multiply." When he spoke thus he must have addressed the soul as well as the body; for the body alone is incapable of either understanding or executing a command. It is, therefore, highly reasonable to conclude that the *whole* man, by virtue of the Divine appointment and blessing, can "be fruitful and multiply," and that our souls as well as our bodies come into existence by *traduction*.

(5.) Hence Moses informs us that "Adam begat a son in his own likeness, after his image." But had he generated a body without a soul he would not have begotten "a son in his own likeness," since he was not a mere mortal body, but a fallen *embodied spirit*.

The usual objection to the doctrine of traduction is, that it tends to materialism. But this arises from a mistaken view of that in which the procreation of a human being lies. It does not consist in the production out of nothing of either of the parts in man's compound nature, but only in the uniting of them substantially with one another. As the matter of the body is not then first made, so neither is the soul by that act first produced. The creation of both belongs to a higher power; and then the question is, whether all souls were created in Adam, and are transmitted by a law which is peculiar to themselves. Since, therefore, the *traduction* of the human soul is more rational and scriptural than its *immediate creation*, the objection which we have been considering is shown to be groundless. But,

2. It is objected to the doctrine of man's total depravity, that we often discover *virtuous traits of character in unregenerate men*.

To this our reply is, that all the moral excellence which can be justly claimed for unregenerate men may be easily accounted for without giving up the doctrine of man's total depravity. In doing this we remark,

(1.) That there is often the appearance of virtue where none really exists. It is well known that various vices may, from their very nature, to some extent counteract one another, and thus produce a kind of negative virtue. The passion of avarice may lead men to the practice of industry, and the love of fame may incline them to perform acts of ostentatious benevolence; but in neither case can there be any real virtue, because the principle of action is not spiritually good.

(2.) That selfish motives may sometimes lead men to a course of conduct which may seem to be morally good. A mere love of self-interest induces many to endeavor to establish a good moral character on account of the standing and influence which it will give them in society. All this, however, is perfectly consistent with the view which we have taken of man's moral corruption.

(3.) That the character of men often appears much better than it really is, merely because surrounding circumstances have not called into action the latent principles of the soul. They may have in them the seeds of a thousand evils, but these may lie measurably dormant for the want of exciting causes to call them forth.

(4.) That it does not follow, from the doctrine of man's moral corruption, that there should be nothing virtuous and praiseworthy among men until they are truly regenerated. It is to be remembered that we are not left to ourselves, and to the unrestrained influence of our corrupt nature. In consequence of the atonement made by Christ, a day of grace is given to all men, during which the Holy Spirit operates upon their hearts in various ways, repressing the risings of their native depravity, and moving them to that which is good. In some cases the issue is life, in others an aggravated death. But in nearly all this Divine influence cannot fail to correct and prevent much evil, and to bring into existence some good, though it may be as the morning cloud and the early dew, and to produce civil and social virtues. None of these effects, however, are to be placed to the account of *nature*, or used to soften our views of its entire alienation from God; but they are to be ascribed to the working of Divine *grace*, which is ever employed in seeking and saving the lost, and which alone is the cause of all that is really and spiritually good among men.

CHAPTER IV.

MAN'S MORAL AGENCY.

THE *moral agency of man* is a subject of great interest and importance. Indeed, if men were not free moral agents their actions could not be either virtuous or vicious; they could neither deserve praise nor be justly liable to blame.

Philosophers of every age since the earliest date of metaphysical science have examined this subject with a greater or less degree of particularity, but it must be acknowledged that much of their labor has tended more to darken counsel than to place truth before the mind in a clear and intelligible light. Their metaphysical speculations and finespun theories have so bewildered the public mind that it is exceedingly difficult to exhibit the subject in a clear, concise, and satisfactory manner. Difficult, however, as the task may be, we will try to present such views of man's moral agency as will be found to accord with the word of God and with the principles of sound philosophy. Let us then consider, *first*, its nature; and *secondly*, the proofs by which it is established.

I. THE NATURE OF MAN'S MORAL AGENCY.

A *moral agent* is one who is capable of performing such voluntary actions as are determined by some rule or law to be good or evil. "Moral good and evil," says Locke, "is the conformity or disagreement of our voluntary actions to some law whereby good or evil is drawn upon us from the will or power of the law-maker."

In regard to the simple question of man's *agency* we presume there will be no controversy. We do not contend that he is an *independent agent*. In this sense agency belongs to God alone, for he only possesses the power of action in an underived and independent sense. All created agents derived this power from the Creator, and are dependent on him for its continuance; yet in the exercise of this derived power they are capable of acting. Thus they are distinguished from inanimate matter, which moves only as it is moved by some external force.

That man is a *moral* agent will not be denied by any who believe the holy Scriptures. By these inspired records his actions are determined to be either right or wrong. He is everywhere regarded as being capable of virtue or vice, and susceptible of praise or blame. But in regard to that liberty or freedom which man possesses in the performance of moral actions, very different views have been entertained. Though these views are both numerous and variant, yet upon close examination it will be found that they all harmonize with one or the other of two general or leading theories—that of *necessity*, on the one hand, or that of *free moral agency* on the other. We will notice,

1. *The doctrine of necessity.*—Those who advocate this theory teach that the actions of men are in some way so overruled and directed that they cannot be different from what they are. There is, to be sure, a wide difference in the manner in which this class of writers express themselves upon this subject. Some do it in the most unequivocal terms, openly denying that man has any control whatever over his moral conduct. Others, from the language which they employ, seem to espouse the doctrine of moral liberty in its highest sense; but when their definitions and teachings are scrutinized they are found to result in the doctrine of necessity, or, at least, to be reconciled to it.

Under the general term of *necessity* there are three different schemes of doctrine included, which we should carefully distinguish. The first scheme is called *materialistic fatalism;* the second, *Stoical fatalism;* and the third is that which is now commonly distinguished from the two former as the theory of *moral necessity.*

Materialistic fatalism is based upon the fundamental doctrine that there is nothing in the universe besides matter and motion. This scheme, of course, denies the spirituality of God and of the human soul, and discards all moral distinctions. It is surely not necessary to attempt a refutation of so baseless a theory. A mere statement of its doctrines is enough to convince every sober mind of its extreme absurdity.

Stoical fatalism rises above the former in regard to dignity and purity of character. Its fundamental doctrine is that all things, both in heaven and earth, are bound together by an "implex series and concatenation of causes." The advocates of this theory believe in the existence of God, but they regard him merely as the greatest and brightest link in the adamantine chain of universal necessity. According to this scheme, though it includes the notion of moral distinctions, the idea of moral liberty is inconceivable and impossible.

The theory of *moral necessity*, while it harmonizes with the two former schemes in denying moral freedom to *man,* differs from them in maintaining the absolute freedom of God. Its fundamental doctrine is that God is the central and all-controlling power of the universe; that from all eternity he decreed whatever should come to pass, including even the deliberations and volitions of men; and that by his own power he now executes his decrees. "We do not, with the Stoics," says Calvin, "imagine a necessity arising from a perpetual concatenation and intrinsic series of causes contained in nature; but we make God the arbiter and governor of all things, who, in his own wisdom, has, from all eternity, decreed what he would do, and now by his own power executes what he decreed."*

The great reformers, Calvin and Luther, while they maintained the absolute freedom of God, denied the freedom of the human will. They allowed, indeed, that man, in his original state, possessed freedom. "I admit," says Luther, "that man's will is free in a certain sense; not because it is now in the same state it was in Paradise, but because it was made free originally, and may, through God's grace, become so again."† Man "was endowed with free-will," says Calvin, "by which, if he had chosen, he might have obtained eternal life."‡ But it is well known that Luther wrote a work on the "Bondage of the Human Will," and that Calvin, in his Institutes, has written a chapter to show that "man, in his present state, is despoiled of freedom of will, and subjected to a miserable slavery." Thus, according to both Luther and Calvin, man was by the fall despoiled of freedom of will.

They admit that man is free from compulsion or restraint, but they repudiate the idea of calling this a freedom of the will. "Lombard at length pronounces," says Calvin, "that we are not therefore possessed of free-will because we have an equal power to do or think either good or evil, but *only because we are free from constraint.* And this liberty is not diminished, although we are corrupt, and slaves of sin, *and capable of doing nothing but sin.* Then man," Calvin proceeds, "will be said to possess free-will in this sense, not that he has an equal free election of good and evil, but because he does evil voluntarily, *and not by constraint.* That, indeed, is true; but what end could it answer to deck out a thing so diminutive with a title so superb?"§ And truly, if Lombard meant nothing more by that liberty for which he contended than mere freedom from external restraint, Calvin might well contemptuously exclaim, "Egregious liberty."

It has come to pass, however, since the days of the great reformers, that philosophers and theologians have decked out this very kind of liberty, this diminutive thing, with the superb title of *the freedom of the will,* and have passed it off for the highest and most glorious liberty of which the human mind can form any conception. In this category we

* Institutes. † Scott's Luther and Ref., vol. 1, pp. 70, 71.
‡ Institutes, book 1, chap. 15. § Id., book 2, chap. 2.

may place Sir John Locke and President Edwards. The definition of liberty which is given by Locke, in his "Essays on the Human Understanding," is this: "Liberty is a power to act or not to act, according as the mind directs." President Edwards defines liberty to be the "power, opportunity, or advantage that one has to do as he pleases."* That these two definitions are in perfect harmony will be admitted by every one who weighs the terms in which they are stated. They both teach the doctrine that human liberty consists in a power to act according to the dictates of the mind.

We admit that this theory of liberty rests upon high and distinguished authority; but believing it to be at war with the true doctrine of man's moral agency, we will not shrink from the task of pointing out some of its most obvious errors and defects. And here we may remark,

(1.) That the definition of liberty in which these philosophers agree is no definition of *moral* liberty—it touches not the real question at issue. It evidently confounds moral liberty with the freedom of bodily actions. These philosophers seem to take for granted that if a man has power to conform his actions to the dictates or directions of his mind he possesses moral liberty in its highest sense. But who does not see that if liberty consists in the power to act as the mind directs, or in the power to do as we please, that it can relate to bodily actions alone, as distinguished from those of the mind? In other words, it is made to consist in the unrestrained opportunity of following the directions or volitions of the mind, but not in the power of the mind itself to originate its own volitions.

This may be a correct view of *civil* liberty but not of *moral*. Civil liberty consists in the power or opportunity of doing what we please and of going where we please, so as not to infringe upon the rights of others. Here the external actions of the agents are mainly considered without any reference to the manner in which their volitions originate. In this sense the body might be free to follow the determinations of the mind, though the mind itself should be fast bound in the chains of absolute necessity. This kind of liberty, therefore, has nothing to do with the *freedom of human volitions*, but is confined entirely to the *power or opportunity of acting in accordance with them.*

That this is the only kind of freedom contended for by President Edwards may be seen from his own language. In explaining what he means by the term *liberty*, he says that it is the "power and opportunity for one to do and conduct as he will, or according to his choice; without taking into the meaning of the word anything of the cause of that choice, or at all considering how the person came to have such a volition." In whatever manner a man may come by his choice, "yet, if he is able, and there is nothing in the way to hinder his pursuing and executing his will, the man is perfectly free according to the primary and common notion

* Inquiry, part 1, sec. 5.

of freedom."* This, we repeat it, may be natural or civil liberty, but it cannot be moral liberty. It is that kind of liberty which may be associated with the most absolute fatalism in regard to the volitions of the human mind.

(2.) Another difficulty in this definition of freedom is, that it claims for man what no man ever possessed: a "power to do as he pleases, or as his mind directs." If this is freedom, then it is to be found nowhere but in God; for no one but an independent and omnipotent being can "do as he pleases." Suppose my child falls into the water, where he is in danger of being drowned. The feelings of my nature strongly impel me to save him. Accordingly, I exert myself with all my might to accomplish the desired object, but without being successful. Have I here the power to do as I please? Doubtless I have not, and consequently, according to the definition of President Edwards, I am not at liberty to save my child. I know it may be said that my immediate will is not to save my child, but only to exert myself in order to save him. Such, however, is evidently not the case. My first and governing intention is to save him. This lies at the foundation of all my exertions; for if I did not will to save my child I could not voluntarily exert myself to that end. It follows, then, that no man has the power to "do as he pleases;" and consequently that, in this respect, the definition which we are considering implies too much. But,

(3.) A man may have the power, in certain cases, to "do as he pleases," while at the same time he has no liberty to do otherwise. Suppose a man to be conducted into a room where he meets a friend whom he had long desired to see. Without his knowledge he is locked in; but he is so delighted with his company that he continues in the room most willingly, without any desire to leave it. Will any one pretend to say that his staying with his friend is not voluntary? We think not, and yet he has no liberty to do otherwise. We see, therefore, that a man may do as he pleases in some cases when he has no liberty to act in any other way. Consequently in such cases he cannot be free, unless we confound all language, and say that liberty and necessity are the same thing.

From what we have seen, it is very evident that there is no real difference between the views of President Edwards in regard to human liberty and those of Luther and Calvin. They all agree that in order to man's accountability he must be free from compulsion. Thus, suppose a man wills to perform an external action, but is prevented by some outward restraint; or suppose he is constrained to do an action against his will, he is said to be under compulsion, co-action, or natural necessity, and cannot, therefore, in either case be held accountable. The reformers held this freedom from co-action or compulsion to be consistent with *necessity*, so far as our volitions are concerned, and accord-

* Inquiry, part 1, sec. 5.

ingly they denied the freedom of the human will. President Edwards takes up this same doctrine of freedom from co-action, and expands it into his far-famed theory of the free-agency and accountability of man, a theory which is perfectly consistent with the most absolute necessity in regard to the will itself.

That we do not misrepresent his views in this matter his own language will show. He tells us that "the plain and obvious meaning of the words *freedom* and *liberty*, in common speech, is *power, opportunity, or advantage, that any one has to do as he pleases.* Or, in other words, his being free from hinderance or impediment in the way of doing or conducting in any respect as he wills. And the contrary to liberty, whatever name we call that by, is a person's being hindered or unable to conduct as he will, or being necessitated to do otherwise." Again, "there are two things that are contrary to this which is called liberty in common speech. One is *constraint;* the same is otherwise called force, compulsion, and co-action, which is a person's being necessitated to do a thing contrary to his will. The other is *restraint;* which is his being hindered, and not having power to do according to his will."*

These quotations show that the liberty for which Edwards contends is merely a freedom from co-action and not from necessity. It has no relation to the question as to how a man comes by his volitions; whether they are put forth by the mind itself without being necessitated, or whether they are necessarily produced by some other cause. "Let the person come by his volition or choice HOW HE WILL," says Edwards; let it happen without a cause, let it be determined by an antecedent volition, let it be produced by a direct exertion of Almighty power; "yet if he is able, and there is nothing in the way to hinder his pursuing and executing his will, the man is fully and perfectly free, according to the primary and common notion of freedom."† We see, therefore, that this scheme of moral agency claims for man only that freedom from compulsion or restraint which allows him to act according to his own volitions; and that, so far as these volitions themselves are concerned, it is perfectly reconcilable with the most absolute scheme of necessity or fatalism that the world has ever seen.

Accordingly, it is assumed by Edwards that our volitions are the passive and necessary effects of motives. He tells us that "every act of the will whatever is excited by some motive;" that "if every act of the will is excited by a motive, then that motive is the cause of the act of the will;" and that "volition is *necessary*, and is not from any self-determining power in the will."‡ Thus the human mind is reduced to the condition of a mere machine, capable only of acting as it is acted upon by some external force; and if this is the real state of the case, as the advocates of philosophical necessity must allow, then we have no more to do with our volitions than with the circulation of our blood.

* Inquiry, part 1, sec. 5.   † Ibid.   ‡ Id., part 2, sec. 10.

But as this theory is too absurd to be adopted by any one who believes in moral distinctions, we will direct our attention,

2. *To what we conceive to be the true doctrine of free moral agency.*—
A *free agent* is one who is capable of acting without being necessitated to do so by some cause extrinsic to himself.

That such an agent may exist cannot be denied without denying to God the original power to produce creation. It is admitted that he only existed from eternity. And, as creation was produced by the act of God when nothing had previously existed but himself, it necessarily follows that he could not have been impelled to the work of creation by any extrinsic cause. To suppose that God cannot put forth an act without being impelled thereto by a power back of his own, is to suppose a power greater than his, on which the exercise of his omnipotence depends. By a parity of reason we should be compelled to suppose another power still back of that, and so on, *ad infinitum*, which would be both absurd and impious. Hence we are forced to the conclusion that God is a free agent in the fullest sense of our definition, being self-active, and wholly independent of all extrinsic influences whatever.

Now, it is not difficult to conceive that God should create moral agents, bearing his image in this, namely, the possession of a *self-active power*—agents who are capable of acting without being necessitated to act, by some efficient cause beyond themselves. Nor is it more difficult to conceive that man possesses self-active power than it is to conceive that such a power belongs to God; for though, in the former case, this power is limited and dependent, and in the latter infinite and independent, yet in both, so far as the simple question of free-agency is concerned, it is the same. We must admit the possibility that man should be endowed with self-active power, for to deny this is to deny the omnipotence of God. It follows, therefore, that the great question in regard to free-agency is, whether man, in the exercise of that power with which God has endowed him, is capable of acting, without being efficiently caused to do so by anything extrinsic to himself. If he possesses this self-active power he is a free agent, and is properly the author of his own actions; but if not, he is no more the real author of what he does than a passive machine.

When we claim for man a self-active power in the exercise of volition, we do not mean that the will is altogether uninfluenced by motives and external circumstances. The mind is the efficient agent that wills; but the act itself is performed according to the laws which properly belong to a self-moving and accountable being. Though motives and external circumstances can exercise no efficient agency in reference to the will, yet, speaking figuratively, they may be properly said to influence the mind, and to be conditions or occasions of the mind's action in willing. In this sense they may be said to influence the *will;* but they cannot exercise over it an absolute and irresistible controlling influence. In no case can they efficiently cause an act of volition without destroying its freedom.

Necessitarians seem to have taken for granted, in their arguments upon this subject, that there is no medium between absolute necessity and perfect independency; but the true doctrine of man's free moral agency is at an equal distance from both these extremes. We deny, on the one hand, that the volitions of men are so determined by things external to themselves as to be fast bound in the chain of absolute necessity; and on the other, that they are so perfectly disconnected with surrounding circumstances and things external as to be entirely uninfluenced by them. The point in controversy, therefore, between the advocates of necessity and the defenders of free agency is, not whether man is influenced, in the exercise of volition, by motives and external circumstances, for this is admitted by all; but whether his will is thus necessarily and absolutely controlled, so that his volitions could not be different from what they are.

It is a fact of great importance in the investigation of this subject that there are three leading attributes or faculties of the human mind which are clearly distinguishable from each other, namely, the *intelligence*, the *sensibility*, and the *will*. In other words, the human mind is capable of *thought*, of *feeling*, and of *volition*. Now it will be found, on examination, that the phenomena which pertain to these several departments of capability possess different characteristics, according to the attribute or faculty to which they belong. Of these differences we must form clear conceptions, if we would avoid that obscurity and confusion in which the philosophy of the will is mostly involved.

Let us suppose, for the sake of illustration, that I fix my attention upon an apple. I conclude, in my own mind, that it is round and red. This decision or judgment of the mind is a state of the *intelligence*—a state which does not depend on any effort of my own; for I could not possibly come to any other conclusion respecting the form and color of the apple if I would. Hence this decision, this judgment, this state of the intelligence, is necessitated; and so also is every other perception or state of the intelligence. But while I continue to look upon the apple, I experience a strong desire to eat it. This desire or appetite is a state of the *sensibility*; and in this case, as well as in all our feelings, the mind is as clearly passive as in the former. It follows, therefore, that every state of the intelligence and of the sensibility is a necessary result of its proximate cause, and for this reason it cannot be free.

Again, though I have experienced the judgment that the apple is round and red, and have felt the desire to eat it, yet, hitherto, I have put forth no voluntary effort, except in fixing my attention upon it. But now I determine to eat the apple, and accordingly this determination is carried into effect. Here, then, is an entirely new phenomenon.

It is an *effort*, an *act*, a *volition* of the mind; and my consciousness assures me that in this I am free.

If these remarks are just, it will at once be seen how important it is that we should distinguish the *will* from both the intelligence and the sensibility, in order that we may perceive its true nature, and wherein its liberty consists. Necessitarians have generally confounded these distinct faculties of the human mind; and as their theory is based upon this false psychology, it is not strange that they should deny the proper freedom of the will. "By whatever name we call the act of the will," says Edwards, "choosing, refusing, approving, disapproving, liking, disliking, embracing, rejecting, determining, directing, commanding, forbidding, inclining or being averse, being pleased or displeased with—all may be reduced to this of choosing."* Thus it is manifest, according to the psychology of this author, that the phenomena of the intelligence, the sensibility, and the will are identified, as are also these faculties themselves. With him approving, liking, being pleased or displeased with, and willing, are all the same. His psychology admits of no distinction between the impression which is made on a man's intelligence or sensibility by the presence of an apple, and that act of the will by which he puts forth his hand to eat it. "I humbly conceive," says Edwards, "that the affections of the soul are not properly distinguished from the will, as though there were two faculties."† And again, "all acts of the will are truly acts of the affections."‡ Thus this great metaphysician, by confounding things which are perfectly distinct in their nature, has been led to the adoption of views respecting the human will which are contrary to truth, involved in obscurity, and self-contradictory.

We readily admit that in the perception of truth the intelligence is perfectly passive. The mind can no more avoid the conclusion that two and two are equal to four, than it can determine that white is black, or that light is darkness. We admit also that every state of the sensibility is a passive impression—a necessitated phenomenon of the human mind. No matter what fact or truth may be presented to the mind either by its own voluntary attention or by any other agency, the impression which it makes upon the sensibility is beyond the control of the will, except by refusing to give it the attention of the mind. But in the act of willing the case is very different. Here the mind is perfectly free, because it possesses a power of acting over which there is no controlling power either within or without itself. This is what we understand by the free moral agency of man. Let us consider,

II. THE PROOFS BY WHICH MAN'S FREE MORAL AGENCY IS ESTABLISHED.

In defending the proposition that man is a free moral agent, we may reply,

1. *Upon our own consciousness.*—By this we mean that knowledge

* Edwards's Works, vol. 2, p. 16. † Ibid., vol. 4, p. 82. ‡ Ibid.

which we have of what passes in our own minds. Thus, when we are joyful or sad, when we love or hate, when we hope or fear, we are immediately conscious of the fact. This kind of knowledge is not derived from an investigation of testimony, nor does it result from a course of reasoning, but rises spontaneously in the mind. In regard to things of which we are conscious arguments are superfluous. They can neither strengthen our convictions, nor cause us to doubt. We cannot persuade a man whose heart is elated with joy that he is at the same time oppressed with grief; nor can we convince any one who is writhing under the influence of a painful disease that he is in the enjoyment of perfect health. The reason is that consciousness carries with it its own demonstration, and from it there is no appeal.

What, then, is the testimony of consciousness in regard to the freedom of the human will? It is evidently this, at least, that the mind is not controlled in its volitions by any extrinsic cause. Who can convince me that I have not the power to write, or to refrain from writing; to sit still, or to rise up and walk? And this consciousness of a self-determining power of the mind is universal. A false philosophy may occasionally confuse the understanding in regard to this subject, but still the conviction comes home to every man with resistless force, that he has within himself the power of volition, and that he exercises this power freely.

That we are free to choose either good or evil, and not impelled in our moral actions by any law of absolute necessity, is a position which accords with every man's consciousness, a position which we can no more rationally doubt than we can doubt our own existence. Hence it is that all men have a sense of blame when they do wrong, and of approbation when they do right. If you convince a man who is charged with the commission of a crime that the act was unavoidable, he can no more blame himself for having committed it than he can blame the tree which fell upon his neighbor and killed him. Remorse for past offenses depends, for its very existence, upon a conviction that we are morally free. We conclude, therefore, that our consciousness demonstrates the freedom of the human will. To set aside its testimony would be as unphilosophical as to conclude that it is midnight when we behold the full blaze of the meridian sun. But we argue this doctrine,

2. *From the general history of the world.*—If we turn our attention to any period of the world's history, we will find among all nations, in their language and common modes of speech, terms and phrases which clearly indicate their general belief in the freedom of the human will. Terms expressive of blame and of praise are everywhere employed, clearly recognizing the principle that men have power to control their own actions, and that when they do wrong they are blamed because they *might* and should do otherwise. No one is ever seriously blamed for doing an act which is believed to be unavoidable. The very

idea of blame, therefore, implies the principle for which we are contending.

Again, the laws of all civilized nations punish criminals upon the supposition that they have power to control their own moral conduct. Suppose a man to be accused of homicide. If it could be made appear that in the act in question he was not a voluntary agent, but was constrained by an external force which he had not the power to resist, there is not a government upon the earth that would find him guilty, and for this simple reason, that in the event he was merely a passive instrument.

We know that rewards and punishments are connected with the statutory provisions of all civilized governments, and that they are constantly held out before the community. But why should these sanctions of law be thus exhibited if men are not free moral agents? Can these motives induce men voluntarily to conform their actions to law, if they really possess no such voluntary power? But perhaps it may be said that these motives are designed to determine the will itself, independent of any active agency in the man. This, however, cannot be granted; for if motives are to determine the will, why is the man required to attend to the motives, to weigh them carefully, and to make a correct decision in reference to their real weight? We see, therefore, that all men in all ages of the world, and in all places, have regarded themselves as free moral agents.

If man has not the power to control his own actions, why is he censured for any crime that he may commit? "Why, we might ask, are jails and penitentiaries and various modes of punishment, more or less severe, everywhere prevalent in civilized lands? If the advocates of necessity really believe in the truth of their system let them be consistent, and go throughout the civilized world and plead for the destruction of all terms of language expressive of blame or praise; let them decry the unjustifiable prejudice of nations, by which benevolence and virtue have been applauded, and selfishness and vice contemned. Let them proclaim it abroad that the robber and the murderer are as innocent as the infant or the saint, since all men only act as they are necessarily acted upon; and let them teach all nations to abolish at once and forever every description of punishment for crime or misdemeanor. Such would be the consistent course for sincere necessitarians."* Again, we argue the free moral agency of man,

3. *From the Divine administration toward him, as exhibited in the Holy Scriptures.*—Here we shall see that revelation beautifully harmonizes with nature; and that the evidences of our free-agency which are derived from experience and observation are abundantly confirmed by the book of God. In presenting the argument, which is drawn from the Divine administration, we may remark,

* Ralston's Elements, p. 248.

(1.) That God has placed man under moral government. Immediately after his creation a moral law was given him to keep, and a severe penalty was annexed to its transgression. If man had not been created a free agent, to have given him a moral law for the government of his actions would have been inconsistent with the Divine wisdom; for a moral law commanding what is right and prohibiting what is wrong, can only be adapted to beings capable of doing both right and wrong. Hence we argue, that as God placed man under a moral law he must have been a free moral agent, capable alike of obedience and of disobedience.

To this conclusion we are also conducted by the history of the fall. To suppose that all the volitions and actions of men are absolutely determined by causes over which they have no control, is to suppose that the sin of Adam was absolutely necessary. But to suppose that the penalty of the law was inflicted upon the first transgressor for an act which he could not possibly avoid, is to suppose the Divine administration to be unjust and cruel. Can any rational man believe that God would place Adam in such circumstances as would render his act of disobedience absolutely necessary, and then say to him, "In the day thou eatest thereof thou shalt surely die?" Most certainly not. The whole history of the fall, if viewed in the light of reason, of common-sense, and of what we know of the character and government of God, proclaims, in language clear and forcible, that man is a free moral agent.

Though man is now in a fallen condition, and robbed of his primitive glory, yet he is still under moral government. God has given him a law for the rule of his life. He enforces this law by promises and threatenings, thus proving most clearly that man is in a state of probation. But this implies that he is a free moral agent—that he is capable of conforming his actions to the rule of life under which God has placed him. For, if the volitions and actions of men are necessitated by some power over which they have no control, to suppose them to be in a state of probation is most absurd. We might as well ascribe a probationary state to the beasts of the field, or the fowls of the air. If, then, we are in a state of trial we are free moral agents.

(2.) The freedom of the human will is everywhere acknowledged in the Scriptures. "I call heaven and earth to record this day against you, that I have set before you life and death, blessing and cursing: therefore *choose* life, that both thou and thy seed may live." Deut. xxx, 19. "*Choose* you this day whom you will serve." Josh. xxiv, 15. To *choose* is to *determine* or to *will;* and men are here exhorted to choose for themselves. But if the will is not free—if every volition of the human mind is necessarily determined by a necessary cause, such exhortations are nothing better than solemn mockery.

Our Lord said to the Jews, "How often would I have gathered thy children together, even as a hen gathereth her chickens under her wings, and ye *would not!*" Matt. xviii, 37. And again, "Ye *will not* come to me, that ye might have life." John v, 40. These, and numerous other passages of a similar import, refer expressly to the will of men as being under their own control. And on no other principle could the Saviour of the world upbraid men in terms of the deepest solemnity, and denounce against them the severest punishment for the obstinacy of their will. According to the notion of President Edwards and other necessitarians all our volitions are necessarily fixed by antecedent causes; but if so, they are no more under our control than the motions of the heavenly bodies. It does not require the eye of a philosopher, however, to see the antagonism between this theory and the teachings of the Holy Scriptures, and it cannot be difficult to determine which we should adopt. But we may remark,

(3.) That God holds men to an account for their moral conduct. It is the doctrine of the Bible that "every one of us shall give account of himself to God;" that "we must all appear before the judgment-seat of Christ; that every one may receive the things done in his body, according to that he hath done, whether it be good or bad." These and many other Scriptures clearly set forth the doctrine of a general judgment and of future rewards and punishments. But if man were not *free* in his volitions and moral actions, how could we reconcile the retributions of the great day with the attributes of God? As well might we suppose that an all-wise and merciful Being would reward men for breathing the surrounding atmosphere, or punish them for permitting the blood to circulate in their veins. As well might we suppose that he would punish or reward the fish for swimming in the ocean, or the birds for flying in the air!

President Edwards and others have attempted to reconcile the doctrine of necessity with the proper freedom and accountability of man. They have contended that though the will is necessarily determined, yet man is properly a free moral agent merely because he has a will, acts voluntarily, and is free from constraint. But to say that he enjoys freedom merely because he is at liberty to obey his will, is as absurd as to contend that the man who is subject to the edicts of a cruel tyrant enjoys freedom in a civil sense merely because he is at liberty to obey the laws under which he is placed. Will any man contend that civil liberty consists in the privilege of obeying law? Surely not; for this would be to assume that a man may enjoy civil liberty and at the same time be a slave. No one will deny that even slaves have liberty to obey the law under which they are placed: but can they be persuaded that for this reason they are properly free? We know they cannot. And yet this is the very kind of freedom that President Edwards ascribes to man in a moral sense. The will, according to his theory, is unalterably fixed; but as man has the liberty to do as he wills, he is therefore a free moral agent, and accountable to God for his moral actions.

We deny, however, that this kind of liberty can render its possessor an accountable moral agent. "Indeed, there is no difference between the liberty attributed to man by the learned President of Princeton College, and that possessed by a block of marble as it falls to the earth when let loose from the top of a tower. We may call the man *free*, because he may act according to his will or inclination while that will is determined by necessity; but has not the marble precisely the same freedom? It has perfect liberty to fall; it is not constrained by natural force to move in any other direction. If it falls necessarily, even so, on the principle of Edwards, man acts necessarily. If it be said that the marble cannot avoid falling as it does, even so man cannot avoid acting according to his will, just as he does. If it be said that he has no disposition, and makes no effort to act contrary to his will, even so the marble has no inclination to fall in any other direction than it does. The marble moves *freely*, because it has no inclination to move otherwise; but it moves necessarily, because irresistibly compelled by the law of gravitation. Just so man acts freely, because he acts according to his will; but he acts necessarily, because he can no more change his will than he can make a world. And thus it is plain, that, although necessitarians may say they believe in free-agency and man's accountability, it is a freedom just such as pertains to lifeless matter.

"If, according to Edwards, man is free, and justly accountable for his actions, merely because he acts according to his own will when he has no control over that will, upon the same principle the maniac would be a free, accountable agent. If, in a paroxysm of madness, he murders his father, he acts according to his will. It is a voluntary act, and necessitarians cannot excuse him because his will was not under his control; for, in the view of their system, it was as much so as the will of any man in any case possibly can be. The truth is, it is an abuse of language to call that freedom which binds fast in the chains of necessity. Acting voluntarily amounts to no liberty at all, if I cannot possibly act otherwise than I do. The question is, not whether I have a will, or whether I may act according to my will, but what determines the will? This is the point to be settled in the question of free-agency. It is admitted that the will controls the actions; but who controls the will? As the will controls the actions, it necessarily follows that whatever controls the will must be accountable for the actions. Whoever controls the will must be the proper author of all that necessarily results from it, and consequently should be held accountable for the same." *

From the whole of this reasoning we feel ourselves safe in the conclusion that the theory of moral necessity cannot be reconciled with man's accountability and the retributions of the judgment day. Men may talk as they please about moral agency and the freedom of the human will;

* Ralston's Elements, pp. 252, 253.

but unless man possesses a self-controlling power over his own moral actions, he can no more be justly rewardable or punishable than the beasts that roam in the forest. This controlling power can only be exerted in acts of volition, and hence we contend that the *will of man is free.*

CHAPTER V.

MAN'S MORAL AGENCY: OBJECTIONS.

AGAINST the doctrine of the free moral agency of man, as presented and defended in the preceding chapter, several objections have been urged. We are told that this doctrine is absurd in itself, that it is conflictive with the established doctrine of motives, and that it is irreconcilable with the foreknowledge of God. To each of these grave objections we propose to give our candid attention and to return a suitable reply.

I. IT IS ALLEGED THAT OUR DOCTRINE OF FREE-AGENCY IS ABSURD IN ITSELF.

President Edwards has argued at great length to prove the absurdity of the doctrine, that the human mind in the exercise of volition is self-active. He alleges that it involves the absurdity either of an infinite series of volitions, or of an effect without a cause. Let us then for a moment examine this supposed dilemma. And,

1. It is here assumed that, according to our theory of the freedom of the human will, every act of volition implies a preceding volition by which it is determined. If this were really our doctrine of free-agency; if it implied, as Edwards supposes it does, that "each active volition is necessarily preceded by another," it would, indeed, involve the notion of an infinite series of volitions, the absurdity of which is so obvious that arguments to prove it are altogether unnecessary. But though this has often been asserted of the Arminian system of moral agency, it has never yet been proved and never can be. Our doctrine is, not that one volition determines another, but that the mind itself, as a living, active, and intelligent agent, puts forth its own volitions. When we speak of *free-will* we do not mean that the will is a distinct *agent* of which freedom is an attribute, but that it is an act of the mind, and that the mind, in the act of willing, is free from the control of any efficient cause extrinsic to itself. In other words, the mind is the active intelligent agent, to whom both freedom and volition belong.

Is it then true that, according to the Arminian doctrine of the self-determining power of the mind, every act of volition must be preceded and determined by another act of volition? We think not. We cannot see why there may not be an act of willing performed by the mind itself without any previous act of volition to determine it. To say that there can be no such free act of the mind; that man, in the possession of those powers with which God has endowed him, and independent of any predetermining cause operating upon him, cannot exercise free volition, is the same as to say that he is a slave to the most absolute fatalism.

But this is not all. To say that the doctrine of a self-active power in the exercise of willing is *absurd in itself*, is as much as to say that there is not a free agent in the universe, for this would lead to the fearful conclusion that even God himself has not the power of free volition, but is moved alone by the impulse of fatality. As it is absurd to suppose that every volition of the human mind is determined by a previous volition, so such a supposition must be equally absurd when applied to God. It must, therefore, be admitted, either that the will of God is efficiently determined by external causes, or that in the exercise of volition he possesses a self-determining power. To suppose that his volitions are efficiently determined by external causes, is in effect to suppose that he cannot be the Creator of all things. For, before he exerted creative power he must have willed to do so; but as nothing then existed external to himself, that volition could not have been produced by any external cause. It follows, therefore, that it must have originated in his own self-active nature.

If, then, the Divine mind can will freely without being impelled to do so, either by a previous act of volition or by any extrinsic cause, to suppose that the human mind possesses a similar power cannot be absurd in itself. And if God possesses in himself the power of free volition, the only question is, whether he can confer this exalted ability on created beings. To deny that he possesses this power himself is to deny his independence and free-agency; and to deny that he can confer it on creatures is to deny his omnipotence. But we may proceed to observe,

2. If we avoid the absurdity of an infinite series of volitions by denying that one act of volition is preceded and determined by another, then we are told that, according to our theory of the self-determining power of the mind, volition is an effect without a cause. In replying to this feature of the objection, if we would not dispute about mere words, we should know precisely what is meant by the terms *cause* and *effect*.

President Edwards tells us that he sometimes uses the term *cause* " to signify any antecedent, either natural or moral, positive or negative, on which an event so depends that it is the ground and reason, either in whole or in part, why it is rather than not, or why it is as it is rather than otherwise."* So also he tells us that, 'n accordance with this definition of a cause, he " sometimes uses the word *effect* for the consequence of another thing which is perhaps rather an occasion than a cause, most properly speaking."† But when he employs the term *cause*

* Inquiry, part 2, sec. 3. † Ibid.

in what he regards to be its proper sense, he uses it "to signify only that which has a positive efficiency or influence to produce a thing or bring it to pass."* In other words, he uses the term to indicate what is properly called an *efficient* cause. This is the sense in which he is to be understood when he speaks of motives as being the cause of volition. Consequently, when he calls volition an *effect*, his meaning must be that it is the correlative of an efficient cause.

But now let us ask, Is it indeed true that volition is an *effect?* If we mean by the term whatever comes to pass, of course volition is an effect, for no one can deny that volitions come to pass. Or, if we include in the definition of the term everything which has a sufficient reason and ground of its existence, it will certainly embrace the idea of volition; for, under certain circumstances, the human mind furnishes a sufficient reason and ground for the existence of volition. But if we take the term in its proper sense, as the correlative of an efficient cause, the sense in which it is evidently employed in the objection, we may unhesitatingly deny that volition is an *effect*.

There are no two things in nature which are more perfectly distinct than action and passion. When an effect is produced in anything by the action or influence of something else, the object in which the effect is produced is wholly passive in regard to it. An effect cannot be the act of that in which it is produced, because it results wholly from that which produces it. To say, then, that a thing acts, is the same as to say that its act is not produced by the action or influence of anything else. To suppose that an act is produced by an efficient cause, is to suppose it to be a passive effect, and therefore no act at all.

If these remarks are correct, it will necessarily follow that an act of the mind cannot be the effect of an efficient cause. The ideas of action and passion, of cause and effect, are opposite, and contrary the one to the other. Hence it is absurd to assert that the mind may be caused to act, or that a volition can be produced by anything acting upon the mind as an efficient cause. It is in this restricted sense that we use the term in question when we deny that volition is an *effect*.

It is perhaps impossible to gain a clear conception of the nature of volition, while we continue to view it in the light of that relation which an effect sustains to its efficient cause. The reason is, that volition involves no such relation, and to view it as an effect is to look at it in the light of a false psychology. We know it has been said, and very generally believed, that "all things fall under the one or the other of the two following relations: the relation between subject and attribute, or the relation between cause and effect." It is in this last category that volitions are supposed to be included; but truth requires that they should be placed under a very different relation, namely, the relation of *agent* and *action*. Unless this relation be admitted, and clearly distin-

* Inquiry, part 2, sec. 3.

guished from that of cause and effect, it will be impossible that we should rightly understand the phenomena of the will. Indeed, it may be safely affirmed that the true philosophy of volition is not to be determined by abstract considerations, or alone by the power of words, because it is not so much a question of logic as of psychology. If, therefore, we would really understand the phenomena of the will, we must not undertake to accomplish the end by a mere process of reasoning. We must fix the mind upon its own inward workings, and subject our volitions to a rigid investigation in the light of consciousness.

What, then, is the testimony of consciousness in regard to the nature of volition ? Does it appear to be the passive result of a previous act of the mind, or of motive, or of anything else? In other words, is it properly an *effect?* President Edwards has more than once told us that "the mind can be the cause of no *effect*, except by a preceding act of the mind;" that "an effect results from the action or influence of its cause," and that "nothing is any further an effect than as it proceeds from that action or influence." Does our idea of volition correspond with this notion of an *effect?* Does it appear to us that volition, like the motion of body, is the passive result of something else ? Most assuredly not. Volition is action itself, and not the result of action. It is an act of the mind, and not a passive state. It is a determination, and not that which is determined. It is itself an original producing cause, and not a produced effect. He, therefore, who reflects upon this subject in the light of experience can hardly fail to see that there is a clear and manifest distinction between an ACT and an EFFECT.

Now if volition is *not an effect*, then it will follow that our theory of the self-active power of the mind *does not* involve the absurdity of an effect without a cause; for it does not at all acknowledge the relation of cause and effect in the exercise of volition, but only that of *agent* and *action.* We readily allow that there is in the powers and capabilities of the human mind a sufficient ground or reason for the exercise of volition, but we deny that it is efficiently caused either by a previous volition or by anything else. Thus we think that the doctrine of man's free moral agency is successfully vindicated from the charge of absurdity and self-contradiction.

II. IT IS OBJECTED THAT THE LIBERTARIAN VIEW OF THIS SUBJECT IS CONFLICTIVE WITH THE DOCTRINE OF MOTIVES.

Necessitarians of every class have uniformly regarded motives as being the efficient cause of volition. Dr. Hartley contends that the thoughts and feelings of the soul result from the various vibrations of the brain, and that these vibrations are produced by the influence of motives or surrounding circumstances. He frankly admits that his theory implies "the necessity of human actions," and says, "I am sorry for it, but I cannot help it." Lord Kames represents the universe as "one vast machine composed of innumerable wheels, all closely linked together, and moving as they are moved." He considers man as "one wheel fixed in the middle of a vast automaton, moving just as necessarily as the sun, moon, or earth." President Edwards represents "motives and surrounding objects as reaching through the senses to a finely wrought nervous system, and by the impressions made there necessarily producing thought, volition, and action, according to the fixed laws of cause and effect."

Thus it is assumed, by the advocates of philosophical necessity, that volition is the passive and unavoidable result of motives and surrounding circumstances, or in other words, that it is necessarily determined by the strongest motive. If this is what we are to understand by the doctrine of motives, we are ready to admit the truth of the objection and to declare our opposition to any such doctrine.

But here it may be proper to inquire, What do necessitarians mean by the strongest motive? Is it the motive which has the most weight and importance in itself? Surely not. To say, in this proper sense of the phrase, that the will is always determined by the strongest motive, is the same as to say that it is always determined by the best reason; for motive, being but a reason of action considered in the mind, the best reason, being in the nature of things the strongest, must always predominate. But this is evidently contrary to fact and experience. If it were not, all men would act reasonably and none foolishly; or, at least, there would be no faults among them but those of the understanding, none of the heart and affections. The weakest reason, however, too generally succeeds when appetite and corrupt affections are present; that is to say, the weakest motive. For if this be not allowed, we must say that under the influence of appetite the weakest reason also appears to be the strongest, which is also false in fact, for then there would be no sins committed against *judgment* and *conviction*. But we cannot deny that many of our sins are of this description.

When necessitarians say that the strongest motive always prevails, do they mean, by the strongest motive, that which has the greatest influence on the mind at the time and under all the circumstances of the case? This is doubtless what they mean. But if so, they only utter this simple truism, that the prevailing motive always prevails—a proposition which no one in his senses will deny. What, then, it may be inquired, is the precise question in controversy between us? It is not whether the mind wills and acts under the influence of motives; for this is freely admitted by every libertarian. But it is simply this: Do motives exert an efficient, absolute, and irresistible influence over the will, so as in all cases to make it necessarily what it is? This is the only point in the doctrine of motives on which the controversy turns. Necessitarians affirm, and libertarians deny; and in support of this denial we offer the following remarks:

1. The doctrine of philosophical necessity is based upon the false foundation that volition is the passive result of motive. Its advocates

assume that there is no difference between mind and matter in regard to the attribute of *passivity*. The notion inculcated is, that motives influence the will just as a weight thrown into an even scale poises it, and inclines the beam. This is the grand metaphysical blunder of necessitarians of every school and of every age. The ancient Manichees, the Stoics, the Atheistic and Deistic philosophers, Spinoza, Hobbes, Voltaire, Hume, and others, adopted this principle; and they have been followed in this confounding of mind and matter by many learned and excellent men, such as President Edwards of Princeton, and President Day of Yale College. Indeed, the whole treatise of Edwards on the "Freedom of the Will" is based on this error. He assumes that the mind, like matter, can act only as it is acted upon; and from assumption he infers that the mind, like matter, is governed by necessity, and that the will is therefore necessarily determined by motives.

It must be admitted either that God has created beings capable of acting without being necessarily caused to act by something else, or that he has not. If he has not created such beings, then it will follow that he himself is the only agent in existence, and that angels and men are no more self-active than a clod of lifeless matter. This conclusion is not only subversive of the distinction between matter and mind, but directly repugnant to the whole tenor of Scripture and to the plainest dictates of common-sense. And yet this is the only view of the subject which accords with the scheme of necessity.

But now let us suppose, according to Scripture and common-sense, that God has endowed his intelligent creatures with a self-moving energy; and that, in the exercise of their derived powers, and independent of the absolute control of anything extrinsic to themselves, they are capable of voluntary action, and it will be easy to see that there is an essential distinction in nature between these intelligent beings and mere lifeless matter. And if this distinction be admitted, then it will follow that the laws by which intelligent creatures are regulated must be as different from those which govern mere matter as mind and matter are different in their essential qualities.

2. Another fundamental error involved in the scheme of necessity is, that motives possess an independent and active influence. To see the absurdity of this notion let us thoughtfully inquire, What are motives? Are they created beings endowed with self-moving energy? Are they capable not only of moving themselves, but of imparting their force to what is external to themselves, so as to produce action in that which could not act without them? If we answer these questions in the affirmative, we ascribe to motives all that self-controlling and self-determining energy which libertarians claim for the mind itself; and if a power to act without being acted upon must be ascribed either to mind or to motives in order to account for volition, it is certainly more rational to ascribe it to the former than to the latter.

If it be said that motives do not possess an *independent* influence, but that they derive their power from some antecedent cause, then it will follow either that they are connected with an infinite series of causes, which is absurd in itself, or that they depend upon God alone both for their existence and efficiency. But if motives themselves do not act—if God acts upon man, and determines his volitions by the instrumentality of motives, why is the doctrine still maintained that motives determine the will? This is the same as to say that motives do not act and that they do act at the same time, which is a contradiction. It is, in fact, to give up the argument for necessity, which is founded upon the supposed influence of motives. Again, if motives are only the instruments by which God determines the volitions of his rational creatures, then he is the only agent in the universe; while angels and men are mere passive instruments, acting only as they are acted upon by Divine power.

But now, if we answer these questions in the negative, as truth requires us to do, then we must allow that motives, considered in themselves, can no more act on the mind so as necessarily to determine its volitions, than one portion of inert matter can, of its own accord, act upon another. The truth is, that motives themselves do not act at all. Independent of the mind they can have no existence. It is the mind that acts upon them and gives them all the influence which they possess. But if motives depend upon the mind both for their existence and influence, is it not most unreasonable to suppose that they should control the mind in all its acts of volition? We conclude, therefore, that though the mind acts in view of motives, yet the controlling power is not in the motives, but in the mind itself.

This view of the subject is established by the very nature of motives. " What are they? Are they not arguments, reasons, or persuasions? Now, if the mind can exercise no free-agency of its own, in attending to arguments, examining reasons, or yielding to persuasions, why address them to man, and exhort him to give them their due weight? The very fact that they are motives, arguments, reasons, or persuasions, is proof sufficient that they are designed to influence the will, not necessarily and irresistibly, but only through the agency of man." What, then, is it that gives to motives their prevailing influence? It is not any inherent power in them, but it is the act of the mind itself, by which it yields to that influence in the exercise of free volition. If it should be asked why the mind yields to one motive rather than another, our reply would be that the reason is in the mind itself. God has endowed us with this power, without which we could not be moral and accountable agents.

3. The doctrine of necessity proceeds upon the false assumption that the mind can exercise no agency whatever in regard to motives. The theory is that the will is determined by motives; that motives arise from

circumstances; that circumstances are ordered by a power above us and beyond our control; and that, therefore, our volitions necessarily follow an order and chain of events appointed and decreed by Infinite Wisdom. If this is true, it will necessarily follow that we have no power to displace one motive by another, or to control those circumstances from which motives flow.

But who will say that a person may not shun evil company and fly from many temptations? Either this must be allowed, or else it must be a link in the chain of necessary events, fixed by a superior power, that we should not shun evil company or fly from temptations. Hence it would follow that the exhortations, " when sinners entice thee consent thou not," and "go not in the way of sinners," are very impertinent, and only prove that Solomon was no philosopher. But we are all conscious that we have the power to alter, and control, and avoid the force of motives. If we have no such power, why does a man resist the same temptation at one time to which he yields at another without any visible change in the circumstances? Why does he at one time resist a powerful temptation, which is the same as to resist a powerful motive, and yield, at another time, to one that is feeble, knowing that he does so?

But further, the motive or reason for an action may be a bad one and yet be prevalent for the want of the presence of a better reason or motive to lead to a contrary choice and act; but in how many instances is the true cause why a better reason or stronger motive is not present, that we have lived thoughtlessly and in ignorance? And if so, then the thoughtless might have been more thoughtful, and the ignorant might have acquired better knowledge, and thereby have placed themselves under the influence of stronger and better motives. Thus the theory of necessity does not accord with the facts of our own consciousness, but contradicts them. It is also refuted by every part of the moral history of man, and it may be, therefore, concluded that those speculations on the human will, to which the theory of philosophical necessity has driven its advocates, are equally opposed to the Holy Scriptures, to the philosophy of mind, to our observation of what passes in others, and to our own convictions.

4. The doctrine of motives, as it is held by necessitarians, is disproved by the absurdity of its logical consequences. We will not attempt to push this argument to its utmost extent. It is only necessary that we should notice some of the most obvious absurdities which result from the doctrine that volitions are necessarily determined by motives. And,

(1.) If volitions are efficiently caused by motives, then the dominion of absolute necessity is *universal*. The steps by which we reach this fearful conclusion are few and easily traced. Volitions cannot be produced by motives without being preceded by them, as the effect must always be preceded by its cause. Nor can they exert any influence over the motives by which they are produced; for they do not even come into existence till their producing motives have finished their operation. Indeed, no effect can modify its cause unless it can act before it exists, which is absurd. But if volition cannot influence the motive by which it is produced, it certainly cannot influence the antecedent to that motive; and so of every other antecedent in a retrospective series, until we reach the first cause. If, then, volition sustains a necessary relation to its producing motive, as our opponents assume, there can be no room for freedom between the volition and the first cause; for, if volition is *necessary*, all that precedes it up to the first cause must be so too.

But may there not be freedom between volition and its *effect?* By no means. Both the volition and its sequence, by the theory, are *effects;* and as every effect sustains a necessary relation to its cause, both the volition and all its sequences are necessary. It is, therefore, impossible to avoid the conclusion that all human volitions are only so many links in the adamantine chain of universal necessity. But what renders this conclusion a thousand times more startling is, that it applies to God as well as to man. The theory maintains that volition from its *very nature*, without a motive cause, would be an absurdity. But if the *nature* of volition demands a motive cause, that demand must be as applicable to the volitions of God as to those of his creatures; for, whatever differences may exist between created minds and the Infinite mind, the theory allows none in regard to volition. The very ground on which necessity is predicated of human volition requires that it should also be predicated of *Divine volition*. If motives are the only possible cause of volition in some minds they are so in all minds. And if this motive-control makes the volitions of all minds necessary, it must make all events equally so. The will of God, no less than the will of man, must be passive. Eternal necessity must rule the one no less than the other.

(2.) Another consequence of this doctrine of motives is, that it destroys the very foundation of moral distinctions. If all minds, without exception, are under the control of absolute and eternal necessity, then human virtue and human vice are impossible.

It is one of the plainest dictates of common-sense that the criminality of an evil act is grounded on the power of the agent to refrain from it. But who can contend successfully against an eternal necessity? Indeed, it is impossible that any one should even *attempt* to act otherwise than he does. For if every volition is the necessary effect of some motive, how can the mind command a different volition until it is produced by a different motive? And if this different motive lies entirely beyond the control of the agent, the very *attempt* to act otherwise than he does lies as far beyond his control as are the movements of the heavenly bodies.

Hence we are forced to the conclusion, if we argue correctly, that all moral creatures are equally undeserving of either praise or blame. For, though we are told that the character of an act lies in the *will*, yet the cause of the will lies in the *motive*, and over this the agent has no control. The greatest crimes in the universe are as necessary as the most distinguished virtues; and though we may regard the criminal as being unfortunate, yet in view of this necessity, and of the claims of eternal justice, we dare not pronounce him *guilty*. As well might men be accounted guilty for becoming hungry or thirsty; or for any other effect that is necessarily produced by the established laws of their physical constitution.

(3.) This doctrine of the causality of motives is injurious to the character of God. If motives are the only possible cause of volition, and if an effect sustains a necessary relation to its cause, then we must allow either that God puts forth no volitions at all, which would contradict both Scripture and reason, or that his volitions are caused by motives, and therefore necessary; but in either case we would deny his free-agency. To say that his volitions are determined by motives is to place him under the same law of necessity which is supposed to govern his creatures, and thus to deny his absolute independence. Nay, it is virtually to say that eternal necessity, and not God, governs the world.

But if we suppose God to be the free and independent governor of all things, and confine our notions of moral necessity to the actions of his intelligent creatures, still this scheme is derogatory to the Divine character. If virtue alone existed in the moral world, we could trace with pleasure the necessitating hand of God in the volitions and actions of his intelligent creatures. But when we fix our attention upon the ungodly deeds of wicked men, and are told that these were rendered necessary from all eternity by the immutable decree of God, and secured in time by a necessary chain of causes and effects, we instinctively inquire, Is there not some other solution of this awful subject which would exhibit the Supreme Governor of the moral world in a more amiable and engaging light? Is it not a most fearful conclusion, indeed, that falsehood, treachery, murder, and blasphemy are declarations of the Divine will? Yet such they must be if the doctrine of philosophical necessity is true.

III. *The last objection we will notice is, that* FREE MORAL AGENCY IS IRRECONCILABLE WITH THE FOREKNOWLEDGE OF GOD.

This is the most frequently employed argument of necessitarians against the doctrine of free moral agency, and one on which they rely with the greatest degree of confidence. Luther calls the foreknowledge of God "a thunderbolt, to dash free-will to atoms."* And Dr. Dick, a distinguished Calvinistic divine, has said that if our actions are certainly

* Bondage of the Will.

foreknown, "it is as impossible to avoid them, as it is to pluck the sun from the firmament."* Hence necessitarians tell us that we must either deny the foreknowledge of God or give up the doctrine of man's free moral agency. But our reply is, We will do neither the one nor the other.

As to the Divine foreknowledge, we believe that it extends to all things great and small, whether necessary or free, and that it is perfect and certain. We believe, moreover, that what God foreknows will certainly come to pass. In this respect the conclusion is the same, whether it be deduced from foreknowledge or concomitant knowledge. If a thing is known *now* to exist, it follows, by an absolute *certainty*, that it does exist; for otherwise it could not possibly be known to exist. So, likewise, if an event is certainly foreknown, it follows, with equal *certainty*, that it will come to pass. We conclude, therefore, that what God foreknows will most certainly and infallibly take place; but this infallible certainty has nothing to do with the manner in which future events will be brought about. It does not determine whether they will take their existence on the principle of *necessity* or on that of *free moral agency*.

By the *necessity* of any action or event we are to understand the impossibility that it should *not* be, or that it should be *different* from what it is. It is in this sense the term is employed when necessitarians tell us that Divine prescience implies *necessity*. If anything can be free from this kind of necessity, one would expect to find it in human volition; but according to the theory of President Edwards, the *will* is absolutely and efficiently determined by the influence of motives. So also Dr. Dick tells us that "a man chooses what appears to be good, and he chooses it necessarily, in this sense, that he *could not do* otherwise."† This sense of the term is evidently implied in the objection; for, as our doctrine of free moral agency acknowledges the *certainty* of future events, it cannot be irreconcilable with the foreknowledge of God, unless his foreknowledge is supposed to imply their absolute *necessity*.

But does the foreknowledge of God imply the necessity of all future events? This is what we deny, and what, we believe, can never be proved. Those who take the affirmative of this question are bound to admit one of two things—either that the foreknowledge of God makes future events necessary, or that he cannot foreknow them unless they are necessary. Let us, then, look for a moment at the consequences of each.

1. To say that the Divine prescience makes future events necessary, is the same as to say that necessity governs all things in heaven and earth. It is to say that all the volitions and actions of angels and men are as necessary as the movements of the planets—that the rebellion of holy angels, the sin of our first parents, and all the ungodly deeds that wicked men have ever committed, were rendered necessary by the foreknowl-

* Dick's Theology, Lec. 34.   † Ibid.

edge of God, and could not have been avoided. Moreover, if whatever is foreknown is thereby rendered necessary, and cannot be otherwise, then, as God foreknows from eternity every act that he would perform throughout all duration, he is a necessary agent in all that he does, acting only as he is acted upon by stern necessity. Thus we see that the "thunderbolt" of the great Reformer, which was supposed to "dash free-will to atoms," falls with as destructive weight upon the free-agency of man in Paradise, and even upon the freedom of God himself, as it does upon the free-will of man in his present condition.

But is it not most glaringly absurd to suppose that the great Jehovah, in all his acts, is impelled by necessity? This is to suppose the eternal existence of some superior power, separate and distinct from himself; which is at once to deny his independence and supremacy. It cannot, therefore, be true that all the acts of God are brought about by necessity. Yet they are foreknown; and if the foreknowledge of God does not render his own acts necessary or destroy his free-agency, so neither can it render the actions of his moral creatures necessary, nor destroy their free-agency.

To suppose that the Divine foreknowledge makes future events necessary is incompatible with the very nature of knowledge in general. What is knowledge? Is it an active power, possessing a distinct and independent existence? We answer, No. It is nothing more than a clear and certain perception of truth and fact. It is, therefore, passive in its nature, and possesses only a relative and dependent existence. And though it is often said that "knowledge is power," yet nothing more is intended by this expression than that it directs an active agent in the exertion of his power. What influence can mere knowledge exert upon any event, whether past, present, or future? Evidently none at all; and for this reason, that it is knowledge and not power.

2. But now let us turn our attention to the other alternative, namely, that God cannot foreknow future events unless they are necessary. This seems to be the position which is generally assumed by necessitarians, and which appears to be based upon the supposition that the volitions and actions of free moral agents are in their very nature uncertain. "There must be a certainty in things themselves," says President Edwards, "before they are certainly known."* But what is this certainty in things themselves, or in human volitions, without which they are incapable of being foreknown? The answer is obvious; for Edwards everywhere contends that unless our volitions are brought to pass by the influence of moral causes—that unless they are necessarily produced by an "effectual power and efficacy," they are altogether uncertain. Hence he clearly maintains, that unless human volitions are brought to pass by the necessitating influence of motives, they are not certain in themselves, and are therefore incapable of being foreknown.

* Inquiry, Part 2, sec. 12.

That this mode of reasoning may hold good in regard to human knowledge we will not deny; but that it will apply to the foreknowledge of God is what cannot be shown. If there is anything in us approaching to foreknowledge, it must result from a knowledge of something now existing between which and the event foreknown there is a necessary connection. But is it proper to conclude, because this is the case with man, that it must also be the case with Deity? Shall we make our own limited and feeble intellects the measure of all possible modes of knowledge with God?

We freely admit that an event cannot be foreknown unless it will certainly come to pass. But why may not the free volitions and actions of moral creatures be as certain as those events that are necessary? To say they cannot, is a mere assumption which never can be proved. To suppose them to be certain and uncertain at the same time would involve a contradiction; but there is no contradiction in supposing them to be future, certain, and free.

That we can gain as clear and certain knowledge of a past free action as of one that was necessarily produced, no one will deny. May we not then reasonably suppose that God can foreknow the free volitions and actions of his moral creatures, as well as those events that are necessary? That he cannot, is more than any finite being should presume to declare.

But if all future events must be necessary in order to be foreknown, then it will follow, either that this necessity exists in the very nature of things themselves or in God. To say that this necessity arises from the nature of things themselves, is to take one's stand upon the platform of Stoical fatalism. It is to assume that all things in heaven and earth are bound together by an intricate series and concatenation of causes; that fate and not God governs the world; and that all moral creatures in the universe, with the *Infinite One* in the same category, are bound by the fetters of eternal necessity. These are only some of the absurd and shocking consequences which result from this scheme of necessity, but they are sufficient to refute it.

Are we, then, to place the necessity of all things in God? This is our only alternative; and this, we believe, is what necessitarians maintain. "If we allow the attribute of prescience," says Mr. Buck, "the idea of a decree must certainly be allowed also, for how can an action that is really to come to pass be foreseen if it be not determined? God knew everything from the beginning, but this he could not know if he had not so determined it."* Again: "No effect can be viewed as future," says Dr. Dick, "or, in human language, can be the object of certain expectation, but when considered in relation to its efficient cause, and the cause of all things that ever shall exist is the purpose of God."†

* Theological Dictionary. † Dick's Theology, Lec. 21.

In these two brief quotations we have the fundamental principles of the necessitarian scheme. They are these: 1. That God is the moving and efficient cause of all things; 2. That all things are made necessary by his purpose or determination; and, 3. That he foreknows future events, because he has made them necessary. Neither time nor space will allow us to enter into an extended examination of this theory. We can only glance at some of its consequences. And,

First, If God is the efficient cause of all things, then the horrible consequence must follow, that he is the efficient cause of all the moral evil that ever existed or ever will exist. It is no answer to this difficulty to say that God is only the cause of the *act* that is sinful, but not of its sinfulness. Wherein does the sinfulness of an act lie? Is it not in the will? But according to this theory, God controls the will and makes that as necessary as the act itself.

Secondly, If the purpose or determination of God makes all things necessary, then it will follow that a necessity as absolute as Stoical fatalism governs the moral world; and that falsehood, treachery, blasphemy, and murder are rendered as necessary by the Divine purpose as piety and virtue.

Thirdly, To say that God foreknows future events because he has made them necessary, is to say that an essential *attribute* of Deity is dependent for its existence upon an *act* of the Divine mind, the foreknowledge of God upon his purpose or decree.

The conclusion, then, which we draw from the whole argument is this, that though our doctrine of free moral agency is incompatible with the necessitarian notion of Divine foreknowledge, yet it is in perfect harmony with the true doctrine upon this subject, and so the objection falls to the ground.

BOOK IV.

THE REMEDIAL DISPENSATION.

We have shown from the teachings of the Holy Scriptures that our first parents fell from that state of holiness and happiness in which they were created, and became liable to death temporal, spiritual, and eternal; that all their posterity are born into the world with a corrupt nature, from which rebellion against God universally flows; and that consequently the whole world, as St. Paul forcibly expresses it, "is guilty before God."

Had no method of forgiveness and restoration been devised with respect to human offenders, the penalty of death would have been immediately executed upon the first sinning pair, and with them the human race would have utterly perished. But God, in his infinite benevolence toward his offending creatures, made with Adam a covenant of pardon and salvation, which, however, did not terminate upon himself alone, but comprehended the whole human race.

Since, then, the penalty of death was not immediately executed in all its extent upon the first sinning pair, and is not immediately executed upon their sinning descendants; since they were actually restored to the Divine favor, and the same blessing is offered to us, our inquiries must, in the next place, be directed to the *nature* of that *remedial dispensation* in which God lays aside in so great a measure the sternness and inflexibility of his office as Judge and becomes the dispenser of grace and favor to the guilty. This will lead us to examine the principles of God's moral government, the doctrine of atonement, and the benefits which are derived to man "through the redemption that is in Jesus Christ."

CHAPTER I.

PRINCIPLES OF GOD'S MORAL GOVERNMENT.

In the investigation of the principles of God's moral government it will be necessary to illustrate to some extent the Divine character; to point out the connection which exists between the essential justice of God and the establishment of that legal constitution which requires death as the penalty of sin, and to show that Divine justice requires the execution of the penalty. Let us, then, direct our attention,

I. To the Character of God.

The existence of a Divine law obligatory upon man is not doubted by any who admit the existence and government of God. We have already seen its requirements, its extent, and its sanctions, and have proved that its penalty consists not merely in severe sufferings in this life, but in *death;* that is, the separation of the body and the soul; the former being left under the power of corruption, the latter being separated from God and made liable to punishment in another state of being.

It is, therefore, important to keep in view the extent and severity of the punishment denounced against transgression, as being illustrative of the character of God both with reference to his essential holiness and to his proceedings as governor of the world. The miseries connected with sin, whether as natural consequences or as the results of Divine visitation, must all be regarded as *punitive;* for it would be abhorrent to all our notions of the Divine character to suppose that perfectly *innocent* beings should be subject to such miseries. They are only to be accounted for upon the ground of their being the results of a supreme judicial administration, which bears a strict and often a very terrible character.

Though God has manifested his severity against moral offense quite independent of the Scriptures, yet it is to them that we must resort for the most important illustrations of his character, and especially of his HOLINESS and JUSTICE.

1. With respect to the HOLINESS of God the Scriptures show us that it is something more than a mere absence of moral evil—more than the approval of moral goodness, or even a delight in it. They prove that whatever is opposed to it is the object of an active displacence, of hatred, of opposition and resistance; and that this sentiment is inflexible and eternal. God is " of purer eyes than to behold evil, and cannot look on

iniquity." To him "even the thoughts of the wicked are an abomination." But,

2. With respect to the JUSTICE of God it will be necessary to consider it more at large, since a right conception of this attribute of the Divine nature lies at the foundation of the Christian doctrine of atonement.

Justice is usually considered as universal or particular. *Universal* justice comprehends all the moral attributes of God, and consists in the rectitude of his nature. *Particular* justice consists in a practical conformity to the principles of equity, and is either *commutative*, which respects equals, or *distributive*, which is the dispensing of rewards and punishments, and is exercised only by governors. It is the justice of God in this last view, but still in connection with universal justice, with which we are now concerned—that *rectoral sovereign justice* by which he maintains his own rights and the rights of others and gives to every one his due, according to that legal constitution which he has himself established. And as the legal constitution under which God has placed his creatures is the result of universal justice or righteousness—the holiness, goodness, truth, and wisdom of God united; so his distributive justice, or his respect for the laws which he has established, is, in every respect and degree, faultless and perfect. In this legal constitution nothing is enjoined or prohibited, nothing promised or threatened, but what is conformable to the moral perfections of God. "The law is holy, and the commandment HOLY, and JUST, and GOOD." Rom. vii, 12.

Of the strictness and severity of the punitive justice of God the sentence of death pronounced upon *sin* is sufficient evidence; and the actual infliction of bodily death is the standing proof to the world that the threatening is not a dead-letter, and that in the Divine administration continual and strict regard is had to the claims and dispensations of distributive justice. "Shall not the Judge of all the earth do RIGHT?" Gen. xviii, 25. So St. Paul speaks of "the day of wrath, and revelation of the RIGHTEOUS JUDGMENT OF GOD." Rom. ii, 5.

The legal constitution, then, which we are under secures life to the obedient, but dooms offenders to die. To execute this penalty, as well as to bestow the reward of obedience, is the office of distributive justice; and the appointment of the penalty and the execution of it are both the results of the essential rectitude of God. But we will now proceed to notice,

II. THE CONNECTION BETWEEN THE UNIVERSAL JUSTICE OF GOD AND THIS LEGAL CONSTITUTION WHICH REQUIRES SO SEVERE A PENALTY AGAINST SIN.

Whether we succeed or not in discovering this connection the fact remains the same, firmly grounded on the most explicit testimony of Scripture. But believing that the question is not entirely beyond our grasp, and that it is one of importance, we will give it a brief consideration. And,

1. The creation of beings capable of choice, and endowed with affections, seems necessarily to involve the possibility of volitions and acts contrary to the will of the Creator, and, consequently, a liability to suffer. In the prevention of these evils both justice and benevolence are concerned. That the Creator has an absolute right to the entire obedience of his moral creatures no one will deny. Any delinquency on their part is a violation of this *right*, which violation justice is therefore bound to prevent. But as all opposition to the will of God must be the source of misery to the offender, even independent of direct punishment, the prevention of moral evil is as much the work of *benevolence* as it is of justice.

2. To prevent evil of every kind, and to secure the benevolent purposes for which creative power was exerted, were the ends, therefore, of that administration which arose out of the existence of moral agents. No sooner did they exist than a Divine government was established over them, and to the ends just mentioned all its acts must have been directed. The first act was the publication of the will of God; for where there is no declared law there can be no rational government. The second act was to give motives to obedience; for to creatures liable to evil, though created good, these were necessary. But as they were made *free*, and designed to yield a *willing* service, more than rational inducements, operating through the judgment and affections, could not be applied. These motives were the promise of a happy life, the justice of the service required, and the evil to be feared from disobedience.

3. But now let us suppose that nothing less than a positive penalty of the most tremendous kind could be sufficient to deter free moral creatures from transgression; that even this penalty would not in all cases be sufficient; but that in no case would a less powerful motive prove sufficiently cautionary; then, in such circumstances, the moral perfections of the Divine nature would undoubtedly require the ordination of such a penalty, however tremendous.

It was certainly required by the essential rectitude of God that he should adopt the *most effectual* means of preventing the introduction of moral evil among his rational creatures, and, when introduced, of checking and limiting its progress. If, therefore, there were no means equally effectual for these purposes as the issuing of a law enforced by the penalty of *death*, then the adoption of such a measure was required by the holiness, the justice, and the benevolence of God.

But is the penalty of death, as the punishment of sin, the most effectual means of counteracting moral evil? To all who believe the Bible the answer is, that as this has actually been adopted as the universal penalty of transgression,* and as this is confessedly the highest possible penalty, nothing less than this could be effectual to the purpose of gov-

* See Book iii, chap 3.

ernment and to the manifestation of the Divine rectitude. If it could, then a superfluous and excessive means has been adopted for which no reason can be given, and which impeaches the wisdom of God, the office of which attribute is to adapt means to ends by an exact adjustment; if not, then it was required by all the moral attributes of the Divine nature. But,

III. DOES THE JUSTICE OF GOD OBLIGE HIM TO EXECUTE THE PENALTY OF HIS LAW?

All the opponents of the doctrine of atonement deny this, and argue, *first*, that God has power to give up his own rights and to pardon sin on prerogative; *secondly*, that when repentance succeeds offense there is a moral fitness in forgiveness, since the offender presents a reformed character; and *finally*, that the very affections of goodness and mercy, so eminent in God, require us to conclude that he is always ready, upon the repentance of his creatures, to forgive their delinquencies, or, at most, to make their punishments light and temporary.

1. It is contended that *God may give up his own rights*. This must mean either his right to obedience from his creatures, or his right to punish disobedience when that occurs. With respect to God's right to be obeyed, the perfect rectitude of his nature forbids him to give it up, or in any sense to relax it. No king can morally give up his right to be obeyed in the full degree which may be enjoined by the laws of his kingdom. No parent can give up his right to obedience from his children and be blameless. In both cases, if this be done voluntarily, it argues an indifference to that principle of rectitude on which such duties depend, and, therefore, a moral imperfection. But as this cannot be attributed to God, he never can yield up his right to be obeyed.

But may he not give up his right to punish when disobedience has actually taken place? By no means; for this would be the same as to give up his right to be obeyed. It is only by punitive acts that the Supreme Governor guards this right, and shows that he will not relax it. If sin is not punished, then it will follow that his right to obedience is given up. Again, if impunity were confined to a few offenders there would be partiality in God; but if it were extended to all, then would he renounce his sovereignty, and show himself indifferent to the principles of rectitude and moral order.

In addition to this, we have already seen that, by a formal law, the highest possible penalty has been threatened in all cases of transgression, and that a less awful sanction would have been wholly inadequate to the end intended. If so, then not to exact the penalty would be to repeal the law, to reduce its sanction to an empty threat, incompatible with the veracity of God, and to render it altogether inert; inasmuch as it would soon be seen whether sin is followed by punishment or not.

2. The notion that *repentance, on the part of the offender, renders him a fit object of pardon*, will be found equally fallacious.—This argu-

ment assumes that it is *morally unfit*, that is, *wrong*, to pardon the impenitent; and this is expressly conceded by Socinus, who says, that "not to give pardon, in case of impenitence, is due to the rectitude and equity of God." It follows, then, that those who believe repentance to be necessary, in order to render it morally fit for God to pardon offenders, must give up the doctrine of pardon by mere prerogative. For, according to their own showing, in order to make forgiveness an act of moral fitness, some consideration is required—something which shall make it *right*, as well as *merciful*, in God to forgive. Those who urge that repentance is that *consideration* do thus unwittingly give up their own principle and tacitly adopt that of the satisfactionists, differing only as to what does actually constitute it *right* in God to forgive. We deny, however, that mere repentance is sufficient to render it morally fit for God to pardon offenders; for,

(1.) There is no intimation in the Scriptures that the penalty of the law is not to be executed in case of repentance. There was certainly none given in the promulgation of the law to Adam; none in the decalogue; none in any of those passages which speak of the legal consequences of sin; as, "the soul that sinneth, it shall die,"—"the wages of sin is death." The Scriptures, it is true, enjoin repentance, but then it is in connection with a system of atonement and satisfaction independent of repentance, and of which repentance itself is an *effect*.

(2.) Nor is it true that repentance changes the legal relation of the guilty to God. Nothing but pardon can change that relation; for nothing but pardon can cancel crime, and it is clear that repentance is not pardon. The sentence of the law is directed against transgression, and repentance does not annihilate the fact of that transgression, but, on the contrary, is an acknowledgment of it. The charge lies against the offender; he may be an obdurate or a penitent criminal; but, in either case, he is equally guilty of all for which he stands truly charged; and how then can his relation to the Lawgiver be changed by repentance?

(3.) As repentance cannot produce this change of relation, so neither can it save offenders from the penal consequences of transgression. For, though men are now under a dispensation of grace, yet the Scriptures represent repentance as incapable of turning away deserved vengeance from those who have been obstinately wicked. "Then shall they call upon me, but I will not answer; they shall seek me early, but they shall not find me." Prov. i, 28. Here, to call upon God, and to seek him early—that is, earnestly and carefully—are acts of repentance and reformation too, and yet they have no power to arrest the exercise of punitive justice.

The general course of Providence is also in opposition to the notion that mere repentance can arrest punishment. The sufferings which follow sin in the present life by natural consequence, and the established constitution of things, are as much the effects of God's appointment as the direct penalties attached to the violation of his laws; but repentance does not prevent these penal consequences—it does not restore health injured by intemperance, property wasted by profusion, or character dishonored by vice.

(4.) Those who contend that repentance is a reason for the non-execution of the penalty of the law, seem entirely to overlook or to disregard its true nature. Is it nothing more than a sorrow for sin, merely because of the painful consequences to which the offender is exposed? Every criminal, when convicted and in danger of immediate punishment, would as necessarily repent, in this sense, as he would necessarily be sorry to be liable to pain; and if such sorrow were true repentance it would in all cases, according to this doctrine, render it morally fit and right that forgiveness should be exercised, and consequently wrong that it should be refused. But to grant pardon on such a condition would be tantamount to the entire and absolute repeal of all law, and the annihilation of all government.

If true repentance be allowed to consist in a perception of the evil of sin, and a dislike to it as such, with real remorse and sorrow that the authority of God has been slighted and his goodness abused—and this is certainly the light in which it is exhibited in the Scriptures—then it is forgotten that man in his fallen condition is incapable of penitence of this kind. That repentance which the Scriptures require is said to be *the gift of Christ*, whom "God exalted to be a Prince and a Saviour," that he might "give repentance," as well as "forgiveness of sins,"—a gift quite superfluous, if to repent truly were in the power of man and independent of Christ. To suppose, therefore, that man is capable of evangelical repentance, is to assume human nature to be what it is not.

(5.) With this view of the insufficiency of repentance to obtain pardon the Scriptures agree. John the Baptist was, emphatically, a preacher of repentance; but he gave no intimation that repentance alone would render it morally fit that God should forgive sin. He taught his disciples to look for a higher baptism than that which he administered—the baptism of the Holy Ghost; and to "behold the Lamb of God, which taketh away the sin of the world." Thus he virtually declared, that the repentance which he preached could not take away sin; but that it was taken away by Christ alone, and that in his sacrificial character, as "the Lamb of God." Moreover, he concludes his discourse concerning Jesus with these memorable words: "He that believeth on the Son hath everlasting life; and he that believeth not the Son shall not see life; but the wrath of God abideth on him." John iii, 36. The testimony of John therefore is, that something more than repentance, even *faith in Christ*, is necessary to salvation. Such also is the doctrine both of our Lord and his apostles; for though they declare that men must repent, they no less explicitly teach that they must believe.

CHAPTER II.

THE ATONEMENT: PRIMITIVE SACRIFICES.

HAVING shown that sin is neither forgiven by the mere prerogative of God nor on account of repentance in man, we will proceed to investigate that method of love, wisdom, and justice by which a merciful God justifies the ungodly; or, in other words, the doctrine of *atonement* by the sufferings and death of our Lord Jesus Christ. That we may follow the order in which this doctrine has been gradually unfolded to the world, we will examine it, *first*, in its connection with patriarchal sacrifices; *secondly*, as it is exhibited in the sacrifices of the law; and, *thirdly*, as it is set forth in the Scriptures of the New Testament.

It will be our business, then, in this chapter to consider the doctrine of atonement in its connection with the primitive or patriarchal sacrifices. In doing this we will attempt to show that the antemosaic sacrifices were of *Divine origin*, and that they were *expiatory* in their character.

I. THEY WERE OF DIVINE ORIGIN.

It is admitted that the Scriptures make no mention of the first institution of animal sacrifices, and from this fact some have concluded that they proceeded originally from a dictate of nature, or from a grateful inclination to return unto God some of his own blessings. But this is no argument against the Divine appointment of this rite; for it is to be expected that in so brief an account of so large a portion of time as is included in the antediluvian history many things should be omitted. Thus, Moses says nothing of the prophecy of Enoch, or of the preaching of Noah, though these are both referred to in other parts of Scripture.* The Jews, for whom Moses primarily wrote, knew that their own sacrifices were of Divine institution, and that God in a miraculous manner had manifested his acceptance of them. Nor had they any reason to doubt that the patriarchal sacrifices had been so instituted, and so accepted from the beginning. It was not necessary, therefore, that the sacred historians should expatiate upon a matter which had doubtless descended to them by a clear and uninterrupted tradition. But that the rite of sacrifice was originally of Divine appointment may be argued,

1. *From the impossibility that it should have originated with man.* —Such a system of worship could not have had its origin in *human reason*. It is true, a grateful sense of the blessings of God will incline

* See Jude xiv; and 2 Peter ii, 15.

men at any time to offer him praise and thanksgiving. But what dictate of reason could ever have taught man that to destroy the best of his fruits, or the choicest of his cattle, would be a service acceptable to God? Goodness and mercy and compassion are constantly ascribed to that Infinite Being. Who then could have thought, that putting an innocent and inoffensive animal to torture, spilling its blood upon the earth, and burning its flesh upon an altar, would be either a grateful sight, or "an offering of a sweet smelling savor" to the Most High?

Moreover, that the life of an irrational animal should ransom the life of a man, and that its blood should have any virtue to wash away his sin, to purify his conscience, and to restore him to the favor of an offended God, are not the dictates of reason, or the teachings of the light of nature, but quite the contrary. Nor could man have any right to take the life of an animal, if that right had not been conferred upon him by the Creator. But it is evident that God did not confer this right upon the antediluvians for any other purpose than that of sacrifice. They had no right to take the life of an animal for food, much less for unnecessary torture. It follows, therefore, that for them to have taken away animal life without a positive Divine appointment would have been an act of cruelty and wickedness, and not of acceptable worship.

That this rite did not originate in any *demand of our nature* is undeniable; for no one will say that we have any natural instinct or appetite to gratify in spilling the blood and burning the flesh of innocent creatures. Indeed, the taking of animal life is even now shocking to human nature, though custom has long made it familiar. Nor could the rite have had its foundation in appetite, since it was first observed at a period when the whole sacrifice was consumed by fire, or when, if it had not been so consumed, men wholly abstained from flesh.

Again, the practice cannot be resolved into *priestcraft;* for no order of priests existed when the rite of sacrifice was first observed. And if men resolve it into *superstition*, they must not only suppose that the first family were superstitious, but also that God, by his acceptance of Abel's sacrifice, gave his sanction to a superstitious and irrational practice. But as no one will be thus bold, our only rational conclusion is, that the rite of animal sacrifice is of Divine appointment. This position is indicated,

2. *By the distinction of animals into clean and unclean.*—This distinction cannot be rationally accounted for, unless we admit that God had given commandment for certain kinds of beasts to be offered in sacrifice; and as this distinction existed before the flood, and consequently at a time when the grant of animal food had not been made to man, it presents a strong proof of the Divine appointment of animal sacrifices at that early period. This is corroborated by the fact that Noah was commanded to take with him into the ark a greater number of clean than of unclean animals; the former by *sevens*, and the

latter by *two* of a kind. Now if the clean beasts were such as had been appointed as proper for sacrifice, and if we bear in mind that Noah offered sacrifices immediately on leaving the ark, the propriety of the command is at once manifest, but on no other principle. But the Divine origin of this rite is more fully established,

3. *By a reference to particular cases of patriarchal sacrifice.*—The first act of sacrifice of which we have any express record is that of Cain and Abel in Gen. iv, 3, 4: " Cain brought of the fruits of the ground an offering unto the Lord; and Abel, he also brought of the firstlings of his flock and of the fat thereof;" or, according to the Hebrew idiom, the fattest or best of his flock. With this account of the transaction we ought to connect the comment of St. Paul upon it as it is recorded in Heb. xi, 4: " By faith Abel offered unto God a more excellent sacrifice than Cain, by which he obtained witness that he was righteous, God testifying of his gifts."

Here two things are to be considered. One is that the sacrifice of Abel was offered "*by faith;*" the other, that it was *divinely approved.* When we examine what is said in the eleventh chapter of Hebrews respecting the faith of the ancient worthies, we at once discover that it rested in all cases on some Divine declaration or promise; and the plain inference is, that such must have been the case in regard to the faith of Abel. Indeed, this is clearly implied in the very nature of faith; for the apostle tells us that it comes " by hearing, and hearing by the word of God." If we deny that Abel, in this solemn transaction, was acting under Divine instructions, we see no possible way in which his sacrifice could have been offered "*by faith.*" Hence, we conclude that this act of sacrificial worship was performed in accordance with a previous Divine appointment.

The same conclusion will follow from the fact that the sacrifice of Abel was divinely approved. We need not now inquire into the manner in which God manifested his approbation of this act of religious worship. It affects not the argument whether it was by an internal impression on the mind of the worshiper, by an audible voice, or by sending fire from heaven to consume the sacrifice. The important truth would still be before us, that Abel in this transaction " obtained witness that he was righteous, God testifying of his gifts." But are we to suppose that he obtained this Divine testimony by a means which God had not appointed? If not, the Divine origin of the rite of animal sacrifice must be allowed.

The next instance of patriarchal sacrifice which we shall notice in this connection is that of Noah immediately on his leaving the ark, which is recorded in Gen. viii, 20, 21: "And Noah builded an altar unto the Lord, and took of every clean beast, and of every clean fowl, and offered burnt-offerings on the altar. And the Lord smelled a sweet savor; and the Lord said, I will not again curse the ground any more for man's sake." To see that Noah performed this act of worship in compliance with a previous appointment of God it is only necessary that we should consider a few of the attendant circumstances: 1. He engaged in the work as soon as he came forth from the ark. There was no time for the exercise of his inventive genius, which we may suppose would have been necessary, had he not been previously familiar with this mode of worship. 2. He "took of every clean beast and of every clean fowl;" which shows that the distribution of animals into clean and unclean was an appointment of God in reference to sacrifice, and consequently that the rite itself was divinely appointed. 3. The Lord approved this sacrifice; he "smelled a sweet savor;" which clearly proves that this mode of worship was in accordance with his own institution.

Again, in Gen. xv, 9, 10, we see Abraham on a memorable occasion engaging in the performance of animal sacrifice at the direct command of God and with Divine approbation. "And he said unto him, Take me a heifer of three years old, and a she goat of three years old, and a ram of three years old, and a turtle-dove, and a young pigeon. And he took unto him all these, and divided them in the midst, and laid each piece one against another: but the birds divided he not." In this case there can be no dispute in regard to the Divine appointment of the sacrifice, for it was expressly commanded. And if to this we add that God manifested his acceptance of the offering by the "burning lamp," the symbol of the Divine presence which "passed between" its pieces, our argument is made good.

One other instance only we will adduce in support of the present position. It is the case of Abraham in presenting his son Isaac as a burnt-offering to the Lord on Mount Moriah. In this transaction, which is recorded in the twenty-second chapter of Genesis, we have a clear proof that animal sacrifices were originally instituted by Divine appointment. This will appear if we consider that God expressly commanded Abraham to go to Mount Moriah and there offer a burnt-offering; that Abraham spoke of his intended sacrifice as of a service to which he had been accustomed; that Isaac, by asking the question, "Where is the lamb for a burnt-offering?" discovered a familiarity with that mode of worship, and that God did actually provide the offering which was sacrificed instead of Isaac. All these circumstances testify that sacrificial worship was an institution of God. Believing, therefore, that the point in discussion is fully established, we will pursue it no further.

II. THE ANTEMOSAIC SACRIFICES WERE EXPIATORY.

We have an argument in support of the expiatory character of the patriarchal sacrifices,

1. *In the prohibition of blood*, when the use of animal food was granted to man.—" But flesh with the life thereof, which is the blood thereof, shall ye not eat." Gen. ix, 4. This prohibition is repeated by

Moses to the Israelites with this explanation: "I have given it to you upon the altar, to make an *atonement* for your souls." From this "additional reason," as it has been called, some have argued that the doctrine of the atoning power of blood was then for the first time announced by Moses, otherwise the same reason for the prohibition would have been given to Noah.

To this we reply, 1. That unless the same reason be supposed as the ground of the prohibition to Noah as that which was given by Moses to the Jews, no reason at all can be conceived for this restraint upon the appetite of mankind from Noah to Moses. 2. That it is a mistake to suppose that Moses assigns any reason for the interdiction of blood to the Israelites which is not to be found in the original prohibition to Noah. His language is, "FOR THE LIFE of the flesh is in the blood; and I have given it to you upon the altar, to make an atonement for your souls; *for it is the* BLOOD (or LIFE) that maketh an atonement for the soul." The great reason, then, for the prohibition of blood is, that it is the LIFE; and what follows respecting atonement is *exegetical* of this reason, the life is in the blood, and the blood or life is given as an atonement.

Now, by turning to the original prohibition in Genesis, we find that precisely the same reason is given; and the reason being the same, the question is, whether the exegesis added by Moses must not necessarily be understood in the general reason given for the restraint to Noah. Blood is prohibited for this reason, that it is the LIFE; and Moses adds, that it is "the blood," or *life*, "which makes atonement." We have, however, in the sacrifice of the paschal lamb, and in the sprinkling of its blood, a sufficient proof that before the giving of the law blood was appropriated to a sacred and sacrificial purpose. But again, the doctrine for which we are contending is supported,

2. *By the history of patriarchal sacrifices.*—Here it will be seen that the sacrifices of the patriarchs were those of animal victims, and that they were offered for the purpose of averting the displeasure of God from sinning men. Thus it is evident, from the language of the apostle, that the end of Abel's offering was pardon and acceptance with GOD; and by it this end was realized, for "he obtained witness that he was righteous." Heb. xi, 4.

As to the *matter* of Abel's sacrifice, it was an *animal* offering. He "brought of the firstlings of his flock, and of the fat thereof." And as to the peculiar *nature* of this transaction, the apostle declares that, "By FAITH Abel offered unto God a more excellent sacrifice than Cain, by which he obtained WITNESS that he was *righteous*, GOD testifying of his gifts; and by it he, being dead, yet speaketh." Here the sacred penman evidently assigns a direct efficacy to the faith of Abel, and to the kind of sacrifice by which that faith was expressed and of which his faith was the immediate cause. The faith which he exercised was pleasing to God, and God had respect to his offering because it was the proper expression of that faith. That which vitiated the offering of Cain was the want of faith; for "without faith it is impossible to please" God.

But what does the apostle mean when he says that Abel "obtained witness that he was *righteous?*" Doubtless that he was justified, pardoned, and dealt with as righteous. Thus he argues that *Abraham* "believed God, and it was accounted to him for righteousness"—that "faith was reckoned to Abraham for righteousness"—that "he received the sign of circumcision, a seal," a visible, confirmatory, declaratory, and witnessing mark "of the righteousness which he had by faith." In these two cases we have a similarity so striking that they can scarcely fail to explain each other. In both sinful men are placed in the condition of *righteous* men—the instrument, in both cases, is *faith;* and the transaction is, in both cases also, publicly and sensibly *witnessed.* In the case of Abraham it was witnessed by the sign of circumcision; and in that of Abel by a visible acceptance of his sacrifice, while the offering of Cain was rejected.

Now, that which Abel did "by faith" was, if considered *generally*, to perform an act of solemn worship in the confidence that it would be acceptable to God. This supposed a revelation, either immediate or by tradition, that such acts of worship were acceptable to him; for otherwise his faith could have had no warrant, and would not have been faith, but mere fancy. It is, therefore, impossible to allow that the act of Abel, in this instance, was *an act of faith*, unless we allow that it had respect to a previous revelation which corresponded with *all the parts of that sacrificial action*. Had his sacrifice been merely *eucharistic* it would have expressed gratitude, but not *faith ;* or, if faith in the general sense of confidence in God that he would receive an act of grateful worship and reward the worshiper, it could not have been a stronger expression of faith than the offering of Cain, who surely believed these two points; for otherwise he would not have brought an offering of any kind. But the offering of Abel was evidently *expiatory*, and, on this account, it expressed a faith which Cain had not. It taught the world how guilty men were to approach God, and was a declaration of the necessity of an atonement for sin. By this act of sacrificial worship, therefore, "he being dead yet speaketh."

The same, however, is equally true of other acts of patriarchal sacrifice. Thus the burnt-offerings of Noah, when he left the ark, served to avert the cursing of "the ground any more for man's sake;" that is, for man's sin, and the smiting any more of every living thing.* The burnt-offerings which Job offered for his children, at the close of their festival, were evidently to make an atonement for their sins; for he said, "It may be that my sons have sinned, and cursed God in their hearts."† Thus

* Gen. viii, 20, 21.   † Job i, 4, 5.

also, in the case of Eliphaz and his two friends, the prescribed burnt-offering was to avert the wrath of God which was kindled against them, lest he should deal with them after their folly.*

We will close this chapter by the adduction of one other text of Scripture, which shows most clearly that animal sacrifices among the patriarchs were offered for the purpose of averting the Divine displeasure, and that this notion of sacrifice was entertained by the Israelites *previous* to the giving of the law. "Let us go, we pray thee, three days' journey into the desert, and sacrifice unto the Lord our God, *lest he fall upon us with pestilence or with the sword.*" Exod. v, 3. Here Moses and Aaron speak of sacrificing, not as a new and uncommon thing, but as a usual mode of worship, with which Pharaoh was as well acquainted as themselves.

CHAPTER III.

ATONEMENT: SACRIFICES OF THE LAW.

HAVING shown that the rite of animal sacrifice, as it was observed among the patriarchs, was a divinely-appointed institution; that it was based upon the promise of that Great Deliverer, "*the Seed of the woman;*" and that their offerings were expiatory in their character, we will proceed, in this chapter, to investigate the subject of atonement in the light which is afforded by the sacrifices of the law. This will lead us to consider those passages of Scripture in which the writers of the New Testament use the *sacrificial terms* of the Old with reference to the work of human redemption by our Lord Jesus Christ.

The sacrifices of the law were unquestionably of Divine origin; and as terms taken from them are so frequently applied in the New Testament to Christ and his sufferings, it is very evident that the apostles regarded his death as a *sacrifice of expiation*—as the *sin-offering* for the world. In order to present the argument in as clear a light as possible it will be necessary that we should consider the expiatory nature of the Jewish sacrifices, their typical character, and the manner in which sacrificial terms and allusions are employed in the New Testament to describe the nature and effect of the death of Christ.

I. THE LEVITICAL SACRIFICES WERE EXPIATORY.

It is not necessary to prove that all the Levitical offerings were of this character. It is enough to show that the grand and eminent sacrifices of the Jews were strictly expiatory, and that by them the offerers were released from punishment and death.

* Job xlii, 7, 8.

When we speak of vicarious sacrifices we do not mean either, on the one hand, a substitution which requires the victim to bear the same quantum of pain and suffering that the offender deserves, or, on the other, that the victim is put in the place of the offender as a mere symbolical act by which he confesses his desert of punishment; but a substitution made by Divine appointment, by which the victim is exposed to suffering and death instead of the offender, in virtue of which the offender himself is released. That the sacrifices of the law were thus vicarious and expiatory admits of abundant proof. This is established,

1. *By the general appointment of blood to be an atonement for the soul.*—Here we need do little more than refer to Lev. xvii, 10, 11: "I will even set my face against that soul that eateth blood, and will cut him off from among the people. For the life of the flesh is in the blood; and I have given it to you upon the altar, to make an atonement for YOUR SOULS; for it is the blood that maketh an atonement for THE SOUL." Here, to make an atonement for the soul is the same as to give a ransom for the soul, as will appear by a reference to Exod. xxx, 12; and to give a ransom for the soul is to avert death. "Then shall they give every man a ransom for his soul unto the Lord, that there be no *plague* among them," by which their life might be suddenly taken away. The soul is also here obviously used for the *life*. The blood, or the life of the victims, in all the sacrifices, was substituted for the life of man to preserve him from death, and the victims were therefore vicarious. This view of the subject is proved,

2. *By particular instances.*—Let us refer to Lev. v, 15, 16: "If a soul commit a trespass, and sin through ignorance, in the holy things of the Lord, he shall make amends for the harm that he hath done in the holy things, and shall add the fifth part thereto, and give it unto the priest." Here is the proper fine for the trespass; but then it is added, "he shall bring, for his trespass unto the Lord, a ram without blemish, and the priest shall make an atonement for him with the ram of the trespass-offering, and it shall be *forgiven* him." Thus, then, so far was the sacrifice from being a mere *fine*, as some have supposed, that the fine is distinguished from it; for with the ram only was the atonement made for the trespass.

Nor can the ceremonies with which the trespass and sin-offerings were accompanied agree with any notion but that of their vicarious character. The worshiper, conscious of his trespass, brought an animal, his own property, to the door of the tabernacle. He laid his hands upon its head, the symbolical act in the transfer of punishment, then slew it with his own hand and delivered it to the priest, who burnt the fat and part of the animal upon the altar; and having sprinkled part of the blood upon the altar, and, in some cases, upon the offerer himself, he poured the rest at the bottom of the altar. It is clearly made manifest by these actions, and by the description of their nature and end, that the animal bore the punishment of the offender, and that by this appointment he was reconciled to God and obtained the forgiveness of his offenses. But in proof that the life of animal sacrifices was accepted in place of the life of man, we may observe,

3. *That the law required a sacrificial atonement even for bodily disorders.*—All such unclean persons were liable to death, and were exempted from it only by animal sacrifices. This appears from the conclusion of the Levitical directions concerning the ceremonial which was to be followed in all cases: "Thus shall ye separate the children of Israel from their uncleanness, when they defile my tabernacle that is among them." Lev. xv, 31. So, then, by virtue of sin-offerings the children of Israel were saved from a *death* which otherwise they would have suffered for their uncleanness, and that by substituting the life of the animal for that of the offerer. As a further proof of the vicarious character of the principal sacrifices of the Mosaic economy, we may instance,

4. *Those which were statedly offered for the whole congregation.*— Two lambs were offered every day, one in the morning and the other in the evening, "for a continual burnt-offering." To these daily victims were added, weekly, two other lambs for the burnt-offering of the Sabbath. None of these could be considered in the light of fines for offenses, since they were offered for the whole congregation and not for particular persons. They must therefore be regarded, unless they are resolved into an unmeaning ceremony, as piacular and vicarious.

Passing over, however, the monthly sacrifices, and such as were offered at the great feasts, we will advert to those which were offered on the solemn anniversary of expiation, "to make an atonement for the children of Israel for all their sins." On this day of general expiation two goats were selected as a sin-offering for the people; one of them to be killed, and the other to be "presented alive before the Lord," as the "scape-goat." The high-priest was commanded to offer a bullock for himself, and to "take of the blood, and sprinkle it upon the mercy-seat;" to "kill the goat of the sin-offering for the people, and to do with that blood as he did with the blood of the bullock; to lay both his hands upon the head of the live goat, and confess over him all the iniquities of the children of Israel;" and to send the animal, thus bearing the sins of the people, away into the wilderness. Hence we see, by an action which cannot be misunderstood, that the *atonement* which was effected by the sin-offering consisted in removing from the people their iniquities by transferring them to the animal. We find another most explicit illustration of this doctrine,

5. *In the sacrifice of the* PASSOVER.*—This celebrated feast was instituted in commemoration of the deliverance of the Israelites, when the angel smote the first-born of Egypt, and clearly shows that the life of

* See Exod. xii.

the sinner was preserved by the death of the victim. The lamb was slain, and its blood sprinkled upon the posts of the doors; and wherever the blood was sprinkled the destroying angel passed over and spared the life of all within the house. Thus, by the blood of the slain lamb was human life preserved.

The chief objections made to the doctrine that the Levitical sacrifices were expiatory are, first, that under the law, in all capital cases, the offender, upon legal conviction, was doomed to die, and no sacrifice could exempt him from the penalty. Secondly, that in all lower cases, to which the law had not attached capital punishment, the penalty was to be regarded in the light of a pecuniary fine.

Much of this may be granted without any prejudice to the argument. The law under which the Jews were placed was at once as to them both a *moral* and a *political* law. For the order and benefit of society the Lawgiver required that blasphemy, idolatry, murder, and adultery should be punished with temporal death; and because this was the *state* penalty, he would accept no atonement for such transgressions. But running parallel with this political application of the law to the Jews as subjects of the theocracy, we see the authority of the *moral* law kept over them as moral creatures; and while a few of the more "presumptuous sins" were the only *capital* crimes considered politically, every transgression of the law was a capital crime considered morally, and would have subjected the offender to death but for this provision of expiatory obligations. The true question then is, whether such sacrifices were appointed by God, and accepted instead of the *life* of the offender, which otherwise would have been forfeited as in other cases; and if the life of animal sacrifices was accepted instead of the life of man, then the notion that they were pecuniary fines or penalties falls to the ground, and the *vicarious* nature of most of the Levitical oblations is established.

II. THE LEVITICAL SACRIFICES WERE ALSO TYPES OF A BETTER SACRIFICE.

A *type*, in a theological sense, is a sign or example prepared and designed by God to prefigure some future person or thing. It is required that it should represent this future object with more or less clearness, either by something which it has in common with the antitype, or in being the symbol of some property which it possesses; that it should be *prepared* and *designed* by GOD thus to represent its antitype, which circumstance distinguishes it from a simile and from a hieroglyphic; that it should give place to the antitype as soon as the latter appears; and that the efficacy of the antitype should exist in the type in appearance only, or in a lower degree.

The typical character of the Levitical dispensation and of many events in the Mosaic history, is clearly taught in the New Testament. Thus St. Paul calls the meats and drinks, the holy days and new moons, and the sabbaths of the Jews, including in them the *services* performed in the celebration of these festivals, "*a shadow* of things to come;" the "*body*" of which shadow, whose form the shadow generally and faintly exhibited, "is Christ."* Again, he declares that the Israelites all "drank of that spiritual rock that followed them, and that rock was Christ." And when speaking, in the same connection, of things which happened to them in the wilderness, he calls them "ensamples (τυποὶ) written for our admonition."†

In Hebrews x, 1, the apostle, when discoursing expressly upon the *sacrifices* of the tabernacle, calls them the "shadow (σκιαν) of good things to come," and places them in contrast with "the *very image* of the things" referred to. Now whether we take the word σκιὰ for the shadow of the body of man, or for a faint delineation or sketch, to be succeeded by a finished picture, it is clear that whatever the law was, it was by Divine appointment. And as there is a relation between the shadow and the body which produces it, and between the sketch or outline and the finished picture, so if, by Divine appointment, the law was this shadow of good things to come, which is what the apostle asserts, there was then an intended and typical relation of the former to the latter.

Of this *appointment* and *designation* of the tabernacle service to be a shadow of good things to come, the ninth chapter of Hebrews affords several direct and unequivocal declarations. So verse 7, 8 : "But into the second went the high priest alone once every year, not without blood, which he offered for himself and for the errors of the people; the HOLY GHOST thus SIGNIFYING (*showing, declaring by this type*) that the way into the holiest of all was not YET made manifest." Here we have the *declaration* of a doctrine by type, which is referred to the design and intention of the Holy Ghost himself at the time when the Levitical ritual was prescribed, and this typical declaration was to continue until the new dispensation should be introduced. In verse 9 the tabernacle itself is called a figure or parable? "Which was a figure (πάραβολὴ) for the time then present." It was a *parable* by which the evangelical and spiritual doctrines were taught. It was an *appointed* parable, because it was limited to a certain time; "*for the time then present*," that is, until the bringing in of the things signified, to which it had this *designed* relation. Again, verse 23, the things under the law are called "*patterns* (ὑπόδειγματα, *typical representations*) of things in the heavens ;" and in verse 24, "the holy places made with hands" are denominated "the figures of the true."

The sacrificial ceremonies, then, of the Levitical institute are clearly established to be typical, and to have all the characters of a type in the theological sense. They are represented by St. Paul, in the passages which have been under consideration, as adumbrative, as divinely designed and appointed to be so, as having respect to things future, to

* Col. ii, 17. † 1 Cor. x, 4, 11.

Christ and to his sacerdotal ministry, and as being inferior in efficacy to the antitypes which correspond to them; and they were all displaced by their antitypes, the Levitical ceremonies being repealed by the death and ascension of our Lord.

Having shown that the writers of the New Testament regarded the Jewish sacrifices as being both *expiatory* and *typical*, we will proceed to consider,

III. THE MANNER IN WHICH THEY EMPLOY SACRIFICIAL TERMS AND ALLUSIONS TO DESCRIBE THE NATURE AND EFFECT OF THE DEATH OF CHRIST.

He is called "the LAMB OF GOD;" not with reference to his meekness, or any other moral virtue; but with an accompanying phrase which would communicate to a Jew the full sacrificial sense of the terms employed: "the Lamb of God which TAKETH AWAY the sin of the world." He is called "our PASSOVER SACRIFICED for us." He is said to have given "himself for us, an OFFERING and a SACRIFICE to God for a sweet-smelling savor;" and to have "put away sin by the SACRIFICE OF HIMSELF." To these and many other similar expressions and allusions we may add the argument of St. Paul in his epistle to the Hebrews; in which, by proving at length that the sacrifice of Christ was superior in efficacy to those of the law, he most unequivocally assumes that it was a sacrifice for sin. For if it had no sacrificial character it would no more have been capable of comparison with the Jewish sacrifices than the death of John the Baptist, or of any other martyr for the truth.

Now, as the offering of the animal sacrifices took away sin, that is, obtained remission for offenses against the law, we can be at no loss to know what the Baptist meant when he exclaimed, "Behold the Lamb of God, which *taketh away* the sin of the world!" As there was a transfer of suffering and death from the offender to the legally clean and sound victim, so Christ died, "the *just* for the unjust." As the animal sacrifices were expiatory, so Christ is our ιλασμος, propitiation or expiation; and as by the Levitical oblations men were *reconciled* to GOD, so we, when enemies, "were *reconciled* to God by the death of his Son." As under the law there was no remission without the shedding of blood, so as to Christ we are "justified by his blood," and "have redemption through his blood, the forgiveness of sins." As by the blood of the appointed sacrifices "the holy places made with hands" were made accessible to the Jewish worshipers, that blood being carried into them and sprinkled by the high-priest; so Christ, "by his own blood, entered into the holy place, having obtained eternal redemption for us," and having thus opened up for us a "new and living way" into the celestial sanctuary. As the blood of the Mosaic oblations was the blood of the *Old* Testament, so Christ calls his blood the "blood of the *New* Testament, shed for the remission of sins." And as it was a part of the sacrificial solemnity, in some instances at least, to feast upon the offered victim, so with direct reference to this our Lord declared, "Whoso eateth my flesh and drinketh my blood hath eternal life; for my flesh is meat INDEED, and my blood is drink INDEED;" that is, my flesh and blood are in *truth* and *reality* what the flesh and blood of the Jewish victims were in *type*.

St. Paul, in concluding a discourse upon our reconciliation to GOD, lays it down as the general principle upon which that reconciliation is to be explained and enforced, that Christ, "who knew no sin," was "made to be sin for us; that we might be made the righteousness of God in him." 2 Cor. v, 21. Here, then, the question is, In what sense was Christ MADE SIN for us? Not, certainly, as to the *guilt* of it, for he "knew no sin;" but as to the *expiation* of it by his personal sufferings, by which he delivers the guilty from punishment. He was, therefore, made a *sin-offering* for us.

Again, "Christ also hath loved us, and hath given himself for us, an *offering* and a *sacrifice to God* for a sweet-smelling savor." Eph. v, 2. Here the object of the apostle is, in the first place, to impress the Ephesians with a deep sense of the love of Christ. He "hath LOVED us, and hath *given himself for us.*" He then explains the mode in which Christ gave himself *for* us, that is, by suffering in our room and stead. He was made "an OFFERING and a SACRIFICE to God, for a sweet-smelling savor." Thus the apostle applies to the sacrificial death of our Lord the very terms which are applied to the Jewish sacrifices.

The Socinian pretense is, that the inspired penman used the sacrificial terms which occur in their writings in a figurative sense. We reply, however, that they could not do this honestly without giving notice of this new application of the established terms of Jewish theology. But the apostles have given us no intimation that they applied these terms to the death of Christ in any strange or altered sense. We must therefore conclude that, as honest men, they must have employed them in their true sacrificial import; and, consequently, that they intended to represent the death of our Lord as a *sacrifice for sin*. If this was not their intention, nothing could be more misleading than their employment of those terms and phrases in connection with that event; because such would be the natural and necessary inference from the terms themselves, which had acquired this as their established meaning.

If we assume that the sacred writers used these sacrificial terms and allusions, as applied to Christ, in a figurative sense, then it will necessarily follow that their writings leave us wholly at a loss to discover what they really intended to teach by them. As to this they are themselves utterly silent; and the varying theories of those who reject the doctrine of atonement afford no solution of the difficulty. If, therefore, it is blasphemous to suppose, on the one hand, that inspired men should write on purpose to mislead, so, on the other, it is utterly inconceivable, had they been only ordinary writers, that they should construct a figurative language out of terms which had a definite and established sense, without giving any intimation that they employed them otherwise than in their received meaning; and more especially when they knew that they must be interpreted, both by Jews and Greeks, in a sense which, if the Socinians are right, is in direct opposition to what they intended to convey.

We conclude, therefore, that the sacrificial terms, which the inspired writers apply to the death of Christ, are used *properly* and must be understood *literally*. For, what was an expiatory sacrifice under the law but the offering of the life of an innocent creature in the place of the guilty, and that in order to obtain for the latter exemption from death? And was not the death of Christ as literally an offering of himself, "the just for the unjust," that "we might not perish?" The legal sin-offerings cleansed the body, and qualified men for the ceremonial worship prescribed by the law; and the blood of Christ as truly purifies the conscience, and consecrates men to that spiritual service which the Gospel requires. Indeed, "the offering of the body of Jesus Christ once for all" is the only *true* sacrifice, of which the Levitical sacrifices were but the appointed types, and by which they are to be interpreted.

CHAPTER IV.

ATONEMENT: DEATH OF CHRIST PROPITIATORY.

FROM what has been said in regard to the patriarchal and the Jewish sacrifices we pass to consider the doctrine of atonement as it is set forth in the Scriptures of the New Testament, and to establish the propitiatory character of the death of our Lord Jesus Christ. In the prosecution of our design we will endeavor to prove that our salvation is everywhere ascribed to this grand event, that his death was *necessary* to our salvation, and that he died in our room and stead as a proper substitute for us.

I. OUR SALVATION IS EVERYWHERE ASCRIBED TO THE DEATH OF CHRIST.

This fact must be evident even to the most superficial reader of the New Testament. Christ himself declares, "I lay down my *life* for the sheep." St. Paul tells us that he "*gave himself* for us;" that "Christ was once *offered* to bear the sins of many;" and that "while we were yet sinners Christ *died* for us." So also the song of the redeemed in heaven is, "Unto him that loved us, and washed us from our sins in his *own blood.*" In these and many other passages the entire salvation of man is clearly ascribed to the sacrificial death of our Lord.

This doctrine of the holy Scriptures must, in some way or other, be accounted for and explained. The Socinian attempts to account for it by making the death of Christ the *means by which repentance is produced in man*, so as to make it morally fit that he should be forgiven. The modern Arian connects with this notion that kind of *merit* in the death of Christ which arises from a generous and benevolent self-devotion; and which, when pleaded by him in the way of mediation, God is pleased to honor, by accepting true repentance in place of perfect obedience. But to prove the falsity of both these theories it is only requisite to show,

II. THAT THE DEATH OF CHRIST WAS NECESSARY TO MAN'S SALVATION.

This principle is wholly excluded both by the Socinian and the Arian hypotheses. By the former, the reason for pardon is placed in repentance alone; by the latter, in the right which God has to pardon the penitent, but which he chooses to exercise in honor of the philanthropy of Jesus Christ. Both make the death of Christ, though in a different way and in a very subordinate sense, the means of obtaining forgiveness, because it is the means of bringing men into that state in which they are fit objects of pardon. But the Scripture doctrine is, that the death of Christ is not merely the meritorious *means*, but the meritorious *cause* of the exercise of pardon; and that repentance is only one of the instrumental means of actually obtaining it. In accordance with this view the Scriptures speak of the death of Christ, not as one of many means by which the same end might have been accomplished, but as *necessary*, in the strictest sense, to the salvation of man. This has been considered, even by some divines professing orthodoxy, to be a bold position; but its truthfulness may be argued,

1. *From the Divine character of our Lord.*—It follows, of course, from the Socinian or the Arian hypothesis, that if he were a created being, and if he were the mere messenger of a mercy which might be exercised on prerogative, and not the procuring cause of it, any other creature might have accomplished the work which he came to perform. But when it is admitted that Christ is the Divine Son of God; that he was "God manifest in the flesh;" that the forgiveness of sin required a satisfaction to Divine justice of no less value than the sufferings and death of the incarnate Deity; even from such premises alone it would seem necessarily to follow that sin could not have been forgiven but for the interposition of Christ, unless some other sacrifice of equal merit could have been found. But if no such being existed out of the Godhead, then human hope rested solely on the voluntary incarnation of the Son of God, and the overwhelming fact and mystery of his becoming flesh in order to suffer for us shows that the case to be reme-

died was one of a character absolutely extreme, and, therefore, not otherwise remediable. But this matter is put beyond all reasonable doubt,

2. *By the testimony of Scripture.*—" From that time forth began Jesus to show unto his disciples, how that he *must* go unto Jerusalem and *suffer many things* of the elders and chief priests and scribes, and *be killed*, and *be raised* again the third day." Matt. xvi, 21. "Thus it is written, and thus it *behoved* Christ to *suffer* and to rise from the dead the third day." Luke xxiv, 46. Here a *necessity* for the death of Christ is plainly expressed. If it be said that this event was necessary in order to the fulfillment of prophecy, it is only to be remembered that what was predicted on this subject arose out of a previous appointment of God, in whose eternal counsel Christ had been designated as the Redeemer of man. The necessity of this death, then, rested on Divine appointment, and that on the necessity of the case ; and if it was *necessary* for him to die in order that we might live, then we live only in consequence of his death.

The same view is conveyed in a strongly figurative passage from the teachings of our Lord. " Verily, verily, I say unto you, Except a corn of wheat fall into the ground and die, it abideth alone ; but if it die, it bringeth forth much fruit." John xii, 24. From this it inevitably follows, that the death of Christ was as necessary to human salvation as is that change in the sown wheat which is here called dying in order to the production of the harvest. It was so necessary that without it man could not have been saved. Had Christ not died he would have remained " alone," and have brought "no sons to glory." Moreover, the Scriptures teach the doctrine,

III. THAT CHRIST DIED IN OUR ROOM AND STEAD, *or*, AS A PROPER SUBSTITUTE FOR US.

The Socinian scheme makes the death of Christ only an incidental benefit, as sealing the truth of his doctrine, and setting an example of eminent passive virtue. In this sense they acknowledge that he died for men, because in this indirect manner they derive from his death the benefit of instruction, and because some of the motives to virtue are thereby placed in a stronger light.

The modern Arian scheme, sometimes called the *intercession* hypothesis, acknowledges that our Lord acquired by his disinterested and generous sufferings the highest degree of virtue and a powerful interest with God, on account of which his intercession on behalf of penitent sinners is honored by an exercise of higher mercy than would otherwise have taken place. But it by no means follows from this that repentance might not otherwise have taken place, and that mercy might not otherwise have been exercised. According to this view, then, Christ died for the benefit of men somewhat more directly than on the Socinian scheme ; but he did not die in their room and stead. His death was not vicarious, and it is not on that account *directly* that the guilty are absolved from condemnation.

To prove, however, that the death of Christ was vicarious, that he died as a proper substitute for us and in our room and stead, the testimony of the sacred writers must be adduced. This doctrine may be argued,

1. *From all those passages which declare that he died* FOR *men*.—Christ asserts that he came "to give his life a ransom *for* many." Matt. xx, 28. St. Paul tells us that "Christ died *for* the ungodly," Rom. v, 6; that "he died *for* all," 2 Cor. v, 15; that he "gave himself a ransom *for* all," 1 Tim. ii, 6; and that he tasted "death *for* every man," Heb. ii, 9. St. Peter declares that he died, "the just *for* the unjust," and that "he suffered *for* us."

To this argument it has been objected that the Greek prepositions ὑπὲρ and αντὶ, which are rendered *for* in the above quotations, do not always signify substitution, but are sometimes to be rendered *on account of;* as when it is said that "Christ died for our sins," which cannot mean *instead of* our sins. All this may be granted, but it is nevertheless certain that there are numerous texts of Scripture in which these particles can only be interpreted when taken to mean "instead of," or "in the place of." When Caiaphas said, (John xi, 50,) "It is expedient that one man should die (ὑπὲρ) *for* the people, and that the whole nation perish not," he plainly taught that either Christ or the nation must perish; and that to put the former to death would be to cause him to perish *instead of* the latter. In Rom. v, 6-8, the sense in which "Christ dies *for* us" is indubitably fixed by the context. "For scarcely for a righteous man will one die, yet peradventure for a good man some would even dare to die; but God commendeth his love toward us in that while we were yet sinners, Christ died *for* us." But who can imagine that any one would die for a good man unless it were to redeem his life by giving up his own?

In this sense, also, αντὶ is used by the LXX, 2 Sam. xviii, 33, where David says concerning Absalom, "would God I had died (αντι σου) for thee." Here he evidently expresses the wish that he had died *instead of* his son. In this sense, too, αντὶ is frequently used in the New Testament; as, "Archelaus did reign in Judea (αντὶ) *in the room of* his father Herod." Matt. ii, 22. "If he ask a fish, will he (αντὶ) for a fish," in place or instead of a fish, "give him a serpent?" Luke xi, 11. When, therefore, the same preposition is employed, (Mark x, 45,) "The Son of man came to give his life a ransom (αντὶ) for many," there can surely be no reason drawn from the meaning of the preposition itself to prevent its being understood in the sense of substitution. But, that Christ died for us directly as a *substitute* is fully proved,

2. *By those Scriptures in which he is said to have borne the punishment due to our offenses*.—It is thus that he is said to have borne our

sins. "Who his own self bare our sins in his own body on the tree." 1 Pet. ii, 24. Here the apostle evidently quotes from Isa. liii, 11, 12: "He shall bear their iniquities,"—"he bare the sin of many." The same expression is used by St. Paul, Heb. ix, 28: "So Christ was once offered to bear the sins of many." Now, to bear sin is, in the language of Scripture, to bear the punishment of sin;* and the use of the compound verb αναφέρω by both the apostles is worthy of notice. St. Peter might have said, simply, ἤνεγκε, *he bore;* but wishing at the same time to signify the *manner* in which Christ bore our sins, he said, ἀνήνεγκε, *he bore up*, meaning, he bore by going up to the cross. St. Paul, too, uses the same verb both with reference to the Levitical sacrifices, which were carried to an elevated altar, and to the sacrifice of Christ. It is also decisive as to the sense in which St. Peter uses the phrase, *to bare sin*, that he quotes from Isa. liii, 11, "He shall bear their iniquities;" where the Hebrew word סבל means, to bear or sustain a burden, and is evidently employed in the sense of bearing the punishment of sin. This may be seen in Lam. v, 7: "Our fathers have sinned, and are not; and (סבלנו) WE HAVE BORNE *their iniquities.*"

Similar to this expression of bearing sins is the declaration of Isaiah in the same chapter: "He was wounded for our transgressions, he was bruised for our iniquities;" and then, to show in what sense he was wounded and bruised *for us*, the prophet adds, "the chastisement of our peace was upon him, and with his stripes we are healed." Now, chastisement is the punishment of a fault; but the sufferer of whom the prophet speaks is wholly free from transgression. He is perfectly and emphatically innocent. This prophecy is applied to Christ by the apostles, whose constant doctrine is the entire immaculateness of their Lord. If "chastisement," therefore, was laid upon him, it could not have been on account of his own faults. His sufferings were the chastisement of *our* faults, the price of *our* peace; and his "stripes," another punitive expression, were borne by him that we might be "healed." These passages, therefore, prove *a substitution—a suffering in our stead.*

The same view is presented to us under another and even still more forcible phrase in the sixth and the seventh verse of the same chapter: "All we like sheep have gone astray; we have turned every one to his own way, and the Lord hath laid on him the iniquity of us all. He was oppressed, and he was afflicted." Bishop Lowth translates this passage, "and Jehovah hath made to light upon him the iniquity of us all; it was exacted, and he was made answerable."

In 2 Cor. v, 21, the apostle uses almost the same language: "For he hath made him to be sin for us, who knew no sin; that we might be made the righteousness of God in him." Here St. Paul places "sin" and "righteousness" in opposition to each other. We are "made the righteousness of God," that is, we are justified and freed from the pen-

* See Lev. xxii, 9; Ezek. xviii, 20.

alty of the law; but, in order to this, Christ was "made sin for us," or bore our punishment. There is another antithesis in the apostle's words. God made him who *knew no sin*, and consequently deserved no punishment, to be sin for *us*, who are really guilty; that is, it pleased the Father that the innocent Redeemer should suffer for guilty man. The antithesis, therefore, requires us to understand that Christ bore the penalty of the law in our room and stead.

That the death of Christ was *penal*, which implies that he took our place and suffered in our stead, is evident also from Gal. iii, 13: " Christ hath redeemed us from the curse of the law, being made a curse for us; for it is written, Cursed is every one that hangeth on a tree." Here the apostle, in order to prove that Christ was made obnoxious to penal suffering, cites the language of Moses, who expressly assents that he who is hanged on a tree, according to the Divine law, "is accursed of God."* Consequently, in the words of the apostle, who quotes the language of Moses and refers it to Christ, we must supply the same circumstance, "accursed of God." The meaning, then, is, that Christ was made "accursed of God;" or, in other words, was made obnoxious to the highest and most ignominious punishment "*for us.*" But the vicarious and sacrificial character of the death of Christ is still further established,

3. *By those Scriptures which connect with it propitiation, redemption, reconciliation, and the making of peace between God and man.*—The Scriptures represent the death of our Lord,

(1.) As a *propitiation.*—To *propitiate* is to appease, to atone, to turn away the wrath of an offended person. In the case before us the wrath turned away is the wrath of God, the person making the propitiation is Christ, and the propitiatory sacrifice is his blood. All this is expressed, in most explicit terms, in the following passages: " Whom God hath set forth to be a *propitiation* through faith *in his blood.*" Rom. iii, 25. " He is the propitiation for our sins." 1 John ii, 2. " God sent his Son to be the *propitiation* for our sins." 1 John iv, 10. The word which is rendered propitiation in the first passage is ἱλαστήριον, in the two latter, ἱλασμός. Both are from the verb ἱλάσκω, a word often used by Greek writers to express the action of a person who, in some appointed way, turned aside the wrath of a deity. It cannot, therefore, bear the sense which Socinus would put upon it, " the destruction of sin;" which is not supported by a single example.

Modern Socinians have conceded, in their note on 1 John ii, 2, in their Improved Version, that ἱλασμός means "the pacifying of an offended party;" but they subjoin that Christ is a propitiation, because " by his Gospel he brings sinners to repentance, and thus averts the Divine displeasure." The concession is important, but the comment is absurd; for in this sense Moses, or any of the apostles, or any minister of the

* Deut. xxi, 22, 23.

Gospel who succeeds in bringing sinners to repentance, is as truly a propitiation for sin as Christ himself.

The authors of the Improved Version translate ιλαστήριον, in Rom. iii, 25, by the phrase "*mercy-seat*," supposing that this rendering removes that countenance to the doctrine of atonement by vicarious suffering which the common translation affords. It is true ιλαστήριον is used in the Septuagint Version, and in the Epistle to the Hebrews, to denote the mercy-seat or covering of the ark; but so little is to be gained by taking the word in this sense in the passage before us that this rendering is adopted by several orthodox commentators as expressing, in a very emphatic manner, by supplying a type to the antitype, the doctrine of our Lord's atonement.

The *mercy-seat* was so called because, under the Old Testament dispensation, it was the place where the high-priest on the feast of expiation sprinkled the blood of the sin-offerings, in order to make an atonement for himself and the whole congregation; and since God accepted the offering which was then made, it is for this reason accounted the medium through which he showed himself propitious to the people. With reference to this Jesus Christ may be fitly called a *mercy-seat*, as being the person through whom God shows himself propitious to mankind. And as under the law God was propitious to those who came to him by appearing before his mercy-seat with the blood of their sin-offerings, so, under the Gospel dispensation, he is propitious to those who come to him through faith in that blood which Jesus shed for the remission of sins. The text, therefore, points us to the *blood of Christ* as the only means of obtaining mercy. "Without shedding of blood is no remission." Heb. ix, 22.

Socinians, in the hope of proving that propitiation in the *proper sense* cannot be the doctrine of the Scriptures, deny the existence of *wrath* in God. In order to give plausibility to their statement they pervert and caricature the orthodox opinion, and argue, as though it formed a part of the doctrine of Christ's propitiation for sin, that God is naturally an implacable and vengeful being, and only disposed to show mercy by satisfaction being made to his displeasure through our Lord's sufferings and death. This is as contrary to Scripture as it is to the opinion of all sober persons who hold the doctrine of Christ's atonement. God is *love;* but it is not necessary in order to support this truth to assume that he is nothing else. He has, as we have seen, other attributes which harmonize with this and with each other; though, assuredly, that harmony cannot be exhibited by any who deny the propitiation for sin made by the death of Christ. Their system, therefore, obliges them to deny the existence of some of the attributes of God, or to explain them away.

The question is not whether God is love, or whether he is of a placable nature, for in this we are agreed; but we are to inquire whether

God is *holy* and *just;* whether we, his creatures, are *under law;* whether this law has any *penalty;* and whether God in his rectoral character is bound to *execute* that law. These are points which have already been established; and as the justice of God is punitive, then is there *wrath* in God; then is God *angry* with the wicked; then is man, as a sinner, obnoxious to this *anger;* and so a propitiation becomes necessary to turn it away from him.

Nor is it unscriptural to ascribe wrath to God. John the Baptist declares that "the *wrath of God* abideth on him" who "believeth not the Son;" and St. Paul, that "the *wrath of God* is revealed from heaven against all ungodliness and unrighteousness of men." So the day of judgment is, with reference to the ungodly, called "the day of *wrath*." It is evident, then, that to deny the existence of wrath in God is to deny the Scriptures. In holding this doctrine, however, we do not ascribe to the Divine Being *vengeful affections.* We only mean by the "wrath of God" that awful attribute of his justice which requires the punishment of the guilty, or satisfaction in order to their forgiveness. To the passages in which Christ is called a propitiation we add,

(2.) Those which ascribe to him our *redemption,* either by employing that word itself or others of the same import. "Being justified freely by his grace, through the *redemption* that is in Christ Jesus." Rom. iii, 24. "Christ hath *redeemed* us from the curse of the law, being made a curse for us." Gal. iii, 13. "In whom we have *redemption* through his blood." Eph. i, 7. "Ye were not *redeemed* with corruptible things, as silver and gold, . . . but with the precious blood of Christ." 1 Peter i, 18, 19. "And ye are not your own, for ye are *bought* with a price." 1 Cor. vi, 19, 20.

By redemption, those who deny the atonement made by Christ wish to understand *deliverance* merely, regarding only the effect, and studiously putting out of sight the cause from which it flows. But the very terms used in the above cited passages, to "*redeem,*" and to be "*bought* with a price,*"* will be found to refute the notion of a gratuitous deliverance, whether from sin or punishment, or both.

Our English word *redeem* literally means to buy back; and $\lambda \acute{v} \tau \rho o \omega$, to *redeem,* and $\alpha \pi o \lambda \acute{v} \tau \rho \omega \sigma \iota \varsigma$, *redemption,* are, both by ancient Greek writers and in the New Testament, used for the act of setting free a captive by paying $\lambda \acute{v} \tau \rho o \nu$, a ransom or redemption price. They signify, moreover, deliverance from exile, death, and every other evil from which we may be freed; and $\lambda \acute{v} \tau \rho o \nu$ signifies whatever satisfies another so as to effect this deliverance.

The nature of this redemption or purchased deliverance is therefore to be ascertained by the circumstances of those who are the subjects of it. In the case before us the subjects are sinful men. They are under guilt, under "the curse of the law," under the power and dominion of the devil, liable to death of the body and to death eternal. To the whole of this case the purchased deliverance of man as proclaimed in the Gospel applies itself. Hence, in opposition to guilt, we are "justified freely through the redemption that is in Jesus Christ." We have redemption "from the curse of the law," through him who was "made a curse for us;" from the power of Satan, by him who came "to destroy the works of the devil;" from death, by a resurrection; and from future wrath, by the gift of eternal life.

Throughout the whole of this glorious scheme of human redemption, as taught in the New Testament, there is a constant reference to the λύτρον, the *redemption price*, which is as constantly declared to be the death of Christ, which he endured in our stead. He gave "his life a *ransom* (λύτρον) for many." "We have redemption (την απολύτρωσιν) through his *blood*." He "gave himself a *ransom* (αντίλυτρον) for all." Our redemption by Christ is not, therefore, a gratuitous deliverance granted without consideration, as an act of mere prerogative; the redemption price was exacted and paid; one thing was given for another—the precious blood of Christ for captive and condemned men.

Of the same import are those passages which represent us as being "*bought*," or *purchased* by Christ. St. Peter speaks of those who denied "the Lord that *bought* them." St. Paul says, "Ye are *bought* with a *price;*" which price is expressly said by St. John (Rev. v, 9) to be the blood of Christ: "Thou wast slain, and hast redeemed us to God by thy *blood*." But we may add,

(3.) That the Scriptures speak of *reconciliation and the establishment of peace between God and man* as the design and direct effect of Christ's death.—Thus: "We are *reconciled* to God by the death of his Son." Rom. v, 10. God "hath *reconciled* us to himself by Jesus Christ." 2 Cor. v, 18. "Having made *peace* through the blood of his cross, by him to *reconcile* all things unto himself." Col. i, 20. "That he might *reconcile* both unto God in one body by the cross, having slain the enmity thereby." Eph. ii, 16. The verbs καταλλάσσω and αποκαταλλάσσω, translated to *reconcile*, denote a change from one state to another; but in these passages they signify a change from enmity to friendship—a reconciliation. In Romans v, 11, the noun καταλλαγὴ is rendered *atonement;* but it is contended that it ought to have been rendered *reconciliation*, unless we take the word atonement in the sense of *being at one*, which is its primitive meaning. It was surely not in this sense, however, that the word was used by our translators, but in that of *propitiation*, in its proper and sacrificial import. But to render καταλλαγὴ *reconciliation* is most agreeable to the context; for in the preceding verse it is said that "we were reconciled to God by the death of his Son," which death, as we have seen, is in other passages of Scripture called a "propitiation." The reconciliation, therefore, of which the apostle speaks is only through the sacrificial death of Christ.

The expressions "reconciliation" and "making peace," necessarily imply a previous state of mutual hostility between God and man. This is sometimes called *enmity*, a term which is rather inappropriate as it respects God, since it is almost exclusively employed to signify a malignant and revengeful feeling. Hence some have argued that as there can be no such affection in the Divine nature, therefore reconciliation in Scripture does not mean the reconciliation of God to man, but only of man to God. It is, indeed, a sad and humbling truth, that human nature is malignantly hostile to God, and to the control of his law; but this is far from expressing the whole of that relation of man to God which requires a reconciliation. The relation is a legal one; for God is to be regarded as a sovereign in his judicial capacity, and man as a criminal who has violated his law and who is therefore treated as an enemy. It is this judicial variance and opposition between God and man which is referred to in the term "reconciliation," and in the phrase "making peace;" and the hostility is, therefore, in its own nature *mutual*.

Hence it follows that reconciliation means more than the laying aside of our enmity to God. This is evident from Rom. v, 10, where the apostle shows that "when we were *enemies* we were *reconciled* to God by the death of his Son," that is, when we were objects of Divine judicial displeasure, accounted as enemies, and liable to be treated as such.

Again, "God was in Christ reconciling the world unto himself, not imputing their trespasses unto them." 2 Cor. v, 19. The act of reconciling is here ascribed to God and not to us; but if reconciliation consisted in the laying aside of our own enmity, the act would be ours alone. Moreover, this reconciliation is effected, not by our laying aside our enmity, but by the non-imputation of our trespasses to us by God, or by his becoming propitious to us through Jesus Christ. This previous reconciliation of the world to God by the death of his Son is clearly distinguished by the apostle from our actual reconciliation; for in virtue of it "the word of reconciliation" is proclaimed to the guilty, who are thus entreated to be "reconciled to God."

The same doctrine is taught in Eph. ii, 16: "That he might reconcile both unto God in one body by the cross, having slain the enmity thereby." Here the act of reconciling is attributed to Christ. Man is not spoken of as reconciling himself to God, but Christ is said to reconcile Jews and Gentiles together, and both to God "by his cross." Thus, says the apostle, "he is our peace;" but in what manner is this peace effected? Not, in the first instance, by subduing the enmity of man's heart, but by removing the enmity of "the law." "Having abolished in his flesh the enmity, even the *law of commandments*." The ceremonial law only is here meant; for by its abolition through its fulfillment in Christ the enmity between Jews and Gentiles was taken away. It was necessary, however, not only to reconcile Jews and Gentiles together, but to "reconcile both unto God."

The above passages will show how falsely it has been asserted that the Scriptures nowhere represent God as being reconciled to us. The fact is, that the very phrase, *our being reconciled to God*, imports the turning away of his wrath from us. " If thou bring thy gift to the altar, and there rememberest that thy brother hath aught *against thee*," not that *thou* hast aught against thy *brother*, "first be reconciled to thy brother;" that is, appease and conciliate him; so that the words, in fact, import, *see that thy brother be reconciled to thee*, since that which goes before is not that he has done thee an injury, but thou him.

Thus, then, for us to be reconciled to God is to avail ourselves of the means by which his anger toward us is to be appeased, which the New Testament expressly declares to be generally the *sin-offering* of him "who knew no sin," and instrumentally, as to each individual personally, "faith in his blood." But the propitiatory character of the death of Christ is still further explained in the New Testament,

4. *By the manner in which it connects our justification with "faith in his blood," and both our justification and the death of Christ as its meritorious cause, with the* RIGHTEOUSNESS OF GOD.—The justification of man is an act of the highest grace—a manifestation of the ineffable love of GOD, and is at the same time a strictly RIGHTEOUS proceeding. These views, scattered throughout the books of the New Testament, are summed up in the following explicit language of St. Paul, Rom. iii, 24–26 : " Being justified freely by his grace, through the redemption that is in Jesus Christ; whom God hath set forth to be a propitiation through faith in his blood, to declare his *righteousness* for the remission of sins that are past, through the forbearance of God; to declare, I say, at this time, his *righteousness ;* that he might be *just,* and the justifier of him which believeth in Jesus."

The argument of the apostle is exceedingly lucid. He treats of man's justification before God, of which he mentions two methods. The first is by our own obedience to the law of God. This method of justification he proves to be impossible to man, laying it down as an incontrovertible maxim that "by the deeds of the law there shall no flesh be justified." The other method is justification by the grace of God, as a "free gift," but coming to us through the interposition of the death of Christ as our redemption price and received instrumentally by faith in him.

But the apostle shows, moreover, that while this method of justification displays the grace and mercy of God, it also vindicates his *justice*. Christ is "set forth to be a propitiation," that God "might be *just*, and the justifier of him which believeth in Jesus." Similar language is also used by St. John: "He is faithful and *just* to forgive us our sins." 1 John i, 9. Thus the grand doctrine of Christianity is unequivocally stated by both apostles to be that, according to its constitution, the forgiveness of sin is at once an act of *mercy* and of *justice*, or of strictly righteous government. Nor is it difficult to see how the doctrine of pardon through the propitiatory sacrifice of Christ declares the righteousness of God. For,

(1.) *The law, the rule of the Divine government, is by this means established in its authority and perpetuity.*—For the Christian doctrine of atonement is, that sin cannot go unpunished under the Divine administration. But the hypothesis which rejects the doctrine of atonement repeals the law by granting impunity to transgressors; for if punishment does not follow offense, or if no other term of pardon is required than one which the culprit has it always in his power to offer, then is the law, as to its authority, virtually repealed, and the Divine government over rebellious creatures annihilated.

(2.) This doctrine declares that *God is a holy and righteous being— a strict and exact governor.*—On any other theory there is no manifestation of God's hatred of sin, answering to all that intense holiness of his nature which must lead him to abhor it, and no proof of his rectoral justice as governor of the moral world.

(3.) The doctrine which connects the pardon of the guilty with the meritorious death of Christ *illustrates the attributes of Divine justice* by the very act of connecting and blending it with the attribute of *love*, and the exercise of an effectual compassion. While it guards with so much care the doctrine of non-impunity to sin, it offers impunity to sinners; but the medium through which this offer is made serves to heighten the impression of God's hatred of sin. The person appointed to suffer the penalty of the law for us was the Father's "only begotten Son." In him divinity and humanity were united in one person, so that he was "God manifest in the flesh," assuming our nature in order that he might offer it in death, a sacrifice to GOD. If this was *necessary*, and we have proved that it was, then is sin declared, by the strongest possible demonstration, to be an evil of immeasurable extent; and the justice of GOD is, by a demonstration of equal force, declared to be inflexible and inviolable. God "spared not his own Son, but delivered him up for us all."

(4.) It is further to be considered that though by the death of Christ all men antecedent to their repentance and faith are put into a salvable state, *yet none of them are*, by this act of Christ, *brought from under the authority of the moral law.* This remains in its full and original force; and as all continue under the original obligation of obedience, those who neglect the great salvation offered to them by Christ fall under the full original penalty of the law, and are left to its malediction without obstruction to the exercise of Divine justice. Nor with respect to those who are justified by faith in Christ is there any repeal, or even relaxation of the law of God. The end of justification is not to set men free from law, but from punishment. It follows, therefore, that in the doctrine of the atonement of Christ the authority of the Divine law is established, the rectoral justice of God is manifested, and the strictness of a righteous government is united with the exercise of mercy.

These views respecting the propitiatory character of the death of Christ will enable us to attach an explicit meaning to the theological phrase, "*satisfaction made to Divine justice,*" by which the *nature* of the atonement is often expressed. This is not a phrase of Holy Writ; but it is not, on this account, to be disregarded, since, like many other theological terms and phrases, it has been found useful as a guard against subtle evasions of the doctrine of Scripture, and in giving explicitness, not indeed to the language of inspiration, but to the *sense* in which that language is interpreted.

The term *satisfaction* is taken from the Roman law, and signifies *to content a person aggrieved*, by doing or offering something which procures liberation from the obligation of debts or the penalties of offenses, not *ipso facto*, but by the will of the aggrieved party admitting the substitution. It is from this use of the term that it has been adopted into theology; and, however its meaning may have been heightened or lowered by the advocates of different systems, it simply indicates the contentment of the injured party by whatever he may choose to accept in place of the enforcement of his obligation upon the party indebted or offending. Accordingly, we call the death of Christ a satisfaction made to Divine justice for the transgressions of men with reference to its *effect upon the mind of the Supreme Lawgiver.* As a *just Governor,* he is *satisfied* with the atonement made by the vicarious death of his Son; and being disposed from the goodness of his nature to show mercy to the guilty, he can now do it consistent with the rectitude of his character and with the authority of his laws.

There are other phrases, such as "a full equivalent," and "an adequate compensation," which theologians have often employed in connection with this subject, and to which, when soberly interpreted, there can be no reasonable objection. "A full equivalent" is something equal in value, or of equal force and power to something else; but here the phrase is to be understood in a *judicial sense*. The meaning is, that the death of Christ for sinners as a means of a righteous government was determined in the infallible judgment of God to be a demonstration of his justice, fully equal to the personal and extreme punishment of offenders themselves.

So, also, as to the term "compensation," which signifies the weighing of one thing against another, the making of amends. If this be interpreted as the former, *judicially*, the death of Christ for sinners is an adequate compensation for their personal punishment in the estimation of Divine justice; because it is, at least, an equally powerful demonstration of the righteousness of God, who only in consideration of that atonement forgives the sins of offending men.

It is objected by those who oppose the doctrine of atonement, that it is unjust to lay the punishment of the guilty upon the innocent. The objection resolves itself into an inquiry how far such benevolent interpositions of one person for another, as involve sacrifice and suffering, may go, without violating justice; and when the subject is followed in this direction it will be found that the objection is of no weight.

It has always been regarded a virtue for men to endure inconveniences, to encounter danger, and even to suffer, in certain circumstances, for the sake of others. Parents and friends not only endure labor and make sacrifices for their children and connections, but often submit to positive pain in accomplishing that to which their affection prompts them. To save a fellow-creature from perishing by water or fire, men of generous minds often expose themselves to great personal risk of life, and even sometimes perish in the attempt; yet the claims of humanity are considered sufficient to justify such deeds, which are never blamed, but always applauded.

No man's life, we grant, is at his own disposal; but in all cases where it is agreed that God has left men at liberty to offer their life for the benefit of others, no one questions the justice of their doing it. Thus, when a patriot army marches to almost certain destruction to defend its coast from foreign invasion and violence, the established notion that the life of every man is at the disposal of his country justifies the hazard. But it is still a clearer instance, because matter of revelation, that there are cases in which we *ought* "to lay down our lives for the brethren;" that is, for the Church and the interests of religion in the world. In times of persecution it is obligatory upon Christians not only to suffer but even to die, rather than deny Christ. No one questions the justice of this, because all see that God has invested men with the right of thus disposing of their life; nor do we ever hear it urged that it is unjust in him to require his servants to submit to racks, and fires, and other modes of violent death, which they certainly do not deserve.

These cases are not adduced as parallel to the death of Christ for sinners; but they agree with it so far that in the ordinary course of Providence, and by express appointment of God, men suffer and even die for the benefit of others. In some cases, too, the morally worthy, the comparatively innocent, die for the benefit of the unworthy and vicious. There is a similarity in the two cases also in other particulars, as that the sufferings of danger or death is in both a matter of choice, not of compulsion or necessity; and that there is a *right* in the parties to choose suffering or death, though, as we shall see, this right in benevolent men is of a different kind from that with which Christ was invested.

In all the cases mentioned above, as most in point in the argument, we grant that there is no instance of satisfaction by vicarious punishment—no legal substitution of one person for another. Indeed, human governments could not justly adopt this principle in any case. They could not oblige an innocent person to suffer for the guilty, for that would be unjust to him; nor could they accept his offer to become the substitute of another, were he even anxious to do so, for that would be unjust to God, since he has given them no authority to take away human life in this manner.

With respect to the Divine government a parallel case is also impossible, because no guilty man could be a substitute for his fellows, his own life being forfeited; and no higher *creature* could be that substitute. For, if it was necessary that Christ, who is infinitely above all creatures, should suffer for us in order that God might be just in justifying the guilty, then his justice could not have been manifested by the interposition of any created being in our behalf, and, therefore, the legal obstacle to our pardon must have remained in full force.

Though there can be no full parallel to this singular and only case, yet, as to the question of justice, which is here the only point under consideration, it rests on the same principle as those before mentioned. In the case of St. Paul we see a willing sufferer. He chooses to suffer and to die "for the elect's sake," and that he might publish the Gospel to the world. Was it unjust in God to accept this offering of generous devotedness for the good of mankind, when it was in obedience to his own will? Certainly not. Was it an unjust act toward God for St. Paul to choose to die for the Gospel? By no means; for God had made it his duty to die for the truth.

The same considerations of choice and right unite in the sufferings of our Lord, though the case itself was one of an infinitely higher nature, a circumstance which strengthens but does not change the principle. He was a willing substitute, and choice was in him abundantly more free and unbiased than it could be in any creature. His incarnation was voluntary; and, when incarnate, his sufferings were still a matter of choice; nor was he, in the same sense as his disciples, under the power of men. "No man taketh my life from me; but I lay it down of myself." He had the right to do so in a sense in which no creature could possess it. To say that anything is *unjust*, is to say that the rights of some one are invaded; but if in this case no right was invaded, than which nothing can be more clear, then was there in the case nothing of injustice as assumed in the objection.

But the difficulty of reconciling the sufferings of Christ with Divine justice lies with those who deny the doctrine of atonement, and not with us. We who regard him as suffering by virtue of a voluntary substitution of himself in our room and stead can account for his agonies, and, by the foregoing arguments, can reconcile them to justice; but, as our Lord was perfectly and absolutely innocent and holy, how will they reconcile it to Divine justice that he should be as pre-eminent in suffering as he was in virtue, when, according to them, he sustained a personal character only, and not a vicarious one? For this difficulty they have no rational solution.

We have now adduced the scriptural evidence of the atonement made by the death of Christ for the sins of the world; and we have seen the agreement of the three grand dispensations of religion to man, the PATRIARCHAL, the LEVITICAL, and the CHRISTIAN, in the great principle that "without shedding of blood there is no remission." Indeed, only one religion has been given to man since the fall, though gradually communicated. This is fitly denominated "THE MINISTRY OF RECONCILIATION;" for its exclusive object is, however modified externally, to reconcile an apostate race to their offended Creator.

CHAPTER V.

EXTENT OF THE ATONEMENT.

HAVING established, as we believe, the doctrine of the atonement by the vicarious sufferings and death of our Lord Jesus Christ, we will proceed in the next place to inquire into its *extent*, or to examine the question, *For whom are the benefits of the death of Christ designed?* This inquiry will lead us into what is called the Calvinistic controversy; with respect to which we may observe that it forms a clear case of appeal to the Scriptures. For, whether the benefits of Christ's death are extended to the whole of our race or only to a part, must be a matter of Divine revelation.

But before we attempt to vindicate what we believe to be the doctrine of Scripture in regard to the *extent* of the atonement, we will present a brief view of the several leading theories which have been entertained respecting it. These we will denominate the *Calvinistic*, the *Universal*, and the *Arminian*.

I. THE CALVINISTIC THEORY.

All genuine Calvinists agree in believing that Christ did not so die for man as to make it possible for *all men* to be saved—in other words, that the saving benefits of Christ's death are confined to those of mankind whom God "predestinated unto everlasting life." It is true Calvinistic divines have expressed themselves upon this subject in a very diversified manner; and we may rationally conclude, judging from their language, that they have differed, at least in some respects, from one another. But when we come to the real question, Did Christ so die for all men as to make their salvation possible? every Calvinist will answer in the negative.

It will be proper, however, in order that we may do justice to all, to state some of the principal views which have been propagated by theologians under the general name of Calvinism. We will notice,

1. What may be called *the strict Calvinistic view*, that the atonement of Christ is limited in its *nature, design*, and *benefits* to the elect, so that Christ died for them alone; that he represented them alone in the covenant of redemption; and, consequently, that none but the elect can possibly be saved.

This view was held by Calvin himself, and is set forth in the "Westminster Confession of Faith," which is the standard of nearly all the Calvinistic Churches both in Europe and America. It is held, however, by the abettors of this system, that all men, by virtue of the atonement of Christ, are favored with temporal mercies, and with what they term a "common call" of the Gospel; but they deny that these benefits were designed to eventuate in their eternal salvation, or that it is possible they should.

2. Another scheme is that the atonement of Christ possessed sufficient value in its nature to redeem the whole world; but that it was designed to be applied only to the elect, and cannot possibly be extended in its application to any others.

The only point in which this system seems to differ from the first is that it allows a sufficiency in the *nature* of the atonement to avail for the salvation of all; but that sufficiency in nature is completely neutralized by the declaration that, according to the purpose of God, the application cannot possibly be made to any but the elect. This system has sometimes been called "*general redemption* with a *particular application*." But to call it a scheme of general redemption is obviously an abuse of language; for if none but the elect can possibly obtain the benefits of the atonement, the work of redemption, so far as others are concerned, is only in name, and amounts to a perfect nullity. There is, therefore, no real difference between this scheme and the one preceding.

3. Again, it is taught by some that the atonement is not only *sufficient*, but was also *designed* for the salvation of all men; and that the Gospel should therefore be preached with sincerity alike to all. But they hold at the same time that none but the elect can possibly be saved, because men cannot be saved unless they believe the Gospel, and men cannot believe unless God gives them faith; and this he has decreed from all eternity to withhold from those who are not elected. The substance of this theory is, that Christ has purchased for all men a conditional salvation; that faith in Christ is this condition; but that, according to the Divine purpose, none but the elect can possibly obtain this faith.

This is substantially the scheme which was advocated by the pious

Baxter, with the avowed purpose of steering a middle course between Arminianism and rigid Calvinism. It differs little from the views entertained by Dr. Samuel Hopkins and many other divines of the last and the present century, both in Europe and America. Calvinists of this class feel themselves warranted in offering salvation to all men, in urging all to repent and believe the Gospel, and in assuring all that they have a sufficiency of grace to enable them to comply with the Gospel call, and that if any are not saved the fault is their own. Indeed, they appear to those who are not well versed in the technicalities of their theological system to exhibit the benefits of the atonement with as much unrestrained fullness to all mankind as it would be possible for Arminians to do. It is, therefore, not surprising that many should be unable to distinguish their views in regard to the extent of the atonement from genuine Arminianism. But, though we freely exonerate them from any intention to give their trumpet "an uncertain sound," yet it is most evident, if we take their language as they themselves understand it, that their views, so far from being Arminian, are reconcilable with the most rigid Calvinism.

When they say that all men have a sufficiency of grace to enable them to repent and believe the Gospel, we must not overlook their own interpretation of the term SUFFICIENCY. By the phrase "SUFFICIENT GRACE," as used in reference to the non-elect, we are not to understand *invincible effectual* grace, such as is given to the elect, but merely "sufficient ineffectual grace," as Baxter himself termed it. What he understood by this phrase is evident from his own language : "I say it again, confidently, all men that perish (who have the use of reason) do perish directly for rejecting sufficient recovering grace. By *grace* I mean mercy contrary to merit. By *recovering* I mean such as *tendeth* in its own nature toward their recovery and leadeth or helpeth them thereto. By *sufficient* I mean *not sufficient directly to save them*, (for such none of the elect have till they are saved,) *nor yet sufficient to give them faith, or cause them savingly to believe*. But it is sufficient to bring them *nearer* Christ than they are, though not to put them into immediate possession of Christ by union with him, as faith would do."*

We may regard these words of Baxter as a just comment on the language of all Calvinists who tell us that a sufficiency of grace is given to all men. They mean a sufficiency to do them some good, "to bring them nearer Christ than they are," and even a sufficiency to save them if they would believe ; but this they cannot do, because God withholds saving faith from all but the elect. It is impossible, therefore, to understand the phrase "sufficient grace," as employed by Baxter and others, to signify anything more than *insufficient* grace. So far as the non-elect are concerned, the term *sufficient* is entirely explained away, and the system falls back on the platform of rigid Calvinism.

* Universal Redemption, page 434.

Again, when Calvinists say that all men have the ability to believe and be saved, they do not understand the term *ability* according to the full import of the word as it is commonly used. They make a distinction between *natural* and *moral* ability. By the former they mean the physical power necessary to the performance of any specific act. By the latter, that mental state or condition of the will which is necessary to the performance of an action. When they say that all men *may* believe, they only mean that all men have the natural powers necessary to saving faith. But they hold that these powers cannot be exerted without the moral ability; which, nevertheless, God has determined to withhold from all who are not elected to eternal life. "It is admitted by Calvinists," says Dr. Hill, "that the moral inability in those who are not elected is of such a kind as will infallibly prevent their obeying the commands of God; and it is a part of their system, that the Being who issues these commands has resolved to withhold from such persons the grace which alone is sufficient to remove that inability."*

It follows, therefore, from what we have seen, that however Calvinists may differ from one another on points of little or no importance, in regard to the extent of the atonement, and however diversified may be their language and modes of reasoning upon the subject, when they come to the main question in controversy they all harmonize. Whether they speak of the atonement as being universal or limited; whether they present the offer of Gospel grace in terms the most general, or with marked restriction; whether they are supralapsarian or sublapsarian in their peculiar views of the covenant of redemption; whether they are Antinomians or moderate Calvinists; whether they are Baxterians, Hopkinsians, Old School or New School; whether they dwell mostly on free-agency and sufficient grace, or on Divine sovereignty and philosophic necessity; or in whatever else they may differ, they arrive at the same ultimate conclusion, that the atonement of Christ did not so extend to all men as to make their salvation possible.

II. THE THEORY OF UNIVERSALISM.

This theory has for its starting point the Calvinistic tenet, that the atonement will infallibly be applied to all for whom it was intended. Universalists reason thus: All for whom Christ made an atonement will infallibly be saved. But the Scriptures teach that Christ made an atonement for all men; therefore, all men will infallibly be saved. If the propositions in this argument are both true the conclusion is unavoidable, and Universalism is the true theory of the atonement. Calvinists oppose the argument by attempting to disprove the second proposition, while Arminians overthrow it by disproving the first.

It is not our intention in this place to enter into an investigation of the general system of Universalism. A brief consideration of its fundamental principle is all that we suppose to be necessary. The scheme

* Hill's Lectures.

itself is evidently based upon an erroneous view in regard to the *nature of the atonement*. Universalists represent the work of redemption as a *commercial transaction* between the Father and the Son, by which the Son made a fair purchase of the human family by paying down, in his sufferings and death, an adequate price for the unconditional salvation of all men; and that, consequently, justice can have no claim upon any man, to punish him hereafter. It is true that many Calvinists take the same view of the atonement, so far as its *nature* is concerned. The only difference is that they limit its saving benefits to the elect, by which their salvation is absolutely and unconditionally secured, while others are left to perish in their sins, without the possibility of escape.

But this whole scheme, whether advocated by Universalists or Calvinists, is based upon a false assumption. The Scriptures everywhere represent the atonement, not as a *commercial transaction*, but as a *governmental arrangement*. According to the commercial view of the *nature* of the atonement it would inevitably follow that all for whom the atonement was made would infallibly be saved. Consequently, the only point of controversy between Calvinists and Universalists would be, whether Christ made an atonement for the elect only, or for all mankind; as both parties would be compelled to admit that all for whom the atonement was made would most assuredly be saved.

That this commercial view of the subject is erroneous and unscriptural will be obvious when we reflect that it tends directly to banish from the scheme of human redemption the whole system of *grace*. If Christ has purchased, by the payment of an equivalent, the absolute and unconditional salvation of all for whom he died, then it follows that the Father is under obligations, in strict justice, to save them. Consequently their salvation, so far as God the Father is concerned, is not of *grace*, but of *debt;* and the entire display of the Divine benevolence in the eternal salvation of sinners is reduced to a fiction.

It is incorrect to suppose that the atonement, of itself, brings the Almighty under obligations to save men. It is true that without the atonement none could be saved; but *that alone* does not inevitably and necessarily secure the salvation of any. It only removes the obstructions which stood in the way of man's salvation. These obstructions were, *a broken law, and the unsatisfied claims of Divine justice.* While these barriers were in the way God could not, consistent with his nature and the rectitude of his moral government, extend mercy to man. But though the atonement has removed every obstruction to the exercise of Divine mercy toward man, it does not necessarily follow that God is under obligations to extend mercy to him. It only follows that he MAY. The atonement, then, considered in the abstract, leaves God free either to extend or withhold pardoning mercy; whereas, without this provision, he was not free to extend mercy, but was bound to withhold it. All the obligations which God is under to save sinners arise, not from the fact of the atonement, but from his own gracious promises. Hence it follows that God is under no obligations, merely on account of the atonement of Christ, to save any man; much less to save all men unconditionally.

If, then, God is free to extend or withhold mercy according to his own good pleasure, it necessarily follows that he has a right to fix the conditions of our salvation. And as he has promised salvation to those who repent and believe the Gospel, and threatened eternal destruction to the impenitent and unbelieving, those who reject the conditions of salvation must perish everlastingly, and with them must perish also the dream of Universalism.

Having presented the true attitude and the essential agreement of Calvinists in regard to the main question of controversy, and having pointed out the sandy foundation of Universalism, we will turn our attention,

III. To the Arminian theory.

Arminianism, strictly speaking, is that system of religious doctrine which was taught by Dr. James Arminius, Professor of Divinity in the University of Leyden. If, therefore, we would learn precisely what Arminianism is, we must have recourse to the writings of that great divine. This, however, will by no means give us an accurate idea of that which, since his time, has been usually denominated Arminianism. On examination it will be found that, in many important particulars, those who have called themselves Arminians, or have been accounted such by others, differ as widely from Arminius as he himself differed from Calvin and other doctors of Geneva.

The leading tenets of the Arminian system may be comprised in the following five articles:

" (1.) That God from all eternity determined to bestow salvation on those whom he foresaw would persevere unto the end in their faith in Christ Jesus, and to inflict everlasting punishment on those who should continue in their unbelief, and resist unto the end his Divine succors; so that election was conditional, and reprobation in like manner the result of foreseen infidelity and persevering wickedness.

" (2.) That Jesus Christ, by his sufferings and death, made an atonement for the sins of all mankind in general, and of every individual in particular; that, however, none but those who believe in him can be partakers of the Divine benefits.

" (3.) That true faith cannot proceed from the exercise of our natural faculties and powers, nor from the force and operation of free-will; since man, in consequence of his natural corruption, is incapable either of thinking or doing any good thing; and that, therefore, it is necessary, in order to his salvation, that he be regenerated and renewed by the operation of the Holy Ghost, which is the gift of God through Jesus Christ.

" (4.) That this Divine grace or energy of the Holy Ghost begins and perfects everything that can be called good in man, and consequently all good works are to be attributed to God alone; that, nevertheless, this grace is offered to all, and does not force men to act against their inclinations, but may be resisted and rendered ineffectual by the perverse wills of impenitent sinners.

"(5.) That God gives to the truly faithful, who are regenerated by his grace, the means of preserving themselves in this state; and though the first Arminians made some doubt with respect to the closing part of this article, their followers uniformly maintain that the regenerate may lose true justifying faith, forfeit their state of grace, and die in their sins." *

From this statement of the general principles of Arminianism we may conclude that all genuine Arminians agree, 1. That, though the atonement has been made, those to whom the Gospel is addressed cannot be saved without faith in Christ; 2. That mankind, by the exercise of their own natural powers, are incapable of believing in Christ unto salvation without the supernatural influence of Divine grace; and, 3. That the assisting grace of God is, through the atonement, so extended to every man as to enable him to partake of salvation.

We see, then, that while Arminians discard the merit of works, or ability to save themselves, they agree in believing that the atonement of Christ so extends to all men as to make their salvation possible; and as the substance of the controversy between Calvinists and Arminians is plainly involved in this single question, we are now prepared to appeal "to the law and to the testimony." On a subject so important as this we cannot confidently rely on anything short of "Thus saith the Lord;" and, happy for us, there is no subject on which the Holy Scriptures are more copious and explicit.

CHAPTER VI.

EXTENT OF THE ATONEMENT.

THE question now before us, and which we propose to discuss in this chapter, is simply this: *Did Christ so die for all men as to make salvation attainable by all?* That the affirmative of this question is the real doctrine of Scripture, we will at once proceed to prove. But, before we adduce the arguments in support of our proposition, we may be allowed to premise that the saving benefits of the atonement are nowhere limited in the sacred Scriptures to a part of mankind. No

* Watson's Biblical Dictionary.

advocate of a limited atonement will pretend that there is a single passage which directly declares, either that Christ *did not* die for all men, or that he died *only for some.* This is an important fact in the argument, and with this advantage it will be easy to establish our position. That Christ so died for all mankind as to render their salvation possible, may be argued,

I. FROM ALL THOSE PASSAGES OF SCRIPTURE WHICH DESIGNATE THE OBJECTS OF REDEMPTION BY UNIVERSAL TERMS.

We have already seen that the phrase, to die "*for* us," signifies to die in our room and stead, as a sacrificial oblation, by which satisfaction is made for our sins, so that they become remissible upon the terms of the evangelical covenant. When, therefore, it is said that Christ, "by the grace of God, tasted death *for every man;*" and that "he is the propitiation for our sins, and not for ours only, but also *for the sins of the whole world;*" it can only, we think, be fairly concluded from such declarations, that by the death of Christ the sins of every man are rendered remissible, and that salvation is consequently attainable by every man.

Again, St. John testifies, "that the Father sent the Son to be the Saviour of *the world;*" and our Lord himself declares, "God so loved *the world* that he gave his only begotten Son, that *whosoever* believeth in him should not perish, but have everlasting life, for God sent not his Son into the world to condemn the world; but that *the world* through him might be saved." St. Paul tells us that "he died for *all,*" and that he is "the Saviour of *all men.*"

To this class of texts it is objected, that the phrases "*all men,*" "*the world,*" and "*the whole world,*" are sometimes used in Scripture in a limited sense. This, however, may be granted without any injury to our argument. For, though in Scripture, as in common language, *all* and *every,* and such universals, are occasionally used in a limited sense, when the connection prevents any misunderstanding, yet they are strictly universal terms, and are most frequently used in this manner. The true question then is, whether in the passages above cited the phrases "every man," "all men," "the world," and "the whole world," can be understood except in their largest sense, whether they can be interpreted of the elect only. This we very confidently deny, because,

1. *Their universal sense is confirmed, either by the context of the passages in which they occur, or by other Scriptures.*—When Isaiah says, "All we, like sheep, have gone astray, and the Lord hath laid on him the iniquity of us all," he affirms that the iniquity of all who had gone astray was laid on Christ. When St. Paul says, "We thus judge that if one died for all, then were all dead," he argues the universality of spiritual death from the universality of the means adopted for raising men to spiritual life, a plain proof that Christ's dying for all men is taken in its utmost latitude, or else it could not be made the basis of the

apostle's argument. When he says that Christ is "the Saviour of all men, specially of those that believe," he manifestly includes all mankind as being interested in this salvation, though the full benefits of it are received only by them that believe.

When the apostle declares that, "AS by the offense of one judgment came upon all men to condemnation, EVEN SO by the righteousness of one the free gift came upon all men" εις, *in order to* "justification of life," the force of the comparison would be lost if the term "all men" were not taken in its widest sense. Nor can it be objected, that the apostle uses the terms "many" and "all men" indiscriminately in this chapter, for in this there is no contradiction. All men are *many*, though many in numerous cases are not *all*. But it is evident that he uses the term "many" in the sense of *all*, as appears from the following parallels: "Through the offense of one *many* be dead;" "death passed upon *all men*." "The gift by grace hath abounded unto *many*, the free gift came upon *all men*."

It is equally impracticable to restrict the phrases "the world," and "the whole world," and to paraphrase them *the world of the elect*. And yet there is no other alternative; for, either "the world" means those elected out of it, or else Christ died in an equal sense for every man. The elect, however, are never called "the world" in Scripture, but are everywhere distinguished from it. "If ye were of the world," said our Saviour to his disciples, "the world would love his own; but because ye are not of the world, but I have chosen you out of the world, therefore the world hateth you." John xv, 19. "We know that we are of God, and the whole world lieth in wickedness." 1 John v, 19. But we deny this restrictive interpretation, because,

2. *It leads, in many cases, to gross absurdity.*—"God so loved the world that he gave his only begotten Son, that whosoever believeth in him should not perish." Now, if the world here means the elect, then it is affirmed that whosoever of this elect world believeth shall not perish; which plainly implies, that some of the elect may not believe, and may therefore perish. The same absurdity will follow from a like interpretation of the great Gospel commission. If "all the world," and "every creature," mean the elect only, then he of the elect who believes "shall be saved," and he of the elect who believes not "shall be damned." Passages so plain and explicit cannot be turned into any such consequences by any true method of interpretation. They must, therefore, be taken in their obvious sense, which unequivocally expresses the universality of the atonement.

It has been urged by the advocates of a limited atonement that our Lord himself says, John xvii, 9: "I pray for them: I pray not for the world, but for them which thou hast given me." Do they interpret "the world" here to be the elect? If so, they cut off even them from the benefit of Christ's prayer. If they say it means the non-elect, then they must allow that one end which our Lord had in view in this prayer was that this non-elect world might believe, verse 21. They may choose either side of the alternative.

It may be affirmed, therefore, that a restrictive interpretation of this class of texts contradicts the plainest declarations of God's own word. For it is not true, upon this interpretation, that "God loved the world," nor is it true that Christ was "not sent to condemn the world," if his coming only enhanced its condemnation; nor that the Gospel, as "good tidings of great joy," can be preached to "every creature," for it is sad and doleful tidings to all who are shut out from the benefits of the atonement. But our view of this question is supported,

II. BY THOSE PASSAGES WHICH ASCRIBE AN EQUAL EXTENT TO THE EFFECTS OF THE DEATH OF CHRIST, AS TO THE EFFECTS OF THE FALL.

The apostle argues thus: "For as in Adam *all die*, even so in Christ shall *all be made alive*." 1 Cor. xv, 22. It is admitted that in this passage the resurrection of the body is the main topic of discussion; nevertheless, there is here a clear inferential proof that Christ died for all men so as to make salvation attainable by all. For, if by virtue of the death and resurrection of Christ all men are to be redeemed from the grave, then it will follow that all men were represented by him in the covenant of redemption. And if so, he must have died as an expiation for their sins.

Again: "Not as the offense, so also is the free gift. For if through the offense of one many be dead, much more the grace of God, and the gift by grace, which is by one man, Jesus Christ, hath abounded unto many. Therefore, as by the offense of one judgment came upon all men to condemnation; even so, by the righteousness of one the free gift came upon all men unto justification of life." Rom. v, 15, 18. Here the "free gift" is represented as even going beyond the "offense," which it could not do if it were only designed to make salvation possible to a part of our race. Moreover, as "all men" are said to be brought into condemnation by the "offense of one," even so "the free gift" is said to come "upon all men," $\varepsilon\iota\varsigma$, *in order to* "justification of life." This implies a possibility of salvation, and from this passage alone it is just as plain that all men may be saved through Christ as that all are condemned in Adam. We prove our position,

III. BY PASSAGES OF SCRIPTURE WHICH DECLARE THAT CHRIST DIED FOR THOSE WHO MAY PERISH.

"Destroy not him with thy meat, *for whom Christ died*." Rom. xiv, 15. Him, says Pool, for whom, "in the judgment of charity," we are to presume Christ died.* To say nothing of the danger of such unlicensed paraphrases in the interpretation of Scripture, it is obvious that this exposition entirely annuls the motive by which the apostle enforces his exhortation. For if I admit that none can be destroyed for whom Christ died, then, in proportion to the charity of my judgment

* Pool's Annotations.

that any one is of this number, I may be the less cautious of ensnaring his conscience in indifferent matters; since at least this is certain, that he cannot perish, and I cannot be guilty of destroying him. Would the apostle thus counteract his own design? Would he seriously admonish his readers not to do that which he knew to be impossible?

Mr. Scott, feeling how difficult it is to reconcile this passage of Scripture with his own theological system, charges the inspired penman with careless writing. "The apostles," he observes, "did not write in that exact systematical style which some affect, otherwise they would *scrupulously have avoided such expressions*."* This is rather in the manner of Priestley or Belsham than that of an orthodox commentator; but it does homage to the force of truth by turning away from it, and by tacitly acknowledging that the Scriptures cannot be Calvinistically interpreted.

Again: "And through thy knowledge shall the weak brother perish *for whom Christ died*." 1 Cor. viii, 11. "Of how much sorer punishment, suppose ye, shall he be thought worthy, who hath trodden under foot the Son of God, and hath counted the blood of the covenant, *wherewith he was sanctified*, an unholy thing, and hath done despite unto the Spirit of grace." Heb. x, 29. "But there were false prophets also among the people, even as there shall be false teachers among you, who privily shall bring in damnable heresies, even denying the Lord that *bought* them, and bring upon themselves swift destruction." 2 Peter ii, 1.

Mr. Scott observes on this last passage "that Christ's ransom was of infinite sufficiency, and the proposal of it in Scripture general; so that men are addressed according to their profession; but that Christ only *intended* to redeem those whom he foresaw would eventually be saved." On this we may remark, 1. That the sufficiency of Christ's redemption is not the question with the apostle, but the actual redemption of these deniers of Christ. He is called "the Lord that *bought* them;" but if he did not *intend* to redeem them, he did not buy them at all; which contradicts the apostle. 2. That the proposal of Christ's ransom is general, and that all men are addressed as being interested in it, we grant, and see how well this accords with the doctrine of general redemption; but the difficulty lies with those who limit the atonement of Christ to the elect, to explain, not merely how men can be addressed generally, but how the sins of those who perish can be aggravated by the circumstance of Christ's having bought them, if he did not buy them; and how they can be justly punished for rejecting him, if they never could receive him so as to be saved by him.

Other passages of this class might be adduced, but these are sufficient to show that some for whom Christ died may perish, and, consequently, that it cannot be argued from the actual condemnation of men that they were, from all eternity, excluded from the saving benefits of the atone-

* Rev. T. Scott's Notes.

ment. But if Christ died for them that may perish, the reasonable inference is that he died for all mankind. This doctrine is further supported,

IV. BY THOSE SCRIPTURES WHICH AUTHORIZE THE PREACHING OF THE GOSPEL TO ALL MEN.

That our Lord intended the Gospel to be proclaimed throughout the whole world, and to every human being, is evident from the grand commission which he gave to his apostles: " Go ye, therefore, and teach *all nations*, baptizing them in the name of the Father, and of the Son, and of the Holy Ghost; teaching them to observe all things whatsoever I have commanded you; and lo! I am with you alway, even unto the end of the world." Matt. xxviii, 19, 20. " Go ye into *all the world*, and preach the Gospel to every creature." Mark xvi, 15. In addition to this, our Lord has declared that "this Gospel of the kingdom shall be preached in all the world for a witness unto all nations." Matt. xxiv, 14. " And that repentance and remission of sins should be preached in his name, among all nations." Luke xxiv, 47.

But in order that we may perceive the force of the argument which these Scriptures furnish, it will be necessary to consider,

1. *The universal terms in which the Gospel commission is expressed.*—The apostles are commanded, by an authority as high as heaven, to " go into *all the world*" and to " preach the Gospel to *every creature*." They are commanded to go and " teach *all nations*," and to teach them " to observe *all things* whatsoever " Christ has commanded. The fact, then, is fully established, that the Gospel is to be preached, indiscriminately, to all men. But let us now consider,

2. *The nature of the Gospel message.*—What is the Gospel? It is emphatically GOOD NEWS; or, as it is defined in Scripture, it is " *good tidings of great joy*, which shall be *to all people*." It is a message of mercy and salvation—a proclamation of peace on earth and " good-will toward men." Now, if the redeeming work of Christ made it possible for every man to be saved, there is a perfect consistency between the provisions of the atonement and the proclamation of the Gospel to all men. But if the possibility of salvation is confined to a *part* of the human family, as Calvinism evidently teaches, the Gospel cannot be " good tidings to all people." It surely cannot be " good tidings " to those whose salvation was never made possible.

Here it may be said, in justification of the unrestricted publication of the Gospel, that the atonement has secured to all men temporal mercies, and the common " ineffectual " calls of the Gospel and of the Holy Spirit. But to this we reply, that, according to Calvinism, these advantages, so far from rendering the condition of the non-elect more tolerable, or furnishing the least evidence that the Gospel can be good news to them, only aggravate their hopeless condition, and afford additional evidence that the Gospel cannot be to them good tidings of great joy."

If all our temporal blessings flow from the covenant of redemption, as Calvinists will readily allow, then it will follow that if Christ had not made an atonement for man, no one, except the first sinning pair, could ever have enjoyed the blessing of personal existence, and consequently, that none others could ever have been exposed to personal suffering. And as it is clear that non-existence itself would be preferable to a state of inevitable and eternal misery, so it is equally clear, if Calvinistic reprobation were true, that life with all its attendant mercies would be to the non-elect not a blessing, but a curse.

Again, if, as Calvinism teaches, these temporal mercies, and the calls of the Gospel and influences of the Spirit, cannot possibly be effectual to the salvation of any but the elect, and if the rejection of these calls and influences tends to greater condemnation and misery, then it will follow that as the non-elect cannot possibly avoid this rejection, the mercies of life and the gracious privileges of the Gospel tend inevitably to the aggravation of their unavoidable misery, and must be to them a real curse. If, then, we are to regard the Gospel as an unequivocal expression of the Divine will respecting the recovery of our race; if we would not turn it into mere mockery so far as the non-elect are concerned; if we would not make it to them an engine of torture, instead of "good tidings of great joy," we must allow that it proclaims a salvation which is, through the atonement of Christ, made possible to all men.

We have abundant proof that the most intelligent Calvinists feel themselves unable to reconcile the unlimited calls and invitations of the Gospel with the truth and sincerity of God. The Rev. Dr. Dick, after stating some of the attempts which are made to solve this difficulty, comes to the following conclusion: "We may pronounce, I think, these attempts to reconcile the universal call of the Gospel with the sincerity of God to be a faint struggle to extricate ourselves from the profundities of theology. They are far, indeed, from removing the difficulty. We believe, on the authority of Scripture, that God has decreed to give salvation to some and to withhold it from others. We know, at the same time, that he offers salvation to all in the Gospel, and to suppose that he is not sincere would be to deny him to be God. It may be right to endeavor to reconcile these things, because knowledge is always desirable, and it is our duty to seek it as far as it can be attained. But if we find that beyond a certain limit we cannot go, let us be content to remain in ignorance. Let us reflect, however, that we are ignorant in the present case only of the connection between two truths, and not of the truths themselves, for these are clearly stated in the Scriptures. We ought, therefore, to believe both although we cannot reconcile them."*

Here it may be observed that the doctor fully admits the universality of the calls and invitations of the Gospel, but contends "that God has

* Dick's Theology, Lecture 65.

decreed to give salvation to some, and to *withhold it from others.*" To reconcile this with the sincerity of God, he intimates, is beyond the powers of man, and he pronounces the attempt to be "a faint struggle to extricate ourselves from the profundities of theology." This, while it shows the candor of the learned author, is a fair acknowledgment that human reason cannot reconcile the leading principle of Calvinism, namely, that *salvation is not made possible to all men*, with the undeniable fact that *salvation is offered to all men.* To reconcile these two points with one another, and both with the sincerity of God, is, we readily admit, beyond the power of human reason; not, however, on account of the profundity of the subject, but because the task would require us to reconcile truth with falsehood, which is impossible. That salvation is not attainable by all men is a proposition which, though assumed by Calvinists, has never been proved; and until this doctrine is clearly established from the Bible their efforts to reconcile it with the offer of salvation to all men are only faint struggles to extricate themselves, not from "the profundities of theology," but from the "absurdities of Calvinism." We conclude, therefore, that the only rational solution of this question is found in the doctrine that Christ so died for all mankind as to render their salvation possible. Of this we have additional proof,

V. IN ALL THOSE PASSAGES OF SCRIPTURE WHICH REQUIRE MEN TO REPENT AND BELIEVE THE GOSPEL.

"And the times of this ignorance God winked at, but now commandeth all men everywhere to repent." Acts xvii, 30. "Repent ye, and believe the Gospel." Mark i, 15. "He that believeth and is baptized shall be saved; but he that believeth not shall be damned." Mark xvi, 16. "He that believeth on the Son hath everlasting life; and he that believeth not the Son shall not see life; but the wrath of God abideth on him." John iii, 36.

The plain inference from all such passages is, that the Gospel is preached to all men in order that they may repent and believe in Christ; that repentance and faith are required of them, in order to their salvation; that they have power to "believe to the saving of the soul," for those who believe not incur the wrath of God; that, having power to believe unto salvation, they must have an interest in the merits of Christ's death; and that, consequently, the atonement of Christ, through which alone salvation can be obtained, embraces all mankind.

The same conclusion follows, also, from the nature of that faith which the Gospel requires in order to salvation. This always includes a *personal trust* in the sacrificial death of Christ. But a God of truth could not require men for whose salvation the atonement of Christ made no provision to exercise such a trust. Nor could they be guilty for refusing to trust in an atonement from the saving benefits of which they were entirely excluded.

Either it is the duty of all men to believe the Gospel, or it is not. If we say it is not, we plainly contradict the Bible. If we say it is, then it will follow, either that it is possible for all men to believe, or that it is the duty of some men to do what is absolutely impossible; and as the latter alternative is absurd, the former must be admitted. But if we admit that it is possible for all men to believe, then it will follow, either that those for whom Christ made no atonement may believe, or that he made an atonement for all men. To admit the former proposition implies a contradiction; to admit the latter destroys Calvinism and establishes the Arminian theory.

That repentance and faith are required of all men will not be denied by any who believe the Scriptures. And if so, we may then be allowed to ask, For what purpose, according to Calvinism, is this requirement made? If the salvation of the non-elect is absolutely impossible, how could they be saved even if they were to believe? Could their faith effect that which God has decreed shall never be effected? Surely not. And how, we ask, can salvation be promised on the condition of faith, and damnation threatened as the consequence of unbelief, if neither the one nor the other has any dependence whatever upon man's moral agency? If, according to Calvinism, both *salvation*, the END, and *faith*, the MEANS, are absolutely impossible to the non-elect, we must either deny that the Gospel makes it their duty to repent and believe, or admit that God will punish them eternally for not attaining an impossible end by the use of impossible means. The former alternative contradicts the Scriptures, the latter involves horrible absurdities; and for those who hold the doctrine of a limited atonement there is no middle ground. Again, the extent of the atonement to all mankind may be argued,

VI. FROM THOSE SCRIPTURES WHICH SHOW THAT MEN'S FAILURE TO OBTAIN SALVATION IS ATTRIBUTABLE TO THEIR OWN FAULT.

"Because I have called, and ye refused; I have stretched out my hand, and no man regarded; but ye have set at naught all my counsel, and would none of my reproof: I also will laugh at your calamity; I will mock when your fear cometh." Prov. i, 24–26. "How often would I have gathered thy children together, even as a hen gathereth her chickens under her wings, and ye would not!" Matt. xxiii, 37. "And this is the condemnation, that light is come into the world, and men loved darkness rather than light, because their deeds were evil." John iii, 19. "And ye will not come to me that ye might have life." John v, 40.

It is unnecessary here to multiply quotations, since the Scriptures so constantly exhort men to obedience, reprove them for their folly, and threaten them with the penal consequences of their evil doings. It must therefore be admitted that the sole bar to the salvation of those who are lost is in themselves, and not in any such limitation of Christ's redemption as supposes that they were excluded from its efficacy and gracious intention. Indeed, every Scripture which proves that men's failure to obtain salvation is attributable to themselves, is a proof also that the atonement of Christ has made salvation obtainable by all men. For, on what other ground can any man's destruction be justly regarded as self-secured? He who never had it in his power to avoid the destruction which comes upon him, as Calvinism supposes to be the case with every reprobate, cannot, by any fair construction of language, be called his own destroyer. We conclude, therefore, that it would be incompatible with the justice of God to punish men in hell forever for not exercising a power which they never possessed, or for rejecting a remedy which was never provided for them. The very idea of future punishment presupposes the possibility of salvation in time. But man's salvation is only possible through the atonement of Christ; and if those who are finally lost perish from a state in which their salvation is possible, then it will follow that Christ died for them; and if he died for them he died for all.

Calvinists tell us that "the moral inability in those who are not elected is of such a kind as will infallibly prevent their obeying the commands of God; and that the Being who issues these commands has resolved to withhold from such persons the grace which alone is sufficient to remove that inability."* But they contend, nevertheless, that the non-elect are justly punishable because they continue in unbelief willingly, and act according to their own choice in rejecting the Gospel remedy. This, however, instead of removing the difficulty, only shifts it to another point; for if, as Calvinists allow, they have no power to will, or to choose different from what they do, they can no more be justly punishable for their perverse will and wicked choice than for any other unavoidable act. Our last argument on this subject is drawn,

VII. FROM THOSE SCRIPTURES WHICH DECLARE THE WILL OF GOD RESPECTING THE SALVATION OF ALL MEN.

"For I have no pleasure in the death of him that died, saith the Lord God; wherefore turn yourselves, and live ye." Ezek. xviii, 32. "As I live, saith the Lord God, I have no pleasure in the death of the wicked; but that the wicked turn from his way and live." Ezek. xxxiii, 11. "For this is good and acceptable in the sight of God our Saviour; who will have all men to be saved, and to come unto the knowledge of the truth." 1 Tim. ii, 3, 4. "The Lord is not slack concerning his promise, as some men count slackness; but is long-suffering to us-ward, not willing that any should perish, but that all should come to repentance." 1 Pet. iii, 9.

These Scriptures speak so plainly for themselves that comments are unnecessary. They prove beyond successful contradiction, *first*, that God takes no pleasure in the eternal death of any human being. This he has declared in the most impressive manner. "*As I live*, saith the Lord

---

* Hill's Lectures in Divinity.

God, I have no pleasure in the death of the wicked." But they as plainly prove, *secondly*, that God wills the eternal salvation of all men. He is willing "that all should come to repentance," and to "the knowledge of the truth;" and also, that all men should "be saved." But if God is "not willing that any should perish;" if he is willing that all men should be saved; and if the atonement which was made for man's salvation is in accordance with the Divine will, then it will necessarily follow that the atonement was made for all mankind. Or, in the language of the proposition with which we set out, that Christ so died for all mankind as to render their salvation possible.

We have now shown that this proposition is established,

1. By those texts of Scripture which designate the objects of redemption by universal terms.
2. By those which ascribe an equal extent to the effects of the death of Christ as to the effects of the fall.
3. By those which declare that Christ died for such as may perish.
4. By those which authorize the preaching of the Gospel to all men.
5. By those which require men to repent and believe the Gospel.
6. By those which show that men's failure to obtain salvation is attributable to their own fault. And,
7. By those which declare the will of God respecting the salvation of all men.

These numerous Scriptures we have endeavored to understand, according to their plain and unsophisticated meaning. If they do not prove that Christ made an atonement for all men, we may well despair of ever being able to prove any proposition from the inspired volume.

CHAPTER VII.

PREDESTINATION.

THE doctrine of *Predestination*, as it is commonly understood, has an intimate connection with the doctrine of the atonement in regard to the extent of its benefits—the subject discussed in our last chapter—and it seems proper, therefore, that we should now offer some remarks upon this topic. Calvinists understand this doctrine in a sense which harmonizes with their peculiar views of particular redemption, and a special provision for the salvation of the elect to the exclusion of any possibility of salvation to the rest of mankind; while Arminians believe that predestination, as presented in the Scriptures, is in perfect accordance with the great doctrine of general atonement, which makes salvation possible to all men.

Whether Calvinists can really establish their peculiar views of predestination from the Scriptures we shall presently see; but in order that we may discuss the subject with all due fairness, we will, in the first place, briefly state the leading features of their system in the language of their own acknowledged standards.

"Predestination," says Calvin, "we call the eternal decree of God, by which he has determined in himself what he would have to become of every individual of mankind. For they are not all created with a similar destiny; but eternal life is foreordained for some, and eternal damnation for others. Every man, therefore, being *created for one or the other of these ends*, we say he is predestinated either to life or to death."* Again: "In conformity, therefore, to the clear doctrine of Scripture, we assert that, by an eternal and immutable counsel, God has once for all determined both whom he would admit to salvation and whom he would condemn to destruction."†

The doctrine of predestination is set forth in the Westminster Confession of Faith in the following terms: "By the decree of God for the manifestation of his glory, some men and angels are predestinated unto everlasting life, and others foreordained to everlasting death.

"These men and angels, thus predestinated and foreordained, are particularly and unchangeably designed; and their number is so certain and definite that it cannot be either increased or diminished.

"Those of mankind that are predestinated unto life God, before the foundation of the world was laid according to his eternal and immutable purpose, and the secret counsel and good pleasure of his will, hath chosen in Christ unto everlasting glory, out of his mere free grace and love, without any foresight of faith or good works, or perseverance in either of them or any other thing in the creature, as conditions or causes moving him thereunto, and all to the praise of his glorious grace.

"As God hath appointed the elect unto glory, so hath he, by the eternal and most free purpose of his will, foreordained all the means thereunto. Wherefore, they who are elected being fallen in Adam are redeemed by Christ, are effectually called unto faith in Christ by his Spirit working in due season; are justified, adopted, sanctified, and kept by his power through faith unto salvation. Neither are any other redeemed by Christ effectually called, justified, adopted, sanctified, and saved but the elect only.

"The rest of mankind God was pleased, according to the unsearchable counsel of his own will, whereby he extendeth or withholdeth mercy as he pleaseth, for the glory of his sovereign power over his creatures, to pass by, and to ordain to dishonor and wrath for their sin, to the praise of his glorious justice."

It is evident, from these quotations, that the following are leading tenets in the Calvinistic scheme of predestination:

* Institutes, Book 3, chap. 21. † Ibid.

1. That all things, whether great or small, whether good or evil, whether they relate to the physical or to the moral world, to the history of angels or to the actions of men, were from all eternity firmly and unalterably determined by the immutable decree of God.

2. That by this decree "some men and angels" were elected or chosen to everlasting life, and others foreordained to everlasting death.

3. That the decree of election and reprobation is *unconditicnal;* God having had no regard to faith, obedience, "or any other thing in the creature."

4. That the predestination of moral creatures to everlasting life, or to everlasting death, is *personal* and *absolute.* They "are particularly and unchangeably designed; and their number is so certain and definite that it cannot be either increased or diminished."

5. That the election of some is the sole originating cause of their faith and obedience, and that the reprobation of others is the sole cause of their lack of faith and obedience.

To sustain the peculiarities of the system which we have thus briefly sketched, Calvinists appeal to the Scriptures in which they suppose the doctrine of predestination to be taught, and institute a course of reasoning founded mainly on the prescience and sovereignty of God.

But before we enter upon the discussion of this subject it may be proper to remark, for the sake of clearness and precision, that the term *predestination* is employed by Calvinistic divines in rather a generic sense. "It is applicable," says Dr. Dick, "according to the import of the term, to all the purposes of God which determine beforehand what is to come to pass; but it is usually limited to those purposes of which the spiritual and eternal state of man is the object."* Hence predestination, in this last sense, resolves itself into the two great branches of the Divine purpose toward man—*Election* and *Reprobation.* To these doctrines, then, let us now turn our attention, and examine them in the light of inspired truth.

§ 1. *The Doctrine of Election.*

Election, in the Calvinistic sense, may be defined to be that "choice which God, in the exercise of sovereign grace, made of certain individuals of mankind to enjoy salvation by Jesus Christ."† The Greek term which is rendered ELECTION is εκλογη, *a choice;* from the verb εκλεγω, *to choose.* Hence the import of the verb *to elect* is *to choose;* and the noun *election* signifies *a choice.*

In opening the Bible upon this subject we find that there are three different kinds of election spoken of. These are, 1. The election of individuals to perform some special service; 2. That of nations or bodies of

* Dick's Theology, Lecture 25.   † Id., Lecture 35.

men to eminent religious privileges; and, 3. That of individuals to be the children of God and heirs of eternal life.

I. THE ELECTION OF INDIVIDUALS TO PERFORM SOME PARTICULAR AND SPECIAL SERVICE.

Thus Cyrus was "elected" to build the temple; the twelve apostles were "chosen" to their office by Christ; St. Paul was a "chosen vessel," to be the apostle of the Gentiles. This kind of election has, however, manifestly no relation to the limitation of eternal salvation. It did not confer upon the persons so chosen an absolute security. One of the elected apostles was Judas, who fell and was lost; and St. Paul confesses his own personal liability to become "a castaway." It did not exclude others from the saving grace of God, for the apostles were "elected" to preach the Gospel in order to their salvation.

II. THE ELECTION OF NATIONS OR BODIES OF MEN TO EMINENT RELIGIOUS PRIVILEGES, AND IN ORDER TO ACCOMPLISH, BY THEIR SUPERIOR ILLUMINATION, THE MERCIFUL PURPOSES OF GOD TO OTHERS.

Of this kind of election we have an example,

1. *In the history of the Jews.*—They were chosen to receive special revelations of truth, to be the "people of God," to be his visible Church, and publicly to observe and uphold his worship. "The Lord had a delight in thy fathers to love them, even you above all people." Deut. x, 15. It was on account of the application of the terms ELECT, CHOSEN, and PECULIAR to the Jewish people that they were so frequently applied by the apostles to the members of the Christian Church; for we may remark,

2. *That Christians were also subjects of this second kind of election.*— They became, though in a more special and exalted sense, the chosen people, the elect of GOD. We say, in a more special and exalted sense; because, while the entrance into the Jewish Church was by natural birth, the entrance into the Christian Church, properly so called, is by faith and a spiritual birth. These terms, therefore, as used in the New Testament, have generally respect to true believers.

This "election" is sometimes applied to particular bodies of Christians, as when Peter says, "The Church which is at Babylon, *elected together* with you;" and sometimes to the whole body of believers in every place. To understand its nature, as also the reason of the frequent use of the term election, it is to be remembered, that in the days of the apostles the CHURCH STATE of the Jews, which had continued for so many ages, was abrogated. They had been the only visibly acknowledged people of God in all the nations of the earth; but this distinguished honor they were about to lose. There was then a NEW ELECTION of a NEW PEOPLE of God, to be composed of Jews, not by virtue of their *natural descent*, but of their faith in Christ, and of believing gentiles of all nations, put on equal ground with the believing Jews. And there was also a REJECTION, a *reprobation*, if the term pleases any one better, but not an absolute one; for the ELECTION was offered to the Jews first, in every place, by offering them the Gospel. Some embraced it, and became the elect people of God, on the new ground of faith, instead of the old ground of natural descent; and therefore the apostle (Romans xi, 7) calls the believing part of the Jews "the election," in opposition to those who opposed this "election of grace," and still clung to their former and now repealed election as Jews and the descendants of Abraham.

As the Gospel was preached to the whole Jewish nation, they all might have united with the one new body of believing Jews and Gentiles; but a majority of them made light of it, and refused that election which placed the relation of "the people of God" upon spiritual attainments, and offered them only spiritual blessings. They were therefore deprived of election and Church relationship of every kind. Their temple was destroyed, their political state abolished, their genealogies confounded, and their worship annihilated. God's visible acknowledgment of them as a Church was withdrawn, and transferred to a Church thenceforward to be composed chiefly of Gentiles.

We see, then, that "the calling" and "the election" of the Christian Church, as spoken of in the New Testament, was not the calling and the electing of one nation in particular to succeed the Jews; but it was the calling and the electing of believers in all nations, wherever the Gospel should be preached, to be in reality what the Jews had been but typically, the visible Church of God.

This second kind of election being thus explained, we may now inquire whether anything arises out of it, either as it respects the Jewish or the Christian Church, which obliges us in any degree to limit the explicit declarations of Scripture in regard to the universal extent of the intentional benefits of the atonement of Christ. To place this question in its true light we may observe,

(1.) That this kind of election does not infallibly secure the salvation of every elected person. The Jews were elected to be the peculiar people and visible Church of God; but that did not secure the salvation of every Jew individually. This will be acknowledged by all; for, as the foundation of their Church state was their natural relation to Abraham, and as "that which is born of the flesh is flesh," none of them could be saved merely by virtue of their being "Jews outwardly." The apostle says, that "with many of them God was not well pleased, for they were overthrown in the wilderness." He specified that some of them were "idolaters," some were "fornicators," some "tempted Christ," and that God "sware in his wrath that they should not enter into his rest." Yet these were the "chosen," the "elected," and the "peculiar people" of God.

Nor does the election of the Christian Church absolutely secure the eternal salvation of those thus elected. That this is true, so far as it regards an election to the external privileges of the Gospel, Calvinists themselves will admit; and that it is also true, as applied to the election of believers to the spiritual as well as to the outward privileges of the Gospel, is evident from the numerous warnings given to such persons against turning "back unto perdition," making "shipwreck of faith," or "departing from the living God." Especially is it evident from the language of St. Peter when he exhorts believers to "give diligence to make their calling and election sure." For if it had been made sure from all eternity their diligence could have no tendency to make it sure. We have seen, moreover, in the case of the apostates mentioned in Hebrews, that, in point of fact, some of those who had thus been actually elected and brought into a state of salvation fell away into a condition of utter hopelessness.

(2.) *That this election concludes nothing against the salvability of those who are not thus elected.*—The election of the Jews as the peculiar people of God did not exclude the non-elected Gentiles from the possibility of salvation.—St. Paul, in the second chapter of his Epistle to the Romans, clearly shows us that "the Gentiles, which have not the law," may "do by nature (that is, by the assistance which God affords them independent of the written law) the things contained in the law;" and that thus acting up to the requirements of "their conscience," they may be esteemed as "just before God." That the Gentiles were not precluded from all possibility of salvation, is further evident from several instances recorded in Scripture of pious heathens; such as Melchizedek, Job, and Cornelius. But the language of Peter ought forever to settle this question: "Of a truth I perceive that God is no respecter of persons; but in every nation he that feareth him, and worketh righteousness, is accepted with him." Acts x, 34, 35.

The Calvinistic view of election absolutely precludes the non-elect from all possibility of salvation; but nothing of this kind is implied in the collective election of persons to the enjoyment of Gospel privileges. Thousands who were not thus elected, or who were not of the Church in the days of the apostles, have been brought in in subsequent times. And it will not be denied, even by Calvinists themselves, that thousands who are not now members of the visible and true Church of Christ may yet be called and chosen into that body, and thus partake of an election of which while they are notoriously wicked they cannot be the subjects, whatever may be the secret purpose of God concerning them.

(3.) *That the election of which we speak, so far from dragging along with it Calvinistic reprobation, was intended for the salvation even of the non-elect.*—The establishment of the true worship in the family of Abraham was designed not only to preserve truth, but to diffuse it, and to counteract the spread of superstition and idolatry. The miracles wrought from age to age among the Jews exalted Jehovah above the gods of the heathen. Rays of light from their sacred books and institutions spread far beyond themselves. The temple of Solomon had its court of the Gentiles, and the "stranger" from "a far country" had access to it, and enjoyed the right of praying to the true God. Jerusalem was, in an important sense, literally "the joy of the whole earth;" and in the seed of Abraham "all the families of the earth" have, in some degree, been blessed.

In like manner the election of persons to membership in the Church of Christ does not exclude others from an interest in the mercy of God, but was designed for their benefit and salvation, that they also may be called into the fellowship of the Gospel. Hence, the Church is called "the light of the world" and "the salt of the earth." But in what sense could this be true if there were no capacity in the world to be enlightened and saved? Yet if such a capacity exists in the world it must be derived from the grace of God, and not from nature—a grace which can be imparted to the world only in consequence of the death of Christ. Thus, we fairly arrive at the conclusion that the election of nations or large bodies of people to the enjoyment of peculiar privileges affords no support to the doctrine of Calvinian election.

III. PERSONAL ELECTION, *or the election of individuals to be the children of God and heirs of eternal life.*

It is not at all disputed between us and those who hold the Calvinistic view of election, whether true believers are called THE ELECT with reference to their individual state and individual relation to God as his people. Such passages as "the elect of God," "chosen of God," "elect according to the foreknowledge of God the Father," and many others, we allow to be descriptive of an act of grace in favor of certain persons considered individually.

What, then, is the import of that act of grace which we call *personal election to eternal life?* It is not the choosing of individuals to perform some special and particular service, which is the first kind of election mentioned; nor is it that collective election to religious privileges and a visible Church state on which we have more largely dwelt. For though "the elect" have an interest in this election, individually, as parts of the collective body, yet many others have the same advantages who still remain in sin and unbelief. But those who are properly called "the elect" *have been made partakers of the grace and saving efficacy of the Gospel.* "Many," says our Lord, "are *called*, but few CHOSEN."

What true personal election is we may learn from the sacred Scriptures. It is explained by our Lord where he says to his disciples, "I have chosen you out of the world." John xv, 19. It is explained by St. Paul when he says, "God hath from the beginning chosen you to salvation, through sanctification of the Spirit and belief of the truth." 2 Thess. ii, 13. It is also explained by St. Peter when he says of his Christian brethren that they are "elect, according to the foreknowledge of God the Father, through sanctification of the Spirit unto obedience, and sprinkling of the blood of Jesus Christ." 1 Peter i, 2.

To this scriptural view of the doctrine of personal election we most heartily subscribe; but when it is contended that God has, from all eternity, chosen to salvation a definite number of men, not upon foresight of faith, obedience, or anything else in them as a cause or condition of their being chosen, but unto faith, obedience, and holiness, the doctrine presents itself under a very different aspect, and requires an appeal to the word of God.

This view of election unfolds three leading points: 1. It is *eternal;* 2. It is the choosing of a *determinate number* which cannot be increased or diminished; and, 3. It is *unconditional.* Let us briefly examine each of these particulars.

1. It is assumed that *men are elected to everlasting life from all eternity.*—This is a position which we cannot admit, except so far as the foreknowledge of God, and his purpose to choose men in time, may be termed election. To suppose that actual election can be "from all eternity," is manifestly absurd. To elect signifies to choose, which implies an act of the mind; and every act implies a time in which it took place, and, consequently, a time before it took place. Hence, unless we make the act of election an essential part of the Divine nature (which would be absurd) it cannot be eternal; for the attribute of eternity will properly apply to the Divine essence only.

Again, the eternity of actual election is not only absurd in itself, but it is contrary to Scripture. Here we are taught, not only that it is an act of God done in *time,* but also that it takes place subsequent to the administration of the means of salvation. The "calling" goes before the "election," and men are elected or chosen through "belief of the truth," the "sanctification of the Spirit," and the "sprinkling of the blood of Jesus Christ." The doctrine of *eternal election* is thus brought down to its true meaning. The phrase "eternal election," and "eternal decree of election," so often in the lips of Calvinists, can, therefore, in common sense, mean only an eternal *purpose,* or a purpose formed *in eternity,* to elect or choose men out of the world, and to sanctify them *in time*—a doctrine this which we will not dispute.

2. It is claimed that this election consists *in the choosing of a determinate number.*—This notion rests upon the basis of mere inference; for there is not a text of Scripture which declares that a fixed and determinate number of men are elected to eternal life. But while there is no Scripture in favor of the opinion, there is much against it; and to this test it must therefore be brought.

We have before shown that eternal election can only mean a purpose formed in eternity of electing in time. But of God's eternal purpose to elect we can know nothing except from his own revelation. We take, then, the matter on this ground. A purpose to elect is a purpose to save;

and when it is declared that God is " not willing that any should perish," but " will have all men to be saved," either we must say that his will is contrary to his purpose, which would be to charge God foolishly, or it agrees with his purpose. If the latter, his purpose to save was not confined to a determinate number of men, but extended to all who should believe that they might be elected and saved.

Again, we have shown that Christ died for all men, that all through him might be saved. But if he died in order to their salvation through faith, he died in order to their election through faith; and God must have purposed this from eternity.

Further, in that Gospel which is to be preached "to every creature," Christ has declared, " He that believeth shall be saved, but he that believeth not shall be damned." This is an unquestionable decree of God in time; and if he is unchangeable, it was his decree, in regard to this matter, from all eternity. But this decree cannot be reconciled with the doctrine of an eternal purpose to elect only a determinate number of men. For, if those who believe not " shall be damned," it must be possible for them to believe and be saved. To admit this is to give up the doctrine that the number of the elect " is so certain and definite that it cannot be increased." To deny it is to allow that God commands his creatures to do what is utterly impossible, and then punishes them with eternal damnation for not doing it. If the reason of men's condemnation lies in themselves, and not in the want of sufficient means to save them, as we have shown in a former chapter, then the number of the elect might be *increased*. And if it is true, as the Scriptures evidently teach, that those for whom Christ died may " perish," and that true believers may " draw back unto perdition," and fall into a state in which it were " better for them not to have known the way of righteousness," then the number of the elect may be *diminished*.

3. It is held that *election to eternal life is unconditional.*—It is a gracious act of God in choosing a definite number of men, " without any foresight of faith or good works, or perseverance in either of them, or any other thing in the creature, as conditions or causes moving him thereunto."

We have already seen that *actual* election from eternity is impossible, and that, therefore, election must be either God's purpose in eternity to elect in time, or actual election in time. To affirm that in *purpose* men were elected from eternity, " without foresight of faith or good works," is to say, that from eternity God purposed to constitute his Church of persons to whose faith and obedience he had no respect. He eternally purposed to make Peter, James, and John members of his Church, without respect to their faith or obedience, or anything else in them. His Church is, therefore, constituted on the sole principle of this purpose, not on the basis of faith and obedience: and the persons chosen into it in time, are chosen because they are included in this eternal purpose.

How manifestly this scheme opposes the Word of God we need

scarcely stay to point out. It contradicts that specific distinction which is constantly made in Scripture between the true Church and the world, the only marks of distinction being, as to the former, faith and obedience, and as to the latter, unbelief and disobedience; in other words, the Church is composed not merely of men, as Peter, James, and John; but of Peter, James, and John as obedient believers; while all who believe not and obey not are of "the world." Thus the Scriptures make the essential elements of the Church to be believing and obeying men; but the theory in question makes them to be men in the simple condition of being included in a determinate number, chosen without any respect to faith and obedience.

This view of election contradicts also the history of the commencement and first constitution of the Church of Christ. Peter, James, and John did not become disciples of Christ in unbelief and disobedience. The very act of their becoming his disciples unequivocally implied some degree both of faith and obedience. They were chosen, not as men, but as believing men. This is indicated also by the grand rite of baptism, the initiating ordinance into the Christian Church; for in order to this, a previous faith is always required. We see, therefore, that men are chosen out of the world, and chosen into the Church with respect to their faith. But if actual election in time has respect to faith, God's eternal purpose in regard to election must have had respect to faith also, unless it can be shown that this purpose is at variance with actual election.

It is true, we are told that election is "unto faith and obedience." But we have no such doctrine in the Scriptures as the election of individuals *unto* faith, and it is inconsistent with several passages which expressly speak of personal election. See 1 Peter i, 2: "Elect, according to the foreknowledge of God the Father, through sanctification of the Spirit unto obedience and sprinkling of the blood of Jesus Christ." Here we are clearly taught that the work of the Spirit which produces obedience, and the "sprinkling of the blood of Jesus Christ," are the *media* through which our election is effected. Obedience, then, is not the end of election, but of the "sanctification of the Spirit." Nor can election be *unto* faith; for we are elected through the "sprinkling of the blood of Jesus Christ," which, in all cases, is apprehended by faith.

Very similar to this passage is 2 Thess. ii, 13, 14: "God hath from the beginning chosen you to salvation through sanctification of the Spirit and belief of the truth; whereunto he called you by our Gospel." When Calvinistic commentators interpret the phrase, "from the beginning," to mean from all eternity, they make a gratuitous assumption which has nothing in the scope of the passage to warrant it. The Thessalonians were elected "through sanctification of the Spirit and belief of the truth;" and to this sanctification and faith they were called by the Gospel. But if sanctification and faith are *means* of election, as is here taught, election cannot be "*unto* faith and obedience." It is an election *through* faith and obedience; or, in other words, a choice of obedient believers into the family of God.

In proof of the doctrine that personal election is unto faith and obedience, Calvinists rely mainly upon Ephesians i, 4, 5, 6: "According as he hath chosen us in him before the foundation of the world, that we should be holy and without blame before him in love: having predestinated us unto the adoption of children by Jesus Christ to himself, according to the good pleasure of his will, to the praise of the glory of his grace, wherein he hath made us accepted in the beloved." The context, however, bears unequivocal proof that the apostle is here speaking, not of personal but of collective election to Gospel privileges. Hence, he speaks of election as the *means* of the personal salvation of the Ephesians, and of their salvation as the *end* of election or predestination, an order which is reversed when the election of *individuals*, or of any body of believers considered *distributively* and *personally*, is the subject of discourse.

To be convinced that the passage has no reference to personal election, we need only follow the apostle's argument. He speaks first of the election of Christians in general, whether Jews or Gentiles; using the pronouns "us" and "we" as comprehending himself and all others. He then proceeds to the "predestination" of those "who *first* trusted in Christ," plainly meaning himself and other believing Jews. He goes on to say, that the Ephesians were made partakers of the same faith, and, therefore, were the subjects of the same election and predestination: "in whom ye also trusted after that ye heard the word of truth." He then informs us that the preaching of this truth to them as Gentiles, by himself and his coadjutors, was in consequence of God's "having made known unto them the mystery of his will, that in the dispensation of the fullness of times he might *gather together in one* all things in Christ." This, in the next chapter, a manifest continuation of the same subject, is explained to mean the calling in of the Gentiles with the believing Jews, reconciling "both unto God in one body by the cross." He pursues the same subject in the third chapter also, representing this union of believing Jews and Gentiles in one Church as the revelation of that mystery which had been hid "from the beginning of the world;" but was now manifested "according to the eternal purpose which he purposed in Christ Jesus our Lord."

Here, then, we have the true meaning of the election and predestination of the Ephesians spoken of in the opening of the Epistle. It was their election, as Gentiles, to be, along with the believing Jews, the Church of God, his acknowledged people on earth; which election was, "according to the eternal purpose" of God, to change the constitution of his Church, to establish it on the ground of faith in Christ, and thus to extend it into all nations. So far as this respected the

Ephesians in general, their election to hear the Gospel sooner than many other Gentiles was unconditional and sovereign, and was an election "*unto* faith and obedience;" that is to say, these were the *ends* of that election. But so far as they were concerned individually they were actually chosen into the Church of Christ as its vital members *on their believing*. So, then, election to the saving benefits of the Gospel was a *consequence of their faith*, and not the *cause* of it, and was, therefore, conditional. "In whom ye also trusted, after that ye heard the word of truth, the Gospel of your salvation; in whom also, *after that ye believed*, ye were sealed with the Holy Spirit of promise."

The Calvinistic doctrine of election *unto* faith has no stronger passage than this to lean upon for support, and this manifestly fails them; while other passages in which the terms *election* and *chosen* occur all favor a very different view of the subject. When we are commanded to be diligent "to make our calling and *election* sure," it is evidently implied that it may be rendered nugatory by want of diligence, a doctrine which cannot comport with the Calvinistic theory of election. When believers are called "a *chosen* generation," they are also called "a royal priesthood, a holy nation;" and if the latter characteristics depend upon *faith*, and are consequences of it, so the former depends upon a previous faith, and is the consequence of it.

Finally, in all the passages of Scripture in which these terms relate to the Christian experience of individuals, the previous condition of faith is either expressed or necessarily implied; and though such passages are comparatively few, there are many others which embody the same doctrine in different terms. The phrases to be "IN Christ" and to be "CHRIST's" are doubtless equivalent to the personal election of believers. Though these and similar modes of expression are constantly occurring in the New Testament, indicative of a personal and saving relation to Christ, yet no one is ever represented as being taken into this relation by an eternal election *unto* faith; but, on the contrary, through personal faith alone. The Scriptures know no such distinctions as *elect believers* and *elect unbelievers;* but all unbelievers are represented as being "of the world," under "the wrath of God," and liable to eternal ruin. But if Calvinistic election is true, then there are *elect unbelievers*, and with respect to these the Scriptures are contradicted. They cannot be "of the world," though now in a state of unbelief; since, from all eternity, they were chosen "out of the world." They are not under "the wrath of God," for they are the objects of an eternal and unchangeable love. They cannot be liable to eternal ruin, for God has decreed to bestow upon them, unconditionally, everlasting life. In regard to them, therefore, the threatenings of God are without meaning; and to suppose the Holy Spirit to "convince them of sin" and of danger, is to adopt the monstrous conclusion that he is employed in exciting fears which have no foundation.

§ 2. *The Doctrine of Reprobation.*

The doctrine of the election to eternal life of only a certain number of men, necessarily involves the absolute and unconditional reprobation of all the rest. Let us, then, inquire into the nature of this Divine act of reprobation as it is understood by Calvinists themselves. In the language of the Westminster Confession it is stated thus: "The rest of mankind God was pleased, according to the unsearchable counsel of his own will, whereby he extendeth or withholdeth mercy as he pleaseth, for the glory of his sovereign power over his creatures, to pass by, and to ordain them to dishonor and wrath for their sin, to the praise of his glorious justice."

We have a more extended and very clear statement of this doctrine in the language of Dr. Hill. "From the election of certain persons," says he, "it necessarily follows that all the rest of the race of Adam are left in guilt and misery. The exercise of the Divine sovereignty in regard to those who are not elected is called reprobation; and the condition of all having been originally the same, reprobation is called absolute in the same sense with election. In reprobation there are two acts which the Calvinists are careful to distinguish. The one is called preterition, the passing by of those who are not elected, and withholding from them those means of grace which are provided for the elect. The other is called condemnation, the act of condemning those who have been passed by for the sins which they commit. In the former act God exercises his good pleasure, dispensing his benefits as he will; in the latter act he appears as a judge, inflicting upon men that sentence which their sins deserve. If he had bestowed upon them the same assistance which he prepared for others they would have been preserved from that sentence; but as their sins proceeded from their own corruption, they are thereby rendered worthy of punishment, and the justice of the Supreme Ruler is manifested in condemning them, as his mercy is manifested in saving the elect."*

Regarding these authorities as a clear and faithful exposition of Calvinian reprobation, we may feel ourselves safe in concluding that it involves the two following propositions: 1. That God, from all eternity, unchangeably foreordained a definite number of the human family to everlasting death; and, 2. That this decree of reprobation is absolute and unconditional—resting on no other ground than the mere sovereignty of God. That the first of these propositions is fairly contained in the theory no one will deny; and that the second is also may be established by the testimony of Calvinistic divines. Dr. Dick, in arguing that the ground of reprobation is not in men's moral character, reasons thus: "Although their fall is presupposed to their reprobation, it will appear that the former

* Hill's Lectures, book 4, chap. 7, sec. 3.

was not the reason of the latter, if we recollect that those who were chosen to salvation were exactly in the same situation. Both classes appeared in the eyes of God to be guilty, polluted, and worthy of death. Their sinfulness, therefore, could not be the reason of rejection in the one case, since it did not cause rejection in the other. If it was the reason why some were passed by, it would have been a reason why all should be passed by. As, then, it did not hinder the election of some, it could not be the cause which hindered the election of others. As the moral state of all was the same, it could not be the cause of the difference in their destination. If there was sin in the reprobate, there was sin also in the elect, and we must therefore resolve their opposite allotment into the will of God, who gives and withholds his favor according to his pleasure."*

Having thus stated the Calvinistic view in regard to the awful subject of eternal and unconditional reprobation, we feel ourselves called upon to record our most hearty dissent from any such doctrine. It is not only unsupported by a single passage of inspired truth, rightly interpreted, but it is obviously incompatible both with the character of God as it is revealed in his word, and with many declarations of Scripture. It cannot, we may confidently affirm, be reconciled,

1. To the WISDOM of God. For the bringing into existence of a vast number of intelligent creatures under a necessity of sinning and of being eternally lost, teaches no moral lesson to the world; while it contradicts all those notions of wisdom in the ends and processes of government which we derive, not only from natural reason, but from the Scriptures.

2. Nor can this doctrine be reconciled to the Divine BENEVOLENCE. "God is love." He "is good to *all;* and his tender mercies are over all his works." He has "no pleasure in the death of him that dieth." "The Lord is long-suffering to us-ward, not willing that *any* should perish, but that *all* should come to repentance." But in opposition to this scriptural view of the Divine benevolence, the doctrine of reprobation is that God takes pleasure in the eternal destruction of his moral creatures. According to Calvinism, he might save those whom he dooms to everlasting death upon the very same principle that he saves the elect. For, as Dr. Hill says, "If he had bestowed upon them the same assistance which he prepared for others, they would have been preserved from that sentence." Hence the theory clearly implies that God would rather damn many of his helpless creatures than save them.

3. Equally impossible is it to reconcile this notion to the SINCERITY of God in offering salvation to all men through Jesus Christ, since it supposes that there are many whom he never designed to save. The Gospel, as we have seen, is to be preached "to every creature;" and is, from its very nature, an offer of salvation to every man. But to assume that God has determined, by an unalterable decree, that many to whom he offers salvation, and whom he invites to receive it, shall never be

---

* Dick's Theology, Lecture 36.

saved, and that he will consider their sins aggravated by their rejection of that Gospel which they never could receive, and which he never *designed* them to receive, involves a reflection upon his truth and sincerity at which men ought to shudder.

It is no answer to this to say that God offers his mercy to many, knowing, by virtue of his prescience, that they will not receive it. We grant this; but, not now to enter upon the question of foreknowledge, it is enough to reply that here there is no insincerity. On the Calvinistic scheme the offer of salvation is made to those for whom Christ made no atonement; but on ours he made atonement for all. On the former the offer is made to those whom God never designed to embrace it; but on ours it is the will of God that all to whom the offer is made should embrace it. On their theory the bar to the salvation of the non-elect lies in the want of a provided sacrifice for sin; while on ours it rests solely in men themselves. One is, therefore, consistent with a perfect sincerity of offer; but the other cannot be maintained without bringing the sincerity of God into question, and fixing a stigma upon his moral truth.

4. It is manifestly contrary to Divine JUSTICE. God himself has appealed to those established notions of justice and equity which obtained among all enlightened persons as the measure and rule of his own. "Shall not the Judge of all the earth do *right?*" "Are not my ways *equal?*" We may conclude, therefore, that justice and equity in God are what they are taken to be among reasonable men. If a sovereign should condemn to death a number of his subjects for not obeying a law which it is absolutely impossible for them to obey, and should require them, on pain of aggravated punishment, to do something in order to the pardon of their offenses, which he knows they cannot do, say to stop the tide or to remove a mountain; would not all men everywhere condemn such a procedure as most contrary to justice and right?

But Calvinistic reprobation implies a charge as obviously and awfully unjust against God. It supposes him to pass by and reject men without any avoidable fault of their own, and to destroy them by the simple rule of his own sovereignty; or, in other words, to show that he has power to do it. In whatever light the subject may be viewed, no fault, in any right construction, can be chargeable upon the persons so punished, or, as we may rather say, *destroyed*, since punishment supposes a judicial proceeding which this act shuts out. For either the reprobates are destroyed for a pure reason of sovereignty without any reference to their sinfulness, and thus all criminality is left out of the question, or they are destroyed for the sin of Adam, to which they were not consenting; or for personal faults resulting from an innate corruption of nature, which God wills not to correct, and which they themselves have no power to correct.

To say that reprobates are doomed to "dishonor and wrath *for their sin*," is a mere subterfuge to conceal the deformity of the "horrible decree;" for, according to Calvinism, their doom was fixed from all eternity before they had committed any sin. To say that reprobates are doomed to "dishonor and wrath for their sin," has in it the sound of justice, and seems to some extent to cover up the deformities of reprobation. But the question arises, Was not their sin as much included in the Divine purpose as their final doom? It certainly was, if it is indeed true that God did "freely and unchangeably ordain whatsoever comes to pass." It follows, therefore, that reprobates can no more avoid the sin for which they are doomed to wrath than they can overturn the Divine decree; and that there is really no reason for their eternal destruction but the sovereign will of God.

Another expedient by which this doctrine is kept in countenance is, to represent the decree of reprobation as having respect to men in their fallen and sinful state. "God found men in sin," says Dr. Dick, "and in leaving them there he did no wrong, and was chargeable with no cruelty."* This might indeed be allowed, if the purpose of God had nothing to do with man previous to his fall, and if men were involved in their fallen and sinful condition by their own personal and avoidable transgressions. But if these are not admitted the argument is a mere sophism. The true state of the case is this: Can God bring men into existence in a fallen and sinful state, and under circumstances which render their actual transgression unavoidable; can he withhold from them the only means by which it is possible for them to be saved from their sinful condition, and then *justly* punish them with everlasting misery for their unavoidable transgressions? Such is the course of procedure which the doctrine of unconditional reprobation ascribes to God; but as it is obviously contrary to every one's sense of justice, it proves the doctrine to be false.

5. The doctrine of absolute reprobation destroys the *end* of PUNITIVE *justice*. That end can only be to deter men from sin, and to add strength to the law of God. But if reprobates are left to the influence of their fallen nature without any remedy, they cannot be deterred from sin by threats of inevitable punishment, nor can they ever submit to the dominion of the Divine law. Their doom is fixed, and threats and examples can avail nothing.

6. This doctrine cannot be reconciled with the apostle's declaration, that "GOD IS NO RESPECTER OF PERSONS." This passage, we grant, is not to be interpreted as though the bounties of the Almighty were dispensed in equal measure to all. In the administration of favor there is room for the exercise of that prerogative which, in a just sense, is called the sovereignty of God. Justice, however, knows only one rule; it is in its nature settled and fixed, and respects not the PERSON but the CASE.

* Dick's Theology, Lecture 36.

The phrase *to respect persons*, when it refers to judicial proceedings, signifies to judge from partiality or affection, and not from the merits of the case. It is used by St. Peter with reference to the acceptance of Cornelius, where it evidently means to accept or reject men, not on the ground of moral qualities, but on some prejudice or partiality which forms no moral rule.

If from eternity men are loved or hated, elected or reprobated, before they have done either " good or evil," then it necessarily follows that there is precisely this kind of respect of persons with God; for his acceptance or rejection of them cannot be resolved into any *moral rule*. But Scripture affirms that there is no such respect of persons with God, and, therefore, the doctrine which implies it is contradicted by inspired authority.

CHAPTER VIII.

JUSTIFICATION.

HAVING discussed the subject of the atonement at some considerable length, and having presented and defended the doctrine, that by this wonderful expedient of the Divine benevolence salvation is made possible to all men, we come now to examine some of the leading benefits which are derived to man "through the redemption that is in Jesus Christ."

When we speak of benefits received by the human race in consequence of the atonement of Christ, the truth is, that man having forfeited good of every kind, and even life itself, by his transgression, all that remains to him more than evil in the natural world, and in the dispensations of general and particular Providence, as well as all spiritual blessings put within his reach by the Gospel, are to be considered as the fruits of the death and intercession of Christ, and ought to be gratefully acknowledged as such.

We now, however, speak in particular of those benefits which immediately relate to what in Scripture is called our SALVATION, or in which this *salvation* consists. By this term is meant the deliverance of man from the penalty, dominion, and pollution of his sins; his introduction into the Divine favor in this life, and his future and eternal felicity in the life to come. The sum of this salvation, so far as it regards a qualification for eternal life, consists in justification, regeneration, adoption, and sanctification. But before we enter upon a particular discussion of each of these gracious benefits we will offer a few preliminary remarks. And,

1. The grand object of our redemption was to accomplish human salvation; and the first effect of Christ's atonement, whether anticipated before his coming, as "the Lamb slain from the foundation of the world," or when effected by his passion, was to place man in that new relation from which salvation might be derived to the offender.

The only relation in which an offended sovereign and a guilty subject can stand in mere justice, is that of a judge and a convicted criminal. But the new relation effected by the death of Christ is, as to God, that of an offended sovereign having devised honorable means to suspend the execution of the penalty of death, and to offer terms of pardon to the condemned; and, as to man, that of an offender having assurance of the placableness of God, his readiness to forgive all his offenses, and that he may, by the use of the prescribed means, actually obtain this favor. But,

2. To this is to be added another consideration. God is not merely disposed to forgive the offenses of men upon their application; but the Scriptures ascribed to his compassion an affecting *activity*. The atonement of Christ having made it morally practicable for God to exercise mercy, he pours that mercy forth in ardent and ceaseless efforts to accomplish his gracious purposes; and, not content with waiting the return of men in penitence and prayer, he employs various means to awaken them to a due sense of their fallen and endangered condition, and to prompt and influence them, sometimes even with mighty efficacy, to seek his grace and favor. This activity of the love of God to man displays itself,

(1.) *In the variety of the Divine dispensations.*—That providential arrangement which is seen in the mixed and checkered circumstances of human life is to be attributed to this design; and viewed under this aspect, it throws an interesting light upon the condition of man. By many the infliction of labor, and sorrow, and disappointment upon fallen man, and the shortening of the term of human life, are considered chiefly, if not exclusively, as measures adopted to prevent evil, or to restrain its overflow in society. Such ends are, doubtless, by the wisdom of God, thus effected to a great and beneficial extent; but there is a still higher design. These dispensations are not only instruments of prevention, but designed means of salvation, co-operating with those agencies by which that result can only be directly produced.

(2.) *In a revelation of the will of God, and a declaration of his purposes of grace.*—These purposes have been declared to man with great inequality, we grant, a mystery which we are not able to explain; but we have the testimony of God in his own word, that in no case, that in no nation, has "he left himself without witness." To the Jews he was pleased to give a written record of his will; and the possession of this in its perfect evangelical form has become the distinguished privilege of all Christian nations who are now exerting themselves to make the blessing universal.

By this direct benefit of the atonement of Christ, the *law* under which we are all placed is exhibited in its full, though reproving perfection ; the character of " Him with whom we have to do " is unvailed ; and the redeeming acts of our Saviour are recorded. Here his example, his sufferings and death, his resurrection, his intercession, the terms of our pardon, the process of our regeneration, the bright and attractive path of obedience, are all presented to our meditations; and surmounting the whole is that " IMMORTALITY " which has been brought " to light through the Gospel."

(3.) *In the institution of the Christian ministry.*—To the great religious advantage of a Divine revelation we are to add the appointment of men, who have themselves been reconciled to God, to preach the word of reconciliation to others. It is made their duty to study the word of God themselves ; faithfully and affectionately to administer it to persons of all conditions, and in every place to which they can have access ; and thus, by a constant activity, to keep the light of truth before the eyes of men, and to impress it upon their conscience.

(4.) *In the influences of the Holy Spirit.*—It is the constant doctrine of the Scriptures, that men are not left to the mere influence of a revelation of truth and the means of salvation, but are graciously excited and effectually aided in all their endeavors to avail themselves of both. Before the flood the Holy Spirit strove with men to restrain them from wickedness, and to lead them to repentance. He strove with them under the *law;* for the wicked are said to have resisted " the Holy Ghost." The moral effects flowing from Messiah's dominion are ascribed by the prophets to the pouring out of the Spirit as rain upon the parched ground, and as the opening of rivers in the desert.

In our Lord's discourse with Nicodemus he declares that the regenerate man is " born of the Spirit." It is by the Spirit that he represents himself as carrying on the work of human salvation after his return to heaven ; and in this sense he promises to be with his disciples, " even unto the end of the world." In accordance with this, the apostles ascribed the success of their preaching, in producing moral changes in the hearts of men, to the same Divine influence. It is the Spirit that gives life to the dead souls of men; the moral virtues are called " the fruits of the Spirit ;" and to be " led by the Spirit" is made the proof of our being the sons of GOD.

To this operation, this working of God in man in conjunction with the written and preached word and other means of grace, is to be attributed that view of the spiritual nature of the law under which we are placed, and the extent of its demands, which produces conviction of sin, and at once annihilates all self-righteousness, and all palliations of offense ; which withers the goodly show of supposititious virtues, and brings the convicted transgressor, whatever his character may be before men, to say before God, "Behold, I am vile, what shall I answer thee?" or with the publican to exclaim, " God be merciful to me a sinner!"

That which every such awakened sinner needs is *mercy*—the remission of his sins and consequent exemption from their penalty. It is only this that can take him from under the malediction of the law which he has violated, and bring him into a state of reconciliation with God. This act of mercy is, in the New Testament, called JUSTIFICATION, to the consideration of which doctrine we will now direct our attention. This will lead us, 1. To inquire into its nature; 2. To show how it may be obtained; and, 3. To meet some objections that are urged against our view of the doctrine.

§ 1. *The Nature of Justification.*

I. *Justification* may be defined to be an act of God's free grace, by which he absolves a sinner from guilt and punishment and accepts him as righteous on account of the atonement of Christ.

The original term rendered justification in the New Testament is δικαίωσις, which means absolution, acquittal, remission of sin. The verb is δικάζω, which signifies to judge, to render sentence, to pronounce just. *To justify*, then, in the Bible acceptation of the term, is *to acquit by a judicial sentence or decision.* The term is evidently forensic, having reference to law and judicial proceedings; and in this sense justification may take place in three different ways:

1. A person may be arraigned at the bar of justice to answer to a specific accusation, but on examination of the testimony in the case it may appear that he is not guilty of the crime alleged against him. Here he is justified by the *force of testimony*, and the law acquits him by declaring the charge to be unfounded; or, in the language of Scripture, by " bringing forth his righteousness as the noonday."

2. A person may be arraigned before the bar of justice to answer to a certain accusation, and it may appear in the course of investigation that though the evidence clearly establishes the fact on which the charge is founded, yet the fact itself is contrary to no law. In this case he is justified by the force of *law*, and a correct administration will so declare the decision.

3. A man may be arraigned before his proper tribunal for a specified crime, tried, and condemned; but the person in whose hands the administration of justice and mercy is lodged may remit the penalty. Here he is justified on the principle of *pardon.*

A person may be justified in a *civil* sense, according to any of these three plans. But in a *scriptural* sense, no man can be justified either by the force of testimony or the force of law; for all men stand justly charged with the violation of God's holy law, and condemned to suffer its penalty. The Bible declares that "all have sinned;" that "all the world are guilty before God;" and that "the soul that sinneth it shall die." It follows, therefore, that if any man obtains justification it must be *on the ground of* PARDON. This is the only door of hope to our fallen and guilty race; but it is one which is thrown open to every sinner by Him who "tasted death for every man."

II. Let us now inquire more particularly into the nature of that justification on the ground of *pardon* which the Scriptures unfold. "To justify a sinner," says Dr. Bunting, in an able sermon on this important subject, "is to account and consider him relatively righteous, and to deal with him as such, notwithstanding his past unrighteousness, by clearing, absolving, discharging, and releasing him from various penal evils, and especially from the wrath of God, and the liability to eternal death, which by that past unrighteousness he had deserved; and by accepting him as if just, and admitting him to the state, the privileges, and the rewards of righteousness." Hence, it appears that justification and the remission or forgiveness of sin are substantially the same.

It is clearly established by the language of the New Testament that justification, the pardon or remission of sins, the non-imputation of sin, and the imputation of righteousness, are terms and phrases of the same import. In proof of this the following passages of Scripture may be consulted:

Luke xviii, 14: "This man went down to his house *justified* rather than the other." Here the term "justified" must be taken in the sense of pardon, since the publican confessed himself to be "a sinner," and in this relation prayed for mercy.

Acts xiii, 38, 39: "Be it known unto you therefore, men and brethren, that through this man is preached unto you *the forgiveness of sins;* and by him all that believe are *justified* from all things." Here, also, it is plain that forgiveness of sins and justification mean the same thing, one term being used as explanatory of the other.

Rom. iv, 5–8: "To him that worketh not, but believeth on him that *justifieth the ungodly*, his faith is counted for righteousness: even as David describeth the blessedness of the man unto whom God *imputeth righteousness* without works, saying, Blessed are they whose *iniquities are forgiven*, and whose *sins are covered*. Blessèd is the man to whom the Lord *will not impute sin*." This passage shows clearly that the apostle considered justification, the imputing of righteousness, the forgiveness of iniquities, the covering of sin, and the non-imputation of sin, as of the same import. They are acts substantially equivalent one to another, and they are therefore expressed by convertible terms, though under views somewhat different.

It is abundantly evident, then, from these passages of Scripture, and from many others that might be adduced, that the justification of a sinner before God is to be understood in the sense of *pardon* or "*the remission of sins;*" and the importance of acquiring and of maintaining this simple and distinct view of the subject will appear from the following considerations:

1. *The pardon of sin is not an act of mere prerogative, done* ABOVE *law, but a judicial process, done* CONSISTENT *with law.*—For in this transaction there are three parties: God as sovereign; "It is God that justifieth." Christ as advocate; not to defend the guilty, but to intercede for them. "If any man sin, we have an *advocate* with the Father, Jesus Christ the righteous." The third party is man, who is, by his own confession, guilty, sinful, and ungodly; for that repentance which in all cases precedes the remission of sins is a confession both of offense and desert of punishment. But as justification does not take place except through the propitiation and intercession of Jesus Christ, and on condition, on the part of the guilty, of faith in his sacrificial death, it is not an act of mere mercy or prerogative, but one which is consistent with a perfectly righteous government and with the justice of God.

2. *Justification has respect to particular individuals.*—It is therefore to be distinguished from " that gracious constitution of God, by which, for the sake of Jesus Christ, he so far delivers all mankind from the guilt of Adam's sin as to place them in a salvable state. Justification is a blessing of a much higher and more perfect character, and is not common to the human race at large, but experienced by a certain description of persons in particular."* It is therefore a subject of personal concern, personal prayer, and personal seeking; and it is to be personally experienced. Nor can any one be safe in trusting to that general gracious constitution under which all men are placed, since that was established in order to the personal and particular justification of those who believe.

3. *Justification being a sentence of pardon, the Antinomian notion of eternal justification becomes a manifest absurdity.*—It supposes the grant of pardon before man was created, when no sin had been committed, no law published, no Saviour promised, no faith exercised, which is not only absurd but impossible. If it be said that the sentence was passed in eternity, but manifested in time, we might as well argue that the world was created from eternity, and that the work of creation in the beginning of time was only a manifestation of that which was from everlasting.

Moreover, it is "the ungodly who are justified;" and, therefore, guilt precedes pardon. But a state of justification is incompatible with a state of guilt; so that the advocates of this wild notion must either give up justification in eternity, or a state of condemnation in time. If they

* Bunting on Justification.

hold the former, they contradict common-sense; if they deny the latter, they deny the Scriptures.

4. *Justification being the pardon of sin, it is not a work by which we are made actually just or righteous.*—It changes our relation to law, it removes condemnation, but it does not change our nature or make us holy. "This is sanctification; which is, indeed, in some degree the immediate fruit of justification; but, nevertheless, is a distinct gift of God, and of a totally different nature. The one implies what GOD '*does for us*' through his Son; the other, what he '*works in us*' by his Spirit. So that, although some rare instances may be found wherein the term justified or justification is used in so wide a sense as to include sanctification also, yet in general use they are sufficiently distinguished from each other both by St. Paul and the other inspired writers."*

Keeping in view, then, what has been said in regard to the nature of justification, it will not be difficult to distinguish between this blessing and the work of regeneration, which, properly speaking, is sanctification in its incipient stage. By justification we are released from the guilt and the penalty of past offenses; but by regeneration we are made new creatures, being "created in Christ Jesus unto good works," that we may "go in peace, and sin no more."

We are not to conclude, however, because God justifies us "freely by his grace, through the redemption that is in Jesus Christ," that our past offenses are less odious in his sight than they were previous to our justification. Pardon cannot change the nature of sin; nor can God ever view it in any other than its true character. By no fiction of law can it be supposed that God ever looks upon sin as not being sin, or that he ever regards the pardoned offender as having never transgressed his commandments. The justified man is, therefore, still viewed as having sinned, though now graciously forgiven; nor will this fact be forgotten even by the redeemed in heaven. Their songs and services will be dedicated "unto Him that loved us, and washed us from our sins in his own blood."

§ 2. *How Justification may be obtained.*

Among those who profess to be guided by the Scriptures several different theories have obtained in regard to the manner in which men are put in possession of the blessing of justification. The *first* theory which we will notice is, that we are justified by the imputation of Christ's active obedience; the *second*, that we are justified by the imputation of Christ's active and passive obedience, taken together; and the *third*, that we are justified by the imputation of faith for righteousness. The last is the scheme which we believe to be taught in the

* Wesley's Sermons.

Scriptures; but we will examine each of them in the order in which they are stated.

I. JUSTIFICATION BY THE IMPUTATION OF CHRIST'S ACTIVE OBEDIENCE.

This may be called the high Calvinistic or Antinomian scheme. It is that the active obedience of Christ is so imputed to the elect as to become theirs in legal construction, and render them as legally righteous as if they had been perfectly obedient to the law of GOD. The plain answer to this is,

1. *That it is wholly gratuitous.*—That the active obedience of Christ is imputed to us for justification is nowhere stated in the Holy Scriptures. It is indeed said, in reference to the Messiah, (Jeremiah xxiii, 6,) that "he shall be called the Lord our *righteousness;*" and St. Paul says (1 Corinthians i, 30) that Christ "is made unto us wisdom, and *righteousness,* and sanctification, and redemption." But there is no evidence that Christ's personal righteousness is here referred to at all. It is rather "his obedience unto *death,* even *the death of the cross.*" Nor is it asserted in these Scriptures that Christ's righteousness shall be ours, or that it shall be imputed to us. Their plain and most obvious meaning is that Christ is the source or fountain whence our righteousness or justification is derived.

2. *That the doctrine involves a fiction and impossibility incompatible with the Divine perfections.*—" The judgment of the all-wise God is always according to truth; neither can it ever consist with his unerring wisdom to think that I am innocent, to judge that I am righteous or holy because another is so. He can no more confound me with Christ than with David or Abraham."* Again, if the obedience of Christ is to be accounted ours in the sense of this theory, then it must be supposed that we never sinned because Christ never sinned; and yet we must ask for pardon, though we are accounted to have perfectly fulfilled in Christ the whole law of God. If it should be said that when we ask for pardon we only ask for a revelation to us of our eternal justification, the matter is not altered; for what need is there of pardon in time or eternity if we are accounted to have perfectly obeyed God's holy law? And why should we be accounted also to have suffered in Christ the penalty of sins which we are accounted never to have committed?

3. *That the personal acts of Christ were of too lofty a character to be imputed to mere creatures.*—He was God and man united in one person,—a circumstance which gave a peculiar character of fullness and perfection to his obedience, beyond the reach of man even in his state of innocence. He that assumes to himself the righteousness of Christ, presents himself to God, not in the habit of a righteous man, but in the glorious attire of the great Mediator of the world. Now, for a worm

* Wesley's Sermons.

of the dust to take this robe of immeasurable majesty upon him, and to suppose himself to be as holy and righteous as Jesus Christ, is what no sober man can imagine to be right.

4. *That there are duties which Christ never personally performed, and in regard to which, therefore, his obedience cannot be imputed to us.*— Suppose that we are guilty of violating the paternal or the conjugal duties, the duties of magistrates or of servants, with many others; the theory is that we are justified by the imputation of Christ's personal acts of righteousness to us, and that they are reckoned to us as though we ourselves had performed them. But our Lord having never stood in any of these relations, never acquired a personal righteousness of this kind; and as that which was never done by him cannot be imputed to us, so it would follow that for such delinquencies there could be no forgiveness.

5. *That this doctrine stands opposed to the moral government of* GOD *and shuts out the obligation of personal obedience to his law.*—So far is it from being a demonstration of God's righteousness that it transfers the obligation of obedience from the subjects of the Divine government to Christ, and thus it leaves man without law, and GOD without dominion.

6. But a crowning and most fatal objection to this theory is *that it shifts the meritorious cause of man's justification from Christ's " obedience unto death,"* where the Scriptures place it, *to Christ's active obedience to the precepts of the law,* and leaves no rational account of the reason of Christ's vicarious sufferings. To the "blood" of Christ the New Testament writers ascribe our redemption; and "faith in his blood" is as clearly held out as the instrumental cause of our justification. But by this doctrine the attention and hope of men are perversely turned away from his sacrificial death to his holy life, which, though necessary, both as an example to us and also to qualify his sacrifice that his blood should be that of "a lamb without spot," is nowhere represented as that on account of which men are pardoned.

If the active obedience of Christ is imputed for justification to all for whom he died, then it will follow, 1. That he died for the *just* and not for the *unjust,* as the Scriptures declare. 2. That his death was unnecessary; for those for whom he died are made perfectly righteous without it. "If righteousness come by the law, then Christ is dead in vain." Gal. ii, 21. And, 3. That men are still under the covenant of works, and are justified by an obedience to the law; though St. Paul declares that "by the deeds of the law there shall no flesh be justified in" the sight of God. Rom. iii, 20.

II. JUSTIFICATION BY THE IMPUTATION OF CHRIST'S ACTIVE AND PASSIVE OBEDIENCE TAKEN TOGETHER.

This is the theory which was held by Mr. Calvin, whose sentiments may be collected with sufficient accuracy from the following passages in the third book of his Institutes:

"We simply explain justification to be an acceptance by which GOD receives us into his favor, and esteems us as righteous persons; and we say it consists in the remission of sins, and the imputation of the righteousness of Christ."* "But this is a wonderful method of justification, that sinners, being invested with the righteousness of Christ, dread not the judgment which they have deserved."† "Man is righteous, not in himself, but because the righteousness of Christ is communicated to him by imputation." And again, "What is placing our righteousness in the obedience of Christ, but asserting that we are accounted righteous only because his obedience is accepted for us as if it were our own."‡

The language which Mr. Calvin employs in these passages seems, at first sight, to favor the Antinomian opinion which we have just refuted; but between that theory and the views which he entertained there is this marked difference, that in the latter there is no separation made between the active and the passive righteousness of Christ; in other words, between his obedience to the precepts of the moral law and his obedience to its penalty. But the obedience of Christ is considered as ONE; his holy life and sacrificial death being regarded as constituting that perfect righteousness which is imputed to us for justification before God.

The view taken by Mr. Calvin of the imputation of Christ's righteousness in justification is, obviously, that his entire obedience to the will of the Father, both in doing and suffering, is, as he says, "accepted for us as if it were our own;" so that, in virtue of this obedience, upon our believing we are accounted righteous, not personally, but by the remission or non-imputation of our sins. Thus he observes on Acts xiii, 38, 39: "The justification which we have by Christ in the Gospel is not a justification *with righteousness*, properly so called, but a justification from sin and from the guilt of sin and condemnation due to it. So when Christ said to men and women in the Gospel, 'Thy sins are forgiven thee,' then he justified them—the forgiveness of their sins was their justification." Again, "Those whom God receives are made righteous no otherwise than as they are purified by being cleansed from all their defilements by the remission of sins."§

So little can be objected to Calvin's doctrine of imputed righteousness that many divines, opposed to the Calvinian theory in general, have not hesitated to assent to it in substance; reserving to themselves some liberty in the use of the terms in which it is often enveloped, either to modify, explain, or reject them.

Thus Arminius: "I believe that sinners are accounted righteous solely by the obedience of Christ; and that the righteousness of Christ is the only meritorious cause on account of which God pardons the sins

---

* Institutes, book 3, chap. 11. † Ibid. ‡ Ibid. § Ibid.

of believers and reckons them as righteous as if they had perfectly fulfilled the law. But since God imputes the righteousness of Christ to none except believers, I conclude that, in this sense, it may be well and properly said, *To a man who believes faith is imputed for righteousness through grace;* because God hath set forth his Son, Jesus Christ, to be a propitiation, a throne of grace, (or mercy-seat,) through faith in his blood."*

So also Mr. Wesley: "As the active and passive righteousness of Christ were never in fact separated from each other, so we never need separate them at all, either in speaking or even in thinking. And it is with regard to both these conjointly that Jesus is called 'The Lord our Righteousness.' But in what sense is this righteousness imputed to believers? In this: All believers are forgiven and accepted, not for the sake of anything in them, or of anything that ever was, that is, or ever can be done by them, but wholly and solely for the sake of what Christ hath done and suffered for them."†

Though these eminent divines seem to agree substantially with Calvin as to the meritorious cause of our justification, yet it is clear that in their interpretation of the phrase, "the imputed righteousness of Christ," they do not entirely follow him. With Calvin the notion of imputation seems to be that the righteousness of Christ, that is, his entire obedience to the will of the Father, both in doing and suffering, is, upon our believing, imputed or accounted to us, or accepted for us, "as if it were OUR OWN." From which we may conclude that he admitted some kind of transfer of the righteousness of Christ to our account; and that believers are considered so to be in Christ as that he should answer for them in law, and plead his righteousness in default of theirs.

The opinion of some professedly Calvinistic divines, as of Baxter and his followers, and of the majority of evangelical Arminians is, that the righteousness of Christ is imputed to believers in the sense of its being accounted of God the valuable consideration, satisfaction, and merit, for the sake of which alone he justifies them freely, and admits them to all the privileges of the covenant of grace.

Between these two theories there is a manifest difference, which arises from the different senses in which the term *imputation* is taken. In the latter it is taken in the sense of accounting or allowing to believers the *benefits* of redemption, through the righteousness of Christ, as the only meritorious cause; but in the former, in the sense of reckoning or accounting *the righteousness of Christ* as ours; that is, what he did and suffered is regarded as done and suffered by us. "His obedience is accepted," says Calvin, "as if it were our own." So then, though Calvin does not divide the active and passive obedience of Christ; though he does not make justification anything more than the remission of sins, yet his opinion easily slides into the Antinomian notion,

* Works of Arminius, vol. i, p. 264. † Wesley's Works, vol. i, pp. 171, 172.

and is open to several of the same objections. It is without any foundation in the word of God;* and it also involves the impossibility that what Christ did and suffered can be considered, in any sense, by him who knows all things as they are, as being done and suffered by us.

But the strongest objection to this theory of imputation is, that it is absurd in itself. For, if the righteousness of Christ is made ours by imputation, and if this righteousness includes both his active and passive obedience to the law of God, then these consequences will follow: 1. That in our justification there is no room for pardon, for it is absurd to suppose that pardon and perfect obedience can meet in the same person. 2. That we are furnished with both an active and a passive justification, which is more than the case demands; unless we are required perfectly to obey the law, and to suffer its penalty also, which would be both unjust and absurd.

It is admitted by the best Arminian writers, that the active and the passive righteousness of Christ are not separated in the Scriptures, and that we ought not to separate them. But though they are united, and though both are essential to the accomplishment of human redemption, yet they are not essential precisely in the same sense. The passive obedience of Christ was *directly* essential, as a satisfaction to the claims of justice; but the active obedience of Christ was essential *indirectly*, as giving perfection and dignity to the sufferer. Hence, properly speaking, the moral obedience of Christ was essential in making satisfaction to justice, only so far as it was necessary that he should possess absolute perfection, in order to render his sufferings available. His active obedience sustained the same relation to his redeeming work as his supreme divinity. Both gave dignity and value to that "obedience unto death" which made an atonement for sin, but they constituted no part of the penalty which justice inflicted. To obey the law, and possess divinity, were essential to his character as Mediator; and we have no more right to suppose that his active obedience is imputed to us as our own, than that his Divine nature is.

In no other sense, then, can the righteousness of Christ be imputed to us than in its benefits and effects; that is, in the blessings and privileges purchased by it. And though we may use the phrase in this qualified sense, yet, since this manner of speaking has no foundation in Scripture, and must generally lead to misapprehension, it will be found more conducive to the cause of truth to confine ourselves to the language of the inspired writers. According to them, there is no fictitious accounting either of what Christ did or suffered, or of both united, to us as being done and suffered by us, through our union with him, or

---

* In support of this theory of imputation the following texts are usually quoted: Isa. xlv, 24; Jer. xxiii, 6; Rom. iii, 21, 22; iv, 6; v, 18, 19; 2 Cor. v, 21. A slight examination, however, will clearly show that these passages prove no such doctrine.

through his becoming our legal representative. But his righteousness, both active and passive, heightened in dignity by its union with the Divine nature, is the true meritorious cause of our justification. It is that great consideration, in view of which the offended but merciful Governor of the world has determined it to be just and righteous, as well as merciful, to justify the ungodly. And, for the sake of this perfect obedience of our Lord to the will of the Father, to every penitent sinner who believes in him, but considered still in his own person as "ungodly," his faith is imputed for "righteousness." It is followed by the remission of his sins, and all the benefits of the evangelical covenant. This leads us to consider,

III. THE DOCTRINE OF JUSTIFICATION BY THE IMPUTATION OF FAITH FOR RIGHTEOUSNESS.

This is the only view of the subject which perfectly harmonizes with the teachings of the Holy Scriptures, and with that great tenet of the Reformation, that we are justified by *faith alone*. The doctrine is thus set forth in our ninth article of religion: "We are accounted righteous before God, only for the merit of our Lord and Saviour Jesus Christ *by faith*, and not for our own works or deservings: Wherefore, that we are justified *by faith only* is a most wholesome doctrine, and very full of comfort."

We will now proceed to give a scriptural view of this doctrine; and to show that faith is the condition, and the only condition of our justification before God.

1. *A scriptural view of the doctrine, that faith is imputed to us for righteousness.*—On this, as well as on every other doctrine of Christianity, the teachings of the Bible must be our guide; and we now appeal to this infallible standard of truth, with the strongest confidence of finding a satisfactory account of the doctrine before us.

That this is the doctrine taught by the express letter of the Scriptures no one can deny; and, as has been well observed, "what that is which is imputed for righteousness in justification, all the wisdom and learning of men are not so fit or able to determine as the Holy Ghost." The apostle tells us that "Abraham believed God, and it was counted ($ελογισθη$, *imputed*) unto him for righteousness." Rom. iv, 3. So verse 5: "To him that worketh not, but believeth on him that justifieth the ungodly, his faith is counted for righteousness." So also in verse 9: "We say that faith was reckoned (*imputed*) to Abraham for righteousness." "Now, it was not written for his sake alone, that it was imputed to him; but for us also, to whom it shall be imputed, if we believe on him that raised up Jesus our Lord from the dead." (Verses 23, 24.)

The testimony of the apostle, then, being so express on this point, the imputation of faith for righteousness must be taken to be the doctrine of the New Testament, unless we admit, with the advocates of the imputation of Christ's righteousness, that faith is here used metonymically for the *object* of faith, that is, the righteousness of Christ. The context of the above passages, however, sufficiently refutes this, and makes it indubitable that the apostle uses the term *faith* in its proper and literal sense. In verse 5 he calls the faith of him that believeth, and which is imputed to him for righteousness, " HIS FAITH ;" but in what sense could this be taken if St. Paul meant by "his faith" the object of his faith, namely, the righteousness of Christ? And how could that be *his* before the imputation is made to him?

Again, the faith spoken of is opposed to works. "To him that *worketh* not, but *believeth* on him that justifieth the ungodly, his *faith* is counted for righteousness." In verse 21 the apostle represents that faith which was imputed to Abraham for righteousness as consisting in a firm reliance on the ability of God to perform his gracious promises. " And being fully persuaded, that what he had promised, he was able also to perform. And therefore, it was imputed to him for righteousness." Finally, in verse 24, the faith which shall be imputed to us for righteousness is described to be our believing " on him that raised up Jesus our Lord from the dead." By these explanations the apostle has rendered it most indubitable, that by the term faith he means the act of believing.

Some further observations may be necessary, however, for the clear apprehension of this doctrine in its true scriptural light.

The apostle, in treating the subject of justification, lays it down as a great and fundamental axiom, that *by the works of the law no man can be justified.* His doctrine is, that all men are sinners; that they must confess themselves such and join to this confession a true repentance; that justification is a gratuitous act of God's mercy, a procedure of pure grace, not of debt; that in order to the exercise of this grace on the part of God, Christ was set forth as a propitiation for sin ; that his death under this character is a " demonstration of the righteousness of God" in the free and gratuitous remission of sins, and that this actual remission or justification follows upon our believing in Christ, because faith under this gracious constitution and method of justification is accounted to men for righteousness; in other words, that righteousness is imputed to them upon their believing, which imputation of righteousness consists in the forgiveness of sins.

The apostle shows also, from the justification of Abraham, that this is no new doctrine: " Abraham believed God, and it was counted unto him for righteousness." Rom. iv, 3. " Know ye, therefore, that they which are of faith, the same are the children of Abraham. And the Scripture, foreseeing that God would justify the heathen through faith, preached before the Gospel unto Abraham, saying, In thee shall all nations be blessed. So, then, they which be of faith are blessed with faithful Abraham." Gal. iii, 7-9.

When, however, we say that faith is imputed for righteousness, in order to prevent misapprehension and fully to answer the objections raised on the other side, the meaning of the different terms of this proposition ought to be explained. They are RIGHTEOUSNESS, FAITH, and IMPUTATION.

(1.) With regard to the first, it may be observed that the apostle often uses the term δικαιοσυνη, *righteousness*, in a passive sense for justification itself. Thus: "If righteousness (*justification*) come by the law, then Christ is dead in vain." Gal. ii, 21. "For if there had been a law given which could have given life, verily, righteousness (*justification*) should have been by the law." Gal. iii, 21. "The Gentiles have attained to righteousness, (*justification*,) even the righteousness (*justification*) which is of faith." Rom. ix, 30. "Christ is the end of the law for righteousness (*justification*) to every one that believeth." Rom. x, 4. It may be seen from Romans v, 18, 19, that with the apostle, to "be made righteous" and to be justified signify the same thing; for "justification of life," in the eighteenth verse, is called in the nineteenth being "made righteous." To be accounted righteous is, then, in the apostle's style, where there has been personal guilt, to be justified; and what is accounted or imputed to us for righteousness, is accounted or imputed to us for justification.

(2.) The next term which it is necessary to explain is FAITH. The true nature of justifying faith will be explained in another place. All that is necessary here is to remark, that it is not every act of faith, nor faith in the general truths of revelation, which is imputed for righteousness, though it supposes the *latter*, and is the completion of it. "Through faith we understand that the worlds were framed by the word of God," but it is not our faith in creation which is imputed to us for righteousness. So in the case of Abraham, he not only had faith in the truths of the religion of which he was the teacher and guardian, but had exercised affiance, also, in some particular promises of God before he exhibited that great act of faith which was "counted to him for righteousness," and which made his justification the pattern of the justification of sinful men in all ages. But having received the promise of a son, from whom the Messiah should spring, in whom all nations were to be blessed, "he staggered not at the promise of God," even in view of seeming impossibilities, "but was strong in faith, giving glory to God; and being fully persuaded, that what he had promised, he was able also to perform. *And therefore it was imputed to him for righteousness.*" Rom. iv, 20–22. His faith had Messiah for its ultimate object, and in its nature it was an entire affiance in the promise and faithfulness of God, with reference to the holy seed.

So, likewise, the object of that faith which is imputed to us for righteousness is Christ—Christ as having made atonement for our sins; for it is "through faith *in his blood*" that we obtain remission. This faith is, therefore, an entire affiance in God's promise of pardon, made to us through the atonement of Christ, and founded upon it. This view of faith excludes all notion of its meritoriousness. It is not faith, generally considered, which is imputed to us for righteousness, but *trust* in an atonement offered by another in our behalf; by which trust in something without us we acknowledge our own insufficiency, guilt, and unworthiness, and directly ascribe the merit to that in which we trust, and which is not our own, namely, the propitiation of the blood of Christ.

(3.) The last term to be explained is IMPUTATION. The original verb (λογιζομαι) is well enough translated to impute in the sense of *to reckon, to account;* but it is never used to signify imputation in the sense of accounting the actions of one person to have been performed by another.

A man's sin or righteousness is imputed to him when he is considered as actually the doer of sinful or of righteous acts, in which sense the word *repute* is more commonly used; and he is consequently reputed a vicious or a holy man. A man's sin or righteousness is imputed to him in its *legal consequences*, under a government of rewards and punishments; and then to impute sin or righteousness signifies, in a legal sense, to reckon or account it, to acquit or to condemn, and forthwith to punish or exempt from punishment. Thus Shimei entreated David not to "impute iniquity unto" him, that is, not to punish him for his iniquity.

In this sense, too, David speaks of the blessedness of the man "unto whom the Lord imputeth not iniquity," that is, whom he forgives, so that the legal consequences of his sin shall not fall upon him. This non-imputation of sin to a sinner is expressly called the "imputation of righteousness *without works*." The imputation of righteousness is, then, the non-punishment or pardon of sin; and if this passage be read in its connection, it will also be seen that by the imputing of faith for righteousness, the apostle means precisely the same thing. "To him that worketh not, but believeth on him that justified the ungodly, *his faith is counted for righteousness;* even as David, also, described the man unto whom God *imputeth righteousness* without works, saying, Blessed are they whose *iniquities are forgiven*, and whose sins are covered. Blessed is the man to whom the Lord *will not impute sin*."

This quotation from David would have been nothing to the apostle's purpose unless he had understood the forgiveness of sins, the imputation of righteousness, and the non-imputation of sin, to signify the same thing as the accounting of faith for righteousness, with only this difference, that the introduction of the term *faith* marks the manner in which the forgiveness of sin is obtained. To impute faith for righteousness is nothing more than to be justified by faith; which is also called by St. Paul, "being made righteous," that is, being placed by an act of free forgiveness, through faith in Christ, in the condition of righteous men in this respect, that the penalty of the law does not lie against them, and that they are restored to the Divine favor.

From this brief but, it is hoped, clear explanation of these terms, righteousness, faith, and imputation, it will appear that it is not quite correct in the advocates of the Scripture doctrine of the imputation of faith for righteousness to say that our faith in Christ is accepted in the place of personal obedience to the law; except, indeed, in this loose sense, that our faith in Christ as effectually exempts us from punishment as if we had been personally obedient. The scriptural doctrine is rather that *the death of Christ* is accepted in the place of our *personal punishment* on condition of our faith in him; and that when this faith is actually exercised, then comes in, on the part of God, the act of imputing or reckoning righteousness to us; or, what is the same thing, accounting faith for righteousness; that is, pardoning our offenses through faith, and treating us as the objects of his restored favor. Hence we arrive at the conclusion,

2. *That faith is the condition, and the only condition, of our justification before God.*—This view of the subject is very clearly established by numerous passages of Scripture. We remark, then,

(1.) It is the evangelical condition of justification. "He that believeth on him is not condemned;" that is, he is justified, for justification is the opposite of condemnation. "He that believeth on the Son hath everlasting life." John iii, 36. "Believe on the Lord Jesus Christ, and thou shalt be saved." Acts xvi, 31. It is a *necessary* condition. "He that believeth not shall be damned." Mark xvi, 16. "He that believeth not is condemned already;" and he is condemned "*because* he hath not believed in the name of the only-begotten Son of God." John iii, 18. "He that believeth not the Son, shall not see life; but the wrath of God abideth on him." John iii, 18, 36. As there is no "other name under heaven given among men whereby we must be saved," but the name of Jesus Christ, so there is no way by which we can obtain the salvation which Christ has purchased for us but by believing in his name. While we are destitute of this faith we are "without Christ, being aliens from the commonwealth of Israel, and strangers from the covenants of promise, having no hope, and without God in the world."

(2.) Faith is the *only* necessary condition. It is the "only thing without which no one is justified; the only thing that is immediately, indispensably, absolutely requisite in order to pardon. As on the one hand, though a man should have everything else, yet without faith he cannot be justified; so, on the other, though he be supposed to want everything else, yet if he has faith he cannot but be justified. For suppose a sinner of any kind or degree, in a full sense of his total ungodliness, of his utter inability to think, speak, or do good, and his absolute meetness for hell fire: suppose I say, this sinner, helpless and hopeless, casts himself wholly on the mercy of God in Christ, (which indeed he cannot do but by the grace of God,) who can doubt but he is forgiven in that moment? Who will affirm that any more is *indispensably required* before the sinner can be justified?"*

Faith, then, is the condition to which the promise of God annexes justification; that without which justification would not take place, and in this sense it is that we are justified by faith; not by the *merit* of faith, but by faith *instrumentally* as this condition, for its connection with the benefit arises from the merits of Christ and the promise of God. "If Christ had not merited, God had not promised; if God had not promised, justification had never followed upon this faith; so that the indissoluble connection of faith and justification is from God's institution, whereby he has bound himself to give the benefit upon performance of the condition."†

This reliance upon the promise of God, made to us through the mediation of Jesus Christ, is at once an acknowledgment of our guilt, and that we have no righteousness of our own. It honors God the Father and Christ the Redeemer. It acknowledges on earth what will forever be acknowledged in heaven, that the whole of our salvation, from its beginning to its last degree, is a work of God's free grace, effected through the merits and intercession of Christ, and by the power of the Holy Spirit.

From this plain and scriptural account of the doctrine of justification by faith we may infer, 1. That the faith by which we are justified is not a mere assent to the doctrines of the Gospel, which leaves the heart unmoved and unaffected by a sense of the evil and danger of sin, though it supposes this assent; nor, 2. Is it that more lively and cordial belief of the Gospel, touching our sinful and lost condition, which is wrought in the heart by the Holy Spirit, and from which springs repentance, though this must precede it; nor, 3. Is it only the assent of the mind to the method by which God justifies the ungodly by faith in the sacrifice of his Son, though this is an element in it; but, 4. That it is a hearty concurrence of the WILL and AFFECTIONS with this plan of salvation, which implies a renunciation of every other refuge, an actual trust in the Saviour, and a personal apprehension of his merits. It is "such a belief of the Gospel as leads us to come to Christ, to trust in Christ, and to commit the keeping of our souls into his hands, in humble confidence of his ability and his willingness to save us."‡

§ 3. *Objections Answered.*

To the doctrine of justification by faith alone some objections have been made, the most important of which we will now consider. It is objected,

* Wesley's Works, vol. i, p. 51.   † Lawson.   ‡ Dr. Bunting.

1. That *if faith is imputed to us for righteousness, then justification is by works, or by somewhat in ourselves.*—In this objection the term *works* is equivocal. If it means works of obedience to the moral law the objection is unfounded, for faith is not a work of this kind. If it means the *merit* of works of any kind it is equally without foundation, for no merit is allowed to faith. Indeed, faith, in the sense of exclusive affiance, or trusting in the merits of Christ, shuts out, by its very nature, all assumption of merit to ourselves; otherwise, there would be no need of resorting to the merits of another. But if the term means that faith or believing is doing something in order to our justification, it is, in this view, the performance of a condition, a *sine qua non*, which is not only not forbidden in Scripture, but required of us. "This is the work of God, that ye believe on him whom he hath sent." "He that believeth shall be saved; but he that believeth not shall be damned." And so far is this from being incompatible with the free grace of God in our justification, that St. Paul makes our justification by faith the proof of its gratuitous nature; "for by *grace* are ye saved through *faith*." "Therefore, it is by *faith* that it might be by *grace*."

2. Another objection is, that *the imputation of faith for righteousness gives occasion to boasting, which is condemned by the Gospel.*—The answer to this is, 1. That the objection lies with equal strength against the theory of the imputation of Christ's righteousness, since faith is required in order to that imputation. 2. Boasting of our faith is cut off by the consideration that the power to believe is the gift of God. 3. If it were not, yet the blessings which follow upon our faith are not given with reference to any compensative worth or merit which there may be in our believing, but are given with respect to the death of Christ, from the bounty and grace of God. 4. St. Paul was clearly of the contrary opinion, who tells us that "boasting is excluded *by the law of faith;*" the reason of which has been already stated, that trust in another for salvation does, *ipso facto*, attribute the power, and consequently the honor of our salvation to another, and denies both to ourselves.

3. It is still further objected, that *the doctrine of justification by faith alone is unfavorable to morality.*—To this the answer is, that though we are justified by faith *alone*, the faith by which we are justified is *not alone* in the heart which exercises it. In receiving Christ, as the writers of the Reformation often say, "faith is *sola*, yet not *solitaria*." It is not the trust of a man asleep and secure, but the trust of one awakened, and aware of the peril of eternal death as the wages of sin. It is not the trust of a man ignorant of the spiritual meaning of God's holy law, but of one who is convinced and slain by it. It is, in a word, the trust of one who feels through the convincing power of the word and Spirit of God that he is justly exposed to wrath, and in

whom this conviction produces a genuine sorrow for sin, and an intense and supreme desire to be delivered from its penalty and dominion. As this is proved by the seventh chapter of Paul's Epistle to the Romans, so the former part of the eighth shows the moral state which is the immediate result of "being in Christ Jesus," through the exercise of that faith which alone, as we have seen, can give us a personal interest in him. "There is now no condemnation to them which are in Christ Jesus." This exemption from condemnation is the first result of justification by faith. The next is manifestly concomitant with it, "who walk not after the flesh, but *after the Spirit*." This is the effect of the faith that justifies; from which alone, as it brings us to Christ our deliverer, our entire deliverance from sin can follow. "What shall we say then? Shall we continue in sin, that grace may abound? God forbid: how shall we, that are dead to sin, live any longer therein?" Rom. vi, 1, 2. Thus the apostle himself meets this very objection, by showing that the doctrine of justification by faith is the doctrine of holiness, and points out the only remedy for sin's dominion.

4. It is objected, that *the doctrine of justification by faith alone is inconsistent with what the Scriptures teach in reference to justification by evangelical obedience.*—It is proper to observe here, that the word *justify* is used in Scripture in reference to that sentence of acquittal which shall be pronounced upon men at the day of judgment. Thus: "By *thy words thou shalt be justified*, and by thy words thou shalt be condemned." Matt. xii, 37. As the term "*words*," in the text, denotes the entire moral conduct, this justification is in a certain sense by works. It is not, however, by the *merit* of works, but by their *testimony*, as the proof of our true moral character. Hence it is declared, that every man shall be rewarded "*according to his* works." Nor are the works according to which men shall be justified in the last day to be considered in the abstract, but only as resulting from an evangelical faith.

The theory assumed in the objection is substantially that of justification by works, with these qualifications, that the works are evangelical, or such as proceed from faith; that they are done by Divine assistance; and that such works, though not meritorious, are a necessary condition of justification. The advocates of this scheme rely mainly upon the testimony of St. James, supposing him to teach the doctrine that a man is justified before God by evangelical obedience. Instead of reconciling St. James to St. Paul, the course which commentators usually pursue, they attempt to reconcile the latter to the former. They suppose, therefore, that when St. Paul denies the possibility of justification by works he refers simply to works of obedience to the Mosaic law, and that by the faith which justifies, he means the works which spring from faith. A few remarks, however, will be sufficient to show that these theorists have misinterpreted both St. Paul and St. James, and that there is really no discrepancy between them.

(1.) They seem to disagree only in what they testify respecting the justification of Abraham. But they do not refer to the same event. St. Paul speaks of Abraham's justification when, before the birth of Isaac, his faith in the promise of God was counted "to him for righteousness;" St. James, of his justification when he "offered Isaac his son upon the altar." Hence, as they speak of entirely different transactions, separated in time by about twenty-five years, they cannot contradict one another.

(2.) The two apostles do not use the term *faith* in the same sense. St. Paul speaks of that faith which "works by love and purifies the heart." St. James speaks of faith as a mere assent of the understanding; of that faith which is "dead," and "alone," and such as "devils" possess. St. Paul nowhere affirms that we are justified by such a faith as this. The faith of which he speaks is never "alone," though it alone justifies. Hence, when St. James asks the question, "Can faith save him?" he means a very different faith from that of which St. Paul speaks when he concludes "that a man is justified by *faith* without the deeds of the law." Rom. iii, 28.

(3.) Nor do these apostles use the term *justification* in the same sense. That St. Paul uses it in the sense of pardon, or the remission of sins, has been clearly proved. But that St. James does not use it in this sense is most evident from his reference to the case of Abraham. "Was not Abraham, our father, justified by works, when he had offered Isaac his son upon the altar?" Does St. James mean that Abraham was then justified in the sense of being forgiven? Certainly not; for in this sense he had been justified, according to the testimony of Moses, not less than twenty-five years before.* To suppose, then, that St. James speaks of this kind of justification, is to suppose him to teach the doctrine that Abraham was not pardoned and received into the favor of God until he had offered his son upon the altar; but as this would contradict both Moses and St. Paul, it cannot be admitted. Hence we conclude, that St. James, in what he assumes respecting the justification of Abraham by works, means no more than that his obedience was a manifestation or proof of his former justification by faith. By the astonishing act of his obedience in offering his son upon the altar "the Scripture was fulfilled," that is, it was *illustrated* and *confirmed*, "which saith, Abraham believed God, and it was imputed unto him for righteousness." James ii, 23.

* Gen. xv, 4–6.

CHAPTER IX.

REGENERATION.

CONCOMITANT with justification, which we have just considered, are the two great blessings of the remedial system,—REGENERATION and ADOPTION. With respect to these we may observe, that though we must distinguish them as being different from each other, and from justification, yet they are not to be separated. They all occur at the same time, and they all enter into the experience of the same person; so that no man is justified without being regenerated and adopted, and no man is regenerated and made a child of God who is not justified. Whenever, therefore, they are mentioned in Scripture, they involve and imply one another,—a remark which may preserve us from some error.

Thus, with respect to our heirship or title to eternal life, it may be inferred from our *justification*. "That, being justified by his grace, we should be made heirs according to the hope of eternal life." Titus iii, 7. It is also connected with our *regeneration*. "Blessed be the God and Father of our Lord Jesus Christ, which according to his abundant mercy hath begotten us again unto a lively hope by the resurrection of Jesus Christ from the dead, to an inheritance incorruptible," etc. 1 Peter i, 3. It is, however, mainly grounded upon our *adoption*. "And if children, then heirs; heirs of God and joint heirs with Christ." Rom. viii, 17.

These passages are a sufficient proof, that justification, regeneration, and adoption are all taken together as the ground of our title, through the gift of God in Christ Jesus, to the heavenly inheritance. They are attained, too, by the same faith. We are "justified by faith;" and we are "the children of God by faith in Christ Jesus." Accordingly, in the following passage they are all united as the effect of the same faith. "But as many as received him, to them gave he power to become the *sons of God*, even to them that *believe* on his name; which were *born*, not of blood, nor of the will of the flesh, nor of the will of man, but of God." John i, 12, 13.

Having made these general remarks, we will now proceed to inquire into the Nature, the Necessity, and the Means of Regeneration.

I. THE NATURE OF REGENERATION.

The Greek word παλιγγενεσία, which is rendered *regeneration*, is compounded of πάλιν, *again*, and γένεσις, *birth*, *nativity*, *origin*. It literally signifies reproduction; the act of forming a thing into a new and better state. The term is used by Greek writers to express that renovation of the face of nature which is produced by the return of spring, when the earth sends forth her vegetables, flowers, and fruits. So, by a strong metaphor, Cicero, writing to Atticus, expresses the state and dignity to which he was reappointed after his return from exile, by the term *regeneration*. Josephus also calls the rebuilding and restoration of Jerusalem, after the Babylonian captivity, the *regeneration* of his country.

There are only two passages of Scripture in the New Testament in which the term regeneration is employed. These are Matthew xix, 28, and Titus iii, 5. Some commentators refer the term, as employed by Matthew, to the millennial state; some, to the general resurrection; but others, to the Gospel dispensation in its perfected state. It must, however, be admitted by all, that "regeneration," in this passage, has no direct reference to that moral renovation by which men are constituted the children of God.

The passage in Titus reads thus: "Not by works of righteousness which we have done, but according to his mercy he saved us, by the washing of regeneration, and renewing of the Holy Ghost." Here, it is generally understood, that the phrase "washing of regeneration" refers to the rite of baptism; and that this rite is so denominated, because it is the symbol or emblem of that Divine influence by which the soul is truly regenerated. Hence the apostle adds, "and renewing of the Holy Ghost;" which is intimately connected with what goes before, and is exegetical of it. We must conclude, therefore, that the term "regeneration," in this passage, is applied to that moral change by which a man is constituted a child of God and an heir of eternal life.

REGENERATION may be defined to be that moral change in man, wrought by the Holy Spirit, by which he is saved from the love, the practice, and the dominion of sin, and enabled, with full choice of will and the energy of right affections, to love God and to keep his commandments.

In considering more fully the nature of this great moral change, we may remark,

1. *That* REPENTANCE *is not regeneration.*—It is only that preparatory process which leads to regeneration as it leads to pardon; but it is a process without which regeneration does not take place. Conviction, then, of the evil and danger of an unregenerate state must first be felt. It is true that repentance itself implies a work of God in the heart, and an important moral change; but it is not *this* change, because regeneration is that renewal of our nature which gives us dominion over sin, and enables us to serve God from love, and not merely from fear. This, with all true penitents, is still the object of search and eager desire, and is, therefore, confessedly unattained. They are not yet "created in Christ Jesus unto good works," which is as special and instant a work of God as justification.

2. *That regeneration is a supernatural work.*—It is everywhere in Scripture ascribed to Divine agency. The regenerate are born "not of blood, nor of the will of the flesh, nor of the will of man, but *of God.*" John i, 13. It is sometimes ascribed to the Father : " Of his own will begat he us with the word of truth." James i, 18. Of this great change Christ is the meritorious cause; but it is especially attributed to the Holy Spirit as the efficient cause. In our Lord's conversation with Nicodemus he declares that " except a man be born of water and of the *Spirit,* he cannot enter into the kingdom of heaven ;" that " that which is born of the *Spirit* is spirit ;" and that " so is every one that is born of the *Spirit.*" John iii, 5, 6, 8. So also St. Paul teaches us, in 2 Thessalonians ii, 13, that we are chosen to salvation " through sanctification of the Spirit ;" and in Titus iii, 5, that we are regenerated " by the renewing of the Holy Ghost." These are only a few of the many passages which ascribe our moral renovation to the Holy Spirit, but they are sufficient to establish the point.

3. *That regeneration is an inward and spiritual change.*—To be convinced that this is an inward and thorough renovation of our moral being, it is only necessary that we should consider the many plain and impressive figures which the sacred writers employ illustrative of its nature.

It is the bestowment of a *new heart* and a *new spirit.* " Then will I sprinkle clean water upon you, and ye shall be clean: from all your filthiness and from all your idols will I cleanse you. A new heart also will I give you, and a new spirit will I put within you; and I will take away the stony heart out of your flesh, and I will give you a heart of flesh." Ezek. xxxvi, 25, 26.

It is the *circumcision of the heart.* " The Lord thy God will circumcise thy heart, and the heart of thy seed, to love the Lord thy God with all thy heart, and with all thy soul, that thou mayest live." Deut. xxx, 6. Again: " He is a Jew, which is one inwardly ; and circumcision is that of the heart, in the spirit, and not in the letter ; whose praise is not of men, but of God." Rom. ii, 29.

It is a *new birth.* " Except a man be *born again,* he cannot see the kingdom of God." " Marvel not that I said unto thee, Ye must be *born again.*" John iii, 3, 7. " Being *born again,* not of corruptible seed, but of incorruptible." 1 Peter i, 23.

It is a *new creation.* " If any man be in Christ he is a *new creature:* (or, there is a new creation:) old things are passed away; behold, all things are become new." 2 Cor. v, 17. So also, " We are his workmanship, created in Christ Jesus unto good works." Eph. ii, 10.

It is the *image of God on the soul.* "And that ye put on the new man, which after God is created in righteousness and true holiness." Eph. iv, 24. Again : " And have put on the new man, which is renewed in knowledge after the image of him that created him." Col. iii, 10.

It is *Christ formed in the heart.* "My little children, of whom I travail in birth again until *Christ be formed in you.*" Gal. iv, 19. "To whom God would make known what is the riches of the glory of this mystery among the Gentiles; which is *Christ in you,* the hope of glory." Col. i, 27.

And, finally, it is *freedom from the dominion of sin.* "For sin shall not have dominion over you; for ye are not under the law, but under grace." Rom. vi, 14. "Whosoever is born of God *doth not commit sin;* for his seed remaineth in him, and he *cannot sin,* because he is born of God." 1 John iii, 9.

From these Scriptures it manifestly appears what is the true nature of regeneration. "It is that great change which God works in the soul when he brings it into life; when he raises it from the death of sin to the life of righteousness. It is the change wrought in the whole soul by the Almighty Spirit of God when it is 'created anew in Christ Jesus;' when it is 'renewed after the image of God, in righteousness and true holiness;' when the love of the world is changed into the love of God; pride into humility; passion into meekness; hatred, envy, malice, into a sincere, tender, disinterested love for all mankind. In a word, it is that change whereby the earthly, sensual, devilish mind is turned into the 'mind which was in Christ Jesus.'"* "So is every one that is born of the Spirit."

4. *That regeneration always accompanies justification.*—This may be proved,

(1.) From the nature of justification itself, which takes away the penalty of sin: that penalty in not only obligation to punishment, but also the loss of the sanctifying Spirit, and the curse of being left under the slavery of sin and the dominion of Satan.—Regeneration is effected by this Spirit restored to us, and is a consequence of our pardon; for though justification in itself is the remission of sin, yet a justified *state* implies a change, both in our condition and disposition: in our *condition,* as we are in a state of life, not of death; of safety, not of condemnation and danger: in our *disposition,* as regenerate and new creatures.

(2.) From Scripture, which affords us direct proof that regeneration is concomitant with justification. "If any man be IN CHRIST, he is a new creature." 2 Cor. v, 17. The meaning of the phrase "IN CHRIST" is explained by Romans viii, 1, considered in connection with the preceding chapter, to which it properly belongs. That chapter describes the state of one convinced and slain by the law. We may discover in this description certain moral changes, as consenting to the law that it is good; delight in it after the inward man; strong desires, and a humble confession. The state represented is, however, one of guilt, spiritual captivity, helplessness, and misery; a state of *condemnation,*

---
* Wesley's Works, vol. i, p. 403.

and of *bondage to sin.* The opposite condition is that of a man "IN CHRIST JESUS." To him "there is no *condemnation;*" he is forgiven; the bondage to sin is broken; he "walks not after the flesh, but after the Spirit." To be "IN CHRIST" is, therefore, to be justified; and regeneration instantly follows. We see, then, the order of the Divine operation in individual experience: conviction of sin, helplessness, and danger; faith in Christ, justification, and regeneration.

II. THE NECESSITY OF REGENERATION.

The great proof of the necessity of regeneration lies in the depravity of our moral nature. This doctrine St. Paul teaches in the most explicit manner in the first three chapters of his Epistle to the Romans; and, commenting on his own arguments, he says, "We have proved both JEWS *and* Gentiles, that they are all under sin." Considering this point as fully established, we will proceed to argue the necessity of regeneration,

1. *From express declarations of Scripture.*—"Except ye be converted, and become as little children, ye shall not enter into the kingdom of heaven." Matt. xviii, 3. "Except a man be born again, he cannot see the kingdom of God." "Ye must be born again." John iii, 3, 7. "Know ye not that the unrighteous shall not inherit the kingdom of God." 1 Cor. vi, 9. But this necessity may be argued,

2. *From the holiness of God.*—God is a perfectly holy Being, and must, therefore, regard sin with hatred and abhorrence. "Every sinner opposes his whole character, law, designs, and government; loves what he hates, hates what he loves, and labors to dishonor his name and to frustrate his purposes. This character of the sinner God discerns with clear and unerring certainty. Both his guilt and its desert are naked to the Omniscient eye. It is impossible, therefore, that he should not regard it with abhorrence. To suppose him, then, to approve and love such a character, is to suppose him to approve of that which he sees to be deserving of his absolute reprobation, and to love that which he knows merits nothing but his hatred."* Such a course of procedure cannot be ascribed to a God of infinite purity, and hence none but the regenerate shall enter into life eternal. But this necessity is evident,

3. *From the character of God as a righteous Governor.*—Were he to confer upon the unregenerate the blessings which are promised to the virtuous as their proper reward, he would equally desert his character and his government, and would overthrow the wisdom, the equity, and the benevolent end of his moral administration. To crown the unregenerate with eternal life would be a declaration on the part of God that they deserved the same proofs of his favor as his obedient children, and were therefore of the same character; that rebels were faithful subjects; that enemies were friends; and that, though he had denounced

* Dwight's Theology, vol. 2, p. 407.

them as objects of his wrath, they were nevertheless the objects of his infinite complacency. "This would be no other than a final declaration on his part that right and wrong, holiness and sin, were the same things; that his law, and the government founded on it, were introduced to no purpose, unless to excite wonder and fear in his intelligent creatures; that the redemption of Christ was accomplished to no end; and that all the Divine conduct, solemn, awful, and sublime as it has appeared, was wholly destitute of any object, and really of no importance in the view of the Infinite mind."* If we would avoid these and similar absurdities, we must admit the necessity of regeneration and holiness of character in order to the rewards of eternal life. But regeneration is necessary,

4. *To qualify men for the* HAPPINESS *of heaven.*—"Heaven is the seat of supreme and unmingled happiness; of enjoyment solid, sincere, and eternal; the foundation on which, so far as creatures are concerned, this happiness ultimately rests, is their holy or virtuous character. All their affections, all their pursuits, all their enjoyments, are virtuous without a mixture. Hence heaven is called *the high* and *holy place*, and, from the dispensations of God toward these unspotted beings, is termed *the habitation of his holiness.* With such companions a sinner could not accord, such affections he could not exercise, in such pursuits he could not unite, in such enjoyments he could not share. This is easily and familiarly demonstrated. Sinners do not love virtuous persons here; they exercise no virtuous affections, engage in no virtuous pursuits, and relish no virtuous enjoyments. Sinners in the present world love not God, trust not in the Redeemer, delight not in Christians, and regard neither the law of God nor the Gospel of his Son with complacency of heart. Sinners in this world find no pleasure in the Sabbath, nor in the sanctuary; and never cordially unite either in the prayers or the praises then and there offered up to their Maker.

"How, then, could sinners find happiness in heaven? That glorious world is one vast sanctuary; and the endless succession of ages which roll over its happy inhabitants are an everlasting sabbath. 'They rest not day and night, saying, Holy, holy, holy, Lord God Almighty, which was, and is, and is to come.' As the worship of God is uniformly burdensome to sinners here, the same worship must be at least equally burdensome to them there. If, then, a sinner is to be admitted into heaven, it is absolutely necessary that he should have a new heart, a new disposition. Otherwise it is plain, that amid all the blessings of that delightful world, he would find nothing but disgust, mortification, and sorrow."†

III. THE MEANS OF REGENERATION.

The regeneration of a sinner is emphatically a work of the Holy Spirit. In the performance of this work, however, he is not bound by any

* Dwight's Theology, vol. 2, p. 408. † Ibid., vol. 2, pp. 408, 409.

specific rules or mode of procedure; for he performs his operations in a sovereign manner, and can work without the intervention of any visible means whatever. But there are certain ordinances of Divine appointment which were evidently intended to be the means of our salvation, and consequently, the means of our regeneration. Connected with these Divine institutions are "exceeding great and precious promises;" so that in the proper use of them we may expect to escape from our moral corruption, and to be made "partakers of the Divine nature." As means, therefore, of regeneration, we may notice,

1. *The inspired* Word.—"The law of the Lord is perfect," says David, "converting the soul." Psa. xix, 7. St. Paul in addressing Timothy says, "From a child thou hast known the Holy Scriptures, which are able to make thee wise unto salvation through faith which is in Christ Jesus." And then he immediately adds this very important testimony respecting the saving efficacy of the inspired word: "All Scripture is given by inspiration of God, and is profitable for doctrine, for reproof, for correction, for instruction in righteousness; that the man of God may be perfect, thoroughly furnished unto all good works." 2 Tim. iii, 15. Of the same import is the testimony of St. James and St. Peter. "Of his own will begat he us with the word of truth." James i, 18. "Being born again, not of corruptible seed, but of incorruptible by the word of God, which liveth and abideth forever." 1 Peter i, 23. How appropriate, then, is the exhortation of our Lord: "Search the Scriptures; for in them ye think ye have eternal life."

2. *The Ministry of the Gospel.*—This is the great instrument that God has appointed to turn sinners "from darkness to light, and from the power of Satan unto God." Hence, St. Paul declares of the Gospel, that "it is the power of God unto salvation to every one that believeth;" and speaks of it as "the sword of the Spirit." The numerous conversions recorded in the New Testament were chiefly effected through the preaching of the Gospel. It came to them who heard it, as the apostle says, "not in word only, but also in power, and in the Holy Ghost, and in much assurance." It was while Peter preached the Gospel on the day of Pentecost that the multitude cried out, under penitential awakenings, "Men and brethren, what shall we do?" It was while Philip "preached Jesus" that the eunuch believed; and while Paul "spake unto the women" by the river side that Lydia's heart was opened. In speaking of his success among the Corinthians he says, "In Christ Jesus I have begotten you through the Gospel." 1 Cor. xiv, 15; and on the same ground he calls Onesimus his *son*, whom he had "begotten" in his bonds. (Philemon 10.) It was, therefore, with great confidence that St. Paul could say, "The weapons of our warfare are not carnal, but *mighty through* God." 2 Cor. x, 4.

3. *Prayer.*—The Holy Spirit is expressly promised to those who seek, in the exercise of prayer, for his saving influences. "If ye then, being

evil, know how to give good gifts unto your children; how much more shall your heavenly Father give the Holy Spirit to them that ask him?" Luke xi, 13. Whatever means of regeneration may be employed, none can supersede the use of prayer. It is indispensably requisite in all cases, and if persisted in with importunity and humble dependence upon God it will infallibly prevail. It is not possible that he should mock us by exciting our desires and encouraging our supplications, and then disappointing and rejecting us. When the penitent thief prayed, "Lord, remember me," our Lord replied, "To-day shalt thou be with me in paradise;" which clearly involves the regeneration of the suppliant. The prayer of the publican was, "God be merciful to me a sinner;" but he "went down to his house justified," and, consequently, regenerated. We have therefore great encouragement to pray, in the language of David, "Create in me a clean heart, O God; and renew a right spirit within me. Cast me not away from thy presence; and take not thy Holy Spirit from me." Psa. li, 10, 11.

These are the ordinary means through which and by which the Holy Spirit operates upon the human mind, and produces in man that moral change which is denominated regeneration or the new birth. And though we would not attempt to confine the Holy Spirit to any definite mode of operation, yet, so far as we are concerned, we have no right to expect the regeneration of our souls, except by a believing application to the Father of our spirits, through the mediation of Christ and in the use of these and other divinely appointed means. We are not to suppose, however, that the efficiency by which this great moral renovation is effected is in the means themselves. If we are "*born again*" we are "BORN OF THE SPIRIT," by whose direct agency alone we can be made the children of God.

We will close this chapter by subjoining a few inferences which naturally follow from the preceding discussion. And,

(1.) It follows that baptism is not regeneration.* We mean not to derogate from the honor of that Divine ordinance when we assert that too much dependence has been placed upon it. Being an institution of Christ, it ought to be religiously observed, not only as the appointed mode of admission into the visible Church, but as a means in which we may ask and expect the communication of that grace of which it is so significant an emblem. But it ought not to be forgotten, that it is only an emblem or outward sign of an inward work; and for this very reason it cannot be regeneration. It is "not the putting away of the filth of the flesh" which saves us, "but the answer of a good conscience

* We admit that the term "regeneration" may be properly applied to water baptism. This follows from the language of our Lord, "*born of water*," and from the use of the term "*regeneratio*," by the Christian Fathers, as expressive of this ordinance. But we must make a distinction between regeneration as a mere outward sign, and regeneration as an inward and spiritual grace. It is in the latter sense we employ the term.

toward God;" and this is not to be attained without a spiritual renovation. It is therefore manifest that baptism is an outward and visible sign, while regeneration is an inward and spiritual grace. The former is the act of man purifying the body; the latter, a change divinely wrought in the soul. The one is therefore as distinguishable from the other as the soul is from the body, or as water is from the Holy Spirit. But we may observe,

(2.) That " as the new birth is not the same thing with baptism, so it does not always accompany baptism: they do not constantly go together. A man may possibly be 'born of water,' and yet not be 'born of the Spirit.' There may sometimes be the outward sign where there is not the inward grace. 'The tree is known by its fruits:' and hereby it appears too plain to be denied, that divers of those who were children of the devil before they were baptized continue the same after baptism; 'for the works of their father they do.' They continue servants of sin, without any pretense to either inward or outward holiness."* Like Simon Magus, though they have received the outward washing, yet they are still " in the gall of bitterness, and in the bond of iniquity." But we infer,

(3.) That regeneration is not the same with sanctification. This is indeed taken for granted by many, who therefore speak of regeneration as a *progressive work*. But though this is true of sanctification, it is not true of regeneration, which is at once complete. Regeneration "is a part of sanctification, not the whole; it is the gate to it, the entrance into it. When we are born again then our sanctification, our inward and outward holiness, begins; and thenceforward we are gradually to 'grow up into him who is our head.' This expression of the apostle admirably illustrates the difference between one and the other, and further points out the exact analogy there is between natural and spiritual things. A child is born of a woman in a moment, or at least in a very short time: afterward he gradually and slowly grows, till he attains to the stature of a man. In like manner a child is born of God in a short time, if not in a moment. But it is by slow degrees that he afterward grows up to the measure of the full stature of Christ. The same relation, therefore, which there is between our natural birth and our growth, there is also between our new birth and our sanctification." † This, however, will be more clearly seen when we come to speak of the latter.

* Wesley's Works, vol. i, p. 405. † Ibid., vol. i, p. 406.

CHAPTER X.

ADOPTION.

HAVING considered, to some extent, the subject of regeneration, we will now direct our attention to that of adoption, which is a large and comprehensive blessing, concomitant with justification. What we shall say upon this subject will be included under the three following heads: 1. The nature of adoption; 2. Its evidence; and, 3. The benefits which it secures. We will consider,

I. THE NATURE OF ADOPTION.

Adoption, in its literal sense, signifies the act of receiving a stranger into a family, and conveying to him all the rights, privileges, and benefits belonging to a natural or legitimate child. To adopt children in this manner has, it is well known, been a custom generally prevailing in all ages, and probably in all nations. Thus children were adopted among the Egyptians, the Jews, the Romans, and other ancient nations; and the same custom exists in the Christian nations of Europe and in our own country.

Among the Romans the ceremony of adoption consisted in buying the child to be adopted from his parents for a sum of money formally given and taken. The parties appeared before the magistrate in the presence of five Roman citizens; and the adopting father said to the child, "Art thou willing to become my son?" to which the child replied, "I am willing." Then the adopter, holding the money in his hand, and at the same time taking hold of the child, said, "I declare this child to be my son according to the Roman law, and he is bought with this money," which was given to the father as the price of his son. Thus the relation was formed according to law; and the adopted son entered into the family of his new father, assumed his name, became subject to his authority, and was made a legal heir to the whole of the inheritance, or to a share of it if there were any other sons.*

Of the same nature is that transaction in the Divine economy by which men are acknowledged to be the children of God. We may, therefore, define *adoption*, according to the scriptural sense of the term, to be that gracious act of God by which we are acknowledged to be of the number and become entitled to all the privileges of his children.

It is supposed by some that adoption is virtually the same with justification—that it differs from the latter only in the manner in which it exhibits the relation of believers to God. It is admitted that adoption, as well as justification, is a *relative* change, and that the same general

---

* See Kennet's Roman Antiquities.

idea is involved in both; for whether we say that a sinner passes from a state of guilt and condemnation to a state of justification, or that he is taken from the kingdom of darkness and adopted into the family of God, we express the same fact, only in different terms. But adoption implies something more than the pardon of sin, which is the central thought in justification. It is more particularly expressive of that *covenant relation* into which God graciously receives those who become justified and regenerated by acknowledging them to be his people, and declaring himself to be their God.

The term is applied to the Israelites in their collective capacity, "to whom," as St. Paul says, "pertaineth the *adoption*," because God had acknowledged them as his children, and had entered into a covenant with them;* but in its proper and fullest import it is applied only to believers in Christ. "God sent forth his Son, made of a woman, made under the law, to redeem them that were under the law, that we might receive the adoption of sons." Gal. iv, 4, 5. Those who are made the subjects of this adoption "are no more strangers and foreigners, but fellow-citizens with the saints, and of the household of God." Eph. ii, 19. They are taken into that covenant relation which is so clearly and forcibly described by the prophet, as quoted by St. Paul: "For this is the covenant that I will make with the house of Israel after those days, saith the Lord; I will put my laws into their mind, and write them in their hearts; and I will be to them a God, and they shall be to me a people." Heb. viii, 10.

Though justification, regeneration, and adoption are in some respects so blended, like the colors of the bow in the heavens, that their precise boundaries cannot be ascertained, yet there is this general distinction to be observed, that justification consists in the pardon of the guilty, regeneration in the moral renovation of the unholy, and adoption in the gracious reception of those who are alienated from God and disinherited, as his acknowledged children. Adoption is, therefore, sufficiently distinct from justification, and from every other display of Divine grace in the remedial system, to require a distinct consideration. It is a subject, moreover, which involves some of the most interesting and encouraging views that are anywhere revealed in the system of saving grace.

As in civil adoption the adopted son originally belonged to a different family from that into which he was received, so mankind are by nature strangers to the family of God. They are "aliens from the commonwealth of Israel, and strangers from the covenants of promise, having no hope, and without God in the world." Eph. ii, 12. Our Lord said to the unbelieving Jews, "Ye are of your father the devil, and the lusts of your father ye will do." John viii, 44. And the apostle declares, "He that committeth sin, is of the devil." 1 John iii, 8. But even to such the Gospel holds out the glorious privilege of becoming the sons of

---

* See Exod. iv, 22; Deut. v, 2, 3; xiv, 1, 2; Jer. xxxi, 9.

God. Let them but renounce their allegiance to the prince of darkness, and believe in the Lord Jesus Christ, and they will at once be admitted into God's own family, and be entitled to all the privileges of his children.

We have seen that in civil adoption the consent of the person to be adopted was demanded and publicly expressed. So also in spiritual adoption, though the privilege is freely offered to us in the Gospel, yet it does not become ours until we personally accept it; which implies the exercise of justifying faith. "As many as received him, to them gave he power to become the sons of God, even to them that believe on his name." John i, 12. Those who thus receive Christ are made partakers of the grace of adoption, to which belong freedom from a servile spirit, the special love and care of God, a filial confidence in him, free access to him at all times and under all circumstances, a title to the heavenly inheritance, and the Spirit of adoption. This leads us to consider,

II. The evidence of Adoption.

It is allowed by all sober divines that some comfortable persuasion, or at least hope of the Divine favor, is attainable by true Christians and is actually possessed by them, except under the influence of bodily infirmities, and in peculiar seasons of temptation, and that all true faith is in some degree personal and appropriating.

By those who admit, that upon previous contrition and faith in Christ an act of justification takes place by which we are reconciled to God and adopted into his family, a doctrine which has been established, it must also be admitted, either that this act of mercy on the part of God is entirely kept secret from us, or that there is some means by which we may know it. If the former, there is no remedy for doubt and fear and tormenting anticipation, which must be great, as our repentance is deep and genuine; and so there can be no comfort, no freedom, no cheerfulness of spirit in religion; which contradicts the sentiments of all Churches and all their theologians. What is still more important, it contradicts the word of God.*

If, then, we come to know that we are justified, by what means do we obtain this knowledge? We believe the doctrine of Scripture to be, that the children of God have the inward witness or testimony of the Holy Spirit to their adoption or sonship; from which flows a comfortable *persuasion* or *conviction* of their present acceptance with God, and the hope of future and eternal glory.

The apostle says, "Ye have not received the spirit of bondage again to fear; but ye have received the Spirit of adoption, whereby we cry, Abba, Father. The Spirit itself beareth witness with our spirit, that we are the children of God." Rom. viii, 15, 16. Again: "God sent forth his Son, made of a woman, made under the law, to redeem them that were under the law, that we might receive the adoption of sons.

* See Rom. v, 1, 2, 11; 1 Peter i, 8.

And because ye are sons, God hath sent forth the Spirit of his Son into your hearts, crying, Abba, Father." Gal. iv, 4–6.

On these two passages we may remark: 1. That the Spirit here spoken of as being "sent forth," and as witnessing "with our spirit," is not the personified spirit or genius of the Gospel, as some would have it, but the Spirit of God; and hence he is called "*the Spirit itself*," or himself, and "*the Spirit of his Son.*" 2. That upon our obtaining pardon or actual redemption from the curse of the law, the Spirit is sent forth into our hearts. 3. That the office of the Spirit is, to remove servile fear; to inspire filial confidence in God as our Father, which stands opposed to the fear produced by the "spirit of bondage;" and to bear a direct testimony to our adoption, or to "witness with our spirit *that we are the children of God.*"

On the subject of this witness or testimony of the Spirit there are four different opinions. These, in the first place, we will briefly state, and then offer such remarks upon them as the case may seem to require.

1. *A brief statement of different opinions in regard to the witness of the Spirit.*—And,

(1.) It is the opinion of some, that the testimony which the Holy Spirit bears to our adoption consists alone in the moral effects which he produces within us; and that the witness of our own spirit is nothing more than a consciousness of possessing faith. This is called the reflex act of faith, by which a person, conscious of believing, reasons in this manner: "I know that I believe in Christ, therefore I know that I shall obtain everlasting life."*

(2.) Another opinion is, that there is but one witness, the Holy Spirit, acting concurrently with our own spirit. "The Spirit of God," says Bishop Bull, "produces those graces in us which are the evidences of our adoption. It is he who, as occasion requires, illuminates our understanding, and assists our memory in discovering and recollecting those arguments of hope and comfort within ourselves. But God's Spirit doth witness with, not without our spirit and understanding, in making use of our reason in considering and reflecting upon those grounds of comfort which the Spirit of God hath wrought in us, and from them drawing this comfortable conclusion to ourselves, that 'we are the sons of God.'" With this notion is generally connected that of the entire imperceptibility of the Spirit's operations as distinguished from the operations of our own mind.

(3.) The third opinion which we will notice is, that the Spirit of God bears a direct testimony to the mind of the believer that he is a child of God, but that this is the privilege of only a few favored persons. Of this notion it is a sufficient refutation, that the apostle, in the texts before quoted, speaks of believers in general, and does not restrain the

* Hill's Lectures, book 5, chap. 2.

attainment from any who seek it. He places it, in this respect, on the ground of all the other blessings of the new covenant.

(4.) The fourth opinion, and the one which we believe to be in accordance with the Scriptures, is, that the evidence of our adoption is twofold: a direct testimony of the Holy Spirit, bearing witness, by an "inward impression on the soul," that we are the children of God, and are reconciled to him; and an indirect testimony, arising from the work of the Spirit in the heart and life, which St. Paul calls the testimony of our own spirit; for this is clearly inferred from his expression, "the Spirit itself beareth witness *with* our spirit." The compound verb συμμαρτυρει, which the apostle uses in this place, literally signifies to testify or bear witness together, or at the same time with another, or to add one's testimony to that of another. It agrees, therefore, with the literal rendering of the word, as it does also with other passages, to conjoin this testimony of the Holy Spirit with those confirmatory proofs of our adoption which arise from his work within us, and which may, upon examination of our state, be called the testimony of our own spirit or conscience. To this testimony the apostle refers in the same chapter: "But ye are not in the flesh, but in the Spirit, if so be that the Spirit of God dwell in you. Now if any man have not the Spirit of Christ, he is none of his; for as many as are led by the Spirit of God, they are the sons of God." Rom. viii, 9, 14.

This testimony of our own spirit, or indirect testimony of the Holy Spirit by and through our own spirit, is considered, then, as confirmatory of the direct testimony of the Spirit of God. "How am I assured," says Mr. Wesley, "that I do not mistake the voice of the Spirit? Even by the testimony of my own spirit; by 'the answer of a good conscience toward God.' Hereby I shall know that I am in no delusion, that I have not deceived my own soul. The immediate fruits of the Spirit, ruling in the heart, are 'love, joy, peace, bowels of mercies, humbleness of mind, meekness, gentleness, long-suffering.' And the outward fruits are the doing of good to all men, and a uniform obedience to all the commandments of God."*

2. *We will now offer a few remarks upon these opinions, and for the establishment of the one last presented.*—And,

(1.) It must be evident, from what has already been said, that to the fact of our adoption two witnesses and a twofold testimony must be allowed. But the main consideration is, whether the Holy Spirit gives his testimony *directly* to the mind by impression, suggestion, or otherwise, or *mediately* by our own spirit, in some such way as is described by Bishop Bull in the extract above given; by "illuminating our understanding, and assisting our memory in discovering and recollecting those arguments of hope and comfort within ourselves," which arise from "the graces which he has produced in us." But to this statement

* Wesley's Works, vol. i, page 92.

of the doctrine we object, that it makes the testimony of the Holy Spirit, in point of fact, nothing different from the testimony of our own spirit; and that by holding but *one* witness it contradicts St. Paul, who, as we have seen, holds *two*. For, the testimony is that of our own consciousness of certain moral changes which have taken place, no other is admitted; and, therefore, it is but one testimony. Nor is the Holy Spirit brought in at all, except to qualify our own spirit to give witness. The argument is, that the Holy Spirit works certain moral changes in the heart, and these are the evidence of our sonship. The Spirit is, therefore, entirely excluded as a *witness*, although the apostle declares explicitly that he gives witness to the fact, not of a moral change, but of our adoption.

(2.) Further: suppose our mind to be so assisted by the Holy Spirit as to discern the reality of his work in us, and suppose this to be taken as the evidence of our adoption, to what degree must this work of the Spirit advance before it can be evidence of this fact? It were absurd to allege *penitence* as the proof of our pardon, since that supposes that we are still under condemnation. What further work of the Spirit, then, is the proof? The reply to this usually is, that though repentance should not be evidence of pardon, yet when faith is added this becomes evidence, since God has declared in his word that we are "justified by faith," and that whosoever "believeth shall be saved."

To this we reply, that though we should become conscious of both repentance and faith, either by a "reflex act of our own mind," or by the assistance of the Spirit, this would be no evidence of our forgiveness. Justification is an act of God which passes in his own mind, and is declared by no outward sign. It follows, therefore, that no one can know when he is justified without some direct testimony from God, unless it had been stated in his word that in every case pardon is dispensed when repentance and faith have reached some definite degree clearly pointed out; and, also, unless we were expressly authorized to judge when they have reached this degree, and thence to conclude our justification. But we have no such particular description of faith, nor are we authorized to make ourselves judges of the fact, whether the act of pardon as to us has passed the mind of God. The apostle in the passages quoted above has assigned that office to the Holy Spirit; but it is in no part of Scripture ascribed to us.

If, then, we have no authority from God to conclude that we are pardoned when faith is added to repentance, the whole becomes a matter of mere *inference;* and we argue, that having "repentance and faith," we are forgiven; in other words, that these are sufficient evidences of pardon. But repentance and faith are exercised IN ORDER TO pardon. How, then, can they be the evidences of it? We have, through the mercy of God, the promise of pardon to all who repent and believe; but repentance is not pardon, and faith is not pardon. They are only its prerequisites. Each is a *sine qua non*, but surely not the pardon itself, nor can either be considered the evidence of pardon without an absurdity. As pardon, therefore, must have an attestation of higher authority, and of a distinct kind, the only attestation conceivable which remains is, the direct witness of the Holy Spirit. Either this must be acknowledged, or a painful uncertainty as to the *genuineness* or the required *measure* or *degree* of our repentance and faith, quite destructive of comfort, must remain throughout life.

(3.) But if neither our repentance, nor even a consciousness of faith, when joined with it, can be the evidence of our adoption, it has been urged that the fruits of the Spirit, when found in our experience, must be sufficient evidence of the fact, without supposing a more direct testimony of the Holy Spirit. The "fruits" thus referred to are those enumerated by St. Paul, Galatians v, 22, 23. They are, "love, joy, peace, long-suffering, gentleness, goodness, faith, meekness, temperance."

Two things will here be granted, and they greatly strengthen the argument for a direct testimony of the Holy Spirit: *first*, that these fruits are found only in those who have been received, by the remission of their sins, into the Divine favor. This is proved from what immediately follows: "And they that ARE CHRIST's have crucified the flesh with the affections and lusts." For to be "*Christ's*," and to be "*in Christ*," are the same as to be in a justified state: "There is no condemnation to them which are *in Christ Jesus*." *Secondly*, that these graces are fruits of the Spirit of adoption. This is proved by the connection of the words with verse 18, "But if ye be led by the Spirit, ye are not under the law;" which passage is exactly parallel to the fifth and sixth verses of chapter four: "To redeem them that were under the law, that we might receive the adoption of sons; and because ye are sons, God hath sent forth the Spirit of his Son into your hearts, crying, Abba, Father." These fruits of the Spirit, then, presuppose not only our pardon, but pardon previously attested and made known to us, the persuasion of which conveyed to the mind, not by them, but by the Spirit of adoption, is the foundation of these fruits; at least, of that "love, joy," and "peace," which are mentioned first, and which must not be separated in the argument from the others.

Nor can these fruits result from anything but manifested pardon. They cannot themselves manifest our pardon, for they cannot exist till it is manifested. If we "love God," it is because we know him as God reconciled. If we have "joy in God," it is because "we have received the atonement." If we have "peace," it is because we are "justified by faith." God, conceived of as angry, cannot be the object of filial love. Pardon unfelt supposes guilt and fear still to burden the mind, in which case "joy" and "peace" cannot exist. But by the argument of those who make these fruits of the Spirit the *media* of ascertaining the fact of our forgiveness and adoption, we must be supposed to love God, while yet we feel him to be angry with us; to rejoice and have peace, while the fearful apprehensions of the consequences of unremitted sins are not removed. If this is impossible, as it certainly is, then the ground of our love, peace, and joy is pardon revealed and witnessed, directly and immediately, by the Spirit of adoption. Thus it is established, that the witness of the Spirit is *direct* and not mediate.

(4.) This doctrine has been generally termed the doctrine of *assurance;* and perhaps the expressions of St. Paul, the "full assurance of faith," and the "full assurance of hope," may warrant the use of the word. But as there is a current and generally understood sense of this term among persons of the Calvinistic persuasion, implying that the assurance of our present acceptance and sonship is an assurance of our final perseverance, and of our indefeasible title to heaven, the phrase, a comfortable persuasion or conviction of our justification and adoption, arising out of the Spirit's inward and direct testimony, is to be preferred.

There is another reason for the sparing and cautious use of the term assurance, which is, that it seems to imply, though not necessarily, the absence of all doubt, and to shut out all those lower degrees of persuasion which may exist in the experience of Christians. For, as our faith may not at first, or at all times, be equally strong, the testimony of the Spirit may have its degrees of strength, and our persuasion or conviction be proportionately regulated. Yet if faith is genuine, God respects even its weaker exercises, and encourages its growth by affording measures of comfort and degrees of this testimony. Nevertheless, while this is allowed, the fullness of this attainment is to be pressed upon every one that believes. "Let us draw near," says the apostle, "with full assurance of faith."

(5.) It may serve to remove an objection which is sometimes made to this doctrine, and to correct an error into which some have fallen in stating it, to observe, that this assurance, persuasion, or conviction is not of the essence of justifying faith; that is, justifying faith does not consist in the assurance of our being forgiven through Christ. If we are justified *by faith,* as the Scriptures declare, that faith must evidently precede our justification; and it is equally evident that we must be justified before we can have any assurance of it. To say that we must be persuaded of our acceptance with God in order to our justification, is the same as to say, that we are justified by believing what is false. We conclude, therefore, that this inward and direct testimony of the Spirit to our adoption follows justification, and is one of its results.

(6.) The *second* testimony is that of our own spirit, and consists in "a consciousness of our having received, in and by the Spirit of adoption, the tempers mentioned in the word of God as belonging to his adopted children: a consciousness that we are inwardly conformed, by the Spirit of God, to the image of his Son, and that we walk before him in justice, mercy, and truth, doing the things which are pleasing in his sight."* But this testimony, let it be observed, is not to the fact of our adoption *directly*, but to the fact that we have, in truth, received the Spirit of adoption, and that we are under no delusive impressions.

Our own spirit can take no cognizance of the mind of God as to our actual pardon, and can bear no witness to that fact. The Holy Spirit only, who knows the mind of God, can be this witness; and if the fact that God is reconciled to us can only be known to him, by him only can it be attested to us. But we are competent witnesses, from our own consciousness, that such moral effects have been produced within us as it is the office of the Holy Spirit alone to produce; and thus we have the testimony of our own spirit that the Holy Spirit is with us and in us, and that he who bears witness to our adoption is, in truth, the Spirit of God.

Of the four opinions on this subject which we have noticed, the last only is fully conformable to the Scriptures, and ought, therefore, to be believed and taught. The first opinion is refuted in our examination of the second; for what is called "the reflex act of faith" is only a consciousness of believing, which we have shown must be exercised *in order to* pardon, but cannot be an evidence of it. The second opinion has been examined more at large, and its errors have been pointed out. The third opinion was refuted when it was first stated.

III. THE BENEFITS OF ADOPTION.

The relation between God and his children which is brought into existence by the act of adoption, involves in its consequences a long train of rights and obligations, of duties and blessings. Of these only a few can be mentioned in the present connection, and even these must be mentioned in a very summary manner. The benefits secured to us by adoption are chiefly comprehended under these two leading ideas— reception into the family of God, and a title to all the privileges of his children.

1. *By adoption we are received into the family of God.*—In regard to this benefit, which God so freely bestows upon the returning prodigals of our race, we will offer the following remarks:

(1.) That it has been granted to men in every age of the world. The sacred historian informs us that as early as the birth of Enos, the grandson of Adam, men began "to call upon the name of the Lord;" or, as the margin has it, and perhaps more correctly, "to call themselves *by the name* of the Lord." The meaning seems to be that they began to take upon themselves the name of God, and to be regarded by others as his children; and the title by which they began to be known at this early period has been continued through every succeeding age of the Church.

* Wesley's Works, vol. i, p. 87.

In Genesis vi, 2, we read of "the sons of God," who, in all probability, were the descendants of Seth, and who were thus denominated to distinguish them from the wicked progeny of Cain, and to characterize them as God's adopted children. That such persons were meant by the phrase "sons of God," is sufficiently manifest from the use which is made of it in other passages. In Job i, 6, and xxxviii, 7, it is applied to the holy angels. When, therefore, men receive the same appellation it is because they are supposed to belong to the same family, and to be the children of the same Father.

In the communications which God made to the family of Abraham this relation is more explicitly declared. To say to them as he did, Leviticus xxvi, 12, "I will be your God, and ye shall be my people," was virtually to tell them that he would be their Father, and they should be his children. When God sent Moses to demand the release of his people, he commanded him to say to Pharaoh, "Thus saith the Lord, *Israel is my son*, even my first-born." Exod. iv, 22. In the same manner Moses declared to the same people, "Ye are the children of the Lord your God." Deut. xiv, 1. So also it is said to the rulers of Israel, "All of you are children of the Most High." Psa. lxxxii, 6.

But though this relation is thus clearly recognized in the Scriptures of the Old Testament, yet it is more distinctly revealed in those of the New. "As many as received him, to them gave he power to become the sons of God." John i, 12. "As many as are led by the Spirit of God, they are the sons of God." Rom. viii, 14. "Ye are all the children of God by faith in Christ Jesus." Gal. iii, 26. "Beloved, now are we the sons of God." 1 John iii, 2. Many other passages might be quoted in proof of the fact that God acknowledges all true believers as his children, and members of his household; but these are altogether sufficient for our present purpose. We may, then, proceed to remark,

(2.) That this relation confers upon its subjects great dignity and honor. How glorious is the family with which believers become united! First in dignity and honor is Jesus Christ himself, who, in his divine nature, is the eternal Son of God. But in our own nature he belongs to the heavenly family, in which he claims precedence, and holds the most distinguished place, as "the first-born among many brethren." Next in order are those glorious beings, the holy angels, who, having retained their purity and fidelity, have continued, without interruption, to enjoy the honor and felicity of their primeval state. Added to these are the glorified spirits redeemed from earth. Abraham, Isaac, Jacob, the prophets and apostles, the martyrs and confessors, and believers of every age and nation, are associated in one great brotherhood. When, therefore, we become "the children of God by faith in Christ Jesus," we are introduced into fellowship with the most glorious and dignified creatures in the universe. "Ye are come unto mount Sion, and unto the city of the living God, the heavenly Jerusalem, and to an innumer-

Chap. 10.] ADOPTION. 443

able company of angels, to the general assembly and Church of the firstborn, which are written in heaven, and to God the Judge of all, and to the spirits of just men made perfect, and to Jesus the Mediator of the new covenant, and to the blood of sprinkling, that speaketh better things than that of Abel." Heb. xii, 22-24. Well may the apostle exclaim, "Behold, what manner of love the Father hath bestowed upon us, that we should be called the sons of God!" 1 John iii, 1. But,

2. *By adoption we become entitled to all the privileges of the children of God.*—In consequence of this relation, he is to us all that is implied in the character of a Father, and will bestow upon us all that this character warrants us to expect. If we are his children, then have we "promise of the life that now is, and of that which is to come." He will,

(1.) *Provide for the wants of his children.*—God does indeed provide for the wants of all his creatures. He feeds the fowls of the air, and "the young lions seek their meat from God." He opens his hand and satisfies "the desire of every living thing." But the provision which he makes for the wants of his children is distinguished from that which he makes for others by this important consideration, that in kind, in degree, and in manner it is exactly such as is most promotive of their real welfare. "No good thing will he withhold from them that walk uprightly." Psa. lxxxiv, 11. "And we know that all things work together for good to them that love God, to them who are called according to his purpose." Rom. viii, 28.

The provision which God makes for his children differs from that which he makes for other men in another important particular. It is secured to them by his own express promise, and rests on the immovable foundation of his immutable veracity. Every one of them may therefore say with the psalmist, "The Lord is my Shepherd; I shall not want. Surely goodness and mercy shall follow me all the days of my life." Psa. xxiii, 1, 6.

(2.) *He will protect them.*—That from the cradle to the grave we are exposed to evil, in an endless variety of forms, is a standing dictate of all human experience; and we know that against this exposure no human foresight can effectually provide. "Except the Lord keep the city, the watchman waketh but in vain." Psa. cxxvii, 1. But God is the keeper of his children. He says to every one of them, "The Lord is thy shade upon thy right hand. The sun shall not smite thee by day, nor the moon by night. The Lord shall preserve thee from all evil; he shall preserve thy soul. The Lord shall preserve thy going out and thy coming in from this time forth, and even for evermore." Psa. cxxi, 5-8. In every situation of life in which the children of God may be placed his eye is upon them for good. "When thou passest through the waters, I will be with thee; and through the rivers, they shall not overflow thee. When thou walkest through the fire thou shalt not be burnt; neither shall the flame kindle upon thee. For I am the Lord thy God, the Holy One of Israel, thy Saviour." Isa. xliii, 2, 3. God may sometimes suffer a pious man to fall into apparent evil for the promotion of his spiritual good, but "though he" thus "fall, he shall not be utterly cast down; for the Lord upholdeth him with his hand." Psa. xxxvii, 24. To all, therefore, who fully trust in God, means of protection and defense are ever provided, even in seasons apparently hopeless, and often in ways utterly unexpected.

(3.) *He will instruct them.*—"This work he accomplishes by his Providence, by his word, by his ordinances, by his ministers, by the life and conversation of Christians, by the Divine example of his Son, and by the peculiar communications of his Spirit. In all these ways he furnishes them with whatever knowledge and whatever useful impressions they need to receive, and trains them up as children, in effectual preparation for the perfect state of manhood to which they will arrive in his heavenly kingdom.

"This, however, is the peculiar office of the Spirit of truth. As he originally revealed the truth of God concerning our salvation, so, throughout their earthly pilgrimage, he discloses to the children of God the Divine import of his own instructions, and gives them eyes to see, ears to hear, and hearts to understand and obey his own glorious precepts. He teaches them the true evangelical use of religious ordinances, of trials, of afflictions, and of blessings; dissolves their doubts, removes their perplexities, shows them the path of life, takes them by the hand and guides them through the mazes of this earthly wilderness to the heavenly Canaan."* "As many as are led by the Spirit of God, they are the sons of God." Rom. viii, 14.

(4.) *He will administer to them suitable correction.*—Of this necessary but benevolent parental office, St. Paul gives us a detailed account in the twelfth chapter of his Epistle to the Hebrews. "My son, despise not thou the chastening of the Lord, nor faint when thou art rebuked of him; for whom the Lord loveth he chasteneth, and scourgeth every son whom he receiveth. If ye endure chastening, God dealeth with you as with sons, for what son is he whom the father chasteneth not? But if ye be without chastisement, whereof all are partakers, then are ye bastards, and not sons. Furthermore, we have had fathers of our flesh, which corrected us; and we gave them reverence. Shall we not much rather be in subjection to the Father of spirits, and live? For they verily for a few days chastened us after their own pleasure; but he for our profit, that we might be partakers of his holiness. Now no chastening for the present seemeth to be joyous, but grievous; nevertheless, afterward it yieldeth the peaceable fruits of righteousness unto them which are exercised thereby."

In this summary account we have a complete view of all that is most

* Dwight's Theology, vol. ii, p. 514.

interesting in this subject. We learn particularly that correction is a distinctive privilege of the children of God, and that those who are not corrected are not his children; that God corrects his children, not arbitrarily, or wantonly, but with a benevolent intention, "that we might be partakers of his holiness and live;" that for this reason, as well as on account of the prerogatives and perfections of God, we are bound to receive our corrections with reverence, submission, patience, and fortitude; and that if we do thus receive them the result will be our present good and eternal felicity.

(5.) *He will bestow upon them a glorious inheritance.*—Children, by the law of nature and of nations, inherit the property of their father; and an adopted son possesses all the rights and privileges of a son by descent. At the death of the person who adopted him he is legally entitled to his property. There is also an inheritance which belongs to the family of God, and every one who is received into it becomes an heir. "If children, then heirs; heirs of God, and joint heirs with Christ." Rom. viii, 17.

The Scriptures everywhere abound in the most encouraging descriptions of that inheritance which awaits the children of God. It is called "a kingdom," and a "better country." It is "eternal life," a "crown of life," a "crown of righteousness," a "crown of glory," an "eternal weight of glory." St. Peter calls it "an inheritance incorruptible, and undefiled, and that fadeth not away." "It doth not yet appear," says the sacred penman, "what we shall be; but we know that when he (Christ) shall appear we shall be like him; for we shall see him as he is."

"Whatever God now is to angels and glorified saints, and whatever he will be to them through an endless duration, for all this the adopted sons of God are authorized to hope. Even in this world, how happy does the earnest of the inheritance make them! How divine the peace which sheds its influence upon their souls! How pure and elevating the joy which, in some select hour, springs up in their bosoms! How are they raised above the pains and the pleasures of life, while, in the contemplations of faith, they anticipate their future abode in the higher regions of the universe! But these are only an earnest."* In due time, however, the full reward will be realized.

* Dick's Theology, Lec. 73.

CHAPTER XI.

ENTIRE SANCTIFICATION.

We have already spoken of justification, regeneration, and adoption, and we come now to consider another benefit of redemption which is distinctly marked and graciously promised in the Holy Scriptures: this is, the ENTIRE SANCTIFICATION or PERFECTED HOLINESS of believers. In the investigation of this subject we will consider the *nature*, the *attainability*, the *time*, and the *manner* of this gracious work, and then answer some objections which are urged against it.

I. THE NATURE OF ENTIRE SANCTIFICATION.

It may be defined to be an entire conformity of heart and life to the will of God, as made known to us in his word. The term "to sanctify," so often employed by the sacred writers, has two leading meanings. 1. It signifies to consecrate, to separate from a common use, and dedicate to God and his service. 2. It signifies to cleanse from moral corruption, to make holy. In both these senses it applies to the subjects of entire sanctification. They are consecrated to God, and cleansed "from all unrighteousness."

This state of grace is also expressed in Scripture by such terms as *purity of heart*, "holiness," and "perfection." Thus, "Blessed are the *pure in heart*." Matt. v, 8. "Being made free from sin, and become servants to God, ye have your fruit unto *holiness*." Rom. vi, 22. "Leaving the principles of the doctrine of Christ, let us go on unto *perfection*." Heb. vi, 1. But that we may guard against improper views respecting the nature of entire sanctification, we remark,

1. *That it does not differ in* ESSENCE *from regeneration.*—It introduces no new principle into the experience of the Christian, but is only the growth and perfection of that moral change which is effected in "every one that is born of the Spirit." Regeneration, says Mr. Wesley, "is a part of sanctification, not the whole; it is the gate to it, the entrance into it. When we are born again then our sanctification, our inward and outward holiness, begins; and thenceforward we are gradually to grow up in Him who is our head."* In regeneration there is an infusion of spiritual life into the soul, in which life all the graces of the Christian character are virtually included; but in the work of sanctification these graces are unfolded and matured.

2. *It does not imply a state of indefectibility.*—Absolute perfection belongs to God alone, and lies infinitely beyond the reach of all created beings. Nor is it possible that we should attain either angelic or

---
* Wesley's Works, vol. i, p. 406.

Adamic perfection. As to angels, they are a superior order of intelligences; and though their knowledge is doubtless limited, yet we must suppose that it is perfect in its kind—that their understanding is as clear as the light, and their judgment always true. And as they have ever maintained that sinless purity in which they were originally created, the fire of their holy affections must burn with an intensity, and their services must be performed with a faultless precision and rectitude, which are not possible to fallen man in his present state of being.

"Neither can any man, while he is in a corruptible body, attain Adamic perfection. Adam, before his fall, was undoubtedly as pure, as free from sin as the holy angels. In like manner his understanding was as clear as theirs, and his affections as regular. In virtue of this, as he always judged right, so he was able always to speak and act right. But since man rebelled against God the case is widely different with him. He is no longer able to avoid falling into innumerable mistakes, consequently he cannot always avoid wrong affections; neither can he always think, speak, and act right. Therefore man, in his present state, can no more attain Adamic than angelic perfection."*

3. *It does not exclude the possibility of temptation.*—To be tempted is reconcilable to the highest degree of moral perfection. This is evident from the history of our first parents. No one will deny that in their primitive state they were perfectly pure and holy; and yet they were subjects of temptation. But it is more strikingly evident from the history of our Lord. Though he was "holy, harmless, undefiled," and "separate from sinners," yet he "was in all points tempted like as we are." It is, therefore, not to be expected that any state of grace which we can attain in this life will place us beyond the reach of temptation. Indeed, a liability to temptation seems to be necessarily involved in the very idea of a probationary state.

What, then, is implied in that state of grace which we call entire sanctification? To this we answer, that it implies the maturity or perfection of all the fruits of the Spirit which compose the Christian character. These are "love, joy, peace, long-suffering, gentleness, goodness, faith, meekness, temperance." Gal. v, 22, 23. It implies obedience to the law of love. "Thou shalt love the Lord thy God with all thy heart, and with all thy soul, and with all thy mind. This is the first and great commandment; and the second is like unto it, Thou shalt love thy neighbor as thyself." Matt. xxii, 37–39. "Love," says St. Paul, "is the fulfilling of the law." Rom. xiii, 10. We conclude, therefore, that the whole of entire sanctification or Christian perfection is included in the phrase, "perfect love," as employed by St. John. He tells us that "there is no fear in love; but *perfect love* casteth out fear."

II. THE ATTAINABILITY OF ENTIRE SANCTIFICATION.

That a state of perfected holiness or entire sanctification is attain-

* Wesley's Works, vol. ii, p. 168.

able may be argued from various considerations drawn from the sacred Scriptures.

1. *Such a state is expressly commanded.*—Thus God said to Abraham, "Walk before me, and be thou *perfect.*" Gen. xvii, 1. And our Lord said to his disciples, "Be ye therefore *perfect*, even as your Father which is in heaven is perfect." Matt. v, 48. These passages are not to be considered as requiring of men a perfection like that of the Deity, unlimited and absolute; but a perfection is certainly required, and it can mean nothing less than an entire conformity of heart and life to the will of God. Hence we are commanded to be "*holy* in all manner of conversation," and to love God with all the heart, soul, and mind, and our neighbor as ourselves.

Are we, then, capable of complying with these requirements? To say we are *not*, is virtually to say, with the slothful servant, that God is a hard master, "reaping where" he has "not sown, and gathering where" he has "not strewed." It is to say that we are held responsible for what is not in our power—that for the non-performance of what is absolutely impossible we are in danger of eternal fire; for it is expressly declared that without *holiness* "no man shall see the Lord." But if it be allowed that we are capable of complying with these injunctions, the *possibility* of holiness or Christian perfection will necessarily follow.

2. *To the obtainment of this state we are frequently exhorted.*—"I beseech you, therefore, brethren, by the mercies of God, that ye present your bodies a living sacrifice, holy, acceptable unto God, which is your reasonable service." Rom. xii, 1. "Having, therefore, these promises, dearly beloved, let us cleanse ourselves from all filthiness of the flesh and spirit, *perfecting holiness* in the fear of God." 2 Cor. vii, 1. In these passages, which are only a specimen of what might be quoted, a full deliverance from sin is clearly indicated. The latter passage especially goes to the extent of the entire sanctification of the whole man, a cleansing "from *all filthiness* of the *flesh* and *spirit;*" the obtainment of *perfect holiness.*

3. *This gracious state is also made the subject of explicit promise.*—"Come now, and let us reason together, saith the Lord. Though your sins be as scarlet, they shall be as white as snow; though they be red like crimson, they shall be as wool." Isa. i, 18. "Then will I sprinkle clean water upon you, and ye shall be clean. From all your filthiness, and from all your idols, will I cleanse you." Ezek. xxxvi, 25. "Thou shalt call his name JESUS; for he shall save his people *from their sins.*" Matt. i, 21. "If we confess our sins, he is faithful and just to forgive us our sins, and to cleanse us *from all unrighteousness.*" 1 John i, 9. "The blood of Jesus Christ cleanseth us *from all sin.*" It must be evident to every candid mind that these Scriptures hold out a deliverance from the very *inbeing* of sin, as well as from its guilt and domin-

ion. It follows, therefore, that if we would not charge God with tantalizing man by such "great and precious promises," we must admit the attainability of entire sanctification.

4. *It is, moreover, the object of special prayer.*—David prayed, "Create in me a clean heart, O God; and renew a right spirit within me." Psa. li, 10. Our Lord taught his disciples to pray, that the will of God might "be done in earth as it is in heaven." Here the standard of moral rectitude and service is placed sublimely high. The rule to be observed is the will of God. The manner in which his will should be obeyed is, as it is done in heaven. If angels are sinless and pure, rendering to God a full and consistent obedience, then are we authorized, by the language of our Lord himself, to pray for that degree of sanctity which will at least preserve us from all voluntary transgression. If the attainability of entire holiness is impossible, how can the putting of this prayer into our lips be harmonized with sincerity and truth? But that it is attainable, is manifest from our Lord's own prayer for his beloved disciples. In addressing the Father in their behalf he uses this notable petition: "Sanctify them through thy truth: thy word is truth." John xvii, 17.

We next adduce in this connection the expressions of St. Paul, which exhibit *his* views of this important subject. "Now the God of peace, that brought again from the dead our Lord Jesus, that great Shepherd of the sheep, through the blood of the everlasting covenant, make you *perfect in every good work to do his will,* working in you that which is well-pleasing in his sight through Jesus Christ." Heb. xiii, 20, 21. Again: "The very God of peace *sanctify you wholly;* and I pray God your whole spirit and soul and body be preserved blameless unto the coming of our Lord Jesus Christ." 1 Thess. v, 23. This passage evidently embraces all that is included in the doctrine of holiness; and it therefore follows, either that the apostle prayed for what he believed to be unattainable, or that he believed in the attainability of *entire sanctification.* But as the former is too absurd to be supposed, the latter must be admitted.

To this we add that sublime prayer which the apostle offered for his Ephesian brethren. "For this cause I bow my knees unto the Father of our Lord Jesus Christ, of whom the whole family in heaven and earth is named, that he would grant you according to the riches of his glory, to be strengthened with might by his Spirit in the inner man; that Christ may dwell in your hearts by faith; that ye, being rooted and grounded in love, may be able to comprehend with all saints what is the breadth, and length, and depth, and height; and to know the love of Christ, which passeth knowledge, that ye may be filled with all the fullness of God." Eph. iii, 14–19.

5. *The doctrine of entire holiness is confirmed by personal examples.* —Thus it is said of Noah that he "was a *just* man, and *perfect* in his

generations," and that he "*walked with God.*" Gen. vi, 9. It is also said of Job that he " was *perfect* and *upright,* and one that feared God, and eschewed evil." Job i, 1. And the sacred historian informs us that Zacharias and Elisabeth " were both righteous before God, walking in *all* the commandments and ordinances of the Lord *blameless.*" Luke i, 6. When our blessed Redeemer, who knows the hearts of all men, " saw Nathanael coming to him," he exclaimed, " Behold an *Israelite indeed,* in whom is *no guile!*" John i, 47. In accordance with these examples, St. Paul speaks of those who had attained Christian perfection. " Howbeit we speak wisdom among them that are *perfect.*" 1 Cor. ii, 6. " Let us, therefore, as many as be *perfect,* be thus minded." Phil. iii, 15.

These are some of the leading arguments in support of the attainableness of entire holiness or Christian perfection. He who examines them with care and candor will hardly fail to conclude that it is the Christian's privilege to be cleansed " from all unrighteousness;" to love the Lord with all his heart, and his neighbor as himself; and to perfect " holiness in the fear of God."

III. THE TIME OF THIS GRACIOUS WORK.

The attainableness of entire holiness is not so much a matter of debate among Christians as the *time* when we are authorized to expect it. For, as it is an axiom in Christian doctrine that " without holiness no man shall see the Lord," unless we admit the doctrine of purgatory, the entire sanctification of the soul, and its complete renewal in holiness, must take place in this world.

While this is generally acknowledged, however, among spiritual Christians, it has been warmly contended by many that the final stroke which destroys our natural corruption is only given at death ; and that the soul, when separated from the body, and not before, is capable of that moral purity which the Scriptures exhibit to our hope.

If this view can be refuted, then it must follow, unless a purgatory of some description be allowed after death, that the entire sanctification of believers is attainable at any time previous to their dissolution. To the opinion in question, then, there appear to be the following fatal objections :

1. That we nowhere find the promises of entire sanctification restricted to the article of death, either expressly or in fair inference from any passage of Scripture.

2. That we nowhere find the circumstance of the soul's union with the body represented as a necessary obstacle to its entire sanctification. The principal passage which has been urged in proof of this from the New Testament is that part of the seventh chapter of Romans in which St. Paul, speaking in the first person of the bondage of the flesh, has been supposed to describe his own state as a believer in Christ. But it is evident from the context itself, as well as from many other portions of Scripture, that the apostle is speaking, not of one who is justified by

Chap. 11.] ENTIRE SANCTIFICATION. 451

faith in Christ, but of one struggling in LEGAL BONDAGE, and brought to that point of conviction of sin and self-despair which must always precede an entire trust in the merits of Christ for salvation.

To see the contrast which the apostle draws between one thus held in legal bondage and those who are freely justified, let us turn to the preceding chapter. "Shall we continue in sin, that grace may abound? God forbid! How shall we that are dead to sin, live any longer therein? Know ye not that so many of us as were baptized into Jesus Christ were baptized into his death? Therefore we are buried with him by baptism into death; that like as Christ was raised up from the dead by the glory of the Father, even so we also should walk in newness of life. For if we have been planted together in the likeness of his death, we shall be also in the likeness of his resurrection: knowing this, that OUR OLD MAN is crucified with him, THAT THE BODY OF SIN MIGHT BE DESTROYED, that henceforth we should not serve sin. For he that is dead IS FREED FROM SIN." So clearly does the apostle show that he who is BOUND to the "body of death," as mentioned in the seventh chapter, is not in the state of a believer; and that he who has a true faith in Christ "is FREED from sin."

3. The doctrine before us is disproved by those passages of Scripture which connect our entire sanctification with subsequent habits and acts to be exhibited in the conduct of believers *before death*. Thus, in the quotation just given from Romans vi, "Knowing this, that the body of sin might be destroyed, that *henceforth* we should not serve sin." So the exhortation in 2 Corinthians vii, 1, refers to the present life, and not to the hour of dissolution; and in 1 Thessalonians v, 23, the apostle first prays for the entire sanctification of the Thessalonians, and then for their *preservation* in that holy state "unto the coming of our Lord Jesus Christ."

4. It is disproved, also, by all those passages which require us to bring forth the graces and virtues which are usually called the fruits of the spirit. That these are to be produced during our life, and to be displayed in our spirit and conduct, cannot be doubted; and we may then ask whether they are required of us in perfection and maturity. That they are so required we have already shown; and if so, in this degree of purity and perfection they necessarily suppose the sanctification of the soul from all antagonistic evils. *Meekness* in its perfection supposes the extinction of all sinful anger; perfect *love to God* supposes that no affection remains contrary to it; and so of every other perfect internal virtue.

The inquiry, then, is reduced to this, whether these graces, in such perfection as to exclude the opposite corruptions of the heart, are of possible attainment. If they are not, then we cannot love God with our whole heart; then we must be sometimes sinfully angry; and how, in that case, are we to interpret that *perfectness* in these graces which

God has required of us and promised to us in the Gospel? For if the *perfection* meant be so comparative as that we may be sometimes sinfully angry and may sometimes divide our hearts between God and the creature, we may apply the same comparative sense of the term to our words and actions, as well as to our affections. Thus, when the apostle prays for the Hebrews, that God would make them "*perfect in every good work* to do his will," we must understand this perfection of evangelical good works so that it shall sometimes give place to opposite evil works, just as good affections must sometimes necessarily give place to the opposite evil affections.

This view can scarcely be soberly entertained by any enlightened Christian; and it must, therefore, be concluded that the standard of our attainable Christian perfection, as to the *affections*, is a love of God so perfect as to rule the heart and exclude all rivalry, and a meekness so perfect as to cast out all sinful anger and prevent its return; and that as to *good works*, the rule is that we shall be so "perfect in every good work" as to do the will of God habitually, fully, and constantly. If we fix the standard lower we let in a license totally inconsistent with that Christian purity which is allowed by all to be attainable, and we make every man his own interpreter of that *comparative* perfection which is often contended for as that only which is attainable.

5. The doctrine of the necessary indwelling of sin in the soul till death supposes that the seat of sin is in the flesh, and thus it harmonizes with the pagan philosophy, which attributed all evil to matter. The doctrine of the Bible, on the contrary, is that the seat of sin is in the soul; and it makes it one of the proofs of the fall and corruption of our spiritual nature that we are in bondage to the appetites and motions of the flesh. Nor does the theory which places the necessity of sinning in the connection of the soul with the body account for the whole moral case of man. There are sins, as pride, covetousness, malice, and others, which are wholly spiritual; and yet no exception is made in this doctrine of the necessary continuance till death as to them. There is, surely, no need to wait for the separation of the soul from the body in order to be saved from evils which are the sole offspring of the spirit; and yet these are made as inevitable as the sins which more immediately connect themselves with our animal nature.

We conclude, therefore, as to the TIME of our complete sanctification, that it can neither be referred to the hour of death, nor placed subsequent to the present life. A freedom from the dominion of sin is an attainment which believers are to experience in time, and one which is necessary to that completeness of *holiness*, and of those active and passive graces of Christianity by which alone they are fully qualified to glorify God and edify mankind.

IV. THE MANNER OF SANCTIFICATION.

Not only the time, but the *manner* also, of our sanctification has been matter of controversy. Some contend that all attainable degrees of it are required by the process of gradual mortification and the acquisition of holy habits. Others allege that it is instantaneous, and a fruit of an act of faith in the Divine promises. That the regeneration which accompanies justification is a large approach to this state of perfect holiness, and that all dying to sin and all growth in grace advances us nearer to this point of *entire* sanctity, are points so obvious that in regard to them there can be no reasonable dispute. But these facts are not at all inconsistent with a more instantaneous work, when, the depth of our natural depravity being more painfully felt, we plead in faith the accomplishment of the promises of God. The great question to be settled is, whether the deliverance sighed for is held out to us in these promises as a present blessing. And, from what has already been said, there appears to be no ground to doubt this, since no small violence would be offered to the passages of Scripture already quoted, as well as to many others, by the opposite opinion.

All the promises of God which are not expressly, or from their *order*, referred to future time, are objects of *present trust*, and their fulfillment *now* is made conditional *only* upon our faith. They cannot, therefore, be pleaded in our prayers with an entire reliance upon the truth of God in vain. The general promise that we shall receive "all things whatsoever we ask in prayer, believing," comprehends, of course, all things suited to our case which God has engaged to bestow; and if the entire renewal of our nature is included in the number, without limitation of time, except that in which we ask in faith, then to this faith shall the promise of entire sanctification be given. This, in the nature of the case, supposes an instantaneous work, immediately following our entire and unwavering faith. We are not to suppose, however, that there is any degree of sanctification attainable in this life, whether instantaneously or otherwise, which precludes the possibility of subsequent growth. It is, therefore, proper that we should regard the work of entire sanctification as being both instantaneous and progressive.

V. OBJECTIONS TO THE DOCTRINE OF ENTIRE SANCTIFICATION ANSWERED.

The only plausible objections made to this doctrine may be answered in few words. It has been urged,

1. That this state of entire sanctification supposes future *impeccability*.—Certainly not; for if angels and our first parents fell when in a state of immaculate sanctity, the renovated man cannot be placed, by his entire deliverance from inward sin, beyond the reach of danger. It has been supposed,

2. That this supposed state renders the atonement and intercession of Christ superfluous in future.—But the very contrary of this is manifest when the case of an evangelical renewal of the soul in righteous-

ness is understood. This proceeds from the grace of God in Christ, through the Holy Spirit, as the efficient cause; it is received by faith as the instrumental cause; and the state itself into which we are raised is maintained, not by inherent native power, but by the continual presence and sanctifying influence of the Holy Spirit himself, received and retained in answer to ceaseless prayer, which prayer has respect solely to the merits of the death and intercession of Christ. But it has been further alleged,

3. That a person delivered from all inward and outward sin has no longer need to use the petition of the Lord's prayer, "forgive us our trespasses," because he has no longer need of pardon. To this we reply,

(1.) It would be absurd to suppose that any person is placed under the necessity of sinning in order that a general prayer, designed for men in a mixed condition, might retain its aptness to every particular case.

(2.) Trespassing of every kind and degree is surely not supposed by this prayer to be continued, in order that it might be used always in the same *import;* for otherwise it might be pleaded against the renunciation of any trespass or transgression whatever.

(3.) This petition is still relevant to the case of the entirely sanctified and evangelically perfect Christian, since neither angelic nor Adamic perfection is in question; that is, a perfection measured by the perfect law of God, which in its obligations contemplates all creatures as having sustained no injury by moral lapse, and, therefore, requires perfect obedience. But men, though wholly sanctified, are nevertheless *naturally* weak and *imperfect,* and so liable to mistake and infirmity, as well as to defect, in the *degree* of that absolute obedience which the law of God demands. It may also be remarked that we are not the ultimate judges of our own case as to the defects or fullness of our obedience, and we are not, therefore, to put ourselves in the place of God, who "is greater than our heart." St. Paul says, "I know nothing by myself," that is, I am conscious of no offense, "yet am I not thereby justified, but he that judgeth me is the Lord." To him, therefore, the appeal is every moment to be made through Christ the Mediator, and he, by the renewing testimony of his Spirit, assures every true believer of his acceptance in his sight.

CHAPTER XII.

THE POSSIBILITY OF TOTAL APOSTASY.

WE have examined the leading features of the *remedial system*, so far as it applies to man in his present state of being, beginning with the doctrine of atonement, and concluding with that of entire sanctification. But that Christians may understand the danger to which they are exposed, as well as the nature and extent of that "great salvation" which is provided for them in Christ Jesus, we will now inquire whether it is possible for true believers to fall from their state of grace and perish everlastingly.

This has long been a question of debate between Calvinistic and Arminian divines; the former taking the negative, and the latter the affirmative. That we may examine the subject with all possible fairness, let us ascertain, 1. How far these contending parties agree; 2. The ground on which the Calvinistic theory is based; and, 3. The arguments by which the possibility of total apostasy is supported.

I. HOW FAR THESE CONTENDING PARTIES AGREE.

All genuine Arminians agree with Calvinists in asserting,

1. *That believers are preserved in the way of life and salvation by Divine power.*—Thus St. Peter asserts, that they "are kept by the power of God through faith unto salvation." 1 Peter i, 5. The same doctrine is taught in the doxology with which Jude closes his Epistle. "Now unto him that is able to keep you from falling, and to present you faultless before the presence of his glory with exceeding joy."

2. *That no adverse agency or influence shall ever be able to separate true believers from the love of God.*—Of such our Lord says, "They shall never perish, neither shall any man pluck them out of my hand." John x, 28. "Who shall separate us from the love of Christ? Shall tribulation, or distress, or persecution, or famine, or nakedness, or peril, or sword? Nay, in all these things we are more than conquerors, through him that loved us. For I am persuaded that neither death, nor life, nor angels, nor principalities, nor powers, nor things present, nor things to come, nor height, nor depth, nor any other creature, shall be able to separate us from the love of God, which is in Christ Jesus our Lord." Rom. viii, 35-39.

3. *That God has promised persevering grace to all faithful believers.*—He will present us "holy, and unblamable, and unreprovable in his sight," if we "continue in the faith grounded and settled, and be not moved away from the hope of the Gospel." Col. i, 22, 23. Again,

St. Peter declares, that if we give all diligence to add to our "faith, virtue, knowledge, temperance, patience, godliness, brotherly kindness, and charity," we "shall *never fall.*" 2 Pet. i, 5–7, 10.

4. *That true believers may fall into gross and scandalous sins.*— Thus Lot fell into drunkenness and incest; David, into adultery and murder; Solomon, into gross idolatry; and Peter, into a denial of his Lord, with oaths and imprecations. It is moreover agreed on all hands, that those who commit such horrid sins are guilty in the sight of God, and unfit for the kingdom of heaven, until they are again renewed through repentance and faith. But the Calvinistic theory is, that a truly regenerate man " can neither *totally* nor *finally* fall away from a state of grace; but shall certainly persevere therein to the end, and be eternally saved."* Let us then examine,

II. THE GROUND ON WHICH THIS THEORY IS BASED, *or the arguments by which it is supported.*

1. The doctrine is argued *from the perfections of God.*—It is said that " God, as a being possessed of infinite love, faithfulness, wisdom, and power, can hardly be supposed to suffer any of his people finally to fall into perdition. This would be a reflection on his attributes, and argue him to be worse than a common father. His *love* to his people is unchangeable, and therefore they cannot be the objects of it at one time and not at another. His *faithfulness* to them and to his promise is not founded upon their merit, but on his own will and goodness. This, therefore, cannot be violated. His *wisdom* foresees every obstacle in the way, and is capable of removing it, and of directing them in the right path. It would be a reflection on his wisdom, after choosing a right end, not to choose right means in accomplishing the same. His *power* is insuperable, and is absolutely and perpetually displayed in their preservation and protection."†

In reply to this argument it is only necessary to remark that there is nothing in it that cannot, with equal force, be employed against certain *facts* the existence of which our opponents themselves admit. We refer to the fall of angels and of our first parents. If such perfectly holy beings have fallen, and some of them to rise no more, how can we argue the impossibility of total apostasy from the *perfections* of God? Are not these perfections the same now that they were before the fall of man and angels? The argument, therefore, proves too much, as it proves the impossibility of what has taken place.

But is it indeed true, as this favorite argument assumes, that God's moral creatures cannot be the objects of his love at one time and not at another? If it is, then it will follow either that God never loved " the angels which kept not their first estate," though they were at first his holy and happy creatures, or that he loves them still, though now " reserved in everlasting chains;" both of which are too absurd

---

* Conf., chap. 17, § 1. † Buck's Theological Dictionary.

to be believed. It will follow, moreover, on the same principle, that God must remain perfectly the same to those who are now his regenerate children as he was to them in their unregenerate and rebellious state. But to suppose this is a reflection on the character of God and a contradiction of his word. The key to the whole question is, that God ever loves what is *morally good*, and hates all *moral evil*. Hence, while creatures change, the love of God may be *extended* to them or *withheld* from them, according to their moral character, and yet God remain unchangeable, loving holiness and hating iniquity. But the unfrustrable perseverance of the saints is also argued,

2. *From certain doctrines peculiar to the Calvinistic scheme.*—These are, 1. That some men and angels are unconditionally predestinated to everlasting life; 2. That the covenant which God makes with his people is unconditional; 3. That all for whom Christ died shall infallibly be saved; 4. That the intercession of Christ secures the salvation of all for whom it is made; and, 5. That the Holy Spirit never forsakes any man whom he regenerates. As these are all questions of controversy, it will be time enough to receive them as so many grounds of argument when they are proved to be true. Till then they must be regarded as mere assumptions, and, consequently, as incapable of establishing the doctrine in proof of which they are adduced. But the advocates of the theory which we are considering attempt to support it,

3. *By direct Scripture testimony.*—We will therefore proceed to an examination of the leading passages which they bring forward for this purpose.

Job xvii, 9: "The righteous also shall hold on his way, and he that hath clean hands shall be stronger and stronger." But this is far from saying that no righteous man shall ever become *unrighteous*. If the passage is to be so understood, then we may safely assert, on the same principle, that no evil doer can ever be reformed; for it is expressly said that "evil men and seducers *shall wax worse and worse*."

Psalm lxxxix, 30–35: "If his children forsake my law, and walk not in my judgments; if they break my statutes, and keep not my commandments; then will I visit their transgression with the rod, and their iniquity with stripes. Nevertheless my loving-kindness will I not utterly take from him, nor suffer my faithfulness to fail. My covenant will I not break, nor alter the thing that is gone out of my lips. Once have I sworn by my holiness, that I will not lie unto David."

Every one must see that the covenant here spoken of related wholly to David and his seed. Had it, therefore, been absolute and unconditional, this would not prove that such is God's covenant with all his spiritual children. But that it was a conditional covenant, though expressed in absolute terms, is evident from what follows in the same connection. "But thou hast cast off and abhorred, thou hast been wroth with thine anointed. Thou hast *made void the covenant of thy servant;* thou hast profaned his crown, by casting it to the ground." Thus God did "alter the thing that" had "gone out of his lips," but without any impeachment of his truth.

Jeremiah xxxi, 3: "I have loved thee with an everlasting love; therefore with loving-kindness have I drawn thee." Our opponents seem to quote this passage as an evidence that those whom God loves at one time always *were* and always *will be* the objects of his love. But there is certainly a wide difference between loving "with an everlasting love," in the sense of the text, and loving *everlastingly*, for the passage has no reference whatever to futurity—"I *have loved* thee with an everlasting love." Nor do these words imply that no righteous man will ever turn from his righteousness, and so perish forever. They do not touch that question, but simply declare the strong and abiding love of God to the Jewish Church. To see this it is only necessary to read the passage in connection with the preceding context. "At the same time, saith the Lord, I will be the God of all the families of Israel, and they shall be my people. Thus saith the Lord, The people which were left of the sword found grace in the wilderness; even Israel, when I went to cause him to rest." Then the prophet adds, speaking in the person of Israel, "The Lord hath appeared of old unto me, saying, Yea, I have loved thee with an everlasting love; therefore with loving-kindness have I drawn thee."

Mark xvi, 16: "He that believeth and is baptized shall be saved." Does this mean "he that believeth" at this moment "shall" certainly and inevitably "be saved?" If this interpretation is good, then, by all the rules of speech, the other part of the sentence must mean, "he that believeth not" at this moment "shall" certainly and inevitably "be damned." This interpretation, therefore, cannot be admitted. The obvious meaning of the whole sentence is, "He that believeth," if he continue to believe, "shall be saved; but he that believeth not," if he continue in unbelief, "shall be damned."

John v, 24: "He that heareth my word, and believeth on him that sent me, hath everlasting life, and shall not come into condemnation; but is passed from death unto life." Here we remark, 1. That the present condition of true believers is called in Scripture "everlasting life," or "life eternal," *first*, because it is the same in nature with the life of heaven; and *secondly*, because, in the order of saving grace, it leads to a life of glory. "This is life eternal," said our Lord, "that they might know thee the only true God, and Jesus Christ whom thou hast sent." John xvii, 3. 2. That all who truly believe pass from spiritual death into this state of spiritual life; and, 3. That if they continue steadfast they "shall not come into condemnation;" for surely the passage cannot mean that when believers fall into gross sins, like David, Solomon, and Peter, they incur no condemnation.

John x, 27, 28: "My sheep hear my voice, and I know them, and

Chap. 12.]   THE POSSIBILITY OF TOTAL APOSTASY.   459

they follow me; and I give unto them eternal life; and they shall never perish, neither shall any man pluck them out of my hand." Here we have only to ask, Who "shall never perish?" The answer is, Those who *hear* the *voice* of Christ, and *follow* him. This promise is, therefore, so far from being unconditional, that the condition is clearly expressed.

John xiii, 1: "Having loved his own which were in the world, he loved them unto the end." The passage means nothing more than that our Lord continued to love his disciples "unto the end" of his own life. If it were therefore true that persons once in grace must forever remain in that state the doctrine could derive no support from this passage, except by a false interpretation.

John xvii, 11: "Holy Father, keep through thine own name those whom thou hast given me, that they may be one, as we are." Calvinists have laid great stress upon this text as teaching the doctrine that all whom the Father has given to Christ in the covenant of grace must infallibly persevere to the end. And yet in the very next verse our Lord declares that one of those whom the Father had given him did not persevere to the end, but perished everlastingly. His own words are, "Those that thou gavest me I have kept, and none of them is lost, but the son of perdition." So, then, one of this number was finally lost, which shows very clearly that the phrase "those whom thou hast given me" signifies here, if not in most other places too, the twelve apostles, and them only.

Romans viii, 38, 39: "For I am persuaded, that neither death, nor life, nor angels, nor principalities, nor powers, nor things present, nor things to come, nor height, nor depth, nor any other creature, shall be able to separate us from the love of God which is in Christ Jesus our Lord." But what does this text prove in regard to the perseverance of the saints? It proves that the apostle was at that time fully persuaded of his own perseverance—a persuasion which no doubt many Christians have at the present day called in Scripture "the full assurance of hope." It proves that he had the most unlimited confidence in the faithfulness and power of God to support his people in all the trials of life—a doctrine which we most heartily believe, for it is written, "As thy days, so shall thy strength be." Deut. xxxiii, 25. But it does not prove the absolute and unconditional perseverance of all true believers to the end, for the apostle says, "I keep under my body, and bring it into subjection; lest that by any means, when I have preached to others, I myself should be a castaway." 1 Cor. ix, 27.

These Scriptures, and a few others, have been pressed into the service of the Calvinistic theory of perseverance; but they utterly fail, when fairly interpreted, to establish the doctrine in support of which they are adduced. Nor is there a single passage in the Bible which, in its true import, proves the doctrine in question. But to be fully convinced of this, let us consider,

III. THE ARGUMENTS BY WHICH THE POSSIBILITY OF TOTAL APOSTASY IS SUPPORTED.

The simple question now before us is this: Can a true believer so fall away as to perish everlastingly? Believing the affirmative of this question to be the doctrine of the Bible, we will proceed to adduce some of the numerous arguments by which it is established. We refer,

1. *To those passages of Scripture in which the doctrine is expressly taught.*—Thus Ezekiel xviii, 24: "But when the righteous turneth away from his righteousness, and committeth iniquity, and doeth according to all the abominations that the wicked man doeth, shall he live? All his righteousness that he hath done shall not be mentioned. In his trespass that he hath trespassed, and in his sin that he hath sinned, in them shall he die."

That this is to be understood of eternal death appears evident from the twenty-sixth verse: "When a righteous man turneth away from his righteousness, and committeth iniquity, and dieth in them; (here is temporal death;) for his iniquity that he hath done, shall he die." (Here is death eternal.)

To evade the force of these passages some assert that the righteousness of which the prophet speaks does not imply true piety, but is a mere external or hypocritical righteousness. This, however, is a most unhappy shift, for it turns the language of the prophet into downright nonsense. Thus: When one who is hypocritically "righteous turneth away from his" hypocritical "righteousness, and committeth iniquity, shall he live?" Doubtless he shall not, as the interrogatory clearly implies. But this fact does not depend upon his turning away from his righteousness, unless it can be shown that hypocritical righteousness will secure eternal life. Again, "All his" hypocritical " righteousness that he hath done shall not be mentioned;" that is, shall not be reckoned to him. Happy circumstance! that at least so much of his hypocritical life is to be passed over in silence. But why? Because "he doeth according to all the abominations that the wicked man doeth." To escape these absurdities we must admit that one who is truly righteous may nevertheless so fall away as to perish everlastingly.

John xv, 1, 2, 6: "I am the true vine, and my Father is the husbandman. Every branch in me that beareth not fruit he taketh away. If a man abide not in me, he is cast forth as a branch, and is withered; and men gather them, and cast them into the fire, and they are burned."

Here we may remark, 1. That the persons spoken of are branches in the true Vine, Christ Jesus; 2. That some of these branches abide not in the Vine, but the Father taketh them away; 3. That the branches which abide not are cast forth, cast out from Christ and his Church; 4. That they are withered, and, consequently, are never grafted in again; and, 5. That they are also cast into the fire and burned. It is not possible for words more strongly to declare that even those who

Chap. 12.] THE POSSIBILITY OF TOTAL APOSTASY. 461

are now branches of the true Vine may so fall from God as to perish forever.

Romans xi, 17, 18, 21, 22 : "If some of the branches be broken off, and thou, being a wild olive-tree, wert graffed in among them, and with them partakest of the root and fatness of the olive-tree; boast not against the branches. For if God spared not the *natural* branches, take heed lest he also spare not thee. Behold therefore the goodness and severity of God: on them which fell, severity; but toward thee, goodness, if thou continue in his goodness: otherwise thou also shalt be cut off."

Here we observe, 1. That the olive-tree spoken of is the invisible and spiritual Church of God, consisting of all true believers. For, says the apostle, "If the first fruit be holy, the lump is also holy; and if the root be holy, so are the branches." And again, "Because of *unbelief* they were broken off; and thou *standest by faith*." 2. The persons addressed were actually grafted into this olive-tree, and were therefore *holy branches*. 3. These branches were still liable to be cut off from the olive-tree into which they were then grafted; and, 4. No intimation is given that the broken off branches were ever grafted in again. We conclude, therefore, that those who are members of the spiritual invisible Church may nevertheless so apostatize as to perish everlastingly.

1 Timothy i, 18, 19: "War a good warfare; holding faith, and a good conscience; which some having put away, concerning faith have made shipwreck." Here it is only necessary to remark, 1. That the persons alluded to, such as Hymeneus and Alexander, had once that faith which purifies the heart and produces a good conscience; for otherwise they could not have "put it away." 2. That of this faith they "made shipwreck," which necessarily implies that it was totally and finally lost; for a vessel once wrecked can never be recovered. The apostle himself represents one of these men at least as being irrecoverably lost. His words are, "Alexander the coppersmith did me much evil; the Lord reward him according to his works." 2 Tim. iv, 14. Hence one who possesses faith and a good conscience may so fall away as to perish everlastingly.

Hebrews vi, 4–6 : "For it is impossible for those who were once enlightened, and have tasted of the heavenly gift, and were made partakers of the Holy Ghost, and have tasted the good word of God, and the powers of the world to come, if they shall fall away, to renew them again unto repentance, seeing they crucify to themselves the Son of God afresh, and put him to an open shame."

That the persons whom the apostle describes in this passage were *true believers*, cannot be denied without great absurdity; for it would be a most glaring inconsistency to characterize the unregenerate by the terms and phrases which are here employed. They "were once *enlightened;*" an expression familiar with St. Paul, but which he never applied to those who were not true believers. "The eyes of your understanding being *enlightened;* that ye may know what is the hope of his calling, and what the riches of the glory of his inheritance in the saints." Eph. i, 18. And again, "For God, who commanded the light to shine out of darkness, hath shined into our hearts, to give the light of the knowledge of the glory of God in the face of Jesus Christ." 2 Cor. iv, 6.

They had "*tasted* of the *heavenly gift;*" which was something more than a mere intellectual or sentimental approval of the Gospel, as some would have it. For, the heavenly gift is distinguished both from the Holy Spirit, and from the word of God mentioned afterward, which leaves us no choice but to interpret it of Christ. And then, to taste Christ is to receive his grace and mercy in the remission of sins. "If so be ye have *tasted* that the Lord is gracious." 1 Peter ii, 3.

They "were made *partakers* of the *Holy Ghost;*" which evidently means, in the language of the New Testament, to receive the Holy Ghost in his sanctifying and comforting influences. "Repent, and be baptized every one of you in the name of Jesus Christ, for the remission of sins, and ye shall receive the gift of the Holy Ghost." Acts ii, 38. Again, "The love of God is shed abroad in our hearts, by the Holy Ghost which is given unto us." Rom. v, 5.

They "tasted the good word of God, and the powers of the world to come;" in other words, they heartily embraced the word of truth, and realized the saving power of the Gospel dispensation. And yet these persons, after possessing all these high attainments, so fell away that it was impossible "to renew them again unto repentance." Consequently, their fall was total and final.

But it will be said, the apostle only makes a supposition, "if they shall fall away." We answer, the apostle makes no supposition at all; for there is no *if* in the original. His words are, καὶ παραπεσοντας, *and having fallen away.* We have, therefore, in this passage a proof almost as clear as language can make it, that those who are made the subjects of converting and sanctifying grace may nevertheless so fall away as to perish everlastingly.

Hebrews x, 26–29: "For if we sin willfully after that we have received the knowledge of the truth, there remaineth no more sacrifice for sins, but a certain fearful looking for of judgment, and fiery indignation which shall devour the adversaries. He that despised Moses's law died without mercy under two or three witnesses. Of how much sorer punishment, suppose ye, shall he be thought worthy, who hath trodden under foot the Son of God, and hath counted the blood of the covenant, wherewith he was sanctified an unholy thing, and hath done despite unto the Spirit of grace?"

Here it is undeniably plain, 1. That the person referred to as an example was once *sanctified* by the blood of the covenant; for, to sup-

Chap. 12.] THE POSSIBILITY OF TOTAL APOSTASY. 463

pose, as some have done, that it was Christ himself who was sanctified by this blood, is too absurd to need refutation. 2. That he afterward, by known and willful sin, trod under foot the Son of God; treating his person and authority with the utmost contempt, as did the Jews in his crucifixion. 3. That he counted the blood of Christ, by which the new covenant between God and man was ratified, sealed, and confirmed, "an unholy thing;" regarding it as destitute of any sacrificial or atoning merit. 4. That he insulted the Holy Spirit; and, 5. That by these means he incurred a sorer punishment than temporal death, namely, death eternal. Therefore, those who are sanctified by the blood of Christ may yet fall away and perish forever.

There is one remark which we desire to make in regard to the last two passages quoted. It is this: Though they establish, beyond successful controversy, the possibility of total and final apostasy, yet they do not prove, as some have urged by way of objection to the doctrine, that no apostate can ever be recovered. They do not apply to backsliders of every kind; but only to those who rejected the whole Christian system, abjured Christ, and joined with the blaspheming Jews in calling him an impostor. Thus they rendered their salvation impossible by *willfully* and *maliciously* rejecting the only means of recovery. But these passages do not apply to any apostate who still believes in Christ as the Redeemer of men, and acknowledges Christianity as a Divine revelation. To all such there remains an available "sacrifice for sins," and they may yet be recovered "out of the snare of the devil."

Many other texts of Scripture might be adduced in proof of the doctrine in question; but those which we have quoted are quite sufficient for our present purpose. We will, therefore, proceed to argue the possibility of apostasy,

2. *From Scripture examples.*—We now assume it as a fact, which we think the following cases will prove, that the Scriptures furnish us with examples of total and final apostasy. We refer,

(1.) *To the case of* SAUL, *king of Israel.*—That he was once in a state of grace and favor with God is sufficiently clear from what is recorded of him in 1 Samuel x, 6, 7, 9. Samuel said to him, "The Spirit of the Lord will come upon thee, and thou shalt prophesy with them, and shalt be turned into *another man.* And let it be, when these signs are come unto thee, that thou do as occasion serve thee; for God is with thee. And it was so, that when he had turned his back to go from Samuel, God gave him *another heart.*" Thus we see that God gave Saul "another heart;" that he was "turned into another man;" that he possessed the spirit of prophecy, and that God was with him.

But in 1 Samuel xxviii, 15, Saul tells Samuel, "I am sore distressed; for the Philistines make war against me, and God is departed from me." And in 1 Samuel xxxi, 4, the sacred historian informs us that "Saul took a sword, and fell upon it;" thus destroying his own life. If, therefore, the doctrine of the apostle is true, that "no murderer hath eternal life abiding in him," Saul must have perished in his sins.

(2.) *Solomon.*—It will startle some to hear the name of Solomon among those who are regarded as examples of total and final apostasy. We need not attempt to prove that he once enjoyed the Divine favor, for this is what no one will deny. But it will be asked, What evidence have we of his apostasy? This question may be answered by a reference to the eleventh chapter of the first book of Kings, where his unlawful marriages with strange women and his shameful idolatry are recorded. It is, moreover, plainly declared that "the Lord was angry with Solomon, because his heart was turned from the Lord God of Israel, which had appeared unto him twice, and had commanded him concerning this thing, that he should not go after other gods; but he kept not that which the Lord commanded." True, we are often told that Solomon was reclaimed from all his backslidings; but of this we have no evidence whatever. Indeed, the inspired record seems to contradict it; for according to this, the last act of his life was an attempt to kill Jeroboam. Thus the sacred historian leaves his condition under a dark cloud, which forbids us to believe that he entered into life eternal.

(3.) *Judas Iscariot.*—"But was not Judas a devil from the beginning?" Certainly not. On the contrary, we have reason to believe that he was, when chosen as an apostle, the firm friend of our Lord. The psalmist speaks of him thus: "Yea, mine own familiar friend, in whom I trusted, which did eat of my bread, hath lifted up his heel against me." Psa. xli, 9. That this prophecy refers directly to Judas cannot be doubted, for it is so applied to him by Christ himself. (John xiii, 18.) Can we, then, seriously conclude that our Lord would hold familiar friendship with a devil, that he would receive him into his own family, and that he would send him forth to preach his Gospel and to cast out devils?

But it is said that our Lord called Judas a devil, and that he was, moreover, styled a thief. This is all true; but we must remember that he also applied to Peter the term *Satan*, which is only another name for the same evil spirit. Are we therefore to conclude that Peter had never been in a state of grace? Certainly not. It is also to be remembered that Judas was not called a devil until near the time when he wickedly betrayed his Master. That he became a wicked man is a matter of the clearest record. Hence it is asserted (John xiii, 27) that "Satan entered into him." Moreover, St. Peter declares that "Judas by transgression fell, that he might go to his own place." Acts i, 25. And it is also clear that he died under guilt, for he destroyed his own life.

(4.) *The Israelites who fell in the wilderness.*—Of these we have an account in 1 Corinthians x, 1–5: "Moreover, brethren, I would not that ye should be ignorant, how that all our fathers were under the cloud, and all passed through the sea; and were all baptized unto Moses in the cloud and in the sea; and did all eat the same spiritual meat; and did all drink the same spiritual drink; for they *drank of that spiritual Rock that followed them;* and that Rock was Christ. But with many of them God was not well pleased; for *they were overthrown in the wilderness.*"

(5.) The last case of this kind which we will notice is that of *Hymeneus and Alexander*: "Holding faith, and a good conscience; which some having put away, concerning faith have made shipwreck. Of whom is Hymeneus and Alexander; whom I have delivered unto Satan, that they may learn not to blaspheme." 1 Tim. i, 19, 20. It is sometimes said that the faith which these persons possessed was not a true faith, and that the conscience referred to was not really a good conscience. And, therefore, though they are represented as falling from the favor of God, yet in reality they only fell from a profession of goodness. To this the only necessary reply is, 1. That the conscience spoken of is emphatically called "*a good conscience;*" and, 2. That St. Paul exhorts his son Timothy to hold fast the very same faith and conscience which he ascribes to Hymeneus and Alexander. It follows, therefore, that they are examples of total and final apostasy. But our doctrine may be argued,

3. *From the cautions and warnings of the Scriptures against unfaithfulness and apostasy.*—Thus: "Let him that thinketh he standeth take heed lest he fall." 1 Cor. x, 12. "Therefore we ought to give the more earnest heed to the things which we have heard, lest at any time we should let them slip." Heb. ii, 1. "Take heed, brethren, lest there be in any of you an evil heart of unbelief, in departing from the living God." Heb. iii, 12. "Let us therefore fear, lest a promise being left us of entering into his rest, any of you should seem to come short of it." Heb. iv, 1. "Cast not away therefore your confidence, which hath great recompense of reward." Heb. x, 35. "Now the just shall live by faith; but if any man draw back, (literally, if the *just man* draw back,) my soul shall have no pleasure in him." Heb. x, 38. "Ye therefore, beloved, seeing ye know these things before, beware lest ye also, being led away with the error of the wicked, fall from your own steadfastness." 2 Peter iii, 17.

That these Scriptures are addressed to true believers will hardly be denied; but if it is impossible for them to "fall," to "depart from the living God," to "cast away their confidence," or to "draw back unto perdition," why do the inspired writers use such warnings, cautions, and exhortations? Will the advocates of the unfrustrable perseverance of the saints tell us that this is a means by which believers are preserved from apostasy? This would certainly be in conflict with their own theory, which regards the perseverance of believers as being wholly unconditional. Or, will they say that this system of caution and warning is a means of exciting believers to watchfulness and proper Christian diligence? If so, it will be proper to inquire whether this system is based on truth. If it is, then it will necessarily follow that there is a danger of apostasy, and that our doctrine is true. But if no such danger exists, then we have the absurdity of supposing that the spiritual interests of Christians are promoted by a system of falsehood. The last argument which we will offer in support of our position is derived from the fact,

4. *That the present life is a state of probation.*—A state of probation is one in which the character of men is formed and developed preparatory to a state of retribution. It involves obligations to obedience; commands and prohibitions; inducements to do right, and temptations to sin, with a certainty of final reward or punishment, according to the character which may be formed under the various circumstances of trial. It also enters into the very nature of a probationary state that the erring may be recovered, and that the obedient may go astray; for without this it would not be a state of trial.

To deny that man is now in a state of probation is to deny the doctrine of a final judgment; for, in the economy of the Divine government, the one necessarily implies the other. If man has nothing to do in the formation of his own moral character, why is he required to "give account of himself to God?" and how could God say to any of our race, "Depart, ye cursed, into everlasting fire?" But if man is now in a probationary state there is no degree of saving grace which he may not forfeit; no height of holiness from which he may not fall. This is confirmed by the history of all moral beings with whom we have become acquainted. Angels fell from heaven, and Adam fell from paradisaical holiness. And such is the similarity between all moral beings in a state of trial that the fall of angels and of our first parents is a corroborating fact in support of the doctrine that a state of probation involves the possibility of apostasy.

BOOK V.

MORALS OF CHRISTIANITY.

MORALITY, in a general sense, denotes *virtue*, or *the practice of moral duties*. In a strictly theological sense it means a voluntary conformity of our moral actions to the will of God. By the *morals of* Christianity, therefore, we are to understand the practical duties which Christianity requires. Hence it becomes a matter of importance to know both what these duties are and how they ought to be performed. But before we proceed to investigate them in detail we will offer some remarks in regard to that system of moral law on which they all depend, and by which they are prescribed.

CHAPTER I.

THE MORAL LAW.

BY *moral law* we understand a law which prescribes to men their religious and social duties; or, in other words, the duties which we owe to God and to one another. Such a law, in its highest degree of perfection, is contained in the Scriptures of the Old and New Testament, and in them only, the Divine authority of which has been fully established in our first book.

Philosophers have entertained various and conflicting opinions in regard to what constitutes the *ground of moral obligation;* but all Christians will agree that the will of God, which is ever in perfect accordance with rectitude, is the *standard* of right for all moral creatures, and ought to be obeyed. And as the Holy Scriptures are the only authoritative revelation of the Divine will, we will proceed to inquire into the manner in which they make known to us a system of moral law. To aid those who desire to gain a clear understanding of this subject we will offer the following remarks:

1. *The morals of the Scriptures are not generally proposed to us in*

the form of a regular code.—Even in the books of Moses, which, to a great extent, have the legislative form, all the principles and duties that constitute the full character of *godliness* under that dispensation are not made the subjects of formal injunction by particular precepts. They are partly unfolded in general principles, or often take the form of injunction in an apparently incidental manner, or as matters of obvious inference. A preceding code of traditional moral law is also all along supposed in the writings of Moses and the prophets, as well as a customary ritual and a doctrinal theology, both transmitted from the patriarchs.

This, too, is eminently the case with the Christian Scriptures. They suppose that all who believed in Christ admitted the Divine authority of the Old Testament, and they assume the perpetual authority of its morals as well as the truth of its fundamental theology. The constant allusions in the New Testament to the moral rules of the Jews and patriarchs, either expressly as precepts or as the data of argument, sufficiently guard us against the notion that what has not in so many words been re-enacted by Christ and his apostles is of no authority among Christians. In a great number of instances, however, the form is directly preceptive, so as to have all the explicitness and force of a regular code of law, and is, as much as a regular code could be, a declaration of the sovereign will of Christ, enforced by the sanctions of eternal life and death.

2. *The moral law is summarily comprehended in the Decalogue or Ten Commandments.*—These were written by the finger of God on two tables of stone, and delivered to Moses on Mount Sinai. These tables were deposited in the sacred chest, called the ark of the covenant, but copies of them were transcribed into the Pentateuch in Exodus xx, 1–17, and in Deuteronomy v, 6–21.

The giving of the law on Mount Sinai was the most solemn transaction which ever took place between God and man, and, therefore, it was introduced in the most solemn manner. In the morning of the day on which this law was given the presence of Jehovah became manifest by thunders and lightnings, a dense cloud on the mountain, and a terrific blast of a trumpet, so that the whole assembly were struck with terror and dismay. Shortly after the whole mountain appeared on fire, columns of smoke arose from it as the smoke of a furnace, and an earthquake shook it from top to base; the trumpet continued to sound, and the blast grew longer and louder. Then Jehovah, the sovereign Lawgiver, came down upon the mount and called Moses to ascend to the top that he might receive his law.

In this summary of moral law we have the most complete and perfect arrangement and specification of human duties which has ever been made, and one which will probably never be improved. Its division into two distinct parts or tables was not accidental, but a matter of design, and was made for most important reasons. The first table comprehended the four precepts which enjoin our duty to God, and the second the six which prescribe our duty to men. It is called the moral law because the subject of its injunctions is not ceremonial observances but moral actions, and to distinguish it from the positive laws, which were only of temporary obligation.

3. *The moral precepts of the Old Testament are received into the Christian code.*—When our Lord, in his Sermon on the Mount, says, "Think not that I am come to destroy the law or the prophets. I am not come to destroy, but to fulfill"—that is, to confirm or establish the law—the entire scope of his discourse shows that he is speaking exclusively of the moral precepts of THE LAW, eminently so called, and of the moral injunctions of the prophets founded upon them, and to which he thus gives an equal authority.

In like manner St. Paul, after having strenuously maintained the doctrine of justification by faith alone, anticipates an objection by asking, "Do we then make void the law through faith?" and subjoins, "God forbid; yea, we *establish* the law;" meaning by this term, as the context and his argument show, the *moral* and not the ceremonial law.

After such declarations it is worse than trifling for any one to contend that, in order to establish the authority of the moral law of the Jews over Christians, it ought to have been formally re-enacted. Indeed, the summary of the law and the prophets, which is to love God with all our heart, and to love our neighbor as ourselves, is unquestionably enjoined, and even re-enacted by the Christian Lawgiver. When our Lord was explicitly asked by "one who came unto him and said, Good Master, what good thing shall I do, that I may have eternal life?" the answer shows that the moral law contained in the Decalogue is so in force under the Christian dispensation that obedience to it is necessary to final salvation. "If thou wilt enter into life keep the commandments." And that he refers directly to the Decalogue is manifest from what follows. "He saith unto him, Which? Jesus said, Thou shalt do no murder. Thou shalt not commit adultery. Thou shalt not steal," etc. Matt. xix, 17–19. Here we have all the force of a formal re-enactment of the Decalogue, a part of it being evidently put for the whole.

Nor would it be difficult to produce passages from the discourses of Christ and the writings of the apostles, which enjoin all the precepts of this law separately by their authority, as indispensable parts of Christian duty, and that, too, under their original sanctions of life and death. So, then, the two circumstances which form the true character of LAW in its highest sense, DIVINE AUTHORITY and PENAL SANCTIONS, are found as truly in the New Testament as in the Old. It will not, for instance, be denied that the New Testament enjoins the worship of one God alone; that it prohibits idolatry; that it forbids false and profane swearing; that St. Paul uses the very words of the fifth commandment preceptively when he says, (Ephesians vi, 2,) "Honor thy father and mother, which is the first commandment with promise;" or that murder, adultery, theft, false witness, and covetousness are prohibited under pain of exclusion from the kingdom of God.

Thus, then, we have the whole Decalogue brought into the Christian code of morals by a distinct injunction of its separate precepts, and by their recognition as of permanent and unchangeable obligation; the fourth commandment only being so far excepted that its injunction is not so expressly marked. This, however, is no exception in fact; for, 1. Its original place in the two tables sufficiently distinguishes it from all positive, ceremonial, and typical precepts, and gives it a moral character in respect to its *ends;* which are, first, *mercy* to servants and cattle, and secondly, the undisturbed *worship of God.* 2. It is necessarily included in that "law" which our Lord declares he came "not to destroy," or abrogate; in that "law" which St. Paul declares to be established by faith; and, 3. It was recognized in the practice of the apostles, who did not cease to keep holy one day in seven, but gave "the Lord's day" that eminence and sanctity in the Christian Church, which the seventh day had in the Jewish, by consecrating it to holy uses.

4. *The New Testament contains a fuller revelation of moral law than the Old.*—It is important to remark, that though the moral laws of the Mosaic dispensation pass into the Christian code, yet they stand there in other and higher circumstances. In particular,

(1.) They are more expressly extended to the heart, as by our Lord in his Sermon on the Mount; who teaches us, that the thought and inward purpose of any offense is a violation of the law which prohibits its external and visible commission.

(2.) The principles on which they are founded are carried out in the New Testament into a greater variety of duties, which, by embracing more perfectly the social and civil relations of life, are of a more universal character; and there is an enlarged injunction of positive and particular virtues, especially of such as belong to the Christian temper.

(3.) All overt acts are inseparably connected with those corresponding principles in the heart which are essential to acceptable obedience; which principles suppose the regeneration of the soul by the Holy Spirit. This moral renovation is, therefore, held out as necessary to our salvation, and promised through Christ.

(4.) The precepts of the Gospel are connected with peculiar promises of Divine assistance; are illustrated in the perfect example of our Lord; and are enforced by sanctions derived from the clearer revelation of a future state, and the more explicit promises of eternal life, and threatenings of eternal punishment.

It follows, therefore, that the Gospel contains the most complete and perfect revelation of *moral law* that has ever been given to man. It contains a law which is of universal obligation, the law which was given to Adam in paradise, and from which his subsequent apostasy could not release him. This law has no relation, therefore, to times and places, or to one age or nation more than another; but being founded in the relations of men to their Creator and to one another, it retains its authority under all dispensations.

The great principle involved in all acceptable obedience to moral law is LOVE—*love to God* and *love to man*. When the lawyer inquired, "Master, which is the great commandment of the law? Jesus said unto him, Thou shalt love the Lord thy God with all thy heart, and with all thy soul, and with all thy mind. This is the first and great commandment. And the second is like unto it, Thou shalt love thy neighbor as thyself. On these two commandments hang all the law and the prophets." Matt. xxii, 36–40. So also St. Paul testifies, that "love is the fulfilling of the law." Rom. xiii, 10. It is on this grand principle of universal love that all moral law is founded; and its particular precepts only point out the various ways in which this love is to be manifested.

To the revealed will of God we may now turn for all necessary information on the interesting subject of Christian morality. But as the Gospel is a message of mercy to a sinful and rebellious race, and as it requires of all men, as indispensable conditions of their salvation, "*repentance* toward God and *faith* toward our Lord Jesus Christ," it seems both proper and necessary that we should in the first place direct our attention to a consideration of these important evangelical requirements.

CHAPTER II.

REPENTANCE.

REPENTANCE is a doctrine which presupposes sin. Hence our Lord says, "I came not to call the righteous, but *sinners* to repentance." Mark ii, 17. But as all men are sinners, and as all who continue in a state of impenitence must perish forever, the doctrine of repentance is one in which every man is deeply interested. Let us, therefore, proceed to inquire into the nature, the necessity, and the means of evangelical repentance.

I. ITS NATURE.

Mr. Watson, in his Biblical Dictionary, defines repentance to be "a godly sorrow wrought in the heart of a sinful person by the word and

Spirit of God, whereby, from a sense of his sin, as offensive to God, and defiling and endangering to his own soul, and from an apprehension of the mercy of God in Christ, he, with grief and hatred of all his known sins, turns from them to God as his Saviour and Lord."

There are two distinct words in the Greek Testament which, in our authorized version, are rendered "repent." These are μεταμέλομαι and μετανοέω. The former, *metamelomai*, sometimes signifies merely to change the mind or purpose, as in Matthew xxi, 29: "He answered and said, I will not; but afterward he *repented* (μεταμεληθεὶς) and went." At other times it means to change the mind from a painful motive, to feel sorrow or remorse, as in Matthew xxvii, 3: "Then Judas, when he saw that he was condemned, *repented himself,* (μεταμεληθεὶς,) and brought again the thirty pieces of silver to the priests and elders." The latter term, *metanoeo*, usually signifies to change the mind and reform the life, from feelings of sorrow and remorse. Thus, "*Repent* ye; (μετανοεῖτε;) for the kingdom of heaven is at hand." Matt. iii, 2. "If thy brother trespass against thee, rebuke him; and if he *repent*, (μετανόηση,) forgive him." Luke xvii, 3.

Here it may be observed that though these two words are not exactly synonymous, yet they have no opposition of meaning. The only difference is that one implies more than the other. *Metanoeo* implies all that is meant by *metamelomai*, together with reformation of life. The repentance of Judas, spoken of in Matthew xxvii, 3, is expressed by the verb *metamelomai;* but the expression affords no evidence that his repentance went any further than mere contrition or remorse. But in general, when the Scriptures speak of that repentance which is connected with salvation, they employ *metanoeo*, or some word derived from it. Hence we conclude that the repentance which the Gospel requires consists mainly in *contrition* and *reformation*.

As it regards the nature of repentance, it may be considered both as the gift of God and as the duty of man. That repentance is the gift of God is plainly taught in the Scriptures. One or two passages will establish this point. "Then hath God also to the Gentiles *granted repentance* unto life." Acts xi, 18. Again: "Him hath God exalted to be a Prince, and a Saviour, for to *give repentance* to Israel." Acts v, 31.

It is evident, moreover, from the nature of repentance itself, that it is the gift of God. One of its essential elements, as we have seen both from the above definition and from the etymology of the word, is a deep and heart-felt sorrow for sin. But this we cannot produce in ourselves, as might easily be shown. Nothing short of Divine agency can produce that godly sorrow which "worketh repentance unto life;" and, therefore, repentance is everywhere regarded by evangelical Christians as being, in this respect, eminently the work of the Holy Spirit. We must not suppose, however, that because repentance is the gift of God we have nothing to do in the matter. This would be to contradict the plainest declarations of inspiration, for God commands "all men everywhere to repent." Repentance, then, is both the gift of God and the duty of man; and is, therefore, very properly regarded as consisting in *contrition of spirit* and *reformation of life.*

1. Repentance consists in *contrition*, or *a sincere sorrow for sin.*—A child who disobeys a kind father usually feels, after the fear of punishment is over, sincere regret on account of his disobedience. Let a man be convinced that he has done an injury to a friend, and though the fact should be unknown to all but himself, he will lament in secret his unworthy conduct. In like manner a penitent sinner feels regret and sorrow because he has offended God and injured his fellow-men. Of this contrition or godly sorrow it may be asserted,

(1.) That it always presupposes *conviction.* It has been very generally taught by theologians that conviction of sin constitutes a part of repentance; but this notion, we think, is not well founded. That it must necessarily precede repentance, and is therefore indispensable to its existence, we readily admit; but that it constitutes an essential part of repentance is what we cannot allow. That conviction cannot be a part of repentance will appear evident when we consider that the Scriptures represent it as a common and universal benefit bestowed on mankind through the agency of the Holy Spirit. "He will reprove (convict or convince) *the world* of sin, and of righteousness, and of judgment." John xvi, 8. The enlightening and convicting grace of God leaves all men without excuse for their sin; but it does not imply repentance in any proper sense of the term. Our Lord said of the wicked Jews, "If I had not come and spoken unto them, they had not had sin; but now they have no cloak for their sin." John xv, 22. They were instructed, and convicted of sin, but they were still impenitent.

(2.) That contrition implies a clear discovery of *the great evil of sin.* "Fools make a mock at sin," but to those who are truly of a contrite spirit it appears to be a great and terrible evil, fraught with consequences of the most dreadful nature. They see that sin is an injury done to God; that every transgression of his holy law is an open and causeless affront to his infinite authority. Nor will they fail to recollect that this exalted being is their own supreme benefactor, and that every blessing which they receive comes "down from the Father of lights." With this consideration in view they will be deeply pained by a sense of their ingratitude. They see that sin is the cause, either directly or indirectly, of all the sufferings that exist throughout the world; that it entails on human life a thousand ills, and plunges the soul into eternal ruin. They see, too, the injury which sin has done to themselves; that it has degraded them beneath the proper level of rational beings; that it has occupied their noble faculties only in such pursuits as are unworthy and mischievous; that it has rendered them justly loathsome in the sight of

God, and contemptible in the eyes of all his holy creatures; and that it exposes them to eternal perdition.

(3.) That contrition for sin will prompt the subjects of it to *free confession*. This is the first, the proper, and the natural language of true penitence. David said, " I acknowledge my transgression; and my sin is ever before me." Psa. li, 3. " For innumerable evils have compassed me about; mine iniquities have taken hold upon me, so that I am not able to look up: they are more than the hairs of my head, therefore my heart faileth me." Psa. xl, 12. So also the publican " smote upon his breast, saying, God be merciful to me a sinner." Luke xviii, 13. Thus the contrite heart, in the clear view of its sinful condition, overflows with penitential sorrow; and from the abundance of the heart the mouth is compelled to speak.

2. *Repentance includes reformation.*—Without this there can be no repentance to salvation. " Let the wicked forsake his way, and the unrighteous man his thoughts; and let him return unto the Lord, and he will have mercy upon him; and to our God, for he will abundantly pardon." Isa. lv, 7. " Thus saith the Lord God, Repent, and turn yourselves from all your idols; and turn away your faces from all your abominations." Ezek. xiv, 6.

This doctrine is also strongly inculcated in the New Testament. John the Baptist required those who came to his baptism to " bring forth fruits meet for repentance;" and our Lord said, " If any man will come after me, let him deny himself, and take up his cross, and follow me." Matt. xvi, 24. So also St. Paul tells us that he " showed first unto them of Damascus, and at Jerusalem, and throughout all the coasts of Judea, and then to the Gentiles, that they should repent and turn to God, and do works meet for repentance." Acts xxvi, 20.

It is worthy of remark that true contrition naturally leads to reformation of life. This may be seen in the words of the apostle: " For godly sorrow worketh repentance to salvation not to be repented of." 2 Cor. vii, 10. It is asserted by some that " godly sorrow " is no part of repentance, because it is here said to *work repentance*. Hence it is concluded that as repentance cannot be produced by itself, so " godly sorrow " must be something different from repentance, which it is said to work or produce. We readily admit that a thing cannot be at the same time and in the same sense both effect and cause; and, consequently, in this acceptation repentance cannot be the cause of itself. But one part of repentance may be the cause of another; and this, we believe, is the obvious meaning of the passage in question. Contrition or " godly sorrow," the first part of repentance, works reformation of life, the second part of repentance. Though " godly sorrow " is repentance begun, yet no repentance is " repentance to salvation" until it extends to a thorough reformation of heart and life. It is, therefore, asserted by the apostle that " godly sorrow worketh repentance to salvation." But,

Chap. 2.] REPENTANCE. 475

3. The question is sometimes asked, *What is the order of repentance in its connection with faith and regeneration?*—The Calvinistic view on this subject is, that both faith and repentance follow regeneration, and flow from it. Their theory is clearly expressed by Mr. Buck, in his Theological Dictionary, thus: "1. Regeneration is the work of God enlightening the mind and changing the heart, and in order of time precedes faith. 2. Faith is the consequence of regeneration, and implies the perception of an object. It discerns the evil of sin, the holiness of God, gives credence to the testimony of God in his word, and seems to precede repentance, since we cannot repent of that of which we have no clear perception or no concern about. 3. Repentance is an after thought, or sorrowing for sin, the evil nature of which faith perceives, and which immediately follows faith. Conversion is a turning from sin, which faith sees and repentance sorrows for, and seems to follow and to be the end of all the rest." Thus the order of these graces, in point of time, is supposed to be, 1. Regeneration; 2. Faith; 3. Repentance; and, 4. Conversion.

Arminian divines hold a different order on this subject. They hold that repentance precedes both justifying faith and regeneration, and that the order of these graces, in point of time, is this: 1. Repentance; 2. Faith; 3. Regeneration. Let us then look at this subject in the light of Scripture.

We do not deny that repentance is preceded by the influences of the Holy Spirit, and by some degree of faith. Such is the depravity of our nature that the soul must first be visited by the enlightening and convicting grace of God, and be led to exercise a degree of faith in Divine truth before it can take a single step in the way of evangelical repentance. "For he that cometh to God must believe that he is, and that he is a rewarder of them that diligently seek him." Heb. xi, 6. Nor do we deny that repentance may sometimes follow justifying faith and regeneration. It is freely admitted that true believers may, in some sense and to some extent, be the subjects of repentance. Such they *will* be as long as there are remains of sin in the soul, and such they *may* be even as long as the soul remains in the body; for those who are cleansed "from all unrighteousness" may very properly continue to exercise a sorrowful remembrance of past offenses, which is one part of repentance. But to show that evangelical repentance, in the common acceptation of the term, precedes justifying faith and regeneration, we may notice,

(1.) The order in which these graces are spoken of by the inspired writers. "*Repent* ye, and believe the Gospel." Mark i, 15. "Him hath God exalted with his right hand, to be a prince and a Saviour, for to give *repentance* to Israel, and *forgiveness of sins.*" Acts v, 31. "Testifying both to the Jews, and also to the Greeks, *repentance* toward God, and *faith* toward our Lord Jesus Christ." Acts xx, 21. In these, and many other passages, *repentance* is placed first in order; and though we would not rest our argument on this fact alone, yet if it were always preceded by faith and regeneration, it would be difficult to account for the general observance of this order in the Scriptures. But this question is set at rest,

(2.) By those Scriptures which mark the actual process of the work of saving grace. Peter says, "*Repent*, and be baptized every one of you in the name of Jesus Christ, for the *remission of sins*, and ye shall receive *the gift of the Holy Ghost.*" Acts ii, 38. These persons could not have been regenerated believers, for if so their sins must have been forgiven; but they were commanded to "repent" and to "be baptized" in order to "remission." It is, therefore, clear, that in their case repentance preceded remission. But as justifying faith, remission, and regeneration are always united, their repentance must have preceded both faith and regeneration. Again, "*Repent* ye, therefore, and be converted, that your sins may be blotted out." Acts iii, 19. Here repentance, instead of being "an after-thought," following regeneration and faith, is made a condition of pardon; and, consequently, it must precede regeneration. We have only to add,

(3.) That while the Calvinistic theory is unsupported by Scripture, it is objectionable on other grounds. If men cannot repent until they are regenerated, and if regeneration is a work in which they are altogether passive, as Calvinists teach, then it will follow, 1. That God commands all men everywhere to do what he knows they cannot do, that is, "to repent,"—not after they are regenerated, but now—at this moment. 2. That the finally impenitent may urge a strong plea in extenuation of their impenitence. They may say, "True, we never repented, but we are not to blame. Repentance could not precede regeneration, and of that work we were never made the subjects. Consequently, there never was a time when we could repent." Repentance, then, must be understood to precede both justifying faith and regeneration.

II. THE NECESSITY OF REPENTANCE.

That repentance is necessary, in order to the obtainment of the Divine favor and of everlasting life, is proved,

1. *From the word of God.*—This is clearly taught, 1. In the Scriptures of the Old Testament. "Repent, and turn yourselves from all your transgressions; so iniquity shall not be your ruin." Ezek. xviii, 30. 2. By John the Baptist. "In those days came John the Baptist, preaching in the wilderness of Judea, and saying, Repent ye, for the kingdom of heaven is at hand." Matt. iii, 1, 2. 3. By Jesus Christ. "From that time Jesus began to preach, and to say, Repent, for the kingdom of heaven is at hand." Matt. iv, 17. "Except ye repent, ye shall all likewise perish." Luke xiii, 3. 4. By the apostles. "And they went out, and preached that men should repent." Mark vi, 12. "Repent ye therefore, and be converted, that your sins may be blotted out."

Acts iii, 19. "And the times of this ignorance God winked at, but now commandeth all men everywhere to repent." Acts xvii, 30. But the necessity of repentance may be argued,

2. *From the nature of true religion.*—The religion of the Bible requires the exercise of meekness, humility, faith, hope, and charity; but these can have no place in the experience of impenitent sinners. They are characterized as "hateful and hating one another;" and as being under the control of "the carnal mind," which "is enmity against God." True repentance is therefore necessary, in order that men may be qualified to discharge the duties of religion; but it is equally necessary in order to its *enjoyments*, whether in the present or the future life. For the spiritual and holy joys of Christianity impenitent sinners have no desire. As they "are in the flesh," they "live after the flesh," "fulfilling the desires of the flesh and of the mind." Nor could they, as impenitent sinners, realize enjoyment even in the bliss of heaven itself; for their moral condition would be incongenial to the joys and employments of that holy place. Hence, without repentance there can be no "peace with God" on earth; no "crown of glory" in heaven.

III. THE MEANS OF REPENTANCE.

"In contemplating this subject, we would here endeavor to guard against presumption on the one hand and despair on the other. By the former we may be led to look upon repentance as a work of our own, that we may fully accomplish by the unassisted exercise of our own powers; and thus we may be led to despise the proffered grace of the Gospel, and by scornfully rejecting the aid of heaven, be left to perish in our sins. By the latter we may be led to look upon repentance as a work of God alone, in reference to which the efforts of man are perfectly useless; and thus we may be led to repose our consciences upon the downy pillow of careless indifference, and yield ourselves up to the seducing slumbers of sin, till the door of repentance shall be closed against us forever."

"To suppose that the carnal mind can turn itself to God, and by its own innate, underived energy, work out 'repentance unto salvation,' is to set aside the doctrine of human depravity, and contradict those Scriptures which refer to God as the author of repentance. To suppose that man can have no agency in the work of repentance, is to deny his responsibility for his actions, and discard those Scriptures which call upon 'all men everywhere to repent.' It is true, God is the author of evangelical repentance; but he confers that blessing according to a certain plan, and such as use the prescribed means have the promise that they shall attain the proposed end."* What, then, are the means of repentance? We answer,

1. *Serious consideration.*—The impenitent multitude, immersed in worldly pursuits, and allured by the imposing charms of pleasure, wealth,

* Ralston's Elements, pp. 272, 273.

and honor, seldom take time to inquire whence they came, what they are, or whither bound. How touching is the lamentation of Moses over the thoughtlessness of an ungodly race! "O that they were wise, that they *understood* this, that they would *consider* their latter end!" Deut. xxxii, 29. And how solemn is the accusation which God himself urges against his forgetful and backsliding people: "The ox knoweth his owner, and the ass his master's crib; but Israel doth not know, my people doth not *consider*." Isa. i, 3. The want of consideration has been in every age, and still is, a fruitful cause of impenitence and final ruin. Men "perish for lack of knowledge," and they lack knowledge because they "do not consider." If they could be induced to pause in their headlong rush to destruction, and to consider the claims which the religion of Christ has upon them, their condition would at once become hopeful; for consideration is the first step toward evangelical repentance.

2. *Self-examination.*—There is, perhaps, no work in which sinners are more unwilling to engage than that of self-examination; and yet it is a work of great importance as a means of repentance. We cannot repent of sin, until we know that we are sinners; and we cannot fully understand the nature and extent of our sinfulness, until we examine ourselves in the light of God's law. As a man must know that he is diseased before he will call in a physician, so sinners must see and feel their moral disease and helplessness before they will cry, "Lord, save us; we perish." It is possible for us to suppose, in the absence of self-examination, that we are "rich, and increased with goods, and have need of nothing;" while at the same time we are "wretched, and miserable, and poor, and blind, and naked." St. Paul says, "I was alive without the law once, but when the commandment came, sin revived and I died." Rom. vii, 9. The holy and spiritual law of God convinced him that he was "carnal, sold under sin," and led him to exclaim, in the bitterness of penitential sorrow, "O wretched man that I am! who shall deliver me from the body of this death?"

3. *Meditation on the Divine goodness.*—The Gospel employs every argument that is calculated to enlist our attention and engage our affections. It addresses our hopes and our fears, our reason and our conscience, and often appeals to our *gratitude*. "The goodness of God," says St. Paul, "leadeth thee to repentance." Rom. ii, 4. If earthly parents have a just claim upon our gratitude, how much stronger are the claims of our Father in heaven! "We read his mercy in all his works. It is written upon every leaf, and wafted upon every breeze. It glows in every star, and sparkles in every brook. But, above all, in the unspeakable gift of Christ, in his sufferings and death for our sins, we behold, beyond the power of language to tell, the love of God to us. A consideration of this glorious theme should lead us to repentance. Hard, indeed, must be the heart, and fiend-like the soul, that can contemplate

such a debt of love, and feel no pang in offending against such goodness." Such meditations should lead the soul to God in penitential gratitude.

4. *Prayer for Divine aid.*—As human efforts, without the blessing of God, are unavailing in the common pursuits of life; so, also, we cannot "cease to do evil," and "learn to do well," without the aid of the Holy Spirit. But in regard to this we have most encouraging promises. "If ye then, being evil, know how to give good gifts unto your children, how much more shall your heavenly Father give the Holy Spirit to them that ask him?" Luke xi, 13. And again, our Lord says, "Ask, and it shall be given you; seek, and ye shall find; knock, and it shall be opened unto you." Matt. vii, 7. We have, therefore, a gracious right to "come boldly unto the throne of grace, that we may obtain mercy, and find grace to help in time of need." Heb. iv, 16.

CHAPTER III.

FAITH.

To "believe on the Lord Jesus Christ" is the grand precept of the Gospel. It is a duty inculcated with peculiar earnestness by the inspired writers; it is bound upon us by the strongest obligations; it is connected with the most solid and extensive advantages; and its necessity is universal, perpetual, and indispensable. Faith is, therefore, a subject in the discussion of which all men should feel a lively interest. We propose, then, 1. To offer some remarks on the nature of faith in general; and, 2. To consider more particularly the properties of that faith which is necessary to salvation.

I. WE WILL OFFER SOME REMARKS ON THE NATURE OF FAITH IN GENERAL.

The Greek word which is rendered *faith* in the New Testament is πιστις, from the verb πείθω, which means *to persuade*. Faith, therefore, according to the etymology of the word, is *the persuasion of the truth of a proposition;* or, in other words, faith is the assent of the mind to the truth of a proposition on the ground of evidence.

By *evidence* we mean whatever is a ground or cause of belief. There are various kinds of evidence by which human knowledge is gained and propositions are established. We have the evidence of *sense*, of *reason*, of *consciousness*, and of *testimony*. It is the evidence of testimony alone which produces faith in its strictest acceptation; and faith is therefore more pure and genuine, in proportion as the truth believed possesses less credibility in itself, and rests solely upon the veracity of the testifier. It was this fact that so eminently distinguished the faith of Abraham. "He staggered not at the promise of God through unbelief; but was strong in faith, giving glory to God." Rom. iv, 20. But we may proceed to remark,

1. *That faith implies a previous knowledge of that which is made the subject of belief.*—Hence knowledge has been regarded as an antecedent act of faith; for in order that we might believe, it is necessary that we should have a previous knowledge of what we are to believe. There is, therefore, great propriety in the question of the man who had been healed of his native blindness, when our Lord said to him, "Dost thou believe on the Son of God? He answered and said, Who is he, Lord, that I might believe on him?" John ix, 35, 36.

A proposition to be believed may be either directly expressed or only implied. Of the former we have an example in John iv, 50, when our Lord said to the nobleman of Capernaum, "Thy son liveth," and of the latter in John ix, 7: "Go, wash in the pool of Siloam." Jesus did not tell the blind man that by washing in this pool he should receive sight, but this proposition was plainly implied. "He went his way therefore, and washed, and came seeing."

2. *Faith implies evidence.*—No man can believe a proposition without evidence, either real or supposed; nor can any one withhold his assent to a proposition which, according to his judgment, is sustained by a sufficient amount of evidence. Belief, therefore, is the natural and necessary result of evidence whenever such evidence is apprehended by the mind; for it is impossible that any one should believe a proposition to be both true and false at the same time.

But to this it may be objected, that if a man cannot believe without evidence, and if belief is the natural and necessary result of evidence, then it will follow either that no man ever believed a falsehood, or that falsehood is sometimes supported by evidence; neither of which can be allowed. To this we reply: It is evident that men often believe that which is false; and it is equally evident that falsehood cannot be supported by real evidence, otherwise the distinction between truth and error would be destroyed. But these facts are in perfect harmony with the position which we have assumed. Thus, a man's judgment, through some improper bias, may decide in favor of a proposition for which there is really no evidence; but then we must make a distinction between what is *really* evidence and what is *supposed* to be evidence. A man may take that for evidence which is really no evidence at all, and by this means be led into the belief of error. On the other hand a proposition may be true, and it may be susceptible of the clearest proof; but from some mismanagement of the mind its truth may not be apprehended. Hence it follows that men are responsible for what they believe as well as for what they do.

3. *Faith always operates according to the fact or proposition believed.*
—If the thing proposed appears to be of importance it will, when believed, excite emotion, and perhaps prompt to action; which action is the fruit and external evidence of faith. When God revealed to Noah his determination to destroy mankind by water, and commanded him to prepare an ark as the means of preserving himself and his family, he was "moved with fear:" here was the emotion which his faith produced; and he "prepared an ark to the saving of his house:" here was the action consequent on his faith. When Jonah proclaimed, "Yet forty days, and Nineveh shall be overthrown, the people of Nineveh believed God, and proclaimed a fast, and put on sackcloth, from the greatest of them even to the least of them." Jonah iii, 4, 5. When the multitude on the day of Pentecost believed the preaching of Peter they were "pricked in their heart." This was the emotion which accompanied their faith, and they cried out, "Men and brethren, what shall we do?" Acts ii, 37. Thus they expressed their emotion in a manner which gave evidence of their faith.

4. *Faith may exist in different degrees.*—It may not only be more or less extensive in regard to the truths embraced, but it may vary also in its degree of strength. Our Saviour addresses his disciples, saying, "O ye of *little faith.*" Matt. vi, 30. So St. Paul speaks (Romans xiv, 1) of "him that is *weak* in the *faith.*" On the other hand our Lord says, in regard to the centurion's faith, "I have not found so *great faith*, no, not in Israel." Matt. viii, 10. Again, addressing the woman of Canaan, he says, "O woman, *great* is thy *faith:*" Matt. xv, 28. Here faith is spoken of as being in some cases *little* or *weak*, and in others *great;* hence it must exist in different degrees.

The same doctrine is taught in all those Scriptures which speak of faith as being progressive. The disciples are exhorted to "have faith as a grain of mustard-seed," which clearly implies its growth and expansion. Accordingly, we find the disciples praying, "Lord, *increase* our *faith.*" Luke xvii, 5. St. Paul, when speaking of the Gospel, says, "Therein is the righteousness of God revealed *from faith to faith.*" Rom. i, 17. This can only mean, that faith advances from one degree to another. Again, he says to his brethren, "Your *faith groweth exceedingly.*" 2 Thess. i, 3. It follows, therefore, that there may be degrees in true faith.

II. WE WILL CONSIDER THE PROPERTIES OF THAT FAITH WHICH IS NECESSARY TO SALVATION.

Though much is said in the sacred Scriptures in regard to faith, there is only one passage in which it is particularly defined. This is Hebrews xi, 1: "Now faith is the substance of things hoped for; the evidence of things not seen." As this is the only inspired definition of saving faith, it will be proper to examine with suitable attention the terms in which it is expressed.

The word ὑπόστασις, which is rendered *substance*, means literally something placed under, a basis or foundation. But in its metaphorical application it means a certain persuasion, an assured expectation, a confident anticipation. We think that the last sense, *confident anticipation*, is the true import of the word in the passage before us, as the apostle connects it with "things hoped for." So also, in Hebrews iii, 14, the same original word is rendered *confidence* in our translation.

The term ελέγχος, rendered *evidence*, means primarily whatever serves to convince or confute; an argument, proof, or demonstration. But when it is used by metonymy it means refutation or conviction; firm persuasion. The last we take as the true import of the word in the present case. The apostle's definition, therefore, may be stated thus: Faith is the confident anticipation of things hoped for, the firm persuasion of things invisible. But we will now consider, more directly, the properties of saving faith.

1. *All saving faith is grounded upon revealed truth.*—The apostle tells us that the *Gospel* is "the power of God unto salvation to every one that *believeth*," Romans i, 16; and that men are chosen to eternal life "through sanctification of the Spirit and *belief of the truth*." 2 Thess. ii, 13. He accordingly inquires, "How then shall they call on him in whom they have not believed? and how shall they believe in him of whom they have not heard? and how shall they hear without a preacher? and how shall they preach except they be sent? So then *faith cometh by hearing*, and hearing by the *word of God*." Rom. x, 14, 17. That revealed truth is the ground of saving faith will further appear from the following passages. Our Saviour says, "Neither pray I for these alone, but for them also which shall believe on me *through their word.*" John xvii, 20. "And many other signs truly did Jesus in the presence of his disciples, which are not written in this book. But *these are written that ye might believe* that Jesus is the Christ, the Son of God; and that believing ye might have life through his name." John xx, 30, 31.

It is worthy of remark, that while the Scriptures propose to us truths to be believed, they also afford the evidence on which a rational faith may be founded. This will appear from the following passages: "If I do not the works of my Father, believe me not. But if I do, though you believe not me, believe the works; that ye may know and believe, that the Father is in me, and I in him." John x, 37, 38. "How shall we escape, if we neglect so great salvation; which at the first began to be spoken by the Lord, and was confirmed unto us by them that heard him; God also bearing them witness, both with signs and wonders, and with divers miracles, and gifts of the Holy Ghost, according to his own will?" Heb. ii, 3, 4. Again: "For we have not followed cunningly devised fables, when we made known unto you the power and coming of our Lord Jesus Christ, but were eyewitnesses of his majesty. For

Chap. 3.] FAITH. 483

he received from God the Father honor and glory, when there came such a voice to him from the excellent glory, This is my beloved Son, in whom I am well pleased." 2 Peter i, 16, 17. Thus we see that the faith which the Scriptures require is not a blind assent of the mind without any rational foundation. It is a well-grounded and reasonable confidence, based upon good and sufficient evidence.

2. *Saving faith is something more than a mere intellectual assent to Gospel truth.*—It is admitted that this intellectual assent is included in saving or justifying faith, and that without it there can be no salvation; but that it does, in itself, necessarily produce salvation, is what we deny. So far is this from being the fact, that moral creatures may possess a high degree of intellectual assent to Divine truth, while they are involved in sin and far from God. Thus St. James, in speaking of a mere intellectual and inoperative faith, says, "The devils also believe and tremble." James ii, 19. In accordance with this is the language of one of those wicked spirits, when our Lord was about to cast him out: "I know thee who thou art, the Holy One of God." Mark i, 24. We see, therefore, that devils possess faith; and if the Gospel required nothing more than an intellectual assent to Divine truth, it would only require of men the faith of devils. But as no one can suppose that justifying faith is the same as that which is possessed by devils, the inference is obvious, that it must be something more than the bare assent of the understanding.

It is evident, moreover, that men may be convinced of the Messiahship of Christ and the truth of revealed religion without being the subjects of saving grace. Of Simon Magus it is said that he "*believed,*" and "was baptized;" that is, he "believed Philip preaching the things concerning the kingdom of God, and the name of Jesus Christ." But Peter said to him immediately afterward, "Thou hast neither part nor lot in this matter; for thou art in the gall of bitterness and in the bond of iniquity."* St. Paul, in his defense before Agrippa, said, "King Agrippa, believest thou the prophets? I know that thou believest." Acts xxvi, 27. But did he possess saving faith? Certainly he did not. It follows, therefore, that saving faith is something more than an intellectual assent to the truth.

3. *Saving faith implies a full and hearty consent of the will to the Gospel plan of salvation.*—We are everywhere addressed in the word of God as voluntary agents. "If ye be *willing* and obedient," saith the Lord, "ye shall eat the good of the land." And "if any man *will* come after me," said Christ, "let him deny himself, and take up his cross and follow me." Matt. xvi, 24. When the Ethiopian eunuch desired to be baptized, "Philip said, If thou believest with *all thine heart,* thou mayest." Acts viii, 37. So St. Paul testifies, that "with *the heart* man believeth unto righteousness." Rom. x, 10. It follows, therefore, that

* See Acts viii, 12–23.

true and saving faith implies an enlistment of the whole heart—the will and affections—in the cause of God.

It is said of a certain young man who came to our Lord, saying, "Good Master, what good thing shall I do, that I may have eternal life?" that "he went away sorrowful." But why? Doubtless, because he was not willing to comply with the terms which Christ proposed.* On another occasion "many of his disciples went back, and walked no more with him," because they were offended at his doctrines.† We are moreover informed, that "among the chief rulers many believed on him; but because of the Pharisees they did not confess him, lest they should be put out of the synagogue; for they loved the praise of men more than the praise of God." John xii, 42, 43. These rulers were believers in Christ, but they were not willing to make the sacrifices which the religion of Christ requires; consequently, they did not possess justifying or saving faith. To such our Lord refers when he says, "Whosoever, therefore, shall be ashamed of me and of my words in this adulterous and sinful generation, of him also shall the Son of man be ashamed, when he cometh in the glory of his Father with the holy angels." Mark viii, 38. Thus it is evident that saving faith requires a voluntary and full surrender of ourselves to God. But,

4. *It implies also unshaken* TRUST *in God.*—This refers to whatever is revealed or asserted on Divine authority, whether it relates to the past, the present, or the future. It is very evident, from the testimony of Scripture, that the faith which God requires of men always comprehends *trust* or *reliance*, as well as persuasion and consent. The faith by which "the elders obtained a good report" was clearly of this character, uniting a noble confidence in the word and promises of God with an assent to the truth of his revelations. "Our fathers *trusted* in thee," said David; "they *trusted* in thee, and thou didst deliver them." Psa. xxii, 4. This is the faith which was exercised by Abraham when "he went out, not knowing whither he went;" when he rested in the promise of God, and obtained justification; and when he obeyed the Divine command, in offering up his son Isaac. This faith, too, pious Job possessed when he said, "Though he slay me, yet will I *trust* in him." Job xiii, 15. And the psalmist, in characterizing a good man, says, "His heart is fixed, *trusting* in the Lord." Psa. cxii, 7.

The same view of this subject is fully established in the New Testament. When our Lord said to his disciples, "Have faith in God," he did not question their belief in his existence, but exhorted them to confide or trust in his promises. He therefore adds, "Whosoever shall say unto this mountain, Be thou removed, and be thou cast into the sea; and shall not doubt in his heart, but shall believe that those things

---

* See Matt. xix, 16–22. † See John vi, 60, 66.

which he saith shall come to pass; he shall have whatsoever he saith." Mark xi, 22, 23. It was in reference to the centurion's simple trust in the power of Christ that our Lord so highly commended him, saying, "I have not found so great faith, no, not in Israel." Matt, viii, 10. In all the instances in which persons were miraculously healed by Christ their faith was also of this kind. It was belief in his claims, and trust in his goodness and power.

That faith in Christ which is connected with salvation is clearly of this nature. He is set forth, both to Jews and Gentiles, as a propitiation "through faith in his blood," which faith cannot mean a mere assent, either to the historical fact that his blood was shed by a violent death, or to the doctrine that it possesses an atoning quality. But as all expiatory offerings, both among Jews and Gentiles, were *trusted in* as the means of propitiation, so now we are to trust exclusively in the blood of Christ as the meritorious cause of our salvation. "In his name shall the Gentiles *trust*." Matt. xii, 21. "In whom ye also *trusted*, after that ye heard the word of truth." Eph. i, 13. "We both labor and suffer reproach, because we *trust* in the living God, who is the Saviour of all men, specially of those that believe." 1 Tim. iv, 10. This firm and unshaken trust in God is the crowning exercise of saving faith. It is by this that the humble penitent throws himself upon the mercy of God, through our Lord Jesus Christ, and claims the blessing of pardon. It is by this that the Christian wars a good warfare, overcomes the world, and obtains everlasting life.

It must be remembered, however, that the trust which leads to salvation is not a blind and superstitious trust in the sacrifice of Christ, like that of the heathen in their sacrifices; nor is it the presumptuous trust of wicked and impenitent men, who depend on Christ to save them in their sins; but it is such a trust as is exercised according to the authority and direction of the word of God. To know the Gospel in its leading principles, to assent to its truth, and to comply with its injunctions, are, therefore, necessary to that more specific act of faith which is called *trust* or *reliance;* or, in theological language, *fiducial assent*, of which cometh salvation.

CHAPTER IV.

LOVE TO GOD.

HAVING discussed the two primary Gospel duties, "*repentance* toward God, and *faith* toward our Lord Jesus Christ,"—duties which are prerequisite to the right performance of every other Gospel requirement—we may proceed to consider the great and comprehensive duty of *love to God*. Let us, then, inquire both into its *nature* and its *obligations*.

I. ITS NATURE.

Supreme love to God is the chief of what have been called our *theopathetic* affections. It is the sum and the end of law, and though lost by us in Adam, it is restored to us by Christ. When it regards God absolutely and in himself as a being of infinite and harmonious perfections and moral beauties, it is that movement of the soul toward him which is produced by admiration, approval, and delight. When it regards him relatively, it rests on the ceaseless emanations of his goodness to us in the continuance of our existence, on the circumstances which render this existence felicitous; and, above all, on that "great love wherewith he loved us," manifested in the gift of his Son for our redemption, and in saving us by his grace; or, in the language of St. Paul, on "the exceeding riches of his grace, in his kindness toward us through Christ Jesus." Under all these views an unbounded gratitude overflows the heart which is influenced by this spiritual affection.

But love to God is more than a sentiment of gratitude. It rejoices in all his glorious perfections, and devoutly contemplates them as the highest and most interesting subjects of thought. It keeps the idea of this supremely beloved object constantly present to the mind, turns to it with adoring ardor from the business and distractions of life, and connects it with every scene of majesty and beauty in nature, and with every event of general and particular providence. It brings the soul into fellowship with God, real and sensible, because vital. It moulds the other affections into conformity with what God himself wills or prohibits, loves or hates, and produces an unbounded desire to please him and to be accepted of him in all things. It is jealous of his honor, unwearied in his service, quick to prompt to every necessary sacrifice in his cause, and renders all such sacrifices, even when carried to the extent of suffering and death, unreluctant and cheerful. It chooses God as the chief good of the soul, the enjoyment of which assures its perfect and eternal interest and happiness. "Whom have I in heaven but thee? and there is none upon earth that I desire beside thee," is the language of every heart when its love to God is true in principle and supreme in degree.

With the philosopher the love of God may be the mere approval of the intellect, or a sentiment which results from the contemplation of infinite perfection, manifesting itself in acts of power and goodness. But in Scripture it is much more than either, and is produced and maintained by a different process. We are there taught that "the carnal mind is enmity against God," and is therefore incapable of loving God. Yet this "carnal mind" may consist with deep attainments in philosophy and with strongly impassioned poetic sentiment. The mere approval of the understanding, and the susceptibility of being impressed with feelings of admiration, awe, and even pleasure, when the character of God is manifested in his works, are not the love of God; since both may be found in the "carnal mind," which is "enmity against God." They are principles which enter into that love, and without which it cannot exist; but they may exist without this affection itself, and be found in a vicious and unchanged nature.

The love of God is a fruit of the Holy Spirit; that is, it is implanted by him only in the souls of the regenerate; and, as that which excites its exercise is chiefly, and in the first place, a sense of the benefits bestowed by the grace of God in our redemption, and a well-grounded persuasion of our personal interest in those benefits, it necessarily presupposes our personal reconciliation to God through faith in the atonement of Christ, and the attestation of it by the Spirit of adoption.

Love to God is essential to true obedience; for when the apostle declares this love to be "the fulfilling of the law," he declares in effect that the law cannot be fulfilled without it; and that every action which has not this for its principle, however virtuous in its appearance, fails to meet the claims of the law. But if the will of God is the perfect rule of morals; and if supreme love to God produces prompt, unwearied, and delightful subjection to his will, or rather an entire and most free choice of it as the rule of all our principles, affections, and actions, the importance of this affection in securing that obedience to the law of God in which true morality consists is manifest, and we clearly perceive the reason why an inspired writer has affirmed that "love is the fulfilling of the law."

But this love to God cannot be felt so long as we are conscious of his wrath, and are in dread of his judgments. These feelings are incompatible with each other, and we must be assured of his reconciliation to us before we can love him. Thus the very existence of love to God implies the doctrines of the atonement, repentance, faith, and the gift of the Spirit of adoption to believers; and unless it be taught in this connection, and through this process of experience, it will be exhibited only as a beautiful object to which man has no access, or as a fictitious and delusive sentimentalism.

But that we may have a still clearer view of the nature of that love to God which the Scriptures require, we may remark that it implies,

1. *Submission to God.*—This springs from a due sense of that relation in which we stand to him as creatures. The right of an absolute sovereignty over us must, in the reason of the case, exist exclusively in Him who made us; and it is the perception and recognition of this, as a practical habit of the mind, which renders outward acts of obedience sincere and religious. The will of God is the only rule to man in everything on which that will has been declared; and as it lays its injunctions upon the heart as well as the life, the rule is equally in force when it directs our *opinions,* our *motives,* and our *affections,* as when it enjoins or prohibits external acts. We belong to God, however, not only because he created us, but also because he redeemed us. "Ye are not your own," says the apostle, "for ye are bought with a price; therefore glorify God in your body, and in your spirit, which are God's."

These ideas of absolute right on the part of God, and of absolute obligation to universal obedience on the part of man, are united in the profession of St. Paul, "Whose I am, and whom I serve;" and form the grand fundamental principle of *godliness* both in the Old and New Testament; in each of which the *will of God* is laid down both as the highest *reason,* and the most powerful *motive* to obedience. The application of this principle, so established by the Scriptures, will show how greatly superior is the ground on which Christianity places moral virtue to that of any other system. For,

(1.) The will of God, which is the rule of duty, is authenticated by the whole of that stupendous evidence which proves the Scriptures to be of Divine authority.

(2.) This will at once defines and enforces every branch of inward and outward purity, rectitude, and benevolence.

(3.) It annuls by its authority every other rule of conduct contrary to itself, whether it arises from custom, or from the example, persuasion, or opinions of men.

(4.) It is a rule which cannot be lowered to the weak and fallen state of human nature; but, connecting itself with a gracious dispensation of supernatural help, it directs the morally imbecile to that remedy, and holds them guilty of the violation of its claims if that remedy is neglected.

(5.) It does not accommodate itself to the temporal interests or safety of men, but requires that interest, honor, liberty, and even life itself, should be surrendered, rather than its demands should be violated.

(6.) It admits no exceptions in obedience, but requires it *whole* and *entire;* so that outward virtue cannot be taken in the place of that which has its seat in the heart. It allows no acts to be really virtuous but those which spring from a willing and submissive mind, and are done with a distinct recognition of our rightful subjection to God. Without such feeling of submission, God cannot be the object of our supreme love.

2. *Trust in God.*—We have already shown that trust in God is an essential element of justifying faith; and as none but those who are justified can really love God, the connection between trust and love is at once established. There is, however, a distinction to be made between that trust which is exercised by a believing penitent in order to justification, and the trust which co-exists with genuine love to God. The former necessarily precedes this love, and is the trust of a penitent sinner for pardoning mercy, through the merits of the atonement. The latter is exercised by those only who are "justified by faith," and is the confidence not merely of creatures in a beneficent Creator, nor of subjects in a gracious Sovereign, but of *children* in a reconciled and benevolent Father.

Our trust in God is enjoined in as many respects as he has been pleased to give us in his word assurances of help and promises of favor. It respects the supply of every want, temporal and eternal; the wise and gracious ordering of all our concerns; our preservation from all that can *upon the whole* be injurious to us, our guidance through life, our hope in death, and our eternal felicity in another world.

To trust in God is a *duty*, because it is a subject of express command. "*Trust* in the Lord, and do good." Psa. xxxvii, 3. "*Trust* in the Lord with all thine heart." Prov. iii, 5. From our Lord's Sermon on the Mount it is clear that one end of his teaching was to deliver men from the perplexing anxieties of life by encouraging them to confide in the care and bounty of their "heavenly Father." This duty is also enforced by the consideration that, since God has given us such demonstrations of his kindness, distrust would imply a dishonorable and sinful denial of his love and faithfulness. If, therefore, we *love* God, our *trust* in him will be sincere, universal, and perpetual. But this love implies,

3. *The fear of God.*—This element of true godliness is associated with love and trust in every part of the holy Scriptures, and is enjoined upon us as a leading duty. Let us, then, notice both its nature and its practical influence.

(1.) As to its *nature*, it consists in that profound reverence for God which springs from a just view and sincere love of his character, and which leads the subjects of it to hate and shun everything that is sinful, and to delight in holy obedience. It is, therefore, to be distinguished from that servile passion which consists in painful apprehensions of the Divine displeasure, and a just conviction of personal liability to punishment. Such a fear of God is not designed to be the habit of the mind, nor is it included in the phrase, "the fear of the Lord," when that is used to express the whole of practical religion, or its leading principles.

But though that reverential fear which is implied in love to God excludes all servility of spirit, yet it supposes our *conditional* liability to the Divine displeasure. For since the saving benefits of the atonement are conditional, and since during life we are in a state of trial, there is sufficient reason why we ought to be so impressed with our spiritual danger as to produce in us that cautionary fear of the holiness, justice, and power of God which shall deter us from sin, and lead us often to view with a restraining and salutary dread those consequences of unfaithfulness and disobedience to which we are liable. Powerful, therefore, as are the reasons for our firm affiance in the mercy and benevolence of God, we are nevertheless not beyond the reach of danger. Hence we are exhorted to "fear, lest a promise being left us of entering into rest," we should "come short of it;" and to "pass the time of" our "sojourning here in fear."

(2.) This scriptural view of the fear of God, as combining both reverence for the Divine Majesty, and a suitable apprehension of our *conditional* liability to his displeasure, is of large practical influence. It restrains our faith from degenerating into presumption, our love into familiarity, and our joy into carelessness. It nurtures humility, watchfulness, and the spirit of prayer. It induces a reverent habit of thinking and speaking of God, and gives solemnity to the exercises of devotion. It presents sin to us under its true aspect, as dangerous as well as corrupting to the soul; as darkening our prospects in a future life, as well as injurious to our peace in the present; and it gives strength and efficacy to that most important practical moral principle, the constant reference of our inward habits of thought and feeling, and our outward actions to the approbation of God.

II. OUR OBLIGATIONS TO LOVE GOD.

That it is the duty of all men to love God may be argued from the excellency of his nature, the tendency of this love to promote our happiness, and the positive requirements of the holy Scriptures.

1. *From the excellency of the Divine nature.*—Amid the darkness which involves the movements of the Almighty, we discover qualities in his character infinitely lovely. Though he possesses in himself all that is necessary to constitute him infinitely happy, yet he is continually seeking the welfare of his creatures. Of this fact we have ample evidence in our own history. Short-sighted as we are, we clearly discover in every dispensation of his providence beneficence and kindness. Notwithstanding our ingratitude and sins, every manifestation of his will brings with it fresh indications of his goodness. Little as we understand of the designs of Providence, its long and complicated chain of causes and effects, its amazing process of abstracting good from evil, and the ultimate objects of its operations, we cannot but exclaim with David, "O that men would praise the Lord for his goodness, and for his wonderful works to the children of men!" Psa. cvii, 8. Wonderful,

however, as are the exhibitions of Divine goodness in the works of creation and providence, they are still greater in the work of redemption. The incarnation of the Son of God, his obedience to the Divine law in our behalf, and his sufferings and death for our redemption, prove in the highest degree the riches of his goodness, and demand our warmest gratitude and love.

2. *From the tendency of the love of God to promote our happiness.*—To have the energies of our nature directed to their proper object, to accomplish the high destiny of our moral being, to possess feelings in harmony with the principles of eternal excellence, to contemplate with rapture and admiration the primary qualities of all beauty, are the effects of loving God, and these effects are the elements of all true happiness. But in connection with these enjoyments we have the pleasure of knowing, that while we love God he also loves us; and surely nothing can contribute more to our happiness than a persuasion of this kind. To believe that He who holds in his hands the destinies of all intelligent creatures is our friend and benefactor, cannot fail, even in the darkest periods of human life, to afford hope, to alleviate affliction, and to promote real happiness. This, then, is another strong reason why we should love God.

3. *From the positive injunctions of Scripture.*—The first and great commandment is, "Thou shalt love the Lord thy God with all thine heart, and with all thy soul, and with all thy might." Deut. vi, 5. "I have," said Moses to the Hebrews, "set before thee this day life and good, and death and evil; in that I command thee this day to love the Lord thy God, to walk in his ways, and to keep his commandments and his statutes and his judgments, that thou mayest live and multiply; and the Lord thy God shall bless thee in the land whither thou goest to possess it." Deut xxx, 15, 16. It is not necessary, however, to multiply quotations in proof of our obligation to love God, for it is well known that this is everywhere taught, both in the Old and the New Testament.

We remark in conclusion, that upon these internal principles of piety—love, submission, trust, and filial fear—rests that moral habit or state of the mind which is often expressed by the term HOLINESS. Separate from these principles, our morality can only consist in visible acts, imperfect in themselves because not vital; and however commended by men, abominable to God, who searches the heart. But when our moral acts proceed from these sources they are proportioned to the strength and purity of the principle which originates them, except as in some cases they may be influenced and deteriorated by an uninformed or weak judgment. But supreme love to God, entire submission to him, firm affiance in his covenant engagements, and that fear which abases the spirit before him, and departs even from "the appearance of evil," when joined with a right understanding of Divine truth, render the man of God "perfect, thoroughly furnished unto all good works."

CHAPTER V.

THE DUTY OF PRAYER.

HAVING considered those internal principles which are essential to true piety, we will in the next place direct our attention to some of the external duties which we owe to God. The first in order is that of *prayer*, which we will make the subject of the present chapter by considering its *nature*, its *obligation*, and its *utility*.

I. THE NATURE OF PRAYER.

Under this head we may notice, 1. The general character of **prayer**; and, 2. Its various kinds.

1. *Its general character.*—Prayer is the offering of our desires to God through the mediation of Jesus Christ, under the influence of the Holy Spirit, and with suitable dispositions, for things agreeable to his will.

(1.) Prayer is the act of an indigent creature seeking relief from the fountain of mercy. A sense of want excites *desire*, and desire is the very essence of prayer. "One thing have I *desired* of the Lord," says David, "that will I seek after." Psa. xxvii, 4. And again, "My heart and my flesh *crieth out* for the living God." Psa. lxxxiv, 2. We may assume the most humble attitude, employ the most appropriate and impressive language, and join in the most scriptural and elevated forms of worship, but if we do not properly appreciate the importance of the Divine blessings, if we do not "*hunger* and *thirst* after righteousness," our prayers will be unavailing. "The kingdom of heaven suffereth violence, and the violent take it by force." Prayer without *desire* is like a sacrifice without the fire from heaven to consume it.

(2.) Prayer consists in *offering* our desires to God. The supposition of some, that the worship of God is merely passive, or consists only in meditation, is without any foundation in truth. Jacob not only felt his need of the blessings which he sought, but even *wrestled* for them till they were bestowed. When the angel said, "Let me go, the day breaketh," his reply was, "I will not let thee go except thou bless me." Gen. xxxii, 26. So also the language of our Lord is, "*Ask*, and it shall be given you; *seek*, and ye shall find; *knock*, and it shall be opened to you." Matt. vii, 7.

(3.) The only object to whom our prayers should be addressed is *God*. Neither saints, nor angels, nor any created beings are permitted to be the objects of religious worship. So long as the first two commandments remain to be a part of the Decalogue, so long will it be the duty of men to offer their prayers to God alone. In the system of redemption each Person of the adorable Trinity has his appropriate office; and though the Scriptures prove it to be right that we should pray directly to the Son or to the Holy Ghost, yet they evidently teach the doctrine that our prayers are ordinarily to be addressed to God the Father. St. Paul says, "I bow my knees unto the Father of our Lord Jesus Christ;" and St. Peter, "Blessed be the God and Father of our Lord Jesus Christ."

(4.) Our prayers must be offered to God through the mediation of Christ. He himself declares, "I am the way, and the truth, and the life: no man cometh unto the Father but by me." John xiv, 6. Again, he says to the apostles, "I have chosen you, and ordained you, that you should go and bring forth fruit, and that your fruit should remain; that whatsoever ye shall *ask of the Father in my name*, he may give it you." John xv, 16. St. Paul testifies of our Lord that "through him we both (Jews and Gentiles) have an access by one Spirit unto the Father;"* and that there is "one Mediator between God and men, the man Christ Jesus."†

(5.) But to present our prayers acceptably to the Father, through the Son, we must offer them under the influence of the Holy Spirit. Though we are not authorized to look for those immediate and sensible inspirations which the prophets, and apostles, and many of the primitive Christians possessed, yet we may expect, from the unction of "the Holy One," that earnestness, and fervor, and penitence, and trust which are necessary to acceptable devotion. The Holy Spirit is the great agent in the world of grace, and without his influence there can be no spiritual worship. Hence he is called "the Spirit of grace and of supplication." Zech. xii, 10. And St. Paul says, Rom. viii, 26, "The Spirit also helpeth our infirmities; for we know not what we should pray for as we ought; but the Spirit itself maketh intercession for us with groanings which cannot be uttered."

(6.) But again: our prayers, in order to be acceptable, must be offered with suitable dispositions. Every unholy motive and every improper disposition must, without reluctance or reserve, be given up. "If I regard iniquity in my heart," says David, "the Lord will not hear me." Psa. lxvi, 18. And the apostle requires "that men pray everywhere, lifting up holy hands, without wrath and doubting." 1 Tim. ii, 8. Our prayers should be offered, 1. Without *ostentation*. "When thou prayest," says our Lord, "thou shalt not be as the hypocrites are; for they love to pray standing in the synagogues and in the corners of the streets, that they may be seen of men. Verily I say unto you, They have their reward." Matt. vi, 5. 2. In the *spirit of forgiveness*. "If ye forgive men their trespasses, your heavenly Father will also forgive you; but if ye forgive not men their trespasses, neither will your Father forgive

* Eph. ii, 18. † 1 Tim. ii, 5.

your trespasses." Matt. vi, 14, 15. Therefore, " when ye stand praying, forgive, if ye have aught against any; that your Father also which is in heaven may forgive you your trespasses." Mark xi, 25. " Forgive, and ye shall be forgiven." Luke vi, 37. 3. In the spirit of *humility and confession.* Of this we have a striking example in the case of the publican. He " would not lift up so much as his eyes unto heaven, but smote upon his breast, saying, God be merciful to me a sinner. I tell you," says our Lord, " this man went down to his house justified rather than the other. For every one that exalteth himself shall be abased; and he that humbleth himself shall be exalted." Luke xviii, 13, 14. 4. In the spirit of *resignation.* That submission which distinguished the Son of God in all the changes through which he passed should characterize his people. In every petition which is offered to God, the language of the heart should be, "not as I will, but as THOU wilt." 5. In *faith.* Without this it is impossible to please God. But our Lord says, "What things' soever ye desire when ye pray, believe that ye receive them, and ye shall have them." Mark xi, 24.

(7.) Our prayers must be offered for things agreeable to the will of God. As we have forfeited, by wicked works, every title to the blessings of heaven, we can expect to receive them only on the ground of unmerited goodness. It would, therefore, be presumptuous in us to ask God for what he has never promised to bestow; or to ask even his promised blessings at a time, or in a degree, which is not in accordance with his will. In all our addresses to God we should remember that *sovereignty* belongs to him, and that *submission* is appropriate to us.

But we should be unfeignedly thankful to God that we are not straitened in the scope of our petitions. Everything calculated to promote our happiness, both in this world and in that which is to come, is made a subject of gracious promise, and may, therefore, be an object of prayer. "The Lord God is a sun and shield; the Lord will give grace and glory: no good thing will he withhold from them that walk uprightly." Psa. lxxxiv, 11. The exhortation of the apostle is, "Be careful for nothing; but in *everything* by prayer and supplication, with thanksgiving, let your requests be made known unto God." Phil. iv, 6.

2. *The various kinds of prayer.*—The general duty of prayer is usually distributed into four kinds, *ejaculatory, private, social,* and *public;* each of which is of sufficient importance to require a separate consideration.

(1.) EJACULATORY *prayer.*—This term is given to those secret and frequent aspirations of the heart to God for general or particular blessings, by which a just sense of our habitual dependence upon God and of our wants and dangers may be expressed while we are employed in the common affairs of life. It includes, too, all those short and occasional effusions of gratitude and silent ascriptions of praise, which the remembrance of the mercies of God will excite in a devotional spirit under the same circumstances. Both, however, presuppose what divines call "the spirit of prayer;" which springs from a sense of our dependence upon God, and is a breathing of the desires after intercourse of thought and affection with him, accompanied with a reverential and encouraging sense of his constant presence with us.

The cultivation of this spirit is clearly enjoined upon us as a duty by St. Paul, who exhorts us to "pray without ceasing," and "in everything" to "give thanks;" and also to set our "affection on things above,"—exhortations which imply a holy and devotional frame and temper of mind, and not merely acts of prayer performed at intervals. The high and unspeakable advantages of this habit are, that it induces a watchful and guarded mind; prevents religion from deteriorating into a lifeless form; unites the soul to God; induces continual supplies of Divine influence; and opposes an effectual barrier, by the grace thus acquired, against the encroachments of worldly anxieties and the force of temptations. The existence of this spirit of prayer and thanksgiving is one of the grand distinctions between nominal and real Christians; and by it the measure of vital and effective Christianity enjoyed by any individual may ordinarily be determined.

(2.) PRIVATE *prayer.*—This, as a duty, rests upon the express words of our Lord, which, while they suppose the practice of individual prayer to have been generally acknowledged as obligatory, enjoin that it should be strictly *private.* "But thou, when thou prayest, enter into thy closet, and when thou hast shut thy door, pray to thy Father which is in secret; and thy Father which seeth in secret, shall reward thee openly." Matt. vi, 6. The duty of private prayer is also enforced by our Lord's own example; who, on several occasions, retired into absolute privacy that he might "pray."*

The reason for this institution of private devotion appears to have been, to incite us to a friendly and confiding intercourse with God, in all those particular cases which most concern our feelings and our interests. Hence, when this duty is enjoined upon us by our Lord, he presents the Divine Being before us under a relation most of all adapted to inspire that unlimited confidence with which he would have us to approach him: "Pray to thy FATHER which is in secret." Thus the dread of his omniscience, indicated by his *seeing in secret,* and of those other overwhelming attributes which omnipresence and omniscience cannot fail to suggest, is mitigated, or only employed to inspire greater freedom and a stronger affiance.

(3.) FAMILY *prayer.*—The absence of an *express precept* for family worship has been urged against its obligation, even by some who have considered it to be a prudential and useful practice. But the strict obligation of so important a duty is not to be given up merely on this

* See Matt. xiv, 23; Luke vi, 12.

account. As well might we conclude that we are under no obligation to feed and clothe our children, to teach them the use of letters, or to train them to some lawful employment or profession. The obligation of family prayer arises out of the very constitution of a family, and is confirmed by Scripture examples.

First, It arises out of the very constitution of a family. It will not be denied by any Christian parent, that his obligation to the members of his family should be measured by the extent of his *capacity* to do them good, and that he is bound to honor God to the utmost extent of this capacity. In the providence of God he is placed at the head of a family; and, therefore, in possession of a sacred trust, he has the care of *souls*. If, then, his responsibility is measured by his capacity, and if there is real utility in family prayer, both of which must be admitted, he is morally bound to perform this duty, even if the Scriptures were entirely silent upon the subject. But,

Secondly, This duty has the authority of Scripture examples. A great part of the worship of patriarchal times was *domestic*. The worship of God was observed in the family of Abraham, Jacob, and Job; nay, the highest species of worship—the offering of sacrifices—which it could not have been without Divine appointment. It arose, therefore, out of the original constitution of a family, that the father and natural head was invested with a sacred and religious character; and as this has never been revoked, the family priesthood continues in force, and stands on the same ground as several other religious obligations which have passed from one dispensation of revealed religion to another without express re-enactment.

The existence of family religion and family worship is distinctly marked in the history of the Jews. The passover was a solemn religious institution, comprehending several direct acts of worship; but it was placed in the hands of the heads of families, and was, therefore, clearly of a domestic nature. The religious instruction of the family was also, in the law of Moses, enjoined upon the father. He was required to teach his children the commandments of the Lord, and the import of the different festivals and commemorative institutions.* So, also, the family of Jesse had a yearly sacrifice;† and of David it is said, that he "returned to bless his household." 2 Sam. vi, 20. But perhaps the clearest example of family devotion recorded in the Old Testament is in the case of Daniel. The history informs us that "he kneeled upon his knees three times a day and prayed, and gave thanks before his God." Dan. vi, 10. That this refers to domestic worship, is evident from all the attendant circumstances. It was performed in his own house, not privately, but with his windows "open in his chamber toward Jerusalem;" so that when his enemies assembled at the hour of devotion they "found Daniel praying and making supplication before

* Exod. xii, 26; Deut. vi, 7; Josh. iv, 6. † 1 Sam. xx, 6.

his God." It was performed, too, not merely on the occasion of its being interdicted by the king's decree, but according to his regular custom, and in obedience to what he regarded to be "the law of his God;" and such was the value which he attached to this observance, that he was willing to make a sacrifice of all that was dear to him on earth, rather than to lay it aside even "for thirty days." Let Christians who neglect family prayer look at this and blush!

The sacred office of the father or master of a household passed from Judaism into Christianity. And a duty so well understood among the Jews, as that the head of the family ought to influence and control its religious character, needed no special injunction under the new dispensation. Our Lord himself filled the office of the master of a family, as appears from his eating the passover with his disciples, and presiding as such over the whole rite. In the early spread of Christianity the father or master who believed was baptized, and "all his house." The first religious societies were chiefly domestic; and the antiquity of domestic religious service among Christians leaves it unquestionable, that when their number so increased as to require them to assemble in some common room or Church, the domestic worship was not superseded.

(4.) PUBLIC *prayer.*—Under this head is included every branch of public worship; the principal part of which are, prayer, praise, and the reading of the holy Scriptures. It is evident that *praise* and *thanksgiving* are implied in prayer, and included in our definition of that duty. But besides those ascriptions of praise, and expressions of gratitude, which are to be mingled with the precatory part of our devotions, solemn psalms and hymns of praise, to be sung with the voice, and accompanied with the melody of the heart, are of an apostolic injunction, and form an important part of the worship of God, whether public or social.

II. THE OBLIGATION OF PRAYER.

The question now before us is this: Why ought we to offer prayer and supplication to God? And in answer to this question we offer the following remarks:

1. *Prayer is urged upon us by a sense of dependence.*—If the duty were no otherwise enforced, the fact of our entire dependence upon God is quite sufficient to show its reasonableness. From him, and him alone, flow all the blessings we now enjoy, or ever can enjoy. We are always, entirely, and absolutely dependent on him for every breath we breathe, for every word we speak, for every act we do, and for every favor we enjoy. To know this, is to know a most solemn and important truth; and to *feel* our dependence on God, and confess this feeling in the exercise of prayer, is at once to conform in our feelings and actions to that state of things which is agreeable to the Divine will, and, consequently, to absolute rectitude.

2. *Prayer is demanded by our sinful condition.*—Our conduct has been deeply marked in every period of our being with crime and imperfection. Long, indeed, is the catalogue of sins charged against us in the book of God's remembrance—a catalogue whose items defy our memory to recall or our intellect to enumerate. Having rendered ourselves guilty before God, we are exposed to his wrath and the penalty of his law; and being thus exposed, we ought surely to ask him for mercy and forgiveness. Every compunctious pang we feel, every discovery of peril we make, and every temptation with which we are assailed, should urge us to the throne of God for that assistance which he alone can afford.

3. *Prayer is expressly enjoined in the holy Scriptures.*—Thus: "Seek the Lord and his strength; seek his face evermore." Psa. cv, 4. "Seek ye the Lord while he may be found, call ye upon him while he is near." Isa. lv, 6. "Let us lift our hearts with our hands unto God in the heavens." Lam. iii, 41. This duty is enjoined, with equal clearness, by Christ and his apostles: "And he spake a parable unto them to this end, that men ought always to pray, and not to faint." Luke xviii, 1. So also St. Paul: "In everything by prayer and supplication, with thanksgiving, let your requests be made known unto God." Phil. iv, 6. "Continue in prayer, and watch in the same with thanksgiving." Col. iv, 2. "I will, therefore, that men pray everywhere, lifting up holy hands, without wrath and doubting." 1 Tim. ii, 8. Many other passages of the same import might be adduced, but these are sufficient to show that prayer is of Divine appointment.

4. *This duty is also enforced by Scripture examples.*—The pious in all ages have practically acknowledged the obligation of prayer, commending it by their example. Under the patriarchal dispensation altars were erected to the God of heaven, and men called upon his name. It was in the exercise of prayer that Jacob, as a prince, prevailed with God, and thus inherited the name of Israel. So Samuel, David, Solomon, Daniel, and many others are spoken of in the Scriptures as men of prayer. Even Christ himself, though "holy, harmless, and separate from sinners," was attentive to this duty. He often retired to some lonely place, where no mortal eye could see him, and there poured out his supplications to the Father. St. Paul testifies of him that "in the days of his flesh" he "offered up prayers and supplications, with strong crying and tears." Heb. v, 7. He prayed for his disciples; he prayed for his murderers; and the last words that trembled on his dying lips were words of prayer addressed to the Father: "My God, my God, why hast thou forsaken me?" This example is not only a pattern and motive, but it has all the force of positive law, binding us with Divine authority to the performance of prayer to God.

5. As to the scriptural obligations of *public* worship, it is based,

(1.) Upon *example.*—The institution of public worship under the law, the practice of synagogue worship among the Jews, and the sanction which was given to both these by the practice of our Lord and his apostles, cannot be called in question. Indeed, the order of the synagogue worship became the model of that of the Christian Church. It consisted in prayer, reading and explaining the Scriptures, and the singing of psalms; and thus one of the most important means of instructing men, and of spreading and maintaining the influence of morals and religion among them, passed from the Jews into all Christian countries.

(2.) Upon *plain inference.*—The command to publish the Gospel implies the obligation of assembling to hear it. And the very term, *church*, by which a Christian society is usually designated in Scripture, signifies an *assembly* for the transaction of some business. In the case of a Christian assembly the business is necessarily spiritual, including the sacred exercises of prayer, praise, and religious instruction.

(3.) Upon *direct precepts.*—Thus some of the epistles of St. Paul were commanded to be read in the churches. The singing of psalms, hymns, and spiritual songs is enjoined as an act of solemn worship "to the Lord;"* and St. Paul cautions the Hebrews that they forsake not the assembling of themselves together.† Thus primitive Christians were in the constant practice of assembling for public worship; and the Supper of the Lord was celebrated by the body of believers *collectively.*‡

III. THE UTILITY OF PRAYER.

The utility of this Divinely commanded duty may be very justly argued,

1. *From the nature and attributes of God.*—It has been shown that God has made it our duty to pray. But it would be inconsistent with his character and perfections to require us to do any act that would not be for our real good. Every argument, therefore, which proves prayer to be Divinely required is a proof of its utility. But the utility of prayer is clearly seen,

2. *In its connection, as an appointed condition, with the bestowment of Divine blessings.*—Our Lord says, "Every one that asketh receiveth; and he that seeketh findeth; and to him that knocketh it shall be opened." Matt. vii, 8. Again: "Whatsoever ye shall ask in my name, that will I do, that the Father may be glorified in the Son. If ye ask anything in my name, I will do it." John xiv, 13. These are "great and precious promises," and may be justly regarded as securing to those who address God in prayer the bestowment of every blessing for which they ask, in accordance with the Divine will. Prayer, therefore, may be offered up in expectation of an answer; and when it is "the prayer of faith" it is not presented in vain. "The eyes of the Lord are over the righteous, and his ears are open unto their prayers." 1 Peter iii, 12. The utility of prayer is also apparent,

3. *In its direct tendency to promote an inward work of grace.*—

---

* See Eph. v, 19; Col. iii, 16.   † Heb. x, 25.   ‡ 1 Cor. xi.

"Prayer," says Bishop Taylor, "is the peace of our spirit, the stillness of our thoughts, the rest of our cares, the calm of our tempest." The circulation of the vital current through its proper channels is not more essential to life and health than prayer is to a growth of grace in our hearts. In the neglect, or even in the remission of this duty, it is impossible to advance in virtue. The soul, in itself, is like the unsupported vine, which, instead of shooting upward, creeps upon the ground, and exhausts its vigor in unavailing efforts to ascend. But when animated with the spirit of prayer, it is like the same vine fixing its adhesive tendrils to the sturdy oak, rising to its summit, and waving, uninjured, its verdant branches in the blasts of the tempest, or maturing its fruit in the rays of the summer's sun.

Prayer excites in us a vivid sense of our unworthiness, of our entire dependence upon God, and of our absolute need of an interest in the merits of Christ. It awakens holy and elevated feelings, dampens the spirit of levity and vanity and the love of pleasure, weans our affections from worldly objects, and transfers them to "things above." Nothing but fervent and unceasing prayer can bring us near to our heavenly Father, can penetrate the clouds which darken our distant prospects, and disclose to our weary eyes the Sun of Righteousness, shining in his cheering radiance. But when we approach the throne of God with humble and longing hearts heaven opens to our eye of faith, and pours upon our waiting souls its animating glories. When sick with the sins and sorrows of earth; when all the gayeties and pleasures of the present life lose their power to please, we find in prayer a consolation which all the treasure of this world can never equal.

4. The utility of prayer is very obvious, *in the advantages of public worship.*—These are so important that the institution must ever be considered as one of the most condescending and gracious dispensations of God to man. By this means his Church confesses him before the world, and the public teaching of his word is associated with such acts of devotion as prepare the mind for hearing it to edification. It is thus that the ignorant and vicious are called together and instructed and warned, the invitations of mercy are published to the guilty, and the sorrowful and afflicted are comforted. In the assembly of the saints, God, by his Spirit, diffuses his vital and sanctifying influence, imparts to all his people grace according to their need, and affords them a foretaste of the deep and hallowed pleasures which await them in the life to come.

Here prayers and intercessions are heard for national and public interests; and while the benefit of these exercises descends upon a people or country, all are kept sensible of the dependence of every personal and public interest upon God. Praise calls forth grateful emotions, and gives cheerfulness to piety; and that "instruction in righteousness" which is so perpetually repeated diffuses the principles of morality and religion throughout society, enlightens and gives activity to conscience, raises the standard of morals, attaches shame to vice and praise to virtue, and thus exerts a powerfully purifying influence upon mankind. Human laws receive a force which under other circumstances they could not acquire, and thus the administration of justice is aided by the strong sanctions of religion. We conclude, therefore, that piety, benevolence, and patriotism are equally dependent for their purity and vigor upon the regular and devout worship of God, in the simplicity of the Christian dispensation.

CHAPTER VI.

OBSERVANCE OF THE SABBATH.

ANOTHER external duty which we owe to God is the observance of the holy Sabbath—a duty which is of vital importance to the interests of religion. The institution, however, is not only essential to our moral and religious culture, but in perfect accordance with the philosophy of our physical constitution; its observance being found necessary to preserve health, and to recruit our wasted energies. In the discussion of the subject we will consider, 1. The universal and perpetual obligation of the holy Sabbath; 2. Its change from the seventh to the first day of the week; and, 3. The manner in which it is to be observed.

I. ITS UNIVERSAL AND PERPETUAL OBLIGATION.

In considering and establishing the universal and perpetual obligation of the holy Sabbath, it will be necessary to notice,

1. *Its primitive institution.*—This event is recorded in Genesis ii, 2, 3: " And on the seventh day God ended his work which he had made; and he rested on the seventh day from all his work which he had made. And God blessed the seventh day and sanctified it; because that in it he had rested from all his work which God created and made." The testimony which this passage affords in support of the universal and perpetual obligation of the Sabbath arises from the *time* of its appointment, and the *ends* of the institution.

(1.) The *time* of its appointment was the seventh day from the beginning of the creation, and the first after it was ended. At that time the only human beings in existence were our first parents. For *them*, therefore, the Sabbath was instituted; and if for them, for *all* their posterity. If it was not instituted for *all* their posterity, it was not instituted for *any* of them; for surely no reason can be given why it should be instituted for one portion of the race more than for another. " The Sabbath," then, " was made for *man*."

(2.) The *ends* of the institution hold out the same universality of obligation. These are, 1. To commemorate the wisdom, power, and goodness of God in the work of creation; and, 2. To afford mankind an opportunity of resting at suitable intervals from secular employments, and of engaging in the duties of religious worship and instruction. The *sanctification* of the seventh day can mean nothing less than its consecration to religious purposes, for in no proper sense can sanctification or holiness be predicated of a *day*, except with respect to the uses to which it is devoted, and as distinguishing *sacred* from secular time. The sanctification of the Sabbath, therefore, must have been its dedication to religious purposes, involving the prohibition of all secular labor.

2. *Its recognition in the wilderness, as of Divine authority.*—The first explicit notice which we have of the Sabbath, subsequent to its original institution, is in Exodus xvi, 23–30, and in connection with the miracle of the manna. "And it came to pass, that on the sixth day they gathered twice as much bread, two omers for one man; and all the rulers of the congregation came and told Moses. And he said unto them, This is that which the Lord hath said, To-morrow is the rest of the holy Sabbath unto the Lord. Bake that which you will bake to-day, and seethe that ye will seethe; and that which remaineth over lay up for you, to be kept until the morning. And they laid it up till the morning, as Moses bade; and it did not stink, neither was there any worm therein. And Moses said, Eat that to-day, for to-day is a Sabbath unto the Lord. To-day ye shall not find it in the field. Six days ye shall gather it; but on the seventh day, which is the Sabbath, in it there shall be none. And it came to pass, that there went out some of the people on the seventh day for to gather, and they found none. And the Lord said unto Moses, How long refuse ye to keep my commandments and my laws? See, for the Lord hath given you the Sabbath, therefore he giveth you on the sixth day the bread of two days. Abide ye every man in his place; let no man go out of his place on the seventh day. So the people rested on the seventh day."

From this passage Dr. Paley infers that the Sabbath was first instituted, not at the creation, as seems to be clearly indicated in Gen. ii, 2, 3, but in the wilderness; and that it was designed for the Jews alone. His theory is mainly based upon the two following assumptions: 1. That the Sabbath is nowhere mentioned, or even obscurely alluded to, either in the general history of the world before the call of Abraham, or in that of the first three Jewish patriarchs. 2. That in the passage just quoted from the sixteenth chapter of Exodus there is no "intimation that the Sabbath, when appointed to be observed, was only the revival of an ancient institution, which had been neglected, forgotten, or suspended."

Were the first assumption to be fully granted, it would not disprove the existence of the Sabbath previous to the exodus; for it might have been observed by the patriarchs, though no express mention is made of it in their brief history. With the exception of Jacob's supplication at Bethel, scarcely a single allusion to prayer is to be found in all the Pentateuch; and yet, considering the eminent piety of those whose life it records, we cannot doubt the frequency of their devotional exercises. Circumcision, being the sign and seal of God's covenant with Abraham, was beyond all question punctually observed by the Israelites in all their generations; yet from their settlement in Canaan till the time of John the Baptist, a period of about fifteen hundred years, no particular instance of it is recorded.

Nor is the Sabbath itself expressly mentioned in Joshua, Judges, Ruth, the two books of Samuel, or the first book of Kings, though it was doubtless regularly observed all the time included in these histories. In the second book of Kings and the two books of Chronicles it is mentioned only twelve times, some of which are merely repetitions of the same instances. If, then, the Sabbath is so seldom spoken of in this long historical series, is it to be thought strange that it should not be mentioned in the summary account of the patriarchal ages?

But we cannot agree with Dr. Paley, that there is not "even the obscurest allusion" in the patriarchal history to the institution of the Sabbath. We think it is *strongly* alluded to, and even clearly *implied*, in the division of time into weeks or periods of seven days.* The computation of time by days, months, and years arises from obvious revolutions in the planetary system; but its division into periods of seven days has no foundation in any natural or visible septenary change. It must, therefore, have originated in some positive appointment, or in some tradition anterior to the dispersion of mankind; and thus we are at once directed to the Mosaic account of the original institution of the holy Sabbath, as recorded in the second chapter of Genesis.

With regard to Dr. Paley's second assumption we make the following remarks: 1. It is not claimed that the transaction recorded in the sixteenth chapter of Exodus was "the revival of an ancient institution which had been neglected, forgotten, or suspended." It was only the *recognition* of an institution which had been observed from the beginning, and had never been either forgotten or suspended. 2. There is not the slightest intimation in the passage that the event which it records was the original institution of the Sabbath; but, 3. The contrary seems to be the natural inference from the whole narrative. The Sabbath is spoken of exactly in the manner in which a historian would speak of a well-known institution. For instance, when the people were astonished at the double supply of manna on the sixth day, Moses observed, "This is that which the Lord hath said, To-morrow is the rest of the holy Sabbath unto the Lord;" which, as far as we know,

* See Gen. viii, 10, 12; xxix, 27, 28.

was never said previous to this transaction, except at the close of creation. When a double portion of manna was promised on the sixth day, no reason was assigned for so extraordinary a circumstance; which seems to imply that the reason was known to the Israelites. Again: "Six days ye shall gather it; but on the seventh day, which is the Sabbath, in it there shall be none." Here the Sabbath is spoken of as an ordinance with which the people were familiar. It is likewise mentioned in a merely incidental manner, in the recital of the miracle of the manna, without any notice of its being enjoined upon that occasion for the first time; which would be a very surprising circumstance had that been the original establishment of the Sabbath. In short, the whole account of this remarkable transaction accords with the supposition, and with it alone, that the Sabbath had been long established, and was well known to the Israelites.

Dr. Paley attempts to show that the passage in the second chapter of Genesis is consistent with his opinion. "For," says he, "as the seventh day was erected into a Sabbath, on account of God's resting upon that day from the work of creation, it was natural enough in the historian, when he had related the history of the creation, and of God's ceasing from it on the seventh day, to add, 'And God blessed the seventh day, and sanctified it, because that on it he had rested from all his work which God created and made;' although the blessing and sanctification, that is, the religious distinction and appropriation of that day, were not actually made till many ages afterward. The words do not assert that God *then* 'blessed' and 'sanctified' the seventh day, but that he blessed and sanctified it *for that reason;* and if any ask, why the Sabbath, or sanctification of the seventh day, was *then* mentioned, if it was not *then* appointed, the answer is at hand: the order of connection, and not of time, introduced the mention of the Sabbath in the history of the subject which it was ordained to commemorate."*

We can hardly suppose a greater violence to the sacred text than is offered by this interpretation. The historian tells us that "God blessed the *seventh day*, and sanctified it;" but the interpretation assumes that he blessed and sanctified some other day, after the lapse of twenty-five hundred years, and *not* the seventh day, in which he "rested from all his work." Thus, Dr. Paley's interpretation is a direct contradiction of the language of Moses; and it is not difficult to determine, in this case, whose teaching we ought to embrace.

Nor is there the slightest evidence that Moses followed "the order of connection and not of time;" for no reasonable motive can be assigned for his mentioning the Sabbath in connection with the history of creation, if it was not *then* appointed. The resting of God on the seventh day, and the sanctification of that day, are too closely connected to be separated in time. If the former took place immediately after the work

* Moral and Political Philosophy, book 4, chap. 7.

of creation was ended, so did the latter. It was clearly the design of the sacred historian to give a faithful account of the origin of the world, and to this the whole narrative is confined without the most distant allusion to subsequent events. It is, therefore, absurd to suppose that he deserted his grand object to mention a Hebrew ordinance which was not appointed till after a period of more than two thousand years.

3. *Its inclusion in the Decalogue.*—This circumstance, perhaps more than any other, establishes the universal and perpetual obligation of the holy Sabbath. The language of the fourth commandment is, "Remember the Sabbath-day, to keep it holy. Six days shalt thou labor, and do all thy work; but the seventh day is the Sabbath of the Lord thy God. In it thou shalt not do any work, thou, nor thy son, nor thy daughter, thy manservant, nor thy maidservant, nor thy cattle, nor thy stranger that is within thy gates. For in six days the Lord made heaven and earth, the sea, and all that in them is, and rested the seventh day. Wherefore the Lord blessed the Sabbath-day, and hallowed it." Exod. xx, 8–11.

To perceive the light which this commandment throws upon the subject before us we must carefully consider the following remarks:

(1.) We are not to suppose that the Decalogue imposed new duties upon men which had never before been required. It only enjoined those which had been previously instituted. Impiety, idolatry, and profaneness were sins before the delivery of the Ten Commandments as really as since. The same is true of disobedience to parents, of murder, of theft, and of adultery. The giving of the Decalogue, therefore, did not originate the laws which it contains, but was only a republication of them in a new and convenient form, and under circumstances which were calculated to make them most solemnly impressive. The fourth commandment contains two distinct allusions to the previous institution of the Sabbath. The first is in the clause "*Remember* the Sabbath-day," which represents the Sabbath as having been previously instituted, and requires that it should not be forgotten, or suffered to fall into disuse. The second is in the reason assigned for keeping the Sabbath. It is "the Sabbath of the Lord thy God;" the day in which he "rested" from all his creative work. "Wherefore, the Lord *blessed* the Sabbath-day, and *hallowed* it." Thus the seventh day was set apart from the beginning as a holy day of sacred rest.

(2.) The fourth commandment is a part of the *moral law*. This may be argued from the fact that it is united with the other commandments of the Decalogue, which are all acknowledged to be moral precepts. It is placed in the midst of this summary of moral law, being the last precept of the first table, and is therefore included in what our Lord calls "the first and great commandment," namely, "Thou shalt love the Lord thy God with all thy heart, and with all thy soul, and with all thy mind." Matt. xxii, 37, 38. Would it not, then, be most absurd to suppose that this precept should be detached from those with which it is so closely connected, and regarded as merely *ceremonial*, while all the rest are acknowledged to be *moral?*

But that the law of the Sabbath is a *moral* precept may be further argued from the circumstances of solemnity which attended its promulgation. This commandment, together with the other nine, was uttered in an audible and awful voice from the midst of the thunderings and lightnings which crowned the top of Sinai with dreadful glory. Such were the splendor and majesty of this scene that when the people " saw the thunderings, and the lightnings, and the noise of the trumpet, and the mountain smoking, they removed and stood afar off. And they said unto Moses, Speak thou with us, and we will hear; but let not God speak with us, lest we die." Even Moses himself said, "I exceedingly fear and quake." Heb. xii, 21. It is also to be added that this commandment, as well as the other nine, *was written by the finger of God*—a distinction which cannot be claimed for any precept which is merely ceremonial.

Again, this commandment is frequently referred to by the sacred writers as one of moral obligation. Hence the most solemn threatenings are uttered against those who disregard it, while the greatest rewards are promised to those who obey it. "Ye shall keep the Sabbath, therefore, for it is holy unto you. Every one that defileth it shall surely be put to death; for whosoever doeth any work therein, that soul shall be cut off from among his people." Exod. xxxi, 14. "If thou turn away thy foot from the Sabbath, from doing thy pleasure on my holy day; and call the Sabbath a delight, the holy of the Lord, honorable, and shalt honor him, not doing thine own ways, nor finding thine own pleasure, nor speaking thine own words: then shalt thou delight thyself in the Lord; and I will cause thee to ride upon the high places of the earth, and feed thee with the heritage of Jacob thy father, for the mouth of the Lord hath spoken it." Isa. lviii, 13, 14.

(3.) If, then, the fourth commandment is a part of the moral law, it must be of universal and perpetual obligation. This fact is very forcibly indicated by the manner in which the precepts of this law were originally recorded. A table or pillar of stone was in ancient times a direct symbol of the perpetuity of whatever was engraved upon it. This very natural symbol God was pleased to employ in the case before us. Hence it is reasonable to believe that he intended to distinguish the Decalogue from every other part of the Mosaic Law, and to mark its superior importance and perpetuity by writing it with his own hand on tables of stone. It is incredible that God should distinguish the fourth commandment, together with the other nine, in so solemn a manner if he had not intended that all men should regard it as of perpetual obligation.

It is also worthy of remark that this commandment is delivered in the same absolute manner as the other nine. The fifth commandment,

"Honor thy father and thy mother," is obligatory on all children to whom the precept comes. So, likewise, the eighth, "Thou shalt not steal," is binding upon all who know it, whether Jew or Gentile. Accordingly, every one who knows the fourth commandment is bound to "remember the Sabbath-day, to keep it holy."

(4.) If the moral law is the law of all men, it is the law of Christians; and if it is the law of Christians, then is the Sabbath as explicitly enjoined upon us as it was upon the Jews. That the moral law is our law, as well as the law of the Jews, all but Antinomians must acknowledge; and few, we suppose, will be inclined to plunge themselves into the fearful mazes of that error in order to support lax notions respecting the obligation of the Sabbath. That the law of the Decalogue is binding upon us the Scriptures of the New Testament clearly prove.

Our Lord says, "Think not that I am come to destroy the law or the prophets: I am not come to destroy, but to fulfill." Matt. v, 17. If by "the law" he meant both the moral and the ceremonial law, he fulfilled the latter by fulfilling its types, and the former by upholding its authority. A similar distinction may be made in regard to "the prophets." They either enjoined morality, or uttered prophecies respecting Christ. The latter were fulfilled in the sense of accomplishment; the former by being sanctioned and enforced. That the observance of the Sabbath is a part of the moral law we have before shown, and for this reason the injunctions of the prophets respecting the Sabbath are to be regarded as a part of their moral teaching.

The preceding passage from our Lord's Sermon on the Mount, with its context, is a sufficiently explicit enforcement of the moral law generally upon his followers. But when he says, "The Sabbath was made for man," he clearly refers to its original institution as a universal law, and not to its obligation upon the Jews only, in consequence of the enactments of the law of Moses. It "was made for *man*," not as he may be a Jew or a Christian, but as *man*, a creature bound to love, worship, and obey his God and Maker, and on his trial for eternity.

Another explicit proof that the law of the Ten Commandments, and, consequently, the law of the Sabbath, is obligatory on Christians, is found in Romans iii, 31: "Do we then make void the law through faith?" which is equivalent to asking, Does Christianity teach that the law is no longer obligatory on Christians, because it teaches that no man can be justified by it? To this the apostle answers in the most solemn form of expression, "God forbid; yea, we establish the law." Now, the sense in which he uses the phrase, "the law," in this argument, is indubitably marked in Romans vii, 7: "I had not known sin but by *the law;* for I had not known lust, except *the law* had said, Thou shalt not covet." Here the apostle refers directly to one of the precepts of the Decalogue; and this plainly shows that the Decalogue is "*the law*" of which he speaks, and which is "*established*" by the Gospel as the rule of all inward and outward holiness. Whoever, therefore, denies the obligation of the Sabbath on Christians, denies the obligation of the whole Decalogue; and there is no medium between the acknowledgment of the Divine authority of this sacred institution, as a universal law, and that gross corruption of Christianity generally denominated Antinomianism.

II. THE CHANGE OF THE SABBATH FROM THE SEVENTH TO THE FIRST DAY OF THE WEEK.

In giving a satisfactory account of the change of the Sabbath from the seventh to the first day of the week, it will be important to show, 1. That such a change is compatible with the nature of the institution; and, 2. That it was made by Divine authority.

1. *The change is compatible with the nature of the institution.*—To see this in its true light it is only necessary to observe,

(1.) That the law of the Sabbath is partly moral and partly positive. Or in other words, the institution consists of two parts: the *Sabbath*, or *holy rest;* and the *day* on which it is observed. These are plainly alluded to as distinct from each other when it is said that the Lord " rested the *seventh* day," and " blessed the *Sabbath* day, and hallowed it." He did not bless and hallow the day *as the seventh*, but only as being the day on which the *Sabbath*, or *holy rest*, was to be kept. While, therefore, the Sabbath itself is a perpetual institution, morally binding upon all men, the law which determines the *time* of its observance is purely positive, and consequently may be changed. But though the day might be altered, without altering the substance of the institution, yet it could be altered only by Divine authority. The same authority which instituted the Sabbath, appointed also the day on which it was to be observed; and no other authority is competent to change either the one or the other.

(2.) That the same portion of time which constituted the seventh day from the creation could not be observed in all parts of the earth. It is not probable, therefore, that the original law required more than that a seventh day, or one day in seven, the seventh day after six days of labor, should be thus appropriated, from whatever point the hebdomadal cycle might begin. For if more had been intended, then it would have been necessary to establish a rule for the reckoning of days themselves, which has been different in different nations; some reckoning from evening to evening, and others from midnight to midnight. But if we could be absolutely certain as to the mode of reckoning days when the Sabbath was first instituted, the differences of latitude and longitude would throw the whole into disorder; and it is not probable that a universal law should have been fettered with that circumstantial exactness which would have rendered difficult, and sometimes doubtful astronomical calculations necessary, in order to its being obeyed according to the intention of the Lawgiver. Hence we conclude,

(3.) That the precise *time* of the Sabbath is not essential to the institution, and that this may be changed by Divine authority, without making any alteration in the *law* of the Sabbath either as it stands in the second chapter of Genesis, or in the fourth commandment. It is, therefore, as consistent with the nature of the institution for Christians to observe the first day of the week, as it was for Jews to observe the seventh. We are not to suppose, however, that every man has a right to determine which day of the week should be his Sabbath, though he should fulfill the law so far as to abstract the seventh part of his time from labor. It was ordained for *public* worship; and it is, therefore, necessary that it should be uniformly observed by a whole community at the same time. The Divine legislator of the Jews interposed for this end by special direction, as to his people. The first Sabbath kept in the wilderness was calculated from the first day in which the manna fell, and with no apparent reference to the creation of the world. By apostolic authority it is now fixed to be held on the first day of the week, and thus one of the great ends for which it was established, that it should be a day of "holy convocation," is secured.

2. *The change of the Sabbath to the first day of the week was made by Divine authority.*—In order to establish this proposition we offer the following remarks:

(1.) One grand end of the original institution of the Sabbath was, to commemorate the creation of the world. The reason why God chose that the work of creation should be thus commemorated, rather than the deluge, or the deliverance of the Israelites from bondage, was, it is presumed, the peculiar greatness of the work itself, as also the display which it furnished of his glorious perfections. If this be admitted, as it probably will be by every sober man, it must also be admitted that we ought to expect, according to this scheme, that the greater and more glorious work of redemption should be commemorated with equal or greater solemnity. In the accomplishment of this work the resurrection of Christ was the crowning event. It completed the chain of evidence by which his Messiahship was established. It was his triumph over death, and a triumphant vindication of all his claims. Hence, since the resurrection of Christ, the first day of the week has been observed as the Christian Sabbath in honor of that event, and in commemoration of the work of redemption.

It is to be remembered, however, that the original institution is still substantially preserved. The Sabbath still returns upon one day in seven. It is still a memorial of the creation of the world; while the new creation, as its importance demands, takes its own superior place in the commemoration. Thus the institution, instead of being abrogated, is made the memorial of two wonderful works of God, instead of one. While it is a memorial of creation, it is so enlarged as to commemorate also the work of redemption.

(2.) It is admitted that there is not on record any Divine command issued to the apostles to change the Sabbath from the day on which it was held by the Jews to the first day of the week. But when we see that this was done in the apostolic age, and that St. Paul speaks of the Jewish Sabbaths as not being obligatory upon Christians, while he contends that the whole moral law is obligatory upon them, the fair inference is, that this change of the day was made by Divine direction. It will hardly be denied, that the change was made under the sanction of the inspired and divinely appointed rulers of the Church of Christ, whose business it was to "set all things in order" which pertained to its worship and moral government. It follows, therefore, that in observing the first day of the week as the Christian Sabbath we act under apostolic authority.

(3.) The first day of the week was observed by the apostolic Churches as a day of *public worship.* "And upon the first day of the week, when the disciples came together to break bread, Paul preached to them, ready to depart on the morrow, and continued his speech until midnight." Acts xx, 7. This took place at Troas, where Paul and his companions abode seven days; the last of which was the first day of the week. On this day "the disciples came together to break bread;" or, in other words, to partake of the Lord's Supper. But if the seventh day of the week had been the Christian Sabbath, and the day of public worship, the administration of this sacrament would naturally have belonged to that day. Though Paul and his companions were there for several days, yet no mention is made of any religious service on the seventh day of the week; but it is expressly stated that "the disciples came together," and that "Paul preached to them" on "the first day of the week." The object of the meeting is also stated to have been *the breaking of bread,* which clearly indicates that the first day of the week was regarded as the Christian Sabbath.

(4.) The first day of the week is denominated, in the New Testament, *the Lord's day,* in distinction from the Jewish Sabbath, and from all other days. "I was," says St. John, "in the Spirit on the Lord's day." Rev. i, 10. The phrase "Lord's day" is similar to that of "Lord's Supper," which occurs in 1 Corinthians xi, 20. And as the "Lord's Supper" is a sacred supper, so, by the same rule, the "Lord's day" is a sacred day. There would be a manifest impropriety in calling a common supper the Lord's Supper; and a similar impropriety in calling a secular day the Lord's day. St. John uses the phrase "Lord's day" without otherwise indicating which of the seven days of the week he referred to; thus evidently showing that when the Apocalypse was written there was a day known and observed by Christians generally as the "Lord's day." That this was the first day of the week, which was kept in memory of the resurrection of our Lord, is abundantly evident from the history of the Church.

IGNATIUS, a companion of the apostles, says, in so many words, "Let us no more Sabbatize," that is, keep the Jewish Sabbath, "but let us keep the *Lord's day*, on which our Life arose."

IRENÆUS, Bishop of Lyons, who lived in the second century, says, "On the Lord's day every one of us, Christians, keeps the Sabbath; meditating in the law, and rejoicing in the works of God."

DIONYSIUS, Bishop of Corinth, who also lived in the second century, says in his letter to the Church at Rome, "To-day we celebrate the Lord's day when we read your epistle to us."

Other allusions to the Christian Sabbath under the title of the Lord's day occur in the writings of the early Christian fathers. These evidences show clearly, that the day called the Lord's day by St. John was the first day of the week; and that it was set apart and distinguished from the other days, in consideration of its having been the day of Christ's resurrection. The first day of the week, in being thus described as the Lord's day, is evidently distinguished from other days considered as secular days, and marked as a sacred day, or holy Sabbath.

(5.) This day is distinguished from all other days of the week by God's gracious dispensations. The first of these is the resurrection of our Lord. This event raised the drooping hopes of the apostles and other primitive Christians, and laid the foundation for the successful propagation of Christianity. It is customary to observe, annually, days which have been distinguished by public benefits; but so great is the benefit obtained on this day that it demands a weekly commemoration. "Blessed be the God and Father of our Lord Jesus Christ, which according to his abundant mercy hath begotten us again unto a lively hope, by the resurrection of Jesus Christ from the dead."

The first appearances of Christ to his disciples, after his resurrection, were on the morning of the day he rose.* He appeared again to ten of the disciples, Thomas being absent, in the evening of the same day.† On the next first day of the week he appeared to his disciples, and found them all assembled together, as if for religious worship.‡ Thus we have two first days specified as days on which Christ appeared, but there is no such specification in regard to the Jewish Sabbath.

The day of Pentecost, so distinguished by the gift of the Holy Ghost, was also the first day of the week. On this day there was the most remarkable outpouring of the Spirit that ever occurred, in consequence of which about three thousand persons were converted and added to the Church. But why was the honor of the Pentecostal blessing conferred on the *first* day of the week, and not on the seventh? To this question no satisfactory answer can be given, unless we allow that God intended, by this dispensation, to place his seal upon it as a perpetual Christian Sabbath.

---

* Matt. xxviii, 9, 10; Mark xvi, 9, 12.   † John xx, 19-24.   ‡ John xx, 26-29.

(6.) God has signally honored the observance of the Christian Sabbath with his blessing. If it were a human institution, it would be one of great impiety; for to neglect the Sabbath of God's own appointment, and to observe one appointed by man in its place, would be highly dishonorable and offensive to God. It would be virtually to say that God did not appoint the proper day, and that we can improve upon his institutions. But how has God treated the observance of the first day of the week as the Christian Sabbath? Has he refused to bless religious assemblies on this day? Has he visited them with any perceptible marks of his displeasure? By no means. On the contrary, he has crowned the observance of the Christian Sabbath with most distinguished blessings, and has made it subservient to all the great interests of morality and religion. "On this day millions of the human race have been born unto God. From the word and ordinances of God, from the influences of the Holy Spirit, from the presence of Christ in his Church, Christians have derived on this day, more than on all others, the most delightful views of the Divine character, clear apprehensions of their own duty, lively devotion to the service of God, strength to overcome temptations, and glorious anticipations of immortality."* Thus God has set his seal upon the Christian Sabbath as one of the institutions of true religion.

These considerations, when taken together, fully prove that the change of the Sabbath from the seventh to the first day of the week is of Divine authority, and that, consequently, we are under obligation to keep the *Christian* Sabbath and not the Jewish. No change, however, is made in the service required on this day, or in the manner of observing it, except such as necessarily arises from a change of dispensations. Religious worship still continues to be the appropriate business of the Sabbath, as it was formerly; and though it is performed in a different mode, it is the same in spirit and design.

III. THE MANNER IN WHICH THE SABBATH IS TO BE OBSERVED.

The obligation of a Sabbatical observance upon Christians being established, the inquiry which naturally follows is, In what manner is this great festival, at once so ancient and venerable, and intended to commemorate events so illustrious and so important to mankind, to be celebrated? To this a sufficient answer will be found in the Decalogue, in incidental passages of Scripture, and in the discourses and acts of Christ and his apostles.

The fourth commandment refers to this subject in the following terms: "Remember the Sabbath day, to keep it holy. In it thou shalt not do any work, thou, nor thy son, nor thy daughter, thy manservant, nor thy maidservant, nor thy cattle, nor thy stranger that is within thy gates." Hence, the law of the Sabbath may be considered both in regard to what it forbids, and to what it enjoins. We will consider it,

* Dwight's Theology, vol. 3, p. 244.

1. *In regard to what it forbids.*—The law prohibits all kinds of secular labor on the Sabbath. "In it thou shalt not do any work." This prohibition has reference,

(1.) To the government of our own conduct. It forbids all labor, whether manual or mental, which has not for its object the worship of God, or our own religious improvement. The law itself is expressed in the most comprehensive and unlimited terms, prohibiting without exception all manner of labor; but it was certainly not intended by the Lawgiver that it should be interpreted in its strict and literal sense. The prohibition cannot comprehend, in its true interpretation, works of necessity and mercy, because such a prohibition would be wrong. It would be inconsistent with a benevolent provision for the wants and necessities of men, and with the declaration of Christ, that "The Sabbath was made for man, and not man for the Sabbath." Mark ii, 27.

The law, therefore, in its true import, allows several exceptions to the literal requirement, and actually demands them. These exceptions are called *works of necessity and mercy.* The necessity, however, must be one which is imposed by the providence of God, and not by our own will. Thus, a ship, when on a voyage, may sail on the Sabbath as well as on any other day without violating the *rule;* but it would be evidently violated by *commencing* the voyage on the Sabbath, because, in this case, a choice of days is in the power of the master.

The law, then, requires men to refrain from all kinds of work on the Sabbath which can be omitted without essential and necessary injury. It forbids the pursuit of *pleasure,* or of any animal or merely intellectual gratification. An intemperate indulgence of appetite, journeying for amusement, social visiting, the reading of books designed merely to gratify the taste or the imagination, are all violations of the Sabbatic law. But,

(2.) The prohibition has reference to the labor of those who are committed to our charge. It is made the duty of parents to enforce the observance of the Sabbath upon their children, and of masters upon their servants. The duty of sustaining the Sabbath by authority is one of the utmost importance, and especially in the case of parents. If they train up their children in Sabbath-keeping habits, they confer upon them inestimable benefits; but if they neglect to do this, they expose them to incalculable evil. Nor is it enough for parents to advise their children to keep the Sabbath. They ought to *command* them to do it, and to enforce their commands by suitable motives.

A similar authority is to be exercised over servants, as far as they are the subjects of domestic control. But even where the heads of families possess only advisory power, they are required to employ that power in promoting the due observance of the Sabbath. Hence their duty extends to the "*stranger* that is within" their gates, as well as to children and servants.

(3.) *Beasts of burden* employed in our service are also included in that law of the Sabbath which forbids labor and ordains rest to man. They need the repose which it grants, and we are required to let them have it. He who hires out his cattle or horses on the Sabbath day is as guilty of its violation as if he worked with his own hands. But we will consider the law of the Sabbath,

2. *In regard to what it enjoins.*—Though the Sabbath is a day of rest, yet it is not a day of idleness. In it we are to be actively employed in the solemn and immediate duties of religion. "Remember the Sabbath-day, *to keep it holy.*" This is to be done in the use of those means which God has appointed for his own worship, and for our spiritual edification. Such means are to be observed with fervor and constancy in our public assemblies, in our families, and in the closet.

(1.) *In our public assemblies.*—It appears to have been designed, in the institution of the Sabbath, to afford men the most favorable opportunity of uniting together in the public and solemn worship of God. No other day is so well adapted to the purpose. It was therefore commanded in the law, "On the seventh day ye shall have an holy convocation." Num. xxviii, 25. It was the invariable practice of our Lord to attend the services of the synagogue on the Sabbath day. The first Christians also, and after them the whole Christian Church, thus hallowed the first day of the week by coming together for religious services. Can we follow better examples? Let us not be unwilling, but esteem it our highest privilege to wait upon the Lord in the public assembly, and to enjoy communion with him and his people. How encouraging the promise, "'Where two or three are gathered together in my name, there am I in the midst of them!" Matt. xviii, 20.

(2.) *In our families.*—God should be worshiped, not at church only, but in our houses. And in general, there are no opportunities so suitable for attending to the spiritual interests. children and servants as those which the Sabbath affords. If this great concern is neglected then, we may presume that it is neglected during the rest of the week. Let parents and masters, then, consider their important trust. Do they call together their families, and begin the day with praise and prayer? Do they exhort and command those who are committed to their care to improve the sacred season? Do they lead them to the house of God, and teach them to be serious and devout in their deportment? Do they spend part of the day in giving them catechetical instruction on religious subjects? Were the Sabbath to be thus sanctified in every family true religion would revive and spread among us, and blessings would crown the rising generation.

(3.) *In the closet.*—Without private devotion, public ordinances, the most solemn addresses of ministers, or the pious exhortations of parents and friends, will be of no real profit. Retirement after the public duties of the Sabbath is to the soul what digestion after eating is to the body; and every one knows that the most excellent food not properly digested must fail in affording nourishment. In general, men find but little leisure on other days for religious solitude, and for this reason the Sabbath should be to them the more precious. They can then retire to their closets without fear of interruption, and fill up every interval in reading, meditation, and prayer.

CHAPTER VII.

THE LOVE OF OUR NEIGHBOR.

As *love to God* is the sum of the first table of the moral law, so the precepts of the second are all comprised in *love to man*. Hence they are epitomized by our Lord in this one injunction, "Thou shalt love thy neighbor as thyself." Matt. xxii, 39. The whole law, then, is a law of love; and accordingly St. Paul declares, "Love is the fulfilling of the law." Rom. xiii, 10. In the investigation of this law of love, so far as it respects the duties which we owe to our neighbor, we will consider it *first* in its general character as a principle of moral action; and, *secondly*, in its application to particular duties. The former will occupy the present chapter.

In order to understand the nature and general character of that evangelical love of our neighbor which the law of God demands, we must consider it, 1. In its source; 2. In what it excludes; and, 3. In what it requires. We must consider it,

I. IN ITS SOURCE.

The only source of genuine love to our neighbor is a regenerated state of mind. We have shown that the love of *God* springs from the gift of the Holy Spirit to those who are justified by faith in Christ; and that every sentiment which, in any other circumstances, assumes this designation is imperfect or simulated. We make the same remark in regard to the love of our *neighbor*. If it does not flow from the love of God, the only sure mark of a regenerate nature, it is an imperfect or simulated sentiment. Without true love to God there can be no true love to man; nor can there be true love to God without regenerating grace.

The existence of morals without piety is, therefore, not to be presumed. Human nature is too perverse to be restrained independent of religious motives. The instant the doctrine of future retribution is obliterated from the mind the influence of moral obligation ceases to operate. Philosophy may declaim with all her power upon the advantages of virtue in the present life, but, in the absence of Christian motives, she will declaim in vain. It is only the powerful and persuasive influence of Scripture doctrines that will induce a course of moral conduct contributive to social happiness.

We see, therefore, in this view of the subject the superior nature of Christian morals, or of morals when kept in connection, as they should always be, with the doctrines of the Gospel and the regenerating work of the Holy Spirit. There may, indeed, be a degree of natural benevolence which, if aided by well-directed education, may counteract the malevolent and selfish feelings of our nature. Yet love to man, as a religious principle, and in its full operation, can only result from a change of heart by the power of Divine grace, because that only can subdue the affections to the obedience which the law of love requires. But the love of our neighbor is to be considered,

II. IN REGARD TO WHAT IT EXCLUDES.

It is a matter of great importance to Christian morality that we should gain a clear understanding of what is excluded by that love of our neighbor which is enjoined upon us by Christ and his apostles. To aid in the obtainment of this object we may remark,

1. *That it excludes all* ANGER *and* HATRED *toward our fellow-men.*—It is true, these are emotions of which we are necessarily susceptible, and which may exist in perfect harmony with the law of love. They are indeed expressly ascribed in the Scriptures to God himself. It is asserted that he "is *angry* with the wicked every day." Psa. vii, 11. So of Christ it is said, on a certain occasion, that he looked on the people "with *anger*, being grieved for the hardness of their hearts." Mark iii, 5. God declares, "I *hate* robbery for burnt-offering." Isa. lx, 8. And Solomon tells us that "the fear of the Lord is to *hate* evil." Prov. viii, 13.

It follows, therefore, that the emotions of anger and hatred are not sinful in themselves. They only become sinful when they contravene the law of love; and in this sense they are explicitly condemned in the Scriptures. Our Lord says, "Whosoever shall be *angry* with his brother without a cause, shall be in danger of the judgment." Matt. v, 22. So also St. Paul, "Let all bitterness, and *wrath*, and *anger*, and clamor be put away from you, with all *malice*." Ephes. iv, 31. St. John testifies, "He that saith he is in the light, and *hateth* his brother, is in darkness even until now." 1 John ii, 9. Again, "Whosoever *hateth* his brother is a murderer." 1 John iii, 15. "If a man say, I love God, and *hateth* his brother, he is a liar." 1 John iv, 20.

2. *It excludes all* REVENGE.—We must exact no punishment of another for offenses against ourselves. For, though it is lawful and right to inflict penalties upon those who offend against society, yet this is never to be done on the principle of private revenge, but on the public ground that law and government are ordained of God. The Divine injunction is, "Recompense to no man evil for evil;" and again, "Avenge not your-

selves; but rather give place to wrath: for it is written, Vengeance is mine; I will repay, saith the Lord." Rom. xii, 17, 19.

3. *It excludes all* IMPLACABILITY.—This is deemed so great a violation of that law of love which ought to bind all men together, that if we do not promptly and generously forgive our offending neighbor God will not forgive us. "If ye forgive men their trespasses," says our Lord, "your heavenly Father will also forgive you; but if ye forgive not men their trespasses, neither will your Father forgive your trespasses." Matt. vi, 14, 15. When Peter inquired, "Lord, how oft shall my brother sin against me, and I forgive him? till seven times?" Jesus replied, "I say not unto thee, Until seven times; but, Until seventy times seven." Matt. xviii, 21, 22. In agreement with these Scriptures we have the exhortation of the apostle: "Be kind one to another, tender-hearted, forgiving one another, even as God for Christ's sake hath forgiven you." Ephes. iv, 32.

4. *It excludes all* CENSORIOUSNESS *or* EVIL-SPEAKING.—This consists in relating what is improper or wrong in an absent person when duty or truth does not require it. For, whenever the end is merely to lower a person in the estimation of others, it is resolvable into a splenetic and immoral feeling. Hence St. Paul exhorts Christians to let all "*evil speaking* be put away from" them. St. James says, "*Speak not evil* one of another, brethren. He that speaketh evil of his brother, and judgeth his brother, speaketh evil of the law, and judgeth the law." James iv, 11.

5. *It excludes,* as limitations to its exercise, *all those* ADVENTITIOUS DISTINCTIONS *which have been created by men, by providential arrangements, or by accidental circumstances.*—Men of all nations, of all colors, of all conditions, are the objects of the unlimited precept, "Thou shalt love thy neighbor as thyself." Kind feelings produced by natural instincts, by intercourse, by country, may call the love of our neighbor into warmer exercise as individuals or classes of men; or these may be considered as distinct and special, though similar affections superadded to this universal charity; but as to all men this character is an efficient affection, excluding all *ill-will* and all *injury.* Let us, then, consider the love of our neighbor,

III. WITH RESPECT TO WHAT IT REQUIRES.

This love, considered as a general principle of moral action, has respect to those duties which are equally incumbent upon *all men.* These are clearly indicated in few words by the prophet Micah: "He hath showed thee, O man, what is good; and what doth the Lord require of thee, but to *do justly,* and to *love mercy,* and to walk humbly with thy God?" Micah vi, 8. They are also included in our Lord's golden rule: "Therefore all things whatsoever ye would that men should do to you, do ye even so to them; for this is the law and the prophets." Matt. vii, 12. From these Scriptures it is evident that the law of love requires us to exercise *justice* and *benevolence* toward all men.

1. *It requires us "to do* JUSTLY."—This is most obviously implied in doing to others as we would that they should do to us. Justice consists in giving to every one his due, or in acting in all things according to the principles of rectitude. "Render, therefore," says the apostle, "to all their dues; tribute to whom tribute is due; custom to whom custom; fear to whom fear; honor to whom honor." Rom. xiii, 7.

The exercise of universal justice, commonly called *ethical* justice, would secure to all men the enjoyment of their *natural rights*. These are briefly summed up in three—*life, property,* and *liberty*.

(1.) Our natural right to *life* is guarded by the precept "Thou shalt not kill." This right is limited by the still more ancient injunction to the sons of Noah: "Whoso sheddeth man's blood, by man shall his blood be shed." Gen. ix, 6. In a state of society this right may be further limited by a government, and capital punishment may be extended to other crimes, as we see in the laws of Moses. But against all individual authority the life of man is absolutely secured; and not only so, but anger, which is the first principle of violence, and which proceeds first to malignity and revenge and then to personal injuries, is prohibited under the penalty of the Divine wrath—a lofty proof of the superior character of the Christian rule of justice.

But here it may be inquired, Have not men the power of surrendering, at their own option, the right of life? To this we reply,

First, that since government is an institution of God it seems obligatory on all men to live in a social state; and if so, to each is conceded the right of putting his life to hazard when called upon by his government to defend that state from domestic rebellion or foreign war. So, also, we have the power to hazard our life to save a fellow-creature from perishing. In times of persecution for religion we are commanded by our Lord to flee from one city or place to another; but when flight is cut off we have the power to surrender life rather than betray our allegiance to Christ. According to the apostle's rule, "we ought to lay down our lives for the brethren;" that is, for the Church and the cause of religion. In this case, and in some others accompanied with danger to life, when a plain rule of duty is seen to be binding upon us we are not only at liberty to take the risk, but are bound to do it, since it is more our duty to obey God than to take care of our life. But,

Secondly, this power over our life does not extend to self-destruction or suicide. The precept "Thou shalt not kill" must be taken to forbid not only murder properly so called, but the taking away of human life in all cases, except by the authority of human governments proceeding upon the rules and principles of the word of God. It is true, the Mosaic law is entirely silent as to the punishment of suicide. In this, however, there is good reason, for the subject himself is, by his own direful act, put beyond the reach of human authority, and must be left wholly to

Chap. 7.]   THE LOVE OF OUR NEIGHBOR.   519

the retribution of God. Moreover, every dishonor done to the inanimate corpse is only a punishment inflicted upon the innocent survivors, who, in most cases, have a large measure of suffering otherwise inflicted upon them. But we must not suppose that the absence of all *post mortem* penalties against suicide in the Mosaic law is a proof that it is not included in the precept against murder. As well might we suppose, because thefts and other instances of covetousness in *action only* are restrained in the Mosaic law by positive penalties, that the precept "Thou shalt not covet" does not forbid a covetous *disposition*.

That suicide has very deservedly received the *morally descriptive* appellation of *self-murder* will appear from the reason given to Noah for making murder a capital crime. The precept is, "Whoso sheddeth man's blood, by man shall his blood be shed;" and then the reason is added, "*for in the image of God made he man.*" There is in this reason a manifest reference to the dignity put upon human nature by its being endowed with a *rational* and *immortal spirit*. The crime of murder is, therefore, made to lie, not merely in the injury done to a neighbor in depriving him of animal life, but eminently in its contempt of the *image of God* in man, and its interference with man's *immortal* interests and relations as a deathless spirit, accountable in the future state for the actions done in this. If this is allowed then suicide bears upon it these awful characteristics of murder, and is, therefore, an infraction of the law of God as well as the killing of others. Indeed, we cannot well understand the principles of our religion without perceiving that, of all crimes, willful suicide ought most to be dreaded, because it places the criminal at once beyond the reach of mercy.

Thirdly. If, then, no man has a right to dispose of his life by suicide, he has no right to hazard it in *duels*. The sinfulness of dueling is clearly implied in the Christian Scriptures. If I have received a personal injury I am bound to forgive it, unless it is of such a nature as to require punishment by a due course of law; and even then the offender is not to be punished in the spirit of revenge, but out of respect to the peace and welfare of society. If I have given offense I am bound to acknowledge it and to make reparation; and if my adversary will not be satisfied, and insists upon my staking my life against his own, no considerations of reputation or disgrace, or of the good or ill opinion of men who form their judgments in utter disregard to the laws of God, can have any more weight in this than in any other case of immorality.

The sin of dueling unites, in fact, the two crimes of suicide and murder. He who falls in a duel is guilty of suicide by voluntarily exposing himself to be slain; and he by whom he falls is guilty of murder, as having shed man's blood without authority. Nay, the guilt of the two crimes unites in the same person. He who falls is a suicide in fact, and the murderer of another in intention. He by whom he falls is a murderer in fact, and so far a suicide as to have put his own life in imminent peril in contempt of the authority of God over him. He has contemned the image of God in man, both in himself and in his brother. And where duels are not fatal on either side, the whole guilt is chargeable upon the parties as a sin *purposed in the heart;* though in that case there is space left for repentance.

(2.) In *property* lawfully acquired every man has a natural right. Against individual aggression the right of property is secured by the Divine law, "Thou shalt not steal." It is also guarded by another injunction which carries the restraint up to the very principle of justice in the heart, "Thou shalt not covet;" covetousness being that corrupt affection from which arises every injury done to men in their property. The Christian injunction, "Be content with such things as ye have," is another important security in the right of property, in regard to which right the fullest claims of justice would be met if these Scripture precepts were carried out in their spirit and design.

The right of property is of incalculable value to human beings. It enables them to secure happiness in a great measure proportionable to their skill, economy, and moral virtues. It multiplies objects of enjoyment, and lays a foundation for voluntary industry and enterprise. It is one of the main pillars of civilization. It leads to the perfection of all those arts and sciences which are connected with civilized life, and is the basis of all mechanical, mercantile, and manufacturing pursuits. The protection of men by the state in the enjoyment of the rights of property is only second, therefore, to their protection in the enjoyment of personal rights and liberties.

The right of property is violated by theft, robbery, and fraud. *Theft* consists in taking property without the knowledge of the owner, and contrary to his will. *Robbery* consists in taking property from a person having lawful possession of it by violence, or by putting him in fear of some injury. *Fraud* is the injury of our neighbor by deception or artifice in commercial transactions. It is committed by inducing men to part with their property on false pretenses, by selling property for more than an equivalent, by representing articles as better than they really are, and by contracting debts without an intention or ability to pay them. It is also a species of fraud to induce persons to purchase what they do not need, or what they cannot procure without unwarrantable sacrifices.

These are common forms of dishonesty, and are manifestly violations of justice. It is as criminal to obtain our neighbor's property on false pretenses, or by deception and artifice, as by stealing. All dishonesty is of the nature of stealing, and is forbidden in the eighth commandment under this title. No commercial transaction is right which takes away our neighbor's property without giving him a full equivalent for it. "Ye shall do no unrighteousness in judgment, in mete-yard, in weight, or in measure. Just balances, just weights, a just ephah, and a just hin shall ye have." Lev. xix, 35, 36. And St. Paul says, " Let no man go beyond or defraud his brother in any matter; because the Lord is the avenger of all such." 1 Thess. iv, 6.

Nor are we to suppose that *gambling*, which consists in playing games of skill or chance for money, is any more consistent with the claims of justice than theft or fraud. The money which is lost by this means is an entire loss to the man who parts with it without any equivalent, and that which is gained is, therefore, a fraudulent gain to him who obtains it. One gains only by the other's loss. This is not the case in respect to the gains of any lawful business. The gains of the farmer, the mechanic, the merchant, and the banker are for services performed, which contribute to public prosperity by actual production; but the gains of the gambler are for no services rendered, and the result of no production. Games of chance and skill, even without gambling, are objectionable. They waste time, produce a distaste for honest industry, and may lead to gambling in its vilest forms.

Lotteries are a species of gambling, in which a large number of persons hazard small sums for the chance of obtaining greater ones. Lotteries, like private games, produce nothing. They take from the many without any equivalent, and give to the few. They concentrate the small amounts paid by multitudes into a few large sums, which are distributed by chance to a few of the contributors. The many are impoverished, while the few are enriched at their expense. Lotteries, therefore, are as incompatible with justice as fraud in any other form.

(3.) Another natural right which every man may justly claim, and with which no individual authority ought to interfere, is *liberty*. This, in its general acceptation, consists in exemption from compulsion or restraint, and is applicable to both body and mind. A man may therefore be said to enjoy *liberty*, when his volitions and actions are not controlled by any power beyond himself. This natural right comprehends liberty of *person*, the liberty of *speech and of the press*, and liberty of *conscience*.

Liberty of person consists in exemption from the arbitrary will of our fellow-men, or in the privilege of doing as we please, so as not to trespass on the rights of others. This kind of liberty belongs to men in a social state, and can only be maintained by established laws. Hence, liberty of person, as it recognizes the rights of every member of society, and depends upon the restraints of law, is evidently included in what is called *civil liberty*.

Liberty of person must be distinguished from what is sometimes called *natural* liberty. This is supposed to consist in a freedom to do in all things as we please, without any regard to the interests of our fellow-men. To such liberty, however, we have no just right, either natural or acquired. The liberty to rob and to plunder may be the natural right of the wolf or the tiger; but if mankind are by nature fitted and designed for the social state, which will hardly be denied, it cannot be the natural right of men. When, therefore, we speak of liberty as a natural right, we mean that kind of liberty which is in accordance with the rights of all men.

The liberty of *speech and of the press* is the right of every citizen "freely to speak, write, and publish his sentiments" on all suitable subjects. The word *press* is here employed in its most comprehensive sense, denoting the general business of printing and publishing. Hence, the liberty of the press is the liberty to publish books and papers without restraint, except such as may be necessary to guard the rights of others. Men are not at liberty in *all* cases to speak or publish against others what they please. Without *some* restraint they might, by false reports or malicious publications, injure the reputation, the peace, or the property of their fellow-men. It is, therefore, proper, while the civil authority guarantees to every man freedom of speech and of the press, that it should hold him responsible for the *abuse* of this right.

For a person to defame another by a false or malicious statement or report is either slander or libel. When the offense consists in words spoken, it is *slander;* when in words written or printed, it is called *libel.* The latter, because it is generally more widely circulated than the former, and is, therefore, likely to do greater injury, is supposed to be the greater offense.

Liberty of conscience, or religious liberty, consists in the unrestrained privilege of adopting and maintaining whatever religious opinions our judgment may approve, and of worshiping God according to the dictates of our conscience. History informs us of countries in which the people have been denied the enjoyment of this most sacred right. Even in some called Christian, thousands have been put to death for the expression of their religious opinions. Liberty of conscience, however, is now more extensively tolerated than formerly. The laws of our own happy country secure to every religious denomination, "without discrimination or preference, the free exercise and enjoyment of religious worship."

Thus we have seen that the proper administration of justice will secure to us the three great natural rights of man—*life, property,* and *liberty.* But these rights may be forfeited by crime. If a man commits murder he forfeits his life, and lawfully suffers death. If he is guilty of rebellion, his estate may be seized and confiscated. If he steals, he loses his right to liberty, and is justly imprisoned. How far the natural rights of every man may be restrained by public authority is a point, however, on which different opinions have been held.*

Before we dismiss this part of the subject it will be proper to remark, (4.) That justice requires, in all our transactions, a strict conformity to TRUTH. The general law in regard to this is, "Thou shalt not bear false witness against thy neighbor." This precept forbids not only false oaths to deprive our neighbor of his life or of his rights, but all departures from moral truth. Whatever is deposed as a truth which is false in fact, and tends to injure another in his body, goods, or influence, is against the spirit and letter of this law. The violation of promises, the disappointment of hopes which we may have created or cherished, pretending to be what we are not, or not to be what we really are, or any attempt whatever to make an impression upon the mind of another which we know to be contrary to reality and fact, is an infraction of the *spirit* of the law and of the claims of justice.

The nature and character of the Divine being, the interests of individuals and of communities, our own conscience, and the word of God, all demand that we should abstain from every species of falsehood. Solomon tells us that "lying lips are abomination to the Lord." Prov. xii, 22. "Wherefore," says the apostle, "putting away lying, speak every man truth with his neighbor." Eph. iv, 25. Again: "Lie not one to another." Col. iii, 9. It is expressly declared that "all liars shall have their portion in the lake which burneth with fire and brimstone." Rev. xxi, 8. But,

2. *The law of love requires us also to exercise* BENEVOLENCE *toward all men.*—We are not only "to do justly," but "*to love mercy.*" "All the law is fulfilled in one word," says the apostle, "even in this, Thou shalt love thy neighbor as thyself." Gal. v, 14. The terms *mercy, love, kindness,* and *charity* are often used in the Scriptures as synonymous, denoting that good-will toward all men which inclines us to do to others as we would that they should do to us. We shall employ them in this sense in the present discussion, including them all under the term *benevolence,* which may be defined to be the love of mankind, accompanied with a desire to promote their happiness. The following remarks will more fully unfold its nature:

(1.) Benevolence is not merely a negative affection, but brings forth rich and varied fruits. It produces a feeling of *delight* in the happiness of others, and thus destroys envy; it is the source of *sympathy* and *compassion;* it opens its hand in *liberality* to supply the wants of the needy; it gives *cheerfulness* to every service undertaken in the cause of our fellow-men; it resists the wrong which may be inflicted upon them, and it will run hazards of health and life for their sake. Benevolence has special respect to the *spiritual interests* and *salvation* of men. It instructs, persuades, and reproves the ignorant and vicious; it counsels

* See note at the end of the volume, page 664.

the simple; it comforts the doubting and perplexed; and it rejoices in those gifts and graces of others by which society may be enlightened and purified.

(2.) True Christian benevolence is *disinterested:* "Thou shalt love thy neighbor *as thyself.*" We do not say that it implies an absence of all reference to our own good. A total disregard of our own gratification is obviously impossible; for such a state of feeling would contradict the most active and efficient principles of human nature. But though, strictly and philosophically speaking, benevolence may not divest us of all reference to our own interest, yet it implies those feelings which render our happiness dependent on promoting the happiness of others. To be kind to men simply because they are kind to us, or to alleviate their wants merely because it contributes to our own interest, is not benevolence, but selfishness. "If ye love them which love you," says our Lord, "what thank have ye? for sinners also love those that love them. And if ye do good to them which do good to you, what thank have ye? for sinners also do even the same." Luke vi, 32, 33.

(3.) True benevolence is *unrestricted* in its objects. Disdaining the dictates of a narrow and calculating policy, it inclines us, to the utmost of our ability, to promote the happiness of *all men.* The command is, "Thou shalt love thy *neighbor.*" But who is my neighbor? Doubtless every human being. The charity of the Gospel, therefore, requires us to love every human being, whether he is righteous or unrighteous, whether he is a friend or an enemy. It is this charity alone that can induce a compliance with the Divine injunction, "Love your enemies, bless them that curse you, do good to them that hate you, and pray for them which despitefully use you and persecute you." Matt. v, 44. Unrestricted by the ties of consanguinity, the habits of association, circumstances of locality, or natural sympathy, Christian charity extends its benignant wishes to our entire race. Dissolving the fetters of sectarian bigotry, overleaping the boundaries of political proscription, and renouncing the system of a selfish reciprocity, its aspirations are bounded only by the residence of man.

(4.) Benevolence is *self-sacrificing* and *laborious.* The zeal of apostles, the patience of martyrs, the travels and labors of evangelists in the first ages, were all animated by this affection; and the earnestness of Gospel ministers in all ages, and the labors of private Christians for the benefit of the souls of men, with the operations of those voluntary associations which send forth missionaries to the heathen, or distribute Bibles and tracts, or conduct schools, are all its visible expressions before the world. Except in connection with the religion of the heart, wrought and maintained there by the acknowledged influences of the Holy Spirit, the love of mankind has never exhibited itself under such views and acts as those to which we have just referred. It has never been found in persons *naturally* selfish and obdurate; it has never disposed men to make great and painful sacrifices for others; it has never,sympathized with spiritual wretchedness; it has never been called forth into its highest exercises by considerations drawn from the immortal relations of man to eternity; it has never originated large plans for the illumination and moral culture of society; nor has it ever fixed upon the grand object to which Christian benevolence is now bending the hearts, the interests, and the hopes of the universal Church, *the conversion of the world.*

Unlike circles formed upon the surface of the water, which die away as they recede from the center of their movement, true benevolence acquires strength as the sphere of its operation is enlarged. "Many waters cannot quench love, neither can the floods drown it." "Charity," says the apostle, "never faileth." Possessing an energy which grows with the lapse of time, it operates, even in the agonies of death, with increasing vigor. This attribute of charity was illustriously exemplified in the conduct of the primitive Christians. They hazarded life and every earthly consideration to promote the happiness of their fellowmen. And to many Christian philanthropists of the present day this remark is also applicable. Amid the sufferings of burning climes, the ice and snows of polar regions, and the most savage and inhospitable portions of the earth, they are triumphing over human perversity, and erecting monuments of Christian benevolence which shall endure forever. The plains of India, once whitened with the bones of deluded victims, and the cold and sterile mountains of Greenland and Labrador, in consequence of efforts of this description, now sustain a people who "shall be accounted to the Lord for a generation."

(5.) True benevolence manifests itself in acts of practical *mercy* and *liberality* to the needy and the miserable. This fruit of benevolence is more particularly denominated *charity*, the field for the exercise of which is very extensive. It admits of three general divisions: state charity, Church charity, and individual charity. *State* charity embraces the building and supporting of institutions for the instruction of the mute and the blind, and for the cure and care of the insane, and provision for the education of poor children, and for the relief of the poor and infirm generally. The field for the exercise of *Church* charity is the care and instruction of its own poor, who should never become a charge to other institutions where the Church to which they belong has the most moderate ability to afford them support. Individual or private charity is exercised toward all those objects of commiseration which are not duly provided for by the state or the Church.

The general LAW in regard to this branch of benevolence is express and unequivocal. "He that hath two coats, let him impart to him that hath none; and he that hath meat, let him do likewise." Luke iii, 11. "As we have therefore opportunity, let us do good unto all men, especially unto them who are of the household of faith." Gal. vi, 10. "But to do good, and to communicate, forget not; for with such sacrifices God is well pleased." Heb. xiii, 16. A most important and influential principle, to be found in no mere system of ethics, is also drawn from that relation in which we all stand to God, and on which we must be judged at the last day. We are "*stewards* of the manifold grace of God." We are mere "servants," to whom the great Master has committed his "goods," to be used according to his directions. We have nothing, therefore, of our own; no right in property, except under the conditions on which it is committed to us; and we must give an account for our use of it according to these conditions.

As to the *quantum* of our exertions in doing good to others, it is to be determined by a rule of proportion, as several Scriptures clearly indicate. "For unto whomsoever much is given, of him shall be much required." Luke xii, 48. "For if there be first a willing mind, it is accepted according to that a man hath, and not according to that he hath not." 2 Cor. viii, 12. It is a further rule, that our charities should be both cheerful and abundant. The language of St. Paul to his Corinthian brethren is, "See that ye *abound* in this grace also." 2 Cor. viii, 7. And again, "Every man according as he purposeth in his heart, so let him give; *not grudgingly*, or of necessity; for God loveth a *cheerful* giver." 2 Cor. ix, 7.

The entire neglect to exercise this practical benevolence is highly criminal. It involves a degree of selfishness and inhumanity which is entirely inconsistent with the character of a good man. "Whoso hath this world's goods, and seeth his brother have need, and shutteth up his bowels of compassion from him, how dwelleth the love of God in him?" 1 John iii, 17. For an uncharitable man, therefore, to profess the religion of Christ, is the greatest inconsistency. A religion requiring equal love to our neighbor must, in a world like ours of suffering and sorrow, be a religion of active benevolence. Nor would there be any advantage in being exempt from the claims of charity. Its exercise is no less a benefit to the giver than to the receiver. "He that hath pity upon the poor lendeth unto the Lord; and that which he hath given will he pay him again." Prov. xix, 17. That "it is more blessed to give than to receive," is an inspired sentiment with which the experience of every truly benevolent man accords. The compassionate heart finds not only relief, but a real luxury in the exercise of charity. Nothing can be less a task, or more a privilege.

CHAPTER VIII.

DUTIES TO OUR NEIGHBOR.

HAVING viewed the love of our neighbor in its general character, as a principle of moral action, we come now to consider it in its application to particular duties. The *particular* duties which we owe to our fellow-creatures arise from the various modifications of the social state. These modifications, as recognized in the Scriptures, are the *domestic* and the *political*.

I. DOMESTIC RELATIONS.

That modification of the social state which we call *domestic*, has respect to those relations which grow out of the existence of families, and which are, therefore, called domestic relations. They are the *conjugal*, the *parental*, the *filial*, and the *servile* relations.

1. *The conjugal relation.*—This arises out of the institution of marriage; which is the conjunction of one man and one woman, united by their free vows in a bond made by the Divine law indissoluble, except by death or by adultery. That the conjugal relation is agreeable to the will of God is evident from the existence of the sexes, the feelings of human nature, and the requirements of the Scriptures. The duties which arise from this relation are *fidelity* and *mutual affection*.

(1.) It demands *fidelity*. This duty is urged in the Holy Scriptures with uncommon earnestness. In the dispensation of the moral law, amid thunderings and lightnings, and awful manifestations of Divine power, God uttered the command, "Thou shalt not commit adultery." This crime is uniformly treated in the Scriptures as one of the most atrocious of human vices. "The man," says God, "that committeth adultery with another man's wife, the adulterer and the adulteress shall surely be put to death." Lev. xx, 10. Moreover, according to our Lord's exposition of the spirit of the law, it forbids the indulgence even of lustful desires; and thus the purity of the heart is placed under the guardianship of that hallowed fear which his authority inspires.

That the conjugal relation involves perpetual and inviolable obligations to fidelity, is also evident from our Lord's reply to the question of the Pharisees respecting the lawfulness of divorce. "Have ye not read, that he which made them at the beginning, made them male and female; and said, For this cause shall a man leave father and mother, and shall cleave to his wife; and they twain shall be one flesh? Wherefore they are no more twain, but one flesh. What, therefore, God hath joined together, let no man put asunder." Matt. xix, 4-6. From this and similar passages it is evident, that the man and the woman who enter into the marriage relation become *one, never* to be separated in feeling, in interest, or in pursuits, till death dissolves the nuptial contract. Hence this relation demands the duty,

(2.) *Of mutual affection.*—Those who are united in holy wedlock should have but one feeling, one desire, one effort; and that should have for its object the reciprocation of unfeigned love. To the husband his wife should be his light, his joy, and the object of his most tender solicitude; and to the wife her husband should be her solace, her glory, and the object of her unceasing reverence and affection. "Wives," says the apostle, "submit yourselves unto your own husbands, as unto the Lord. For the husband is the head of the wife, even as Christ is the head of the Church." To husbands his command is, "Love your wives, even as Christ also loved the Church, and gave himself for it." And then he adds, "Let every one of you in particular so love his wife even as himself; and the wife see that she reverence her husband." Eph. v, 22, 23, 25, 33.

2. *The parental relation.*—From this arise the duties of parents in regard to their children. In these duties are comprehended love, support, government, education, and a comfortable settlement in life.

(1.) *Love.*—This, though a natural instinct, is yet to be cultivated by Christians as a duty, which may be done by frequent meditation upon all those important and interesting relations in which Christianity has placed them and their offspring.

(2.) *Support.*—The duty of support and care, even under the most trying circumstances, is imperative upon parents. For, though this is not directly enjoined in so many words, yet it is supposed necessarily to follow from true parental love. To deny either support or care to infants would destroy them, and thus the unnatural parent would be involved in the crime of murder. The duty of giving to children an adequate support is a dictate of humanity, of mercy, and of justice. "If any provide not for his own," says the apostle, "and especially for those of his own house, he hath denied the faith, and is worse than an infidel." 1 Tim. v, 8. The kind of support due to children depends upon the circumstances and abilities of the parents. As in providing for themselves, so in providing for their children their obligations are proportionable to their means. The poor discharge their duty by giving their children the best and most appropriate support they can, and the rich only discharge theirs by doing the same.

(3.) *Government.*—This is another great branch of parental duty, in which both the parents are bound cordially to unite. Like all other kinds of government appointed by God, the end is the good of those subject to it; and it, therefore, excludes all caprice, vexation, and tyranny. In the case of parents it is eminently a government of LOVE; and, therefore, although it includes strictness, it necessarily excludes severity. The mild and benevolent character of our holy religion displays itself here, as in every other instance where the heat of temper, the possession of power, or the ebullitions of passion might be turned against the weak and unprotected. "And ye fathers, provoke not your children to wrath; but bring them up in the nurture and admonition of the Lord." Ephes. vi, 4. Again: "Fathers, provoke not your children to anger, lest they be discouraged." Col. iii, 21.

But though the parental government is founded upon kindness, and can never be separated from it when rightly understood and exercised, yet it is *government*, and must be faithfully discharged. It requires, as its basis, a complete and just system of family laws. These laws ought to be few and simple, and to be such, and such only, as are necessary to the peace and comfort of the family and of each individual. To adopt unnecessary rules is as great a fault as to exclude those which are necessary. A careful distinction should be made between the appropriate sphere of family government and that of advice. Many actions may properly be matters of advice which it would not be expedient to enforce. It is, therefore, an error for parents to command when they ought only to advise, or only to advise when they ought to command.

Family government may be lawfully enforced by the hope of reward and the fear of punishment. The proper reward of obedience is the approbation of the parents. To withhold this from obedient children is both wrong and injurious. It is a deviation from the plan of the Divine government, and consequently from that of infinite wisdom and goodness. A word of approbation, or even a kind look, is often of great use to a child in strengthening its principles of obedience, and is often an ample reward for arduous services.

The proper punishments of disobedience in children are, disapprobation and chastisement with the rod. Disapprobation may be expressed by rebuke or admonition, but not by angry scolding. Fretfulness and scolding are a great disadvantage to family government, and are incompatible with its efficient administration. And, besides, they render persons odious and contemptible, and are entirely destructive of all parental dignity. They are, therefore, improper modes of expressing displeasure.

The ultimate resort in family government is to "the rod of correction" when other means are ineffectual. This is explicitly sanctioned in the Scriptures,* and is fully justified by the general experience of mankind. Yet it may be laid down as a certain principle that where the authority of a parent is exercised with constancy and discretion, and enforced by gravity, kindness, and a suitable dignity of character, this kind of punishment will seldom be found necessary. Nor will it need often to be repeated if the steady resolution of the parent to inflict it when it is demanded by the case is once known to the child.

(4.) *Education.*—This, in the full meaning of the term, implies that

---

* See Prov. x, 13; xiii, 24; xxii, 15; and xxiii, 13, 14.

system of culture, whether public or private, which elicits and improves the capabilities of human nature; which calls into salutary exercise and puts under proper discipline the *intellectual*, the *moral*, and the *animal* faculties of man; and which imparts to him power for the *effective* and *graceful* accomplishment of the several duties which, in the order of Divine Providence, he may be called to perform. Anything less than this, however imposing in its pretensions, falls short of an adequate and finished education. But especially should parents be attentive to the religious training of their children. If they would see them prosper in the present life, if they would wish them to close their earthly career under the blessings of their country and their God, and finally to enjoy the felicity of heaven, they should " bring them up in the nurture and admonition of the Lord." "Train up a child," says Solomon, "in the way he should go, and when he is old he will not depart from it." Prov. xxii, 6.

(5.) Another duty of parents is the *comfortable settlement* of their children in the world as far as their ability extends. This includes the discreet choosing of a calling, by which their children may "provide things honest in the sight of all men;" taking special care, however, that their moral safety shall be consulted in the choice—a consideration which too many disregard under the influence of carelessness or a vain ambition. It is taught, both by nature and by our religion, that parents should lay up for their children. But this duty must not interfere with the rational comforts of a parent according to his rank in life, nor with those charities which Christianity requires.

3. *The filial relation.*—This comprehends the duties of children— a branch of Christian morality which receives both illustration and authority in a very remarkable and peculiar manner from the holy Scriptures. "*Honor* thy father and thy mother," is a precept which was written at first by the finger of God, and is, as the apostle declares, "the first commandment with promise," or to which a promise is annexed. The meaning of the term *honor* is comprehensive, and imports *love, reverence,* and *obedience.*

(1.) *Love.*—This is founded upon esteem and reverence, and comprises gratitude also, no small degree of which is obligatory upon every child for the unwearied cares, labors, and kindness of parental affection. In the few instances in which esteem for a parent can have but little place, gratitude, at least, ought to remain; nor can any case arise in which the obligation of *filial love* can be canceled.

(2.) *Reverence.*—This consists in that honorable esteem of parents which children ought to cherish in their hearts, and from which spring on the one hand the desire to please, and on the other the fear to offend. The fear of a child, however, is opposed to the fear of a slave. The latter has respect chiefly to the *punishment* which may be inflicted; but the former, being mixed with love and the desire to be loved, has respect to the *offense* which may be taken by a parent, his grief, and his displeasure. Hence the fear of God, as a grace of the Spirit in the regenerate, is compared to the fear of children.

This reverential regard due to parents has its external expression in all honor and civility, whether in words or actions. The behavior is to be submissive, and the speech respectful. Reproof is to be borne with meekness, and the impatience of parents sustained in silence. Children are bound to close their eyes as much as possible upon the failings and infirmities of the authors of their being, and always to speak of them in terms of respect. In the duty of honoring parents is also included their support when in necessity. This is clearly to be inferred from the teaching of our Lord. (Matt. xv, 4–6.)

(3.) *Obedience.*—The Divine injunction is, "Children, obey your parents in all things; for this is well-pleasing unto the Lord." Col. iii, 20. This obedience is to be universal, with only one restriction, and that respects the conscience, when children are of an age to judge for themselves. The apostle therefore says, "Children, obey your parents *in the Lord.*" Eph. vi, 1. That the phrase "in the Lord" limits the obedience of children to what is *lawful* is clear from the words of our Lord, "He that loveth father or mother more than me is not worthy of me." Matt. x, 37. In all *lawful* things, however, the rule is absolute; and the obedience of children, like that which we owe to God, ought to be cheerful and unwearied. Should parental injunctions chance to cross their inclinations, this will be no excuse for hesitancy, much less for refusal.

4. *The servile relation.*—This relation, which in one form or other seems to be unavoidable in the social state, involves the reciprocal duties of servants and masters—duties which are prescribed in the New Testament with all necessary explicitness. Let us, then, consider,

(1.) The duties of *servants.*—The relation of masters and servants is nearly allied to that of parents and children, though differing from it in several circumstances; and as government in masters, as well as in parents, is an appointment of God, it is therefore to be duly respected. Hence servants are required, 1. To *fear* their masters. To them the inspired injunction is, "Be obedient to them that are your masters, with *fear and trembling.*" Eph. vi, 5. And again: "Be subject to your masters with all *fear.*" 1 Pet. ii, 18. 2. To *honor* them. "Let as many servants as are under the yoke count their own masters worthy of all *honor.*" 1 Tim. vi, 1. This direction enjoins upon servants, not only the cultivation of respect for their masters, but also propriety of external demeanor toward them. 3. To *obey* them. "Servants, be *obedient* to them that are your masters." Again: "Servants, obey in all things your masters according to the flesh; not with eye-service, as men-pleasers, but in singleness of heart, fearing God. And whatsoever ye do, do it heartily, as to the Lord, and not unto men." Col. iii, 22, 23. The obedience of servants, like that of children, is obligatory only in things that are lawful. But with respect to all lawful commands, they are required to obey their masters *universally*, " in all things ;" *faithfully*, "not with eye-service;" *conscientiously*, "fearing God;" and *cheerfully*, doing " it heartily," with alacrity and good feeling.

The duties of servants, thus briefly stated, might easily be shown to comprehend every particular which can be justly required of persons in this station; and the whole is enforced by a sanction which could have no place but in a revelation from God: " Knowing that whatsoever good thing any man doeth, the same shall he receive of the Lord, whether he be bond or free." Eph. vi, 8. Thus we see that even the common duties of servants, when properly performed, are by Christianity made rewardable actions. But we must consider,

(2.) The duties of *masters*. After the apostle lays down the duties of servants, as above described, he then adds, " And ye masters, do *the same things* unto them;" that is, act toward them upon the same equitable, conscientious, and benevolent principles as you exact from them. But again he says, " Masters, give unto your servants that which is just and equal." Col. iv, 1. The terms *just* and *equal*, though of near affinity, have somewhat different signification. To give that which is *just* to a servant is to deal with him according to contract; but to give him what is *equal* is to render him a full compensation for his service, though it should be more than he could demand on legal principles.

Equity here, however, may have respect particularly to that important rule which obliges us to do to others what we would, in similar circumstances, have them do to us. This rule of equity has a large range in the treatment of servants. It excludes all arbitrary and tyrannical government; it teaches masters to respect the strength and capacity of their servants; it represses rage and passion, contumely and insult; and it directs that their labor shall not be so extended as to deprive them of proper time for rest, for recreation, and for attendance upon the worship of God.

Moreover, when the apostle enjoins it on masters to " forbear threatening," he inculcates the treatment of servants with Christian *kindness* as well as with justice and equity. He then enforces these duties by two weighty considerations. The first is, that masters are held accountable to God for the manner in which they treat their servants—" knowing that your Master also is in heaven." The second is, that in the sight of God masters and servants are equal—" neither is there respect of persons with him."

II. POLITICAL RELATIONS.

That modification of the social state which we call *political* has respect to those relations which grow out of the existence of a community under some form of civil government, and hence they are called political relations.

In all civilized countries the people live under government and laws, but their several modes and forms of government are very different; that is, the power or authority to govern is not always placed in the same class of persons, nor exercised in the same manner. There are three distinct forms of civil government, namely, the *monarchical*, the *aristocratical*, and the *republican*.

A *monarchical* government is one in which the supreme power is lodged in the hands of a single person. A government in which *all* power resides in one person is called an *absolute* monarchy; but if the power of the monarch is restrained by fundamental laws, or by some other power, it is a *limited* monarchy.

An *aristocratical* government is one in which the whole supreme power is vested in a few persons of rank and wealth. When the supreme power is exercised by a *very* small number the government is called an *oligarchy*, which term, however, is usually applied to a corrupted form of aristocracy.

A *republican* government is one in which the supreme power is lodged in the hands of the people collectively, or in which the people exercise the powers of legislation by their representatives. Such is the government of the United States of America.

That God intended men to live in society can hardly be doubted. The very laws which he has given them, prescribing their relative duties, assume the permanent existence of social relations, and, therefore, place them under regulation; and from this fact the Divine appointment of government flows as a necessary consequence. A society cannot exist without rules or laws, and it therefore follows that such laws must be upheld by enforcement. Hence an *executive* power in some form must arise to guard, to judge, to reward, to punish. For, if laws were not executed they would become a dead-letter, and, therefore, be the same as none at all.

But we are not left to mere inference. In the first ages of the world government was paternal, and the power of government was vested in parents by the express appointment of God. Among the Jews rulers, judges, and kings were also appointed by God himself; and as for all other nations the New Testament expressly declares that "the powers which be are ordained of God." The origin of power is not, therefore, from man, but from God; and hence it is not left to men as a matter of choice whether they will be governed or not.

But though government is of Divine authority, it appears to be left to men to judge in what FORM its purposes may, in certain circumstances, be most effectually accomplished, since no direction is given on this subject in the Scriptures. It is, therefore, the right of a majority of the people concerned to decide what that *form* shall be.

Civil government necessarily implies two parties, the governing and the governed; and involves, therefore, reciprocal duties correspondent to this relation. We will direct our attention,

1. *To the duties of those who govern.*—In all well-constructed governments the civil power is divided into three departments, which are separated from one another and administered by different persons. These are denominated the *legislative*, the *judicial*, and the *executive*. The *legislative* department is that by which the laws of the state are made; the *judicial*, that which declares and applies them; and the *executive*, that which executes them.

The duties of the sovereign power, whatever the form of government may be, are the enactment of just and equal laws,—the mild but impartial execution of those laws, the protection and sustenance of the poor and helpless, the maintenance of domestic peace, and, as far as the interests of the community will allow, of peace with all nations; the faithful observance of all treaties, an incessant application to the cares of government, without exacting more tribute from the people than is necessary for the real wants of the state, and the honorable maintenance of its officers, the appointment of inferior magistrates of probity and fitness, with a diligent and strict oversight of them; and finally, the encouragement of industry, learning, morality, and the religion of the Holy Scriptures.

These obligations are either plainly expressed, or clearly implied in such passages as the following: "The God of Israel said, the Rock of Israel spake to me, He that ruleth over men must be just, ruling in the fear of God." 2 Sam. xxiii, 3. "Ye shall do no unrighteousness in judgment; thou shalt not respect the person of the poor, nor honor the person of the mighty; but in righteousness shalt thou judge thy neighbor." Lev. xix, 15. "Moreover, thou shalt provide out of all the people able men, such as fear God, men of truth, hating covetousness; and place such over them, to be rulers of thousands, and rulers of hundreds, rulers of fifties, and rulers of tens; and let them judge the people at all seasons." Exod. xviii, 21, 22.

The New Testament directions, though expressed generally, are equally comprehensive; and it is worthy of remark, that while they assert the Divine ordination of "the powers that be," they explicitly mark out for what *ends* they were thus appointed, and allow, therefore, of no plea of Divine right in rulers for anything contrary to them. "For rulers are not a terror to *good works*, but to *the evil*. Wilt thou then not be afraid of the power? do that which is *good* and thou shalt have *praise* of the same; for he is the minister of God to thee *for good*. But if thou do that which is evil, be afraid; for he beareth not the sword in vain; for he is the minister of God, a revenger to execute wrath *upon him that doeth evil*." Rom. xiii, 3, 4. Submit yourselves to every ordinance of man for the Lord's sake; whether it be to the king, as supreme, or unto governors, as unto them that are sent by him for the punishment of *evil doers*, and for the praise of them that *do well.*" 1 Peter ii, 13, 14.

2. *The duties of the governed.*—In the preceding passages, which state the legitimate *ends* of government, the duties of subjects are partially anticipated; but they are capable of a fuller enumeration. These duties are,

(1.) *Patriotism*, or the love of our country.—This species of love is analogous to that of children toward the family. The obligation of citizens to love their country arise from their relations to it, as the objects of its protection, and the subjects of numerous distinguished benefits. Our country is one of the most important and influential agents in the promotion of our prosperity and happiness. Its benefiical agency commences with the protection of our infancy, and continues, in one unremitting stream of benefits, till the latest period of life. It protects our persons and our property. It adopts measures for the encouragement of industry and enterprise, and for the widest possible diffusion of wealth, learning, virtue, and religion. In respect to these and other blessings our country is our parent and friend, and as such it ought to be regarded and loved. Especially are citizens of the United States under obligations to love their country. The blessings which it confers upon them are immense and innumerable; and these benefits demand a return of gratitude and love proportionable to their number and magnitude.

(2.) *Obedience* to civil laws.—These are the rules of action which are prescribed by the proper authority of the state, and which are supposed to have for their *end* the protection of life, liberty, and property, the encouragement of industry and enterprise, and the promotion of general prosperity and happiness. The duty of obedience to all such laws is explicitly enjoined in the Scriptures. "Let every soul," says St. Paul, " be subject unto the higher powers. For there is no power but of God. The powers that be, are ordained of God. Whosoever, therefore, resisteth the power, resisteth the ordinance of God; and they that resist shall receive to themselves damnation." Rom. xiii, 1, 2. The language of Peter is, " Submit yourselves to every ordinance of man for the Lord's sake; whether it be to the king, as supreme, or unto governors, as unto them that are sent by him for the punishment of evil doers, and for the praise of them that do well." 1 Peter ii, 13, 14.

In these passages the duty of obedience to civil authority is clearly and strongly stated, and is therefore a matter of Divine injunction. Its necessity, however, is equally obvious from the nature of the case. For, without obedience to civil law, there could be no civil government; and without civil government, we could enjoy none of the blessings of civilized life. But this law of obedience and submission to " the powers that be," though general and indispensable, has legitimate exceptions. When civil laws command what God forbids, or forbid what he commands, they are not obligatory. When a higher and a lower authority have legitimate jurisdiction, they are both to be respected as far as practicable. But where obedience to both is impossible from their commanding opposite and inconsistent actions, the higher authority alone is to be respected. God's authority is the highest in the universe; and his laws are, therefore, to be obeyed in all cases, human laws to the contrary notwithstanding. This principle is fully established by inspired authority when the apostles declare, "We ought to obey God rather than men." Acts v, 29. It is also exemplified in the case of Daniel and his three companions, and in that of the early Christian martyrs.

(3.) *Pecuniary supplies* for the necessities of government.—As no civil government can be conducted without considerable expense, it becomes the duty of citizens, for whose benefit government exists, to contribute what is necessary for its successful operation. Justice demands that all the necessary agents of government should be liberally rewarded for their faithful services. "For," says the apostle, "for this cause pay you tribute also; for they are God's ministers, attending continually upon this very thing. Render, therefore, to all their dues; tribute to whom tribute is due; custom to whom custom." Rom. xiii, 6, 7.

(4.) *Respect* and *reverence* for rulers.—"It is written, Thou shalt not speak evil of the ruler of thy people." Acts xxiii, 5. "Curse not the king," says Solomon, "no, not in thy thought." Eccl. x, 20. St. Paul teaches us that in rendering to all their dues we must render "fear to whom fear" is due; "honor to whom honor." St. Jude lays it down as characteristic of the ungodly that they "despise dominion, and speak evil of dignities." Rulers are therefore to be duly honored, both by external marks of respect and by being maintained in dignity. Their actions are to be judged of with candor and charity; and when questioned or blamed this is to be done with moderation, and not with invective or ridicule—a mode of speaking evil of dignities which grossly offends against the Christian rule.

(5.) *Prayer* for those in authority and for our country in general.—"I exhort therefore, that, first of all, supplications, prayers, intercessions, and giving of thanks, be made for all men; for kings, and for all that are in authority; that we may lead a quiet and peaceable life, in all godliness and honesty. For this is good and acceptable in the sight of God our Saviour." 1 Tim. ii, 1–3.

This holy and salutary practice is founded upon a recognition of the fact that government is the ordinance of God; and also, that the existing powers in every place are God's ministers. It supposes that all public affairs are under the Divine control; it reminds men of the arduous duties and responsibilities of governors; it prompts a benevolent, grateful, and respectful feeling toward them; and it is a powerful guard against a factious and seditious spirit. These are so evidently the principles and tendencies of this sacred custom that when prayer has been used, as it sometimes has, to convey the feelings of a malignant, factious, or light spirit, every well-disposed mind must have been shocked at so profane a mockery.

BOOK VI.

THE INSTITUTIONS OF CHRISTIANITY.

Since Christ has established a Church in the world, by means of which revealed truth is to be maintained, and the Gospel preached "to every creature;" and since he has ordained that certain religious rites shall be observed by all who become members of his Church, it is necessary that we should inquire into the nature of this religious organization, and of the peculiar rites by which it is distinguished.

CHAPTER I.

THE CHRISTIAN CHURCH.

The Church of Christ, in its largest sense, consists of all who have been baptized in the name of Christ, and have thereby made a public profession of faith in his Divine mission, and in all the doctrines of the Gospel. In a stricter sense it consists of those who are vitally united to Christ as members of his body, and who, being thus imbued with spiritual life, walk no longer "after the flesh, but after the Spirit." Taken in either view it is a visible society, bound to observe the laws of Christ, its only Head and Lord.

Visible fellowship with this Church is the duty of all who profess faith in Christ; for in this in part consists that confession of Christ before men on which so much stress is laid in the discourses of our Lord. It is obligatory on all who are convinced of the truth of Christianity to be baptized, and upon all thus baptized frequently to partake of the Lord's Supper, in order to testify their continued faith in Christ as the Redeemer of the world by his sufferings and death; both of which suppose union with the Church.

The ends of this fellowship or association are, to proclaim our faith in the doctrines of Christ as being Divine in their origin and necessary to salvation; to offer public prayers and thanksgivings to God through

Christ as the only Mediator; to hear God's word expounded and enforced; and to place ourselves under that discipline which consists in the enforcement of the laws of Christ upon the members, not merely by general exhortation, but by kind oversight and personal injunction and admonition of its ministers. All these flow from the original obligation to avow our faith in Christ and our love to him.

The Church in Christ, then, being a visible and permanent society, bound to observe certain rites and certain rules, the existence of government in it is necessarily supposed. All religious rites suppose ORDER, all order DIRECTION and CONTROL, and these a DIRECTING and CONTROLLING POWER. Again, all laws are nugatory without enforcement in the present mixed and imperfect state of society; and all enforcement of law supposes an EXECUTIVE. Thus government follows necessarily from the very nature of the institution of the Christian Church. And since this institution has the authority of Christ and his apostles, it is not to be supposed that they left its government unprovided for; and if they have in fact made such a provision, it is no more a matter of mere option with Christians whether they will be subject to government in the Church, than it is optional with them to confess Christ by becoming its members.

In this chapter there are four points to be examined: 1. The *nature* of this government; 2. The *persons* to whom it is committed; 3. The *share* which the *body of the people* have in their own government; and, 4. The *ends* to which Church authority is legitimately directed.

I. THE NATURE OF CHURCH GOVERNMENT.

As to the *nature* of Church government it is wholly *spiritual.* "My kingdom," says Christ, "is not of this world." This characteristic of the government of the Church is manifest,

1. From the fact that *it is concerned only with spiritual objects.*—The Church is a society founded upon faith, and united by mutual love for the personal edification of its members in holiness, and for the religious benefit of the world. It cannot employ force to compel men into its pale, for the only door of the Church is faith, to which there can be no compulsion. He who believes in Christ, and confesses him in the ordinance of baptism, becomes a member of the Church according to its original constitution. But that the government of the Church is purely of a spiritual nature is further evident,

2. *From the nature of its punitive discipline.*—It cannot inflict pains and penalties upon the disobedient and refractory like civil governments, for the only punitive discipline authorized in the New Testament is comprised in admonition, reproof, sharp rebukes, and, finally, excision from the society. The last will be better understood if we consider the special relations in which true Christians stand to each other, and the duties resulting from them. They are members of one body, and are, therefore, bound to tenderness and sympathy. They are the

conjoint instructors of others, and are, therefore, to strive to be of "one judgment." They are brethren, and they are bound to love one another *as such ;* that is, with an affection more special than that general goodwill which they are commanded to bear to all mankind. They are, therefore, to seek the intimacy of friendly society among themselves, and, except in the ordinary and courteous intercourse of life, they are bound to keep themselves separate from the world. They are enjoined to do good to all men, but "specially to them that are of the household of faith." They are forbidden "to eat" at the Lord's table with those who dishonor their Christian profession by immoral conduct.

With these relations of Christians to one another and to the world, and their correspondent duties before our minds, we may easily interpret the nature of that extreme discipline which is vested in the Church. Persons who will not hear the Church are to be held as heathen men and publicans, as those who are not members of it; that is, they are to be separated from it, and to be regarded as of the world. But still, like heathen men and publicans, they are to be the objects of pity and general benevolence.

Nor is this extreme discipline to be hastily inflicted before a "first and second admonition," nor before attempts are made to restore the brother who may "be overtaken in a fault;" and when the "wicked person" is "put away," still the door is to be kept open for his reception again upon repentance. The true excommunication of the Christian Church is, therefore, a merciful and considerate separation of an incorrigible offender from the body of Christians without any infliction of civil pains or penalties.*

II. THE PERSONS TO WHOM THE GOVERNMENT OF THE CHURCH IS COMMITTED.

In regard to this point it is necessary to consider the composition of the primitive Church as stated in the New Testament. Here it is evident that the great body of believers comprehended both officers and private members, and that the government of the Church mainly devolved upon the former. Let us then consider,

1. *The distinctive offices to which men were appointed in the primitive Church.*—Of these we have full information in Ephesians iv, 11, 12: "And he gave some, apostles; and some, prophets; and some, evangelists; and some, pastors and teachers; for the perfecting of the saints, for the work of the ministry, for the edifying of the body of Christ."

Of these the office of *apostle* is allowed by all to have been confined to those who were immediately commissioned by Christ to witness the fact of his miracles and of his resurrection from the dead, and to reveal the complete system of Christian doctrine and duty, confirming their extraordinary mission by miracles wrought by themselves.

If by *prophets* we are to understand persons who foretold future

* See 1 Cor. v, 5, 11; 2 Thess. iii, 6.

events, then the office was, from its very nature, extraordinary, and the gift of prophecy has passed away with the other miraculous endowments of the first age of Christianity. If, with others, we understand that these prophets were extraordinary teachers, raised up until the Churches were settled under permanent qualified instructors, still the office was temporary.

The *evangelists* are generally understood to be assistants of the apostles, who acted under their especial authority and direction. Of this number were Timothy and Titus; and as the Apostle Paul directed them to ordain bishops or presbyters in the several Churches, but gave them no authority to ordain successors to themselves in their particular office as evangelists, it is clear that the evangelists must also be reckoned among the number of extraordinary and temporary ministers suited to the first age of Christianity.

Whether by "*pastors* and *teachers*" two offices are meant, or only one, has been disputed; but the point is of little consequence. A pastor was a teacher; but teachers were not all necessarily pastors, for in many cases they were confined to the office of subordinate instruction, whether as expounders of doctrine, catechists, or even more private instructors of those who were unacquainted with the first principles of the Gospel of Christ. The term pastor implies the duties both of instruction and government, of feeding and of ruling the flock of Christ; and as presbyters or bishops were ordained in the several Churches, both by the apostles and evangelists, and rules are left by St. Paul as to their appointment, there can be no doubt that these are the pastors spoken of in Ephesians, that they were designed to be the permanent ministers of the Church, and that with them both the government of the Church and the performance of its leading religious services were deposited. Deacons had the charge of the gifts and offerings for charitable purposes, though, as appears from Justin Martyr, not in every instance; for he speaks of the weekly oblations as being deposited with the chief minister, and distributed by him.

Whether bishops and presbyters are the same in office, or whether these appellatives express two distinct sacred orders, is a subject which has been warmly controverted by Episcopalians and Presbyterians. Without pretending to engage in this controversy to any considerable length, it may be proper to offer the following remarks:

(1.) The argument which is drawn from the promiscuous use of these terms in the New Testament to prove that the same *order* of ministers is expressed by them appears to be incontrovertible. When St. Paul, for instance, sends for the elders or presbyters of the Church at Ephesus to meet him at Miletus, he thus charges them: "Take heed to yourselves, and to all the flock, over the which the Holy Ghost hath made you overseers" or bishops. That the elders or presbyters are here called bishops cannot be denied; and the very office assigned to them, to "feed the Church of God," and the injunction, to "take heed to the *flock*," show that the office of elder or presbyter is the same as that of *pastor* in the passage quoted from Ephesians.

Again, St. Paul directs Titus to "ordain elders (*presbyters*) in every city," and then adds, as a directory to ordination, "a *bishop* must be blameless," etc., plainly marking the same office by these two convertible appellations. "Bishops and deacons" are the only classes of ministers addressed in the Epistle to the Philippians; and if the presbyters were not understood to be included under the term bishop, the omission of any notice of this order of ministers is not to be accounted for. As the apostles, when not engaged in their own extraordinary vocation, appear to have filled the office of stated ministers in those Churches in which they occasionally resided for a considerable time, they sometimes called themselves presbyters. "The elder (*presbyter*) unto the elect lady." 2 John i, 1. "The elders (*presbyters*) which are among you I exhort, who am also an elder," (*presbyter*.) 2 Peter v, 1.

The highest offices of teaching and government in the Church were vested in the Presbyters. "*Feed* the flock of God, which is among you, taking the *oversight* thereof." There is, therefore, the most conclusive evidence from the New Testament, that, after the extraordinary ministry vested in the apostles, prophets, and evangelists had ceased, the teaching and government of the Church devolved upon an order of men indiscriminately called pastors, presbyters, and bishops, the two latter names growing into most frequent use.

(2.) It is not indeed to be doubted, that, at a very early period, in some instances probably from the time of the apostles themselves, a distinction arose between bishops and presbyters; in which fact lies the whole strength of the cause of Episcopalians. Still this gives not the least sanction to the notion, that bishops are a superior *order* of ministers to presbyters, invested in virtue of that order, and by Divine right, with powers to govern both presbyters and people, and with exclusive authority to ordain to the sacred offices of the Church. As little, too, will that ancient distinction prove anything in favor of diocesan episcopacy, which is of still later introduction.

(3.) As to the argument from the succession of bishops from the times of the apostles, could the fact be made out, it would only trace diocesan bishops to the bishops of parishes; those, to the bishops of single churches; and bishops of a supposed superior order, to bishops who never thought themselves more than presiding presbyters, *primi inter pares*. This, therefore, would only show that an unscriptural assumption of distinct orders has been made, which that succession, if established, would refute. But the succession itself is imaginary.

(4.) Whether episcopacy may not be a matter of prudential regulation is another question. We think it often may; and that Churches are quite at liberty to adopt this mode, provided they maintain St.

Jerome's distinction, that "bishops are greater than presbyters rather by custom than by appointment of the Lord, and that still the Church ought to be governed in common," that is, by bishops and presbyters united. It was on this ground that Luther placed episcopacy, as useful, though not of Divine right. It was by admitting this liberty in Churches that Calvin and others allowed episcopacy and diocesan Churches to be lawful, there being nothing in Scripture to forbid such an arrangement when placed on the ground of expediency. Indeed, some divines of the English Church have chosen to defend its episcopacy wholly upon this ground, as alone tenable; and, admitting that it is safest to approach as near as possible to primitive practice, have proposed the restoration of presbyters as a senate to the bishops, the contraction of dioceses, the placing of bishops in all great towns, and the holding of provincial synods, thus raising the presbyters to their original rank, as the bishop's "*compresbyters*," as Cyprian calls them, both in government and ordination.

The only scriptural objection to episcopacy, as it is understood in modern times, is its assumption of superiority of *order*, and of an exclusive right to govern the pastors as well as the flock, and to ordain to the Christian ministry. These exclusive powers are nowhere granted to bishops in distinction from presbyters. The government of pastors as well as people was at first in the assembly of presbyters, to which ruling body all were individually accountable. As to ordination, it was a right in each presbyter, though used by several together for better security; and even when the presence of a bishop came to be thought necessary to its validity, presbyters were not excluded.

Having ascertained who are the proper persons to administer the government of the Church, let us direct our attention,

2. *To the* CHURCH *itself*, the body to be governed.—On this subject various and opposite opinions have been held, from that of the Papists, who contend for its visible unity throughout the world under a visible head, to that of the Independents, who consider the universal Church as composed of congregational Churches, each perfect in itself, and entirely independent of every other. Here we remark,

(1.) The opinion of the Papists is contradicted by the language of the apostles, who, while they teach that there is but one Church composed of believers throughout the world, think it not at all inconsistent with this to speak of " the Churches of Judea," " the Churches of Galatia," " the seven Churches which are in Asia," and " the Church at Ephesus." The apostles, among themselves, had no common head; but planted Churches and gave directions for their government, in most cases without any apparent correspondence with each other. The popish doctrine is certainly not found in their writings; and so far were they from making provision for the government of this one supposed Church, by the appointment of one visible head, that they provided for the government of the respective Churches raised up by them in a totally different manner, that is, by the ordination of ministers for each Church, who were indifferently called bishops, presbyters, and pastors.

The only unity of which the apostles speak is the unity of the whole Church in Christ, the invisible head, by faith; and the unity produced by the "fervent charity" of the members toward one another. Nor has the popish doctrine any countenance from antiquity. The best ecclesiastical historians have shown that the Christian Churches were independent of one another during the greater part of the second century, and that no very large association of Churches existed till toward its close. These facts sufficiently refute the papal argument from antiquity.

(2.) The independence of the early Christian Churches was not, however, the same as that of the Churches which in modern times are called independent. During the life of the apostles and evangelists they were certainly subject to their counsel and control, which proves that the independency of separate societies was not the first form of the Church. It may be allowed that some of the smaller and more insulated Churches might, after the death of the apostles and evangelists, have retained this form for some considerable time; but the large Churches in the chief cities, and those planted in populous neighborhoods, had many presbyters, and as the members multiplied they had several separate assemblies or congregations, yet all under the same common government. And when Churches were raised up in the neighborhood of cities, the appointment of *chorepiscopi*, or country bishops, and of visiting presbyters, both acting under the presbytery of the city, with its bishop at its head, is sufficiently in proof that the ancient Churches, especially the larger and more prosperous of them, existed in that form which in modern times we should call a religious connection, subject to a common government.

Having shown that the persons appointed to feed and govern the Church of Christ are those who in the New Testament are called *pastors*, a word which at once imports both *care* and *government*, we will proceed to consider,

III. THE SHARE WHICH THE BODY OF THE PEOPLE HAVE IN THEIR OWN GOVERNMENT.

In the investigation of this point it will be necessary, *first*, to make a few remarks in regard to the general principles of Church associations; and, *secondly*, to apply these principles to particular cases. And,

1. The only view in which the New Testament writers regarded the Churches was that of associations founded on conviction of the truth of Christianity, and the obligatory nature of the commands of Christ. They considered the pastors as dependent for their support on the free contributions of the people, and the people as bound to sustain, love, and obey them in all scriptural requirements; and, in things indifferent,

to pay them a respectful deference. But if any of the pastors or teachers erred in doctrine, the people were commanded not "to receive them," to "turn away" from them, and not even to bid them "god speed." The rule which forbids Christians "to eat," that is, to communicate with an immoral "brother," held good, of course, when that brother was a pastor. Thus pastors were put under the influence of the public opinion of the Churches; and the remedy of separating from them, in manifest defections of doctrine and morals, was afforded to the sound members of a Church, where no power existed able or inclined to silence the offending pastor and his party.

2. A perfect religious liberty is always supposed by the apostles to exist among Christians. No compulsion of the civil power is anywhere assumed by them as the basis of their advices or directions; no binding of the members of one Church, without liberty to join another, by any ties but those involved in moral considerations, of sufficient weight, however, to prevent the evils of action and schism. It was this which created a natural and competent check upon the ministers of the Church, for being only sustained by the opinion of the Churches, they could not but have respect to it; and it was this which gave to the sound part of a fallen Church the advantage of renouncing, upon sufficient and well-weighed grounds, their communion with it, and of kindling up the light of a pure ministry and a holy discipline by forming a separate association, bearing its testimony against errors in doctrine and failures in practice.

3. It is also an important general observation that, in settling the government of a Church, there are pre-existent laws of Christ, which it is not in the option of any to receive or reject. Under whatever form the governing power is arranged, it is bound to execute all the rules left by Christ and his apostles as to doctrine, worship, the sacraments, and discipline; nor is it at liberty to take that office, or to continue to exercise it, if by any restrictions imposed upon it it is prevented from carrying these laws into effect. Government in the Church, as well as in the state, is an ordinance of God; and as it is imperative upon rulers in the state to be "a terror to evil-doers, and a praise to them that do well," so also is it imperative upon the rulers of the Church to banish strange doctrines, to uphold God's ordinances, to reprove and rebuke evil-doers, and, finally, to put them away.

The spirit in which this is to be done is also prescribed. It is to be done in the spirit of meekness, and with long-suffering; but the work must be done upon the responsibility of the pastors to Him who has commissioned them for this purpose, and they have a right to require from the people that in this office and ministry they should not only not be obstructed, but affectionately and zealously aided, as ministering in these duties, sometimes painful, not for themselves, but for the good of the whole.

With respect to the members of a Church, the same remark is applicable as to the members of a state. It is not a matter of option with them whether they will be under government according to the laws of Christ or not, for that is imperative; government in both cases being of Divine appointment. They have, on the other hand, the right to full security that they shall be governed by the laws of Christ; and they have a right to establish as many guards against human infirmity and passion in those who are " set over them " as may be prudently devised, provided these are not carried to such an extent as to be obstructive to the legitimate scriptural discharge of their duties. The true view of the case appears to be, that the government of the Church is in its pastors, open to various modifications as to form, and that it is to be conducted with such a concurrence of the people as shall constitute a sufficient guard against abuse, and yet not prevent the legitimate and efficient exercise of pastoral duties, as these duties are stated in the Scriptures.

This original authority in the pastors and concurrent consent in the people, as exhibited in these general principles, may be thus applied to particular cases:

(1.) *As to the ordination of ministers.*—It will be evident, if we consult the New Testament, that the power of ordination was never conveyed by the people. The apostles were ordained by our Lord, the evangelists by the apostles, and the elders in every Church both by apostles and evangelists. Nothing is clearer in the New Testament than that all the candidates for the ministry were judged of by those who had been placed in that office themselves, and that from them they received their ordination. So also, after the death of the apostles and evangelists, the presbyters of the Church continued to exercise this prerogative.

In the time of the apostles, who were endowed with special gifts, the concurrence of the people in the appointment of men to the sacred office was not, perhaps, always formally taken; but the directions to Timothy and Titus imply a reference to the judgment of the members of the Church, because from them only it could be learned whether the party fixed upon for ordination possessed those qualifications without which ordination was prohibited. When Churches assumed a more regular form, it was usual for the people to be present at ordinations and to ratify the action by their approbation. Sometimes also they nominated persons by suffrages, and thus proposed them for ordination. The mode in which the people shall be made a concurrent party is matter of prudential regulation; but they had an early, and certainly a reasonable right to a voice in the appointment of their ministers, though the power of ordination was vested in ministers alone, to be exercised on their responsibility to Christ.

(2.) *As to the laws by which the* Church is to be governed.—So far as these are expressly laid down in the word of God the rulers of a Church are bound to execute them, and the people to obey them. They cannot be matter of compact on either side, except as the subject of a mutual and solemn engagement to be governed by them, without any modification or appeal to any other standard.

Every Church declares in some way how it understands the doctrine and the disciplinary laws of Christ. This declaration as to doctrine, in modern times, is usually made by confessions or articles of faith; in which, if fundamental error is found, the evil rests upon the head of that Church collectively, and upon the members individually. For men are bound to try all doctrines by the holy Scriptures, nor can any one support an acknowledged system of error without guilt.

The disciplinary laws of Christ relate to the manner in which a Church provides for public worship, the publication of the Gospel, the administration of the sacraments, the instruction of the ignorant, the succor of the distressed, the admonition of the disorderly, and the excision of offenders. On all these points the New Testament has issued express injunctions. The declaration of a Church on the subject of discipline consists, therefore, in its declared interpretation of these injunctions; but it interprets them on its own collective responsibility and that of its members.

When persons unite with a Church which is acknowledged to be substantially correct in its interpretation of doctrine and moral discipline, they bind themselves, by this very act, to comply with the original terms of the communion into which they enter. They have, therefore, as to the doctrines and disciplinary laws of Christ which are to be preached and enforced, no rights of control over ministers which shall prevent, in these respects, the just exercise of their office. They have a right to such regulations and checks as shall secure, in the best possible way, the just and faithful exercise of that office and the honest and impartial use of that power; but this is the limit of their right, and every system of suffrage or popular concurrence which, under pretense of guarding against abuse of ministerial authority, makes its exercise *absolutely* and in *all cases* dependent upon the consent of those over whom it extends, goes beyond that limit and invades that right of pastoral government which the New Testament has established.

(3.) *As to those disciplinary regulations which are subsidiary to the great ends of scriptural communion*, they are matters of mutual agreement, and may be modified by the mutual consent of ministers and people under their common responsibility to Christ, provided they are in harmony with the Scriptures and promotive of the welfare of the Church. To all such regulations the consent of the people is necessary in order to confidence and harmony, and to a proper security for good and orderly government. This consent of the people may be given either tacitly, by their adoption of the regulations in question, or more expressly by the approval of those who, from their age, wisdom, and influence, or from special appointment, are their proper representatives. In this method of bringing in the concurrence of the people, all assemblages of whole societies, or of very large portions of them, are avoided—a popular form of Church government which, however it might be modified so as to accord with the scriptural authority of ministers, could only be tolerable in very small societies, and that in the times of their greatest simplicity and love.

To raise into legislators and censors *all* the members of a Church, the young, the ignorant, and the inexperienced, is to do them great injury. It is the sure way to foster debates, contentions, and self-confidence, to open the door to intrigue and policy, to tempt forward and conceited men to become a kind of religious demagogues, and entirely to destroy the salutary influence of the aged, experienced, and gifted members by placing all that is good, and venerable, and dear to the Church at the feet of a democracy.

(4.) *As to the power of admission into the Church*, that is clearly with ministers. To them is committed the office of baptism, by which the door is opened into the Church universal; and as there can be no visible communion kept up with the universal Church, except by communion with some particular Church, the admission into that particular communion must be in the hands of ministers. But the members of a Church, though they have no right to obstruct the just exercise of this power, have the right to prevent its being unworthily exercised; and their concurrence with the admission of members, in one way or other, is an arrangement supported by analogies drawn from the New Testament and from primitive usages.

The expulsion of unworthy members devolves upon ministers for this reason, that, as "shepherds" of the flock under the "Chief Shepherd," they are charged to carry his laws into effect. These laws it is neither with them nor with the people to modify; they are already declared by superior authority; but the determination of the facts of the case to which they are applied is matter of mutual investigation and decision, in order to prevent an erring or improper exercise of authority. That such an investigation should take place, not before the assembled members of a society, but before a proper and select tribunal, appears to be a regulation which is both proper and necessary.

The trial of unworthy ministers remains to be noticed. This, wherever a number of religious societies exist as one Church, having therefore many pastors, is manifestly most safely placed in the hands of those pastors themselves; not only because the official acts of censure and exclusion lie with them, but also for other reasons. It can scarcely happen that a minister should be under accusation, except in some very particular cases, but that, from his former influence, some faction would be found to support him. In proportion to the ardor of this feeling, the other party would be excited to undue severity and bitterness. To try such a case before a whole society there would not only be the same objection as in the case of private members, but the additional one that parties would be more certainly formed, and be still more violent. If he must be arraigned, then, before some tribunal, the most fitting is that of his brethren, provided the accusing party has the right to bring on such a trial upon the exhibition of probable evidence, and to prosecute it without obstruction.

The preceding remarks contain only a mere sketch of those principles of Church government which appear to be contained in the New Testament, or to be suggested by it. They still leave much liberty to Christians to adapt them in detail to the circumstances in which they are placed. The offices to be created; the meetings necessary for the management of the various affairs of the Church, spiritual and financial; the assembling of ministers in larger or smaller numbers for counsel, and for the oversight of each other and of the Churches to which they belong, are all matters of this kind, and are left to the suggestions of wisdom and piety. The extent to which distinct societies of Christians shall associate in one Church, under a common government, appears also to be a matter of prudence and of circumstances.

IV. THE ENDS TO WHICH CHURCH AUTHORITY IS LEGITIMATELY DIRECTED.

These *ends*, which we will briefly consider, are of the highest importance to mankind. They are,

1. *The preservation and publication of " sound doctrine."*—Against false doctrines, and the men " of corrupt minds" who taught them, the sermons of Christ and the writings of the apostles abound in cautions. And since St. Paul lays it down as a rule as to erring teachers that "their mouths must be stopped," it is evidently implied that the power of declaring what sound doctrine is and of silencing false teachers was confided by the apostles to the Christian Church. The abuse of this power by the ambition of man forms no small part of that antichristian usurpation which characterizes the Church of Rome. But extravagant as are her claims, so that she brings in her traditions as of equal authority with the inspired writings, and denies to men the right of private judgment and of trying her dogmas by the test of the Holy Scriptures, there is nevertheless a sober sense in which this power may be understood.

The great Protestant principle, that the Holy Scriptures are the only standard of doctrine, that the doctrines of every Church must be proved out of them; and that every individual member has a right to bring them to this standard, in order to the confirmation of his own faith, must be held inviolate, if we would not see Divine authority displaced by human. But since men may come to different conclusions in regard to the meaning of Scripture, it has been the practice from primitive times to declare the sense in which Scripture is understood by collective assemblies of ministers, and by the Churches united with them, in order to the enforcement of such interpretations upon Christians generally, by the influence of learning, piety, numbers, and solemn deliberation.

While one of the apostles lived, an appeal could be made to him when any new doctrine sprung up in the Church. After their death, smaller or larger councils, composed of the public teachers of the Churches, were resorted to, that they might pronounce upon these differences of opinion, and by their authority confirm the faithful and silence the propagators of error. Still later, four councils, called general, from the number of persons assembled in them from various parts of Christendom, have peculiar eminence: the Council of Nice in the fourth century, which condemned the Arian heresy, and formed that scriptural and important formulary called the Nicene Creed; the Council of Constantinople, held at the end of the same century, which condemned the errors of Macedonius, and asserted the divinity and personality of the Holy Ghost; and the Councils of Ephesus and Chalcedon, about the middle of the fifth century, which censured the opinions of Nestorius and Eutyches. The decisions of these councils, both from their antiquity and from the manifest conformity of their decisions on these points to the Holy Scriptures, have been received to this day in what have been called the orthodox Churches throughout the world.

This authority of a Church in matters of doctrine appears to be reduced to the following particulars, which, though directly opposed to the assumptions of the Church of Rome, are of great importance:

(1.) To declare the sense in which it interprets the language of Scripture on all the leading doctrines of Christianity; for to contend, as some have done, that no creeds or articles of faith are proper, but that belief in the Scriptures only ought to be required, would be to destroy all doctrinal distinctions, since all interpreters profess to believe the Scriptures.

(2.) To require from all its members, with whom the right of private judgment is by all Protestant Churches left inviolate, to examine such declarations of faith, with modesty and proper respect to those grave and learned assemblies in which all these points have been weighed with deliberation; receiving them as guides to truth, not implicitly, it is true, but still with docility and humility.

(3.) To silence within its own pale the preaching of all doctrines contrary to its received standards. Nor is there anything in the exercise of this authority contrary to Christian liberty; because the members of any communion, and especially the ministers, know beforehand the terms of fellowship with the Churches whose confessions of faith are thus made public; and because also, where conscience is unfettered by public law, they are neither prevented from enjoying their own opinions in peace, nor from propagating them in other assemblies.

2. *The forming of such regulations, in accordance with the principles of the Gospel, as will promote the general interests of the Church.*—This exercise of ecclesiastical authority consists in making *canons* or *rules* for those particular matters which are not provided for in detail by the directions of Scripture. This power, like the former, has sometimes been carried to a culpable excess. The simplicity of Christianity has thus often been destroyed, and mere human opinions have been set up as the " commandments of God."

There is, however, a sound sense in which this power in the Church must be admitted; for when the laws of Christ are both rightly understood and cordially received, the application of them to particular cases is still necessary, and is with the Church. Many regulations also are dictated by inference and by analogies, and appear to be required by the *spirit* of the Gospel, for which there is no provision in the *letter*. For instance, though the obligation of public worship is plainly stated, the seasons of its observance, its frequency, and the mode in which it is to be conducted must be matters of special regulation. Baptism is to be administered; but the manner of this service is not definitely prescribed in Scripture. So also we have no inspired law as to the mode and times of receiving the Lord's supper. In the absence, therefore, of inspired directions in regard to all such matters the regulations of the Church are necessary, that all things may be done " decently and in order."

It is then doubtless competent for the Church to form such regulations for the conduct of its ministers, officers, and members as shall establish a common order for worship; facilitate the management of the affairs of the community, spiritual, economical, and financial; and give a right direction to the general conduct of the whole society. The general principles by which these regulations should be controlled are the *spirituality, simplicity,* and *practical character* of Christianity; and the authority with which they are invested is derived from piety, wisdom, and singleness of heart in those who originate them, and from that docility and submissiveness of Christians to each other which is enforced upon them in the New Testament.

3. *The infliction and removal of censures.*—The abuse of this power of the Church, and the extravagant lengths to which it has occasionally been carried, have led some wholly to deny it, or to treat it slightly; but it is nevertheless a power which is deposited with every scriptural Church. Even associations much less solemn and spiritual in their character have the power to put away their offending members, and to receive them again, upon certain conditions. In the case of a Christian Church, however, the proceeding connects itself with Divine authority. The members have separated themselves from the world, and have placed themselves under the laws of Christ. To him they sustain a special relation so long as they are faithful. They are the

objects of his care and love, as members of his own body; and to them as such great and numerous promises are made. To preserve them in this state of fidelity, to guard them from errors in doctrine and viciousness of practice, and thus to prevent their separation from Christ, the Church with its ministry, its ordinances, and its discipline was established.

But he who becomes unfaithful in opposition to the influence of those edifying and conservatory means, forfeits the favor of Christ even before he is deservedly separated from Church communion. And when he is thus separated from the fellowship of the faithful, he loses also the benefit of all those peculiar means of grace and salvation which Christ bestows upon the Church. He is, by the solemn sentence of a religious tribunal, thrown back upon the *world* as an enemy to God, and as being exposed to the penalty of his violated law. Where the sentence of excision by a Church is erring or vicious, as it may be in some cases, it cannot affect an *innocent* individual. He would remain, notwithstanding the sentence of men, a member of Christ's invisible universal Church. But when it proceeds upon a just application of the laws of Christ, there can be no doubt of its ratification in heaven, though the door is left open to penitence and restoration.

In concluding this chapter it may be observed that however difficult it may be, in some cases, to adjust modes of Church government, so that in the view of all the principles of the New Testament may be fully recognized, and the ends for which Churches are collected may be effectually accomplished, this labor will always be greatly smoothed by a steady regard on all sides to *duties* as well as to *rights*. These are equally imperative upon ministers, upon subordinate officers, and upon the private members of every Church. Charity, candor, humility, public spirit, zeal, a forgiving spirit, and a desire—a strong desire of unity and harmony, ought to pervade all, as well as a constant remembrance of the great and solemn truth that Christ is the *Judge* as well as the *Saviour* of his Churches.

CHAPTER II.

THE SACRAMENTS.

The word used by the Greek fathers for sacrament was $\mu\nu\sigma\tau\acute{\eta}\rho\iota\omicron\nu$. This word, in the New Testament, always means either a secret—something unknown till revealed—or the spiritual meaning of some emblem or type. In both these senses it is rendered, in the Vulgate translation, *sacramentum*, which shows that the latter word was formerly used in a large signification. As the Greek term (μυστήριον) was employed in the New Testament to express the hidden meaning of an external symbol, as in Revelation i, 20, "the *mystery* of the seven stars," it was naturally applied by the early Christians to the symbolical rite of the Lord's supper.

The Latin word *sacramentum*, in its largest sense, may signify a sacred ceremony, and is the appellation, also, of the military oath of fidelity taken by the Roman soldiers. For both these reasons, probably, the term *sacrament* was adopted by the Latin Christians. For the first, because of the peculiar sacredness of the Lord's supper; and for the second, because of that engagement which was implied in this sacred ordinance to be faithful to the commands of Christ. The same term was also applied, at an early period of the Church, to the ordinance of baptism. But in order that we may gain a more distinct knowledge of the Christian sacraments, let us inquire into their *nature* and their *number*.

I. THEIR NATURE.

Of the *nature* of sacraments there are three leading views:

1. *That which is taken by the Church of Rome.*—According to her the sacraments contain the grace which they signify, and confer grace, *ex opere operato*, by the work itself, upon such as do not put an obstruction by mortal sin. "For these sensible and natural things," it is declared, "work by the almighty power of God in the sacraments what they could not do by their own power." Nor is anything more necessary to this effect than that the priest, "who makes and consecrates the sacraments, have an *intention* of doing what the Church doth, and doth intend to do."*

According to this doctrine the matter of the sacrament derives from the action of the priest, in pronouncing certain words, a Divine virtue; and this grace is conveyed to the soul of every person who receives it. Nor is it required of the person receiving a sacrament that he should exercise any good disposition or possess faith; for such is conceived to be the *physical virtue* of a sacrament that, except when opposed by the obstacle of a mortal sin, the act of receiving it is alone sufficient for the experience of its efficacy.

Against this view of the sacraments the following objections may be urged: 1. It has no authority from the sacred Scriptures. 2. It is antiscriptural. It makes the communication of saving grace depend alone upon a sacrament; but the Scriptures declare that it depends upon true faith. 3. It debases an ordinance of God from a rational service into a mere charm. 4. It is of licentious tendency; as venial sins cannot prevent the recipient of a sacrament from receiving the grace which it communicates. And, 5. It makes whatever privileges the sacraments

* Conc. Trid., Can. ii.

are intended to confer depend entirely upon the intention of the administrator.

2. *The Socinian notion.*—The opinion of Socinus and his followers, toward which some orthodox divines have too carelessly leaned, is that the sacraments do not differ *essentially* from other religious rites and ceremonies; but that their peculiarity consists in their emblematic character, under which they represent spiritual and invisible things, and are memorials of past events. Their sole use, therefore, is to cherish pious sentiments by leading the mind to such meditations as are adapted to excite them. Some also add that they are the badges of a Christian profession, and the instituted means by which Christians testify their faith in Christ.

The fault of the popish opinion is superstitious *excess;* the fault of the latter scheme is that of *defect.* The sacraments are emblematical; they are adapted to excite pious sentiments; they are memorials, at least the Lord's supper bears this character; they are badges of profession; they are the appointed means for declaring our faith in Christ; and so far is this view superior to the popish doctrine that it elevates the sacraments from the base and degrading character of a mere incantation to that of a reasonable and spiritual service. It is defective, however, as we will soon show, in not considering the sacraments to be *signs* and *seals* of the covenant of grace.

3. *The true Protestant doctrine respecting the nature of the sacraments.*—This, in the formularies of different Protestant Churches, is variously expressed; but the essential features of the doctrine are all included in the following definition: A sacrament is a holy ordinance formally instituted by Christ in his Church, not only as a badge or token of our Christian profession, but rather as a sign and seal of the covenant of grace, and a means of conveying to us the blessings of the Gospel. The essential characteristics of the sacraments are the following:

(1.) *They are instituted by Christ himself.*—It is this consideration which stamps a peculiar sanctity on these institutions, and binds us so sacredly to the observance of them. It is right that due honor should be given to those ceremonies of human appointment which are calculated to promote the good order and edification of the Church; but let them not be placed on a level with the religious observances which derive their origin immediately from the command of Christ. These are obligatory on the conscience, and none who are faithful to him can treat them with indifference. That baptism and the Lord's supper are express and positive institutions of Christ cannot be denied. He commanded the apostles to disciple all nations, "baptizing them in the name of the Father, and of the Son, and of the Holy Ghost." Matt. xxviii, 19. So, also, when he instituted the supper, he said to his disciples, first with respect to the *bread,* "Take, eat; this is my body;" and then in regard to the *cup,* "Drink ye all of it." Matt. xxvi, 26, 27.

(2.) *They are* SIGNS *of Divine grace.*—As such they are visible and symbolical expositions of the benefits of redemption. In other words, they exhibit to the senses, under appropriate emblems, the same benefits that are exhibited in another form in the doctrine and promises of the word of God. As Augustine said, "*sacramentum esse verbum visibile.*" It is not difficult to see how aptly the water of baptism points out that " washing of regeneration, and renewing of the Holy Ghost," which is promised to all who believe. Thus the prophet seems to allude both to the sign and the thing signified: "Then will I sprinkle clean water upon you, and ye shall be clean." Ezek. xxxvi, 25. So in the feast of the Eucharist the visible elements which are employed point to the broken body and shed blood of the Redeemer. "The cup of blessing which we bless, is it not the communion of the blood of Christ? the bread which we break, is it not the communion of the body of Christ?" 1 Cor. x, 16. Hence says the apostle, "As often as ye eat this bread, and drink this cup, ye do show the Lord's death till he come." 1 Cor. xi, 26. But while we thus gratefully remember the death of our Lord, this sacramental service impresses deeply upon the mind lessons of the most important instruction.

(3.) *They are* SEALS.—A seal is a confirming sign; or, according to theological language, there is in a sacrament a *signum significans* and a *signum confirmans;* the former of which is said (*significare*) to notify or to declare, the latter (*obsignare*) to set one's seal to, to witness. The sacraments are the seal of the covenant of grace, both on the part of God and on the part of men. They are seals on the part of God by which he declares his gracious intention of bestowing his favors upon us, and by which he binds himself to fulfill his covenant engagements. While we look upon these symbols we feel our minds impressed with his condescension and love, our faith in his promises is confirmed, and the most devout affections toward him are excited. On our part also they are seals by which we enter into the most solemn obligations with him, according to the terms of the covenant which he proposes to our acceptance. While, by the reception of these visible tokens, we profess to "lay hold upon the hope set before us," we seal the solemn contract, as with our own signature, that we will dedicate to God ourselves and our all—that we will be his alone, and his forever.

(4.) *The sacraments are* MEANS *of grace*, as well as signs and seals of it.—We do not imagine, with the superstitious devotees of the Church of Rome, that the sacraments contain the grace which they signify, or that any spiritual virtue or real efficacy is necessarily connected with them. But still there is a sober sense in which they may be regarded as means of grace to those who rightly receive them. They stand in intimate connection with the essential doctrines of Christianity, and they can in themselves produce no effect upon those who have no knowledge of these doctrines, or no conviction of their truth. But as the Gospel "is the power of God unto salvation," and as in the sacraments the leading doctrines of the Gospel are taught in the most impressive manner, it would be absurd to suppose that they do not in this way exert a saving influence. In the administration of these sacred rites our faith is called into lively exercise, and our expectations are enlarged. The very act of participating in them implies that the favor which God tenders to us we put forth our hand to receive. Thus, according to our Sixteenth Article, by these sacraments God "doth work invisibly in us, and doth not only quicken, but also strengthen and confirm our faith in him."

The sacraments, then, are federal transactions between God and our souls, and the conveyancers to us of the blessings of the Gospel. To every one who receives the sign a seal and pledge of the invisible grace is also given; and every one who draws near with a true heart and with full assurance of faith does, in *his own person*, enter into God's covenant. Let us, therefore, be mindful of our sacred obligations. Let us give diligence to prove ourselves faithful. God will not forget his engagements; but let us fear lest we aggravate our guilt and condemnation by a species of perjury, of all kinds the most base and detestable. Let every Christian say, in the language of the psalmist, "Thy vows are upon me, O God."

II. THE NUMBER OF THE SACRAMENTS.

The number of sacraments is held by all Protestants to be but two, *baptism* and the *Lord's supper*, because they find no others instituted in the New Testament or practiced in the early Church. The superstition of the Church of Rome has added no fewer than five to the number—*confirmation, penance, orders, matrimony,* and *extreme unction.*

As to these five additional sacraments of the Church of Rome, they have no visible sign ordained of God; nor do they stand in direct connection with any covenant engagement with his creatures. *Confirmation* rests on no scriptural authority whatever. *Penance,* if it means anything more than repentance, is equally unsanctioned by Scripture; and if it means "repentance toward God," it is no more a sacrament than faith. *Orders,* or the ordination of ministers, is an apostolic command, but has in it no greater indication of a sacramental act than any other such command. *Marriage* appears to be made a sacrament for this curious reason, that St. Paul, when speaking of the love and union of husband and wife, and taking occasion from that to allude to the love of Christ to his Church, says, "This is a great mystery;" which the Vulgate translates, "SACRAMENTUM *hoc magnum est.*" Thus they confound the large and the restricted sense of the word sacrament, and forget that the true "mystery" spoken of by the apostle lies not in marriage, but in the union of Christ with his people. As to *extreme unction,* it is nowhere prescribed in Scripture; and if it were, it has clearly nothing in it of a sacramental character.

CHAPTER III.

BAPTISM.

FEW subjects within the range of theology have given rise to a greater amount of controversy than that of Christian baptism; and perhaps it is one on which we may not hope for a general agreement of sentiment. But as baptism is an ordinance of the New Testament, and as every one is required to examine the doctrines and institutions of Christianity for himself, it will be proper for us to investigate this subject in the light of revealed truth. Three things will require examination: 1. The *nature* of baptism; 2. Its *subjects;* and, 3. Its *mode.*

§ 1. *The Nature of Baptism.*

Baptism, as a Christian ordinance, may be defined to be the application of pure water to a proper subject, by a lawful administrator, in the name of the sacred Trinity. 1. It is the application of pure water, as the language of the apostle clearly indicates. "Having our hearts sprinkled from an evil conscience, and our bodies washed with *pure water.*" 2. The water must be applied to a proper subject; not to an inanimate object, but to a human being under certain circumstances. 3. The ordinance must be performed by a lawful administrator; and as the commission to baptize was given to ministers of the Gospel alone, no others have a right to perform this office. And, 4. It must be administered in the name of the sacred Trinity, "baptizing them in the name of the Father, and of the Son, and of the Holy Ghost."

In considering more particularly the *nature* of baptism, two things will demand our attention; 1. Its universal obligation; and, 2. Its sacramental import.

I. ITS UNIVERSAL OBLIGATION.

There are those who deny that we are under any obligation to observe the rite of water baptism under the Christian dispensation. Some of these persons, to support their opinion, adduce Hebrews ix, 10: "Which stood only in meats, and drinks, and divers washings, and carnal ordinances, imposed on them until the time of reformation." From this it has been argued that baptism was among those carnal ordinances that were to be done away in Christ. That the term *washings*, in the texts, means *baptisms*, is admitted; but it by no means follows that the baptism of the Gospel is included. The apostle in the passage is referring to the Jewish worship, as may be seen by the context. Of whatever nature those *washings* were, and to whatever extent they were used in the Jewish worship, they, together with every other rite and ceremony attached to the Jewish dispensation, were in *fact* done away at the opening of the Gospel dispensation. Therefore, though the unbelieving Jews retained those ceremonies, yet it must be admitted that *Christians* rejected them. But as water baptism was administered by the apostles after the opening of the Christian dispensation, it clearly follows that Christian baptism was not embraced in the *washings* of which the apostle here speaks.

Some argue against the use of baptism under the Christian dispensation from the language of John the Baptist: "I indeed baptize you with water unto repentance: but he (Christ) shall baptize you with the Holy Ghost." Matt. iii, 11. From this the inference is drawn that under the new dispensation water baptism was to be discontinued, and the baptism of the Spirit to take its place. It is true, John's baptism may have been done away when Christ baptized with the Holy Ghost; but that proves nothing against the institution and perpetuation of the Christian ordinance. Hence this text, as well as the other, fails to afford any warrant for rejecting water baptism.

That baptism is of universal and perpetual obligation may be proved,

1. *From our Lord's express command.*—He said to his apostles, "Go ye, therefore, and teach all nations, baptizing them in the name of the Father, and of the Son, and of the Holy Ghost; teaching them to observe all things whatsoever I have commanded you; and lo, I am with you alway, even unto the end of the world." Matt. xxviii, 19, 20. This passage contains a general command to make disciples of all nations, and two specific directions how this is to be accomplished: 1. By baptizing them in the name of the Holy Trinity; and, 2. By teaching them to observe whatsoever Christ had commanded. It is also very clearly implied in the passage, that the observance of baptism is to be coextensive with the preaching of the Gospel, and to be continued to "the end of the world." Of the same import is the parallel passage in Mark xvi, 15, 16: "Go ye into all the world, and preach the Gospel to every creature. He that believeth and is baptized shall be saved; but he that believeth not shall be damned."

2. *From the words of Christ to Nicodemus.*—"Except a man be born of water and of the Spirit, he cannot enter into the kingdom of God." John iii, 5. If by the phrase "*born of water*" our Lord did not allude to baptism, it would be difficult, if not impossible, to determine what the meaning of the passage is. But if he refers to this, then it will follow that he recognizes baptism as an ordinance of his religion, for if not, why does he thus speak of it? Why connect it in any

respect with *entering into the kingdom of God?* Though we would not affirm that no man can be saved without being baptized, yet we think our Lord may be fairly understood as teaching the doctrine that this is the regularly instituted means by which we make a public profession of his religion and enter into his visible kingdom, and that those who neglect this when the duty is made known to them neglect a plain command of God.

3. *From apostolic practice.*—The history of the Church shows that the apostles uniformly baptized all who believed. Thus Peter, on the day of Pentecost, exhorted the people, "Repent, and be baptized every one of you, for the remission of sins." "Then they that gladly received his word were baptized." Acts ii, 38, 41. "But when they believed Philip preaching the things concerning the kingdom of God, and the name of Jesus Christ, they were baptized, both men and women." Acts viii, 12.

Let no one say that water baptism is not intended in these passages. We admit that through the laying on of the hands of the apostles the Holy Ghost was given; but by whom? ' We answer, Not by the apostles, but by God himself, whose prerogative alone it is to "give the Holy Spirit to them that ask him." If, then, the apostles did not baptize with the Holy Ghost, they must have baptized with water; for it is positively asserted that they did baptize.

But that they baptized with water is put beyond all dispute by the sacred history. Take, for instance, the case of Philip and the eunuch. "They came unto a certain water; and the eunuch said, See, here is water, what doth hinder me to be baptized?" Acts viii, 36. Did the eunuch suppose that the presence of water was necessary, in order that he might be baptized with the Spirit? But further: "They went down both into the water, both Philip and the eunuch, and he baptized him." Why did they both go down into the water if that was not the element to be employed in administering the sacred ordinance?

Again, let us consider the language of Peter in the house of Cornelius: "Can any man forbid water, that these should not be baptized, which have received the Holy Ghost as well as we?" Acts x, 47. Here the apostle marks an evident distinction between water baptism and that of the Spirit. These persons had "received the Holy Ghost." This baptism of the Spirit was poured out upon them while Peter was preaching the word; but after all this he inquires, "Can any man forbid water?" When, therefore, "he commanded them to be baptized in the name of the Lord," he commanded water baptism, and not the baptism of the Spirit. Hence we have clear and positive testimony that the apostles baptized with water; and consequently, that baptism under the Christian dispensation is of Divine authority, and of perpetual obligation.

II. Its Sacramental Import.

Baptism, in its sacramental import, is the initiatory ordinance into the visible Church of Christ, and a sign and seal of the covenant of grace.

1. *It is initiatory.*—That the Church of Christ, as a visible society, must have some mode of admitting members, is generally conceded. This mode must be either the requisition of a spiritual qualification or the performance of some visible act. It cannot be the former, for of that qualification the Church is not competent to judge. As the form of initiation must therefore be a *visible act*, what can that act be? It is not the act of attending public worship, for many do this who are confessedly not members of the Church. Nor does it consist in a public avowal of religion, for this would preclude all infants. It is not the celebration of the eucharist; for this, as it is to be often repeated, cannot be an initiatory rite. It follows, therefore, that it must be baptism, which has been regarded as initiatory from the earliest ages of Christianity. To deny this is the same as to affirm that Christianity has no initiatory ordinance.

But that our Lord intended baptism to be the initiating ordinance into his visible Church is evident from the fact that he connected it, by positive injunction, with that grand commission which he gave to his apostles to "preach the Gospel to every creature." This initiatory character of baptism is alluded to by the apostle when he inquires of the Corinthians, "Were ye baptized in the name of Paul?" 1 Cor. i, 13. Here he evidently assumes the principle that if he had baptized any persons in his own name, he would thereby have represented himself as the head of a sect. But as they were baptized in the name of *Christ*, they were thereby united to *his* Church by this initiatory rite.

2. *Baptism is a sign.*—As such, it holds out to our view all the provisions and promises of the covenant of grace. It is a symbolic representation,

(1.) Of our spiritual purification. As water is universally employed to cleanse things from external impurity, it is most appropriately used as the symbol of that gracious influence by which the soul is cleansed from its moral defilement. While baptism, therefore, is an acknowledgment of that guilt and moral pollution in which all are involved, it is a recognition of the placability of God to man, the cleansing efficacy of the blood of Christ, and the regenerating power of the Holy Spirit. The promise of God is, "I will pour water upon him that is thirsty, and floods upon the dry ground; I will pour my Spirit upon thy seed, and my blessing upon their offspring." Isa. xliv, 3. "Then will I sprinkle clean water upon you, and ye shall be clean: from all your filthiness and from all your idols will I cleanse you. A new heart also will I give you, and a new spirit will I put within you." Ezek. xxxvi, 25, 26. In exact accordance with these predictions our Lord declares, "Except a man be born of water and of the Spirit, he cannot enter into the king-

Chap. 3, § 2.]   THE NATURE OF BAPTISM.   561

dom of God." So also the apostle: "According to his mercy he saved us, by the washing of regeneration, and the renewing of the Holy Ghost." Whenever, therefore, this ordinance is administered, it enforces this exhortation both upon the subject and upon every spectator: "Let us draw near with a true heart, in full assurance of faith, having our hearts sprinkled from an evil conscience, and our bodies washed with pure water." Heb. x, 22. But,

(2.) As a *sign*, baptism is especially emblematical of that effusion of the Spirit which is peculiar to the Gospel dispensation. This is perhaps one of the principal reasons why it was substituted for circumcision; for in baptism by *affusion* (the New Testament mode of baptizing, as we shall show in the proper place) we have a natural symbol of this heavenly gift. Accordingly, the pouring out of the "Spirit upon all flesh," which is spoken of by the prophet Joel, is in the New Testament called a BAPTISM. To this baptism of the Spirit John had reference when he said of Christ, "He shall baptize you with the Holy Ghost." Matt. iii, 11. To this our Lord himself also alluded when he said to his disciples, after his resurrection, "Ye shall be baptized with the Holy Ghost not many days hence." Acts i, 5. These predictions were gloriously fulfilled on the day of Pentecost, when "they were all filled with the Holy Ghost." It was then that the Holy Spirit, in all his fullness, was "shed forth" upon the Church of God. For this reason Christianity is called "the ministration of the Spirit;" and so far is this from being confined to the miraculous gifts in the first age of the Church, that to be "led by the Spirit" is made the standing and prominent test of true Christianity: "If any man have not the Spirit of Christ, he is none of his." Rom. viii, 9. Of this great new covenant blessing, baptism, in its true mode of administration, is eminently the *sign*, as it represents the *pouring out* of the Spirit, the *descending* of the Spirit, and the *falling* of the Spirit upon men.

3. *Baptism is a seal.*—It is, on the part of God, a visible assurance of his faithfulness to his covenant stipulations. Thus he condescends to bind himself by a perpetual ceremony—a ceremony to which the weak and wavering may ever appeal, as a sensible pledge of his unwavering fidelity. But it is *our seal* also. It is that act by which we make ourselves a party to the covenant, and thus "set to our seal that God is true." In this respect it binds us, as, in the other, GOD mercifully binds himself for the stronger assurance of our faith. We *pledge* ourselves to trust wholly in Christ for pardon and salvation, and to obey his laws: "teaching them," says Christ, "to observe all things whatsoever I have commanded you."

§ 2. *The Subjects of Baptism.*

The *nature* of baptism having been explained, we may proceed to consider who are its proper *subjects*. This question has long been, and still continues to be, a fruitful source of controversy; but if we view it in the light both of the Old and the New Testament, it will not be a difficult matter to arrive at true and satisfactory conclusions. Relying, therefore, upon the teachings of God's word, we affirm that the proper subjects of Christian baptism are,

I. BELIEVERS IN CHRIST.

That religious instruction, in the case of adults, is prerequisite in order to baptism, is evident from the language of the great commission in which this rite was instituted: " Go ye, therefore, and *teach* all nations, baptizing them in the name of the Father, and of the Son, and of the Holy Ghost." Here *teaching* precedes baptism, and prepares the subjects for the reception of the ordinance. It is also evident that faith is a necessary qualification. The eunuch said to Philip, " See, here is water; what doth hinder me to be baptized ?" To this Philip responded, " If thou believest with all thine heart thou mayest. And he answered and said, I believe that Jesus Christ is the Son of God." Thus it is evident from the language of Philip that the want of faith, in the case of adults, is an insuperable bar to this sacrament.

That believers are proper subjects of baptism is established by the language of Christ. "He that believeth, and is baptized, shall be saved." Mark xvi, 16. The same fact is taught in Acts x, 46-48. "Then answered Peter, Can any man forbid water, that these should not be baptized, which have received the Holy Ghost as well as we? And he commanded them to be baptized in the name of the Lord." This passage proves, in addition to the object for which it is here adduced, that men may receive the Holy Ghost, and, consequently, may be regenerated without being baptized. Therefore, baptism cannot be the regenerating act, as is so confidently affirmed by some.

II. THE INFANT CHILDREN OF BELIEVING PARENTS.

But here we are met, at the very threshhold of our argument, by various objections. It will, therefore, be proper, 1. To obviate the objections that are usually urged against the position here assumed; and, 2. To support it by direct arguments.

First, then, we will consider and obviate the objections to infant baptism. Those commonly urged are,

(1.) That it has no express warrant in the word of God. How far this objection is founded in truth we will consider in another place. But supposing it, for the sake of the argument, to be true, does it, therefore, follow that infants ought not to be baptized? To draw this conclusion is to assume the principle that, so far as religious observances are concerned, whatever is not expressly enjoined in the word of God ought not to be done. If so, then females ought not to be admitted to the Lord's supper, for there is certainly no express warrant for female communion. The word $ἄνθρωπος$, in 1 Corinthians xi, 28, cannot be pleaded as a warrant, because it is commonly applied to males, and sometimes means males in opposition to females: as, "For this cause shall a man (*anthropos*) leave father and mother, and shall cleave to his wife." Matt. xix, 5. So our Lord is called "the man (*anthropos*) Christ Jesus." 1 Tim. ii, 5.

Again, according to this mode of reasoning, we ought not to keep the first day of the week as a holy Sabbath, for this rests on no express warrant in the word of God. The same is also true in regard to the duty of family prayer; and yet who that believes in the truth of Christianity will dare affirm that it ought not to be observed? Indeed, there are many duties incumbent on us which are not *expressly* commanded, but rest upon the ground of inference alone. We conclude, therefore, that if there were even no express warrant in the Scriptures for the baptism of infants it would not thence follow that they ought to be shut out from the ordinance. As well might we conclude that females ought to be prevented from coming to the table of the Lord, parents exempted from praying with their families, or those exculpated from crime who disregard the sanctity of the Christian Sabbath.

(2.) That infants cannot believe, and, therefore, should not be baptized.—We have already shown that *faith*, in a greater or less degree, in the case of adults, is an indispensable qualification for baptism; but that infants are to be shut out from the ordinance because they cannot believe is what we deny. To assume this position is to take for granted what is not true, namely, that the seal of God's covenant is not to be placed on any who are incapable of faith. This condition is connected with baptism precisely as it was with circumcision. When Abraham was circumcised it was "a seal of the righteousness of the *faith* which he had" previously exercised; but when Isaac was to be circumcised no faith on his part was required, for of this he was incapable. So, likewise, in reference to baptism, faith is necessary; but it is only required of those who are capable of exercising it, while their infant children become proper subjects of the ordinance in consequence of the faith of the parents. The objection, therefore, is a mere sophism. But in addition to this it proves as much against the *salvation* of infants as it does against their admission to the ordinance of baptism. Our Lord has positively declared, "He that believeth not shall be damned." But infants do not believe; and, therefore, according to the doctrine of the objection, infants shall be damned. Thus we see that the objection proves too much, and, consequently, it proves nothing at all. But it is objected,

(3.) That as Christ places teaching before baptism, and as infants are incapable of being taught, therefore they ought not to be baptized.— To this our reply is, that no sound argument can be based upon the mere *order* in which events are recorded in the Scriptures, except so far as the order of those events is a matter of record. The sacred writer tells us that "John baptized in the wilderness, and preached the baptism of repentance." And again, "they were baptized of him in Jordan confessing their sins." Mark i, 4, 5. Are we to conclude that John baptized the people before he preached to them? or that he baptized them before they confessed their sins? By no means; and yet these conclusions would be legitimate according to the principle assumed in the objection. If a man were to affirm that in the antediluvian families all the daughters were younger than the sons, and were to adduce as the proof of his theory the oft-repeated clause, "and begat sons and daughters," would not such an argument provoke a smile? But who does not see that it would be quite as rational as the objection which we are considering? It is also objected,

(4.) That infants should not be bound by this ordinance, because they cannot consent to the covenant of which it is the seal.—To suppose that parents have no right to bind their children in covenant engagements is contrary to the common consent of all men and to the daily course of human events. This right is involved in every act of civil legislation, in every conveyance of real estate, and in almost every pecuniary transaction. Thus men bind themselves, their heirs and assigns forever.

But the principle assumed in the objection is refuted by the testimony of sacred history. "Ye stand this day all of you," said Moses, "before the Lord your God; your captains of your tribes, your elders, and your officers, with all the men of Israel, your *little ones*, your wives, and thy stranger that is in thy camp, from the hewer of thy wood unto the drawer of thy water : that thou shouldst enter into covenant with the Lord thy God, and into his oath, which the Lord thy God maketh with thee this day." Deut. xxix, 10–12. Here it is obvious, that not only the parents, but also their "little ones," entered into covenant with God. To this we may add the remark, that the obligations of religion do not depend on our voluntary consent; and this one consideration is, in itself, a sufficient refutation of the objection. It is moreover objected,

(5.) That baptism can do infants no good, and, therefore, they ought not to be baptized. Of all the objections to infant baptism this is the most flimsy, and yet the most common; especially among the less informed. They ask with an air of contempt, what good can it do them? and seem to think that they have effectually exploded the doctrine by this simple question. But suppose we cannot see how baptism can do infants any good, would we thereby be justified in rejecting it? Certainly not; for this would be to make our ignorance the rule of duty and not our knowledge. We cannot subscribe to the doctrine, either that infants are regenerated by baptism, or that the want of it will exclude them from the kingdom of God; but who can say that they will not in riper years be influenced by their baptismal dedication to God on being duly informed of the fact? and who can tell how far God may answer the prayers directed to his throne at the time of that solemn dedication? Until we can fully answer these questions we should not be too loud and positive in our declaration, that baptism can do infants no good.

Having thus considered the objections usually urged against infant baptism, we will proceed, in the *second* place, to present some arguments in its support. That the infant children of believing parents are proper subjects of baptism may be proved,

1. FROM THEIR BEING ADMITTED TO MEMBERSHIP IN THE CHURCH OF GOD UNDER THE ABRAHAMIC COVENANT.

To perceive the force of this argument in its true light several things must be taken into the account. It must be understood that the Church of God took its visible form in the covenant which he made with Abraham, that of that covenant circumcision was the sign and seal, that the Christian Church is a continuation of the Abrahamic covenant, and that baptism has taken the place of circumcision, and is to Christianity what circumcision was to the former covenant. These points are all susceptible of the clearest proof, as we will now proceed to show.

(1.) *The Church of God took its visible form in the Abrahamic covenant.*—That the covenant which God made with Abraham was the *general covenant of grace*, and not wholly, or even chiefly, a political and national covenant, is abundantly evident from the terms in which it is expressed.*

The first engagement in it was, that God would *greatly bless* Abraham; which promise, though it comprehended temporal blessings, referred more especially, as we learn from St. Paul, to the blessing of justification by the imputation of his faith for righteousness, with all the spiritual advantages consequent upon the relation which was thus established between him and God in time and eternity.†

The second promise in the covenant was, that he should be "a father of many nations;" which, according to St. Paul, refers more particularly to his spiritual seed than to his natural descendants. That "the promise might be sure to all the seed; not to that only which is of the law, but to that also which is of the faith of Abraham, who is the father of us all;" that is, of all believers, whether Jews or Gentiles.

The third promise was, "to be a God unto Abraham, and to his seed after him," a promise which implies the highest spiritual blessings, such as the remission of sins and the sanctification of our nature; as also a visible Church state. It is even used to express the felicitous state of the Church in heaven. "And God himself shall be with them, and be their God." Rev. xxi, 3.

The fourth stipulation in God's covenant with the patriarch was, to give to him, and to his seed after him, "all the land of Canaan, for an everlasting possession." But this temporal promise was manifestly the type of the higher promise of a heavenly inheritance. Hence St.

* See Gen. xii, 1-3; xvii, 1-8; xxii, 17, 18. † See Gal. iii, 14.

Paul says, "By *faith* he sojourned in the land of promise, as in a strange country, dwelling in tabernacles with Isaac and Jacob, the heirs with him of the same promise." But this faith did not respect the fulfillment of the *temporal* promise; for the apostle adds, "He looked for a city which hath foundations, whose builder and maker is God." Heb. xi, 9, 10.

The final engagement in this covenant was, that in the seed of Abraham "all the nations of the earth should be blessed;" and this blessing, we are taught by St. Paul, was nothing less than the justification of all believers in all nations, by faith in Christ: "And the Scripture, foreseeing that God would justify the heathen through faith, preached before the Gospel unto Abraham, saying, In thee shall all nations be blessed. So then they which be of faith are blessed with faithful Abraham." Gal. iii, 8, 9.

This covenant with Abraham, therefore, though it had respect to a natural seed, *Isaac*, from whom a numerous progeny was to spring, and to an earthly inheritance provided for this issue, *the land of Canaan*, was nevertheless, under these temporal advantages, to all intents and purposes *the covenant of grace*, embodying itself under these circumstances, as types of a dispensation of salvation and eternal life, to all who should follow the faith of Abraham, whose justification before God was the pattern of the justification of every man in all ages, whether Jew or Gentile. This covenant was perpetuated in its visible form by that special covenant which God made with the descendants of Abraham, in the line of Isaac and Jacob, whom he acknowledged as his visible Church.

But here it is objected by some, that God had no Church in the world until the day of Pentecost; and in support of this opinion they adduce the language of our Lord to Peter, Matthew xvi, 18, "Upon this rock I will build my Church." In reply to this it is only necessary to remark, that the objection contradicts the Scriptures. David says, "In the midst of the *congregation* (*Church*) will I praise thee." Psa. xxii, 22. And Stephen says of Christ, "This is he that was in the *Church* in the wilderness." Acts vii, 38. In these passages, therefore, the Church-state of the Jews is fully acknowledged.

(2.) *Of the Abrahamic covenant circumcision was the sign and seal.* —God said to Abraham, "This is my covenant, which ye shall keep between me and you, and thy seed after thee; every man child among you shall be circumcised. And it shall be a token of the covenant between me and you." Gen. xvii, 10, 11. St. Paul says, "And he received the SIGN of circumcision; a SEAL of the righteousness of the faith which he had yet being uncircumcised." Rom. iv, 11. This rite was enjoined upon the posterity of Abraham under this solemn consideration, that every man child who was not circumcised on the eighth day was to be cut off from his people by the special judgment of God for having broken the covenant. Hence it follows that this sacrament was a constant *publication* of God's covenant of grace among the descendants of Abraham, and its repetition a continual *confirmation* of that covenant on the part of God to all practicing it in that faith of which it was the ostensible expression.

(3.) *The Christian Church is a continuation of the Abrahamic covenant.*—This appears to be undeniable when we consider,

First, that the covenant which God made with Abraham, and of which circumcision was the sign and seal, was to be everlasting in its duration and universal in its blessings. "I will establish my covenant between me and thee, and thy seed after thee, in their generations, for *an everlasting covenant.*" Gen. xvii, 7. "And in thy seed shall *all the nations of the earth* be blessed." Gen. xxii, 18. Hence this covenant, in its highest sense, is carried out in the Gospel dispensation.

Secondly, that Abraham is recognized in the sacred Scriptures as the father of all true believers. Thus St. Paul tell us that "he received the sign of circumcision, a seal of the righteousness of the faith which he had yet being uncircumcised: that he might be *the father of all them that believe*, though they be not circumcised, that righteousness might be imputed to them also; and the father of circumcision to them who are not of the circumcision only, but who also walk in the steps of that faith of our father Abraham, which he had being yet uncircumcised." Rom. iv, 11, 12.

Thirdly, that Christ came to sit upon the throne of David. It is to this the prophet had reference when he said, "Of the increase of his government and peace there shall be no end, upon the throne of David, and upon his kingdom, to order it, and to establish it with judgment and with justice, from henceforth even forever." Isa. ix, 7. In exact accordance with this prediction is the language of Zacharias, the father of John the Baptist. "Blessed be the Lord God of Israel; for he hath visited and redeemed his people, and hath raised up an horn of salvation for us in the house of his servant David; as he spake by the mouth of his holy prophets, which have been since the world began; that we should be saved from our enemies, and from the hand of all that hate us. To perform the mercy promised to our fathers, and to remember his holy covenant, the oath which he sware to our father Abraham, that he would grant unto us, that we, being delivered out of the hands of our enemies, might serve him without fear, in holiness and righteousness before him, all the days of our life." Luke i, 68–75.

These quotations are so full and explicit that hardly another word is necessary to point out and establish the intimate connection between the covenant which God made with Abraham and the Gospel dispensation. That covenant, in its visible form, was perpetuated in the Church-state of the Jews until the coming of Christ, who claimed to be "the King of Israel," and was so acknowledged by his disciples. He therefore took his seat, in the language of the prophet, "upon the throne of David," not in a literal but in a spiritual and ecclesiastical sense, as the King and Head of that Church which had existed from the days of Abraham, "to order it, and to establish it even forever." Accordingly, our Lord claimed the Jews as his own people. John says, "He came to his own."

Fourthly, that the Abrahamic covenant was not annulled by the promulgation of the Gospel, but was thereby extended to all nations, according to its original intention. Hence the visible Church of God, which for ages had been confined to a single nation, instead of being dissolved was opened for the reception of believing Gentiles, without any respect to national distinctions. This is beautifully illustrated by St. Paul in the eleventh chapter of Romans. He compares the believing portion of the Jewish Church—the true sons of Abraham—to a "good olive-tree." By the breaking off of some of its natural branches he represents the rejection of the unbelieving Jews; and by the grafting in of others from the wild olive-tree, the reception of the believing Gentiles. In all this it is taken for granted by the apostle that the "good olive-tree," the true Abrahamic Church, is still standing. He, therefore, adds, that if the broken-off branches "abide not still in unbelief," they shall be again united to the same olive-tree.

Thus the unity of the Church under the former and the present dispensation is fully established. The very covenant which God made with Abraham was an epitome of the Gospel. Hence says the apostle, "The Scripture, foreseeing that God would justify the heathen through faith, preached before the *Gospel unto Abraham*, saying, In thee shall all nations be blessed." Gal. iii, 8. He says of the Israelites, also, that "they drank of that spiritual Rock that followed them; and that Rock was Christ." 1 Cor. x, 4.

(4.) *Baptism has taken the place of circumcision, and is to Christianity what circumcision was to the former covenant.*—At the introduction of the new dispensation the peculiar rites and ceremonies of the Old Testament Church passed away, and with them the initiatory rite of circumcision ceased. But that baptism has precisely the same federal and initiatory character as circumcision, and that it was instituted for the same ends, and in its place, we have full proof in Colossians ii, 10-12: "And ye are complete in him, which is the head of all principality and power; in whom also ye are circumcised with the circumcision made without hands, in putting off the body of the sins of the flesh by *the circumcision of Christ*, buried with him in *baptism*." Here baptism is made the initiatory rite of the new dispensation. By it the Colossians were joined to Christ, *in* whom they are said to be "*complete;*" and so certain is it that baptism has the same office and importance as circumcision formerly, that the apostle expressly calls it "*the circumcision of Christ;*" which phrase he puts out of the reach of frivolous criticism by adding exegetically, "buried with him in *baptism.*" For, unless the apostle here calls *baptism* "the circumcision of Christ," he asserts that we "put off the body of the sins of the flesh," that is, become new creatures by virtue of our Lord's own personal circumcision; but if this is absurd, then the only reason for which he can call baptism "the circumcision of Christ," or Christian circumcision, is, that it has taken the place of the Abrahamic circumcision, and fulfills the same office of introducing persons into God's covenant, and of entitling them to the enjoyment of spiritual blessings.

But of this we have additional proof in Galatians iii, 27–29: "For as many of you as have been baptized INTO Christ, have put on Christ. There is neither Jew nor Greek, there is neither bond nor free, there is neither male nor female, for ye are all one in Christ Jesus. And if ye be Christ's," by thus being *baptized* and by *putting on Christ*, "then are ye Abraham's seed, and heirs according to the promise." The argument here is also decisive. It cannot be denied that it was by circumcision, believingly received, that strangers or heathens, as well as Jews, became the spiritual "*seed* of Abraham," and heirs of the same spiritual and heavenly promises. But in this passage the very same office is ascribed to baptism; and the conclusion is therefore inevitable, that baptism is to us what circumcision was to the former dispensation.

This view of the subject is corroborated by the consideration that both these rites are symbolical of the same moral change. St. Paul tells us that "circumcision is that of the heart, in the spirit, and not in the letter; whose praise is not of men, but of God." Rom. ii, 29. In like manner he speaks of baptism as being emblematical of a death to sin, and a new spiritual life. "Therefore we are buried with him by baptism into death; that like as Christ was raised up from the dead by the glory of the Father, even so also we should walk in newness of life." Rom. vi, 4.

To the substitution of baptism for circumcision it is sometimes objected that as the latter was restricted to males, the former would be placed under the same restriction, if it had been put in the place of circumcision. This objection, however, can have no force, except with the uninformed. Circumcision and baptism are both what we denominate *positive* institutions. Who then will dare to affirm that God had not a right to determine the peculiar circumstances under which they should be signs and seals of his covenant?

Let us now sum up our argument and see whether it does not amount to a SCRIPTURAL WARRANT for the practice of infant baptism. We have shown that the Abrahamic covenant was the general covenant of grace; that children were embraced in that covenant, and were admitted into the visible Church by circumcision; that Christianity is but a continuation, under a new form, of that covenant which God made with Abraham; and that baptism is now the sign and seal of the covenant of grace, as circumcision was under the former dispensation. From these premises it necessarily follows that as the infant children of believing parents, under the Old Testament, were proper subjects of circumcision, so the infant children of Christian believers are proper subjects of baptism.

The only means by which this argument can be set aside, is the adduction of some scriptural prohibition of infant baptism. But such a prohibition does not exist; and this single fact is a sufficient proof, under all the circumstances of the case, that infants have a right to this sealing ordinance. Had it been intended to exclude them from entering into the new covenant by baptism, the absence of every prohibitory expression to this effect in the New Testament must have been misleading to all men, and especially to the Jewish believers. To prohibit infants from entering into God's covenant by baptism, when they had always been entitled to enter into it by circumcision, is therefore a censurable interference with the authority of God—a presumptuous attempt to fashion the new dispensation, in this respect, so as to conform to a mere human opinion of fitness and propriety.

2. From Scripture Testimony.

There are many Scriptures that might be adduced in support of infant baptism, but we will confine ourselves to two single passages. The first is Mark x, 14: "Suffer the little children to come unto me, and forbid them not; for of such is the kingdom of God."

This passage is not brought forward to prove that the children spoken of were brought to Christ for the purpose of baptism. We do not know that he ever administered the ordinance himself, either to adults or infants. But we adduce it as direct and unequivocal testimony that *children belong to the kingdom of God.* The opposers of infant baptism allege that the phrase " of such," means, of such like; that is, of adults being of a childlike disposition, a criticism which takes away all meaning from the words of our Lord. For what kind of reason was it to offer for permitting children to come to Christ for his blessing, that persons, not children, but who were of a childlike disposition, were subjects of the kingdom of God? The absurdity of this notion is its own refutation, since the reason for permitting them to come to Christ must be found in themselves and not in others.

Another way to evade the argument from this passage is to understand the phrase, " kingdom of God," exclusively of the heavenly state. We gladly admit that all children dying in infancy are, through the merits of Christ, admitted to heaven. But for this very reason it follows that infants are proper subjects to be introduced into the Church of Christ on earth; unless it can be shown that more is required in order to admission into the *visible* Church than into the Church *triumphant*. It is well known, however, to those who are acquainted with the phraseology of the New Testament, that the phrases, " the kingdom of God," and "the kingdom of heaven," are more frequently employed by our Lord to denote the Church in this present world than in its state of glory. Accordingly, in the above passage, his meaning evidently is that children belong to his Church on earth; and if so, they are proper subjects of baptism, which is the initiatory rite into every portion of that Church which is visible.

The next passage which we adduce is Acts ii, 39: "For the promise is to you, and to your children, and to all that are afar off, even as many as the Lord our God shall call."

In order to perceive the bearing of this passage upon the question before us, it is only necessary to consider the resemblance that there is between the declaration of Peter, "the promise is to you, and to your children," and the promise of God to Abraham. This resemblance is seen in two particulars: 1. Each stands connected with an ordinance by which persons were to be admitted into the visible Church; in the one case by circumcision, in the other by baptism. 2. Both agree in phraseology. The one is, "unto thee, and to thy seed;" the other, "unto you, and to your children." Every one knows that *seed* and *children* are terms of the same import. It follows, therefore, from these two points of resemblance, that the subjects in both cases are the same; and as it is certain that in the promise of God to Abraham both parents and infant children were included, it must be equally certain that both are included in the announcement of Peter. Here, then, we have an *express warrant* for infant baptism.

It is sometimes urged, by way of objection, that if infants are baptized they should also be admitted to the Lord's supper. To this our reply is, that as baptism is passively received, it may be administered to all infants; but to partake of the supper requires an agency of which many of them are physically incapable. Again, as the Lord's supper is to be a memorial to each participant, infants are intellectually incapable of receiving it according to its intention. To this we have an exact parallel in the Jewish passover; and though all Jewish children were circumcised at eight days old, yet they did not eat the passover until they could comprehend its design.

3. FROM APOSTOLIC PRACTICE.

Though we admit that nothing positive in regard to the baptism of infants can be collected from the practice of the apostles, yet there is, in their practice, strong presumptive evidence in our favor. We have on record at least four cases of family baptism: the household of Lydia, the house of the Philippian jailer, the house of Crispus, and the house Stephanas.* Without dwelling upon these cases individually and at length, it is only necessary to remark, 1. That the word οἶκος, rendered *house* and *household*, means in general household, family, posterity, lineage, and agrees with the idea of children. 2. That these household baptisms

* Acts xvi, 13, 33; xviii, 8; 1 Cor. i, 16.

appear to have taken place through the faith of the parents or heads of families. This is especially evident in the case of Lydia and her family. Though her reception of the Gospel is particularly spoken of, not a word is said respecting the faith of her household. Hence it is very clearly implied that they were baptized on the ground of her faith. 3. That the accounts which the sacred writers give of these cases are just such records as we should expect to be made of the baptism of whole families, including infant children. And, 4. That there is no fact, in the administration of this ordinance by the apostles, that stands opposed to the practice of infant baptism. Whatever testimony arises from apostolic practice is therefore in favor of the doctrine that the infant children of believing parents are proper subjects of baptism.

4. From the History of the Church.

That the practice of infant baptism has existed in the Church for many centuries is a fixed fact, which no one will deny who has any knowledge of ecclesiastical history. It must therefore be allowed, either that this practice was established by the apostles themselves, and from them has been handed down to us, or that it was introduced at a period subsequent to apostolic times. If the latter be assumed, we may then be allowed to ask, When and where did the practice commence? Who introduced it? Who opposed it? By what council was it adopted? To these questions no answer can be given, for, in regard to the points which they involve, the history of the Church affords no information. The practice, according to Baptist writers, is an innovation, not upon the *circumstances* of a sacrament, but upon its *essential principle;* and yet its introduction produced no struggle, was never noticed by any general or provincial council, and excited no controversy. This itself is sufficient to refute the notion that it was introduced at any period subsequent to the days of the apostles, and is therefore a strong presumptive proof that infant baptism rests upon apostolic authority. That it was generally practiced in the Church in the first centuries of the Christian era, is supported by the most ample testimony.

Justin Martyr, who was born about the time of St. John's death, says, when speaking of the members of the Church in his day, that "there were many of both sexes, some sixty, and some seventy years old, who were made disciples to Christ *in their infancy.*" In this he must have had reference to baptism, for in no other way could infants have been made disciples.

Origen, born of Christian parents about the year 184, and a man of more information than any other of his day, says, "Infants are baptized for the remission of sins." And again: "The Church hath received the tradition from the apostles, that baptism ought to be administered to infants."

In the middle of the third century Fidus, an African bishop, applied to Cyprian, Bishop of Carthage, to know if children might be baptized before the eighth day. The question was referred to a council of sixty-six bishops met at Carthage, who decided *unanimously* that they might be baptized at any time.

AUGUSTINE, who lived in the fourth century, says, "The whole Church practices infant baptism. It was not instituted by councils, but was always in use." Again: "I do not remember to have read of any person, whether Catholic or heretic, who maintained that baptism ought to be denied to infants."

PELAGIUS, a man of great learning, about the close of the fourth century, after having traveled through France, Italy, Egypt, and Africa, says, "I never heard of even an impious heretic who asserted that infants are not to be baptized."

Dr. WALL, who examined this subject more extensively, perhaps, than any other man, sums up his history thus: "First, during the first four hundred years from the formation of the Christian Church *Tertullian* only urged the delay of baptism to infants, and that only in some cases; and *Gregory* only delayed it, perhaps, to his own children. But neither any society of men, nor any individual, denied the lawfulness of baptizing infants. Secondly, in the next seven hundred years there was not a society nor an individual who even pleaded for this delay; much less any who denied the right or the duty of infant baptism. Thirdly, in the year eleven hundred and twenty, one sect of the Waldenses denied baptism to infants, because they supposed them to be incapable of salvation. But the main body of that people rejected the opinion as heretical, and the sect which held it soon came to nothing. Fourthly, the next appearance of this opinion was in the year fifteen hundred and twenty-two."

We think it impossible to account for these testimonies on rational principles, without admitting that the practice of infant baptism has come down to us from the days of the apostles.

§ 3. *The Mode of Baptism.*

On this question the Christian world has long been divided. Some assert that baptism can only be performed by *immersing* the whole body of the subject in water; while others maintain that it may be scripturally administered by *sprinkling* or *pouring;* or, to use a term which includes both, by *affusion.* The precise question, therefore, to which our attention is now to be directed is this: Is *immersion* essential to Christian baptism? Of the question thus stated we take the negative, and will proceed, 1. To examine the arguments which are usually employed in favor of *immersion* as the only mode; and, 2. To adduce arguments in support of *affusion.*

I. ARGUMENTS FOR IMMERSION.

We will not promise to notice *all* the arguments which immersionists employ in proof of their theory; but we will consider those which they most frequently use, and on which they most confidently rely. It is common for them to draw an argument,

1. *From the meaning of* βαπτίζω, *to baptize;* the word which is used in the New Testament to designate this ordinance.—Immersionists assert that "all lexicographers define BAPTIZO to mean to *immerse*, to *dip*, to *plunge;* not one to sprinkle, or to pour. Whether this assertion is true or false we will leave to be determined by the lexicographers themselves.

Schrevelius, that great master of the Greek language, whose Lexicon has been a standard work for nearly two hundred years, defines BAPTIZO by *mergo, abluo, lavo;* that is, to immerse, to wash, to *sprinkle*, to moisten or wet. The same definitions are given both by *Scapula* and *Hendericus*, only one of which denotes exclusive immersion, the others signifying the application of water by other modes.

Schleusner, in his Lexicon of the New Testament, a work of the highest authority, defines BAPTIZO, 1. "To immerse in water; 2. To wash, *sprinkle*, or cleanse with water; 3. To baptize; 4. To pour out largely." Only one of these definitions restricts the meaning to immersion. Three of them denote the application of water by affusion.

Cole defines BAPTIZO, to baptize, to wash, to *sprinkle;* and *Passor* defines it to immerse, to wash, to *sprinkle*.

Suidas defines BAPTIZO by *mergo, madefacio, lavo, abluo, purgo, mundo;* that is, to immerse, moisten, *sprinkle*, wash, purge, cleanse.

Conlor defines it by *mersione, ablutione, et aspersione;* that is, immersion, washing, sprinkling or wetting.

The learned *Dr. Dwight* tells us that the original meaning of BAPTO, the root from which *baptizo* is derived, is "to tinge, stain, dye, or color;" and *Grove* defines it "to dip, plunge, immerse, wash, wet, moisten, stain, sprinkle, steep, imbue, dye, or color."

Thus we see that lexicographers *do not* confine themselves to the idea of immersion in defining BAPTIZO, but that they embrace also that of *affusion*. It follows, therefore, that, so far as *their* authority is concerned, the *mode* of baptism is still an open question.

To this we may add that the Greek word βάπτω, and its derivative βαπτίζω, are sometimes so employed in the sacred Scriptures as evidently to convey the idea of affusion and exclude that of immersion. Hence,

(1.) We read, Lev. xiv, 6: "As for the living bird, he (the priest) shall take it, and the cedar wood, and the scarlet, and the hyssop, and shall (BAPSEI) *dip* (or *tinge*) them and the living bird in the blood of the bird that was killed over the running water." Here it is evident that BAPSEI, which is an inflection of BAPTO, cannot mean to *immerse*, for it is impossible that the "living bird, and the cedar wood, and the scarlet, and the hyssop," should *all* have been totally immersed in the blood of one bird.

(2.) In Daniel iv, 33, it is recorded that Nebuchadnezzar's body was (EBAPHE) "*wet* with the dew of heaven." Now what is the action which is here expressed by EBAPHE, an inflection of BAPTO? Was the king *dipped* or *plunged* into the dew of heaven? If we allow the Scriptures to explain their own phraseology, they will determine this to be a clear case of *affusion*, and not of immersion. Thus, "The dew *fell upon* the camp in the night." Num. xi, 9. "His heavens *drop down* dew." Deut. xxxiii, 28. "As the dew *falleth on* the ground." 2 Sam. xvii, 12.

(3.) It is stated, Mark vii, 3, 4, that "the Pharisees, and all the Jews, except they wash their hands oft, eat not, holding the tradition of the elders. And when they come from the market, except they wash, (BAPTIZE *themselves*,) they eat not." Here we see that to "*wash their hands*," and to *baptize themselves*, are synonymous phrases; and that an application of water to a part of the person is truly and properly *baptism*. It is moreover well known that among the Jews their customary mode of washing hands was by affusion; as in 2 Kings iii, 11: "Here is Elisha the son of Shaphat, which *poured water* on the *hands* of Elijah." It would, indeed, be absurd to suppose, unless the fact could be clearly proved, that "all the Jews" were in the habit of immersing themselves in water before they could partake of any food.

(4.) St. Paul tells us, 1 Corinthians x, 2, that the Israelites "were all *baptized* unto Moses in the cloud and in the sea." Was this baptism an immersion? The history of the case, as it is recorded in the fourteenth chapter of Exodus, will teach a very different lesson. We will present the leading facts as they took place. It was late in the day when the Egyptians overtook the Israelites. The first thing that took place was, "The pillar of the cloud went from before their face, and stood behind them," even "between the camp of the Egyptians and the camp of Israel." Verses 19, 20. And it was here—on *dry land—before* the sea was divided, that the Israelites were, as Paul expresses it, "under the cloud." The next event that took place was the dividing of the waters. "Moses stretched out his hand over the sea; and the Lord caused the sea to go back by a strong east wind all that night, and made the sea dry land, and the waters were divided." Verse 21. Thirdly, "the children of Israel," in the morning, "went into the midst of the sea upon dry ground; and the waters were a wall unto them on their right hand, and on their left." Verse 22.

It is therefore evident from the very face of this account that the Israelites were not *immersed;* and yet, according to St. Paul, they were *baptized*. They were not *under* the water—they were not *in* the water —they were not "in the sea" and "under the cloud" at the same time; but they were all the time in the *open air*, with their feet on *dry ground*, and with a *wall of water* on either hand. There was, however, a real immersion on the occasion. The Egyptians were immersed, "for the waters returned, and covered the chariots, and the horsemen, and all the host of Pharaoh that came into the sea after them." Verse 28.

As, then, it is absolutely certain that the Israelites were not *immersed*, how were they baptized? This may be clearly gathered from the history of the event. We have seen that before they went into the sea the cloud passed over them, to take its place between them and the Egyptians—a position which it seems to have occupied until the Israelites had passed over to the other shore. It was only then that they were "under the cloud;" and it was then, in all probability, that they were baptized with it. And as the wind which had driven back the waters no doubt continued while they were passing over, it was perfectly natural that they should be sprinkled with the spray from the sea, which stood as a wall on each side of them. Here, then, we have a rational account of the manner in which they were baptized, that is, with water from the cloud and from the sea; and a complete type of Christian baptism in regard to its *mode*—they were baptized by *affusion*.

(5.) The apostle, in speaking of the ceremonial purifications of the law, calls them divers *baptisms*. "Which stood only in meats and drinks, and divers *washings*, (βαπτισμοῖς, *baptisms*,) and carnal ordinances." Heb. ix, 10. Were these divers baptisms performed by *immersion?* The local circumstances of the Jews in regard to a supply of water, both at the time that their laws of purification were first appointed, and during their entire journey through the wilderness, are decidedly against such a supposition. A frequent scarcity of water is one of the notable facts in their history; and for such a vast number of people to immerse themselves as frequently as the law demanded their purifications, and that for forty years in the desert, was a thing utterly impracticable. Yet when Moses commanded the people to cleanse, wash, or bathe themselves, it was never objected to as impossible; nor is there the least intimation that it was ever neglected under any circumstances.

The term which the sacred historian employed to designate those ceremonial purifications is also against the supposition that they were performed by immersion. In Leviticus xv, 5, 8, 11, 13, 21, 22, 27; and in Numbers xix, 7, 8, 19, we read of a ceremonial bathing of the body. In all these passages the Hebrew word rendered *bathe* is RACHATZ, to *wash;* and is translated by λουο in the Greek, and by *lavo* in the Latin. In Exodus xxix, 4; xl, 12, 32; Leviticus xiv, 8, 9, and many other passages, the same Hebrew word is rendered *wash* in our English Bible. To suppose, therefore, that Moses commanded the people to immerse themselves, or one another, for legal impurities, is in direct opposition to the plain letter of the Scriptures. Indeed, it may be safely affirmed, that so far as the ceremonial washings of the Jews required an administrator they were always performed by *affusion;* nor is there the least evidence that any of them required the plunging of the whole body in water.

We conclude, therefore, that the baptisms of which the apostle speaks consisted in *affusing* the people with blood, oil, or water, either pure or impregnated with the ashes of the red heifer; and that he calls them "divers washings," not because they varied in *mode*, but because they were performed for various ceremonial purposes. In explaining himself in the context he mentions no other mode than that of *sprinkling*. "For if the blood of bulls and of goats, and the ashes of an heifer *sprinkling* the unclean, sanctifieth to the purifying of the flesh: how much more shall the blood of Christ?" "For when Moses had spoken every precept to all the people according to the law, he took the blood of calves and of goats, with water, and scarlet wool, and hyssop, and *sprinkled* both the book and all the people." "Moreover, he *sprinkled* likewise with blood both the tabernacle, and all the vessels of the ministry." Heb. ix, 13, 14, 19, 21. Here, then, according to the testimony of St. Paul, *sprinkling* is *baptism*. But immersionists argue,

2. *From the circumstances connected with many of the baptisms recorded in the New Testament.*—They direct our attention, 1. To John's baptizing in Jordan, Matthew iii, 5, 6: "Then went out to him Jerusalem, and all Judea, and all the region round about Jordan, and were baptized of him in Jordan." 2. To the baptism of our Lord, Matthew iii, 16: "And Jesus, when he was baptized, went up straightway *out of* the water." 3. To the baptism of the eunuch, Acts viii, 38, 39: "And they went down both *into* the water, both Philip and the eunuch; and he baptized him. And when they were come up *out of* the water, the Spirit of the Lord caught away Philip."

The whole strength of the argument in favor of immersion which is deduced from these Scriptures, is based upon four Greek prepositions: EN, EIS, EK, and APO. The first is translated *in;* the second, *into;* and the other two, *out of;* as, "*in* Jordan," "*into* the water," "*out of* the water." Now, were we to grant that these prepositions are invariable in their meaning, and that they are always to be understood as they are translated in the preceding passages, would it necessarily follow that the baptisms referred to were administered by immersion? It certainly would not.

We are not now inquiring whether John baptized his disciples and our Lord "*in* Jordan," nor whether Philip and the eunuch "went down *into* the water," and "came up *out of* the water;" but the question is this: Did John and Philip administer the ordinance by *dipping* or *plunging* the subjects into the water? To this question these prepositions furnish no reply; for every one knows that it is possible for persons to go "down into the water," and "to come up out of the water," when no immersion occurs; and that, too, in connection with the ordinance of baptism.

Will any one contend that the act of going "down into the water" implies immersion? If he does he must allow that Philip was immersed as well as the eunuch, for it is said that "they *both* went down into the water;" and for anything that appears in the record, the one was as deep in the water as the other. Were we, therefore, to grant immersionists all they claim, in regard to the meaning of these words, they could not thereby establish a single case of baptism by immersion. The record only says that the persons "were *baptized*"—not that they were immersed, or dipped, or plunged.

The next step in the argument is to show that these prepositions have more meanings than one—in other words, that EN does not always mean *in*, EIS, *into*, and EK and APO, *out of*. Schleusner, in his celebrated Lexicon of the New Testament, tells us that EN has thirty-six distinct meanings; EIS, twenty-six; EK, twenty-four; and APO, twenty. According to Greenfield, Grove, and others, EN means in, at, by, near to, etc.; EIS, in, to, unto, near to, toward, etc.; EK, from, out of, away from, etc.; and APO, from, out of, away from, etc. It would be easy to illustrate all these meanings by Scripture examples, but this is not necessary, as they will be admitted by every man of common intelligence.

There is, therefore, an entire want of proof that ever any of the New Testament baptisms were actually administered in the water. For, as EN means *at* or *near to*, as well as *in*, nothing more can be inferred from John's baptizing "*in* Jordan" than that he baptized *at* or *near to* it. And that the language of the evangelist is so to be understood, is evident from other passages of Scripture. Accordingly, it is said, Mark i, 4, that "John did baptize in the wilderness." But if we conclude, according to Baptist logic, that John was actually in the water of Jordan when he baptized those who went out to him from the surrounding region, how are we to reconcile this conclusion with the unequivocal declaration that he baptized in the wilderness? Are we to suppose that the wilderness in which he baptized extended into the river, so that he could baptize "in Jordan" and "in the wilderness" at the same time? or that he was capable of baptizing, at the same time, in two different places? or that he baptized the multitudes twice: *first*, "in the wilderness," and *secondly*, "in Jordan?" As these suppositions are evidently absurd, the only just conclusion is that John baptized "in the wilderness" *at, near to*, or in the neighborhood of Jordan.

This conclusion is corroborated by John i, 28: "These things were done *in* Bethabara, beyond Jordan, *where* John was baptizing." Here it is only necessary to remark that the persons whom John baptized in Bethabara could not, according to the argument of immersionists, have been baptized "in Jordan," for Bethabara was not *in* Jordan, but *beyond* it. This subject receives additional light from John x, 40, where it is stated that Jesus "went away again beyond Jordan into the place where John at first baptized; and there he abode." But when our Lord "went away *into* the place where John at first baptized," did he go into Jordan? The text teaches us most clearly that the place to which he went, and in which he took up his abode, was *beyond* Jordan. It cannot be supposed that he went into "the river of Jordan," and took up his residence in its waters; and yet this would be the legitimate conclusion from the argument which we are opposing. Thus, Jesus "went into the place where John at first baptized, and there he abode." But John at first baptized "in the river of Jordan;" therefore, Jesus "went into the river of Jordan," and "there he abode." The only way to escape this conclusion is to admit what the Scriptures most obviously teach, that John at first baptized in Bethabara *beyond* Jordan, and not in its waters.

It only remains for us to observe that as APO means *from* far more frequently than it does *out of*, to say that "Jesus, when he was baptized, went up straightway" *from* "the water," would be a faithful translation of the original. So, likewise, as EIS means *to* or *unto*, as well as *into*, and EK, *from*, as well as *out of*, nothing more can be proved in regard to Philip and the eunuch than that they went down *to* the water, and after the eunuch was baptized they came up *from* the water.

There is one other passage which we will notice in this connection, and on which immersionists greatly rely as a proof of the correctness of their theory. It is this: "And John also was baptizing in Ænon, near to Salim, because there was *much water* there." John iii, 23.

Here it is assumed that the "*much* water" spoken of was required *only* for baptism, and could not be necessary for any other purpose; and that as "John was baptizing in Ænon *because* there was much water there," he must therefore have immersed his disciples. But is it not the language of common sense that for the accommodation of the vast multitudes that attended his ministry "much water" was necessary, even if he had not baptized any of them? And if there are other obvious reasons, besides that of immersion, for his requiring "much water," we are at perfect liberty to conclude that these alone influenced him in the selection of Ænon. It was on this principle that king Hezekiah, in order to arrest the invasive movements of Sennacherib, "stopped all the fountains, and the brook that ran through the midst of the land, saying, Why should the kings of Assyria come and find *much water?*" 2 Chron. xxxii, 4. Surely no one will allow that the Assyrian king needed "much water" for the purpose of baptizing his soldiers.

But is it indeed true, that there was at Ænon that quantity or collection of water which immersionists seem to suppose? They have harped so long and loudly upon the "*much* water" of Ænon that many have magnified it into the notion of an extensive lake or mighty river.

But will any one tell us where these swelling floods are to be found? Will he point to some ancient or modern geographer who has described this great water? Josephus, who was coeval with the apostles, and who notices almost every fountain or water of any magnitude in the Holy Land, does not say a word respecting Ænon in any of his writings. This evidently shows that, in his day, it was a place of but little notoriety, and unnoticed for its waters, except in the passage under consideration. Accordingly, of all the modern travelers who have visited the place, no one has ever discovered a lake or river, or anything more than what is common to a well or fountain of water.

The meaning of the terms employed in the original is in perfect accordance with these facts. Ænon is derived from the Hebrew AYIN, the *eye*, and signifies, according to Parkhurst and others, a well, a fountain, or a spring of water. In the Greek phrase HUDATA POLLA, which is rendered "much water," both terms are plural, and signify, not "much water," but *many waters;* conveying the idea of many fountains or springs, rather than a great quantity of water. The use of POLLA in the sense of *many* is very common in the New Testament. Thus, Matthew xiii, 3: "And he spake (POLLA, not *much*, but) *many* things unto them." Mark i, 34: "And cast out (POLLA) *many* devils." John viii, 26: "I have (POLLA) *many* things to say." Acts ii, 43: "And (POLLA) *many* wonders and signs were done." Revelation i, 15: "And his voice as the sound of (HUDATON POLLON) *many waters.*" We are, therefore, safe in the conclusion that Ænon did not contain a large quantity of water, and that it was insufficient for the numerous immersions which are supposed to have taken place in it. But immersionists argue the correctness of their theory,

3. *From those passages of Scripture which speak of baptism as a burial.*—"Know ye not that so many of us as were baptized into Jesus Christ, were baptized into his death? Therefore we are *buried with him* by baptism into death; that like as Christ was raised up from the dead by the glory of the Father, even so we also should walk in newness of life." Rom. vi, 3, 4. And again: "*Buried with him* in baptism, wherein also ye are risen with him, through the faith of the operation of God, who hath raised him from the dead." Col. ii, 12.

The argument for immersion which is drawn from these passages rests entirely upon the words "*buried with him* BY or IN *baptism.*" It is assumed that the apostle is here speaking of water baptism, and that he defines the mode by comparing it to a burial. Assuming these things, and supposing that there is a striking similarity between an immersion in water and the burial of our Lord, immersionists infer that theirs is the only true mode of baptism. The inference, however, rests on mere assumptions, for which there is not the least shadow of **proof.**

Those who suppose the apostle to speak of water baptism as a burial, and consequently by immersion, must admit the following consequences: 1. That it is possible for persons to be dipped or plunged "into Jesus Christ," or "into his death." 2. That St. Paul and those to whom he wrote were at that very time living in the watery grave; for he does not say, *we* WERE *buried*, but "*we* ARE *buried* with him by baptism." Is it possible for a person to be buried and exhumed at the same time? 3. That if the burial of which the apostle speaks is a baptism, then one baptism is made to perform another; for " we are buried BY *baptism ;*" or in other words, and in Baptist language, we are immersed by an immersion. Thus, one immersion is made to perform the other. 4. That the term *death* is only another name for *water ;* for the text says, "we are buried by baptism into *death.*" Is there no difference between water and death? 5. That our Lord himself is immersed with each one of his disciples, and rises with him from the watery grave; for " we are buried *with him* in baptism," and " are risen *with him.*" And, 6. That those who are immersed rise from the water by an exercise of *faith*, and not by the arm of the administrator; for the apostle says, that in baptism we "are risen through the faith of the operation of God." If these consequences are absurd and ridiculous, so is that theory of which they are the legitimate results.

But there is really no analogy between immersion and the burial of Christ. Indeed, it can hardly be supposed that any one would ever have thought of such analogy had he not taken the idea from the modern mode of burial. The grave in which our Lord was buried was a tomb or vault hewn out of a rock, having a door or way of entrance, and being of sufficient capacity to contain several persons. Accordingly, the women that came to embalm his body, and the angel that appeared to them, were all in it at the same time. (See Mark xvi, 1, 5.) The floor of it must have been on a level with the surface of the earth, or only a little below it. Hence we are told, John xx, 5, that one of the disciples " stooping down and looking in, saw the linen clothes."

In this house for the dead our Lord was quietly laid by at least two of his disciples; and there he remained until the morning of the third day, when he rose from the grave by his own power, and not by the power of those who buried him. Moreover, the disciples who placed our Lord in the tomb must themselves have gone into it in performing their solemn office, for we cannot suppose that they rudely cast him into it while they remained without. We conclude, therefore, from all these facts, that he who can see any analogy between a burial under these circumstances, and the plunging of a person into a lake or river, after the manner of Baptist immersions, must possess the wonderful faculty of discerning that which has no existence. Were we to carry our neighbor to the grave, cover him up in it, the next moment raise him out of it, take him home with us, and then declare that he is buried, would not such a transaction be most ridiculous? And yet this is the only kind of burial to which baptism by immersion bears any resemblance.

We conclude, therefore, from a careful examination of the whole subject, that in the passages under consideration the apostle has no allusion whatever either to water baptism itself or to its mode; but that he is speaking of a *spiritual death, burial, resurrection,* and *life*. He inquires, Romans vi, 2: "How shall we that are *dead to sin,* live any longer therein?" and in this question he gives us a key to the whole passage, "*dead* to sin." And, therefore, being thus "*dead to sin,*" we should not "*continue in sin.*" "Know ye not that so many of us as were baptized into Jesus Christ, were baptized into his death?" that is, "so many of us as were" united to Jesus Christ by the baptism of the Holy Spirit were made partakers of the benefits of his death. "For by one Spirit are we all baptized into one body." 1 Cor. xii, 13. This moral change by which believers are united to Christ, and constituted living branches in "the True Vine," includes in it a death to sin, a burial of "the old man," and a resurrection from spiritual death to a new life of holy obedience. "Therefore we are buried with him *by* baptism *into death;*" that is, as Christ was buried in the grave, so we, by the baptism of the Spirit, are brought into this state of *death to sin,* "that like as Christ was *raised up from the dead* by the glory of the Father, even so we also should walk *in newness of life.*"

Indeed, the whole argument of the apostle shows that he is speaking of the work of the Spirit, and not of water baptism. "For if we have been planted together in the likeness of his death, we shall be also in the likeness of his resurrection: knowing this, that our old man is crucified with him, that the body of sin might be destroyed, that henceforth we should not serve sin." And again, "Likewise reckon ye yourselves also to be dead indeed unto sin, but alive unto God through Jesus Christ our Lord." Can water baptism accomplish the moral change of which the apostle is here speaking? Surely no one will affirm this, unless he has adopted the wild notion that "immersion is the *regenerating act.*"

In regard to Colossians ii, 12, it is only necessary to say that it is a parallel passage to Romans vi, 4. "Buried with him in baptism, wherein also ye are risen with him through the faith of the operation of God, who hath raised him from the dead." The meaning evidently is that as Christ was buried in the grave, so we, by the baptism of the Holy Spirit, are also buried—"our old man" being crucified, and "the body of sin" being destroyed; and that as Christ was "raised up from the dead," so we, by this same baptism, and "through the faith of the operation of God," are risen to a new and spiritual life.

Having noticed the leading arguments of immersionists in support of their theory, and having shown that they fail to establish the doctrine which they are brought to prove, we will proceed,

II. TO ADDUCE ARGUMENTS TO PROVE THAT AFFUSION IS THE SCRIPTURAL MODE OF BAPTISM.

This will be established beyond every reasonable doubt if we consider,

1. *That affusion is the only mode which is suited to universal practice.*—The apostolic commission provides for the baptism of " all nations ;" but men may *exist, repent,* and *believe* under circumstances in which immersion is utterly impossible. It would be impossible, for instance, to immerse the inhabitants of a *sandy desert;* of a *besieged city,* within which there was great scarcity of water; of *many countries* in the time of great drouth; or of the more *northern regions* during the *severity of winter.* Some are brought to true repentance and faith in Christ on a *sick* and *dying* bed, when, to all human appearance, to immerse them would be instant death. Must they, nevertheless, be plunged into a lake or river? Does God require murder for sacrifice? Shall we not rather conclude that the God of wisdom, who has commanded his ministers to *baptize* ALL NATIONS, would adopt a mode which can be employed under all circumstances? But we remark,

2. *That affusion is supported by the history of baptism as recorded in the New Testament.*—We have already shown that the circumstances of John's baptism do not afford the least evidence in support of immersion. But a further consideration of this subject will convince every impartial reader that, in the baptism which he administered, immersion was impracticable, and that, consequently, he must have baptized by *affusion.* Let us notice,

(1.) The length of his ministry. By carefully following the evangelical history we shall arrive at a reasonable certainty that it could not have been continued longer than about nine months. The facts are these: At the time of our Lord's baptism John had been officiating about six months. Jesus, after he was baptized, went immediately into Galilee, where, on the third day after his arrival, he attended the marriage at Cana; John ii, 1. " After this he went down to Capernaum, and continued there not many days;" verse 12. He thence " went up to Jerusalem," to attend the Passover; verse 13. Leaving the city of Jerusalem, he went out into the country of Judea, and baptized; chapter iii, 22. At this time "John also was baptizing in Ænon, near to Salim;" verse 23. When our "Lord knew how the Pharisees had heard that Jesus made and baptized more disciples than John . . . he left Judea, and departed again into Galilee;" chapter iv, 1, 3. But it was not until "he had heard that John was cast into prison." Matt. iv, 12.

We conclude, therefore, that John was arrested while at Ænon, shortly after the passover to which we have referred, or in the latter part of March, A. D. 27, and only about nine months after he had commenced his public ministry. That his ministerial career was of longer duration cannot be proved from the Scriptures. But let us now turn our attention,

(2.) To the number that must have received John's baptism. The inspired record is, "Then went out to him Jerusalem, and all Judea, and all the region round about Jordan, and were baptized of him in Jordan." Matt. iii, 5, 6. Now, according to Josephus, there were then not less than five millions of people in the land of Judea; and it would be a very moderate calculation to suppose that at least one fifth of them were baptized by John. But is it possible that he could have immersed so many in the short period of nine months? This would have required him to immerse at least three thousand seven hundred persons per day, which is utterly impossible without an absolute miracle. But as John's baptism was a kind of ceremonial purifying, as we learn from John iii, 25, it was perfectly easy to accomplish his work in the given time by taking a bunch of hyssop, according to the Jewish custom, and baptizing the people by *sprinkling*, as Moses baptized the congregation of Israel. (Heb. ix, 19.)

But let us now consider the baptisms that occurred under the administration of the apostles. The first instance is that of the three thousand who were baptized on the day of Pentecost in the city of Jerusalem. "Then they that gladly received his word were baptized; and the same day there were added unto them about three thousand souls." Acts ii, 41. Is there any evidence that these three thousand persons were immersed? There certainly is not; but the very reverse is evident from all the circumstances of the case.

(1.) The time was too short for twelve men to immerse so many. It was the third hour of the day, or nine o'clock, when Peter began his discourse. This, together with the subsequent transactions which are recorded, and the examination of the three thousand candidates for baptism, could not have occupied less than four hours, and then only five hours of the day remained in which to baptize them. Could each of the apostles have immersed two hundred and fifty persons in five hours? The thing is perfectly incredible.

We know some have said that they were not *all* baptized on the same day; but this, being a direct contradiction of the word of God, merits no reply. Others assert that the seventy disciples assisted the apostles on the occasion; but there is just as much evidence to prove that they were assisted by the scribes and the Pharisees. It has been asserted also that *affusion* requires as much time as *immersion;* but this, to every impartial mind, is its own refutation.

(2.) It is impossible that suitable places could have been found in the city of Jerusalem for the immersion of so great a multitude. Immersionists tell us that John was under the necessity of going to Jordan or

Ænon in order to find water in sufficient quantity to immerse his disciples. But all at once, in their imagination, Jerusalem is so well supplied with water that the apostles, in the course of five or six hours, could immerse three thousand persons. If this is true, their "much water" argument falls to the ground; for if so many, in so short a time, could be immersed in the city of Jerusalem, it was surely unnecessary for all her inhabitants to make a journey of more than twenty miles in order to be immersed by John in Jordan.

But it is not true that the city was thus supplied with water. There was no river nigher than Jordan, which was some twenty-five miles distant; nor was there in its vicinity any fountain, except that of Siloam, or any stream of water, except the brook Kedron, which was always dry at the time of Pentecost. Harmer says, " that pure water, and such as people might drink, was exceedingly scarce and precious in Jerusalem and its vicinity; what the inhabitants procured for use being preserved with the utmost care in domestic reservoirs, made at great expense, and filled chiefly by the rains and snows which fell in the wet and winter seasons."* It cannot, therefore, be supposed, without great extravagance, that the three thousand were immersed. But,

(3.) If there had been a sufficient number of bathing places in Jerusalem for the immersion of so many, is it at all probable that they could have been obtained for the purpose of Christian baptism? It certainly is not; for those in power, and the leading men in general, were violently opposed to the apostles and to the Christian religion. Can we suppose that the very men who a few days before had "killed the Lord of life and glory," and were then persecuting his followers, would offer the apostles the use of the brazen sea, and of their private baths and reservoirs, in order to serve the Christian cause? The supposition would be absurd in the extreme. And,

(4.) Besides all this, it must not be forgotten that neither the apostles nor the assembled multitude expected the ordinance of baptism to be administered on the occasion, and hence no preparations had been made for such an event. It is, therefore, highly improbable that those who were baptized had with them changes of raiment; and to immerse them in their ordinary garments, when no such change could be procured, would have produced in many certain disease, and in some, at least, premature death. Had they been immersed, such a change of clothing would, therefore, have been indispensable; unless, as some have supposed, they were immersed *naked.*

But if they had even possessed the necessary change of raiment, where could the change have been made? Surely not in the presence of a promiscuous multitude of males and females. And yet not a word is said about suitable apartments at the pools in Jerusalem, in which men and women might separately change their clothing; but the whole

*Harmer's Observations, chap. 1, article 21.

account seems to proceed on the principle that they heard the discourse of Peter, became truly penitent and were baptized, without ever leaving the place in which they had assembled. If, then, we take all these circumstances together, we can come to no other conclusion than that the three thousand who were admitted to the fellowship of the Church on the day of Pentecost were baptized by *affusion*.

In the eighth chapter of Acts we have an account of the baptism of the Ethiopian eunuch, which is the only case under the administration of the apostles in which baptism took place at a stream of water, and in which the candidate is said to have gone *down into the water* for that purpose. It is, therefore, a case on which immersionists greatly rely; but an examination of its attendant circumstances will show that it affords no evidence in support of their theory. We have, on a previous page, met the argument which immersionists draw from the use of the Greek prepositions EIS and EK, the former of which is here rendered *into*, and the latter *out of*. We have shown that the phrases " EIS TO HUDOR " and " EK TOU HUDATOS " may be justly rendered, *to the water*, and *from the water*, without conveying any idea at all of being *in* the water. It is, therefore, only necessary to inquire,

(1.) Whether the " certain water " spoken of by the sacred writer was of sufficient depth for immersion. The phrase " EPI TI HUDOR," " *unto a certain water*," may be as correctly, and even more correctly rendered *to some water*, or *to a little water*, TI having sometimes a diminutive sense. Again, the phrase " *see here is water*," is in the original " IDOU HUDOR," *behold water!* and is evidently the language of emotion, showing the surprise of the eunuch at finding water so unexpectedly. He does not say, " See, here is a *river*," or " here is *much* water," but " Behold water," without any reference to its quantity or depth. But what is the testimony of travelers in regard to this matter? Jerome, Sandys, and others tell us that no stream can be found in those parts which is at any time more than ankle deep; and consequently, none deep enough for immersion. But,

(2.) What was there in the text, and in the sermon of Philip, that could have directed the mind of the eunuch to the subject of baptism? There was nothing in the text, so far as we can see, except the clause, " So shall he *sprinkle* many nations." Isa. lii, 15. It was from that portion of Scripture with which this passage stands connected that Philip " preached unto him Jesus ;" and it is but reasonable to conclude that, in his exposition of the prophecy, he called the attention of the eunuch to this clause as well as to others. But in what manner does Christ sprinkle the nations? Doubtless by the efficacy of his atoning blood, of which water baptism is the appointed symbol. If by this means the eunuch arrived at a knowledge of the ordinance of baptism, (and the history points out no other,) it is not to be supposed that he made so egregious a blunder as to substitute immersion for *sprinkling*, which is so clearly spoken of in the text. All the circumstances of the case unite, therefore, in proving that the eunuch must have been baptized by *affusion*.

We come to consider, in the next place, the baptism of Saul of Tarsus. This is recorded in Acts ix, 18: "And he received sight forthwith, and arose and was baptized." What evidence have we that Saul was immersed? Why, there was a river near Damascus, and, therefore, he must have been baptized in this manner. Wonderful logic this! We might as well argue, that because London lies upon the Thames, therefore all the ministers in that vast city baptize by immersion.

Some think that the phrase "wash away thy sins" refers to water baptism, and points out the mode to be that of immersion. But besides the absurdity of supposing that sin can be washed away by water, this wild notion is refuted by the obvious meaning of the phrase in connection with the context. The language of Ananias is, "Arise and be baptized; and wash away thy sins, *calling on the name of the Lord Jesus.*" It was not, then, by the water of baptism that his sins were to be washed away, but by calling on that Saviour who alone can wash "us from our sins in his own blood."

But let us now inquire whether the circumstances in this case afford any light in regard to the *mode* of baptism. When Ananias found Saul in the house of Judas he seems to have been, perhaps from long fasting and penitential sorrow, confined to his bed or couch; for when he was restored to sight he "looked *up* upon" Ananias. Acts xxii, 13. As soon as Ananias had delivered to him his message he "arose and was baptized." Not a word is said about leaving the house, or going to the water; and it would be the conclusion of every impartial reader, that he was baptized in the room where Ananias found him. But this is not all. The language of the inspired penman directs our attention to the very attitude in which he received the ordinance. The words of the original are ἀναστὰς ἐβαπτίσθη; literally, *standing up he was baptized*. It is, therefore, as clear as language can make it, that Saul was baptized in an erect position; and as this occurred in the very place where Ananias first saw him, he must have been baptized by *affusion*.

In Acts x, 47, 48, we have an account of the baptism of Cornelius and his friends. "Can any man forbid water," said Peter, "that these should not be baptized, which have received the Holy Ghost as well as we? and he commanded them to be baptized in the name of the Lord." Here we may remark, 1. That when Peter entered into the house of Cornelius he "found many that were come together." 2. That they did not leave the house to go in search of water, but were evidently baptized in the same place where the Holy Ghost fell on them. And, 3. That the language of Peter proves that the baptismal water was to be brought to them, instead of their being taken to the water. "Can any man forbid water?"—that is, to be *brought*, and that, too, in a reasonable way. No one could be so awfully stupid as to suppose that Peter intended to have a cistern of water brought into the house in order that the candidates might be immersed. Judging, then, from all the facts in the case, we are compelled to conclude that Cornelius and his friends were baptized by *affusion*.

The last case which we will notice in this connection is that of the jailer and his family. This case of baptism, and its attendant circumstances, are recorded in Acts xvi, 24–34. To place the matter in its true light it may be necessary to notice a few particulars, all of which are clearly sustained by the history. And, 1. The jail itself consisted of at least two apartments, the outer or common prison, and what is called "the inner prison;" verse 24. 2. The house of the jailer was either a part of the prison building, or joined to it, so that from its door or window the prison doors were in full view; for when the jailer awoke he saw "the prison doors open;" verse 27. 3. There was light in the house of the jailer, but none in the inner prison; for though he saw the prison doors open, he could not discern the prisoners, and supposed, therefore, that they had fled. But they could see him, for when he was about to kill himself, "Paul cried out, Do thyself no harm; for we are all here;" verses 27, 28. 4. "Then he called for a light, and sprang in" to the inner prison, and "brought them out" to the outer or common prison; verses 29, 30. 5. Here it was that the jailer made the inquiry, "Sirs, what must I do to be saved?" Here Paul preached Christ unto him; and it was here, and nowhere else, that he and his family were baptized; verses 30–33.

To suppose that the parties left the prison for the purpose of attending to the ordinance is to suppose, 1. That the jailer was baptized while wickedly violating the laws of his country and the most sacred duty of his office. 2. That Paul and Silas encouraged him in this open violation of law, and were therefore no better than he. And, 3. That they hypocritically pretended, when morning came, that they had not been out of the prison, for they refused to leave it until the magistrates should come and take them out; verse 37. These suppositions being evidently absurd, it necessarily follows that the jailer and his family were baptized in the prison; and as it does not appear that there was in the prison any convenience for immersion, the conclusion is that they were baptized by *affusion*. That this is the true scriptural mode of baptism may be argued,

3. *From its emblematical import.*—It is "an outward and visible sign of an inward and spiritual grace." It symbolizes the cleansing efficacy of the blood of Christ, and the regenerating influences of the Holy Spirit. These Gospel blessings are constantly spoken of under the figure of *sprinkling* or *pouring*, but never under that of *immersion*. Thus Isaiah, in speaking of the glorious effects that should follow the sufferings of Christ, says, "So shall he *sprinkle* many nations." Isa. lii, 15. This

promise must relate either to the gracious influences which Christ bestows upon the nations of the earth, "through the redemption of his blood," called "the blood of *sprinkling*," or to the admission of men into his visible Church by the ordinance of baptism. If to the former, these gracious influences are designated by the term "*sprinkle*," to which baptism, the outward sign, should surely correspond; but if to the latter, it fixes the mode of baptism to be by *affusion*, and not by immersion. The prophet does not say, "So shall he" *immerse* "many nations."

We have a similar promise, but one which is still more definite, in Ezekiel xxxvi, 25 : "Then will I *sprinkle clean water* upon you, and ye shall be clean : from all your filthiness, and from all your idols will I cleanse you." This passage, which doubtless refers to Gospel times, marks most distinctly both the purifying influence of Divine grace upon the heart, "from all your filthiness, and from all your idols will I cleanse you," and the outward sign of this inward grace, "then will I sprinkle clean water upon you." St. Paul, in addressing the Hebrew Christians, who were well acquainted with the prophetic Scriptures, refers, no doubt, to this very promise. "Let us draw near with a true heart, in full assurance of faith, having our hearts *sprinkled* from an evil conscience, and our *bodies* washed with *pure water*." Heb. x, 22. By the phrase, "our bodies washed with pure water," the apostle refers to their Christian baptism, which was the fulfillment of the promise, "then will I *sprinkle clean water* upon you."

The New Testament Scriptures speak of the cleansing effects of the blood of Christ under the idea of *sprinkling*. Hence St. Paul says that we are come "to the blood of *sprinkling*, that speaketh better things than that of Abel." Heb. xii, 24. St. Peter also speaks of the "*sprinkling* of the blood of Jesus Christ." 1 Peter i, 2. But if our moral cleansing by the blood of Christ is called a *sprinkling* by the pen of inspiration, we have in this very fact a strong indication that the outward ordinance which is intended to be symbolical of this inward cleansing should be administered by *affusion*.

The manner in which the baptism of the Spirit is spoken of in the sacred Scriptures should settle forever the mode of Christian baptism. As the baptism of the Spirit is the real and essential baptism, and water baptism only figurative or symbolical, the mode of the former must, in all fairness, determine the mode of the latter. What, then, is the mode of the baptism of the Spirit? We will let inspiration answer the question.

"Behold, I will *pour out* my Spirit unto you." Prov. i, 23. "I will *pour* my Spirit *upon* thy seed." Isa. xliv, 3. "I will *pour out* my Spirit *upon* all flesh; and also upon the servants, and upon the handmaidens in those days will I *pour out* my Spirit." Joel ii, 28, 29. This prediction was fulfilled on the day of Pentecost, when the disciples were "all filled with Holy Ghost, and began to speak with tongues, as the Spirit gave them utterance." Acts ii, 4. And the apostle says that Christ "having received of the Father the promise of the Holy Ghost, he hath *shed forth* this, which ye now see and hear." Verse 33.

While Peter was preaching to those who were assembled in the house of Cornelius, " the Holy Ghost *fell on* all them which heard the word;" and Peter's companions were astonished, " because on the Gentiles also was *poured out* the gift of the Holy Ghost." Acts x, 44, 45. When on another occasion Peter is rehearsing this event, he says, " As I began to speak, the Holy Ghost *fell on* all them, as on us at the beginning;" that is, on the day of Pentecost. " Then remembered I the word of the Lord, how that he said, John indeed baptized with *water;* but ye shall be baptized with the Holy Ghost." Acts xi, 15, 16. Here, then, let it be observed that the gift of the Holy Spirit is, by Divine authority, declared to be a *baptism*, and that the *mode* of this baptism is that of *affusion*.

We have now shown, beyond successful controversy, that there is not a solitary proof in the Bible for *immersion;* that the circumstances connected with the administration of baptism, as recorded in the New Testament, are all in favor of *affusion;* and that the baptism of the Holy Spirit, of which water baptism is the symbol, is defined, in regard to its *mode*, by the phrases *pour out, pour upon, shed forth,* and *fell on.* It is, therefore, clear as a mathematical demonstration, that *affusion* is the scriptural mode of Christian baptism.

CHAPTER IV.

THE LORD'S SUPPER.

HAVING considered at some length the nature, the subjects, and the mode of baptism, we shall now proceed to examine the other sacramental ordinance of the Christian Church—the *Lord's supper.*

This sacrament is called the *Lord's supper* because the Lord himself appointed it, and because it was first instituted in the evening, and at the close of the paschal supper. It is called the *communion*, as herein we hold communion with Christ and with his people. It is also called the *eucharist*, a thanksgiving, because Christ, in the institution of it, gave thanks; and because we, in the participation of it, are required to be thankful.

Baptism and the Lord's supper agree in the following respects: "The author of both is God; the spiritual part of both is Christ and his benefits; both are seals of the same covenant, are to be dispensed by ministers of the Gospel and by none other, and to be continued in the Church of Christ until his second coming." Their difference is, "that baptism is to be administered but *once* with *water*, to be a sign and seal of our regeneration and engrafting into Christ, and that even to infants; whereas the Lord's supper is to be administered *often*, in the elements of *bread* and *wine*, to represent and exhibit Christ as spiritual nourishment to the soul, and to confirm our continuance and growth in him, and that only to such as are of years and ability to examine themselves."*

In the further examination of this subject we propose to consider, 1. The institution of the ordinance; 2. Its perpetual obligation; and, 3. Its nature; and then to conclude the chapter by a few general observations.

I. THE INSTITUTION OF THE ORDINANCE.

As baptism was substituted for circumcision, so the Lord's supper was placed by our Saviour in the room of the Passover. This Jewish sacrament was an eminent type of the sacrificial death of our Lord for the redemption of man. But since he was about to fulfill the symbolical rite which from age to age had continued to exhibit him to the faith and hope of ancient saints, it could have no place under the new dispensation. Christ in person became the true Passover; and a new rite was necessary to commemorate the spiritual deliverance of men, and to confirm its benefits.

The circumstances attending the original institution of the Christian eucharist were deeply impressive. Our Lord was on the point of closing his life by an ignominious and agonizing death. He was just entering on the bloody conflict, and having assembled his disciples to partake of his last supper, he apprized them of his approaching departure, and delivered to them appropriate instructions for their own private consolation, and for the public discharge of their ministry. At that solemn moment, with the typical representation of his sacrifice before them, "He took bread," the bread then on the table, "and when he had given thanks, he brake it and said, Take, eat; this is my body, which is broken for you; this do in remembrance of me. After the same manner also he took the cup when he had supped, saying, This cup is the New Testament in my blood; this do ye, as oft as ye drink it in remembrance of me;" or, as it is expressed by St. Matthew, "And he took the cup, and gave thanks, and gave it to them, saying, Drink ye all of it; for this is my blood of the New Testament, which is shed for many for the remission of sins." 1 Cor. xi, 23–25; Matt. xxvi, 27, 28.

II. ITS PERPETUAL OBLIGATION.

That the Lord's supper was intended to be a standing rite in the Christian Church, and not a temporary institution, to be confined to the disciples then present, is evident from the testimony of St. Paul respect-

* Larger Catechism; answer to questions 176, 177.

ing it, as recorded in 1 Corinthians xi, 23–26. From this passage we learn,

1. That the apostle received a special revelation as to this ordinance, which must have had a higher object than the mere commemoration of a historical fact, and must be supposed to have been made for the purpose of enjoining it upon him to establish this rite in the Churches raised up by him, and of enabling him rightly to understand its authority and purport, where he found it already appointed by the founders of the first Churches.

2. That the command of Christ, "This do in remembrance of me," which was originally given to the disciples present with our Lord at the last Passover, is laid upon St. Paul and upon the Corinthians. This is, therefore, in proof of the perpetuation of the ordinance. And,

3. That the apostle regarded the Lord's supper as a rite to be frequently celebrated, and that in all future time, until the Lord himself should come to judge the world. "For as often as ye eat this bread, and drink this cup, ye do show the Lord's death till he come." The perpetual obligation of this ordinance cannot, therefore, be reasonably disputed.

III. THE NATURE OF THE LORD'S SUPPER.

Of the *nature* of this great and affecting rite of Christianity different and very opposite opinions have been formed, arising partly from the elliptical and figurative modes of expression adopted by Christ at its institution, but more especially from the influence of superstition upon some, and the extreme of affected rationalism upon others. We will first present a brief statement of the leading theories in regard to the nature of this ordinance, and then establish its true sacramental character.

1. *Theories respecting the nature of the* Lord's supper.—Of these we notice,

(1.) The doctrine of *transubstantiation.*—It is conceived by those who hold this doctrine that the words, "This is my body, this is my blood," are to be taken in their most literal sense; that when our Lord pronounced these words he changed, by his almighty power, the bread upon the table into his body and the wine into his blood, and really delivered his body and blood into the hands of the apostles; and that at all times when the Lord's supper is administered, the priest, by pronouncing these words with a good intention, has the power of making a similar change. They conceive further, that the bread and wine thus changed are presented by the priest to God as a sacrifice; which, though it is distinguished from all others by being without the shedding of blood, is a true propitiatory sacrifice for the sins of the dead and the living. It is conceived that the materials of this sacrifice, being truly the body and blood of Christ, possess an intrinsic virtue, which does not depend upon the disposition of him who receive them, but operates immediately upon all who do not obstruct the operation by a mortal sin. It is conceived, moreover, that as the elements of the supper, when converted into the body and blood of Christ, are natural objects of reverence and adoration to Christians, it is highly proper to worship them upon the altar; and that it is expedient to carry them about in solemn procession, that they may receive the homage of all who meet them.

This monstrous theory of the Church of Rome is as contradictory to the holy Scriptures, whose words it professes to receive in their literal meaning, as it is revolting to the senses and reason of mankind. Had it not been for the ignorance and superstition of Europe during the middle ages this perversion of the rite could not have been effected; and even then it was not established as an article of faith without many struggles. Almost all writers on the Protestant controversy will furnish a sufficient confutation of this capital attempt to impose upon the credulity of mankind; and to them, should it need any refutation, the reader may be referred.

(2.) *Consubstantiation.*—This is the designation of that theory which was adopted by Luther respecting the presence of Christ in the Lord's supper. He denied that the elements were changed by consecration, and therefore taught that the bread and wine remained the same, but that *with them* the body and blood of Christ were *really* present in this sacrament, and were *literally* received by the communicants. Some of his immediate followers did not, however, admit more on this point than that the body and blood of Christ were really present in the sacrament; but that the manner of that presence was an inexplicable mystery. But we notice,

(3.) That theory which regards the Lord's supper as merely an impressive commemorative rite.—Carolostadt, a professor with Luther in the University of Wittenberg, and Zuinglius, a native of Switzerland, the founder of the Protestant Churches which are not Lutheran, taught that the bread and the wine in the Lord's supper are the signs of the absent body and blood of Christ; that when Jesus said, "This is my body, this is my blood," he employed a common figure of speech, in which the sign is put for the thing signified. Thus the Lord's supper is regarded as a mere religious commemoration of the death of Christ, with this addition, that it has a *natural fitness* to produce salutary emotions, to possess our minds with religious reflections, and to strengthen virtuous resolutions.

This is the view of the subject which is generally entertained by Socinians; and though it avoids the absurdities of transubstantiation, and escapes the difficulties in which the theory of Luther is involved, yet, with much truth, it falls short of the whole truth. Hence we present as the true theory,

(4.) The opinion of the Reformed Churches, as taught by Calvin.— "As he agreed with Zuinglius, in thinking that the bread and wine were the *signs* of the body and blood of Christ, which were not locally present, he renounced both transubstantiation and consubstantiation. He agreed further with Zuinglius, in thinking that the use of these signs, being a memorial of the sacrifice once offered on the cross, was intended to produce a moral effect. But he taught that to all who remember the death of Christ in a proper manner, Christ, by the use of these signs, is *spiritually present*—present to their minds; and he considered this spiritual presence as giving a significancy that goes far beyond the Socinian sense to these words of St. Paul: 'The cup of blessing which we bless, is it not the communion of the blood of Christ? The bread which we break, is it not the communion of the body of Christ?' It is not the blessing pronounced which makes any change upon the cup; but to all who join with becoming affection in the thanksgiving then uttered, in the name of the congregation, Christ is spiritually present, so that they may truly and emphatically be said to be partakers of his body and blood; because his body and blood being spiritually present, convey the same nourishment to their souls, the same quickening to the spiritual life, as bread and wine do to the natural life. According to this system the full benefit of the Lord's supper is peculiar to those who partake worthily. For while all who eat the bread and drink the wine may be said to show the Lord's death, and may also receive some devout impressions, they only to whom Jesus is spiritually present share in that spiritual nourishment which arises from partaking of his body and blood."* But that we may understand more fully the nature and importance of this ordinance, let us consider,

2. *Its true sacramental character.*—The Lord's supper is more than a commemorative rite. It is a commemorative rite *sacramentally;* in other words, it is a commemorative *sign* and *seal* of the covenant of our redemption. It is,

(1.) A SIGN.—As such it exhibits, 1. The infinite love of God to the world in giving "his only-begotten Son, that whosoever believeth in him should not perish, but have everlasting life." 2. The love of Christ who "died the just for the unjust, that he might bring us to God." 3. The extreme nature of his sufferings, which were unto *death.* 4. The vicarious and sacrificial character of that death as a sin-offering and a propitiation, in virtue of which only a covenant of grace was entered into with man by the offended God. 5. The benefits derived from it through believing—" remission of sins," the nourishment of the soul in spiritual life, and its growth and perfection in holiness.

(2.) It is A SEAL.—As such it is, 1. A constant assurance, on the part of God, of the continuance of his covenant of redemption in full and undiminished force from age to age. 2. It is a pledge to every believing penitent who receives this sacrament, with entire reliance on the merits of Christ's passion for forgiveness, that he is an object of merci-

* Hill's Lectures.

ful regard and acceptance. 3. It is a constant exhibition of Christ as the food of the soul, to be received by faith. 4. It is an assurance of the bestowment of all the blessings of the new covenant, both in regard to this life and to that which is to come.

In every celebration of the Lord's supper, the *sign* of all these gracious acts, provisions, and hopes is exhibited, and God condescends thus to repeat his *pledges* of faithfulness and love to his Church. On the other hand, the members of the Church renew their acceptance of the covenant of grace; they publish their faith in Christ; they glory in his *cross*, his sacrificial though shameful death, as the wisdom of God and the power of God; and they feast by faith on Christ, the true Passover with *joy and thanksgiving*, on account of their great deliverance.

IV. WE WILL CONCLUDE WITH A FEW GENERAL OBSERVATIONS.

1. The very nature of this ordinance excludes from a participation in it not only open unbelievers, but all who reject the doctrine of atonement by the vicarious sufferings and death of Christ. If the Lord's supper is something more than a mere commemoration of the fact of Christ's death; if it recognizes the sacrificial character of his death, and the doctrine of "faith in his blood," as necessary to our salvation, this is "an altar of which they have no right to eat" who reject these doctrines.

2. It is equally clear that persons who have never truly repented, and have no desire for salvation according to the terms of the Gospel, are utterly disqualified to partake at "the table of the Lord." They would eat and drink unworthily, and would therefore fall into condemnation. Such persons are expressly prohibited from communicating with the Church by apostolic authority as well as by the original institution of this sacrament, which was confined to Christ's disciples; and ministers would be partakers of "other men's sins" if they were knowingly to admit to the supper of the Lord those who in their spirit and lives deny him.

3. On the other hand, the table of the Lord is not to be surrounded with superstitious terrors. To it all are welcome to come who truly love Christ, and all who sincerely desire to love, serve, and obey him. All truly penitent persons, all who take Christ as the sole foundation of their hope, and are ready to commit their eternal interests to the merits of his sacrifice and intercession, are to be encouraged to "draw near with faith, and to take this holy sacrament to their comfort." In it God visibly exhibits and confirms his covenant to them, and he invites them to become parties to it, by the act of their receiving the elements of the sacrament *in faith*.

4. For the frequency of celebrating this ordinance we have no rule in the New Testament. The early Christians observed it every Sabbath, and exclusion from it was considered a severe sentence of the Church when only temporary. The expression of the apostle, "as *often* as ye eat this bread," intimates that the practice of communion was frequent;

and perhaps the custom of monthly administration will come up to the spirit of the original institution. That it was designed, like the Passover, to be an annual celebration only, has no evidence from Scripture, and is contradicted by the most ancient practice.

5. The habitual neglect of this ordinance by persons who profess a true faith in Christ is highly censurable. In this case a plain command of Christ is violated, though not perhaps with direct intention; and the benefit of this singularly affecting means of grace is lost, in which our Saviour renews to us the pledges of his love, repeats the promises of his covenant, and calls for invigorated exercises of our faith, only to feed us more richly with the bread that comes down from heaven. If a peculiar condemnation falls upon them who partake "unworthily," then a peculiar blessing must follow from partaking worthily; and it therefore becomes the duty of every minister to explain the obligation, and to show the advantages of this sacrament, and earnestly to enforce its regular observance upon all those who give satisfactory evidence of "repentance toward God, and faith in our Lord Jesus Christ."

BOOK VII.

THE FUTURE STATE.

WE come now to consider some of the leading doctrines of the Scriptures in regard to a future state. This is the last general division of Christian theology, and includes the immortality of the human soul, the resurrection of the body, a general judgment, the eternal blessedness of the saints, and the endless punishment of the wicked.

CHAPTER I.

THE IMMORTALITY OF THE SOUL.

THAT the human soul is a spiritual and immaterial substance, distinct from the body, is a doctrine which we believe to be taught both by reason and revelation. But when we speak of its *immortality* we do not claim that this results from its immateriality, or that it is necessarily immortal and indestructible merely because it is immaterial. Such a conclusion would compel us to ascribe immortality to the brute creation also; for, that the spirit of a beast is purely immaterial will hardly be denied by any one who believes that matter cannot think. God alone has a necessary existence, and is absolutely, and independently, and of himself immortal. All other beings, whether material or immaterial, have a *borrowed* existence, for the continuance of which they are entirely dependent upon God; and this is as true of our souls as it is of our bodies—of the whole universe as of a single atom. When, therefore, we ascribe immortality to the soul, we base it, not on the soul's inherent nature, but on the will and appointment of God. With this restriction, our meaning is that when the body dies, the soul, by the order and appointment of God, still lives separate from it; that it retains its natural and moral attributes; and that it is capable of happiness or misery in its absence from the body.

That the human soul survives the body and is immortal might be argued with a good degree of plausibility from the general consent of the best informed of mankind in all ages; from the vast powers of the soul itself; from its ardent desire for immortality; and from the unequal distribution of good and evil in the present life. But as this is eminently a doctrine of divine revelation, and can only be established by an appeal to the Scriptures, we will bring the question at once to this standard, and examine it in the light of what God himself has declared upon the subject. This is the more necessary since it is contended by many that the Scriptures determine death to be the complete destruction of the whole man—the extinction of the soul, as well as the body.

The theory of *destructionism* or *annihilationism*, to which we here allude, is in direct opposition to the commonly received doctrine respecting the soul's immortality. In order, therefore, to present the whole subject in as clear a light as our limited space will allow, we will, 1. Offer some remarks in regard to this theory; and, 2. Adduce arguments in support of the immortality of the soul.

I. THE THEORY OF DESTRUCTIONISM.

In the few remarks which we propose to make upon this theory we must confine ourselves to its history, its fundamental principles, and the mode of argumentation by which it is defended.

1. *Its history.*—That the soul dies with the body, and will be raised with it at the last day, is no new doctrine, but was maintained by an Arabian teacher as early as the third century, against whom Origen wrote. The same doctrine was taught in the twelfth century, and was condemned by Innocent III. In the sixteenth century it was advocated again by some Anabaptists and Socinians. In the close of the seventeenth century it was revived, with considerable popularity, by William Coward, an eminent physician and psychologist of London; and in the eighteenth century the doctrine had a strong advocate in Mr. John Taylor of Norwich. In all these cases, however, it was so successfully resisted by the force of argument that it was repudiated by the great body of the Church as a dangerous error. But not discouraged by former defeats, the theory in the present century is marshaling its forces anew; and seems to be determined, at all hazards, to storm the citadel of man's immortality. Some of the commanders of this army of annihilation are Whately, Dobney, Ham, Hudson, Ellis, Read, and Storrs, whose writings, with those of many others, are now everywhere flooding the Christian world. Let us then notice,

2. *Some of the fundamental principles of this system.*—In regard to many points, annihilationists differ among themselves. In presenting an outline of their system, therefore, we will state only those leading principles respecting which there seems to be a general agreement. They hold,

(1.) That man is *wholly material;* the soul being merely the result of organization, and therefore incapable of a separate existence. In this they are in perfect agreement with Epicurus, Lucretius, and other ancient atheistic philosophers; and also with Spinosa, Toland, Hobbes, Voltaire, and Volney.

(2.) That *death*, as the penalty of the law, consists in the utter destruction or annihilation of the whole man. "Any torment or punishment," say they, "that comes short of terminating the very being of the sufferer, is not death, and therefore is not the penalty of the law."* Here also the philosophy of the annihilationists agrees perfectly with that of Voltaire and other French atheists, and the Robert Owen school of infidels. The only difference is, that the latter oppose their philosophy to the Bible, and to the possibility of a future life; while the former attempt to reconcile their doctrines with the Bible, and with the future life of the righteous.

(3.) That all men shall be raised from that state of non-existence into which they pass at death; but they deny that the same soul or animating principle will be restored to the body.

(4.) That after the general resurrection the wicked will again be annihilated, or blotted out of existence a second time; which they call "the second death," or "eternal destruction." "The future punishment," says J. P. Ham, "will not be an endless preservation in misery, but a total destruction or annihilation."†

(5.) That there is now no hell or place of torment in existence. "It is too commonly taken for granted," says the writer last quoted, "that *place and elements of torment are actually in existence*, and that the wicked, the moment of their decease, are transferred thither." Again, "the fire of hell is not yet kindled, and will not be until after the wicked are raised from the dead, and the processes of the great judgment are completed."‡ And,

(6.) That the righteous, after they are raised from a state of annihilation, shall be endowed with endless life, and rewarded with eternal blessedness in heaven.

Such are the general and fundamental principles of the annihilation theory, and they will very naturally lead us to inquire,

3. *By what mode of argumentation is this system defended?*—We are not to forget that annihilationists regard the Bible as we do, to be a divinely inspired book, and the ultimate ground of appeal in all theological questions. Hence it is to be understood that they claim to be fully sustained in their peculiar views by the teachings of the holy Scriptures. It will appear, however, in the course of this investigation, that their system is supported not by the plain and obvious meaning of inspired truth, but by their own false interpretations. Their fundamental error consists in adopting the atheistic notion, that man is wholly material, and that the human soul is merely the result of animal organization. From this they very naturally draw the conclusion that

* The Bible *versus* Tradition.   † Life and Death, p. 143.   ‡ Ibid.

death is the destruction of the whole man; and as this is the leading and distinguishing tenet of their system, their whole strength of argument is directed to its support.

(1.) They contend that this doctrine is clearly implied in the original penalty, "In the day thou eatest thereof *thou shalt surely die.*" Gen. ii, 17. This, it is asserted, was addressed to the "*whole man;*" and the conclusion is, that the death here spoken of includes the extinction of the *soul*, as well as that of the body. We do not deny that the penalty of the law, as expressed in this passage, implies the death of the *whole man;* but we do deny that it applies to the soul in the same sense that it does to the body, and that it consists in the *destruction* of the whole man. Indeed, the very reverse of this is evident from the case before us. God said to Adam, "Of the tree of the knowledge of good and evil, thou shalt not eat of it; for in the day thou eatest thereof thou shalt surely die." The history tells us that Adam did eat of the forbidden fruit. Did he die in the sense of the Divine threatening "*in the day*" that he transgressed? To say he did *not*, is to charge God with uttering a falsehood. To say that he *did*, is to give up the doctrine that the penalty of the law consists in annihilation; for Adam was not annihilated "in the day" that he fell, but lived nine hundred and thirty years. It follows, therefore, from this very passage, that the annihilation theory is false, and that we must seek some other interpretation of the term *death*, as expressive of the penalty of the law.*

(2.) Annihilationists attempt to support their theory by adducing those Scriptures which compare the mortality of man to that of beasts. "Man being in honor abideth not; *he is like the beasts that perish.* Like sheep they are laid in the grave." Psa. xlix, 12, 14. Here it is asked, "How do the beasts perish? Does the whole beast perish, or only a part of it? If the whole beast perishes, the whole man must perish." This, however, is based upon an entire misapprehension of the passage. The psalmist teaches no other lesson than that the ungodly, notwithstanding all their wealth and pride, must be separated by death from their earthly possessions, and shall as certainly return to the dust as do "the beasts that perish." Again,

Ecclesiastes iii, 19, 20: "For that which befalleth the sons of men befalleth beasts; even one thing befalleth them. As one dieth, so dieth the other; yea, they have all one breath; so that a man hath no pre-eminence above a beast; for all is vanity. All go unto one place; all are of the dust, and all turn to dust again." This passage is perpetually quoted and insisted on by our opponents as a proof of the utter destruction of man at death. But is it indeed true in every respect, that "a man hath no pre-eminence above a beast?" Destructionists themselves do not believe this; and surely our Lord taught a very different lesson when he said, "How much then is a man better than a sheep?" The

* See book 3, chap. 3, § 1.

text proves, however, that a man, so far as his mere *animal existence* is concerned, has "no pre-eminence above a beast." In both, animal life is the same. They breathe the same vital air, and live by the same natural means. They are equally mortal; "as one dieth, so dieth the other." They both return to dust, and thus "go unto one place." But in all this there is nothing to disprove the immortality of the human soul. On the contrary, the doctrine is virtually affirmed in this very connection, when "*the spirit of man that goeth upward*" is distinguished from that of "the beast that goeth downward to the earth."

(3.) They claim that the Scriptures support the doctrine of annihilation by denying to man a state of consciousness after death. In proof of this they cite Psalm cxlvi, 4: "His breath goeth forth, he returneth to his earth; in that very day his thoughts perish." This passage destructionists regard as conclusive proof that the dead are entirely unconscious, and, therefore, entirely extinct. Hence they ask with an air of triumph, "How can a thing be tormented that has no thoughts?" And again: "Will our antagonists explain how it can harmonize with their theory of a state of consciousness after death, that in the day of death a man's 'thoughts perish?'" This, however, is certainly not a difficult matter to explain, when we understand that the term *thoughts*, in this connection, means simply *purposes*, *desires*, or *expectations* connected with the present life—a sense in which the word is often employed. Take, for example, Psalm xlix, 11: "Their inward *thought* (*desire*) is, that their houses shall continue forever." Isaiah lv, 7: "Let the wicked forsake his way, and the unrighteous man his *thoughts ;*" surely not his *thinking* or his *consciousness*, but his purposes or desires. Acts viii, 22: "And pray God, if perhaps the *thought* (*purpose*) of thine heart may be forgiven thee." Indeed, so evidently are the terms thought and purpose used synonymously that we find one employed as exegetical of the other; as in Job xvii, 11: "My *purposes* are broken off, even the thoughts of my heart." We see, therefore, that the passage under consideration is perfectly consistent with the doctrine of the soul's uninterrupted immortality.

Another proof-text of this class is Ecclesiastes ix, 5: "For the living know that they must die; but the dead know not anything, neither have they any more reward." Is this passage to be literally applied to the whole man, as destructionists contend? If so, it will prove not only that the dead have no knowledge, and are therefore extinct, but that there will be no future retribution. For the passage evidently speaks of *all* the dead, without distinction of character; and while it declares that they "*know not anything*," it assures us with the same degree of solemnity that "neither have they *any more a reward*." Thus, by this mode of interpretation the text is made to prove that "death is an eternal sleep." What, then, is its true meaning? Evidently this, that the dead have no knowledge of "anything that is done under the sun;" and that, as their day of probation is ended, no change can ever be effected in regard to their future retribution.

Very similar to this passage is the tenth verse of the same chapter: "Whatsoever thy hand findeth to do, do it with thy might; for there is no work, nor device, nor knowledge, nor wisdom, in the grave whither thou goest." Whether we understand the term which is translated *grave* as denoting the resting-place of the body, or as having reference to the future state of the soul, there is nothing in the passage which militates against the doctrine of immortality. The latter clause assigns the reason for what is enjoined in the former. Why should men do *with their might* the work which is here referred to? Because it can only be done in the present life. For if men die in their sins, "there is no work, nor device, nor knowledge, nor wisdom" in the future state to change their moral condition, or to save them from the penalty of the law.

(4.) Another argument in support of destructionism is drawn from the fact that the Scriptures speak of death as *a state of sleep*. Thus, "David *slept* with his fathers, and was buried in the city of David;" "Many of them that *sleep* in the dust of the earth shall awake;" "Many bodies of saints which *slept* arose;" and numerous other instances. But it is only necessary to remark here that when the dead are said to sleep a metaphor is used, founded upon the striking resemblance between sleep and death; and at the same time, by another trope, a part is spoken of as the whole—the *body* as the entire man. This mode of speaking was not only employed by the sacred writers, but is in common use among ourselves; though we believe, as well as they, in the immortality of the soul. Hence we say of our departed friends, They sleep in death; They are silent in the grave. Must not every one, therefore, perceive the folly of interpreting such figurative language, when used in the Scriptures, in a literal sense? As well might we conclude that the sun performs his journey round the earth every twenty-four hours.

But now let us suppose, for the sake of argument, that the whole man literally sleeps after death. Is such a supposition consistent with the notion of annihilation? It certainly is not. Sleep is a state of being, and necessarily implies the existence of that which sleeps. If the whole man sleeps after death, the whole man must continue to exist. If the soul sleeps as well as the body, it must sleep either *in* the body or *out* of it. If *in* the body, and if, as annihilationists affirm, the soul is the *life* of the body, how can the body be dead while the life is in it? Again, how can the soul sleep in a body which has been utterly destroyed, as in the case of Wiclif and other martyrs? But if the soul sleeps *out* of the body, it must be *separable* from the body, and therefore cannot be the mere result of organization, as is claimed by the annihilation theory. There is nothing, then, in the representation of death as a state of sleep that is at all incompatible with the doctrine of the soul's immortality.

(5.) There are two passages in the New Testament which are urged by destructionists with great confidence as being directly confirmatory of their theory. The first is Acts ii, 34: "For David is not ascended into the heavens." From this it is argued that the soul cannot be immortal—that if David is "both dead and buried," as the apostle asserts, and "is not ascended into the heavens," he must have perished soul and body at death. But to show that this conclusion rests upon a sandy foundation it is only necessary to remark, that though proper names are usually applied to men in their compound and perfect state, yet they are sometimes applied to the body alone, as when it is said that "devout men carried *Stephen* to his burial;" and at other times to the spirit alone, as when the sacred writer tells us that *Moses* appeared on the mount of transfiguration.

The apostle does not say that the *soul* of "David is not ascended into the heavens," but only that *David* is not so ascended. And this is strictly true, whether we understand him to speak of the *body* of David, which is still under the power of death, or of David in his *compound and perfect state*. But that we are to understand the apostle in the latter sense is evident from the context. His theme is the resurrection and ascension of Christ. To prove that Christ had risen from the dead and was glorified in heaven, he quotes the prophetic language of David. But as David had uttered this prediction in the first person, it was necessary for the apostle to show that it had respect to Christ, and not to the prophet himself. Hence he argues that it could not have its fulfillment in David, because he, not having risen from the dead, had not ascended into heaven, in the sense of the prediction. It is plain, therefore, that the ascension of which the apostle speaks implies the resurrection of the body, and glorification of the whole man in heaven. In this sense "David is not ascended into the heavens;" but this is no proof that his soul is not in a state of conscious enjoyment.

The other passage referred to is 1 Corinthians xv, 16–18: "For if the dead rise not, then is not Christ raised. And if Christ be not raised, your faith is vain; ye are yet in your sins. Then they also which are fallen asleep in Christ are perished." There is perhaps no passage of Scripture more frequently quoted by annihilationists than this; but it is certainly not very easy to perceive its relevancy to their purpose. It contains, however, the term "*perished*," which they all understand to mean TOTAL EXTINCTION. But what is the argument of the apostle in this connection? Evidently this, that *if Christ is not risen*, then they who have fallen asleep in him *have perished;* which clearly implies that since he *has* risen they have *not* perished. Now, if *to perish* means to become totally extinct, as destructionists contend, *not to perish* must mean, to continue in a state of conscious being. It follows, therefore, annihilationists themselves being judges, that since Christ has risen from the dead, and has thus declared himself to be the promised Messiah, those who sleep in him have *not* perished, but continue in a state of conscious existence.

Having then exposed, as we think, the futility of the arguments usually urged by annihilationists in vindication of their theory, we will proceed to consider,

II. The testimony of Scripture in regard to the immortality of the soul.

In our inquiries respecting the future state Divine revelation is our only sure guide. No human eye can penetrate the vail that separates us from the unknown world to which we journey. Reason, though a most valuable endowment, can only form conjectures in regard to another life. Imagination may amuse itself in flights of fancy through the spirit-world, but it can ascertain no truth respecting what awaits us beyond the grave. But the Bible, as a revelation from God, brings life and immortality to light, and explains to man in most explicit terms the nature and circumstances of his future destiny. That it teaches the doctrine of the uninterrupted immortality of the human soul is what we believe, and what we now propose to prove. In doing this, we think it best to present the argument under the two following heads: 1. The soul is distinct from the body, and capable of a separate existence. And, 2. It exists after death in an uninterrupted state of consciousness, and will so exist forever.*

1. *The soul is distinct from the body, and capable of a separate existence.*—When we say that the soul is distinct from the body, we do not mean that it is independent of the body in our present mode of existence; but only that it is different from the body in its attributes and functions. The attributes of the soul are not those of matter; such as solidity, magnitude, and figure. These, however, belong to the body, which is therefore material. But man possesses attributes which cannot be ascribed to matter, as consciousness, thought, desire; and hence there must be connected with his being something distinct from matter to which these attributes belong, and this we call the soul. The *functions* of the soul are also distinct from those of the body. Among the latter are circulation, nutrition, motion, and respiration; among the former, conception, volition, and reasoning. But that the soul is distinct from the body, and therefore capable of a separate existence, may be argued,

(1.) From the history of man's creation.—The record is, that "the Lord God formed man of the dust of the ground, and breathed into his nostrils the breath of life, (or *lives*, as the margin has it,) and man

---

* For the endless existence of the soul in a state of retribution, see chapters 4 and 5 of this book.

became *a living soul*." Here it is distinctly stated, that after God had formed from the dust of the ground the corporeal part of man, the soul was superadded as a distinct creation. And, as it is thus distinguished from the body, and was added to the body after it had been formed or organized, it cannot be the mere result of organization; nor can there be any rational ground for the opinion, that it must necessarily perish with the body. Solomon, however, settles the question of the soul's distinct existence. His language is, referring no doubt to man's original creation, " Then shall the dust return to the earth as it was ; and the spirit shall return unto God who gave it." Eccles. xii, 7. Here the sacred penman makes a clear distinction between the body and the soul. The former returns " to the earth *as it was*," according to the Divine announcement, " Dust thou art, and unto dust shalt thou return ;" while the latter returns, not to the earth, as materialism would teach, but "*unto God who* GAVE *it*."

(2.) The committing of the soul to God in the prospect of death is another proof of its separability from the body.—David said, in view of the separation of soul and body in death, " Into thine hand I commit *my spirit*." Psa. xxxi, 5. Our Lord exclaimed, when about to expire on the cross, " Father, into thy hands I commend *my spirit*." Luke xxiii, 46. So likewise the martyr Stephen, when in the agonies of death, uttered the solemn prayer, " Lord Jesus, receive *my spirit*." Acts vii, 59. What was it, then, that the inspired prophet and our dying Lord committed into the hands of God ? And what was it that the expiring Stephen besought the Lord Jesus to receive ? Was it the body? Certainly not. Was it the breath ? Surely no one can seriously suppose that they wished to commit the last portion of air which they breathed to the care of God. What concern could they have about what would become of their last breath ? " Air is air, whether breathed first or last, or not at all; and has no more to do with the spirit than earth or water." Was it the mere animal life which passes into nonentity at death ? To suppose this, would be to suppose that they solemnly committed a nonentity to the care of God, which would be shockingly absurd. The only true answer to the question is that it was the SPIRIT, as the passages declare; the *immaterial* and *immortal* part. It follows, therefore, that the spirit is distinct from the body, and survives its dissolution.

(3.) The same doctrine is taught when death is spoken of as *a giving up of the ghost*, a form of expression which is employed both in the Old and the New Testament.—Thus it is said of Jacob, that " he yielded up the ghost, and was gathered unto his people." Gen. xlix, 33. " Man giveth up the ghost," says Job, " and where is he ?" Job xiv, 10. So also it is said of our Lord that he " yielded up the ghost," or *dismissed the spirit*. Matt. xxvii, 50. Annihilationists do not hesitate to say that this is a " very awkward expression;" and certainly it does not at all suit their theory. But the phrase expresses the exact sense of the original, while it is in perfect harmony with the doctrine, that when the body dies the soul returns to God who gave it. If, however, the soul were not separable from the body, it would be hard to determine the import of such language. But,

(4.) Our position may be further argued from the fact that man has no power to kill the soul.—Our Lord said to his apostles, in order to encourage them against persecution, "Fear not them which kill the body, but are not able to kill the soul; but rather fear him which is able to destroy both soul and body in hell." Matt. x, 28. That persecutors have power to kill the body will not be denied, and therefore needs no proof; but have they power to kill the soul? Our Lord says *they have not.* If, however, destructionism were true, and if the soul were "simply the *life*," as Mr. Ham contends, they would be as able to kill the soul as to kill the body; unless it can be shown by some strange process that the body can be killed without destroying the life.

One of the latest and most popular expositions of the annihilation school on this passage is the following: "Although wicked men and devils can extinguish this life and reduce the being of man to dust, they have no more that they can do; they cannot prevent the resurrection, and therefore cannot *destroy* our being or life." They can " ONLY SUSPEND OUR BEING UNTIL THE RESURRECTION."* But how can such a criticism be reconciled to the language of Christ? It assumes that wicked men have power to extinguish life, to reduce the whole man to dust, and thus to suspend his "being until the resurrection." Consequently, if this is true, they have power to kill the soul in precisely the same sense in which they have power to kill the body. But our Lord says, in direct opposition to this exposition, that they "are *not* able to kill the *soul*." This text, therefore, must continue to stand as an irrefragable proof of the immortality of the human soul, and an unanswerable refutation of the annihilation theory. But we will now proceed to prove,

2. *That the soul exists after death in an uninterrupted state of consciousness.*—There are many passages of Scripture which clearly sustain this doctrine, a few of which we will quote.

(1.) Matthew xvii, 3: "And, behold, there appeared unto them Moses and Elias, talking with him."—As to Elias, he no doubt appeared in the same body that was translated. His appearance, therefore, has no direct bearing upon the question before us. But with Moses the case was very different, for he had died and was buried "in the land of Moab." When, therefore, he appeared to the disciples of our Lord on the mount of transfiguration, he must have appeared as a disembodied spirit, and hence this fact establishes the conscious existence of the soul

* Is man immortal?

after death. To evade the force of this argument annihilationists have indulged in various conjectures. Mr. Z. Campbell supposes the passage to afford "no evidence that either Moses or Elias was ever on that mountain," and concludes that "the whole was a vision."* This he infers from the ninth verse: "Tell the vision to no man." It is fatal to his theory, however, that the word ὅραμα, here rendered "vision," usually signifies *sight, appearance, a thing seen;* and that the parallel passage in Mark determines this to be the true sense: "He charged them that they should tell no man *what things they had seen.*" The vision, therefore, was a real *sight*, Christ himself being judge.

Mr. Storrs, not being satisfied with the *vision* theory, assumes that Moses, on this occasion, "was raised from the dead." The first objection to this view is that it is wholly gratuitous. Of the death and burial of Moses we have positive proof; but there is no intimation in the sacred volume that he was ever raised from the dead. The second objection is that it contradicts the word of God. St. Paul tells us that Christ is "the first-fruits of them that slept,"—"the first-born from the dead;" which would not be true if Moses had risen from the dead when he appeared on the mount. Mr. Storrs attempts to obviate this objection by saying, "It is not true, in an absolute sense, that Christ was the first-born from the dead; for Elisha raised the widow's son. Our Lord also raised several from the dead before his resurrection." But these cases are entirely irrelevant, because the persons alluded to were not raised to a life of immortality. They again died a natural death, and will, with the rest of mankind, be subjects of the resurrection at the last day. If, then, Christ is the first who rose from the dead to die no more, as the Scriptures evidently teach, Moses had not thus risen when he appeared on the mount; and, consequently, his appearance on that occasion and his conversing with our Lord demonstrate the consciousness and activity of departed and disembodied spirits.

(2.) Matthew xxii, 32: "I am the God of Abraham, and the God of Isaac, and the God of Jacob. God is not the God of the dead, but of the living."—This argument of our Lord was intended to refute the error of the Sadducees in regard to the resurrection of the body. But as their denial of this was based upon another fundamental error, namely, the denial of the existence of disembodied spirits, he wisely framed his argument to meet both. The Sadducees professed to believe the writings of Moses, and could not object to the ground of the argument. Our Lord therefore proceeds to draw the conclusion, since God has declared, "*I am the God* of Abraham, and the God of Isaac, and the God of Jacob," that these patriarchs, though long since dead as to the body, must still live; for "God is not the God of the *dead*, but of the *living*." And then, as if intending to place on record an everlasting testimony against annihilationism, he adds, "for ALL *live unto him.*"

* Age of Gospel Light, pp. 34, 35.

Not only do the patriarchs live in the world of spirits, but in like manner all that have died. It follows, therefore, that the conscious existence of the soul is not interrupted by death.

(3.) Luke xvi, 22, 23: "And it came to pass, that the beggar died, and was carried by angels into Abraham's bosom. The rich man also died, and was buried; and in hell he lifted up his eyes, being in torments, and seeth Abraham afar off, and Lazarus in his bosom."—By the phrase *Abraham's bosom*, the Jews understood the resting-place of the pious dead. The word translated *hell* is ᾅδης, which is equivalent to the Hebrew שְׁאוֹל, (SHEOL,) and means simply the place of departed spirits, without any reference to their happiness or misery. It may therefore be employed, in connection with a qualifying term, to designate the place either of future enjoyment or torment.

It is a matter of but little consequence whether we regard this portion of Scripture as a parable or as a real history; for in either case its doctrinal import is the same. If it is a history, it relates what has actually taken place; but if a parable, it is an illustration of what does or may occur. It would be as profane to suppose that Christ conveyed false impressions to mankind under the guise of a parable, as that he deviated from the truth in his plain and positive declarations. He employed parables to illustrate the truth and make it more forcible—not to misrepresent and weaken it. If, then, this is a parable, what does it most naturally and clearly teach? To this there can be but one reply, and that is, It shows that the souls of the righteous enter immediately after death into a state of felicity, and the souls of the wicked into torment; and that there will be no subsequent reversion of their condition. "It cannot be made the representation of anything in this world, because the persons concerned are said to have died, and the world of spirits is clearly designated as the scene of the transaction described. Nor does it represent anything *beyond the judgment;* because, while the one was comforted and the other tormented, the rich man had five brethren alive on the earth under the tuition of Moses and the prophets, and, therefore, eligible to salvation. We take this account, then, as the unequivocal testimony of Infinite Truth to the consciousness of the dead and the diversity of their condition, according to their probationary deportment."*

(4.) Luke xxiii, 43: "Jesus said unto him, Verily I say unto thee, to-day shalt thou be with me in paradise."—This passage expresses, in the clearest possible manner, the immediate entrance of the dying thief into a state of happiness after death, and is, in its most obvious sense, perfectly incompatible with the doctrine of annihilationism. Some of the advocates of this theory wisely pass it over in silence; while others make a most vigorous effort so to explain away its meaning as to reconcile it to their own peculiar views. They assert, for instance,

---

* Methodist Quarterly for 1850, p. 119.

that the adverb *to-day* is used to qualify the verb *say*, and not the verb *shalt be;* and that, therefore, the comma should be placed after the adverb, and not after the pronoun *thee*, as in our authorized version. Thus: " Verily I say unto thee to-day, thou shalt be with me in paradise ;" that is, " thou shalt be with me " after the resurrection.

To justify this change in the punctuation, it is asserted that "the location of the comma is no part of inspired testimony, but a thing of modern invention." And what then? Does this fact give men liberty to turn the Scriptures into nonsense by placing points at random? Or does it not rather say, that the plain and obvious meaning of every inspired passage should determine its punctuation? What a wonderful discovery was made to the dying penitent, according to the notion of annihilationists, when our Lord informed him that he was uttering the language of the text the *very day* he uttered it, and not the day before or the day after! Most men would conclude that he knew this fact, without being so emphatically informed of it. This view of the passage is therefore incompatible with common sense, and must be rejected.

If, then, we understand the text as its common punctuation requires, it must be regarded as the clearest possible announcement of the uninterrupted immortality of the human soul. The Jews employed the term *paradise* to designate the resting-place of the pious dead; and the thief, who was a Jew, could understand the term in no other sense. When, therefore, our Lord said to him, " *To-day* shalt thou be with me in paradise," he must have expected to enter immediately into that place of rest. But this gracious assurance given to the expiring penitent was also backed by that most solemn form of asseveration, ἀμήν, AMEN, *verily*, —a form of expression which the sacred writers never employ, except when they affirm a thing in the most direct and earnest manner. It is even employed as one of the names of Christ: " The *Amen*, the faithful and true witness." Rev. iii, 14.

(5.) 2 Cor. v, 6-8 : " Therefore we are always confident, knowing that, while we are at home in the body, we are absent from the Lord ; (for we walk by faith, not by sight.) We are confident, I say, and willing rather to be absent from the body, and to be present with the Lord."

Here the apostle most evidently teaches, that to be absent from the body is to be present with the Lord; and it is equally evident, that by absence from the body he means the separation of the soul from the body at death. Consequently, the souls of the pious dead are with the Lord; which clearly implies, that they are subjects of uninterrupted immortality. This passage, therefore, is sufficient of itself to settle the question of the soul's conscious existence after death. "There is not the slightest intimation here," says Dr. Clarke, "that the soul sleeps, or, rather, that there is no soul; and when the body is decomposed, that there is no more of the man till the resurrection. I mean according to the sentiments of those who do condescend to allow us a resurrection, though they deny us a soul. But this is a philosophy in which St. Paul got no lessons, either from Gamaliel, Jesus Christ, the Holy Ghost, or in the third heavens, where he heard even unutterable things."

(6.) Phil. i, 21: "For me to live is Christ, and to die is gain."—One would think this to be a difficult passage for annihilationists to interpret. Mr. Storrs, however, explains it thus: "'For me to live is Christ, (is to *magnify* Christ,) and to die is *gain*.' Gain for whom? I answer, *for Christ;* for thereby Christ will be magnified even more than by my life." This is perhaps as plausible an exegesis as this school can afford; but it is liable to one insuperable objection—it contradicts the language of the apostle. He says, "*For* ME to live is Christ, and to die is *gain;*" that is, to die is gain for *me*. And that he considers the gain to be to himself, and not to Christ, is evident from what follows in the same connection. "For I am in a strait betwixt two, having a desire to depart and to *be with Christ;* which is *far better:* nevertheless to abide in the flesh is more needful for you." Thus he believed it to be for the good of the Church that he should live; but for himself it was more desirable that he should die. But why so? *Because* he expected then to be with Christ, in a state of conscious existence and exquisite enjoyment. Who can suppose that St. Paul, with all his burning zeal for Christ and his ardent love for the Church, would rather yield up his whole being to utter destruction, than to live and labor in the cause of God and for the salvation of his fellow-men? Such a supposition would be most unreasonable; and hence this passage must stand as the ever-abiding testimony of the Holy Spirit against the destructive error of annihilationism.

The preceding passages of Scripture are only a few of the many that might be adduced in support of the uninterrupted immortality of the human soul; but they are sufficient, if candidly considered, to establish the doctrine beyond successful controversy. Those who reject their testimony would reject the testimony of a thousand more. It may be proper, however, before we leave this part of the subject, to notice an objection which destructionists often urge against the view of immortality which we have defended. It is this: "If the righteous exist after death in a state of happiness, and the wicked in a state of misery, then men are to be judged twice: first, at death; and secondly, in the judgment of the great day."

To this we reply, 1. That the disembodied spirit, independent of any formal judgment, must, in the very nature of the case, be either in a happy or a miserable condition. Its conscious existence and moral character alone involve this necessity. But, 2. If the doctrine of the uninterrupted immortality of the soul even necessarily implied a twofold judgment, this circumstance would not disprove it. For, what is true of the Divine administration in regard to *angels*, might also be true in regard to *men*. The Scriptures inform us that "God spared not the angels that sinned, but *cast them down to hell;*" or, in other words, adjudged them to their merited punishment; and not only this, but that they are "reserved in everlasting chains under darkness *unto the judgment of the great day.*" If, therefore, the fallen angels can be made the subjects of a twofold judgment, why may not men?

CHAPTER II.

THE RESURRECTION OF THE BODY.

HAVING considered, in the preceding chapter, the doctrine of the soul's immortality, our next subject of investigation is, the resurrection of the human body. This will lead us to examine, 1. Its nature; 2. Its certainty; and, 3. The properties of the body that shall be raised.

I. THE NATURE OF THE RESURRECTION.

By the *resurrection* of the dead we understand the revivification of the body which dies, and its reunion with the immortal spirit; so that after the resurrection every human being will be substantially the same person as in the present life.

The doctrine of the resurrection is purely a doctrine of Divine revelation. Reason does not suggest it; or rather, in the eye of reason it seems incredible. To those, therefore, who have no other guide it is wholly unknown, and when first proposed to such it is usually rejected. When St. Paul delivered his discourse before the Athenian philosophers, and "preached unto them Jesus and the *resurrection,*" they contemptuously called him a "babbler," and said, "Thou bringest certain strange things to our ears."

But though this is a doctrine which reason could not discover, yet, since God has revealed it in his word, reason confirms the dictates of revelation. Reason assures us that the power of God is able to execute the purposes of his will. "Why should it be thought a thing incredible with you that God should raise the dead?" is a question which ought to silence all infidel objectors. As the resurrection does not imply a contradiction, it is possible, and may therefore be effected by Almighty power. He who at first fashioned the human body out of the dust can surely raise it from the dust again. It is therefore unreasonable to hesitate for a moment about the possibility of an event which God has signified his intention to accomplish, merely because we do not understand how it can be effected. To do so is nothing less than to measure the power of God by our own weakness and ignorance.

Assuming, then, for the present, that the resurrection of the human body is a doctrine of the Bible, we will proceed briefly to consider what the Scriptures teach respecting its *nature*. From them we learn,

1. *That it is a resurrection of the same body that dies.*—The identity of the risen body with that which is laid in the grave, may be argued from various considerations.

(1.) It is implied in the very idea of a resurrection.—The word ἔγερσις, which is rendered resurrection, and the corresponding term ἀνάστασις, both signify the rising or standing up of that which had fallen or lain down. Unless the same body which dies is again raised up, the term resurrection is an absurdity. For God to give us a new body—one which the spirit never inhabited, would be a creation, and not a resurrection. Moreover, to suppose that the soul is hereafter to be united to a body which is different from the present, is to suppose that the inspired writers made choice of language to designate this important event, which conveys a fallacious idea. The same body, then, from which the spirit is separated by death, is the body which rises from the dead, and with which the soul is reunited.

(2.) It is explicitly taught in many passages of Scripture.—Thus we read in Daniel xii, 2 : " And many of them that sleep in the dust of the earth shall awake." This cannot be predicated of the soul, for it does not sleep in the dust. It may be also observed, that the terms *sleep* and *awake* imply that when we arise again from the dead our bodies will be as really the same as when we awake from natural sleep. Again, our Lord affirms, John v, 28, 29, " All that are in the graves shall hear his voice, and shall come forth." But if the same body which is laid in the grave does not rise again, how shall they " that are in the graves come forth ?" The graves can give up no bodies but those which were laid in them. It is also expressly taught by St. Paul, that the body which is raised in incorruption, glory, and power, is the very same body that is sown in corruption, dishonor, and weakness;* and that Christ " shall change our vile body, that it may be fashioned like unto his glorious body." Phil. iii, 21. It follows, therefore, that " our vile body," which can be no other than that body with which we are now clothed, is to be made the subject of the resurrection.

(3.) *The same truth is taught in the resurrection of our Lord.*—As he is " the first-fruits of them that slept," his resurrection is to be regarded both as the pledge and the pattern of ours. But it is evident that he did not assume a different body from the one which he had before his death. On the contrary, he proves the fact of his resurrection from his personal identity. " Behold my hands and my feet, that it is I myself;

* See 1 Cor. xv, 42, 43.

handle me, and see." Luke xxiv, 39. Hence, as our Lord rose from the dead in the very same body that was put to death, so we may expect that these mortal bodies of ours "shall put on immortality" in the morning of the resurrection.

An objection to the resurrection of the same body has been drawn from the supposed changes of its substance during life. It is assumed that the body, between youth and old age, changes its entire substance several times; and then it is asserted that if the resurrection body were to include all the matter that ever belonged to it it would necessarily be a monster. The answer to this is, that allowing a frequent and total change of the substance of the body to take place, (which, however, is only a mere hypothesis,) it affects not the doctrine of Scripture, which is, that the body which is laid in the grave shall be raised up.

But then we are told that if our bodies have in fact undergone successive changes during life, the bodies in which we have sinned or performed rewardable actions may not be, in many instances, the same bodies as those which will be actually rewarded or punished. We answer, that rewards and punishments have their relation to the body, not so much as it is the *subject* of them as it is the *instrument*. It is the soul only which perceives pain or pleasure, which suffers or enjoys, and which is, in reality, the only rewardable *subject*. Were we, therefore, to admit such corporeal mutations as are assumed in the objection, they would not affect the case of our accountability.

But who is prepared to prove that what properly constitutes the identity of the body is not continued through the whole of human life? Though we allow the grosser parts of the body to be continually passing away, yet we never suppose that we have lost our body or received a new one. In respect to these grosser parts, our body in infancy was totally different from our present body; and in old age it will be different from what it is now. Still we call it through these different periods *our* body, and regard it as being the *same*. Indeed, if the human body, amid all these supposed changes, does not preserve its personal identity, the common forms of speech, our own consciousness, and the civil jurisprudence of all countries are calculated to mislead; for they all involve the fact that every human being continues to be the same person through every period of life.

Another objection to the resurrection of the same body is, that the same matter may enter successively into the composition of several bodies. "Human bodies may not only become the food of animals which are eaten by men, but they are occasionally devoured by cannibals, and thus converted into a part of their bodies. And if that which was part of one man's body becomes afterward part of the body of another, how can both rise with the same bodies which they had before?" Two things are supposed in this objection: first, that all the particles which have ever belonged to the body will be included in its future composition; and, secondly, that a part of one human body may become a part of another. It is evident, however, that if the first supposition is true the second is false; and if the second is true the first is false; but we cannot affirm anything certainly concerning either. It is enough for us to know that the all-wise and almighty God is able to perform what he has promised.

2. *The resurrection is to be universal.*—It will include the whole human family that have lived and died, from the father of the race to his youngest son. "For the hour is coming, in the which all that are in the graves shall hear his voice, and shall come forth; they that have done good unto the resurrection of life; and they that have done evil, unto the resurrection of damnation." John v, 28, 29. So St. John tells us that "he saw the dead, small and great, stand before God." Rev. xx, 12. How vast will be the assemblage! How sublime the scene! "In a moment, in the twinkling of an eye, at the last trump," all, from the earth and from the sea, from Asia, Africa, Europe, and America, and from the scattered isles that spot the ocean, shall then come forth to life.

The transmutation of the living shall immediately succeed the resurrection of the dead. "Behold," says St. Paul, "I show you a mystery: We shall not all sleep, but we shall all be changed. For this corruptible must put on incorruption, and this mortal must put on immortality." 1 Cor. xv, 51, 53. And again, after speaking of the rising of the dead in Christ, he says: "Then we which are alive and remain, shall be caught up together with them in the clouds, to meet the Lord in the air; and so shall we ever be with the Lord." 1 Thess. iv, 17.

II. THE CERTAINTY OF THE RESURRECTION.

"That there shall be a resurrection of the dead, both of the just and unjust," is the common faith of Jews and Christians. Some, it is true, have supposed the doctrine of the resurrection to be peculiar to the New Testament; but this is obviously an error. We readily admit that it is more clearly revealed in the Christian Scriptures than in those of the Old Testament; but whoever will examine the latter on the subject may easily perceive that, though the Sadducees denied the resurrection of the dead, yet the doctrine was believed by the ancient patriarchs and prophets, and by the Jews in general. This article of the Jewish faith is clearly expressed by Martha when speaking of Lazarus, her departed brother: "I know that he shall rise again in the resurrection at the last day." John xi, 24.

To this doctrine there are many philosophical objections. Some have been noticed, and others might be named; but the wisdom and power of God answer all objections and remove all difficulties. The great question is, whether the resurrection of the dead is a doctrine of Divine revelation. If it is, its truth follows of course. To say that it implies a contradiction is to say that God has formed a world to frustrate his own purposes; which would be to charge the God of nature with folly. Certainly matter, in all its forms, must be under the control of him who created it. When, therefore, he gives the word to raise the human body no obstacle can prevent its resurrection, for it is effected by Almighty power. And does not the power of God effect things as really wonderful every day? "The only difference between these daily occurrences and a miracle is, that the miracle does not occur every day. It is as great a miracle that men breathe, or that the sun rises, as that the dead body shall be raised. It is as great a miracle that men exist now, as that they shall exist again."

There are various analogies in the operations of nature and Providence by which this subject may be illustrated. "What is night but the death of day? What is morning but its resurrection from the shades of darkness? What is winter but the death of the year? In the dead leaves you see emblems of death scattered wherever you go. What is spring but a resurrection? Look at the unsightly seed without any appearance of life, thrown into the earth, and then the particles separating, there springs up a plant! Behold it unfolding, and budding, and blossoming, and casting its fragrance all around: that is its resurrection. We see the insect tribe give their evidence; living frequently and absolutely in different states and elements, sometimes crawling as a worm, then lying in apparent torpor, then bursting the shell and with wings of beauty and activity skimming the atmosphere."* These, however, are merely illustrations, and not adduced as proofs; for as the resurrection of the dead is purely a doctrine of the *Bible*, by no other testimony can it be established.

Having made these remarks as preparatory to the adduction of Bible testimony, we will now proceed to show that the certainty of the resurrection is fully established,

1. *By plain and positive declarations of Scripture.*—"I know," said Job, "that my Redeemer liveth, and that he shall stand at the latter day upon the earth: and though, after my skin, worms destroy this body, yet *in my flesh* shall I see God." Job xix, 25, 26. So also the evangelical prophet speaks in the following animated strain: "Thy dead men shall live, together with my dead body shall they arise. Awake and sing, ye that dwell in dust; for thy dew is as the dew of herbs, and the earth shall cast out the dead." Isa. xxvi, 19. "And many of them that sleep in the dust of the earth shall awake, some to everlasting life, and some to shame and everlasting contempt." Dan. xii, 2. These passages from the Old Testament show that the saints of God, under the former dispensation, looked beyond this world of mortality to the unfolding glories of the resurrection morn.

But this doctrine is still more explicitly declared in the New Testament. Our Lord asserts, that "all that are in the graves shall hear his

* Watson's Sermons, vol. 1, p. 252.

voice, and shall come forth." John v, 28, 29. Again: "This is the Father's will which hath sent me, That of all which he hath given me I should lose nothing, but should *raise it up again at the last day.*" John vi, 39. St. Paul asserts, that "as in Adam all die, even so in Christ shall all be *made alive.* But every man in his own order, Christ the first-fruits; afterward they that are Christ's *at his coming.*" And again: "The trumpet shall sound, and the dead shall be raised incorruptible, and we shall be changed." 1 Cor. xv, 22, 23, 52. Still further: "He which raised up the Lord Jesus, shall raise up us also by Jesus, and shall present us with you." 2 Cor. iv, 14. But this event is secured,

2. *By the resurrection of Jesus Christ himself.*—The sacred writers speak of this fact as being connected with a train of most important consequences, and especially as being connected with the resurrection of the whole human race. Hence Christ is spoken of as "the first-fruits of them that slept." The first-fruits were by the command of God presented to him at a stated season, both as a token of the gratitude of the Israelites for his bounty, and as an earnest of the approaching harvest. In allusion to this rite, Christ is called the first-fruits of the dead. He was first in the order of time; for, though some were restored to life by the prophets and by himself during his personal ministry, none were raised to an immortal life till after his resurrection. And as he was thus first in the order of time, so he was first as an earnest of the resurrection of others. All the saints follow him, as the harvest followed the presentation of the first-fruits in the temple. Go ye, therefore, and search the tomb of Christ, and see in his vacated sepulcher an infallible pledge that your graves shall give you up, and that you, if believers in him, shall be gathered in the general harvest. "Because I live," says Christ, "ye shall live also." The interval between death and the resurrection may be long, and the dreary sterility of the grave may seem to justify the thought that the dust committed to it has perished forever. But our faith rests upon the power of him who can make the wilderness blossom as the rose; and at whose command the charnel house shall give birth to immortality, and death itself shall teem with life. But of this doctrine we have another proof,

3. *In the preaching of the apostles.*—With them, to preach the Gospel was to preach Christ and the resurrection. Thus we learn that Peter and John were cast into prison because " they taught the people, and preached through Jesus the resurrection from the dead." Acts iv, 2. So, also, Paul preached to the Athenians " Jesus and the resurrection ;" and on another occasion, when defending himself before the Jewish council, he exclaimed, " Men and brethren, I am a Pharisee, the son of a Pharisee : of the hope and resurrection of the dead I am called in question." Acts xxiii, 6. We see, therefore, that the apostles made the doctrine of the resurrection of the dead a leading theme in their

public administrations; everywhere insisting on the resurrection of Jesus Christ as "the first-fruits of them that slept," and the consequent resurrection of all the human race. This doctrine is also established,

4. *By a consideration of the nature and extent of redemption.*—Redemption is the payment of a price in order to the liberation of a captive, an idea which is clearly involved in the sacrifice of Christ. Our redemption is twofold, *virtual* and *actual.* Virtual redemption is redemption by price. Actual redemption is redemption in fact—the actual claiming of the captive. Virtual redemption in regard to its extent, includes the whole human family; for Christ tasted "death for every man." It includes also the whole of man's nature—the body as well as the soul. This is evident from what the apostle says: "Ye are not your own, for ye are bought with a price; therefore glorify God in your body, and in your spirit, which are God's." 1 Cor. vi, 19, 20. Hence the bodies of the saints, as well as their souls, have been purchased by Christ. Their members, though dissolved by death, are still written in his book, and will in due time be raised in beauty and immortality, "according to the working whereby he is able even to subdue all things unto himself."

In regard to the soul, every true believer is actually redeemed in the present life; but not so with respect to the body. For, though it is *virtually* redeemed, its *actual* redemption lies beyond the present state of being. That can only be fully accomplished when our Redeemer shall break the iron grasp of death, and liberate the captives of the grave. Till then we must wait for the crowning blessing of our "adoption, to wit, the *redemption of our body.*" Till then the purposes of Christ's mediation will not be fully accomplished; "for he must reign till he hath put all enemies under his feet. The last enemy that shall be destroyed is death." This, therefore, clearly and necessarily implies the resurrection of the human race. And "then shall be brought to pass the saying that is written, Death is swallowed up in victory. O death! where is thy sting? O grave! where is thy victory?" 1 Cor. xv, 54, 55.

III. THE PROPERTIES OF THE RESURRECTION BODY.

This subject is particularly alluded to by St. Paul in the fifteenth chapter of his first epistle to the Corinthians. Some, it is true, suppose that the apostle is here attempting to *prove* the doctrine of the resurrection by arguments drawn from natural things; but as Mr. Watson remarks, "He does no such thing. He never could do it. He was too wise a man to attempt it. He knew it rested on the testimony of Jesus, and not on anything in nature. To deduce from reason the doctrine of the resurrection, is left to half-infidel divines."

The key to the whole argument of the apostle is found in the two following questions: "How are the dead raised up? and with what body do they come?" The first relates merely to the *possibility* of the resurrection, and implies a denial of the fact; or at least, a strong doubt concerning it.* To this he replies, not by attempting to prove that the resurrection is possible, but by showing the folly of denying it; while we are compelled to acknowledge the equally mysterious fact, that in the order of nature the dying seed produces the living plant. "Thou fool! that which thou sowest is not quickened, except it die; and that which thou sowest, thou sowest not that body that shall be, but bare grain, it may chance of wheat, or of some other grain; but God giveth it a body as it hath pleased him, and to every seed his own body." It cannot be shown that the resurrection of the human body is any more wonderful than the process of vegetation, since both must be referred to Divine agency.

The second question, "With what body do they come?" refers to the properties of the resurrection body; but, like the former, it is a question of denial, or at least of strong doubt, and not of mere inquiry. It imports that the objector, even if he allowed the possibility of the resurrection, could form no idea of any material body which would not in its reunion with the spirit be an *evil* instead of a blessing. It was the philosophy of the age, that the body is the prison of the soul; and that the greatest deliverance which men can experience is, to be eternally freed from their connection with matter. Hence the early philosophizing sects in the Christian Church, as the Gnostics and Marcionites, denied the resurrection on the same ground as the philosophers, and thought it opposed to that perfection which they hoped to enjoy in another world.

In reply to this objection the apostle shows that God is able, not only to raise the human body, but so to modify and change its properties as to render it a fit temple for the glorified spirit. He directs our attention to some of the various modifications of matter which have already resulted from the forming hand of the Creator. "All flesh is not the same flesh; but there is one kind of flesh of men, another flesh of beasts, another of fishes, and another of birds. There are also celestial bodies, and bodies terrestrial; but the glory of the celestial is one, and the glory of the terrestrial is another. There is one glory of the sun, and another glory of the moon, and another glory of the stars; for one star differeth from another star in glory." Hence it follows, that as the sun, in all his glorious dress, is as really material as a clod of earth,

---

* The adverb πῶς, *how*, is very frequently employed by the inspired writers in questions which imply negation, as Matthew xii, 26: "If Satan cast out Satan, he is divided against himself; (πῶς) *how* shall then his kingdom stand?" that is, it cannot stand. John v, 47: "If ye believe not his writings, (πῶς) *how* shall ye believe my words?" 1 Tim. iii, 5: "For if a man know not how to rule his own house, (πῶς) *how* shall he take care of the Church of God?" In these and many other passages the word πῶς is evidently used in a negative sense, and in this sense it is to be taken in the question, "How are the dead raised up?"

these bodies of ours, though now humbled in the dust, may be hereafter raised to "glory and honor and immortality."

In the next place, the apostle calls our attention to the contrast between the properties of the body, as it returns to the earth, and those with which it shall be invested in the resurrection. "It is sown in corruption; it is raised in *incorruption*. It is sown in dishonor; it is raised in *glory*. It is sown in weakness; it is raised in *power*. It is sown a natural body; it is raised a *spiritual body*." Though in regard to the resurrection body we cannot fully comprehend what we shall be, yet the language of the apostle places the subject before us in a very satisfactory and engaging light.

1. *Our bodies will be* INCORRUPTIBLE *and* IMMORTAL.—In the present state the human body is liable to dissolution, and contains in itself the principles of decay. It is subject to acute and chronic disease, by which life is suddenly or slowly extinguished; and then the process of putrefaction begins, which terminates in the destruction of its organization and the separation of its parts. But in the future state it will be incapable of waste, disease, or death. The body will be as immortal as the soul; "for this corruptible must put on incorruption, and this mortal must put on immortality." This signifies, not only that we shall die no more, for in this sense the wicked will be incorruptible and immortal, but that we shall be perfectly free from all the bodily evils which result from sin. "There shall be no more death, neither sorrow, nor crying, neither shall there be any more pain." Rev. xxi, 4.

2. *Our bodies will be* GLORIOUS.—Though sown in dishonor, they shall be "raised in *glory*." The word *glory*, when applied to the body, suggests the idea of brightness or splendor; and in this sense we speak of the glory of the sun, and of the stars. It is expressly declared that Christ "shall change our vile body, that it may be fashioned like unto his glorious body." Phil. iii, 20. Mark, then, the *model* of our resurrection bodies: it is the body of Jesus Christ; not as he tabernacled among men; not as he appeared to the disciples between his resurrection and ascension; but in his glorified state, "his *glorious* body." The glory of our Lord's humanity was shadowed forth on the mount of transfiguration, when "his face did shine as the sun, and his raiment was white as the light." It was seen by Saul of Tarsus in its meridian splendor, when he was arrested in his career of persecution. He was on his way to Damascus. The noon-day sun was shining in the cloudless brilliancy of an Asiatic sky. But he was suddenly astonished by a light from heaven "*above the brightness of the sun*." It was *Jesus* that appeared to him in "his glorious body."* So also, when St. John, in the isle of Patmos, beheld his glorified Lord, "his eyes were as a flame of fire, his feet like unto fine brass, as if they burned in a furnace; and his countenance was as the sun shineth in his strength."†

* See Acts ix, 17; xxvi, 16; and 1 Cor. xv, 8. † See Rev. i, 10–16.

How glorious, then, will be the bodies of the saints in the future life! "They that be wise," says Daniel, "shall shine as the *brightness of the firmament;* and they that turn many to righteousness, as the *stars* for ever and ever." And Jesus declares, when speaking of the solemn transactions of the great day, "Then shall the righteous shine forth as the *sun,* in the kingdom of their Father." Matt. xiii, 43. Of this future glory we have a faint resemblance in the luster of the face of Moses, after he had been with God in the holy mount. Such was the glory of his countenance, that the children of Israel "were afraid to come nigh him," until "he put a vail on his face." And that extraordinary majesty which characterized the face of holy Stephen, seemed to be an earnest of his coming glory. "All that sat in the council, looking steadfastly on him, saw his face as it had been the face of an angel." Acts vi, 15. If mortal bodies have been clothed with so much glory, what shall be the future glory of the saints when their bodies shall be fashioned like the glorious body of Jesus Christ!

3. *Our bodies will be* POWERFUL.—Though sown in weakness, they shall be "raised in power." In the present life they are subject to many infirmities. Their strength is soon exhausted, and they require food, and rest, and other means, to restore them. But in the future state languor and weariness will be unknown. We have no means to estimate the strength of the glorified body, as we know of no resistance which it will have to overcome; but we may perhaps judge of it from a circumstance which is revealed concerning the righteous in heaven, that they will be uninterruptedly engaged in the service of God. Constant employment will cause no fatigue, and sleep will not be necessary to renovate their powers. It is plain, therefore, that their bodies will possess a degree of vigor and activity of which we can now form no conception.

4. *Our bodies will be* SPIRITUAL.—It is a remark which must occur to every person, that a *spiritual body* is an apparent contradiction; and we are therefore under the necessity of taking the word *spiritual* in an unusual sense. The apostle does not mean that the resurrection body, like the immortal spirit, will be immaterial; for then it could not be the same body that dies. Nor does he mean that it will be so sublimated or etherialized as not to be *a body* in the proper sense of the word. It will be "a body" (σῶμα), but it will be so far spiritual as to be without the mere animal functions which are essential to the *natural* body. The meaning of the apostle seems to be this: As the soul has an existence independent of animal functions, living without nourishment, and incapable of decay, sickness, or death, so will be the body in the resurrection. It will be destitute of the peculiar physical organization of flesh and blood; for "flesh and blood cannot inherit the kingdom of God." It must therefore undergo a new modification, in consequence of which, though still material, it will be very different from what it now is. It

will be a body without the vital functions of the animal economy, living in the manner in which we conceive spirits to live, and sustaining and exercising its powers without waste, weariness, decay, or the necessity of having them recruited by food and sleep.

We ought to be reminded that there will be a resurrection "both of the just and unjust." But with regard to the wicked, the Scriptures give us no detailed account of the state and qualities of their bodies. We only know that they shall rise "to shame and everlasting contempt." Hence we may infer, that for *them* there will be no glorious body; that they will be dragged from their graves by the messengers of wrath to the throne of judgment; and that their whole external appearance will correspond with their moral degradation, and be expressive of their mental agony. Well may we say, "Gather not my soul with sinners, nor my life with bloody men." When we open our eyes on the morning of the resurrection may we behold a smiling Judge!

The doctrine of the resurrection should fortify Christians against the fear of death. This last enemy is now disarmed, and can do them no hurt. As God said to Jacob, "Fear not to go down into Egypt, for I will go down with thee into Egypt; and I will also surely bring thee up again;" so we may say to all the children of God, Fear not to go down into the grave; for he who watches over your dust will surely bring you up again, and clothe you with immortality. What brighter hope can Christians possess, than this doctrine inspires? It directs the eye of faith to "a house not made with hands, eternal in the heavens;" it pours a heavenly radiance on the dark and lonely tomb; it lights up the smile of joy on the lip of death; and, in accents sweet as angels' voices, it whispers in the ear of the disconsolate mourner, as he follows to the grave the pale remains of the object of his affections, "Thy friend 'shall rise again!'" "Thanks be to God, which giveth us the victory through our Lord Jesus Christ!"

CHAPTER III.

THE GENERAL JUDGMENT.

THE next grand event in the Divine administration toward man, subsequent to the resurrection of the dead, is that of the general judgment — an event which shall terminate the remedial dispensation, put an end to time, and introduce the eternal destinies of men and angels. This, therefore, is one of the most solemn and deeply interesting subjects revealed in the Book of God. Let us consider, 1. The certainty of a general judgment; and, 2. The solemn transactions of the judgment itself.

I. THE CERTAINTY OF A GENERAL JUDGMENT.

There is scarcely a religious truth, except the being of a God, in which mankind have been more universally agreed than in the doctrine of a future judgment. That we are responsible to God for our moral conduct, and that our present state of trial must be followed by one of retribution, are dictates of reason as well as of revelation. The certainty of a future judgment may be argued,

1. *From the justice of God.*—It must be evident to every attentive observer, that, in the present state, the justice of God is only partially exercised; and that the common course of things is conducted without any marked regard to the character and actions of men. Those whom we call good, because their actions are conformable to moral distinctions, are often left to struggle with poverty and to pine in affliction. Even the most illustrious saints, "of whom the world was not worthy," were exposed to penury and contempt, as well as to the violence of ungodly men. They "had trial of cruel mockings and scourgings, yea, moreover, of bonds and imprisonment. They were stoned, they were sawn asunder, were tempted, were slain with the sword. They wandered about in sheep-skins and goat-skins; being destitute, afflicted, tormented."

On the other hand it has been observed, that, in many cases, bold transgressors—men who set their mouths against the heavens, and give loose reins to their appetites and passions, enjoy outward peace, and pass their days in the possession of all that earth can afford to make them happy. "I was envious at the foolish," says the psalmist, "when I saw the prosperity of the wicked. For there are no bands in their death; but their strength is firm. They are not in trouble as other men; neither are they plagued like other men. Their eyes stand out with fatness; they have more than heart could wish." What, then, is the result of this view of the present state of human affairs? The conclusion is inevitable, if we allow God to be just, that, since justice is not at present fully displayed, another dispensation will follow, under which there will be an exact and impartial retribution; that a time will come when the wrongs of the injured shall be redressed, and proud transgressors shall bear the punishment due to their crimes.

2. *From the dictates of conscience.*—By a law of our nature we are compelled to pass sentence on our own moral actions, and to determine whether they are right or wrong. This is what we call conscience, which is simply the exercise of the judgment upon moral subjects. If conscience determines our conduct to be right, we realize a greater or less degree of pleasure, satisfaction, or confidence. To this St. John alludes when he says, "If our heart condemn us not, then have we confidence toward God." 1 John iii, 21. But if it determines our conduct

to be wrong, we become the subjects of guilt, shame, and fear. Nor do these effects arise from the hope of reward or the fear of punishment in the present life; for they follow the most secret acts of our life, as well as those that are done before the world. Moreover, the nearer we approach to our latter end, the more impressive is the voice of conscience. It is then, especially, that the sinner reflects with horror upon his past life, and dreads the consequences of his evil doings. But why should the consciousness of a wicked action make a man fear when no one knows it but himself? Why should reflection upon a life spent in sin fill him with horror and amazement when he is about to leave the world? Why should this happen, we say, if conscience did not strongly suggest that God will judge the world in righteousness?

3. *From the Testimony of Scripture.*—To the preceding arguments no person of candor will object, so far as they go to prove a future retribution. If there is a just God, and if conscience is not a delusive faculty, it must ultimately be well with the righteous and ill with the wicked. Accordingly, a recompense in another state was expected even by those who did not enjoy the benefit of Divine revelation. But the reasoning serves only to establish the fact, that men will be recompensed in another life, not that they will be recompensed by a procedure carried on in the presence of assembled generations. It is to revelation alone that we are indebted for the knowledge of a *general* judgment, in which the proceedings will take place in the sight of angels and men; when all shall be witnesses of the Divine justice in the reward of the righteous and the punishment of the wicked.

The certainty of this grand and solemn event is evident from the following Scriptures: "Our God shall come, and shall not keep silence. A fire shall devour before him, and it shall be very tempestuous round about him. He shall call to the heavens from above, and to the earth, that he may judge his people." Psa. l, 3, 4. "For God shall bring every work into judgment, with every secret thing, whether it be good, or whether it be evil." Eccles. xii, 14. "When the Son of man shall come in his glory, and all the holy angels with him, then shall he sit upon the throne of his glory. And before him shall be gathered all nations; and he shall separate them one from another, as a shepherd divideth his sheep from the goats." Matt. xxv, 31, 32. "For we must all stand before the judgment-seat of Christ." Rom. xiv, 10. "It is appointed unto men once to die, but after this the judgment." Heb. ix, 27. "And I saw the dead, small and great, stand before God; and the books were opened: and another book was opened, which is the book of life: and the dead were judged out of those things which were written in the books, according to their works." Rev. xx, 12. These are only a few of the Scriptures that touch upon this subject, but they are sufficient to show that God has appointed a day in which he will judge the world.

II. The solemn transactions of the judgment itself.

In describing the scenes and transactions of the great assize, we must be guided alone by the teachings of the holy Scriptures; for, though it is a subject which can hardly fail to rouse the imagination, yet nothing but revealed truth can conduct us to sober and safe results. To understand, therefore, the nature, extent, and leading circumstances of the general judgment, we must consider,

1. *Its immediate precursors.*—God has declared, "I will show wonders in heaven above, and signs in the earth beneath; blood, and fire, and vapor of smoke. The sun shall be turned into darkness, and the moon into blood, before that great and notable day of the Lord come." Acts ii, 19, 20. "And there shall be signs in the sun, and in the moon, and in the stars; and upon the earth distress of nations, with perplexity; the sea and the waves roaring; men's hearts failing them for fear, and for looking after those things which are coming on the earth; for the powers of heaven shall be shaken." Luke xxi, 25, 26. Thus the earth, the ocean, and the surrounding atmosphere will be thrown into universal agitation, and men shall wail because of the approaching judgment. But the commotion will extend to the whole planetary system. The sun, the moon, and the stars will all exhibit signs of nature's approaching dissolution.

Then "the Lord himself shall descend from heaven with a shout, with the voice of the archangel, and with the trump of God." 1 Thess. iv, 16. And then "all that are in the graves shall hear his voice, and shall come forth."* "The sea shall give up the dead which are in it; and death and hell shall deliver up the dead which are in them."† Then also shall the living "be changed, in a moment, in the twinkling of an eye;" and pass from a mortal to an immortal state.‡

At the same time Christ "shall send his angels with a great sound of a trumpet; and they shall gather together his elect from the four winds, from one end of heaven to the other." Matt. xxiv, 31. Not only so, "Before him shall be gathered *all nations;*" and he shall place the righteous on his right hand, and the wicked on his left. St. John says, "I saw the dead small and great stand before God." These are the chief circumstances which are recorded in the Scriptures as immediately preceding the general judgment.

2. *The Judge.*—The person by whom God will judge the world is his only begotten Son. Our Lord himself declares, "The Father judgeth no man, but hath committed all judgment to the Son; that all men might honor the Son, even as they honor the Father." John v, 22, 23. St. Luke asserts that Christ commanded his apostles to testify, "that it is he which was ordained of God to be the judge of quick and dead." Acts x, 42. With equal clearness St. Paul teaches us that "God shall judge the secrets of men, by Jesus Christ;" Rom. ii, 16; and that

---

* John v, 28, 29. † See Rev. xx, 13. ‡ See 1 Cor. xv, 52.

Christ " shall judge the quick and the dead at his appearing and kingdom." 2 Tim. iv, 1.

It is manifestly proper that he who is the Saviour of men should be their final judge. It is fit that the promises which he has made and the threatenings which he has uttered should be carried into effect by himself; that from his hand those who have submitted to his law should receive their reward, and those who have been disobedient their punishment. It is fit that he should bring to a close the remedial dispensation which he established by his own personal interposition. But in addition to this, as the general judgment is intended to be a public manifestation of the righteousness of the Divine administration, it will be necessary that there should be a visible judge, whose proceedings all shall see, and whose voice all shall hear. The proper person, therefore, is Jesus Christ, who, being both God and man, will appear as our visible judge in his glorified humanity. Though the Israelites beheld the awful tokens of the Divine presence on Mount Sinai, they only heard the voice of their Lawgiver; but when Jesus shall come in the clouds of heaven to judge the human race, "every eye shall see him." Very different, however, will be his appearance then from what it was when he lay an infant in the manger of Bethlehem! when he was seen in the form of a servant! when he stood at Pilate's bar! or when he hung as a malefactor on the cross! "Behold, he cometh with clouds," invested with power and ineffable glory! He "shall be revealed from heaven with his mighty angels, *in flaming fire,*" surrounded by "ten thousand of his saints;" and his countenance shall be like the sun in his meridian strength.

3. *The persons to be judged.*—These, according to the Scriptures, are angels and men. That the fallen angels will be subjects of the general judgment is evident from 2 Peter ii, 4 : " God spared not the angels that sinned, but cast them down to hell, and delivered them into chains of darkness, to be reserved unto judgment." This fact is still more explicitly stated in the sixth verse of Jude: "The angels which kept not their first estate, but left their own habitation, he hath reserved in everlasting chains, under darkness, *unto the judgment of the great day,*"—the day of final retribution.

But at the judgment-seat of Christ will be assembled all men, to be judged according to the deeds done in the body; from Adam, the first of the human race, down to the very last one of his numerous posterity. All, all will be there. In that vast multitude ranks and distinctions, such as now exist, will be unknown. Those whom birth, or office, or wealth, or talents placed at a distance from one another, will then stand upon the same level. The great will be without their ensigns of dignity, and the poor without their marks of abasement; for then moral distinctions alone will be regarded. The oppressor and the oppressed will be there; the former that his violence may be returned upon his own head, and the latter that his wrongs may be redressed. Jews and

Gentiles, Mohammedans and Christians, the learned and the illiterate, the bond and the free, the high and the low will be there, to render an account to Him who is no respecter of persons, and whose omniscient eye will distinguish each individual in the immense throng as easily as if he were alone. Not one of the righteous will there be forgotten, and not one of the wicked shall find a hiding-place from the eye of the Judge.

4. *The rule of judgment.*—That the judgment will be conducted according to some rule or standard seems to be indicated by St. John when he says, "I saw the dead, small and great, stand before God; and the books were opened; and another book was opened, which is the book of life; and the dead were judged out of those things which were written in the books, according to their works." Rev. xx, 12. No one will suppose that books will be literally used on that occasion. It is more likely that the term refers to the different dispensations under which men have been placed, according to which justice requires that they should be tried. That portion of the Divine will which men know, or might know, will therefore be the standard according to which they shall be finally judged.

(1.) The heathen will be judged by the law of nature, or the law originally given to man as the rule of his conduct.—Some portion of this law has been preserved among them, partly by tradition and partly by reason; and though the traces of it are in some instances obliterated, and in others greatly obscured, yet enough remains to render them accountable beings, and to be the foundation of a judicial trial. St. Paul says, "When the Gentiles which have not the law," that is, the written law, as the Jews had it, "do by nature the things contained in the law, these having not the law, are a law unto themselves: which show the work of the law written in their hearts, their conscience also bearing witness, and their thoughts the meanwhile accusing or else excusing one another." Rom. ii, 14, 15.

(2.) The Jews shall be judged by the law of Moses and the teaching of the prophets.—These Scriptures placed them in much more favorable circumstances than the Gentiles for acquiring a knowledge of their duty, and for becoming wise unto salvation. They knew their Master's will; and if they did it not, they "shall be beaten with many stripes." For, "as many as have sinned in the law, shall be judged by the law." Rom. ii, 12.

(3.) Christians in general will be judged by the Scriptures of the Old and the New Testament; but the Gospel especially, as it confers on men superior privileges, will be the standard of their final trial.—The apostle informs us that "God shall judge the secrets of men by Jesus Christ, according to the Gospel;" and that vengeance shall fall upon them who "obey not the Gospel of our Lord Jesus Christ." How great will be the account which those will have to render who live under the Gospel dispensation. If the Gentile who sins against the light of nature is justly punishable; if he who despised the law of Moses "died without mercy, of how much sorer punishment shall he be thought worthy" who disregards the Gospel? "This is the condemnation," says our Lord, "that light is come into the world, and men loved darkness rather than light, because their deeds were evil." John iii, 19.

5. *The cause to be tried.*—This will be the entire moral conduct and character of every human being. The investigation will have respect, 1. To our actions; "for God will bring every work into judgment with every secret thing, whether it be good, or whether it be evil." 2. To our words. "Every idle word that men shall speak, they shall give account thereof in the day of judgment; for by thy words thou shalt be justified, and by thy words thou shalt be condemned." Matt. xii, 36, 37. And, 3. To our thoughts. Hence Solomon tells us that "the thoughts of the righteous are right," and that "the thoughts of the wicked are an abomination to the Lord." It is, therefore, evident that our thoughts have a moral character, and will be recognized in the judgment of the great day.

But will the sins of the redeemed be remembered in that day, and made known in the great congregation? Some suppose they will not, as they are all forgiven in Christ; and as the Scriptures represent them as being blotted out, covered, cast into the depths of the sea, and remembered no more. Others suppose that they will be published to the assembled universe, that all may know from what a depth of sin and misery the grace of God had delivered them. Of this much, however, we may be sure, that the righteous will be far from feeling any painful sorrow or shame for past transgressions. It will be enough for them to know that these were all washed away in the blood of the Lamb, and that they shall be remembered against them no more.

6. *The time of the judgment.*—With respect to this three things are to be observed: 1. That its time is unknown to all created intelligences. "Of that day and hour knoweth no man; no, not the angels of heaven." Matt. xxiv, 36. Accordingly St. Peter tells us that "the day of the Lord will come as a thief in the night." 2 Pet. iii, 10. 2. That its time is certain and determined; for God "hath appointed a day in the which he will judge the world in righteousness, by that man whom he hath ordained." Acts xvii, 31. Hence this important period is often spoken of in the Scriptures as "the day of judgment," "the day of the Lord," and "the great and terrible day." 3. That its time is associated with the resurrection of the dead and the end of the world.

But why, it may be asked, might not every one receive his final sentence at death, and enter at once upon his endless destiny? To this it would be enough to reply, that God has otherwise ordered it. But if we may be allowed to infer, from apparent fitness, the reasons of the Divine conduct, we think there are several considerations which indicate the propriety of placing the general judgment at the end of the world. And,

(1.) It will be promotive of the declarative glory of God.—In the presence of an assembled universe it will then be shown that "the Judge of all the earth" is possessed of every possible perfection. No other exhibition of the Divine character will equal this in glory. Wisdom, justice, goodness, and truth will never be so divinely illustrated as in the allotments of the righteous and the wicked. And the sentence of the Judge, whether for acquittal or condemnation, will then be sanctioned by the countless millions of angels and redeemed spirits.

(2.) It is a notorious fact, that the influence of a man's actions may continue to operate long after his earthly career is closed. Take, for example, such men as St. Paul, Luther, and Wesley. These men, though dead, still speak. Their influence lives, and will continue to live and bless the world till the latest generation. On the other hand, though Hume, Bolingbroke, and Volney have passed away from the stage of action, their writings still continue to exert a soul-destroying influence among men, and will curse the world through generations yet unborn. It is reasonable, therefore, that the judgment should be deferred till the end of time; when the actual influence which every man has exerted, as well as his personal doings, can be fully exhibited in the view of an intelligent universe.

7. *The final decision.*—The declaration of the Judge concerning those on his right hand, that they are righteous, and those on his left, that they are wicked, will be sufficient to convince all in the immense assembly that the sentence is just. There will be no need of witnesses, as in human courts, because the Judge is omniscient and unerring in his decisions; and to their rectitude there will be a testimony in the bosom of every man. All his past actions will be recalled, with all their circumstances, and will pass before his mind in rapid succession. His conscience will re-echo the voice of the Judge, and all shall acknowledge the rectitude of the Divine decision.

When the investigation is closed, and all are prepared to hear the final award, the Judge will say to those on his right hand, "Come, ye blessed of my Father, inherit the kingdom prepared for you from the foundation of the world." And to those on the left, "Depart from me, ye cursed, into everlasting fire, prepared for the devil and his angels." Then the wicked "shall go away into everlasting punishment; but the righteous into life eternal." Matt. xxv, 34, 41, 46.

In that dreadful hour sentence will also be passed on the angels who kept not their first estate, and who are reserved in chains of darkness unto the judgment of the great day. The peculiar circumstances of their transgression, and the process of judgment in reference to them, we do not pretend to know; but the fact that they will be summoned to the general judgment is clearly revealed. We know that they, like men, are moral agents; and they will therefore be judged for their voluntary conduct in reference to the will of God. They, too, shall go away from the judgment-seat to the place of punishment prepared for them, and, with the ungodly of our race, shall suffer "the vengeance of eternal fire."

8. *The general conflagration.*—The day of *judgment* will be the dying day of this great world; the day in which its groans of dissolution will be heard, and its knell sounded, through the entire universe; the day in which its obsequies will be celebrated with most awful pomp, and with supreme, as well as melancholy, grandeur. No sooner will the final allotments of angels and men be determined, than flaming fire from the presence of the Almighty Judge will sweep in one continued volume over our globe, involving it in universal conflagration. "All the works of man: his palaces, towers, and temples; his villages, towns, and cities; his wonderful displays of art, his haughty piles of grandeur, and his vast labors of defense and dominion, will be lighted up in a single blaze," and vanish forever.

"Nor will the desolation be limited to the works of men. The earth on which they stand; the hills and mountains, the valleys and plains; the lakes, the rivers, and the ocean, will all in a moment become one blazing ruin. The very *elements* of which they are composed will *melt with fervent heat;* and the world itself, so long the seat of sin and sorrow, be finally destroyed."* The visible heavens, too, will catch the flame, and be converted into a concave of liquid fire, surrounding the dissolving earth. Thus Peter tells us that "the heavens shall pass away with a great noise, and the elements shall melt with fervent heat; the earth also, and the works that are therein, shall be burned up." 2 Pet. iii, 10.

From this scene of wide-spread destruction the Judge, together with all the redeemed from earth, will ascend to the heaven of heavens; where he will present them before his Father as his faithful servants, and will crown them with everlasting life. And then will the Judge proclaim to the listening universe, "IT IS DONE," and the curtain will be drawn forever.

* Dr. Dwight.

CHAPTER IV.

ETERNAL BLESSEDNESS OF THE SAINTS.

HAVING presented, to some extent, the testimony of the Scriptures in regard to the great assize; and having briefly adverted to the final allotments of the righteous and the wicked, we propose, in this chapter, to consider more fully the future state of the former. In doing this we will call attention, 1. To the place of their future abode; 2. To the nature of their enjoyments; and 3. To their endless duration.

I. THE PLACE OF THE FUTURE ABODE OF THE RIGHTEOUS.

On this, as well as on every other point respecting a future state, we are indebted alone to the holy Scriptures for all reliable information. The representations which they make of the heavenly world are doubtless figurative, as in the nature of the case they must be; but they are nevertheless intended by the Holy Ghost, as all must admit, to be the foundation of our faith and hope in regard to our future home. We may therefore safely assert, the Scriptures being our guide, that *heaven is a place of unspeakable glory.*

1. *It is a* PLACE.—We know that this comes in collision with a modern refinement, which denies the locality of heaven, supposing it to be a *state* of enjoyment, and not a *place*. But that heaven is a *place* of enjoyment, as well as a *state*, is evident,

(1.) From the language of Scripture.—Our Saviour said to his disciples, "I go to prepare a *place* for you. And if I go and prepare a *place* for you, I will come again and receive you unto myself, that *where* I am, *there* ye may be also." John xiv, 2, 3. Now, to say that the home of the blessed is not a local heaven, is either directly to contradict the teachings of Christ, or to say that the language which he employed in relation to this subject is calculated to deceive us. To avoid these results we must admit that heaven is a *place*. It is undeniable that God can make any place a heaven, by there revealing himself and communicating the fullness of his love; but this is nothing to the purpose. Our business is not with speculations respecting his power, but with the declarations of his word; and the Scriptures uniformly suppose that there is a particular place, which is appointed to be the final abode of the righteous. The same fact is evident,

(2.) From circumstances connected with the future existence of the saints.—Were we to think of men in their future state as pure spirits, immaterial beings, yet would we be compelled to assign to them both individuality and locality. Whatever exists at all, must either exist in some portion of space, or it must fill immensity. But no one in his right mind will predicate omnipresence of human spirits: this belongs to God alone. It follows, therefore, that the spirits of just men made perfect will enjoy a *place* of happiness, as well as a state. But this fact appears still more evident when we consider that the glorified saints shall possess material bodies. True, the apostle tells us that the natural body which dies shall be raised a "*spiritual* body;" but we must not suppose that it will be spiritual in the sense of *immaterial.* It will be a *body*—the *same* body, and therefore material. When Christ rose from the dead, he appeared in the same body in which he had been put to death on the cross; and in this body he ascended to heaven. In like manner shall the bodies of the saints be raised from the dead, and glorified in heaven.

But to complete the argument it remains to be observed, that the glorified saints will constitute one vast *assembly.* The Saviour asserts that "they shall come from the east, and from the west, and from the north, and from the south, and shall sit down in the kingdom of God." Luke xiii, 29. St. John represents this assembly as an innumerable multitude, "of all nations, and kindreds, and people, and tongues," standing "before the throne, and before the Lamb."

We will not undertake to determine in what part of God's vast dominion the future abode of the righteous is located. We speak of it as being above us; but this language conveys no definite idea. The point that is now directly over our heads will, in a few hours, in consequence of the earth's revolution, be beneath our feet. Some have conjectured that the home of the glorified will be in the sun; while others think that this earth will be restored to its paradisaical state, and become the future home of the redeemed. But these and all such conjectures are more curious than useful; and as Divine revelation affords no certain light upon this point, it becomes us to restrain our imagination, and to be content with what God has seen proper to reveal. The only conclusion which the Scriptures seem to warrant in relation to the locality of heaven is, that it is entirely beyond the limits of the visible creation. Thus St. Paul teaches that Christ "ascended up far above all heavens." Eph. iv, 10. By the term heavens, here, we are doubtless to understand, according to the notions of the Jews, the aerial and the starry heavens. Beyond these, therefore, is the home of the blessed; and to this the apostle alludes when he informs us that he was "caught up to the *third heaven.*"

That there is a place where God eminently dwells, and where he reveals himself to his intelligent creatures in a most glorious manner, is an opinion which has prevailed among Jews and Christians, Greeks and Romans; in a word, among all nations and in every age. This opinion is confirmed by Divine revelation. "I dwell," saith the Almighty, "in the *high* and *holy place.*" This is what our Saviour calls his "Father's house," the immediate habitation of the Deity. It is the place into which Jesus entered after his resurrection, and where he reigns King upon the holy hill of Zion. And this is the place, in whatever part of the universe it may be, into which the righteous shall be admitted after death, and in which, after the general judgment, they shall enjoy a blissful immortality. Our Lord says, "Where I am, there shall also my servants be."

2. *Heaven is a place of* UNSPEAKABLE GLORY.—The most striking figures are employed by the sacred writers to convey to our minds some adequate conception of the glory and grandeur of the heavenly world. Have we felt a deep interest in the account which the sacred historian gives of the original Paradise? Has our imagination lingered with inspiring delight upon its verdant fields, its flowery meads, its delicious fruits, and its limpid streams? Have the serenity of its sky, the splendor of its sunshine, the sweetness of its atmosphere, and the beauty of its scenery, awakened in us the most romantic visions? All this, and a thousand times more, we may associate with the home of the redeemed. "To him that overcometh," says Christ, "I will give to eat of the tree of life, which is in the midst of the paradise of God." Rev. ii, 7.

St. John gives a most glowing and sublime description of the heavenly Paradise. He speaks of it as an extensive and magnificent city. Its foundations are garnished with all manner of precious stones. It extends twelve thousand furlongs in every direction. Its walls are of jasper, and its buildings and streets are of pure and pellucid gold. Its gates are pearls, and its watchmen angels. "The Lord God Almighty and the Lamb are the temple of it." The throne of God is in the midst of it. Out of this throne proceeds a pure river of water, on the banks of which grow the trees of immortality. It needs not the light of the sun, nor of the moon; for the glory of God and the presence of the Lamb shall enlighten it with everlasting day.*

Allowing these representations of the heavenly world to be entirely figurative, we are nevertheless bound to conclude, if we would not charge God with deceiving us, that it is a place of unspeakable glory and grandeur; and that it is eminently fitted to afford delight to its holy inhabitants. Below the inspired description it cannot fall; but it may rise infinitely above it; for human language is too poor fully to describe heavenly things.

II. THE NATURE OF HEAVENLY ENJOYMENTS.

On this subject we have no very clear and definite knowledge; and from the nature of things it must be expected that much obscurity will rest upon it, until these mortal bodies shall have put on immortality. Men are naturally inclined to think that the joys of heaven will somewhat resemble the pleasures of the present life. Hence many hope to obtain and enjoy beyond the grave that kind of gratification which they

* See Rev. xxi, 10-26.

hold most dear on earth. The untaught Indian supposes that heaven is a place abounding in game, and affording every desirable facility in his hunting excursions. The enslaved African expects after death to visit his native land, and to enjoy the society of his relatives. Men who live in the indulgence of passion and appetite expect to find a heaven of sensual delights. The indolent, and those who are exhausted by labor, regard rest, or freedom from employment, as the greatest good, and they therefore suppose that the bliss of heaven will consist in a state of quiescence; while the man of science, eagerly bent upon mental improvement, promises himself rich enjoyment in the acquisition of knowledge.

It must be admitted, however, that the happiness of heaven, though sometimes represented by earthly pleasures, must be of a nature entirely different from the happiness of earth. The richest pleasures of earth are insufficient to satisfy an immortal spirit. Experience shows that all earthly joys are of such a nature, that after they have been possessed for a short time they lose their power to please, and are followed by satiety, if not disgust. We conclude, therefore, that the future happiness of the saints will be more pure, more spiritual, and of an infinitely higher nature, than anything that earth can afford.

Now, though the nature of future happiness can be known by us only in part while we sojourn below, yet from the holy Scriptures we may form such ideas of it as are in a good degree satisfactory. Two things, at least, are evident: *first*, that we shall be entirely delivered from the evils of this life; and, *secondly*, that we shall be made partakers of a large amount of positive good.

1. *The saints shall be entirely delivered from the evils of this life.*—They shall be delivered,

(1.) From bodily infirmities.—These bodies of ours are the seat of much affliction. They are subjected to hunger and thirst, to weariness and pain, and are liable to a thousand accidents, that often render human life a burden. But they who shall be accounted worthy to attain to the resurrection of the just shall be entirely freed from all these evils. Their bodies shall be refined, immortalized, and glorified; affording ample capacity for holy action and high enjoyment. "They shall hunger no more, neither thirst any more." Rev. vii, 16. "God shall wipe away all tears from their eyes; and there shall be no more death, neither sorrow, nor crying, neither shall there be any more pain." Rev. xxi, 4. No helpless infant shall there be seen, demanding the anxious care of a fond parent—no decrepid man, bowing under the weight of toilsome years—no emaciated frame or pallid countenance; but eternal youth and blooming health shall be enjoyed alike by all.

(2.) From mental imbecilities.—That the effects of the fall have very much abridged the intellectual powers of man admits of no doubt. Our scanty minds, even at the expense of much labor and study, can gain a knowledge of but a few things, and these are known very imperfectly. But in heaven the soul will commence its career anew. It will not only be restored to that intellectual strength and clearness of mental vision which Adam possessed in his state of innocence, but it will, in all probability, be elevated far above his primitive capability. "Now we see through a glass, darkly; but then face to face. Now we know in part; but then shall we know *even as also we are known.*"

(3.) From all moral depravation.—It is the duty of the Christian, and it is also his privilege, even on earth, to love God supremely, and to obey his commandments. But though he may, through grace, arrive at this exalted state of holiness, yet he feels the need of continual watchfulness and constant exertion against the proneness of his nature to wander from God. But in heaven this shall not exist. There the redeemed shall enjoy a confirmed state of holiness, without a single disposition contrary to the will of God. They shall be pillars in the temple of God, to go no more out. The whole man, body and soul, shall be perfectly delivered from the corruptions of the fall, and shall be restored to the highest possible state of moral purity. Their robes shall be made "white in the blood of the Lamb."

(4.) From the society of the wicked, and from beholding their ungodly deeds.—That the company and practice of the ungodly are a most fruitful source of affliction to the pious, both Scripture and experience declare. They cannot hear the name of God blasphemed, or see his holy Sabbaths profaned, without feeling deeply pained. They cannot witness the gross inattention to our holy religion, which almost everywhere abounds, without dropping a tear. They cannot look upon their fellow-men, who are every moment exposed to eternal death, without heaving a sigh. But in that better land all these causes of affliction shall be forever removed. The heavenly society will be of one heart, and will all be engaged in one employment. "There the wicked shall cease from troubling."

(5.) From the temptations of the devil.—The holiest of men, while on earth, are exposed to his fiery darts. The language of Christ to the disciples is true in regard to all Christians: "Satan desires to have you, that he might sift you as wheat." Luke xxii, 31. Even Christ himself did not escape his hellish malice; and in this respect the servant may not hope to be above his Lord. But when we turn our attention to the citizens of the heavenly Jerusalem, we behold a company of redeemed and triumphant spirits who are forever beyond the reach and power of Satan. He may follow the good man to the very verge of the grave, but beyond this he cannot go. The hour of dissolution is the hour of the Christian's victory—the hour in which he shall be placed beyond the power of infernal agency.

2. *The saints in heaven shall be made partakers of a large amount of positive good.*—To deliver men from all the evils of the present life,

would be to confer upon them a great salvation. But the abounding grace of God stops not here. He himself becomes the portion of his people, and whatever he can bestow to heighten and perfect their bliss will be most freely given. Christ declares that his servants shall enter into the *joy of their Lord*, and shall wear a *crown of life*. St. Paul speaks of the positive bliss of heaven as an "*eternal weight of glory;*" and St. Peter represents it under the figure of an inheritance which is *incorruptible* and *undefiled*, and that "*fadeth not away.*" But there is perhaps no passage of Scripture in which it is more forcibly represented than in Psalm xvi, 11: "In thy presence is *fullness of joy;* at thy right hand there are *pleasures* for evermore."

(1.) Glorified saints will enjoy *pleasures;* by which we are to understand the perfect gratification of all their desires, whether of body or mind.—There will be no desires among them but such as are in strict accordance with the will of God, and they shall be gratified to their full extent. They will derive pleasure, 1. From social intercourse; for "they shall sit down with Abraham, and Isaac, and Jacob, in the kingdom of heaven." Matt. viii, 11. They shall be associated with Enoch, and Moses, and Job, and Isaiah, and David, and the apostles of our Lord, and all the glorified from earth, together with the angels that kept their first estate. 2. From the employments of heaven; for they shall "serve God day and night in his temple." Rev. vii, 15. To worship and adore the Triune God will be at once their leading employment and their highest bliss. 3. From the visions of heaven. Whithersoever the eye is directed, it will light upon objects of symmetry, beauty, glory, and grandeur; but the most entrancing object of the heavenly world will be the Lord Jesus Christ in his glorified humanity. According to his own prayer addressed to the Father, his people shall be with him where he is, that they may behold his glory;* and St. John declares expressly that they "shall see him as he is." 1 John iii, 2. He "shall dwell among them;" and he "shall feed them, and shall lead them unto living fountains of waters." Rev. vii, 17.

(2.) They will realize a *fullness of joy*.—Joy consists in that vivid pleasure or delight which results from the reception and possession of what is peculiarly grateful. The humble Christian, even in this vale of tears, may sometimes possess a "joy unspeakable and full of glory;" but the glorified in heaven shall realize a *fullness* of joy which never can be experienced in this life. It will be joy raised to its highest degree of perfection, and expressing itself in songs of heaven-inspired rapture and delight. They will unite in ascribing "glory and dominion unto him that loved us, and washed us from our sins in his own blood;" while the chorus of that vast multitude shall be heard "as the voice of many waters, and as the voice of mighty thunderings, saying, Alleluia; for the Lord God omnipotent reigneth." But,

* See John xvii, 24.

III. THE BLESSEDNESS OF THE SAINTS IN HEAVEN WILL BE ENDLESS IN ITS DURATION.

The *endless duration* of the future life is as necessary as the life itself; because all that we have stated respecting it could not amount to true felicity if we had not an absolute security of its endless continuance. The very possibility of an end would mar the felicity of heaven; but it is an eternal redemption, of which Jesus Christ is the author. When the saints ascend to heaven in their glorified bodies, they enter upon a career that shall never be finished. Ages will run on more rapidly than hours among mortals; but thousands of ages will take nothing from their felicity. It will then be as true of them as it is of God himself, that their "years shall have no end."

That the future life will be eternal, is most explicitly taught in the Scriptures. He who purchased it for us, and has promised it to us, frequently calls it *eternal life*. It is described as "everlasting habitations," Luke xvi, 9; as a "house eternal in the heavens," 2 Corinthians v, 1; and as a "continuing city," Hebrews xiii, 14: it is expressed by "eternal salvation," Hebrews v, 9; "eternal glory," 1 Peter v, 10; and by "the everlasting kingdom of our Lord and Saviour Jesus Christ." 2 Peter i, 11. And lest we should be discouraged by any lame or equivocal interpretation of this subject, it is further explained in such terms as cannot be mistaken. Our Saviour says, "If a man keep my saying, he shall never see death." John viii, 51. And again: "Whosoever liveth and believeth in me shall never die." John xi, 26. The life, therefore, of the saints in heaven will be endless in its duration.

It is highly probable that the happiness of the redeemed in heaven, however full and perfect at first, will nevertheless be progressive. We know that the capacities of the soul for holy enjoyment are increased on earth by holy exercises; and may we not conclude that the continuance of such exercises, under more favorable circumstances, will still enlarge these capacities? Again, the desires of the soul for happiness are constantly increasing in this life, and will probably increase in eternity. Hence, as the capacities for enjoyment will be progressive, and the sources of gratification inexhaustible, an ever-growing happiness will necessarily follow.

Here the question is sometimes asked, Will the saints in heaven know one another? To this we answer in the affirmative; for, *first*, they will certainly retain a remembrance of their past life. Without this they would not know that they had lived on earth at all. Nor can we conceive how they should celebrate the praise of God for his redeeming grace if they did not remember that they formerly lived in this world, and that they derived the knowledge of Christ from the preaching of the Gospel, and were members of his Church; all of which suppose the remembrance of time, places, persons, and other circumstances. But, *secondly*, this knowledge is clearly implied in the language of St. Paul: "For what is our hope, or joy, or crown of rejoicing? Are not even ye in the presence of our Lord Jesus Christ at his coming?" 1 Thess. ii, 19. He must therefore have expected to know the persons whom he addressed in the kingdom of heaven; and if so, we too may indulge the rational and scriptural hope of recognizing, in that better land, the associates of our earthly pilgrimage.

CHAPTER V.

ENDLESS PUNISHMENT OF THE WICKED.

WE come now to the investigation of one of the most solemn subjects within the entire range of Christian theology—the endless punishment of the finally impenitent. In order to present the doctrine in as clear a light as our limits will allow, we will consider the three following questions: 1. Will the finally impenitent be punished in a future state? 2. What will be the nature of the future punishment of the wicked? and, 3. Will it be endless?

I. WILL THE FINALLY IMPENITENT BE PUNISHED IN A FUTURE STATE?

Universalists teach that all punishment for sin is restricted to the present life. They hold that all the judgment taught in the Scriptures takes place in this world, and that every sinner is punished here in exact proportion to the number and magnitude of his sins, according to the decisions of Divine justice. That this theory of retribution is contrary to truth may be shown by various considerations.

1. *It is disproved by daily matters of fact.*—It is most evident, so far as our knowledge and observation extend, that God does *not* reward men in this world according to their works. It is true, he so administers his government as to show, in many instances even in this life, his approbation of righteousness and disapprobation of sin; but the sinner is not always the most wretched here, nor is the saint always the most happy. Who does not know that ungodly men sometimes enjoy a long life of health, outward peace, and worldly prosperity; while many of the most pious, so far as we can judge, pass all their days in poverty and affliction? To suppose, therefore, that what men suffer or enjoy in the present life is an index to their true moral character, is to ignore all acknowledged distinctions in morals, and to set aside our Lord's rule of judging, "By their fruits ye shall know them," not by what they suffer or enjoy.

2. *It is in direct opposition to the testimony of Scripture.*—"Wherefore do the wicked live, become old, yea, are mighty in power? Their seed is established in their sight with them, and their offspring before their eyes. Their houses are safe from fear, neither is the *rod of God upon them.*" Job xxi, 7-9. "I was envious," says the psalmist, "at the pros-

perity of the wicked. For there are no bands in their death; but their strength is firm. They are not in trouble as other men; neither are they plagued like other men." Psa. lxxiii, 3-5. And so far was David from believing that God punishes all sin in the present life, that he plainly declares, "He hath *not* dealt with us after our sins, nor rewarded us according to our iniquities." Psa. ciii, 5, 6. We see, therefore, both from matters of fact and from the testimony of the Scriptures, that the wicked are not punished in this life according to the number and magnitude of their sins. Nor will it relieve the case to say, that though God does not fully punish sinners during life, he does it in death, by suddenly cutting them off and destroying them from the earth. For, if the death of the wicked were more sudden than that of others, which it generally is not, this circumstance, instead of being any punishment for sin, would only favor them with a more sudden transition from the sorrows of earth to the joys of heaven.

But it is assumed by Universalists that men suffer the full penalty of all their crimes in the compunctions of conscience. To this assumption, however, there are insuperable objections: 1. It is wholly gratuitous, as there is not a single passage of Scripture in which the doctrine is asserted. 2. It is a question which cannot be determined by the human mind in the absence of Divine revelation; for *God only* knows the demerit of sin, and what is, in every case, its just and full penalty. Nor is any man capable of comprehending the consciousness of another, or of rightly estimating the real quantum of his suffering or enjoyment. To assert, therefore, that every man suffers in this life in exact proportion to the number and magnitude of his sins, is to assert what God has not revealed, and what no man knows or can know. 3. The theory is contradicted by human experience; for many a scrupulous saint suffers more in his moral feelings for inadvertent errors, or even for unavoidable imperfections, than he did in an unconverted state for his most heinous crimes. The youth suffers more from the compunctions of conscience on account of the first profane oath, than he does on account of a score when he becomes practiced in profanity. Indeed, the universal experience of the world is, that continuance in crime weakens the voice of conscience, hardens the heart, and makes it more and more unfeeling, as if "seared with a hot iron."

3. *It is absurd in itself.*—It restricts the punishment of sin to the present life, and maintains, at the same time, that every sin is punished according to the full demand of Divine justice. But it will not be denied that men sometimes die in the very act of transgression, without a single moment to suffer for their crimes. Nay, in many cases, their very last act is the wicked and sudden destruction of their own life. Where, then, do such persons bear the full penalty of those acts of wickedness? To say that they do not suffer for them according to their demerit, contradicts Universalism; and to say, according to this

theory, that they suffer for them in this life, contradicts matter of fact and common sense. It follows, therefore, that Universalism must either deny the criminality of suicide and other acts of wickedness which men commit in the moment of death, or admit the doctrine of future retribution.

4. *It subverts the whole scheme of salvation by grace, through faith in Jesus Christ.*—In proof of this it is only necessary to remark, 1. That the Scriptures everywhere represent our salvation as a gracious act on the part of God—a free and unmerited gift. But if men suffer in this life the full penalty of all their evil doings, to talk of salvation by grace is most absurd; unless we confound the Divine attributes, and say that grace and justice are the same thing. According to this theory, God could not inflict upon men any kind or degree of suffering in the future life without being unjust; consequently, their eternal salvation results from the *justice* of God, and not from Divine grace. 2. That the Scriptures teach the doctrine of salvation by *faith;* but if Universalism is true, faith can no more secure our eternal happiness than the most inveterate infidelity. Though the Bible declares, "He that believeth not shall be damned," yet, according to Universalism, a man may despise Jesus Christ, blaspheme the Holy Ghost, reject the entire system of revealed religion, curse God in death, and be as sure of holiness and happiness in heaven after death as was St. John or St. Paul. 3. That the Scriptures declare Christ to be our Saviour; but the theory which we oppose sets aside this important truth of the Gospel. Indeed, it is perfectly absurd to talk of salvation in any way on the ground taken by Universalists. For, according to every rational definition of the term, as used in theology, salvation is altogether excluded by the supposition that God deals with sinners here as their sins deserve.

Salvation necessarily presupposes loss, suffering, or danger; for it is absurd to talk of salvation from evils which have no existence. As sin is the great evil on account of which man needs a Saviour, if he is actually saved by Christ, it must be either from the love and practice of sin in this life, or from its penal consequences, or both. But, according to Universalism, Christ does not save men in any of these respects. *First*, he does not save them from the love and practice of sin in this life; for we have the testimony of facts everywhere before our eyes, that many live in the habit of vice and die in rebellion against God. *Secondly*, he does not save men from the penal consequences of sin, for these are inflicted upon every sinner in exact proportion to the number and magnitude of his sins. And as all punishment for sin is restricted to this life, no man can be saved from a liability to *future* punishment, because no such liability ever did or ever can exist. It follows, therefore, according to Universalist principles, that the happiness of heaven will be independent of Divine grace, of faith in Christ, and of salvation from sin.

Now, since there is grace, mercy, and forgiveness in our salvation;

since these are exercised through Christ as our *Saviour*, and received by faith; and since many die in sin and unbelief, the conclusion is irresistible, that men do *not* suffer the just penalty of their sins in the present life, but that their final award will be in another world. Hence the finally impenitent will be punished in a future state. The truth of this proposition is manifest even from what has already been said; but we will further support it by the two following arguments:

(1.) The Scriptures speak of retribution as being subsequent to the general resurrection.—" And many of them that sleep in the dust of the earth shall awake; some to everlasting life, and some to *shame* and *everlasting contempt*." Dan. xii, 2. It is not possible that the prophet is here speaking of a spiritual resurrection; for certainly none of the subjects of a spiritual resurrection are raised to "*shame* and *everlasting contempt*."*

"The hour is coming," says our Lord, "in which all that are in the graves shall hear his voice, and come forth; they that have done good unto the resurrection of life; and they that have *done evil*, unto the resurrection of *damnation*." John v, 28, 29. Hence says the apostle, "There shall be a resurrection of the dead, both of the just and unjust." Acts xxiv, 15. To apply these Scriptures to anything else than the general resurrection of the dead at the last day is to wrest them from their plain and most obvious meaning, and to adopt a mode of interpretation which would unsettle the meaning of almost every passage in the Bible. But as they evidently refer to this grand event, they must settle forever, in the mind of every one who is willing to be governed in his faith by inspired testimony, the question of future retribution.

(2.) The Scriptures connect future rewards and punishments with the general judgment.—They teach us that "when the Son of Man shall come in his glory, and all the holy angels with him," he will separate the righteous from the wicked. And he will say to the former, "Come, ye blessed of my Father, inherit the kingdom prepared for you from the foundation of the world;" and to the latter, "Depart from me, ye cursed, into everlasting fire prepared for the devil and his angels."†

"The Lord knoweth how to deliver the godly out of temptations, and to reserve the unjust unto the day of judgment to be punished." And again, "The heavens and the earth, which are now, by the same word are kept in store, reserved unto fire against the day of judgment and perdition of ungodly men."‡

We are aware that Universalists, in order to evade the force of this argument, reject the doctrine of a general judgment; but this only proves that they are prepared to reject any doctrine or fact which

---

* Though the term "many," used by the prophet, might not seem, at first sight, to embrace all mankind, yet such must be its import; and in this sense it is employed in Romans v, 15, 19, and in Hebrews ix, 28.

† See Matt. xxv, 31–46.   ‡ 2 Peter ii, 9; iii, 7.

stands opposed to their theory. It is impossible, however, to confine all judgment to the present life, while it stands recorded that "it is appointed unto men once to die, but *after this the* judgment." Heb. ix, 27. Moreover, it is expressly taught in Scripture that Jesus Christ is to be the judge of the *dead* as well as of the living. Thus Peter says, "He commanded us to preach unto the people, and to testify that it is he which was ordained of God to be the judge of quick and dead." Acts x, 42. And St. Paul informs us that he "shall judge the quick and the dead at his appearing and his kingdom." 2 Tim. iv, 1. This passage, while it ascribes the final judgment of all mankind to Jesus Christ, also specifies the time—"at his appearing and kingdom."

We have thus traced the punishment of the wicked to another world. We have seen them rise in the general resurrection to shame, contempt, and condemnation. We have seen them at "the judgment of the great day," sentenced with awful solemnity, and with the curse of the Judge resting upon them, to dwell in "everlasting fire." And now the question arises,

II. WHAT WILL BE THE NATURE OF THEIR FUTURE PUNISHMENT?

In replying to this question it will be proper, in the first place, to consider the terms in which the future punishment of the wicked is expressed in the sacred Scriptures; and secondly, to deduce from the inspired account of this awful subject some sober and legitimate conclusions in regard to its nature. And,

1. *The terms in which future punishment is expressed in the sacred Scriptures.*—A state of future punishment is so different from anything with which we are acquainted in the present world, that it can only be described by comparing it with such things as are within our reach. It is therefore necessarily exhibited to us in language which is at least partly figurative; but the figures employed give us a most terrible description of the future condition of the wicked.

(1.) It is called "the *second death.*"—Death is the most distressing evil that men suffer in the present world. It is, therefore, made by every nation the last infliction of punitive justice for crimes committed against human government. It is surrounded with gloom and terror, and replete with agony. It probably creates more anxiety in the human mind than all the other calamities which exist in this world of suffering. What, then, must it be to die forever, to suffer the pangs of death through days, and years, and centuries, and thus to spend eternity in dying?

(2.) It is called "*darkness,*" and "the *blackness of darkness;*" Jude vi, 13. Our Lord calls it "*outer darkness;*" Matthew viii, 12. And St. Peter describes it by "*chains of darkness,*" and "the *mist of darkness,*" which is "reserved forever" for the ungodly; 2 Peter ii, 4, 7.—Thus the Scriptures represent the melancholy lot of the wicked in the future world as a state of eternal darkness; of darkness resembling the deep midnight of the grave, lengthening onward from age to age, and terminated by no succeeding day.

(3.) It is spoken of as a state of suffering from the action of fire.—Hence our Lord informs us that the wicked shall be cast into "a furnace of fire," Matthew xiii, 42; and St. John, that they "shall have their part in the lake which burneth with fire and brimstone." Rev. xxi, 8. This fire is spoken of as being "everlasting," Matthew xxv, 41; "unquenchable," Luke iii, 17; and "eternal," Jude vii.

Such are the representations which the Holy Ghost has seen proper to make, of the future condition of the finally impenitent. Let us then proceed,

2. *To deduce from this inspired description a few sober and legitimate conclusions in regard to the nature of future punishment.*—We have already admitted that the language of Scripture on this subject is more or less figurative; but whether it is figurative or otherwise, of one thing we may be sure, that it was intended to convey ideas strictly conformable to truth. God can no more make a false impression on the human mind by the use of figures, than he can lead men into error by the plainest and most positive declarations; for both would be alike contrary to the Divine veracity. Nor will his goodness, any more than his truth, allow him to alarm his moral creatures with groundless fears, or to represent the consequences of sin as more dreadful than they really are. We may therefore safely conclude, that the future state of the wicked, as to its general character, will be one of intense suffering; for, to suppose that it will be more tolerable than absolute darkness, the agonies of death, and the action of fire, is virtually to charge God with the utterance of falsehood, and to set up our own standard in opposition to Divine revelation. This intense suffering, which will be the future portion of the ungodly, will arise,

(1.) From what is called the *punishment of* LOSS.—They shall be cut off from all the enjoyments of earth, from all good and agreeable society, and from all happiness, and ease, and rest, and hope. They shall be excluded from all the means of grace, and from heaven and all its joys. "He that believeth not the Son shall not see life." John iii, 36. "The unrighteous shall not inherit the kingdom of God." 1 Cor. vi, 9. They shall be separated from God, which is clearly indicated in the language of Christ, "Depart from me, ye cursed." Thus the wicked shall be driven away in their wickedness "from the presence of the Lord." What thought can be more insupportable than this, that all good is forever lost? Yet such will be the loss of all who die in sin.

(2.) From the *punishment of* SENSE.—To a consciousness of the loss of all good is to be added the endurance of extreme positive misery. Accordingly we are taught, that "at the end of the world," when the wicked shall be "cast into the furnace of fire, there shall be *wailing* and *gnashing of teeth*." Matt. xiii, 50. This awful truth is also set forth in the declaration, " Their worm dieth not, and the fire is not quenched," Mark ix, 44; and in our Lord's assertion respecting the rich man, " In hell he lifted up his eyes, being in *torments*." Luke xvi, 23. These positive sufferings will result from remorse of conscience, from the place of their abode, from wicked society, from a sense of the wrath of God, which will be the most dreadful ingredient in their cup of misery, and from utter despair. But we now inquire,

III. WILL THE FUTURE PUNISHMENT OF THE WICKED BE ENDLESS?

The affirmative of this question is evidently the doctrine of the Bible, as we shall soon prove; but before we do this it will be proper to notice two different theories respecting future punishment which stand opposed to the orthodox view. These are restorationism and annihilationism. We will consider,

1. *The theory of the restorationists.*—They maintain that all future punishment is disciplinary and reformatory; and that, however long and intensely sinners may be punished in the world to come, they shall ultimately be brought to a state of holiness and happiness in heaven. Those who adopt this notion are called restorationists, to distinguish them from that class of Universalists who restrict all punishment for sin to the present life. That this theory is untenable the following remarks will show.

(1.) It is based upon the mere assumption that all future punishment is disciplinary and reformatory, a doctrine which is nowhere taught in the Scriptures.—But this is not all; it supposes that men may be in a state of retribution and of probation at the same time. For, it would be absurd to talk of discipline and reformation in regard to those who are not in a probationary state; but it is equally absurd to suppose that men who are in a state of retribution can be at the same time on trial. We might as well suppose that the redeemed in heaven are still in a state of probation, and may therefore fall, as that sinners in hell are in this state, and may therefore rise to the joys of heaven.

But this supposed reformatory tendency of penal sufferings is in opposition to the teachings of the Bible, as is evident from what is said concerning the fallen angels. When the Gospel was written, they had been suffering punishment at least four thousand years. Yet they were then no less hostile to their Creator, and actuated by no less malice against his moral creatures than at the beginning. Moreover, men of all succeeding ages are warned by Christ and his apostles against their falsehood and seduction, because in every age they would be false and seductive. And at the judgment of the great day they will be consigned to "everlasting fire;" consequently, until that period, their punishment will have no good effect upon their moral character. Nor have we any reason to believe that penal sufferings will exert a more salutary influence upon *men* than upon fallen angels; and if so, restorationism is indeed a hopeless theory.

That the punishment of sinners is not always disciplinary, is fully established by the course of the Divine administration in this world. To place this beyond doubt it is only necessary to refer to the deluge, to the destruction of Sodom and Gomorrah and of Pharaoh and his host, and to the cases of Nadab and Abihu, of Achan, of the house of Eli, and of Ananias and Sapphira. But if God inflicts punishments upon sinners in this world which are evidently not intended to be reformatory, as these references prove, such punishments cannot be inconsistent with the principles of the Divine government; and if not, what right have we to suppose that future punishments will be of an opposite character? They are certainly not exhibited in the Scriptures as disciplinary, but as penal.

(2.) Restorationists assume that the Scriptures teach the doctrine of the final salvation of all mankind.—This they attempt to prove by quoting those passages which declare, 1. That all men shall be blessed in the seed of Abraham.* 2. That Christ died for all men, and is the Saviour of all men.† 3. That God wills the salvation of all.‡ 4. That to him every knee shall bow, and every tongue confess.§ And, 5. That death itself shall be destroyed.‖

It would be easy to show, however, by a careful examination of all such passages, that they do *not* prove the doctrine in support of which they are adduced; but such an examination is uncalled for at this point. It is only necessary to remark, 1. That the blessing which comes upon all men through the seed of Abraham, does not necessarily imply the actual salvation of all. 2. That though Christ died for all men, and is, in this respect as well as in others, the Saviour of all men, yet he is the special Saviour only " of those that believe." 3. That God wills the salvation of all men, but only in the appointed way, that is, "through sanctification of the Spirit and belief of the truth," and not whether they believe in Christ or not. 4. That all men shall bow to Christ and acknowledge him, either by a voluntary reception of his grace and salvation, or by a constrained subjection to his avenging justice; and, 5. That death shall be destroyed when "all that are in the graves shall hear" the voice of Christ "and come forth; they that have done good, unto the resurrection of life; and they that have done evil, unto the resurrection of damnation."

(3.) Restorationists attempt to support their theory by the allegation, that endless punishment is incompatible with the Divine perfections.—It would be *unjust*, say they, for God to inflict on men endless punishment for temporary crimes. To this opinion it is a sufficient reply, that it is founded on ignorance. No finite mind can fully com-

---

* Gen. xxii, 17, 18; xxvi, 4; xxviii, 14; Gal. iii, 8–16.
† 2 Cor. iv, 14, 15; 1 Tim. iv, 10; Heb. ii, 9.
‡ Ezek. xxxiii, 11; 1 Tim. ii, 4; 1 Pet. iii, 9.
§ Isa. xlv, 23; Phil. ii, 10, 11.   ‖ Isa. xxv, 8; 1 Cor. xv, 26, 54.

prehend the demerit of sin; and therefore, for aught we know to the contrary, every sin may justly deserve endless punishment. God has taught us, by his moral administration, that sin both deserves and receives punishment; and as to the intensity and duration of this punishment, he alone is competent to determine.

But it is said that endless punishment is inconsistent with the *mercy* of God. We must not forget, however, that God is *just*, as well as *merciful*. Nor are we to suppose that the mercy of God is a passion by which he is so moved and overcome by seeing a creature in misery that he cannot bear to see justice fully executed. Such a supposition would be derogatory to the Divine character, and contrary to facts; for we see that God, in his providence, inflicts upon men great calamities even in the present life. But the exercise of justice, so far from being conflictive with Divine *mercy*, is to be regarded as a proof of it. Hence, the psalmist gives thanks " to Him that smote Egypt in their firstborn; for his *mercy endureth forever*." That " overthrew Pharaoh and his host in the Red Sea; for his *mercy endureth forever*." But why were those events a proof of the mercy of God? Surely not because there was any mixture of mercy toward the sufferers, but because God wrought a merciful deliverance for his people by the infliction of just punishment upon their enemies.

Here it may be said, that *limited* punishment is consistent with the mercy of God, because he will overrule it for the greater good of the sufferers. To this notion our reply is, that it destroys entirely the penal sanctions of God's law. It virtually says to men, If you sin, you shall indeed be punished; but only in such a manner as shall, in the end, make you the happier for all your sufferings. Who does not see that this is holding out a reward for transgression, rather than a penalty? But further, cannot God make men as happy without suffering as with it? To say he cannot, is to limit his power. To say he has the power but not the will, is to limit his goodness. And if it be said that God, for reasons known to himself, sees it best to permit suffering in his moral government, and to overrule it all for the general good, it is only necessary to add, that for all this reasoning proves to the contrary, God sees it best to punish the finally impenitent with " *everlasting destruction*."

It is further urged, in vindication of the doctrine of Restorationism, that as endless punishment is abhorrent to the feelings of humanity, it must be inconsistent with the Divine *benevolence*. " How," say the advocates of this system, " could you bear to see a fellow, a neighbor, a child, endure such torment? Would you not do the utmost in your power to rescue such a sufferer? Surely you would. And is not God better than man? is he not more benevolent than the best of earthly parents? Certainly he is. How then can we suppose that he will forever punish any of his creatures?"

It would not be proper to call this an argument; it is a mere trick played upon the unreflecting, the fallacy of which may be easily shown. It leaves wholly out of the account the dignity of God's character as Lawgiver and Governor of the world, and the ends of his moral government, and attempts to settle a question of retributive justice by an appeal to human sympathies. On the ground taken by such reasoners we would be compelled to deny many of the facts recorded in Scripture. It will be admitted by all, that no benevolent father could drown his children, or burn them to death. But God is a benevolent father; therefore he could not have destroyed the inhabitants of the old world by water, nor those of Sodom and Gomorrah by fire. But further: no benevolent father could cause his children to suffer poverty, and want, and bodily affliction. But many of the children of God do thus suffer; therefore, God cannot be a benevolent father. Why, then, should any one argue against the doctrine of endless punishment from a principle which leads to such fearful consequences? Indeed, if it were carried out to its legitimate results it would set aside all government, both human and Divine.

(4.) Restorationism is both absurd in itself, and contrary to the doctrine of salvation by grace, through the merits of the atonement.—To suppose that men who despise all the means of salvation in this life, and die in sin, shall nevertheless be brought, by means of penal suffering, to a state of holiness and happiness in heaven, involves the absurdity, that the penalty of sin in the future world will be to sinners the greatest possible blessing. For, if future punishment be instrumental in raising them to the joys of endless life, it will accomplish for them what Christ and all the means of grace failed to do on earth. It is obvious, moreover, according to this theory, that there is, in reality, no salvation for sinners. If they obtain eternal life, it is not by being *saved*, but by suffering the full penalty of the law; not by the obtainment of a gracious pardon through the atonement of Christ, but by paying the debt. This, of course, turns into nonsense all that the Bible declares respecting the salvation of sinners by the grace and mercy of God. How could such persons truthfully unite in ascribing salvation to Him who "washed us from our sins in his own blood?" Would they not rather feel themselves indebted to hell-fire, and the curse of the law?

2. *The theory of Annihilationism.*—The advocates of this theory maintain that the wicked, after the general resurrection, shall suffer the whole penalty of the law; not, however, in a state of endless misery, but by the endurance of a penal process which shall terminate in their utter destruction or annihilation. They assume that the term *death*, as applied to man in the Scriptures, means annihilation, or the extinction of conscious existence; that as death is the penalty of the law, that penalty must consist in annihilation; and that as the annihilation of the finally impenitent will be irreversible, it will be to them an endless punishment. Thus they attempt to reconcile their theory to the doctrine of

the endless *punishment* of the wicked, while they deny a state of endless *suffering*. But it is not our intention, in this place, to enter upon an extended examination of the peculiarities of annihilationism. On this question enough has been said in the first chapter of this book, to which the reader is referred. We only intend to point out, in a few remarks, the erroneousness of the theory in its relation to future punishment. And,

(1.) That the term *death*, as applied to man in the Scriptures, ever means annihilation, and that annihilation is the penalty of the Divine law, are mere assumptions for which there is not the shadow of proof, and which we may very confidently deny.—Indeed, to understand the term death in the sense of annihilation would turn many passages of Scripture into downright nonsense, as a few examples will show. Thus: " Precious in the sight of the Lord is the *death* (*annihilation*) of his saints." Psa. cxvi, 15. " We were reconciled to God by the *death* of his Son." Rom. v, 10. " Who shall deliver me from the body of this *death ?*" Rom. vii, 24. " He that loveth not his brother, abideth in *death*." 1 John iii, 14.

And equally unfounded is the assumption, that the penalty of the law consists in annihilation, as we have shown in another place;* or that annihilation will constitute the future punishment of the wicked. It is asserted, we know, that this doctrine is clearly taught in the Scriptures, by the employment of such terms as perish, consume, destroy, and destruction, in connection with the punishment of the wicked; but this is only to support one baseless assumption by another equally destitute of proof. " Where there is no vision," says Solomon, " the people *perish*." Prov. xxix, 18. Are they annihilated? " I am *consumed* (but not annihilated) by the blow of thine hand." Psa. xxxix, 10. " He sent frogs among them that *destroyed* them." Psa. lxxviii, 43. " The *destruction* of the poor is their poverty." Prov. x, 15.

(2.) The theory is inconsistent with itself.—Its advocates teach, not only that annihilation is the penalty of the law, but that it is the most dreadful of all punishments, even worse than endless suffering; and yet they maintain that the annihilation of the righteous between death and the resurrection is no punishment at all, but a real *gain*.† Will the wicked suffer any more from annihilation between death and the resurrection than the righteous? Certainly not. And if the annihilation of the righteous at death is not the penalty of the law, how can the annihilation of the wicked be? If in the former case there is no infliction of punishment, how can the punishment be so dreadful in the latter? The system teaches, therefore, that annihilation is the penalty of the law and not the penalty; that it is a most dreadful punishment, and no punishment at all; and that the only difference between the righteous and the

* See page 600.
† See "Age of Gospel Light," p. 40; "Debt and Grace," p. 256.

wicked, as far as this matter is concerned, is, that the former shall be annihilated *once*, the latter *twice*.

(3.) That annihilation will not be the future punishment of the wicked is evident from the absurdity of supposing that they shall be raised again into existence merely to be annihilated.—If annihilationism is true, all men lose their personal identity at death; for it would be perfect folly to talk about the continued existence of persons who are annihilated. If death is annihilation, a resurrection is impossible. There might be other moral beings created, but they could not be justly rewardable or punishable for the moral conduct of the annihilated generations of men. And to suppose that God would create moral beings and then annihilate them, merely to show the penal consequences of guilt, with which they had no connection whatever, would be to impugn his wisdom, his goodness, and his justice.

(4.) If the future punishment of the wicked is to consist in annihilation, then all sinners will be punished alike; which is both unreasonable and unscriptural.*—But as there will be different degrees of future punishment, and as there cannot be different degrees of annihilation, therefore annihilation cannot be that punishment. It may be said that the different degrees of punishment spoken of in Scripture refer to that punitive process which will result in annihilation, and that some will suffer therein longer and more intensely than others, according to the number and magnitude of their sins. This mode of avoiding the difficulty, however, only leads to others; for, if the penalty of sin lies in the sufferings which precede annihilation, then annihilation cannot be that penalty. Again, to those who are suffering these supposed torments, annihilation would either be a curse or a blessing. If the former, a state of endless torment would be better for the sinner than a release from all suffering by annihilation; and if the latter, annihilation cannot be the penalty of the law, unless it can be made to appear that a penalty and a blessing are the same thing.

(5.) That the future punishment of the wicked will not consist in annihilation is manifest from the case of the fallen angels.—No one dare assert that they have been annihilated; and that they will not be annihilated is plain from their apprehensions of future punishment. "Art thou come to *torment* us before the time?" said they to our Lord. Hence it is *torment*, and not annihilation, that they expect to suffer; and the Scriptures expressly declare that wicked men shall partake with them in their final punishment. "Depart from me, ye cursed, into everlasting fire, prepared for the devil and his angels." Matt. xxv, 41. With these remarks respecting the inconsistencies of annihilationism we will dismiss the subject, and proceed to consider,

3. *The doctrine of endless punishment.*—That the future punishment

* See Matt. v, 22; xi, 21-24; xxiii, 14; Luke xii, 47, 48.

Chap. 5.] ENDLESS PUNISHMENT OF THE WICKED. 649

of the wicked will be *endless* may be established by the following arguments:

(1.) It is expressly declared in Scripture to be everlasting, eternal, and to endure for ever and ever. Thus Daniel tells us that the wicked shall rise " to shame and *everlasting* contempt." Dan. xii, 2. Our Lord asserts that they " shall go away into *everlasting* punishment," Matt. xxv, 46; and St. Paul, that they "shall be punished with *everlasting* destruction." 2 Thess. i, 9. The means of their punishment is spoken of as "*everlasting* fire," Matt. xxv, 41; and " the fire that *never shall be quenched.*" Mark ix, 43. And the destruction of the wicked is called "*eternal* damnation." Mark iii, 29.

To this argument it is objected, that all terms and phrases of this nature are often employed to denote a limited period, and that therefore they do not prove the endless punishment of the wicked. To this we reply, that though the terms *everlasting, forever,* and *eternal,* are sometimes employed to denote a limited period, yet they most obviously convey the idea of endless duration. They always denote the longest period of which the subjects united with them are capable. Thus a *servant forever* is a servant during life. The *everlasting hills* and the *everlasting mountains,* denote hills and mountains which continue to exist while the earth endures. And, unless it can be proved that the endless existence of the wicked is impossible, these terms will prove their endless punishment.

Eternity is not divided into parts and periods; and therefore, as these words refer to eternity, their meaning must run parallel with the state to which they refer. " The things that are seen," says the apostle, "are temporal, but the things that are not seen are eternal." That is, the things which are seen endure for a time, but the things which are not seen endure forever. But the future state of the wicked is among the things unseen, as their retribution lies in the eternal world. To say that punishment in *eternity* will endure but for a *time,* involves a contradiction. With as much consistency might it be said, that punishment in *time* may be *eternal.*

(2.) The duration of the punishment of the wicked is expressed by the same terms as that of the future happiness of the righteous.—" And these (the wicked) shall go away into everlasting punishment; but the righteous into life eternal." Matt. xxv, 46. Here it is only necessary to remark, that the Greek word αἰώνιος, which is rendered *everlasting* in one case and *eternal* in the other, means unlimited duration; and that it is applied in both cases in exactly the same manner, without the least hint of any diversity of meaning. We have, therefore, no right to conclude that the punishment of the wicked will be of shorter duration than the happiness of the righteous. If the latter be endless, so will the former. If one is " everlasting life," the other is " everlasting punishment." If one is " eternal life," the other is " eternal damnation." If it is said of the righteous in the future world that "they shall reign *for ever and ever*," it is also said of those who worship the beast and his image that " the smoke of their torment ascendeth up *for ever and ever.*"

(3.) The future punishment of the wicked is sometimes spoken of in such terms and under such circumstances as necessarily imply its endless duration.—In the eighteenth chapter of Matthew we have the parable of the servant who owed ten thousand talents and had nothing to pay. This servant was committed to prison, and was there to be confined till he should pay the debt. Is it not evident that he could never make the required payment? And if so, his case is to be regarded as hopeless.

In Mark ix, 45, our Lord informs us, that "to be cast into hell" is to be cast "into the fire that never shall be quenched;" or as it is expressed in Matthew iii, 12, " unquenchable fire." But this representation of the punishment of the wicked is incompatible with the notion that it will ever be terminated; for if the fire shall never be quenched, their punishment shall never end.

In Mark xiv, 21, our Saviour says, " Woe to that man by whom the Son of man is betrayed! good were it for that man if he had never been born." But if Judas should be miserable through any limited duration, however long, and should afterward be admitted to endless happiness, the event would be a direct contradiction of this passage; for he should still have an eternity of blessedness before him. Nor can his punishment consist in annihilation; for the text assures us that non-existence would be *better* than his future condition.

Our Lord says, Mark iii, 29, " He that blasphemeth against the Holy Ghost hath never forgiveness, but is in danger of eternal damnation." The parallel passage in Luke says, " it shall not be forgiven." Now it must be evident that these two evangelists considered not to be forgiven at all, and to be eternally punished, as implying each other; and an eternal punishment for a sin that shall not be forgiven will be necessarily endless.

To these passages might be added many others, declaring the same doctrine in the same unambiguous manner; but we deem it unnecessary to pursue the subject any further. If what has been said will not establish the doctrine of endless punishment, it is to be feared that additional arguments would be unavailing.

TEXTS MORE OR LESS ILLUSTRATED.

Ch.	Ver.	Page
GENESIS.		
1	2	231
1	6	248
1	26	182
3	7–9	416
3	15	223
3	22	182
4	3, 4	345
5	3	304
6	5	299
6	5, 12, 13	300
6	9	450
8	20, 21	345
8	21	348
9	4	345
9	6	518
15	9, 10	346
17	1	448
17	6	214
17	10, 11	566
18	25	338
18	33	190
22	15, 16	191
22	18	223, 467
28	12	255
31	11, 12	191
32	2	254
32	26	492
48	15, 16	191
49	33	605
50	20	273
EXODUS.		
3	6	191
3	14	191
4	2	434, 442
5	3	349
10	21, 23	84
12	23	252
12	26	496
12	29, 30	84
14	21–23	84
16	23–30	502
18	21, 22	534
20	1–17	468
20	8–11	505
20	12	270
20	24	200
22	20	209
23	20	193
30	12	350
31	14	506
34	6	172
LEVITICUS.		
5	15, 16	350
14	6	574
15	31	351
19	2	169
19	15	534
19	35, 36	521
20	10	527
26	12	442
NUMBERS.		
6	24–27	183
8	17, 18	65
11	9	575
21	14	59
23	19	163
27	21	64
DEUTERONOMY.		
4	33	191
5	6–21	468
6	4	140, 182
6	7	496
10	15	390
11	18, 19	64
14	1	42
18	15	223
18	18	64
25	4	75
29	10–12	564
30	6	426
30	15, 16	491
32	29	478
33	25	459
33	28	575
JOSHUA.		
3	5	66
3	15	66
4	6	496
4	18	66
10	13	59
7	25	293
10	6, 7, 9	463
1 SAMUEL.		
20	6	496
28	15	463
31	4	463
2 SAMUEL.		
6	20	496
14	20	575
18	33	359
20	9	16
23	3	534
24	12–15	270
1 KINGS.		
8	27	149
8	39	200
2 KINGS.		
3	11	575
5	27	293
20	18	214
25	5–7	117
1 CHRONICLES.		
16	34	172
29	29	59
2 CHRONICLES.		
32	4	579
JOB.		
1	1	450
1	4, 5	348
1	6	442
10	8, 11, 12	269
11	7	178
11	7–9	140
11	12	304
12	13	159
13	15	484
14	4	304
14	5	270
14	10	605
15	14	304
17	9	459
17	11	601
23	13	236
24	7	254
26	6	152
26	7–10	147
26	13	231
26	14	148
28	24–27	159
33	4	231
34	12	166
36	5	159
38	4	246
38	7	442
42	7, 8	349
PSALMS.		
5	4	272
7	11	516
8	5	279
9	5	199
16	11	635
19	1	147
19	7	430
22	4	484
22	22	566
23	1, 6	443
27	4	492
30	11	157
31	5	605
33	4	162
33	5	172
33	6	331
33	9	147
33	11	236
34	7	255
36	6	203, 268
37	24	444
38	4, 7	251
39	10	647
40	12	474
41	9	464
49	11	600
49	12, 14	600
50	3, 4	623
51	3	474
51	5	304
51	10	449
51	10, 11	431
55	23	270
57	3	304
66	18	493
68	17	254
72	18, 19	178
73	3–5	638
75	6, 7	271
76	10	272
78	43	647
81	11, 12	272
82	6	442
83	18	196
84	2	492
84	11	274, 443
86	5	172
86	10	140
89	30–35	457
89	34	163
90	2	145, 198
90	3	270
90	10	270
91	10, 11	255
99	9	169
102	25–27	145, 157
103	5, 6	638
103	21	253
104	4	252
104	24	159, 249
104	30	231
105	4	498
112	7	484
116	15	647
117	2	163
121	5–8	443
127	1	443
138	6	268
139	1, 2, 11, 12	152
139	7–10	149
139	15, 16	269
145	3	178
145	9	172
145	15, 16	264
147	5	152
PROVERBS.		
1	23	589
1	24–26	385
1	28	341
3	5	489
8	13	516
10	15	647
12	22	523
15	3	264

TEXTS MORE OR LESS ILLUSTRATED.

Ch.	Ver.	Page
19	17	526
19	18	647
22	6	530
22	15	304
29	15	304
30	4	214

ECCLESIASTES.

Ch.	Ver.	Page
3	19, 20	600
7	29	279
9	5	601
10	20	536
12	14	623

ISAIAH.

Ch.	Ver.	Page
1	3	478
1	18	448
6	3	169, 183
8	13	168
9	6	200
9	7	567
33	22	204
40	3	195, 197
40	12	147
40	13, 14	236
40	17	147
43	2	274
43	2, 3	444
43	10	200
44	3	589
44	6	200
45	22	140
46	9, 10	201
46	10	236
54	5	182
55	6	498
55	7	474, 601
58	13, 14	516
60	8	516

JEREMIAH.

Ch.	Ver.	Page
17	5	212, 304
17	10	200
23	5, 6	196
23	24	149
31	3	458
31	31, 32	194
52	10, 11	117

LAMENTATIONS.

Ch.	Ver.	Page
3	41	498
5	7	360

EZEKIEL.

Ch.	Ver.	Page
14	6	474
18	24	460
18	26, 27	158
18	32	386
33	7–9	17
33	11	386
36	25	448, 589
36	25, 26	426, 560

DANIEL.

Ch.	Ver.	Page
4	33	575
4	35	159
6	10	496
12	2	612
12	2	640, 649

HOSEA.

Ch.	Ver.	Page
12	3–5	191

JOEL.

Ch.	Ver.	Page
2	28, 29	589
2	32	197

JONAH.

Ch.	Ver.	Page
3	4, 5	481
3	10	237

MICAH.

Ch.	Ver.	Page
5	2	213
6	8	517

HABAKKUK.

Ch.	Ver.	Page
3	6	147

ZECHARIAH.

Ch.	Ver.	Page
12	10	493

MALACHI.

Ch.	Ver.	Page
1	6	182
3	1	194
3	6	157

MATTHEW.

Ch.	Ver.	Page
1	21	448
1	23	198
2	22	359
3	1, 2	476
3	2	472
3	5, 6	577, 584
3	11	558, 561
3	16	577
3	16, 17	215, 229
3	17	193, 212
4	12	583
4	17	475
5	8	145, 446
5	17	507
5	22	516
5	44	524
5	48	448
6	5	493
6	6	495
6	10	253
6	14, 15	494, 517
6	25–32	264
6	30	481
7	7	479, 492
7	8	499
7	12	517
7	21	16
8	10	481, 485
8	11	635
9	2	203
9	2–8	67
9	6	204
10	1–7	68
10	20	79, 228
10	28	279, 606
10	29, 30	268
10	29–31	264
10	30	153
10	37	531
12	21	485
12	32	233
12	36, 37	627
13	3	580
13	42	642
13	43	620
13	50	642
14	15–21	67
14	23	495
14	33	205
15	4–6	531
15	28	481
16	18	566
16	21	358
16	24	474, 483
17	3	606
17	5	193
18	3	428
18	18–20	68
18	20	200
18	37	320
19	4, 5	282
19	5	563
19	16–22	517
19	17	239
19	17–19	469
19	4–6	527
20	1–16	167
21	29	472
22	32	607
22	36–40	471
22	37, 38	505
22	37–39	147, 276
22	39	515
22	42	223
23	37	385
24	14	382
24	29	148
24	31	256, 624
25	31	253
25	31, 32	623
25	32	148, 204
25	34	628
25	41	642, 648
25	46	148, 649
26	26, 27	554
26	27, 28	591
26	53	254
27	3	472
27	42	199
27	50	605
28	19	232, 558
28	20	200

MARK.

Ch.	Ver.	Page
1	2	194
1	4, 5	564, 581
1	15	384, 475
1	24	483
2	27	513
3	5	516
3	29	649, 650
6	12	476
7	3, 4	575
7	21–23	305
8	38	484
9	43	649
9	44	642
9	45	650
10	14	570
10	45	359
11	24	494
11	25	494
14	21	650
16	15, 16	558
16	16	239, 384, 458, 562

LUKE.

Ch.	Ver.	Page
1	6	450
1	68–75	567
2	14	253
3	17	642
4	8	208
6	12	495
6	37	494
7	3	472
7	11–15	67
10	7	75
11	11	359
11	13	232, 431
12	6	153
12	11, 12	79
12	48	526
13	3	239, 476
13	29	631
15	10	253
16	9	636
16	22	255
16	23	643
17	5	481
18	13	474
18	13, 14	494
20	36	251
21	25, 26	624
22	31	259 634
22	70	217
23	43	608
23	46	605
24	39	251, 613
24	46	358
24	47	382
24	51, 52	206

JOHN.

Ch.	Ver.	Page
1	3	216
1	12	442
1	14	216
1	15	187
1	28	578
1	47	450
1	49	199
2	1	582
2	1–10	67
2	24, 25	201
3	2	89
3	3, 7	426, 427
3	5	558
3	5, 6, 8	230, 426
3	13	177, 200
3	17	216
3	18	419
3	19	627
3	23	579
3	36	384, 419
4	9, 10, 14	216
4	24	143
4	50	480
5	4, 18	230
5	17, 18	217
5	18, 29	216
5	19	201
5	20	199
5	21	204
5	22, 23	624
5	24	458
5	28	148
5	28, 29	204, 612, 616, 640
5	37	215
5	40	220, 385
6	39	616
6	62	189
6	63	231
6	64	201
8	7	187
8	26	580
8	44	256, 434
8	51	291, 636
9	7	480
9	35, 36	480
9	35–38	205
10	18	212
10	27, 28	458
10	28	455
10	31–33	217
10	37, 38	482
10	40	578
11	24	614
11	25	204
11	26	636
12	24	358
12	42, 43	484
13	1	459
13	2	259
13	17	10
13	18	464
13	27	464

TEXTS MORE OR LESS ILLUSTRATED.

Ch.	Ver.	Page	Ch.	Ver.	Page	Ch.	Ver.	Page	Ch.	Ver.	Page
14	2, 3	249, 630	16	31	419	8	35–39	455	5	10	204, 365
14	6	493	17	24–28	264	8	38, 39	459	5	17	426
14	16, 26	229	17	27, 28	149	9	30	417	5	18	364
14	26	78	17	29	278	10	4	417	5	19	365
15	1, 2, 6	460	17	30	384, 477	10	10	483	5	21	360
15	18	187	17	31	627	10	13	197	7	1	448, 451
15	19	393	19	2	229	10	14, 17	482	8	7	526
15	22	473	20	21	475	11	7	391	8	12	526
15	26	228	23	5	536	11	17, 18, 21, 22	461	9	7	526
16	8	473	23	6	616				10	4	111, 430
16	13	78	24	15	640	12	1	448	11	3	282
16	15	201	26	20	474	12	17, 19	517	12	7–9	206
17	3	458	26	27	483	13	1, 2	535	13	14	185, 232
17	5	189	28	25, 26	184	13	3, 4	534			
17	9	379				14	1	481			
17	11	459	**ROMANS.**			14	10	623	**GALATIANS.**		
17	17	449	1	7	207	14	12	204	1	12	81
17	20	482	1	16	482				2	21	417
18	36	111	1	17	481	**1 CORINTHIANS.**			3	8	568
20	4, 8	187	1	25	208	1	2	206	3	8, 9	566
20	5	581	2	4	478	1	13	560	3	13	177, 363
20	28	188	2	5	338	1	27–29	113	3	26	442
20	30, 31	482	2	6	166	2	6	450	4	4	216
			2	14, 15	263	2	9, 10	81	4	4–6	436
ACTS.			2	14, 15	626	2	10	230	4	5	434
1	5	561	2	16	624	2	12	228	4	6	228
1	24	205	2	29	426, 569	4	11, 13	70	4	19	427
1	25	464	3	24	363	5	21	355	5	14	523
2	19, 20	624	3	24–26	366	6	9	428	5	22, 23	439
2	23	235	3	25	362	6	19	230	5	25	232
2	33	230	3	28	361, 423	6	19, 20	363, 617	6	10	526
2	34	603	3	31	507	8	6	140			
2	37	480	4	3	415, 416	8	11	381	**EPHESIANS.**		
2	38	462, 475	4	11	566	9	27	459	1	4–6	397
2	38, 41	559	4	11, 12	567	10	1–5	464	1	5	235
2	43	580	4	20	480	10	2	575	1	7	363
5	3	259	4	20–22	417	10	4	568	1	9	234
5	3, 4	230	5	5	462	10	4, 11	353	1	11	158
5	29	536	5	6–8	359	10	9	195	1	13	485
5	31	475	5	10	364, 647	10	12	465	1	18	462
6	15	620	5	12	278, 291	10	16	555	1	21	203
7	38	566	5	15, 18	380	11	23–25	591	2	1	291
7	59	605	6	1, 2	422	11	26	555	2	7	177
7	59, 60	206	6	2	582	12	6–11	230	2	10	426
8	12	559	6	3, 4	580	12	13	582	2	12	434
8	22	601	6	4	569	14	15	430	2	16	364, 365
8	29	229	6	14	427	14	37	76	2	18	493
8	36	559	6	22	446	15	16–18	603	2	19	434
8	37	483	7	7	507	15	22	292, 380	3	2–5	77
8	38, 39	577	7	9	478	15	22, 23, 52	616	3	3–5	81
9	18	587	7	12	169, 338	15	51, 53	614	3	11	236
10	34, 35	392	7	24	647	15	54, 55	617	3	14–19	449
10	36	197	8	3	219				4	10	631
10	42	624, 641	8	7	518	**2 CORINTHIANS.**			4	24	279, 426
10	44	590	8	9	228, 561	1	1	235	4	25	523
10	46–48	562	8	10	515	2	11	259	4	32	517
10	47, 48	587	8	11	231	3	17	143, 230	5	2	355
11	15	590	8	13, 14	232	4	6	462	5	22, 23, 25, 33	528
11	18	472	8	14	230, 444	4	7	113	6	1	531
11	33	212	8	15–16	435	4	14	616	6	2	470
14	16	272	8	17	424, 445	5	1	636	6	5	531
14	17	175	8	26	493	5	6–8	609	6	8	532
15	18	152, 235	8	28	235, 443						
16	24–34	588	8	29	239						

PHILIPPIANS.

Ch.	Ver.	Page
1	21	610
2	7, 8	177
2	12, 13	271
3	15	450
3	20	619
3	21	612
4	6	494, 498

COLOSSIANS.

Ch.	Ver.	Page
1	14, 15	227
1	16, 17	203
1	20	364
1	22, 23	455
1	27	427
2	10	203
2	10, 12	580
2	17	353
3	10	278, 426
3	20	531
3	21	529
4	1	532
4	2	498
4	16	59

1 THESS.

Ch.	Ver.	Page
4	6	521
4	16	624
4	17	614
5	23	449, 451

2 THESS.

Ch.	Ver.	Page
1	3	481
1	7	252
1	9	649
2	8	498
2	13	393, 482
2	13, 14	396

1 TIMOTHY.

Ch.	Ver.	Page
1	17	159
1	18, 19	461
1	19, 20	465
2	1–3	536
2	3, 4	386
2	5	493, 563
2	8	493
3	6	257
4	10	485
5	8	528

2 TIMOTHY.

Ch.	Ver.	Page
3	15	430
4	1	625, 641
4	14	461

TITUS.

Ch.	Ver.	Page
1	9	16
2	11, 12	16
2	13	199
3	7	428

PHILEMON.

Ch.	Ver.	Page
10		430

TEXTS MORE OR LESS ILLUSTRATED.

HEBREWS.			Ch.	Ver.	Page	1 PETER.			Ch.	Ver.	Page	JUDE.		
			9	28	360				2	1	381			
Ch.	Ver.	Page	10	1	353	Ch.	Ver.	Page	2	4	148	Ch.	Ver.	Page
1	1	231	10	22	561, 589	1	2	239, 394	2	4	256, 625		7	642
1	2	202, 216	10	26–29	462	1	3	424	2	4–7	641		13	641
1	3	203, 262	10	29	381	1	5	455	3	10	229, 627			
1	5	213	10	35	465	1	11	74, 231	3	17	465			
1	6	207	10	38	465	1	11	82	5	1	542	REVELATION.		
1	7	147, 251	11	1	481	1	12	253				1	5, 6	207
1	8	199, 219	11	3	202, 242	1	13	168	1 JOHN.			1	8	201
2	1	465	11	4	345, 347	1	18, 19	363				1	10	510
2	3, 4	482	11	6	475	1	23	426	1	5	163	1	15	280
2	9	359	11	9, 10	566	1	23	430	1	8, 17	200	1	20	553
3	12	465	12	6	274	2	3	462	1	9	166, 367	2	7	632
3	14	255, 482	12	21	506	2	13, 14	534	1	9	448	2	23	201
4	1	465	12	22–24	443	2	13, 14	535	2	2	361	3	14	609
4	15	224	12	24	589	2	18	531	2	9	516	5	9	364
4	16	479	13	16	526	2	24	360	3	2	442, 635	5	11	254
5	7	498	13	20, 21	449	3	9	386	3	9	427	7	15	635
5	9	636				3	12	499	3	14	647	7	16	633
6	1	446	JAMES.			3	18	231	3	15	516	7	17	635
6	4–6	461	1	13	272, 426	5	8	259	3	17	526	19	10	208
6	18	163	1	15	284	5	10	636	3	21	622	20	12	623
8	8–13	194	1	17	157				4	8	169	20	12	613
8	10	434	1	18	426	2 PETER.			4	8	184	21	3	565
9	14	230	1	22	10	1	5–7, 10	456	4	10	360	21	4	619
9	22	362	2	19	483	1	11	636				21	8	523
9	27	623	2	23	423	1	16, 17	482	2 JOHN.			21	8	642
9	27	641	4	11	517	1	21	74, 231		1	542			

INDEX TO SUBJECTS.

	PAGE
Abel's sacrifice...................	347
Ability, natural and moral..........	374
Abraham's sacrifice...............	346
—— offering up of Isaac............	346
Adam, legal relation of, to his posterity	292
Adam's sin imputed to his posterity...	293
Administration of God toward man, of a mixed nature...................	100
Admission into the Church, power of, with ministers....................	548
Adoption, benefits of...............	441
——, defined......................	433
——, evidences of..................	435
——, evidences of, different theories respecting........................	436
——, nature of	433
Adultery, criminality of.............	527
Affection, mutual, demanded by the conjugal relation	528
Affusion the proper mode of Christian baptism	583
Age, Augustan, one of great learning..	70
Agency, man's moral................	308

	PAGE
Agency, man's moral, proofs of	316
——, man's moral, true doctrine of ...	314
——, moral, defined................	308
Alexander, an example of total apostasy	465
All-sufficiency of God	177
Ancient writers testify to the existence and antiquity of Moses............	52
Angel, import of the term...........	250
"Angel of the Lord," a designation of Christ...........................	199
Angels, creation of.................	250
——, holy, employment of...........	254
——, holy, great number of	254
——, holy, moral condition of........	252
——, holy, natural attributes of......	254
——, unholy, employment of	258
——, unholy, fall of	256
——, unholy, final destiny of........	259
——, unholy, moral condition of	257
——, unholy, various titles of........	258
——, unholy, why not redeemed	260
Animals, distinction of, into clean and unclean	344

INDEX OF SUBJECTS. 655

Annihilation not the penalty of the law 647
—— not the future punishment of the wicked 647
Annihilationism, theory of 598
—— inconsistent with itself 647
Antiquity of the Holy Scriptures 53
Apollinarians, doctrine of 221
Apostasy, Calvinistic theory respecting 456
——, general agreement respecting... 455
——, total, arguments in support of... 460
——, total, examples of 463
——, total, possibility of 455
——, total, Calvinistic arguments against, considered 456
Apostles, office of 540
Arguments for the existence of God... 130
Arianism 222
Aristocratical government, what...... 533
Arminianism 376
Atmosphere, creation of 248
Atonement 343, 349, 356
——, Arminian view of 376
——, Calvinistic theory of 371
——, doctrine of 101
——, extent of 377
——, sacrificial, for bodily disorders .. 351
——, supposed injustice of 369
——, Universalist notion of 374
Attributes of God 139
——, Divine, ascribed to Christ 199
Authority, Church, ends of 549
——, Divine, of the sacred Scriptures 71 98, 109

Baptism a seal 561
—— a sign 560
—— by affusion, proofs for 583
—— by immersion, arguments for, refuted 573
——, emblematical import of 588
——, infant, arguments in support of.. 565
——, infant, objections to, obviated... 562
—— initiatory 560
—— in the room of circumcision 568
——, John's, circumstances of 583
——, mode of 573
——, nature of 557
—— not regeneration 431
—— of Cornelius 587
—— of the eunuch 586
—— of Saul of Tarsus 587
—— of the jailer 588
—— of the three thousand 584
——, sacramental import of 560
——, subjects of 561
——, universal obligation of 557
Baxter's theory of the extent of the atonement 372
Believers proper subjects of baptism .. 562
Benedictions, origin and nature of 207
Benefits of the atonement, general view of 403
Benevolence required by the law of love 523
Bible, supposed demoralizing influence of 118

Bishop, office of 541
Blessedness of the saints in heaven endless 636
Blood, why prohibited 350
Body, human, a proof of the Divine existence 136
Cain and Abel, sacrifice of 345
Calvin denied the freedom of the will.. 310
——, theory of, respecting the Lord's Supper 593
Calvinism, brief view of 371
Canon, sacred, how determined 62
——, sacred, integrity of 58
——, sacred, term defined 62
Catalogues, early, of Christian Scriptures 56
Cause, as defined by Edwards 323
Causes, classification of 131
Cautions prove the possibility of apostasy 465
Change of the Sabbath from the seventh to the first day of the week 508
Character of God 337
Children, duties of, to parents 530
—— of believers proper subjects of baptism 562
Christ a propitiation 356, 361
—— a reconciler 364
—— a redeemer 363
—— came down from heaven 188
——, creation ascribed to 201
——, death of, necessary to man's salvation 357
——, death of, propitiatory 356
——, death of, vicarious 358
—— died for all men 378
—— died for those who may perish... 380
——, Divine attributes ascribed to.... 199
——, Divine titles ascribed to 195
——, Divine works ascribed to 201
——, Divine worship paid to 205
——, Divinity of 187
——, errors respecting the Divine nature of 222
——, errors respecting the human nature of 221
——, eternity ascribed to 200
—— existed before the world 189
——, existence and antiquity of 52
—— is called God 197
—— is called Jehovah 196
—— is called King of Israel 199
—— is called Lord 196
——, miracles of 85
——, omnipresence ascribed to 201
——, omniscience ascribed to 200
—— our final Judge 204, 624
——, person of 221
——, pre-existence of 187
——, preservation ascribed to 203
——, raising the dead ascribed to ... 204
——, real existence of 52
——, resurrection of 86

INDEX OF SUBJECTS.

Christ, Semiarian doctrine respecting.. 222
———, sinlessness of.................. 224
———, Sonship of.................... 210
——— subject to innocent infirmities ... 224
——— the Jehovah of the Old Testament 190
———, the two natures of, constitute one person.......................... 224
——— was before Abraham............ 188
——— was truly man 223
——— worshiped by heavenly beings .. 207
——— worshiped by his disciples...... 205
———, worship of, a proof of his Divinity 208
Christianity, ameliorating influence of. 113
———, institutions of 538
———, instruments employed in the propagation of 112
———, marvelous diffusion of, in the first three centuries 109
———, morals of..................... 467
——— not suited to the carnal mind.... 112
——— strongly opposed in the beginning 111
Christians, relation of, to one another.. 539
Church, constitution of.............. 543
———, Christian, a continuation of the Abrahamic covenant.............. 567
———, Christian, officers of the........ 540
———, Christian, punitive discipline of the 539
———, Christian, what 538
Circumcision a sign and seal of the Abrahamic covenant............... 566
Clarke, Samuel, theory of, respecting Christ......................... 222
Compensation, adequate, meaning of the phrase...................... 368
Condition, moral, in which men are born into the world................... 296
Confession an element of true repentance 474
Conflagration, general................ 629
Conformity to truth required by justice 523
Connection between Divine justice and the penalty of the law 338
Conscience, liberty of................ 522
Consciousness a proof of man's moral agency......................... 316
Consent, common, a proof of the Divine existence....................... 131
——— of the will essential to saving faith 483
Consideration a means of repentance.. 477
Consubstantiation, doctrine of........ 593
Contents, table of................... 5
Contrition essential to true repentance 473
Conviction precedes repentance....... 473
Correction, Divine, a privilege of God's people 444
Covenant, Abrahamic, the covenant of grace......................... 565
Creation ascribed to Christ........... 201
——— ascribed to the Holy Ghost..... 231
——— a proof of the Divine goodness .. 172
———, date of...................... 245
———, extent of..................... 248

Creation in general.................. 242
——— in particular................... 249
——— of angels..................... 250
——— of man, history of.............. 277
——— of the world not discoverable by reason 25
Credibility of the sacred writers...... 68
Darkness, plague of................. 84
Days of the creation literal days...... 247
Dead, resurrection of the, ascribed to the Holy Ghost.................. 231
Death, nature of that, which was made the penalty of the law............ 291
——— not annihilation................ 598
——— of Christ necessary to man's salvation 357
——— of Christ propitiatory 356
——— of Christ, reality of the 86
——— of Christ rendered the salvation of all men possible............... 378
——— of Christ vicarious............. 359
Decalogue binding on all Christians... 507
——— imposed no new duties......... 505
Decrees of God..................... 234
———, existence of the 234
———, nature and properties of the.... 235
Deity and personality of the Holy Ghost 227
Depravity, human, degree of......... 298
———, human, nature of............. 297
———, human, proofs of 299
———, human, objections to, obviated.. 306
Design a proof of the Divine existence 134
———, examples of.................. 136
Destructionism, how defended 599
——— refuted 604
———, theory of..................... 598
Destruction of the first-born.......... 84
Devil, the real agent in man's original temptation 285
Diffusion of Christianity an evidence of its Divine authority............ 111
——— in the first three centuries 109
Dispensation, the remedial 336
Divinity of Christ................... 187
Doctor S. Clarke's theory respecting Christ......................... 222
Doctrine of atonement 101
——— of Divine influence 104
——— of the Trinity, importance of 180
Doctrines of Scripture, excellency of... 98
Dueling, criminality of.............. 519
Duties of children to parents 530
——— of masters.................... 532
——— of parents to their children 528
——— of rulers 534
——— of servants................... 531
——— of the subjects of government ... 535
——— to our neighbor 527

Education of children, duty of........ 599
Effects of Christ's death 380
——— of the fall 290
Elders, office of..................... 541

INDEX OF SUBJECTS. 657

Election, Calvinistic view of 394
—— defined 389
—— of bodies of men to eminent privileges 390
—— of persons to eternal life 393
—— of persons to perform special services 390
Elevation, inspiration of 80
Enemies of Christianity, testimonies of the 57
Enjoyments, heavenly, nature of 632
——, heavenly, will be endless 636
Episcopacy may be a matter of expediency 542
Equivalent, a full, meaning of the phrase 368
Errors respecting Christ's Divine nature 222
—— respecting Christ's human nature. 221
Eternity ascribed to Christ 200
—— of God, proofs of the 145
—— of God not inconsistent with successive time 145
—— of matter refuted 243
—— of the world in its organized state refuted 244
Evangelists, office of 541
Evidence, collateral 50, 109
——, different kinds of 40
——, external 40
——, internal 48, 98
——, internal, nature of 48
——, internal, rank of 48
Evidences necessary to authenticate a revelation 40
Existence of God argued from common consent 131
—— of God argued from marks of design 134
—— of things a proof of the Divine existence 133
Expulsion from the Church, power of, with ministers 548
Extent of the Atonement 371, 377
——, Calvinistic theory of the 371
——, Universalist theory of 374
Eye, human, a proof of the Divine existence 136

Failure to obtain salvation man's own fault 385
Faith defined 417
—— implies previous knowledge 480
—— imputed for righteousness 415
—— is based on evidence 480
——, justifying, what 481
—— may exist in different degrees ... 481
——, nature of, in general 479
—— operates according to the fact believed 481
——, saving, properties of 481
—— the only condition of justification. 419
Faithfulness of God, what 165
Fall of man 281
——, effects of 290

Fall, history of, to be taken literally ... 282
Fatalism, materialistic 309
——, stoical 309
Fathers, Christian, testimony of, to the inspiration of the Scriptures 73
Fear of God, implied in love to him ... 489
——, nature of the 489
Fellowship with the Church, the duty of all 538
Fidelity, a duty demanded by the conjugal relation 527
First-born, destruction of 84
Foreknowledge of God 153
—— consistent with man's moral agency 331
—— does not imply necessity 332
—— not dependent upon his decrees . . 135
——, objects of 153
——, theories respecting 154
Forgiveness of sins ascribed to Christ. 203
Fraud, what 520
Functions, animal, prove design 137

Gambling, injustice of 521
Genuineness of a book, what 51
—— of the Scriptures, how established 51
Geologists, notions of, respecting the date of creation 245
Gilgal, the twelve stones of 66
Gnostics, doctrines of, respecting Christ 221
God, a knowledge of, fundamental to religion 180
——, arguments for the existence of .. 130
——, a title given to Christ 197
——, attributes of 139
——, benevolence of, manifested in our creation 174
——, character of 337
——, decrees of 234
—— defined 125
——, derivation of the term 125
——, doctrines respecting 124
——, existence of 124
——, existence of, not discoverable by reason 23
——, general Providence of 268
——, idea of, derived alone from revelation 130
——, idea of, not acquired by rational induction 126
——, idea of, not innate 126
——, immutability of 156
—— is all-sufficient 177
—— is perfect 177
—— is unsearchable 178
——, prescience of 153
——, secret and revealed will of 241
——, special Providence of 269
——, unity of 140
God's moral government, principles of. 337
Goodness of God 170
Government, Church, nature of 539
——, Church, necessity of 539
——, Church, to whom committed 540

INDEX OF SUBJECTS.

	PAGE
Government, civil, different kinds of	533
——, civil, of Divine authority	533
——, Divine, included in the idea of Providence	266
—— of children a parental duty	528
Governors, duties of	534
Gospel, a means of regeneration	430
——, Christians shall be judged by the	626
—— to be preached to all men	382
Heathen shall be judged by the law of nature	626
Heaven, a place	630
——, the glory of	632
Heavens, creation of	247
——, what they include	248
Hebrew ceased to be a living language soon after the captivity	54
History, evangelical, impressed with marks of credibility	70
—— of the world a proof of man's moral agency	317
Holiness of God	167
Holy Ghost, Arius's opinion respecting	228
——, Deity of	230
——, designated by Divine titles	230
——, Divine works ascribed to	231
——, personality of	228
——, possesses Divine attributes	230
——, procession of	228
—— the object of supreme worship	233
—— the source of inspiration	231
——, works of	231
Hymeneus an example of total apostasy	465
Image of God in which man was created	277
Immersion, arguments for, examined	573
Immortality of the soul	597
—— not understood by the heathen	27
Immutability of God	156
Impossibility of corrupting the sacred Scriptures	59
Imputation, doctrine of	292
—— of Adam's sin to his posterity	293
—— of Christ's righteousness	410
—— of faith for righteousness	415
——, the term explained	418
Infants, objections to the baptism of, obviated	562
——, proofs for the baptism of	565
Infidelity, moral effects of	118
Influence of the Holy Spirit	104
Inspiration ascribed to the sacred penmen	73
—— a work of the Holy Spirit	23
—— claimed by the sacred penmen	74
——, defined	71
——, different opinions respecting	77
——, extent of	77
——, necessity of	72
—— of elevation	80
—— of suggestion	81
—— of superintendence	79

	PAGE
Inspiration, plenary, import of	78
——, possibility of	72
——, reasonableness of	72
——, testimony of the Fathers respecting	73
Instinct and appetite govern the lower animals	267
Institutions of Christianity	538
Instruction, Divine, a privilege of God's people	444
Integrity of the Scriptures	58
Introduction	3
Israelites who fell in the wilderness, examples of total apostasy	464
Jehovah, a title given to Christ	196
Jews, apostasies of, predicted	94
——, final restoration of	96
——, prophecies respecting	94
—— shall be judged by Moses and the prophets	626
——, threatened punishments of	95
Judas an example of apostasy	464
Judgment, final, ascribed to Christ	204
——, general, rule of	626
——, general, time of	627
Justice, general	165
——, judicial	166
——, legislative	165
—— of God	165, 338
—— of God requires the penalty of sin to be executed	340
——, particular	165, 338
——, universal	338
——, vindictive or punitive	166
Justification, Antinomian scheme of	410
——, Arminian doctrine of	415
——, Calvinistic theory of	411
—— distinguished from sanctification	409
—— does not make men actually righteous	409
——, eternal, absurdity of	408
——, how obtained	409
—— is by faith alone	419
——, is by faith in the blood of Christ	366
——, method of, peculiar to the Scriptures	409
——, nature of	406
——, preliminary remarks concerning	403
"King of Israel," a title given to Christ	199
Knowledge of God	152
Law, Adamic, nature of	275
——, moral, how made known in the Scriptures	467
——, moral, of the New Testament, a fuller revelation than the Old	470
——, moral, of the Old Testament, received into the New	469
——, moral, summarily comprehended in the Decalogue	468
——, moral, what	467
—— of Moses, two Hebrew copies of	54

INDEX OF SUBJECTS. 659

	PAGE
Law of the Sabbath	512
——, sacrifices of the	349
Laws of nature, what	266
Leslie's four rules for determining the truth of history	64
—— four rules applied to the books of Moses	64
—— four rules applied to the Gospel history	67
Liberty a natural right of man	521
—— defined by Locke and Edwards	311
——, natural, what	521
—— of conscience	522
—— of God	158
—— of person	521
—— of speech and of the press	522
Life a natural right of man	518
Light of nature, what	19
Lord Herbert's primary principles of religion	158
Lord's supper	590
——, general observations respecting	595
——, institution of	591
——, nature of	592
——, perpetual obligation of	591
——, theories respecting	592
——, true sacramental character of	594
Lotteries a species of gambling	521
Love, filial	530
—— of our neighbor	515
——, parental	528
—— to God a fruit of the Spirit	487
—— to God essential to obedience	487
—— to God, nature of	486
—— to God, obligations of	490
Man, doctrines respecting	275
——, fall of	281
—— held accountable for his moral actions	318
——, history of the creation of	277
—— in his fallen condition	174
—— made in the image of God	278
——, moral condition of	99
——, primitive state of	275
——, voluntary actions of, governed by moral laws	267
—— was originally in a state of trial	283
——, what God has done for the recovery of	177
Manna, miracle of	85
Manner of observing the Sabbath	512
Man's moral agency	308
—— consistent with Divine foreknowledge	331
——, nature of	308
——, objections to	322
——, proofs of	316
——, true doctrine of	314
Man's original transgression, character of	281
—— true moral condition	296
Manuscripts, ancient, of the Old Testament, agreement of	60

	PAGE
Masters, duties of	532
Matter not eternal	243
Meditation a means of repentance	478
Mercy-seat, as applied to Christ	362
Messiah, prophecies respecting	96
Ministers, unworthy, trial of	548
Ministry, Christian, nature of	14
——, Christian, responsibilities of	17
Miracle of Christ's resurrection	86
Miracles, an external evidence of Divine revelation	41, 42, 83
——, circumstances under which they become an authenticating evidence	42
——, competency of human testimony to establish the credibility of	43
——, how distinguished	41
——, Hume's objection to, answered	44
——, instances of	41
——, nature of	41
—— of Christ	85
—— of Moses	84
——, possibility of	42
Morality, Christian, motives of	106
——, Christian, superior nature of	106
——, Pagan, principles of, mere abstractions	106
——, Pagan, what	28
Morals, a perfect system of, found only in the Bible	106
—— of Christianity	467
—— of the Scriptures, how proposed	467
Monophysites, doctrine of, respecting Christ	221
Moses, existence of	51
——, miracles of	84
Nations rewarded in this life	167
Nature, human, has two essential parts	277
——, laws of, what	266
Necessity defined	332
——, different kinds of	309
——, doctrine of	309
—— incompatible with moral freedom	320
Neighbor, duties to our	527
——, the love of our	515
Nestorians, doctrine of, respecting Christ	221
New Testament Scriptures, ancient date of	56
——, early catalogues of	56
——, quoted by early Christian authors	56
Noah, sacrifice of on leaving the ark	345
Obedience, filial	531
—— to civil laws the duty of subjects	535
Objection to the doctrine of imputation answered	294
Objections to the Bible answered	114
—— to the Divine administration answered	286
—— to the doctrine of justification answered	420
—— to the Mosaic history of the fall	286

INDEX OF SUBJECTS.

	PAGE
Objections to the spirituality of God...	144
Objects of Divine foreknowledge classified..............................	152
Obligations to love God.............	490
Observance of the Sabbath..........	501
——, manner of....................	512
Offense is followed by penal consequences........................	102
Office, sacred, nature and responsibilities of.........................	11
Omnipotence ascribed to Christ......	201
—— of God......................	146
Omnipresence ascribed to Christ.....	200
—— of God......................	149
—— of God, manner of the..........	151
Omniscience ascribed to Christ.......	200
—— of God......................	151
—— of God, objects of	152
Ordination, power of, with presbyters.	546
Pagan religions, demoralizing influence of.............................	33
Pagans have no conception of pure morality........................	10
Paine, objection of, to the truth of prophecy.......................	116
Pardon not an act of mere prerogative....................... 102,	408
—— not secured by mere penitence and reformation................	102
Parents, duties of, to their children...	528
Passover, sacrifice of...............	351
Pastors, Christian, office of..........	541
——, Christian, qualifications of......	12
Patriotism a duty...................	535
Penalty of sin, nature of............	291
Perfection of God...................	177
Personality and Deity of the Holy Ghost..........................	227
Person, as applied to God...........	178
——, liberty of....................	521
—— of Christ.....................	221
—— of Christ, errors respecting	221
—— of Christ, Scriptural doctrine of..	223
Piety necessary to true morality	515
Philosophers, heathen, concessions of..	32
Plague of darkness.................	84
Pleasures, the portion of the saints in heaven........................	635
Polity of the Jews proves the existence and antiquity of Moses	51
Prayer a means of regeneration	430
—— an aid to repentance...........	479
——, duty of.....................	492
—— for rulers, the duty of subjects ..	536
——, nature of....................	492
——, obligations of.................	497
——, private.....................	495
——, public......................	497
——, utility of	499
——, various kinds of..............	494
Precepts, moral and positive.........	287
—— of the Old Testament received into the New.....................	469

	PAGE
Predestination.....................	387
——, Calvinistic view of............	388
—— defined and stated.............	388
Prediction respecting the coming "SHILOH"..........................:	93
Predictions relate chiefly to the scheme of redemption...................	90
Pre-existence of Christ	187
Preface	3
Prescience of God..................	153
Presbyters, office of................	542
Preservation an element of Divine Providence	265
—— ascribed to Christ	203
—— ascribed to the Holy Ghost	231
Press, liberty of....................	522
Probation implies the possibility of apostasy	466
Proofs of the goodness of God	172
Property a natural right............	520
Prophecies respecting the Jewish nation.............................	94
—— respecting the Messiah.........	96
Prophecy a proof of Divine revelation............................	46
——, an objection to, answered	47
——, double sense of...............	92
——, ends of......................	91
——, extent of	90
——, force of the evidence of........	46
—— found only in the Scriptures	91
——, nature of....................	46
—— respecting the coming "SHILOH"	93
—— respecting the seed of the woman	92
——, supposed obscurity of	91
Prophets, office of..................	540
Propitiation, Christ a........... 356,	361
Protection, Divine, a privilege of God's people	443
Providence, Divine, nature of........	265
——, Divine, proofs of..............	261
——, Divine, objects of	268
——, Divine, with regard to moral evil	271
——, doctrine of, not discoverable by reason	26
——, general	268
——, particular...................	273
——, special......................	269
Provision, Divine, a privilege of God's people	443
Punishment, endless, doctrine of	648
——, endless, not incompatible with the Divine perfections	644
——, endless, of the wicked....	637
——, endless, objection to...........	649
——, future, a state of intense suffering	642
——, future, nature of..............	641
——, future, not reformatory	643
——, future, will be endless	643
—— of the Jews predicted..........	95
—— of sinners not always disciplinary	644
Raising the dead ascribed to Christ...	204
Reality of Christ's death........	86

INDEX TO SUBJECTS. 661

	PAGE
Reason a source of theology	18
—— defined	18
——, extent of the discoveries of	18
——, insufficiency of, in religion	23
——, limitations of	22
——, use of, in religion	20
Reconciliation by Christ	364
Redemption by Christ	363
Red Sea, the dividing of the	84
Reformation impossible without grace	102
—— included in true repentance	474
Regeneration a concomitant of justification	427
—— defined	425
——, general remarks respecting	424
——, means of	429
——, nature of	424
——, necessity of	428
Relation, conjugal	527
——, filial	530
——, legal, of Adam to his posterity	292
——, parental	528
——, servile	531
Relations, domestic	527
——, political	532
Religion, as distinguished from theology	10
——, Christian, a proof of the existence and antiquity of Christ	52
——, doctrines of, not presented in the Bible in a systematic form	14
——, natural, articles of	115
—— understood objectively	10
—— understood subjectively	10
Remedial dispensation	336
Repentance alone cannot secure pardon	102, 341
—— and faith required of all men	384
—— includes contrition	473
—— includes reformation	474
—— is the gift of God	472
——, means of	477
——, nature of	471
——, necessity of	476
—— not regeneration	428
——, order of, in its connection with faith and regeneration	475
Reprobation, doctrine of	399
Republican government, what	533
Restoration of the Jews, prophecy respecting	96
Restorationism, theory of	643
——, untenable	643
Resurrection body, properties of	617
——, certainty of	614
——, nature of	611
—— of Christ	86
—— of the human body	611
—— of the same body that dies	612
——, will be universal	614
Retribution, future, connected with the general judgment	640
——, future, subsequent to the general resurrection	640
Revelation as a source of theology	22

	PAGE
Revelation defined	22
——, Divine, evidences of	39, 84
——, Divine, necessary	23, 31
——, Divine, probable character of	35
——, Divine, possible	22
—— is all that could be reasonably expected	36
Righteousness, explanation of the term	417
—— of Christ, how imputed to us	412
Right to liberty	521
—— to life secured by the law of God	518
—— to property, secured by the Divine law	520
Rights, natural, what	518
—— of God cannot be given up	340
Robbery, what	520
Sabbath, change of, from the seventh to the first day of the week	508
——, Christian, honored of God	512
——, inclusion of, in the Decalogue	505
——, law of, what it forbids	513
——, law of, what it requires	514
——, manner of the observance of	512
——, observance of the	501
——, primitive institution of	501
——, recognition of, in the wilderness	502
——, universal and perpetual obligation of	501
Sabellianism	222
Sacraments, Catholic view of	553
——, institution of, by Christ	554
——, nature of	552
——, number of	556
——, Socinian notion of	554
——, true Protestant doctrine respecting	554
Sacrifice of Abraham	346
—— of Cain and Abel	345
—— of Noah on leaving the ark	345
—— of the Passover	351
——, vicarious, what	350
Sacrifices, ante-Mosaic, expiatory	346
——, Levitical, typical character of	349
——, Levitical, types of a better sacrifice	352
—— of the law expiatory	349
——, patriarchal, of Divine appointment	343
Sacrificial terms applied to Christ and his atoning work	354
Saints, eternal blessedness of	630
—— eternal blessedness of the, will be progressive	636
—— will know one another in heaven	636
Salvation ascribed to Christ's death	356
——, failure to obtain, man's own fault	385
—— of all, will of God concerning the	386
—— offered to all men in the Gospel	382
Sanctification, entire, attainability of	447
——, entire, does not differ from regeneration	446
——, entire, does not exclude temptation	447

INDEX TO SUBJECTS.

Sanctification, entire, does not imply indefectibility 446
——, entire, objections to, answered.. 453
——, entire, the manner of.......... 452
——, entire, the nature of........... 446
——, entire, the time of 450
Satan the real tempter of our first parents........................ 285
Satisfaction made to Divine justice, meaning of the phrase............ 368
Saul an example of total apostasy 463
Scape-goat, sacrifice of.............. 351
Scriptures, authenticity of........... 64
——, Divine authority of ... 71, 83, 90, 98
——, genuineness of 51
——, integrity of 58
——, moral tendency of 105
——, moral tendency of, exemplified in the person of Christ 106
—— worthy of God................. 107
——, Jewish, a catalogue of, by Josephus 53
——, Jewish, antiquity of 51
——, Jewish, translated into Greek... 53
——, Jewish, the impossibility of corrupting the 59
——, New Testament, antiquity of.... 56
——, New Testament, catalogues of .. 56
——, New Testament, could not be corrupted...................... 61
——, New Testament, testimonies of enemies to...................... 57
Seed of the woman, promise of....... 92
Self-examination a means of repentance 478
Semiarianism...................... 222
Serpent, sentence pronounced upon the 285
Servants, duties of 531
Settlement of children, a parental duty. 530
Shiloh, prediction respecting......... 93
Sin not pardoned on mere prerogative...................... 102, 408
—— not pardoned on mere repentance 102
—— not pardoned on repentance and reformation 102
——, original, nature of 297
Solomon an example of total apostasy . 464
Son of God, in what sense Christ is the 213
Sonship of Christ 210
——, false theories respecting the 210
——, importance of the orthodox view of the......................... 219
——, true doctrine of the, established . 213
Soul, the, can exist separate from the body.......................... 604
——, the, exists after death in a conscious state..................... 606
——, immortality of the............ 597
——, immortality of the, not understood by the heathen............. 27
——, immortality of the, proved by Scripture 604
——, nature and powers of, a proof of the Divine existence............. 138

Soul, received by traduction 306
Speech, liberty of................... 522
Spine, human, a proof of design 137
Spirituality of God 142
——, several objections to, answered.. 144
State, future 597
Stonehenge, in Salisbury Plain....... 66
Stones set up at Gilgal 66
Style and manner of the sacred writers 108
Subjects, duties of.................. 535
Submission to God implied in love to him........................... 488
Suicide, criminality of 518
Supplies, pecuniary, for the necessities of government, due from subjects... 536
Support of children, the duty of parents 528
Table of contents 5
Teachers, office of.................. 541
Terms, sacrificial, applied to the death of Christ 354
Testament, New, agreement of ancient manuscripts of 61
——, New, agreement of ancient versions of, with quotations made by early Christian writers............ 62
——, New, antiquity of............. 56
——, New, contains the fuller revelation of moral law 470
——, New, early catalogues of the books of the 56
——, New, integrity of 61
——, New, quoted by early Christians . 56
——, Old, antiquity of.............. 56
Testimony of ancient writers, a proof of the genuineness of the Scriptures. 52
—— of the disciples to Christ's resurrection highly credible............ 87
Theft, what 520
Theology a science.................. 10
—— claims universal attention 17
——, didactic 14
——, divisions of 13
—— embraces many controverted subjects 11
——, general utility of.............. 17
——, importance of 11
——, natural...................... 13
——, natural, not to be rejected...... 13
——, natural, principles of, not discovered by reason 29
——, nature of 9
——, objects of.................... 12
——, polemic 15
——, practical.................... 16
——, revealed.................... 13
——, sources of 18
——, term explained 9
—— the Christian minister's profession 67
Theologian, what 10
Time, succession of, ascribed to God .. 145
Titles, Divine, ascribed to Christ 195
Traduction of the soul 306

INDEX TO SUBJECTS. 663

	PAGE
Translation, Greek, of the Old Testament Scriptures a proof of their antiquity	53
Transubstantiation	592
Tribute, the payment of, the duty of subjects	536
Trinity, doctrine of, as affecting our views of God	180
——, doctrine of, essential to the credit of the Scriptures	181
——, doctrine of, importance of the	180
——, doctrine of, lies at the foundation of revealed theology	31
——, doctrine of, intimately connected with morals	180
——, doctrine of, Scripture proofs of the	182
—— in unity	178
——, Sabellian notion of	222
Trust in God implied in love to him	489
—— in God implied in saving faith	484
Truth, conformity to, required by justice	523
—— of God, proofs of	162
——, when assailed, should be defended	16
Type, what	352
Unity of God, proofs of	140
Universalism, brief view of	374
Universalists, doctrine of, contrary to matters of fact	637
——, doctrine of, contrary to Scripture	637
——, doctrine of, respecting the punishment of sin	637
——, doctrine of, self-contradictory	638
——, doctrine of, subverts the whole scheme of salvation by grace	639
Universe, physical, governed by the laws of nature	266
Unsearchableness of God	178
Volition does not imply an infinite series of volitions	322
—— is not an effect	323
—— is not the unavoidable result of motives	326
Voltaire, objection of, to the truth of prophecy	116

	PAGE
Warnings prove apostasy possible	465
Week, first day of the, called Lord's day	510
——, first day of the, distinguished by God's gracious dispensations	511
——, first day of the, observed by the apostolic Churches	510
Will, as distinguished from intelligence and sensibility	316
——, freedom of, everywhere acknowledged in the Scriptures	319
——, how influenced by motives	314
—— of God concerning the salvation of all men	386
—— of God the only ground of moral obligation	467
—— of God, the secret and revealed	241
Wisdom of God	159
—— demonstrated by his works	159
Witness of our own spirit	440
—— of the Spirit to our adoption	437
—— of the Spirit, different theories respecting the	436
Works, Divine, ascribed to Christ	201
—— of God	242
—— of God declare his wisdom	159
World not eternal	243
Worship paid to Christ	205
—— paid to Christ an evidence of his Divinity	208
——, public, obligations of	498
——, supreme and inferior, Arian notion of	209
——, supreme, paid to the Holy Ghost	232
Wrath ascribed to God	363
Writers, sacred, claimed to be inspired	74
——, sacred, credibility of	68
——, sacred, highly circumstantial in their accounts	70
——, sacred, knew what they related	69
——, sacred, style and manner of	108
——, sacred, were men of exemplary virtue and piety	68
——, sacred, were not influenced by worldly motives	69
——, sacred, wonderful agreement of	107
Zuinglius, theory of, respecting the Lord's Supper	593

NOTE TO PAGE 523.

RELATION OF METHODISM TO SLAVERY.—The following statements by Mr. Watson furnish the grounds on which English Methodism stands in regard to slavery:

"As to the existence of slavery in Christian states, every government, as soon as it professes to be Christian, binds itself to be regulated by the principles of the New Testament; and though a part of its subjects should at that time be in a state of servitude, and their sudden emancipation might be obviously an injury to society at large, it is bound to show that its spirit and tendency is as inimical to slavery as is the Christianity which it professes. All the injustice and oppression against which it can guard that condition, and all the mitigating regulations it can adopt, are obligatory upon it; and since also every Christian slave is enjoined by apostolic authority to choose freedom, when it is possible to attain it, as being a better state, and more befitting a Christian man, so is every Christian master bound, by the principle of loving his neighbor, and more especially his 'brother in Christ,' as himself, to promote his passing into that better and more Christian state. To the instruction of the slaves in religion would every such Christian government also be bound, and still further to adopt measures for the final extinction of slavery; the rule of its proceeding in this case being the accomplishment of this object as soon as is compatible with the real welfare of the enslaved portion of its subjects themselves, and not the consideration of the losses which might be sustained by their proprietors, which, however, ought to be compensated by other means, as far as they are just, and equitably estimated.

"If this be the mode of proceeding clearly pointed out by Christianity to a state on its first becoming Christian, when previously, and for ages, the practice of slavery had grown up with it, how much more forcibly does it impose its obligation upon nations involved in the guilt of the modern African slavery! They professed Christianity when they commenced the practice. They entered upon a traffic which *ab initio* was, upon their own principles, unjust and cruel. They had no rights of war to plead against the natural rights of the first captives; who were in fact stolen, or purchased from the stealers, knowing them to be so. The governments themselves never acquired any right of property in the parents; they have none in their descendants, and can acquire none; as the thief who steals cattle cannot, should he feed and defend them, acquire any right of property, either in them or the stock they may produce, although he should be at the charge of rearing them. These governments not having a right of property in their colonial slaves, could not transfer any right of property in them to their present masters, for it could not give what it never had; nor, by its connivance at the robberies and purchases of stolen human beings, alter the essential injustice of the transaction. All such governments are therefore clearly bound, as they fear God and dread his displeasure, to restore all their slaves to the condition of free men. Restoration to their friends and country is now out of the question; they are bound to protect them where they are, and have the right to exact their obedience to good laws in return: but property in them they cannot obtain; their natural right to liberty is untouched and inviolable. The manner in which this right is to be restored, we grant, is in the power of such governments to determine, provided that proceeding be regulated by the principles above laid down: first, that the emancipation be sincerely determined upon at some time future; secondly, that it be not delayed beyond the period which the *general interest of the slaves themselves* prescribes, and which is to be judged of benevolently, and without any bias of judgment, giving the advantage of every doubt to the injured party; thirdly, that all possible means be adopted to render freedom a good to them."

The Methodist Episcopal Church in the United States has long included the buying and selling of human beings among the sins sufficient to exclude the offender from the kingdom of God. It also declared in 1784 of "the practice of holding our fellow-creatures in slavery;" "we view it as contrary to the golden law of God, on which hang all the law and the prophets, and the unalienable rights of mankind." Having so declared, the Discipline has reiterated from 1796 that we are "more than ever," or "as much as ever convinced of the great evil of slavery;" so that in principle the declaration of 1784 has been constantly reaffirmed. From 1796 the question, "What shall be done for the 'extirpation' of slavery?" has been retained, so that such "extirpation" has been unchangeably held as one of the objects for which we exist as a Church.—ED.

THE END.

www.ingramcontent.com/pod-product-compliance
Lightning Source LLC
Chambersburg PA
CBHW071014240426
43661CB00073B/2177